Management Accounting
for Decision Makers

PEARSON
Education

We work with leading authors to develop the
strongest educational materials in accounting,
bringing cutting-edge thinking and best
learning practice to a global market.

Under a range of well-known imprints, including
Financial Times Prentice Hall, we craft high quality print and
electronic publications which help readers to understand
and apply their content, whether studying or at work.

To find out more about the complete range of our
publishing, please visit us on the World Wide Web at:
www.pearsoned.co.uk

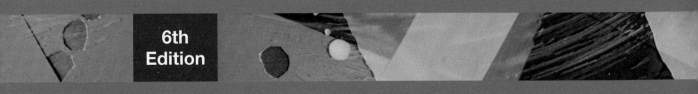

6th Edition

Management Accounting
for Decision Makers

Peter Atrill

and

Eddie McLaney

FT Prentice Hall
FINANCIAL TIMES

An imprint of **Pearson Education**
Harlow, England • London • New York • Boston • San Francisco • Toronto
Sydney • Tokyo • Singapore • Hong Kong • Seoul • Taipei • New Delhi
Cape Town • Madrid • Mexico City • Amsterdam • Munich • Paris • Milan

Pearson Education Limited
Edinburgh Gate
Harlow
Essex CM20 2JE
England

and Associated Companies throughout the world

Visit us on the World Wide Web at:
www.pearsoned.co.uk

First published 1995 by Prentice Hall Europe
Second edition published 1999 by Prentice Hall Europe
Third edition published 2002 by Pearson Education Limited
Fourth edition published 2005
Fifth edition published 2007
Sixth edition published 2009

© Prentice Hall Europe 1995, 1999
© Pearson Education 2002, 2005, 2007, 2009

ISBN: 978-0-273-72362-2

British Library Cataloguing-in-Publication Data
A catalogue record for this book is available from the British Library.

Library of Congress Cataloging-in-Publication Data
Atrill, Peter.
  Management accounting for decision makers / Peter Atrill and Eddie McLaney. — 6th ed.
      p.   cm.
    Includes bibliographical references and index.
    ISBN 978-0-273-72362-2 (pbk. : alk. paper) 1. Managerial accounting.   2. Decision making.
  I. McLaney, Eddie.   II. Title.
  HF5657.4.A873 2009
  658.15′11—dc22

                                                                          2009014455

10 9 8 7 6 5 4 3
11 10

Typeset in 9.5/12.5pt Stone Serif by 35
Printed and bound by Rotolito Lombarda, Italy

The publisher's policy is to use paper manufactured from sustainable forests.

Contents

4   Full costing   92

5   Costing and pricing in a competitive environment   134

6   Budgeting

7 Accounting for control

9 Strategic management accounting 317

Guided tour of the book

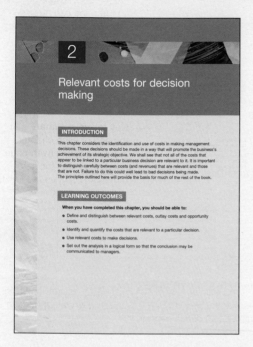

Learning outcomes Bullet points at the start of each chapter show what you can expect to learn from that chapter, and highlight the core coverage.

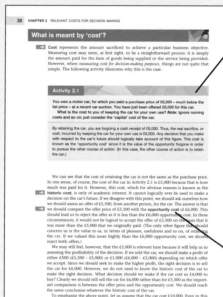

Activities These short questions, integrated throughout each chapter, allow you to check your understanding as you progress through the text. They comprise either a narrative question requiring you to review or critically consider topics, or a numerical problem requiring you to deduce a solution. A suggested answer is given immediately after each activity.

Key terms The key concepts and techniques in each chapter are highlighted in colour where they are first introduced, with an adjacent icon in the margin to help you refer back to the most important points.

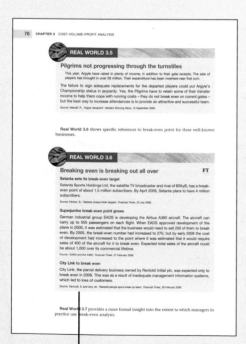

'Real World' illustrations Integrated throughout the text, these illustrative examples highlight the practical application of accounting concepts and techniques by real businesses, including extracts from company reports and financial statements, survey data and other interesting insights from business.

Examples At frequent intervals throughout most chapters, there are numerical examples that give you step-by-step workings to follow through to the solution.

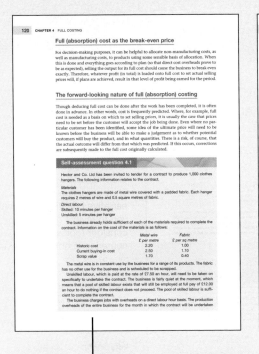

Bullet point chapter summary   Each chapter ends with a 'bullet point' summary. This highlights the material covered in the chapter and can be used as a quick reminder of the main issues.

Key terms summary   At the end of each chapter, there is a listing (with page reference) of all the key terms, allowing you to easily refer back to the most important points.

Self-assessment questions   Towards the end of most chapters you will encounter one of these questions, allowing you to attempt a comprehensive question before tackling the end-of-chapter assessment material. To check your understanding and progress, solutions are provided at the end of the book.

Further reading   This section comprises a listing of relevant chapters in other textbooks that you might refer to in order to pursue a topic in more depth or gain an alternative perspective.

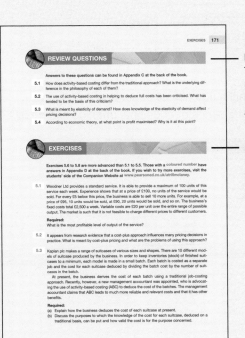

Review questions
These short questions encourage you to review and/or critically discuss your understanding of the main topics covered in each chapter, either individually or in a group. Solutions to these questions can be found at the back of the book in Appendix C.

Exercises   These comprehensive questions appear at the end of most chapters. The more advanced questions are separately identified. Solutions to some of the questions (those with coloured numbers) are provided at the end of the book, enabling you to assess your progress. Solutions to the remaining questions are available online for lecturers only at **www.pearsoned.co.uk/atrillmclaney**.

Guided tour of MyAccountingLab

MyAccountingLab puts students in control of their own learning through a suite of study and practice tools tied to the online e-book and other media tools. At the core of **MyAccountingLab** are the following features:

Practice tests

Practice tests for each section of the textbook enable students to test their understanding and identify the areas in which they need to do further work. Lecturers can customise the practice tests or leave students to use the two pre-built tests per chapter.

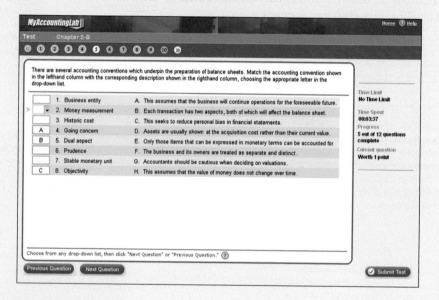

Personalised study plan

Based on a student's performance on a practice test, a personal study plan is generated that shows where further study needs to focus. This study plan consists of a series of additional practice exercises.

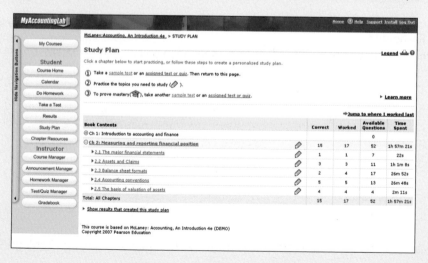

Additional practice exercises

Generated by the student's own performance on a practice test, additional practice exercises are keyed to the textbook and provide extensive practice and link students to the e-book and to other tutorial instruction resources.

Tutorial instruction

Launched from the additional practice exercises, tutorial instruction is provided in the form of solutions to problems, detailed differential feedback, step-by-step explanations, and other media-based explanations, including key concept animations.

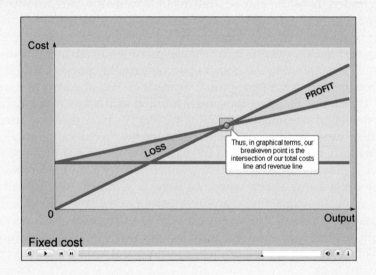

Additional MyAccountingLab tools

1 Interactive study guide
2 Electronic tutorials
3 Glossary – key terms from the textbook
4 Glossary flashcards
5 Links to the most useful accounting data and information sources on the Internet.

Lecturer training and support

We offer lecturers personalised training and support for **MyAccountingLab**. We have a dedicated team of Technology Specialists whose job it is to support lecturers in their use of our media products, including **MyAccountingLab**. To make contact with your Technology Specialist please email **feedback-cw@pearson.com**

For a visual walkthrough of how to make the most of **MyAccountingLab**, visit **www.MyAccountingLab.com**

To find details of your local sales representatives go to **www.pearsoned.co.uk/replocater**

Preface

Management accounting is concerned with ensuring that managers have the information they need to plan and control the direction of their organisation. This book is directed primarily at those following an introductory course in management accounting. Many readers will be studying at a university or college, perhaps majoring in accounting or in another area such as business studies, IT, tourism or engineering. Other readers, however, may be studying independently, perhaps with no qualification in mind.

The book is written in an 'open learning' style, which has been adopted because we believe that readers will find it to be more 'user-friendly' than the traditional approach. Whether they are using the book as part of a taught course or for personal study, we feel that the open learning approach makes it easier for readers to learn.

In writing this book, we have been mindful of the fact that most readers will not have studied management accounting before. We have therefore tried to write in an accessible style, avoiding technical jargon. Where technical terminology is unavoidable, we have tried to give clear explanations. At the end of the book (in Appendix A) there is a glossary of technical terms, which readers can use to refresh their memory if they come across a term whose meaning is in doubt. We have tried to introduce topics gradually, explaining everything as we go. We have also included a number of questions and tasks of various types to try to help readers to understand the subject fully, in much the same way as a good lecturer would do in lectures and tutorials. More detail of the nature and use of these questions and tasks is given in the section 'How to use this book'.

The book covers all the areas required to gain a firm foundation in the subject. Chapter 1 provides a broad introduction to the nature and purpose of management accounting. Chapters 2, 3, 4 and 5 are concerned with identifying cost information and using it to make short-term and medium-term decisions. Chapters 6 and 7 deal with the ways in which management accounting can be used in making plans and in trying to ensure that those plans are actually achieved. Chapter 8 considers the use of management accounting information in making investment decisions, typically long-term ones. Chapter 9 deals with 'strategic management accounting'. This is an increasingly important area of management accounting that focuses on factors outside the organisation but which have a significant effect on its success. Chapter 10 deals with the problems of measuring performance where the business operates through a divisional organisational structure, as most large businesses do. It also considers the use of non-financial measures in measuring performance. Finally, Chapter 11 looks at the way in which management accounting can help in the control of short-term assets, such as inventories (stock) and cash.

In this sixth edition, we have taken the opportunity to improve the book. We have continued to increase the emphasis on the need for businesses to operate within a framework of strategic planning and decision making. This includes greater focus on the business environment and, in particular, on the crucial importance of creating and retaining customers. We have continued to highlight the changing role of management accountants to enable them to retain their place at the centre of the decision-making and planning process. We have also added more examples of management accounting in practice.

We should like to thank those at Pearson Education who were involved with this book, for their support and encouragement. Without their help it would not have materialised.

We hope that readers will find the book readable and helpful.

Peter Atrill
Eddie McLaney

How to use this book

Whether you are using the book as part of a lecture/tutorial-based course or as the basis for a more independent mode of study, the same approach should be broadly followed.

Order of dealing with the material

The contents of the book have been ordered in what is meant to be a logical sequence. For this reason, it is suggested that you work through the book in the order in which it is presented. Every effort has been made to ensure that earlier chapters do not refer to concepts or terms which are not explained until a later chapter. If you work through the chapters in the 'wrong' order, you may encounter points that have been explained in an earlier chapter which you have not read.

Working through the chapters

You are advised to work through the chapters from start to finish, but not necessarily in one sitting. Activities are interspersed within the text. These are meant to be like the sort of questions which a good lecturer will throw at students during a lecture or tutorial. Activities seek to serve two purposes:

1 To give you the opportunity to check that you understand what has been covered so far.
2 To try to encourage you to think beyond the topic that you have just covered, sometimes so that you can see a link between that topic and others with which you are already familiar. Sometimes, activities are used as a means of linking the topic just covered to the next one.

You are strongly advised to do all the activities. The answers are provided immediately after the activity. These answers should be covered up until you have arrived at a solution, which should then be compared with the suggested answer provided.

Towards the end of Chapters 2–11 there is a 'self-assessment question'. This is rather more demanding and comprehensive than any of the activities. It is intended to give you an opportunity to see whether you understand the main body of material covered in the chapter. The solutions to the self-assessment questions are provided in Appendix B at the end of the book. As with the activities, it is very important that you make a thorough attempt at the question before referring to the solution. If you have real difficulty with a self-assessment question you should go over the chapter again, since it should be the case that careful study of the chapter will enable completion of the self-assessment question.

End-of-chapter assessment material

At the end of each chapter, there are four 'review' questions. These are short questions requiring a narrative answer and intended to enable you to assess how well you can recall main points covered in the chapter. Suggested answers to these questions are provided in Appendix C at the end of the book. Again, a serious attempt should be made to answer these questions before referring to the solutions.

At the end of each chapter, there are normally eight exercises. These are more demanding and extensive questions, mostly computational, and should further reinforce your knowledge and understanding. We have attempted to provide questions of varying complexity.

Answers to five out of the eight exercises in each chapter are provided in Appendix D at the end of the book. These exercises are marked with a coloured number. Answers to the three exercises that are not marked with a coloured number are given in a separate teacher's manual. Yet again, a thorough attempt should be made to answer these questions before referring to the answers.

Supplements and website

A comprehensive range of supplementary materials is available to lecturers adopting this text at **www.pearsoned.co.uk/atrillmclaney**.

MyAccountingLab

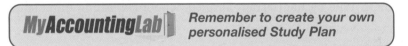
MyAccountingLab | *Remember to create your own personalised Study Plan*

MyAccountingLab supports this book. This banner reminds students to complete the chapter pre-test to create their personal Study Plan. The results of the test determine the Study Plan going forward.

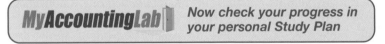
MyAccountingLab | *Now check your progress in your personal Study Plan*

This banner reminds students to complete the chapter post-test in MyAccountingLab to track their progress and mastery of the topics included in each chapter. Their Study plan will adapt according to the results of the test.

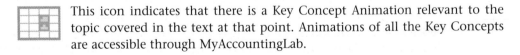
This icon indicates that there is a Key Concept Animation relevant to the topic covered in the text at that point. Animations of all the Key Concepts are accessible through MyAccountingLab.

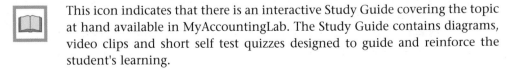
This icon indicates that there is an interactive Study Guide covering the topic at hand available in MyAccountingLab. The Study Guide contains diagrams, video clips and short self test quizzes designed to guide and reinforce the student's learning.

Acknowledgements

We are grateful to the following for permission to reproduce copyright material:

Figures

Figure 5.1 adapted from *Activity Based Costing: A Review with Case Studies*, CIMA Publishing (Innes, J. and Mitchell, F. 1990), this article was published in *Activity Based Costing*, J. Innes and F. Mitchell, Copyright Elsevier 1990; Figure 5.2 from A survey of factors influencing the choice of product costing systems in UK organisations, *Management Accounting Research*, Vol. 18, Issue 4, December, pp. 399–424 (Al-Omiri, M. and Drury, C. 2007), Copyright 2007, with permission from Elsevier; Figure 6.7 from *Financial Management and Working Capital Practices in UK SMEs*, Manchester Business School (Chittenden, F., Poutziouris, P. and Michaelas, N. 1998) Fig. 16, p. 22, Nicos Michaelas, Francis Chittenden, Panikkos Poutziouris; Figure 6.8 from Beyond Budgeting model, Copyright and source Beyond Budgeting Round Table (BBRT) – www.bbrt.org; Figure 9.6 from *The Balanced Scorecard*, Harvard Business School Press (Kaplan, R. and Norton, D. 1996), reprinted by permission of Harvard Business School Press. From *The Balanced Scorecard* by R. Kaplan and D. Norton. Boston, MA 1996. Copyright © 1996 by the Harvard Business School Publishing Corporation; all rights reserved.

Tables

Table on page 187 adapted from *A Survey of Management Accounting Practices in UK Manufacturing Companies*, Chartered Association of Certified Accountants (Drury, C., Braund, S., Osborne, P. and Tayles, M. 1993) ACCA; Table on page 238 from *A Survey of Management Accounting Practices in UK Manufacturing Companies*, Chartered Association of Certified Accountants (Drury, C., Braund, S., Osborne, P. and Tayles, M. 1993) p. 39, Table 5.7, ACCA; Table on page 247 from *A Survey of Management Accounting Practices in UK Manufacturing Companies*, Chartered Association of Certified Accountants (Drury, C., Braund, S., Osborne, P. and Tayles, M. 1993) p. 30, Table 4.4, ACCA; Table on page 384 from *Divisional Performance Measurement: An Examination of Potential Factors*, August, CIMA Research Report (Drury, C. and El-Shishini, E. 2005) p. 30, this table has been reproduced from a CIMA Research Report with kind permission from CIMA; Table on page 395 adapted from *A Survey of Management Accounting Practices in UK Manufacturing Companies*, Chartered Association of Certified Accountants (Drury, C., Braund, S., Osborne, P. and Tayles, M. 1993) p. 66, Table 9.2, ACCA.

Text

Extract on page 7 from easyJet mission statement, www.easyjet.com, with permission from easyJet; Extract on page 7 from Starbucks mission statement, http://starbucks.co.uk/en-GB/_About+Starbucks/Mission+Statement.htm, with kind permission from Starbucks Coffee Company; Extract on page 12 from *Reckitt and Benckiser plc Annual Report 2007*, Reckitt and Benckiser Group PLC; Extract on page 13 from Profit without honour, *Financial Times Weekend*, 29/30 June 2002 (Kay, J.), John Kay; Exhibit 1.13 from Code of Ethics, www.shell.com/codeofethics, Royal Dutch Shell plc; Extract on page 150 from www.renault.com, Renault Group; Extract on page 190 from *Babcock International Group PLC Annual Report 2008*, Babcock International Group PLC; Extract on pages 205–206 from Bunce, P. (2007) Transforming financial planning in small and medium-sized enterprises – September 2007, published in: Horváth, P. (ed.) (2007), *Erfolgstreiber für das Controlling*, Stuttgart, Schäffer-Poeschel Verlag, http://www.bbrt.org/resources/bbrt-pubs.html, Peter Bunce; Extract on page 289 from *Rolls-Royce plc Annual Report and Accounts 2007*, Copyright Rolls-Royce plc; Extract on page 307 from Tesco plc Corporate Governance Report 2008, www.tescocorporate.com, Tesco plc; Exhibit 8.14 adapted from *Eureka Mining plc – Drilling Report*, 26 July 2006, Eureka Mining plc; Extract on page 328 from www.rolls-royce.com, Copyright Rolls-Royce plc; Extract on page 338 from Tesco plc Internal Control and Risk Management 2008, www.tesco.com, Tesco plc; Extract on page 338 from *The Balanced Scorecard*, Harvard Business School Press (Kaplan, R. and Norton, D. 1996) Harvard Business School Publishing Corporation, reprinted by permission of Harvard Business School Press. From *The Balanced Scorecard* by R. Kaplan and D. Norton. Boston, MA 1996. Copyright © 1996 by the Harvard Business School Publishing Corporation; all rights reserved; Extract on page 358 from Hanson plc Annual Report and Form 20-F 2006, www.hanson.biz, Hanson Limited; Extract on page 431 from Top 10 excuses businesses use for not paying invoices, http://www.atradius.us/news/press-releases/, 13 August 2008, Atradius Trade Credit Insurance, Inc; Exhibits 11.12, 11.14 from Dash for Cash, *CFO Europe Magazine*, 8 July 2008 (Karaian, J.), www.cfo.com, © CFO Europe, London (July/August 2008).

The Financial Times

Exhibit 1.5 from Citi looks to sell German retail arm, *Financial Times* (Wilson, J. and Guerrera, F.) © The Financial Times Limited, 17 May 2008; Exhibit 5.8 from Royal following but quality issues remain, *Financial Times* (Reed, J.) © The Financial Times Limited, 3 October 2007; Exhibit 7.1 adapted from Watchdog warns on Olympic costs by Jean Eaglesham, *FT.com* © The Financial Times Limited, 20 July 2007; Exhibit 8.6 adapted from Bond seeks funds in London to mine African diamonds by Rebecca Bream, *FT.com* © The Financial Times Limited, 23 April 2007; Exhibit 8.11 from Satellites need space to earn, *FT.com* (Burt, T.) © The Financial Times Limited, 14 July 2003; Exhibit 8.13 from Easy ride, *FT.com* (Hughes, C.) © The Financial Times Limited, 26 October 2007; Exhibit 9.9 from When misuse leads to failure, *FT.com*, © The Financial Times Limited, 24 May 2006; Exhibit 9.12 from Siemens chief finds himself in a difficult balancing act, *FT.com* (Milne, R.) © The Financial Times Limited, 6 November 2006; Exhibit 10.5 from Transfer pricing abuses criticised, *FT.com* (Politi, J.) © The Financial Times Limited, 13 August 2008; Exhibit 11.4 from Wal-Mart aims for further inventory cuts, *FT.com* (Birchall, J.) © The Financial Times Limited, 19 April 2006; Exhibit 11.8 from Late payment hits small companies, *FT.com* (Chisholm, J.) © The Financial Times Limited, 29 January 2007; Exhibit 11.13 from NHS paying bills late in struggle to balance books, say suppliers, *FT.com* (Timmins, N.) © The Financial Times Limited, 13 February 2007.

In some instances we have been unable to trace the owners of copyright material, and we would appreciate any information that would enable us to do so.

1

Introduction to management accounting

INTRODUCTION

Welcome to the world of management accounting! In this introductory chapter, we examine the role of management accounting within a business. To understand the context for management accounting we begin by considering the nature and purpose of a business. Thus, we first consider what businesses seek to achieve, how they are organised and how they are managed. Having done this, we go on to explore how management accounting information can be used within a business to improve the quality of managers' decisions. We also identify the characteristics that management accounting information must possess to fulfil its role. Management accounting has undergone many changes in response to changes in the business environment and in business methods. In this chapter we shall discuss some of the more important changes that have occurred.

LEARNING OUTCOMES

When you have completed this chapter, you should be able to:

- Identify the purpose of a business and discuss the ways in which a business may be organised and managed.

- Discuss the issues to be considered when setting the financial aims and objectives of a business.

- Explain the role of management accounting within a business and describe the key qualities that management accounting information should possess.

- Explain the changes that have occurred over time in both the role of the management accountant and the type of information provided by management accounting systems.

What is the purpose of a business?

Peter Drucker, an eminent management thinker, has argued that '*The purpose of business is to create and keep a customer*' (see reference 1 at the end of the chapter). Drucker defined the purpose of a business in this way in 1967, at a time when most businesses did not adopt this strong customer focus. His view therefore represented a radical challenge to the accepted view of what businesses do. Forty years on, however, his approach has become part of the conventional wisdom. It is now widely recognised that, in order to succeed, businesses must focus on satisfying the needs of the customer.

Although the customer has always provided the main source of revenue for a business, this has often been taken for granted. In the past, too many businesses have assumed that the customer would readily accept whatever services or products were on offer. When competition was weak and customers were passive, businesses could operate under this assumption and still make a profit. However, the era of weak competition has passed. Today, customers have much greater choice and are much more assertive concerning their needs. They now demand higher quality services and goods at cheaper prices. They also require that services and goods be delivered faster with an increasing emphasis on the product being tailored to their individual needs. If a business cannot meet these needs, a competitor business often can. Thus the business mantra for the current era is '*the customer is king*'; most businesses now recognise this fact and organise themselves accordingly.

Real World 1.1 provides an illustration of how one very successful UK business recognises the supremacy of the customer.

REAL WORLD 1.1

Checking out the customers   **FT**

Tesco plc, the UK supermarket business, has been highly successful at expanding its operations and generating wealth for its owners (the shareholders). In an interview with the *Financial Times*, the business's chief executive (most senior manager) Sir Terry Leahy explained how this profitable expansion is being achieved. He explained:

> The big change for Tesco came when we stopped being a company with a marketing department, and became a marketing company. We put the customer right at the heart of the business and their requirements drove everything we did. It's not too strong to say we became obsessed with customers. Real marketing, that is, understanding people's lives and needs and responding to them with products and services, I believe lies at the heart of business success.

Later in the interview Sir Terry added:

> 'We never forget customers have a choice of stores, and if we don't satisfy them they will go elsewhere.'

Source: 'Ask the expert: Tesco's Sir Terry Leahy', *Financial Times*, 2 June 2006.

How are businesses organised?

Nearly all businesses that involve more than a few owners and/or employees are set up as limited companies. This means that the finance will come from the owners (shareholders) both in the form of a direct cash investment to buy shares (in the ownership of the business) and through the shareholders allowing past profits, which belong to them, to be reinvested in the business. Finance will also come from lenders (banks, for example), who earn interest on their loans, and from suppliers of goods and services being prepared to supply on credit, with payment occurring a month or so after the date of supply, usually on an interest-free basis.

In larger limited companies, the owners (shareholders) are not involved in the daily running of the business; instead they appoint a board of directors to manage the business on their behalf. The board is charged with three major tasks:

- setting the overall direction and strategy for the business;
- monitoring and controlling the activities of the business; and
- communicating with shareholders and others connected with the business.

Each board has a chairman, elected by the directors, who is responsible for running the board in an efficient manner. In addition, each board has a chief executive officer (CEO), or managing director, who is responsible for running the business on a day-to-day basis. Occasionally, the roles of chairman and CEO are combined, although it is usually considered to be a good idea to separate them in order to prevent a single individual having excessive power.

The board of directors represents the most senior level of management. Below this level, managers are employed, with each manager being given responsibility for a particular part of the business's operations.

Activity 1.1

Why aren't most larger businesses managed as a single unit by one manager?

Three common reasons are:

- The sheer volume of activity or number of staff employed makes it impossible for one person to manage them.
- Certain business operations may require specialised knowledge or expertise.
- Geographical remoteness of part of the business operations may make it more practical to manage each location as a separate part, or set of separate parts.

The operations of a business may be divided for management purposes in different ways. For smaller businesses offering a single product or service, separate departments are often created, with each department responsible for a particular function (such as marketing, personnel and finance). The managers of each department will then be accountable to the board of directors. In some cases, individual board members may also be departmental managers.

A typical departmental structure, organised along functional lines, is set out in Figure 1.1.

The structure set out in the figure may be adapted according to the particular needs of the business. Where, for example, a business has few employees, the personnel function may not form a separate department but may form part of another department. Where business operations are specialised, separate departments may be formed to deal with each specialist area. Example 1.1 illustrates how Figure 1.1 may be modified to meet the needs of a particular business.

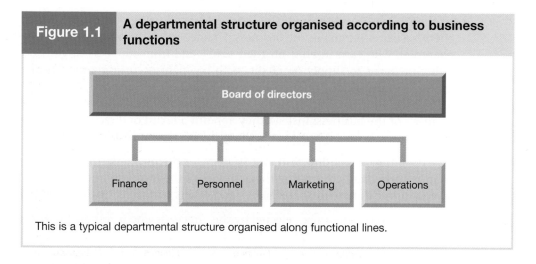

Figure 1.1   **A departmental structure organised according to business functions**

This is a typical departmental structure organised along functional lines.

Example 1.1

Supercoach Ltd owns a small fleet of coaches that it hires out with drivers for private group travel. The business employs about 50 people. It might be departmentalised as follows:

● *Marketing department*, dealing with advertising, dealing with enquiries from potential customers, maintaining good relationships with existing customers and entering into contracts with customers.
● *Routing and personnel department*, responsible for the coach drivers' routes, schedules, staff duties and rotas, and problems that arise during a particular job or contract.
● *Coach maintenance department*, looking after repair and maintenance of the coaches, buying spares, giving advice on the need to replace old or inefficient coaches.
● *Finance department*, responsible for managing the cash flows, borrowing, use of surplus funds, payment of wages and salaries, billing and collecting charges to customers, processing invoices from suppliers and paying suppliers.

For large businesses that have a diverse geographical spread and/or a wide product range, the simple departmental structure set out in Figure 1.1 will usually have to be adapted. Separate divisions are often created for each geographical area and/or major product group. Each division will be managed separately and will usually enjoy a degree of autonomy. Within each division, however, departments will often be created and organised along functional lines. Some functions providing support across the various divisions, such as personnel, may be undertaken at head office to avoid duplication. The managers of each division will be accountable to the board of directors. In some cases, individual board members may also be divisional managers. A typical divisional organisational structure is set out in Figure 1.2. Here the main basis of the structure is geographical. North division deals with production and sales in the north and so on.

Once a particular divisional structure has been established, it by no means needs to be permanent. Successful businesses are likely to be innovative and progressive and so

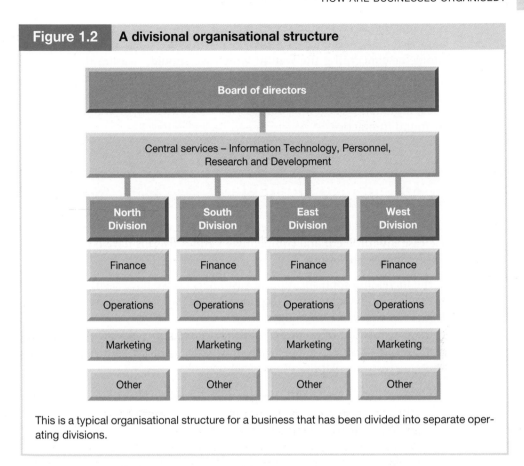

Figure 1.2 **A divisional organisational structure**

This is a typical organisational structure for a business that has been divided into separate operating divisions.

are always looking for ways to improve the way in which they operate. This may well include revising their divisional structure. Take for example the business whose structure is depicted in Figure 1.2. At a later stage, senior management may well conclude that the needs of customers and/or operational efficiency would be better served by having a structure that was based more on product types and less on geographical areas. This might lead to it reorganising into a structure with a separate division for each type of product, irrespective of where production takes place and/or customers are based.

Real World 1.2 provides an example of a reorganisation at a well-known international financial services provider.

REAL WORLD 1.2

Banking on a reorganisation   **FT**

Citigroup Inc., a financial services organisation (Citibank etc.) based in New York, recently reorganised its Asia-Pacific operation in an attempt to refocus on serving customers better. The operation is to be managed as four geographical divisions: Japan, North Asia, South Asia and Southeast Asia. The operation had previously been organised along product lines, from New York.

Asia-Pacific accounts for about 20 per cent of Citigroup's income.

Source: Tucker, S., 'Pandit shake-up shifts responsibility to regional heads', *Financial Times*, 19 August 2008.

Managing large businesses through a group of divisions can be a very effective approach. The existence of a divisional structure does, however, pose a number of problems concerning the way in which we should measure the performance of the various operating divisions. This topic will be considered in detail in Chapter 10. Both the divisional structure and departmental structure just described appear to be widely used, although it should be emphasised that other organisational structures may also be found in practice.

How are businesses managed?

Over the past two decades, the environment in which businesses operate has become increasingly turbulent and competitive. Various reasons have been identified to explain these changes, including:

● the increasing sophistication of customers (as we have seen);
● the development of a global economy where national frontiers become less important;
● rapid changes in technology;
● the deregulation of domestic markets (for example, electricity, water and gas);
● increasing pressure from owners (shareholders) for competitive economic returns; and
● the increasing volatility of financial markets.

The effect of these environmental changes has been to make the role of managers more complex and demanding. It has meant that managers have had to find new ways to manage their business. This has increasingly led to the introduction of **strategic management**.

Strategic management is designed to provide a business with a clear sense of purpose and to ensure that appropriate action is taken to achieve that purpose. The action taken should link the internal resources of the business to the external environment of competitors, suppliers, customers and so on. This should be done in such a way that any business strengths, such as having a skilled workforce, are exploited and any weaknesses, such as being short of investment finance, are not exposed. To achieve this requires the development of strategies and plans that take account of the business's strengths and weaknesses, as well as the opportunities offered and threats posed by the external environment. Access to a new, expanding market is an example of an opportunity; the decision of a major competitor to reduce prices is an example of a threat.

Real World 1.3 indicates the importance attached by senior management to strategic planning.

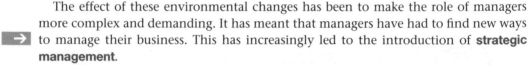

REAL WORLD 1.3

Strategy on board

A recent survey assessed what proportion of their time senior managers (boards of directors) spend on developing strategies for their businesses. McKinsey, the management consultancy organisation, conducted the survey in February 2008, and 586 directors from businesses all over the world responded.

It was found that directors spend 24 per cent of their time at board meetings developing strategies. Half of the managers surveyed said that they would prefer to spend more time on this activity than they currently do. Only one manager in six felt that too much time was spent on it.

Most of the remainder of the time at board meetings was spent on issues concerning actual performance.

Clearly senior managers take strategic planning very seriously.

Source: 'Making the board more strategic', *The McKinsey Quarterly*, March 2008.

The strategic management process can be approached in different ways. To gain an insight into how this might be done, one well-established approach, involving five steps, is now described.

1 Establish mission and objectives

The first step is to establish the mission of a business, which may be set out in the form of a **mission statement**. This normally provides a concise statement of the overall aims, or intentions, of the business. It will often emphasise a clear customer focus, as discussed earlier, and may identify the activities that the business undertakes. It may also identify the values and beliefs that are held. The mission is usually established on a 'once and for all' basis. It is relatively rare for businesses to alter their mission statements. **Real World 1.4** provides examples of mission statements.

REAL WORLD 1.4

On a mission

Mission statements often set ambitious aims for the business. Here are two examples of mission statements.

The budget airline easyJet plc has a mission

> To provide our customers with safe, good value, point-to-point air services. To effect and to offer a consistent and reliable product and fares appealing to leisure and business markets on a range of European routes. To achieve this we will develop our people and establish lasting relationships with our suppliers.

The coffee business Starbucks states its mission as:

> Establish Starbucks as the premier purveyor of the finest coffee in the world while maintaining our uncompromising principles while we grow.

Starbucks went on to say:

> The Starbucks mission is more than just a piece of paper – it's the philosophy that guides how we do business every day.

Sources: www.easyjet.com; www.starbucks.co.uk.

Businesses often publish their mission statements on their websites and, less frequently, in their annual reports.

Having established the broad aims, objectives must then be developed to translate these aims into specific commitments. The objectives should provide clear targets, or outcomes, which are both challenging and achievable and which can provide a basis for assessing actual performance. Although quantifiable objectives provide the clearest targets, some areas of performance, such as employee satisfaction, may only be capable of partial quantification, and other areas, such as business ethics, may be impossible to quantify.

In practice, the objectives set by a business are likely to range across all key areas and may include a commitment to achieve:

● a specified percentage share of the market in which the business competes;
● an increase in customer satisfaction;
● an increase in employee satisfaction;
● improvements in internal business processes;
● high standards of ethical behaviour in business dealings;
● a specified percentage operating profit margin (operating profit as a percentage of sales revenue);
● a specified percentage return on capital employed.

Businesses tend not to make their statement of objectives public, often because they do not wish to make their intentions clear to their competitors.

2 Undertake a position analysis

→ With the **position analysis**, the business is seeking to establish how it is placed relative to its environment (customers, competitors, suppliers, technology, the economy, political climate and so on) given the business's mission and objectives. This is often approached within the framework of an analysis of the business's strengths, weak-
→ nesses, opportunities and threats (a **SWOT analysis**). A SWOT analysis involves identifying the business's strengths and weaknesses as well as the opportunities provided and threats posed by the world outside the business. Strengths and weaknesses are internal factors that are attributes of the business itself, whereas opportunities and threats are factors expected to be present in the environment in which the business operates.

Activity 1.2

Ryanair plc is a highly successful 'no-frills' airline. Can you suggest some factors that could be strengths, weaknesses, opportunities and threats for this business? Try to think of two for each of these (eight in all).

Strengths could include such things as:

● a strong, well-recognised brand name
● a modern fleet of aircraft requiring less maintenance
● reliable customer service concerning punctuality and baggage loss
● internet booking facility used by virtually all passengers, which reduces administration costs.

Weaknesses might include:

● limited range of destinations
● use of secondary airports situated some distance from city centres
● poor facilities at secondary airports.

Opportunities might include:

- new destinations becoming available, particularly in eastern Europe
- increasing acceptance of 'no-frills' air travel among business travellers
- the development of new fuel-efficient aircraft.

Threats to the business might come from:

- increased competition – either new low-fare competitors entering the market or traditional airlines reducing fares to compete
- fuel price rises
- increasing congestion at airports, making it more difficult to turn aircraft around quickly
- changes in the regulatory environment (for example, changes in EU laws concerning the maximum monthly flying hours for a pilot) making it harder to operate
- vulnerability to a downturn in economic conditions.

You may have thought of others.

The SWOT framework is not the only possible approach to undertaking a position analysis, but it seems to be a very popular one.

3 Identify and assess the strategic options

This involves attempting to identify possible courses of action that will enable the business to reach its objectives through using its strengths to exploit opportunities, at the same time avoiding exposing its weaknesses to threats. The strengths, weaknesses, opportunities and threats are, of course, those identified by the SWOT analysis. Having identified the possible options, each will then be assessed according to agreed criteria.

4 Select strategic options and formulate plans

The business will select what appears to be the best of the courses of action or strategies (identified in step 3) available. When making a selection, the implications of the choice for the mission and objectives should be considered as, at times, they might require some adjustment. The strategies selected will provide the general way forward but a plan will be required to specify the particular actions that must be taken. This overall plan will normally be broken down into a series of plans, one for each element of the business.

Sometimes a business may select a strategic option that results in the sale of a part, or all, of its operations. **Real World 1.5** provides an example of this. Here, Citigroup, the business that we met in Real World 1.2, sold a part of its business that it felt lacked 'strategic fit'.

REAL WORLD 1.5

Business is not a hobby for Citigroup

FT

Citigroup is looking to sell its German retail banking operations as part of the radical steps being taken by Vikram Pandit, chief executive, to shrink his bank's balance sheet in the wake of the credit crisis.

The business is one of the most successful consumer banking operations in Germany and analysts said a sale could raise €4–5 billion ($6.2–7.8 billion).

A sale, which would attract interest from domestic rivals as well as international banks keen for a foothold in the country, would make Citi the first bank to withdraw from an important territory in the aftermath of the global financial crisis.

The German operation is among Citi assets deemed non-core by Mr Pandit, who said this month he intended to cut the bank's assets by up to $500 billion in an attempt to increase returns.

'The process has been initiated,' said a person familiar with the plan.

Citi has been in Germany since 1926 but Mr Pandit has repeatedly said the bank cannot afford 'hobbies' – businesses that lack critical mass or a strategic fit with the rest of the conglomerate.

The sale would be one of the largest disposals to date. A bank spokesman in Germany said: 'We are exploring a variety of options for our retail banking business in Germany . . . No decision has been made.'

Citi also runs Frankfurt-based corporate and investment banking operations, which are not being considered for disposal.

The bank has about 3.25m retail customers in Germany and claims a leading position in the consumer credit market. It made net income in 2007 of €365 million.

Source: 'Citi looks to sell German retail arm', *Financial Times* (Wilson, J. and Guerrera, F.), © The Financial Times Limited, 17 May 2008.

5 Perform, review and control

Here the business implements the plans derived in step 4. The actual outcome will be monitored and compared with the plans to see whether things are progressing satisfactorily. Steps should be taken to exercise control where actual performance does not appear to be matching plans.

Figure 1.3 shows the strategic management framework in diagrammatic form. This framework will be considered further as the book develops. We shall see how the business's mission links, through objectives and long-term plans, to detailed budgets, in Chapters 6 and 7.

Real World 1.6 provides an indication of the extent that strategic planning is carried out in practice.

REAL WORLD 1.6

Strategic planning at the top of the list

A recent survey was carried out of 960 large businesses throughout the world. About 20 per cent were in North America, 30 per cent in Europe, 30 per cent in Asia-Pacific and 10 per cent in Latin America, with the remaining 10 per cent elsewhere. The survey found that strategic planning is used by 79 per cent of the businesses. This made strategic planning the single most popular management tool. Strategic planning had occupied first place for the previous eight years and its pre-eminence was similar throughout the world.

Source: Rigby, D. and Bilodeau, B., *The Bain 2005 Management Tool Study*, Bain and Company, 2005.

| **Figure 1.3** | **The strategic management framework** |

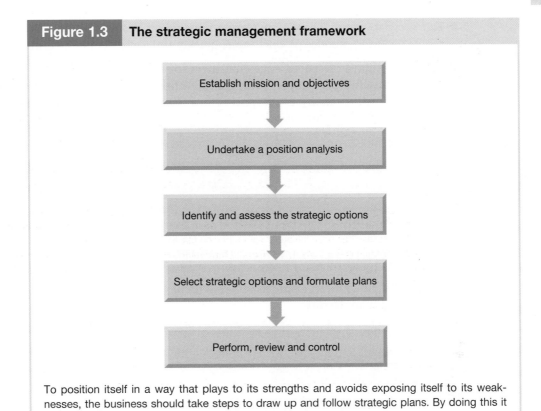

To position itself in a way that plays to its strengths and avoids exposing itself to its weaknesses, the business should take steps to draw up and follow strategic plans. By doing this it should most effectively work towards its objectives and mission.

The changing business landscape

Factors such as increased global competition and advances in technology, which were mentioned earlier, have had a tremendous impact on the types of businesses that survive and prosper, as well as the business structures and processes adopted. Important changes that have occurred in the UK in recent years include:

- *The growth of the service sector.* This includes businesses such as financial services, communications, tourism, transportation, consultancy, leisure and so on. This growth of the service sector has been matched by the decline of the manufacturing sector.
- *The emergence of new industries.* This includes science-based industries such as genetic engineering and biotechnology.
- *The growth of e-commerce.* Consumers are increasingly drawn to buying on-line a wide range of goods including groceries, books, CDs and computers. Businesses also use e-commerce to order supplies, monitor deliveries and distribute products.
- *Automated manufacturing.* Many manufacturing processes are now fully automated and computers are used to control the production process.
- *Lean manufacturing.* This involves a systematic attempt to identify and eliminate waste in the production process through storing excess materials, excess production, delays, defects and so on.
- *Greater product innovation.* There is much greater pressure to produce new, innovative products. The effect has been to increase the range of products available and to shorten the life cycles of many products.

● *Faster response times.* There is increasing pressure on businesses to develop products more quickly, to produce products more quickly and to deliver products more quickly.

These changes have presented huge challenges for the management accountant. New techniques have been developed and existing techniques adapted to ensure that management accounting retains its relevance. These issues will be considered in more detail as we progress through the book.

Setting financial aims and objectives

Enhancing the owners' wealth

Businesses are created by their owners (shareholders) with the intention of enhancing those owners' wealth.

Real World 1.7 gives an example of a statement of objectives by a major UK household products manufacturer.

REAL WORLD 1.7

Cleaning up for the shareholders

Reckitt Benckiser Group plc makes a number of cleaning and household products including Vanish, Dettol, Air Wick and Nurofen. In its 2007 annual report the business stated its primary objective as follows:

> Reckitt Benckiser's vision is to deliver better consumer solutions in household cleaning and health and personal care for the ultimate purpose of creating shareholder value.

Source: Reckitt and Benckiser Group plc Annual Report 2007.

Within a market economy there are strong competitive forces at work to ensure that failure to enhance shareholder wealth will not be tolerated for long. Competition for the funds provided by shareholders and competition for managers' jobs will normally mean that shareholders' interests will prevail. If the managers do not provide the expected increase in shareholder wealth, the shareholders have the power to replace the existing management team with a new team that is more responsive to shareholders' needs. Does this mean that the needs of other groups associated with the business (employees, customers, suppliers, the community and so on) are not really important? The answer to this question is certainly no, if the business wishes to survive and prosper over the longer term. Satisfying the needs of other groups will normally be consistent with increasing the wealth of the owners over the longer term. Dissatisfied customers will take their business to another supplier and this will lead to a loss of wealth for the shareholders. A dissatisfied workforce, for example, may result in low productivity, strikes and so forth, which will in turn have an adverse effect on shareholders' wealth. Similarly, a business that upsets the local community by polluting the environment may attract bad publicity, resulting in a loss of customers, and heavy fines.

Real World 1.8 provides an example of how two businesses responded to potentially damaging allegations.

REAL WORLD 1.8

The price of clothes

FT

US clothing and sportswear manufacturers Gap and Nike have much of their clothes produced in Asia where labour tends to be cheap. However, some of the contractors that produce clothes on behalf of the two companies have been accused of unacceptable practices.

Campaigners visited the factories and came up with damaging allegations. The factories were employing minors, they said, and managers were harassing female employees. Nike and Gap reacted by allowing independent inspectors into the factories. They promised to ensure their contractors obeyed minimum standards of employment. Earlier this year, Nike took the extraordinary step of publishing the names and addresses of all its contractors' factories on the internet. The company said it could not be sure all the abuse had stopped. It said that if campaigners visited its contractors' factories and found examples of continued malpractice, it would take action.

Nike and Gap said the approach made business sense. They needed society's approval if they were to prosper. Nike said it was concerned about the reaction of potential US recruits to the campaigners' allegations. They would not want to work for a company that was constantly in the news because of the allegedly cruel treatment of those who made its products.

Source: Michael Skapinker, 'Fair shares?', ft.com, 11 June 2005.

It is important to recognise that generating wealth for the owners is not the same as seeking to maximise the current year's profit. Wealth creation is a longer-term concept, which relates not only to this year's profit but to that of future years as well. In the short term, corners can be cut and risks taken that improve current profit at the expense of future profit.

Real World 1.9 provides an example of a well-known retailer that suffered from not paying sufficient attention to these other groups. It also raises questions about businesses in other industries.

REAL WORLD 1.9

Short-term gains, long-term problems

FT

In recent years, many businesses have been criticised for failing to consider the long-term implications of their policies on the wealth of the owners. John Kay argues that some businesses have achieved growth and short-term increases in wealth by sacrificing their longer-term prosperity. He points out that

The business of Marks and Spencer, the retailer, was unparalleled in reputation but mature. To achieve earnings growth consistent with a glamour rating the company squeezed suppliers, gave less value for money, spent less on stores. In 1998, it achieved the highest [profit] margin in sales in the history of the business. It had also compromised its position to the point where sales and profits plummeted.

Banks and insurance companies have taken staff out of branches and retrained those that remain as sales people. The pharmaceuticals industry has taken advantage of mergers to consolidate its research and development facilities. Energy companies have cut back on exploration.

We know that these actions increased corporate earnings. We do not know what effect they have on the long-run strength of the business – and this is the key point – do the companies themselves know? Some rationalisations will genuinely lead to more productive businesses. Other companies will suffer the fate of Marks and Spencer.

Source: John Kay, 'Profit without honour', *Financial Times Weekend*, 29/30 June 2002.

Though enhancing the wealth of the owners may not be a perfect description of what businesses seek to achieve, it is certainly something that businesses cannot ignore for the reasons mentioned. For the remainder of this book enhancement/maximisation of shareholders' (owners') wealth is treated as the key financial objective against which decisions will be assessed. There will usually be other non-financial/non-economic factors that will also tend to bear on decisions. The final decision may well involve some compromise.

Balancing risk and return

All decision making involves the future. We can only make decisions about the future; no matter how much we may regret it, we cannot alter the past. Business decision making is no exception to this general rule. There is only one thing certain about the future, which is that we cannot be sure what is going to happen. Sometimes we may be able to predict with confidence that what actually occurs will be one of a limited range of possibilities. We may even feel able to ascribe statistical probabilities to the likelihood of occurrence of each possible outcome, but we can never be completely certain of the future. Risk is therefore an important factor in all financial decision making, and one that must be considered explicitly in all cases.

As in other aspects of life, risk and return tend to be related. Evidence shows that returns relate to risk in something like the way shown in Figure 1.4.

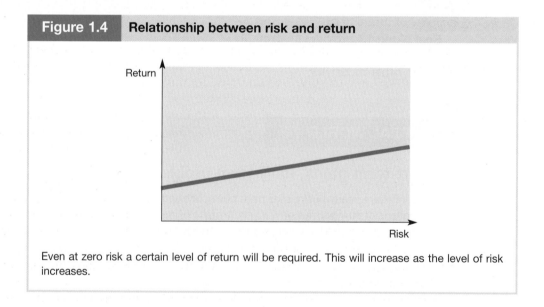

| Figure 1.4 | Relationship between risk and return |

Even at zero risk a certain level of return will be required. This will increase as the level of risk increases.

This relationship between risk and return has important implications for setting financial objectives for a business. The owners (shareholders) will require a minimum return to induce them to invest at all, but will require an additional return to compensate for taking risks; the higher the risk, the higher the required return. Managers must be aware of this and must strike the appropriate balance between risk and return when setting objectives and pursuing particular courses of action.

Real World 1.10 describes how some businesses have been making higher-risk investments in pursuit of higher returns.

REAL WORLD 1.10

Appetite for risk drives businesses   **FT**

Over the last few years, companies from the US and western Europe, joined increasingly by competitors from China and India, have looked to new markets abroad both to source and sell their products.

Driven by intensifying competition at home, companies have been drawn into direct investment in markets that not long ago were considered beyond the pale. But in the drive to increase returns, they have also been forced to accept higher risks.

Over time, the balance between risk and reward changes. For example, companies flooded into Russia early in the decade. But recently returns have fallen, largely due to booming raw materials prices. Meanwhile the apparent risk of investing in Russia has grown significantly.

As the risk–reward calculation has changed in Russia, companies have looked to other countries such as Libya and Vietnam where the rewards may be substantial, and the threats, though high, may be more manageable.

Source: Adapted from Stephen Fidler, 'Appetite for risk drives industry', ft.com, 27 June 2007.

What is management accounting?

Having considered what businesses are and how they are organised and managed, we can now turn our attention to the role of **management accounting**. A useful starting point for our discussion is to acknowledge the general role of accounting, which is to help people make informed business decisions. All forms of accounting, including management accounting, are concerned with collecting and analysing financial information and then communicating this information to those making decisions. This decision-making perspective of accounting provides the theme for the book and shapes the way that we deal with each topic.

For accounting information to be useful for decision making, the accountant must be clear about *for whom* the information is being prepared and *for what purpose* it will be used. In practice there are various groups of people (known as 'user groups') with an interest in a particular organisation, in the sense of needing to make decisions about that organisation. For the typical private sector business, the most important of these groups are shown in Figure 1.5. Each of these groups will have different needs for accounting information.

This book is concerned with providing accounting information for only one of the groups identified – the managers. This, however, is a particularly important user group. Managers are responsible for running the business, and their decisions and actions play an important role in determining its success. Planning for the future and exercising day-to-day control over a business involves a wide range of decisions being made. For example, managers may need information to help them decide whether to:

- develop new products or services (as with a computer manufacturer developing a new range of computers);
- increase or decrease the price or quantity of existing products or services (as with a telecommunications business changing its mobile phone call and text charges);

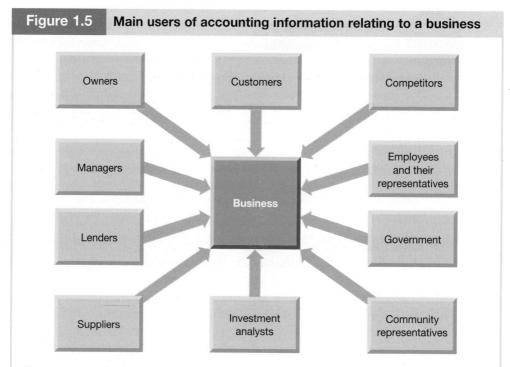

Figure 1.5 **Main users of accounting information relating to a business**

There are several user groups with an interest in the accounting information relating to a business. The majority of these are outside the business but, nevertheless, they have a stake in the business. The above is not meant to be an exhaustive list of potential users; however, the groups identified are normally the most important.

- borrow money to help finance the business (as with a supermarket wishing to increase the number of stores it owns);
- increase or decrease the operating capacity of the business (as with a beef farming business reviewing the size of its herd);
- change the methods of purchasing, production or distribution (as with a clothes retailer switching from UK to overseas suppliers).

As management decisions are broad in scope, the accounting information provided to managers must also be wide-ranging. Accounting information should help in identifying and assessing the financial consequences of decisions such as those listed above. In later chapters, we shall consider each of the types of decisions in the list and see how their financial consequences can be assessed.

How useful is management accounting information?

There are arguments and convincing evidence that management accounting information is regarded by managers as being useful to them. There have been numerous research surveys that have asked managers to rank the importance of management accounting information, in relation to other sources of information, for decision-making purposes. Generally speaking, these studies have found that managers rank accounting information very highly. Broadly, there is no legal compulsion for businesses to produce management accounting information, yet virtually all businesses do so. Presumably, the cost of producing this information is justified on the grounds that managers believe it to be useful to them. Such arguments and evidence, however, leave unanswered the question as to whether the information produced actually is being used for decision-making purposes: that is, does the information affect managers' behaviour?

It is impossible to measure just how useful management accounting information is to managers. We should remember that it will usually represent only one input to a particular decision, and the precise weight attached to that information by the manager and the benefits which flow as a result cannot be accurately assessed. We shall see below, however, that it is at least possible to identify the kinds of qualities that accounting information must possess in order to be useful. Where these qualities are lacking, the usefulness of the information will be diminished.

Providing a service

One way of viewing management accounting is as a form of service. Management accountants provide economic information to their 'clients', the managers. The quality of the service provided would be determined by the extent to which the managers' information needs have been met. It is generally accepted that, to be useful, management accounting information should possess certain key qualities, or characteristics. These are:

- **Relevance.** Management accounting information must have the ability to influence decisions. Unless this characteristic is present, there is really no point in producing the information. This means that the information should be targeted at the requirements of the individual manager for whom it is being provided. Reports that are general in nature are likely to be unhelpful to most managers. To be able to influence a decision, the information must be available when the decision needs to be made. To be relevant, therefore, information must be timely.

- **Reliability.** Management accounting should be free from significant errors or bias. It should be capable of being relied upon by managers to represent what it is supposed to represent. Though both relevance and reliability are very important, the problem that we often face in accounting is that information that is highly relevant may not be very reliable, and that which is reliable may not be very relevant.

Activity 1.3

To illustrate this last point, let us assume that a manager has to sell a custom-built machine owned by the business and has recently received a bid for it. This machine is very unusual and there is no ready market for it.

What information would be relevant to the manager when deciding whether to accept the bid? How reliable would that information be?

The manager would probably like to know the current market value of the machine before deciding whether or not to accept the bid. The current market value would be highly relevant to the final decision, but it might not be very reliable because the machine is unique and there is likely to be little information concerning market values.

Where a choice has to be made between providing information that has either more relevance or more reliability, the maximisation of relevance tends to be the guiding rule.

➔ ● **Comparability**. This quality will enable managers to identify changes in the business over time (for example, the trend in sales revenue over the past five years). It will also help them to evaluate the performance of the business in relation to other similar businesses. Comparability is achieved by treating items that are basically the same in the same manner for management accounting purposes. Comparability tends also to be enhanced by making clear the policies that have been adopted in measuring and presenting the information.

➔ ● **Understandability**. Management accounting reports should be expressed as clearly as possible and should be understood by those managers at whom the information is aimed.

But . . . is it material?

The qualities, or characteristics, that have just been described will help us to decide whether management accounting information is potentially useful. If a particular piece of information has these qualities then it may be useful. However, in making a final decision, we also have to consider whether the information is material, or significant. This means that we should ask whether its omission or misrepresentation in the management accounting reports would really alter the decisions that managers make. Thus, in addition to possessing the characteristics mentioned above, management account-➔ ing information must also achieve a threshold of **materiality**. If the information is not regarded as material, it should not be included within the reports as it will merely clutter them up and, perhaps, interfere with the managers' ability to interpret the financial results. The type of information and amounts involved will normally determine whether it is material.

Weighing up the costs and benefits

Having read the previous sections you may feel that, when considering a piece of management accounting information, provided the four main qualities identified are present and it is material it should be gathered and made available to managers. Unfortunately, there is one more hurdle to jump. Something may still exclude a piece of management accounting information from the reports even when it is considered to be useful. Consider Activity 1.4.

Activity 1.4

Suppose an item of information is capable of being provided. It is relevant to a particular decision; it is also reliable and comparable; it can be understood by the manager concerned and is material.

Can you think of a reason why, in practice, you might choose not to produce the information?

The reason that you may decide not to produce, or discover, the information is that you judge the cost of doing so to be greater than the potential benefit of having the information. This cost–benefit issue will limit the extent to which management accounting information is provided.

In theory, a particular item of management accounting information should only be produced if the costs of providing it are less than the benefits, or value, to be derived from its use. Figure 1.6 shows the relationship between the costs and value of providing additional management accounting information.

| Figure 1.6 | Relationship between cost and the value of providing additional management accounting information |

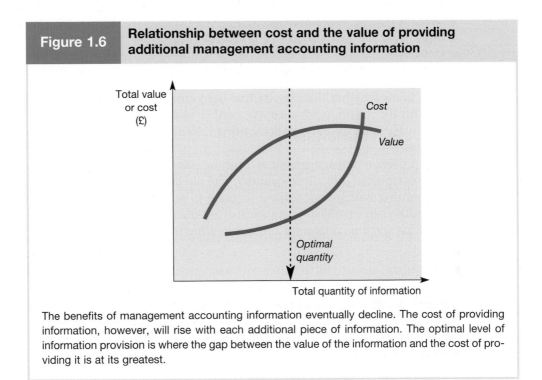

The benefits of management accounting information eventually decline. The cost of providing information, however, will rise with each additional piece of information. The optimal level of information provision is where the gap between the value of the information and the cost of providing it is at its greatest.

The figure shows how the total value of information received by the decision maker eventually begins to decline. This is, perhaps, because additional information becomes less relevant, or because of the problems that a decision maker may have in processing the sheer quantity of information provided. The total cost of providing the information, however, will increase with each additional piece of information. The broken line indicates the point at which the gap between the value of information and the cost of providing that information is at its greatest. This represents the optimal amount of information that can be provided. Beyond this optimal level, each additional piece of information will cost more than the value of having it. This theoretical model, however, poses a number of problems in practice, as discussed below.

To illustrate the practical problems of establishing the value of information, suppose that we wish to have a car repaired at a local garage. We know that the nearest garage would charge £250 but believe that other local garages may offer the same service for a lower price. The only ways of finding out the prices at other garages are either to telephone or visit them. Both, however, cost money and may involve some of our time. Is it worth the cost of finding out the price of the car repair at the various local garages? The answer, as we have seen, is that if the cost of discovering the price is less than the potential benefit, it is worth having that information.

To identify the various prices for the car repair, there are various points to be considered, including:

- How many garages shall we telephone or visit?
- What is the cost of each telephone call or visit?

● How long will it take to make all the telephone calls or visits?
● How much do we value our time?

The economic benefit of having the information on the price of the car repair is probably even harder to assess, and the following points need to be considered:

● What is the cheapest price that we might be quoted for the car repair?
● How likely is it that we shall be quoted prices cheaper than £250?

As we can imagine, the answers to these questions may be far from clear.

Of course, were we to contact all of the garages and find out all of the prices, we should know whether the exercise had been cost-effective. Unfortunately we cannot know this for certain in advance. We need to make a judgement.

When assessing the value of accounting information we are confronted with similar problems.

The provision of management accounting information can be very costly; however, the costs are often difficult to quantify. The direct, out-of-pocket costs such as salaries of accounting staff are not really a problem to put a price on, but these are only part of the total costs involved. There are also less direct costs such as the costs of the manager's time spent on analysing and interpreting the information contained in reports.

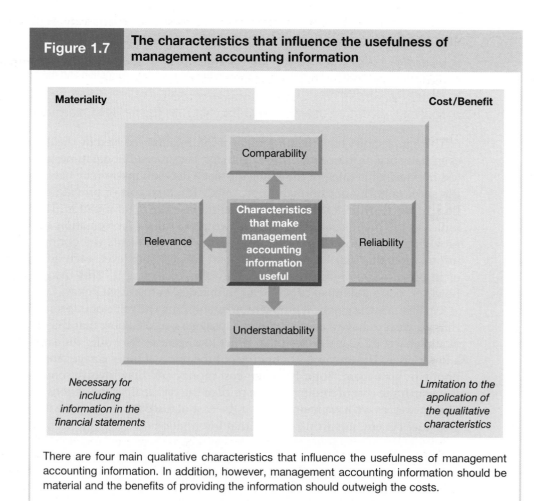

Figure 1.7 **The characteristics that influence the usefulness of management accounting information**

There are four main qualitative characteristics that influence the usefulness of management accounting information. In addition, however, management accounting information should be material and the benefits of providing the information should outweigh the costs.

The economic benefit of having management accounting information is even harder to assess. It is possible to apply some 'science' to the problem of weighing the costs and benefits, but a lot of subjective judgement is likely to be involved. Whilst no one would seriously advocate that the typical business should produce no management accounting information, at the same time, no one would advocate that every item of information that could be seen as possessing one or more of the key characteristics should be produced, irrespective of the cost of producing it.

The characteristics that influence the usefulness of management accounting information and which have been discussed in this section and the preceding section are set out in Figure 1.7.

Management accounting as an information system

Management accounting is a part of the business's total information system. Managers have to make decisions concerning the allocation of scarce economic resources. To try to ensure that these resources are allocated in an efficient manner, managers require economic information on which to base their decisions. It is the role of the management accounting system to provide that information and this will involve information gathering and communication.

The **management accounting information system** has certain features that are common to all information systems within a business. These are:

- identifying and capturing relevant information (in this case economic information);
- recording the information collected in a systematic manner;
- analysing and interpreting the information collected;
- reporting the information in a manner that suits the needs of individual managers.

The relationship between these features is set out in Figure 1.8.

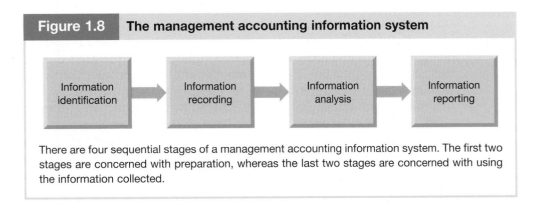

Figure 1.8	The management accounting information system

There are four sequential stages of a management accounting information system. The first two stages are concerned with preparation, whereas the last two stages are concerned with using the information collected.

Given the decision-making emphasis of this book, we shall be concerned primarily with the final two elements of the process – the analysis and reporting of management accounting information. We shall consider the way in which information is used by, and is useful to, managers rather than the way in which it is identified and recorded.

It's just a phase . . .

Though management accounting has always been concerned with helping managers to manage, the information provided has undergone profound changes over the years. This has been in response to changes in both the business environment and in business methods. The development of management accounting is generally accepted to have had four distinct phases.

Phase 1

Until 1950, or thereabouts, businesses enjoyed a fairly benign economic environment. Competition was weak and, as products could easily be sold, there was no pressing need for product innovation. The main focus of management attention was on the internal processes of the business. In particular, there was a concern for determining the cost of goods and services produced and for exercising financial control over the relatively simple production processes that existed during that period. In this early phase, management accounting information was not a major influence on decision making. Although cost and budget information was produced, it was not widely supplied to managers at all levels of seniority.

Phase 2

During the 1950s and 1960s management accounting information remained inwardly focused; however, the emphasis shifted towards producing information for short-term planning and control purposes. Management accounting came to be seen as an important part of the system of management control and of particular value in controlling the production and other internal processes of the business. The controls developed, however, were largely reactive in nature. Problems were often identified as a result of actual performance deviating from planned performance, and only then would corrective action be taken.

Phase 3

During the 1970s and early 1980s the world experienced considerable upheaval as a result of oil price rises and economic recession. This was also a period of rapid technological change and increased competition. These factors conspired to produce new techniques of production, such as robotics and computer-aided design. These new techniques led to a greater concern for controlling costs, particularly through waste reduction. Waste arising from delays, defects, excess production and so on was identified as a non-value-added activity – that is, an activity that increases costs, but does not generate additional revenue. Various techniques were developed to reduce or eliminate waste. To compete effectively, managers and employees were given greater freedom to make decisions and this in turn has led to the need for management accounting information to be made more widely available. Advances in computing, such as the personal computer, changed the nature, amount and availability of management accounting information. Increasing the volume and availability of information to managers meant that greater attention had to be paid to the design of management accounting information systems.

Phase 4

During the 1990s and 2000s advances in manufacturing technology and in information technology, such as the World Wide Web, continued unabated. This further increased the level of competition which, in turn, led to a further shift in emphasis. Increased competition provoked a concern for the more effective use of resources, with particular emphasis on creating value for shareholders by understanding customer needs (see reference 2 at the end of the chapter). This change resulted in management accounting information becoming more outwardly focused. The attitudes and behaviour of customers have become the object of much information gathering. Increasingly, successful businesses are those that are able to secure and maintain competitive advantage over their rivals through a greater understanding of customer needs. Thus, information that provides details of customers and the market has become vitally important. Such information might include customers' evaluation of services provided (perhaps through the use of opinion surveys) and data on the share of the market enjoyed by the particular business.

What information do managers need?

We have seen that management accounting can be regarded as a form of service where managers are the 'clients'. This raises the question, however, as to what kind of information these 'clients' require. It is possible to identify four broad areas of decision making where management accounting information is required.

- *Developing objectives and plans.* Managers are responsible for establishing the mission and objectives of the business and then developing strategies and plans to achieve these objectives. Management accounting information can help in gathering information that will be useful in developing appropriate objectives and strategies. It can also generate financial plans that set out the likely outcomes from adopting particular strategies. Managers can then use these financial plans to evaluate each strategy and use this as a basis for deciding between the various strategies on offer.
- *Performance evaluation and control.* Management accounting information can help in reviewing the performance of the business against agreed criteria. We shall see below that non-financial indicators are increasingly used to evaluate performance, along with financial indicators. Controls need to be in place to ensure that actual performance conforms to planned performance. Actual outcomes will, therefore, be compared with plans to see whether the performance is better or worse than expected. Where there is a significant difference, some investigation should be carried out and corrective action taken where necessary.
- *Allocating resources.* Resources available to a business are limited and it is the responsibility of managers to try to ensure that they are used in an efficient and effective manner. Decisions concerning such matters as the optimum level of output, the optimum mix of products and the appropriate type of investment in new equipment will all require management accounting information.
- *Determining costs and benefits.* Many management decisions require knowledge of the costs and benefits of pursuing a particular course of action such as providing a service, producing a new product or closing down a department. The decision will involve weighing the costs against the benefits. The management accountant can help managers by providing details of particular costs and benefits. In some cases, costs and benefits may be extremely difficult to quantify; however, some approximation is usually better than nothing at all.

These areas of management decision making are set out in Figure 1.9.

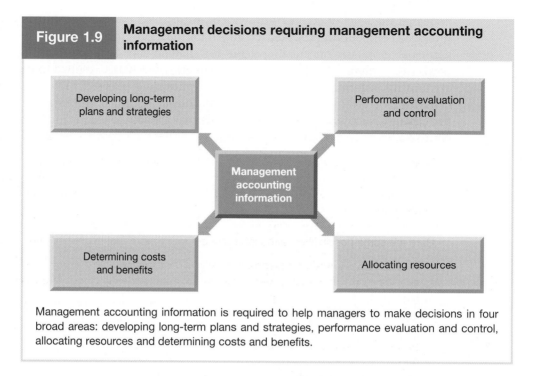

Figure 1.9 **Management decisions requiring management accounting information**

Management accounting information is required to help managers to make decisions in four broad areas: developing long-term plans and strategies, performance evaluation and control, allocating resources and determining costs and benefits.

Reporting non-financial information

Adopting a more strategic and customer-focused approach to running a business has highlighted the fact that many factors, which are often critical to success, cannot be measured in purely financial terms. Many businesses now seek to develop **key performance indicators (KPIs)**. These include the traditional financial measures, such as return on capital employed. KPIs now, however, usually include a significant proportion of non-financial indicators to help assess the prospects of long-term success. To aid decision making, the management accountant has increasingly shouldered responsibility for reporting non-financial measures regarding quality, product innovation, product cycle times, delivery times and so on.

Activity 1.5

It can be argued that non-financial measures, such as those mentioned above, do not, strictly speaking, fall within the scope of accounting information and, therefore, could (or should) be provided by others. What do you think?

It is true that others could collect this kind of information. However, management accountants are major information providers to managers and usually see it as their role to provide a broad range of information for decision making. The boundaries of accounting are not fixed and it is possible to argue that management accountants should collect this kind of information as it is often linked inextricably to financial outcomes.

Activity 1.6 considers the kind of information that may be expressed in non-financial terms and which the management accountant may provide for an airline business.

Activity 1.6

Imagine that you are the chief executive of the 'no-frills' airline Ryanair plc.

What kinds of non-financial information (that is, information not containing monetary values) may be relevant to help you evaluate the performance of the business for a particular period? Try to think of at least six.

Here are some possibilities, although there are many more that might have been chosen:

- volume of passengers transported to various destinations
- average load factor (that is, percentage of total passenger seats occupied) per trip
- market share of air passenger travel
- number of new routes established by Ryanair
- percentage of total passenger volume generated by these new routes
- aircraft turnaround times at airports
- punctuality of flights
- levels of aircraft utilisation
- number of flight cancellations
- percentage of baggage losses
- levels of customer satisfaction
- levels of employee satisfaction
- percentage of bookings made over the internet
- maintenance hours per aircraft.

In Chapter 10 we shall look at some of the financial and non-financial KPIs that are used in practice.

Influencing managers' behaviour

Management accounting information is intended to have an effect on the behaviour of those working in the business. The reason for providing the information is to improve the quality of the decisions. This should lead to actions that better contribute to the fulfilment of the business objectives. In some cases, however, the behaviour change caused by management accounting is not beneficial. One possible effect is that managers and employees will concentrate their attention and efforts on the aspects of the business that are being measured and will give much less attention to the items that are not. It is said that 'the things that count are the things that get counted'. This rather narrow view, however, can have undesirable consequences for the business, which can often arise where a particular measure is being used, or is perceived as being used, as a basis for evaluating performance. This is illustrated in Activity 1.7.

Activity 1.7

A departmental manager has been allocated an amount of money to spend on staff training. How might the manager's focus on 'the things that get counted' result in undesirable consequences? (Hint: Real World 1.9 may give you some ideas for this.)

To demonstrate cost-consciousness, the manager may underspend during the period by cutting back on staff training and development. Though the effect on expenditure incurred may be favourable, the effect on staff morale and longer-term profitability may be extremely unfavourable for the business. These unfavourable effects may go unrecognised, at least in the short term, where the expenditure limit is the focus of attention.

Attempts may be made to manipulate a particular measure where it is seen as important. For example, a manager may continue to use old, fully depreciated pieces of equipment to keep depreciation charges low and, therefore, boost profits. This may be done despite knowledge that the purchase of new equipment would produce higher quality products and help to increase sales revenue over the longer term. Attempts at manipulation are often related to managers' rewards. For example, profit-related bonuses may provide the incentive to manipulate reported profits in the way described.

In some cases, the particular targets against which performance is measured are the objects of manipulation. For example, a sales manager may provide a deliberately low forecast of the size of the potential market for the next period if he or she believes that this forecast will form the basis of future sales targets. This may be done either to increase rewards (for example, where bonuses are awarded for exceeding sales targets) or to ensure that future sales targets can be achieved with relatively little effort.

The management accountant must be aware of the impact of accounting measures of performance on human behaviour. When designing accounting measures, it is important to try to ensure that all key aspects of performance are taken into account, even though certain aspects may be difficult to measure. When operating an accounting measurement system, it is important to be alert to behaviour aimed at manipulating particular measures rather than achieving the goals to which they relate.

Reaping the benefits of IT

The impact of information technology (IT) on the development of management accounting is difficult to overstate. The ability of computers to process large amounts of information means that routine reports can be produced quickly and accurately. Indeed, certain reports may be produced on a daily, or even real-time, basis. This can be vital to businesses operating in a highly competitive environment, which risk the loss of competitive advantage from making decisions based on inaccurate or out-of-date reports. IT has also enabled information to be more widely spread throughout the business. Increasingly, through their personal computers, employees at all levels are able to gain access to relevant information and reports to guide their decisions and actions.

IT has allowed management reports to be produced in greater detail and in greater variety than could be contemplated under a manual system. In addition, it has allowed sophisticated measurement systems to be provided at relatively low cost. Managers can use IT to help assess proposals by allowing variables (such as product price, output, product cost and so on) to be changed easily. With a few key strokes, managers can increase or decrease the size of key variables to create a range of possible scenarios.

The information revolution is gathering pace and so IT is likely to play an increasingly important role in management accounting in the future. Particularly interesting developments are occurring in the area of financial information evaluation. Computers are becoming more capable of making sophisticated judgements that, in the past, only humans were considered capable of doing. Increasingly, in management accounting, IT is viewed not only as a means of improving the timeliness and accuracy of management reports but also as an important source of competitive advantage.

From bean counter to team member

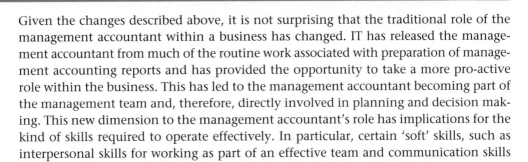

Given the changes described above, it is not surprising that the traditional role of the management accountant within a business has changed. IT has released the management accountant from much of the routine work associated with preparation of management accounting reports and has provided the opportunity to take a more pro-active role within the business. This has led to the management accountant becoming part of the management team and, therefore, directly involved in planning and decision making. This new dimension to the management accountant's role has implications for the kind of skills required to operate effectively. In particular, certain 'soft' skills, such as interpersonal skills for working as part of an effective team and communication skills to help influence the attitudes and behaviour of others, are needed.

This new dimension to the role of the management accountant should have benefits for the development of management accounting as a discipline. When working as part of a cross-functional team, the management accountant should gain a greater awareness of strategic and operational matters, an increased understanding of the information needs of managers and a deeper appreciation of the importance of value creation. This is likely to have a positive effect on the design and development of management accounting systems. As a consequence, we should see increasing evidence that management accounting systems are being designed to fit the particular structure and processes of the business rather than the other way round.

By participating in planning, decision making and control of the business as well as providing management accounting information for these purposes, the management accountant plays a key role in achieving the objectives of the business. It is a role that should add value to the business and improve its competitive position.

Real World 1.11 considers how management accountants are making an impact in the UK National Health Service.

REAL WORLD 1.11

Management accountants operating in the NHS   **FT**

In many ways the National Health Service is in the same position as any private sector organisation. When it comes to running the organisation managers are expected to do more for the same. The expectations of patients rise inexorably.

The limited resource is money. The NHS is a service industry. It is based on delivery and the overwhelming amount of its cost base is people. So the big issues are productivity, getting better value out of capital and getting better value in areas such as drugs.

Real World 1.11 continued

This makes it a classic for treatment by fundamental management accountancy principles. . . .

'The management accountant's role is to bring discipline to the management process,' says Simon Wombwell, deputy chair of CIMA's NHS working group. 'It is not just costing services but also trying to drive down costs. It is the reporting of key performance indicators, for example,' he says, 'and the monitoring of the achievement of productivity and efficiency' . . .

Transparent accounting, rather than the old ways of hushing up the issues, is the best way to achieve long-term results. Increasingly the accountants are working in teams with senior clinicians and senior nurses.

The vast majority of accountants in the NHS have worked within its systems for a good many years.

They do understand the sometimes eccentric ways in which it all works.

In the past the systems stopped them doing much about it.

Now, if the politicians don't get in the way too much, they can bring about the reforms that could create a much more efficient and patient-focused NHS.

Source: Extracts from Bruce, R., 'Physician, heal thyself', *Financial Times*, 6 September 2006.

Reasons to be ethical

The way in which individual businesses operate in terms of the honesty, fairness and transparency with which they treat their stakeholders (customers, employees, suppliers, the community, the shareholders and so on) has become a key issue. There have been many examples of businesses, some of them very well known, acting in ways that most people would regard as unethical and unacceptable. Examples of such actions include:

- paying bribes to encourage employees of other businesses to reveal information about the employee's business that could be useful;
- oppressive treatment of suppliers, for example, making suppliers wait excessive periods before payment; and
- manipulating the financial statements to mislead users of them, for example, to overstate profit so that senior managers become eligible for performance bonuses.

Despite the many examples of unethical acts that have taken place over recent years, it would be very unfair to conclude that most businesses are involved in unethical activities. Nevertheless, revelations of unethical practice can be damaging to the whole business community. Lying, stealing and fraudulent behaviour can lead to a loss of confidence in business and the imposition of tighter regulatory burdens. In response to this threat, businesses often seek to demonstrate their commitment to acting in an honest and ethical way. One way in which this can be done is to produce, and adhere to, a code of ethics concerning business behaviour. **Real World 1.12** provides some interesting food for thought on this topic.

REAL WORLD 1.12

Honesty is the best policy

Some of the largest UK businesses were allocated into two groups: those that had published a code of ethics for their business and those that had not. The commercial success of these two groups of business was then assessed over the five consecutive years ending in 2005. Commercial success was measured by four factors, two linked to the financial (accounting) results and two related to the performance of the businesses' shares on the Stock Exchange.

Overall the businesses with a published ethical statement performed better than the group without such a statement. Of course, it may simply be that the better organised businesses produce both the statement and better performances, but either way it is an interesting finding.

Source: Information taken from Ugoji, K., Dando, N. and Moir, L., *Does Business Ethics Pay? – Revisited*, Institute of Business Ethics, 2007.

Management accountants are likely to find themselves at the forefront with issues relating to business ethics. In the three examples of unethical business activity listed above, a management accountant would probably have to be involved either in helping to commit the unethical act or in covering it up. Management accountants are, therefore, particularly vulnerable to being put under pressure to engage in unethical acts. Some businesses recognise this risk and produce an ethical code for their accounting staff. **Real World 1.13** provides an example of one such code.

REAL WORLD 1.13

Shell's ethical code

Shell plc, the oil and energy business, has a code of ethics for its executive directors and senior financial officers. The key elements of this code are that these individuals should:

- adhere to the highest standards of honesty, integrity and fairness, whilst maintaining a work climate that fosters these standards;
- comply with any codes of conduct or rules concerning dealing in securities;
- avoid involvement in any decisions that could involve a conflict of interest;
- avoid any financial interest in contracts awarded by the company;
- not seek or accept favours from third parties;
- not hold positions in outside businesses that might adversely affect their performance;
- avoid any relationship with contractors or suppliers that might compromise their ability to act impartially;
- ensure full, fair, timely, accurate and understandable disclosure of information that the business communicates to the public or publicly files.

Source: Royal Dutch Shell plc.

Management accounting and financial accounting

Management accounting is one of two main strands in accounting; the other strand is **financial accounting**. The difference between the two is based on the user groups to which each is addressed. Management accounting seeks to meet the needs of managers, whereas financial accounting seeks to meet the accounting needs of the other users that were identified earlier in Figure 1.5 (see p. 16).

The difference in their constituencies has led to each strand of accounting developing along different lines. It is probably worth looking at the ways in which each strand has developed in order to gain a deeper appreciation of how management accounting differs from financial accounting.

- *Nature of the reports produced.* Financial accounting reports tend to be general-purpose. That is, they contain financial information that will be useful for a broad range of users and decisions rather than being specifically designed for the needs of a particular group or set of decisions. Management accounting reports, on the other hand, are often specific-purpose reports. They are designed either with a particular decision in mind or for a particular manager.
- *Level of detail.* Financial accounting reports provide users with a broad overview of the performance and position of the business for a period. As a result, information is aggregated and detail is often lost. Management accounting reports, however, often provide managers with considerable detail to help them with a particular operational decision.
- *Regulations.* Financial accounting reports, for many businesses, are subject to accounting regulations that try to ensure they are produced with standard content and in a standard format. The law and accounting rule makers impose these regulations. As management accounting reports are for internal use only, there are no regulations from external sources concerning the form and content of the reports. They can be designed to meet the needs of particular managers.
- *Reporting interval.* For most businesses, financial accounting reports are produced on an annual basis, though large businesses may produce half-yearly reports, and a few produce quarterly ones. Management accounting reports may be produced as frequently as required by managers. In many businesses, managers are provided with certain reports on a daily, weekly or monthly basis, which allows them to check progress frequently. In addition, special-purpose reports will be prepared when required (for example, to evaluate a proposal to purchase a piece of machinery).
- *Time horizon.* Financial accounting reports reflect the performance and position of the business for the past period. In essence, they are backward-looking. Management accounting reports, on the other hand, often provide information concerning future performance as well as past performance. It is an oversimplification, however, to suggest that financial accounting reports never incorporate expectations concerning the future. Occasionally, businesses will release projected information to other users in an attempt to raise capital or to fight off unwanted takeover bids.
- *Range and quality of information.* Financial accounting reports concentrate on information that can be quantified in monetary terms. Management accounting also produces such reports, but is also more likely to produce reports that contain information of a non-financial nature, as discussed above. Financial accounting places greater emphasis on the use of objective, verifiable evidence when preparing reports. Management accounting reports may use information that is less objective and verifiable, but they provide managers with the information they need.

We can see from this that management accounting is less constrained than financial accounting. It may draw from a variety of sources and use information that has varying degrees of reliability. The only real test to be applied when assessing the value of the information produced for managers is whether or not it improves the quality of the decisions made.

Activity 1.8

Are the information needs of managers and those of other users so very different?
  Is there any overlap between the information needs of managers and the needs of other users?

The distinction between management accounting and financial accounting suggests that there are differences between the information needs of managers and those of other users. Whilst differences undoubtedly exist, there is also a good deal of overlap between these needs. For example, managers will, at times, be interested in receiving a historical overview of business operations of the sort provided to other users. Equally, the other users would be interested in receiving information relating to the future, such as the planned level of profits, and non-financial information, such as the state of the sales order book and the extent of product innovations.

The distinction between the two areas reflects, to some extent, the differences in access to financial information. Managers have much more control over the form and content of information they receive. Other users have to rely on what managers are prepared to provide or what the financial reporting regulations require must be provided. Though the scope of financial accounting reports has increased over time, fears concerning loss of competitive advantage and user ignorance concerning the reliability of forecast data have led businesses to resist providing other users with the detailed and wide-ranging information available to managers.

In the past it has been argued that accounting systems are biased in favour of providing information for external users. Financial accounting requirements have been the main priority and management accounting has suffered as a result. Recent survey evidence suggests, however, that this argument has lost its force. Nowadays, management accounting systems will usually provide managers with information that is relevant to their needs rather than that determined by external reporting requirements. External reporting cycles, however, retain some influence over management accounting, and managers are aware of external users' expectations. (See reference 3 at the end of the chapter.)

Not-for-profit organisations

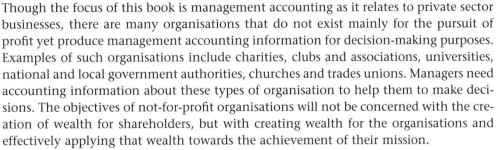

Though the focus of this book is management accounting as it relates to private sector businesses, there are many organisations that do not exist mainly for the pursuit of profit yet produce management accounting information for decision-making purposes. Examples of such organisations include charities, clubs and associations, universities, national and local government authorities, churches and trades unions. Managers need accounting information about these types of organisation to help them to make decisions. The objectives of not-for-profit organisations will not be concerned with the creation of wealth for shareholders, but with creating wealth for the organisations and effectively applying that wealth towards the achievement of their mission.

Not-for-profit organisations are not exempt from the changes that have taken place in the world. They too must be 'customer' orientated and are under increasing pressure to deliver value for money in the manner in which they operate.

Real World 1.14 provides an example of the importance of accounting to relief agencies, which are, of course, not-for-profit organisations.

REAL WORLD 1.14

Accounting for disasters   FT

In the aftermath of the Asian tsunami more than £400m was raised from charitable donations. It was important that this huge amount of money for aid and reconstruction was used as efficiently and effectively as possible. That did not just mean medical staff and engineers. It also meant accountants.

The charity that exerts financial control over aid donations is Mango: Management Accounting for Non-Governmental Organisations (NGOs). It provides accountants in the field and it provides the back-up, such as financial training, and all the other services that should result in really robust financial management in a disaster area.

The world of aid has changed completely as a result of the tsunami. According to Mango's director, Alex Jacobs, 'Accounting is just as important as blankets. Agencies have been aware of this for years. But when you move on to a bigger scale there is more pressure to show the donations are being used appropriately.'

Source: Adapted from Bruce, R., 'Tsunami: finding the right figures for disaster', ft.com, 7 March 2005; Bruce, R., 'The work of Mango: coping with generous donations', ft.com, 27 February 2006.

SUMMARY

The main points of this chapter may be summarised as follows:

What is the purpose of a business?

● To create and keep a customer.

How are businesses organised and managed?

● Most businesses of any size are set up as limited companies.
● A board of directors is appointed by shareholders to oversee the running of the business.
● Businesses are often divided into departments and organised along functional lines; however, larger businesses may be divisionalised along geographical and/or product lines.

Strategic management

● The move to strategic management has been caused by the changing and more competitive nature of business.
● Strategic management involves five steps:
  1 Establish mission and objectives.
  2 Undertake a position analysis (for example, a SWOT analysis).
  3 Identify and assess strategic options.
  4 Select strategic options and formulate plans.
  5 Perform, review and control.

The changing business landscape

● Increased competition and advances in technology have changed the business landscape in the UK.
● There have been changes in the types of businesses operating as well as changes in the ways in which businesses are structured and operate.

Setting financial aims and objectives

● A key financial objective is to enhance/maximise owners' (shareholders') wealth.
● When setting financial objectives the right balance must be struck between risk and return.

What is management accounting?

● All accounting must be useful for decision making and this requires a clear understanding of *for whom* and *for what purpose* the information will be used.
● Management accounting can be viewed as a form of service as it involves providing financial information required by the managers.
● To provide a useful service, management accounting must possess certain qualities, or characteristics. These are relevance, reliability, comparability and understandability. In addition, management accounting information must be material.
● Providing a service to managers can be costly, and financial information should be produced only if the cost of providing the information is less than the benefits gained.

Management accounting information

● Management accounting is part of the total information system within a business. It shares the features that are common to all information systems within a business, which are the identification, recording, analysis and reporting of information.
● Management accounting has changed over the years in response to changes in the business environment and in business methods.
● To meet managers' needs, information relating to the following broad areas is required:
  – developing objectives and plans
  – performance evaluation and control
  – allocating resources
  – determining costs and benefits.
● Providing non-financial information has become an increasingly important part of the management accountant's role.

Influencing behaviour

● The main purpose of management accounting is to affect people's behaviour.
● This effect is not always beneficial.

Reaping the benefits of IT

● IT has had a major effect on the ability to provide accurate, detailed and timely information.
● Developments in IT have enabled information and reports to be more widely disseminated throughout the business.

Changing role of the management accountant

● Less time is spent preparing reports.
● The management accountant is now a key member of the management team.
● This new dimension to the management accountant's role should benefit the design of more relevant management accounting information systems.

Ethical behaviour

- Management accountants may be put under pressure to commit unethical acts.
- Many businesses now publish a code of ethics governing their behaviour.

Management accounting and financial accounting

- Accounting has two main strands – management accounting and financial accounting.
- Management accounting seeks to meet the needs of businesses' managers, and financial accounting seeks to meet the needs of the other user groups.
- These two strands differ in terms of the types of reports produced, the level of reporting detail, the time horizon, the degree of standardisation and the range and quality of information provided.

Not-for-profit organisations

- Not-for-profit organisations also require management accounting information for decision-making purposes.

 Key terms

Strategic management p. 6	**Understandability** p. 18
Mission statement p. 7	**Materiality** p. 18
Position analysis p. 8	**Management accounting information**
SWOT analysis p. 8	**system** p. 21
Management accounting p. 15	**Key performance indicators**
Relevance p. 17	**(KPIs)** p. 24
Reliability p. 17	**Financial accounting** p. 29
Comparability p. 18	

References

1 Drucker, P., *The Effective Executive*, Heinemann, 1967.

2 Abdel-Kader, M. and Luther, R., 'An empirical investigation of the evolution of management accounting practices', University of Essex Working Paper No. 04/06, October 2004.

3 Dugdale, D., Jones, C. and Green, S., *Contemporary Management Accounting Practices in UK Manufacturing*, Elsevier, 2006.

Further reading

If you would like to explore the topics covered in this chapter in more depth, we recommend the following books:

Drury, C., *Management and Cost Accounting*, 7th edn, Cengage Learning, 2007, chapter 1.

Hilton, R., *Managerial Accounting*, 6th edn, McGraw-Hill Irwin, 2005, chapter 1.

Horngren, C., Foster, G., Datar, S., Rajan, M. and Ittner, C., *Cost Accounting: A Managerial Emphasis*, 13th edn, Prentice Hall International, 2008, chapter 1.

Lynch, R., *Corporate Strategy*, FT Prentice Hall, 3rd edn, 2005, chapter 1.

Scapens, R., Ezzamel, M., Burns, J. and Baldvinsdottir, G., *The Future Direction of UK Management Accounting Practice*, CIMA Publishing, Elsevier, 2003.

REVIEW QUESTIONS

Answers to these questions can be found in Appendix C at the back of the book.

1.1 Identify the main users of accounting information for a university. For what purposes would different user groups need information? Do these users differ very much from the users of accounting information for private sector businesses?

1.2 Management accounting has been described as 'the eyes and ears of management'. What do you think this expression means?

1.3 Assume that you are a manager considering the launch of a new service. What accounting information might be useful to help in making a decision?

1.4 'Accounting information should be understandable. As some managers have a poor knowledge of accounting we should produce simplified financial reports to help them.' To what extent do you agree with this view?

EXERCISES

Exercise 1.2 is more advanced than 1.1. Both have answers in Appendix D at the back of the book, starting on p. 480. If you wish to try more exercises, visit the students' side of the Companion Website at **www.pearsoned.co.uk/atrillmclaney**.

1.1 You have been speaking to a friend who owns a small business and she has said that she has read something about strategic management and that no modern business can afford not to get involved with it. Your friend has little idea what strategic management involves.

Required:
Briefly outline the steps in strategic management, summarising what each step tends to involve.

1.2 Jones Dairy Ltd (Jones) operates a 'doorstep' fresh milk delivery service. Two brothers carry on the business that they inherited from their father in the early 1960s. They are the business's only directors. The business operates from a yard on the outskirts of Trepont, a substantial town in mid-Wales.

Jones expanded steadily from when the brothers took over until the early 1980s, by which time it employed 25 full-time rounds staff. This was achieved because of four factors: (i) some expansion of the permanent population of Trepont, (ii) expanding Jones's geographical range to the villages surrounding the town, (iii) an expanding tourist trade in the area and (iv) a positive attitude to 'marketing'.

As an example of the marketing effort, when new residents move into the area, the member of the rounds staff concerned reports this back. One of the directors immediately visits the potential customer with an introductory gift, usually a bottle of milk, a bottle of wine and a bunch of flowers, and attempts to obtain a regular milk order. Similar methods are used to persuade existing residents to place orders for delivered milk.

By the mid 1980s Jones had a monopoly of doorstep delivery in the Trepont area. A combination of losing market share to Jones and the town's relative remoteness had discouraged the national doorstep suppliers. The little, locally-based competition there once was had gone out of business.

Supplies of milk come from a bottling plant, owned by one of the national dairy businesses, which is located 50 miles from Trepont. The bottlers deliver nightly, except Saturday nights, to Jones's depot. Jones delivers daily, except on Sundays.

Profits, after adjusting for inflation, have fallen since the early 1980s. Sales volumes have fallen by about a third, compared with a decline of about 50 per cent for doorstep deliveries nationally over the same period. New customers are increasingly difficult to find, despite a continuing policy of encouraging them. Many existing customers tend to have less milk delivered. A sufficient profit has been made to enable the directors to enjoy a reasonable income compared with their needs, but only by raising prices. Currently Jones charges 40p for a standard pint, delivered. This is fairly typical of doorstep delivery charges around the UK. The Trepont supermarket, which is located in the centre of town, charges 26p a pint and other local stores charge between 35p and 40p.

Currently Jones employs 15 full-time rounds staff, a van maintenance mechanic, a secretary/bookkeeper and the two directors. Jones is regarded locally as a good employer. Regular employment opportunities in the area are generally few. Rounds staff are expected to, and generally do, give customers a friendly, cheerful and helpful service.

The two brothers continue to be the only shareholders and directors and comprise the only level of management. One of the directors devotes most of his time to dealing with the supplier and with issues connected with details of the rounds. The other director looks after administrative matters, such as the accounts and personnel issues. Both directors undertake rounds to cover for sickness and holidays.

Required:
As far as the information given in the question will allow, undertake an analysis of the strengths, weaknesses, opportunities and threats (a SWOT analysis) of the business.

2

Relevant costs for decision making

INTRODUCTION

This chapter considers the identification and use of costs in making management decisions. These decisions should be made in a way that will promote the business's achievement of its strategic objective. We shall see that not all of the costs that appear to be linked to a particular business decision are relevant to it. It is important to distinguish carefully between costs (and revenues) that are relevant and those that are not. Failure to do this could well lead to bad decisions being made. The principles outlined here will provide the basis for much of the rest of the book.

LEARNING OUTCOMES

When you have completed this chapter, you should be able to:

- Define and distinguish between relevant costs, outlay costs and opportunity costs.

- Identify and quantify the costs that are relevant to a particular decision.

- Use relevant costs to make decisions.

- Set out relevant cost analysis in a logical form so that the conclusion may be communicated to managers.

What is meant by 'cost'?

→ **Cost** represents the amount sacrificed to achieve a particular business objective. Measuring cost may seem, at first sight, to be a straightforward process: it is simply the amount paid for the item of goods being supplied or the service being provided. However, when measuring cost *for decision-making purposes*, things are not quite that simple. The following activity illustrates why this is the case.

Activity 2.1

You own a motor car, for which you paid a purchase price of £5,000 – much below the list price – at a recent car auction. You have just been offered £6,000 for this car.

What is the cost to you of keeping the car for your own use? *Note*: Ignore running costs and so on; just consider the 'capital' cost of the car.

By retaining the car, you are forgoing a cash receipt of £6,000. Thus, the real sacrifice, or cost, incurred by keeping the car for your own use is £6,000. Any decision that you make with respect to the car's future should logically take account of this figure. This cost is known as the 'opportunity cost' since it is the value of the opportunity forgone in order to pursue the other course of action. (In this case, the other course of action is to retain the car.)

We can see that the cost of retaining the car is not the same as the purchase price. In one sense, of course, the cost of the car in Activity 2.1 is £5,000 because that is how much was paid for it. However, this cost, which for obvious reasons is known as the → **historic cost**, is only of academic interest. It cannot logically ever be used to make a decision on the car's future. If we disagree with this point, we should ask ourselves how we should assess an offer of £5,500, from another person, for the car. The answer is that → we should compare the offer price of £5,500 with the **opportunity cost** of £6,000. This should lead us to reject the offer as it is less than the £6,000 opportunity cost. In these circumstances, it would not be logical to accept the offer of £5,500 on the basis that it was more than the £5,000 that we originally paid. (The only other figure that should concern us is the value to us, in terms of pleasure, usefulness and so on, of retaining the car. If we valued this more highly than the £6,000 opportunity cost, we should reject both offers.)

We may still feel, however, that the £5,000 is relevant here because it will help us in assessing the profitability of the decision. If we sold the car, we should make a profit of either £500 (£5,500 – £5,000) or £1,000 (£6,000 – £5,000) depending on which offer we accept. Since we should seek to make the higher profit, the right decision is to sell the car for £6,000. However, we do not need to know the historic cost of the car to make the right decision. What decision should we make if the car cost us £4,000 to buy? Clearly we should still sell the car for £6,000 rather than for £5,500 as the important comparison is between the offer price and the opportunity cost. We should reach the same conclusion whatever the historic cost of the car.

To emphasise the above point, let us assume that the car cost £10,000. Even in this case the historic cost would still be irrelevant. If we have just bought a car for £10,000 and found that shortly after it is only worth £6,000, we may well be fuming with rage at our mistake, but this does not make the £10,000 a **relevant cost**. The only relevant factors, in a decision on whether to sell the car or to keep it, are the £6,000 opportunity cost and the value of the benefits of keeping it. Thus, the historic cost can never be relevant to a future decision.

To say that historic cost is an **irrelevant cost** is not to say that *the effects of having incurred that cost* are always irrelevant. The fact that we own the car, and are thus in a position to exercise choice as to how to use it, is not irrelevant.

Opportunity costs are rarely taken into account in the routine accounting process, as they do not involve any out-of-pocket expenditure. They are normally only calculated where they are relevant to a particular management decision. Historic costs, on the other hand, do involve out-of-pocket expenditure and are recorded. They are used in preparing the annual financial statements, such as the statement of financial position (balance sheet) and the income statement. This is logical, however, since these statements are intended to be accounts of what has actually happened and are drawn up after the event.

Real World 2.1 gives an example of linked decisions made by two English football clubs: Manchester City and Chelsea.

REAL WORLD 2.1

Transferring players: a game of two halves

In July 2005, Manchester City Football Club transferred one of its young players, Shaun Wright-Phillips, the England international, to Chelsea Football Club for a reported £21 million. City had signed the player eight years earlier (as a 15-year-old) on a free transfer after Nottingham Forest had released him having decided that he was 'too small' to make a professional footballer.

In August 2008, Chelsea sold Wright-Phillips back to City for a fee believed to be around £8.5 million. During his three seasons with Chelsea, Wright-Phillips started only 43 games, though he was brought on as a substitute in some more.

As the transfer fee from Chelsea to City was rather less than half of the amount originally paid, Chelsea made a huge loss on the transaction. However, to have agreed to the transfer, Chelsea must have viewed the offer of £8.5 million from City as being greater than the sacrifice, or cost, of losing Wright-Phillips's services. The original amount paid for the player's services should not have been a factor in arriving at the agreed transfer price.

Source: http://en.wikipedia.org.

It might be useful to formalise what we have discussed so far.

A definition of cost

Cost may be defined as the amount of resources, usually measured in monetary terms, sacrificed to achieve a particular objective. The objective might be to retain a car, to buy a particular house, to make a particular product, or to render a particular service.

Relevant costs: opportunity and outlay costs

 We have just seen that, when we are making decisions concerning the future, **past costs** (that is, historic costs) are irrelevant. It is future opportunity costs and future **outlay costs** that are of concern. An opportunity cost can be defined as the value in monetary terms of being deprived of the next best opportunity in order to pursue the particular objective. An outlay cost is an amount of money that will have to be spent to achieve that objective. We shall shortly meet plenty of examples of both of these types of future cost.

To be relevant to a particular decision, a future outlay cost, or opportunity cost, must satisfy both of the following criteria:

- *It must relate to the objectives of the business.* Most businesses have enhancing owners' (shareholders') wealth as their key strategic objective. That is to say, they are seeking to become richer (see Chapter 1). Thus, to be relevant to a particular decision, a cost must have an effect on the wealth of the business.
- *It must differ from one possible decision outcome to the next.* Only costs (and revenues) that are different between outcomes can be used to distinguish between them. Thus the reason that the historic cost of the car that we discussed earlier is irrelevant is that it is the same whichever decision is taken about the future of the car. This means that all past costs are irrelevant because what has happened in the past must be the same for all possible future outcomes.

It is not only past costs that are the same from one decision outcome to the next; some future costs may also be the same. Take, for example, a road haulage business that has decided that it will buy a new lorry and the decision lies between two different models. The load capacity, the fuel and maintenance costs are different for each lorry. The potential costs and revenues associated with these are relevant items. The lorry will require a driver, so the business will need to employ one, but a suitably qualified driver could drive either lorry equally well, for the same wage. The cost of employing the driver is thus irrelevant to the decision as to which lorry to buy. This is despite the fact that this cost is a future one.

If, however, the decision did not concern a choice between two models of lorry but rather whether to operate an additional lorry or not, the cost of employing the additional driver would be relevant, because it would then be a cost that would vary with the decision made.

Activity 2.2

A garage business has an old car that it bought several months ago. The car needs a replacement engine before it can be driven. It is possible to buy a reconditioned engine for £300. It would take seven hours for the engine to be fitted by a mechanic who is paid £12 an hour. At present the garage is short of work, but the owners are reluctant to lay off any mechanics or even to cut down their basic working week, because skilled labour is difficult to find and an upturn in repair work is expected soon.

The garage paid £3,000 to buy the car. Without the engine it could be sold for an estimated £3,500. What is the minimum price at which the garage should sell the car with a reconditioned engine fitted?

The minimum price is the amount required to cover the relevant costs of the job. At this price, the business will make neither a profit nor a loss. Any price which is lower than this amount will mean that the wealth of the business is reduced. Thus, the minimum price is:

	£
Opportunity cost of the car	3,500
Cost of the reconditioned engine	300
Total	3,800

The original cost of the car is irrelevant for reasons that have already been discussed; it is the opportunity cost of the car that concerns us. The cost of the new engine is relevant because, if the work is done, the garage will have to pay £300 for the engine; it will pay nothing if the job is not done. The £300 is an example of a future outlay cost.

The labour cost is irrelevant because the same cost will be incurred whether the mechanic undertakes the work or not. This is because the mechanic is being paid to do nothing if this job is not undertaken; thus the additional labour cost arising from this job is zero.

It should be emphasised that the garage will not seek to sell the car with its reconditioned engine for £3,800; it will attempt to charge as much as possible for it. However, any price above £3,800 will make the garage better off financially than it would be by not undertaking the engine replacement.

Activity 2.3

Assume exactly the same circumstances as in Activity 2.2, except that the garage is quite busy at the moment. If a mechanic is to be put on the engine-replacement job, it will mean that other work that the mechanic could have done during the seven hours, all of which could be charged to a customer, will not be undertaken. The garage's labour charge is £40 an hour, though the mechanic is only paid £12 an hour.

What is the minimum price at which the garage should sell the car, with a reconditioned engine fitted, under these altered circumstances?

The minimum price is:

	£
Opportunity cost of the car	3,500
Cost of the reconditioned engine	300
Labour cost (7 × £40)	280
Total	4,080

We can see that the opportunity cost of the car and the cost of the engine are the same as in Activity 2.2 but now a charge for labour has been added to obtain the minimum price. The relevant labour cost here is that which the garage will have to sacrifice in making the time available to undertake the engine replacement job. While the mechanic is working on this job, the garage is losing the opportunity to do work for which a customer would pay £280. Note that the £12 an hour mechanic's wage is still not relevant. The mechanic will be paid £12 an hour irrespective of whether it is the engine-replacement work or some other job that is undertaken.

Activity 2.4

A business is considering making a bid to undertake a contract. Fulfilment of the contract will require the use of two types of raw material. Quantities of both of these materials are held by the business. If it chose to, the business could sell the raw materials in their present state. All of the inventories of these two raw materials will need to be used on the contract. Information on the raw materials concerned is as follows:

Inventories item	Quantity (units)	Historic cost (£/unit)	Sales value (£/unit)	Replacement cost (£/unit)
A1	500	5	3	6
B2	800	7	8	10

Inventories item A1 is in frequent use in the business on a variety of work.

The inventories of item B2 were bought a year ago for a contract that was abandoned. It has recently become obvious that there is no likelihood of ever using this raw material if the contract currently being considered does not proceed.

Management wishes to deduce the minimum price at which the business could undertake the contract without reducing its wealth as a result. This can be used as the baseline in deducing the bid price.

How much should be included in the minimum price in respect of the two inventories items detailed above?

The relevant costs to be included in the minimum price are:

$$\text{Inventories item:} \qquad \text{A1} \qquad £6 \times 500 = £3,000$$
$$\text{B2} \qquad £8 \times 800 = £6,400$$

We are told that the item A1 is in frequent use and so, if it is used on the contract, it will need to be replaced. Sooner or later, the business will have to buy 500 units (currently costing £6 a unit) additional to those which would have been required had the contract not been undertaken.

We are told that item B2 will never be used by the business unless the contract is undertaken. Thus, if the contract is not undertaken, the only reasonable thing for the business to do is to sell the B2. This means that if the contract is undertaken and the B2 is used, it will have an opportunity cost equal to the potential proceeds from disposal, which is £8 a unit.

Note that the historic cost information about both materials is irrelevant and this will always be the case.

Activity 2.5

HLA Ltd is in the process of preparing a quotation for a special job for a customer. The job will have the following material requirements:

Material	Units required	Units currently held in inventories			Replacement cost (£/unit)
		Quantity held	Historic cost (£/unit)	Sales value (£/unit)	
P	400	0	–	–	40
Q	230	100	62	50	64
R	350	200	48	23	59
S	170	140	33	12	49
T	120	120	40	0	68

Material Q is used consistently by the business on various jobs.

The business holds materials R, S and T as the result of previous overbuying. No other use (apart from this special job) can be found for R, but the 140 units of S could be used in another job as a substitute for 225 units of material V that are about to be purchased at a price of £10 a unit. Material T has no other use, it is a dangerous material that is difficult to store and the business has been informed that it will cost £160 to dispose of the material currently held.

If it chose to, the business could sell the raw materials already held in their present state.

What is the relevant cost of the materials for the job specified above?

....

The relevant cost is as follows:

	£
Material P	
This will have to be purchased at £40 a unit (400 × £40).	16,000
Material Q	
This will have to be replaced, therefore the relevant price is (230 × £64).	14,720
Material R	
200 units of this are held and these could be sold. The relevant price of these is the sales revenue forgone (200 × £23).	4,600
The remaining 150 units of R would have to be purchased (150 × £59).	8,850
Material S	
This could be sold or used as a substitute for material V.	
The existing inventories could be sold for £1,680 (140 × £12); however, the saving on material V is higher and therefore should be taken as the relevant amount (225 × £10)	2,250
The remaining units of material S must be purchased (30 × £49)	1,470
A saving on disposal will be made if material T is used	(160)
Total relevant cost	47,730

Real World 2.2 gives an example of how opportunity costs can affect student demand for MBA courses.

REAL WORLD 2.2

MBA = massive bonuses absent   **FT**

By 2008, the slowdown in business in the City (of London) had an effect on the level of recruitment on MBA (Master of Business Administration) courses. When business in the City is booming, many of the people who might be attracted to undertake an MBA feel that the cost of doing so is too great.

When financial markets slow down, the demand for MBA courses tends to pick up. According to Professor Alan Morrison of the Said Business School, University of Oxford, when city bonuses fall, 'the opportunity cost of doing an MBA is reduced'.

Source: Tieman, R., 'Demand hots up despite cool market', *Financial Times*, 16 June 2008.

Sunk costs and committed costs

A **sunk cost** is simply another way of referring to a past cost and so the terms 'sunk cost' and 'past cost' can be used interchangeably. A **committed cost** is also, in effect, a past cost to the extent that an irrevocable decision has been made to incur the cost because, for example, a business has entered into a binding contract. As a result, it is more or less a past cost despite the fact that the cash may not be paid in respect of it until some point in the future. Since the business has no choice as to whether it incurs the cost or not, a committed cost can never be a relevant cost for decision-making purposes.

It is important to remember that, to be relevant, a cost must be capable of varying according to the decision made. If the business is already committed by a legally binding contract to a cost, that cost cannot vary with the decision.

Figure 2.1 summarises the relationship between relevant, irrelevant, opportunity, outlay and past costs.

Activity 2.6

Past costs are irrelevant costs. Does this mean that what happened in the past is irrelevant?

No, it does not mean this. The fact that the business has an asset that it can deploy in the future is highly relevant. What is not relevant is how much it cost to acquire that asset. This point was examined in the discussion that followed Activity 2.1.

Another reason why the past is not irrelevant is that it generally – though not always – provides us with our best guide to the future. Suppose that we need to estimate the cost of doing something in the future to help us to decide whether it is worth doing. In these circumstances our own experience, or that of others, on how much it has cost to do the thing in the past may provide us with a valuable guide to how much it is likely to cost in the future.

Figure 2.1	**Summary of the relationship between relevant and irrelevant costs**

Future costs that vary with the decision under consideration

Costs that are the same irrespective of which decision is made

Relevant costs

Irrelevant costs

The cost of being deprived of the next best option → Opportunity costs

Past costs ← Costs that were incurred as a result of a past decision

Those that vary with the decision → Future outlay costs

Future outlay costs ← Those that do not vary with the decision

Note in particular that future outlay costs may be either relevant or irrelevant costs depending on whether they vary with the decision. Future opportunity costs and outlay costs which vary with the decision are relevant; future outlay costs which do not vary with the decision, and all past costs, are irrelevant.

Qualitative factors of decisions

Though businesses must look closely at the obvious financial effects when making decisions, they must also consider factors that are not directly economic. These are likely to be factors that have a broader, but less immediate, impact on the business. Ultimately, however, these factors are likely to have economic effects – that is, to affect the wealth of the business.

Activity 2.7

Activity 2.3 was concerned with the cost of putting a car into a marketable condition. Apart from whether the car could be sold for more than the relevant cost of doing this, are there any other factors that should be taken into account in making a decision as to whether or not to do the work?

We can think of three points:

● Turning away another job in order to do the engine replacement may lead to customer dissatisfaction.
● On the other hand, having the car available for sale may be useful commercially for the garage, beyond the profit that can be earned from that particular car sale. For example, having a good range of second-hand cars for sale may attract potential customers wanting to buy a car.

→

Activity 2.7 continued

● There is also a more immediate economic point. It has been assumed that the only opportunity cost concerns labour (the charge-out rate for the seven hours concerned). In practice, most car repairs involve the use of some materials and spare parts. These are usually charged to customers at a profit to the garage. Any such profit from a job turned away would be lost to the garage, and this lost profit would be an opportunity cost of the engine replacement and should, therefore, be included in the calculation of the minimum price to be charged for the sale of the car.

You may have thought of additional points.

It is important to consider 'qualitative' factors carefully. There is a risk that they may be given less weight by managers because they are virtually impossible to assess in terms of their ultimate economic effect. This effect can nevertheless be very significant.

Self-assessment question 2.1

JB Limited is a small specialist manufacturer of electronic components. Makers of aircraft, for both civil and military purposes, use much of its output. One of the aircraft makers has offered a contract to JB Limited for the supply, over the next 12 months, of 400 identical components. The data relating to the production of each component are as follows:

(i)   *Material requirements:*
      3 kg of material M1 (see Note 1 below)
      2 kg of material P2 (see Note 2 below)
      1 bought-in component (part number 678) (see Note 3 below)

      Note 1: Material M1 is in continuous use by the business; 1,000 kg are currently held by the business. The original cost was £4.70/kg, but it is known that future purchases will cost £5.50/kg.

      Note 2: 1,200 kg of material P2 are currently held. The original cost of this material was £4.30/kg. The material has not been required for the last two years. Its scrap value is £1.50/kg. The only foreseeable alternative use is as a substitute for material P4 (in constant use) but this would involve further processing costs of £1.60/kg. The current cost of material P4 is £3.60/kg.

      Note 3: It is estimated that the components (part number 678) could be bought in for £50 each.

(ii) *Labour requirements*: Each component would require five hours of skilled labour and five hours of semi-skilled. A skilled employee is available and is currently paid £14/hour. A replacement would, however, have to be obtained at a rate of £12/hour for the work which would otherwise be done by the skilled employee. The current rate for semi-skilled work is £10/hour and an additional employee could be appointed for this work.

(iii) *General manufacturing costs*: It is JB Limited's policy to charge a share of the general costs (rent, heating and so on) to each contract undertaken at the rate of £20 for each machine hour used on the contract. If the contract is undertaken, the general costs are expected to increase as a result of undertaking the contract by £3,200.

Spare machine capacity is available and each component would require four machine hours. A price of £200 a component has been offered by the potential customer.

Required:

(a) Should the contract be accepted? Support your conclusion with appropriate figures to present to management.

(b) What other factors ought management to consider that might influence the decision?

The answer to this question can be found in Appendix B at the back of the book.

To end the chapter, **Real World 2.3** describes another case where the decision makers, quite correctly, ignored past costs and just concentrated on future options for the business concerned.

REAL WORLD 2.3

Pound shop   FT

In 2006 Merchant Equity Partners (MEP), a private equity group, bought the retail arm of MFI (the furniture business) for just £1. MEP planned to revive the loss-making furniture chain and sell it on for up to £500 million in around 2011. MFI management felt at the time that having it taken over by MEP might avoid the retail arm slipping further into financial difficulties.

The buy-out agreement included an arrangement that MFI would pay a 'dowry' of £75 million over three years to encourage MEP to take it off MFI's hands. MFI felt that it would then be able to concentrate on the profitable part of its business, Howden Joinery, which sold kitchen cabinets to the building trade.

In the event, MEP's plans for MFI retail were overtaken by the downturn in furniture sales and MEP allowed the business to be taken over by a group of its managers in 2008.

Source: Taken from Callan, E., 'MFI furniture retail arm bought for £1', ft.com, 12 July 2006, and Braithwaite, T., 'Favell buy-out rescues MFI from administration', *Financial Times*, 28 September 2008.

SUMMARY

The main points in this chapter may be summarised as follows:

Cost = amount of resources, usually measured in monetary terms, sacrificed to achieve a particular objective.

Relevant and irrelevant costs

● Relevant costs must
  – relate to the objective being pursued by the business
  – differ from one possible decision outcome to the next.
● Relevant costs therefore include
  – opportunity costs
  – differential future outlay costs.

- Irrelevant costs therefore include
  - all past (or sunk) costs
  - all committed costs
  - non-differential outlay costs.

Qualitative factors of decisions

- Financial/economic decisions almost inevitably have qualitative aspects that financial analysis cannot really handle, despite their importance.

 Key terms

Cost p. 38	**Past cost** p. 40
Historic cost p. 38	**Outlay cost** p. 40
Opportunity cost p. 38	**Sunk cost** p. 44
Relevant cost p. 39	**Committed cost** p. 44
Irrelevant cost p. 39	

Further reading

If you would like to explore the topics covered in this chapter in more depth, we recommend the following books:

Atkinson, A., Banker, R., Kaplan, R., Young, S. M. and Matsumura, E., *Management Accounting*, 5th edn, Prentice Hall, 2007, chapter 6.

Drury, C., *Management and Cost Accounting*, 7th edn, Cengage Learning, 2007, chapter 9.

Hilton, R., *Managerial Accounting*, 6th edn, McGraw-Hill Irwin, 2005, chapter 14.

Horngren, C., Foster, G., Datar, S., Rajan, M. and Ittner, C., *Cost Accounting: A Managerial Emphasis*, 13th edn, Prentice Hall International, 2008, chapter 11.

REVIEW QUESTIONS

Answers to these questions can be found in Appendix C at the back of the book.

2.1 To be relevant to a particular decision, a cost must have two attributes. What are they?

2.2 Distinguish between a sunk cost and an opportunity cost.

2.3 Define the word 'cost' in the context of management accounting.

2.4 What is meant by the expression 'committed cost'? How do committed costs arise?

EXERCISES

Exercises 2.7 and 2.8 are more advanced than 2.1 to 2.6. Those with coloured numbers have answers in Appendix D at the back of the book. If you wish to try more exercises, visit the students' side of the Companion Website at www.pearson.co.uk/atrillmclaney.

2.1 Lombard Ltd has been offered a contract for which there is available production capacity. The contract is for 20,000 identical items, manufactured by an intricate assembly operation, to be produced and delivered in the next few months at a price of £80 each. The specification for one item is as follows:

Assembly labour	4 hours
Component X	4 units
Component Y	3 units

There would also be the need to hire equipment, for the duration of the contract, at an outlay cost of £200,000.

The assembly is a highly skilled operation and the workforce is currently underutilised. It is the business's policy to retain this workforce on full pay in anticipation of high demand next year, for a new product currently being developed. There is sufficient available skilled labour to undertake the contract now under consideration. Skilled workers are paid £15 an hour.

Component X is used in a number of other subassemblies produced by the business. It is readily available, and 50,000 units of Component X are currently held in inventories. Lombard Ltd made a special purchase of Component Y in anticipation of an order that did not in the end materialise. It is, therefore, surplus to requirements and the 100,000 units that are currently held may have to be sold at a loss. An estimate of various values for Components X and Y provided by the materials planning department is as follows:

Component	X	Y
	£/unit	£/unit
Historic cost	4	10
Replacement cost	5	11
Net realisable value	3	8

It is estimated that any additional relevant costs associated with the contract (beyond the above) will amount to £8 an item.

Required:

Analyse the information and advise Lombard Ltd on the desirability of the contract.

2.2 The local authority of a small town maintains a theatre and arts centre for the use of a local repertory company, other visiting groups and exhibitions. Management decisions are taken by a committee that meets regularly to review the financial statements and to plan the use of the facilities.

The theatre employs a full-time, non-performing staff and a number of artistes at total costs of £9,600 and £35,200 a month, respectively. The theatre mounts a new production every month for 20 performances. Other monthly costs of the theatre are as follows:

	£
Costumes	5,600
Scenery	3,300
Heat and light	10,300
A share of the administration costs of local authority	16,000
Casual staff	3,520
Refreshments	2,360

On average the theatre is half full for the performances of the repertory company. The capacity and seat prices in the theatre are:

200 seats at £24 each
500 seats at £16 each
300 seats at £12 each

In addition, the theatre sells refreshments during the performances for £7,760 a month. Programme sales cover their costs, and advertising in the programme generates £6,720 a month.

The management committee has been approached by a popular touring group, which would like to take over the theatre for one month (25 performances). The group is prepared to pay the local authority half of its ticket income as a fee for the use of the theatre. The group expects to fill the theatre for 10 nights and achieve two-thirds capacity on the remaining 15 nights. The prices charged are £2 less than normally applies in the theatre.

The local authority will, as normal, pay for heat and light costs and will still honour the contracts of all artistes and pay the non-performing employees who will sell refreshments, programmes and so on. The committee does not expect any change in the level of refreshments or programme sales if they agree to this booking.

Note: The committee includes the share of the local authority administration costs when making profit calculations. It assumes occupancy applies equally across all seat prices.

Required:

(a) On financial grounds should the management committee agree to the approach from the touring group? Support your answer with appropriate workings.

(b) What other factors may have a bearing on the decision by the committee?

2.3 Andrews and Co. Ltd has been invited to tender for a contract. It is to produce 10,000 metres of an electrical cable in which the business specialises. The estimating department of the business has produced the following information relating to the contract:

● *Materials*: The cable will require a steel core, which the business buys in. The steel core is to be coated with a special plastic, also bought in, using a special process. Plastic for the covering will be required at the rate of 0.10 kg/metre of completed cable.
● *Direct labour*: Skilled: 10 minutes/metre; Unskilled: 5 minutes/metre.

The business already holds sufficient of each of the materials required to complete the contract. Information on the cost of the inventories is as follows:

	Steel core £/metre	Plastic £/kg
Historic cost	1.50	0.60
Current buying-in cost	2.10	0.70
Scrap value	1.40	0.10

The steel core is in constant use by the business for a variety of work that it regularly undertakes. The plastic is a surplus from a previous contract where a mistake was made and an excess quantity ordered. If the current contract does not go ahead, this plastic will be scrapped.

Unskilled labour, which is paid at the rate of £7.50 an hour, will need to be taken on specifically to undertake the contract. The business is fairly quiet at the moment which means that a pool of skilled labour exists that will still be employed at full pay of £12 an hour to do nothing if the contract does not proceed. The pool of skilled labour is sufficient to complete the contract.

Required:
Indicate the minimum price at which the contract could be undertaken, such that the business would be neither better nor worse off as a result of doing it.

2.4 SJ Services Ltd has been asked to quote a price for a special contract to render a service that will take the business one week to complete. Information relating to labour for the contract is as follows:

Grade of labour	Hours required	Basic rate/hour
Skilled	27	£12
Semi-skilled	14	£9
Unskilled	20	£7

A shortage of skilled labour means that the necessary staff to undertake the contract would have to be moved from other work that is currently yielding an excess of sales revenue over labour and other costs of £8 an hour.

Semi-skilled labour is currently being paid at semi-skilled rates to undertake unskilled work. If the relevant members of staff are moved to work on the contract, unskilled labour will have to be employed for the week to replace them.

The unskilled labour actually needed to work on the contract will be specifically employed for the week of the contract.

All labour is charged to contracts at 50 per cent above the rate paid to the employees, so as to cover the contract's fair share of the business's general costs (rent, heating and so on). It is estimated that these general costs will increase by £50 as a result of undertaking the contract.

Undertaking the contract will require the use of a specialised machine for the week. The business owns such a machine, which it depreciates at the rate of £120 a week. This machine is currently being hired out to another business at a weekly rental of £175 on a week-by-week contract.

To derive the above estimates, the business has had to spend £300 on a specialised study. If the contract does not proceed, the results of the study can be sold for £250.

An estimate of the contract's fair share of the business's rent is £150 a week.

Required:
Deduce the minimum price at which SJ Services Ltd could undertake the contract such that it would be neither better nor worse off as a result of undertaking it.

2.5 A business in the food industry is currently holding 2,000 tonnes of material in bulk storage. This material deteriorates with time, and so in the near future it needs to be repackaged for sale or sold in its present form.

The material was acquired in two batches: 800 tonnes at a price of £40 a tonne and 1,200 tonnes at a price of £44 a tonne. The current market price of any additional purchases is £48 a tonne. If the business were to dispose of the material, it could sell any quantity but only for £36 a tonne; it does not have the contacts or reputation to command a higher price.

Processing this material may be undertaken to develop either Product A or Product X. No weight loss occurs with the processing, that is, one tonne of material will make one tonne of A or X. For Product A, there is an additional cost of £60 a tonne, after which it will sell for £105 a tonne. The marketing department estimates that 500 tonnes could be sold in this way.

With Product X, the business incurs additional costs of £80 a tonne for processing. A market price for X is not known and no minimum price has been agreed. The management is currently engaged in discussions over the minimum price that may be charged for Product X in the current circumstances. Management wants to know the relevant cost per tonne for Product X so as to provide a basis for negotiating a profitable selling price for the product.

Required:

Identify the relevant cost per tonne for Product X, given sales volumes of X of:

(a) up to 1,500 tonnes
(b) over 1,500 tonnes, up to 2,000 tonnes
(c) over 2,000 tonnes.

Explain your answer.

2.6　A local education authority is faced with a predicted decline in the demand for school places in its area. It is believed that some schools will have to close in order to remove up to 800 places from current capacity levels. The schools that may face closure are referenced as A, B, C and D. Their details are as follows:

- *School A* (capacity 200) was built 15 years ago at a cost of £1.2 million. It is situated in a 'socially disadvantaged' community area. The authority has been offered £14 million for the site by a property developer.
- *School B* (capacity 500) was built 20 years ago and cost £1 million. It was renovated only two years ago at a cost of £3 million to improve its facilities. An offer of £8 million has been made for the site by a business planning a shopping complex in this affluent part of the area.
- *School C* (capacity 600) cost £5 million to build five years ago. The land for this school is rented from a local business for an annual cost of £300,000. The land rented for School C is on a 100-year lease. If the school closes, the property reverts immediately to the owner. If School C is not closed, it will require a £3 million investment to improve safety at the school.
- *School D* (capacity 800) cost £7 million to build eight years ago; last year £1.5 million was spent on an extension. It has a considerable amount of grounds, currently used for sporting events. This factor makes it popular with developers, who have recently offered £9 million for the site. If School D is closed, it will be necessary to pay £1.8 million to adapt facilities at other schools to accommodate the change.

In the accounting system, the local authority depreciates non-current assets based on 2 per cent a year on the original cost. It also differentiates between one-off, large items of capital expenditure or revenue, and annually recurring items.

The local authority has a central staff, which includes administrators for each school costing £200,000 a year for each school, and a chief education officer costing £80,000 a year in total.

Required:

(a) Prepare a summary of the relevant cash flows (costs and revenues, relative to not making any closures) under the following options:
　(i)　closure of D only
　(ii)　closure of A and B
　(iii)　closure of A and C.

Show separately the one-off effects and annually recurring items, rank the options open to the local authority, and briefly interpret your answer.

Note: Various approaches are acceptable provided that they are logical.

(b) Identify and comment on any two different types of irrelevant cost contained in the information given in the question.

(c) Discuss other factors that might have a bearing on the decision.

2.7 Rob Otics Ltd, a small business that specialises in building electronic-control equipment, has just received an order from a customer for eight identical robotic units. These will be completed using Rob Otics's own labour force and factory capacity. The product specification prepared by the estimating department shows the following material and labour requirements for each robotic unit:

Component X	2 per unit
Component Y	1 per unit
Component Z	4 per unit
Other miscellaneous items	see below
Assembly labour	25 hours per unit (but see below)
Inspection labour	6 hours per unit

As part of the costing exercise, the business has collected the following information:

- *Component X.* This item is normally held by the business as it is in constant demand. The 10 units currently held were invoiced to Rob Otics at £150 a unit, but the sole supplier has announced a price rise of 20 per cent effective immediately. Rob Otics has not yet paid for the items currently held.
- *Component Y.* 25 units are currently held. This component is not normally used by Rob Otics but the units currently held are because of a cancelled order following the bankruptcy of a customer. The units originally cost the business £4,000 in total, although Rob Otics has recouped £1,500 from the liquidator of the bankrupt business. As Rob Otics can see no use for these units (apart from the possible use of some of them in the order now being considered), the finance director proposes to scrap all 25 units (zero proceeds).
- *Component Z.* This is in regular use by Rob Otics. There is none in inventories but an order is about to be sent to a supplier for 75 units, irrespective of this new proposal. The supplier charges £25 a unit on small orders but will reduce the price to £20 a unit for all units on any order over 100 units.
- Other miscellaneous items. These are expected to cost £250 in total.

Assembly labour is currently in short supply in the area and is paid at £10 an hour. If the order is accepted, all necessary labour will have to be transferred from existing work, and other orders will be lost. It is estimated that for each hour transferred to this contract £38 will be lost (calculated as lost sales revenue £60, less materials £12 and labour £10). The production director suggests that, owing to a learning process, the time taken to make each unit will reduce, from 25 hours to make the first one, by one hour a unit made.

Inspection labour can be provided by paying existing personnel overtime which is at a premium of 50 per cent over the standard rate of £12 an hour.

When the business is working out its contract prices, it normally adds an amount equal to £20 for each assembly hour to cover its general costs (such as rent and electricity). To the resulting total, 40 per cent is normally added as a profit mark-up.

Required:

(a) Prepare an estimate of the minimum price that you would recommend Rob Otics Ltd to charge for the proposed contract such that it would be neither better nor worse off as a result. Provide explanations for any items included.

(b) Identify any other factors that you would consider before fixing the final price.

2.8 A business places substantial emphasis on customer satisfaction and, to this end, delivers its product in special protective containers. These containers have been made in a department within the business. Management has recently become concerned that this internal supply of containers is very expensive. As a result, outside suppliers have been invited to submit tenders for the provision of these containers. A quote of £250,000 a year has been received for a volume that compares with current internal supply.

An investigation into the internal costs of container manufacture has been undertaken and the following emerges:

(a) The annual cost of material is £120,000, according to the stores records maintained, at actual historic cost. Three-quarters (by cost) of this represents material that is regularly stocked and replenished. The remaining 25 per cent of the material cost is a special foaming chemical that is not used for any other purpose. There are 40 tonnes of this chemical currently held. It was bought in bulk for £750 a tonne. Today's replacement price for this material is £1,050 a tonne but it is unlikely that the business could realise more than £600 a tonne if it had to be disposed of owing to the high handling costs and special transport facilities required.

(b) The annual labour cost is £80,000 for this department; however, most workers in the department are casual employees or recent starters, and so, if an outside quote was accepted, little redundancy would be payable. There are, however, two long-serving employees who would each accept as a salary £15,000 a year until they reached retirement age in two years' time.

(c) The department manager has a salary of £30,000 a year. The closure of this department would release him to take over another department for which a vacancy is about to be advertised. The salary, status and prospects are similar.

(d) A rental charge of £9,750 a year, based on floor area, is allocated to the containers department. If the department were closed, the floor space released would be used for warehousing and, as a result, the business would give up the tenancy of an existing warehouse for which it is paying £15,750 a year.

(e) The plant cost £162,000 when it was bought five years ago. Its market value now is £28,000 and it could continue for another two years, at which time its market value would have fallen to zero. (The plant depreciates evenly over time.)

(f) Annual plant maintenance costs are £9,900 and allocated general administrative costs £33,750 for the coming year.

Required:

Calculate the annual cost of manufacturing containers for comparison with the quote using relevant figures for establishing the cost or benefit of accepting the quote. Indicate any assumptions or qualifications you wish to make.

3

Cost–volume–profit analysis

INTRODUCTION

This chapter is concerned with the relationship between volume of activity, cost and profit. Broadly, cost can be analysed between that element that is fixed, relative to the volume of activity, and that element that varies according to the volume of activity. We shall consider how we can use knowledge of this relationship to make decisions and to assess risk, particularly in the context of short-term decisions. This will help the business to work towards its strategic objectives. This continues the theme of Chapter 2, but in this chapter we shall be looking at situations where a whole class of cost – fixed cost – can be treated as being irrelevant for decision-making purposes.

LEARNING OUTCOMES

When you have completed this chapter, you should be able to:

● Distinguish between fixed cost and variable cost and use this distinction to explain the relationship between cost, volume and profit.

● Prepare a break-even chart and deduce the break-even point for some activity.

● Discuss the weaknesses of break-even analysis.

● Demonstrate the way in which marginal analysis can be used when making short-term decisions.

Cost behaviour

We saw in the previous chapter that cost represents the resources that have to be sacrificed to achieve a business objective. The objective may be to make a particular product, to provide a particular service, to operate an IT department and so on. The costs incurred by a business may be classified in various ways and one important way is according to how they behave in relation to changes in the volume of activity. Costs may be classified according to whether they

● remain constant (fixed) when changes occur to the volume of activity, or
● vary according to the volume of activity.

→ These are known as **fixed cost** and **variable cost** respectively. Thus, for example, in the case of a restaurant, the manager's salary would normally be a fixed cost while the unprepared food would be a variable cost.

As we shall see, knowing how much of each type of cost is associated with a particular activity can be of great value to the decision maker.

Fixed cost

The way in which fixed cost behaves can be shown by preparing a graph that plots the fixed cost of a business against the level of activity, as in Figure 3.1. The distance 0F represents the amount of fixed cost, and this stays the same irrespective of the volume of activity.

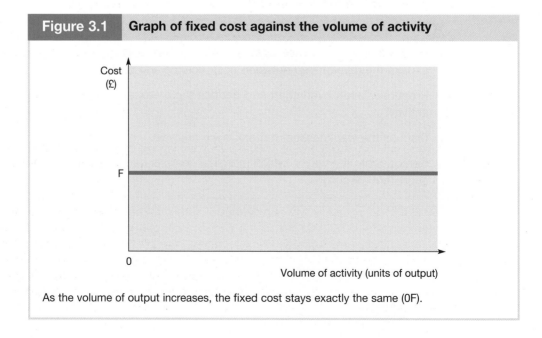

| Figure 3.1 | Graph of fixed cost against the volume of activity |

As the volume of output increases, the fixed cost stays exactly the same (0F).

Activity 3.1

Can you give some examples of items of cost that are likely to be fixed for a hairdressing business?

We came up with the following:

- rent
- insurance
- cleaning cost
- staff salaries.

These items of cost are likely to be the same irrespective of the number of customers having their hair cut or styled.

Staff salaries (or wages) are often assumed to be a variable cost but in practice they tend to be fixed. Members of staff are not normally paid according to volume of output and it is unusual to dismiss staff when there is a short-term downturn in activity. Where there is a long-term downturn, or at least it seems that way to management, redundancies may occur, with fixed-cost savings. This, however, is true of all types of fixed cost. For example, management may also decide to close some branches to make rental cost savings.

There are circumstances in which the labour cost is variable (for example, where staff are paid according to how much output they produce), but this is unusual. Whether labour cost is fixed or variable depends on the circumstances in the particular case concerned.

It is important to be clear that 'fixed', in this context, means only that the cost is unaffected by changes in the volume of activity. Fixed cost is likely to be affected by inflation. If rent (a typical fixed cost) goes up because of inflation, a fixed cost will have increased, but not because of a change in the volume of activity.

Similarly, the level of fixed cost does not stay the same irrespective of the time period involved. Fixed cost elements are almost always *time-based*: that is, they vary with the length of time concerned. The rental charge for two months is normally twice that for one month. Thus, fixed cost normally varies with time, but (of course) not with the volume of output. This means that when we talk of fixed cost being, say, £1,000, we must add the period concerned, say, £1,000 a month.

Activity 3.2

Does fixed cost stay the same irrespective of the volume of output, even where there is a massive rise in that volume? Think in terms of the rent cost for the hairdressing business.

In fact, the rent is only fixed over a particular range (known as the 'relevant' range). If the number of people wanting to have their hair cut by the business increased, and the business wished to meet this increased demand, it would eventually have to expand its physical size. This might be achieved by opening an additional branch, or perhaps by moving the existing business to larger premises nearby. It may be possible to cope with relatively minor increases in activity by using existing space more efficiently, or by having longer opening hours. If activity continued to expand, however, increased rent charges would seem inevitable.

In practice, the situation described in Activity 3.2 would look something like Figure 3.2.

Figure 3.2 **Graph of rent cost against the volume of activity**

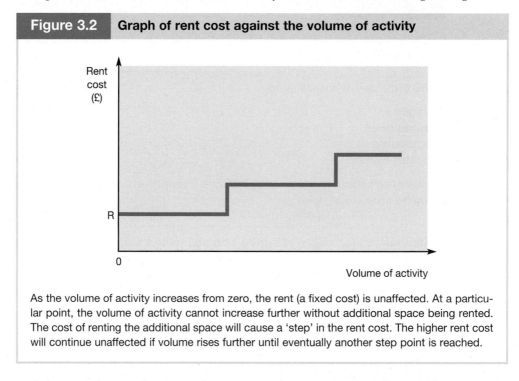

As the volume of activity increases from zero, the rent (a fixed cost) is unaffected. At a particular point, the volume of activity cannot increase further without additional space being rented. The cost of renting the additional space will cause a 'step' in the rent cost. The higher rent cost will continue unaffected if volume rises further until eventually another step point is reached.

 At lower volumes of activity, the rent cost shown in Figure 3.2 would be 0R. As the volume of activity expands, the accommodation becomes inadequate and further expansion requires an increase in premises and, therefore, cost. This higher level of accommodation provision will enable further expansion to take place. Eventually, additional cost will need to be incurred if further expansion is to occur. Elements of fixed cost that behave in this way are often referred to as **stepped fixed cost**.

Variable cost

We saw earlier that variable cost varies with the volume of activity. In a manufacturing business, for example, this would include the cost of raw materials used.

Variable cost can be represented graphically as in Figure 3.3. At zero volume of activity, the variable cost is zero. It then increases in a straight line as activity increases.

Activity 3.3

Can you think of some examples of cost that are likely to be variable for a hairdressing business?

We can think of a couple:

● lotions, sprays and other materials used;
● laundry cost to wash towels used to dry customers' hair.

As with many types of business activity, variable cost incurred by hairdressers tends to be low in comparison with fixed cost: that is, fixed cost tends to make up the bulk of total cost.

| Figure 3.3 | Graph of variable cost against the volume of activity |

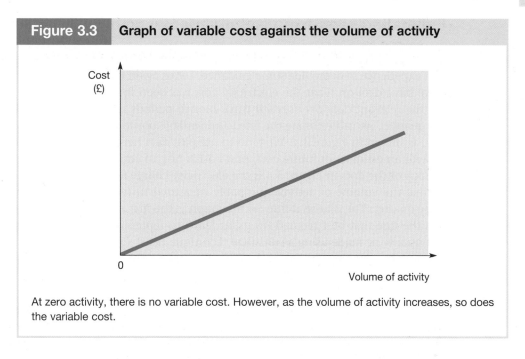

At zero activity, there is no variable cost. However, as the volume of activity increases, so does the variable cost.

The straight line for variable cost on Figure 3.3 implies that this type of cost will be the same per unit of activity, irrespective of the volume of activity. We shall consider the practicality of this assumption a little later in this chapter.

Semi-fixed (semi-variable) cost

In some cases, cost has an element of both fixed and variable cost. It can then be described as **semi-fixed (semi-variable) cost**. An example might be the electricity cost for the hairdressing business. Some of this will be for heating and lighting, and this part is probably fixed, at least until the volume of activity expands to a point where longer opening hours or larger premises are necessary. The other part of the cost will vary with the volume of activity. An example would be power for hairdryers.

| Activity 3.4 |

Can you suggest another cost for a hairdressing business that is likely to be semi-fixed (semi-variable)?

We thought of telephone charges for landlines. These tend to have a rental element, which is fixed, and there may also be certain calls that have to be made irrespective of the volume of activity involved. However, increased business would be likely to lead to the need to make more telephone calls and so to increased call charges.

Estimating semi-fixed (semi-variable) cost

Often, it is not obvious how much of each element a particular cost contains. However, past experience may provide some guidance. Let us again take the example of electricity. If we have data on what the electricity cost has been for various volumes of activity, say the relevant data over several three-month periods (electricity is usually billed by the quarter), we can estimate the fixed and variable portions. This may be done graphically, as shown in Figure 3.4. We tend to use past data here purely because they provide us with an estimate of future cost; past cost is not, of course, relevant for its own sake.

Each of the dots in Figure 3.4 is the electricity charge for a particular quarter plotted against the volume of activity (probably measured in terms of sales revenue) for the same quarter. The diagonal line on the graph is the *line of best fit*. This means that this was the line that best seemed (to us, at least) to represent the data. A better estimate can usually be made using a statistical technique (least squares regression), which does not involve drawing graphs and making estimates. In practice, though, it probably makes little difference which approach is taken.

Figure 3.4	Graph of electricity cost against the volume of activity

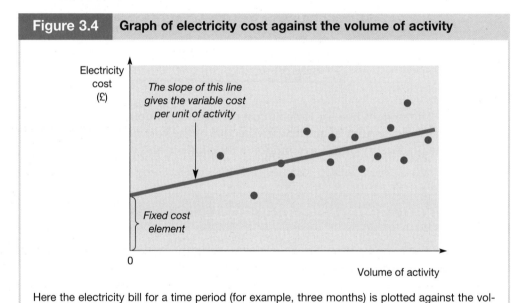

Here the electricity bill for a time period (for example, three months) is plotted against the volume of activity for that same period. This is done for a series of periods. A line is then drawn that best 'fits' the various points on the graph. From this line we can then deduce both the cost at zero activity (the fixed element) and the slope of the line (the variable element).

From the graph we can say that the fixed element of the electricity cost is the amount represented by the vertical distance from the origin at zero (bottom left-hand corner) to the point where the line of best fit crosses the vertical axis of the graph. The variable cost per unit is the amount that the graph rises for each increase in the volume of activity.

By breaking down semi-fixed cost into its fixed and variable elements in this way, we are left with just two types of cost: fixed cost and variable cost.

Armed with knowledge of how much each element of cost represents for a particular product or service, it is possible to make predictions regarding total and per-unit cost at various projected levels of output. Such predictive information can be very useful to decision makers, and much of the rest of this chapter will be devoted to seeing how, starting with **break-even analysis**.

Finding the break-even point

If, for a particular product or service, we know the fixed cost for a period and the variable cost per unit, we can produce a graph like the one shown in Figure 3.5. This graph reveals the total cost over the possible range of volume of activity.

Figure 3.5	Graph of total cost against volume of activity

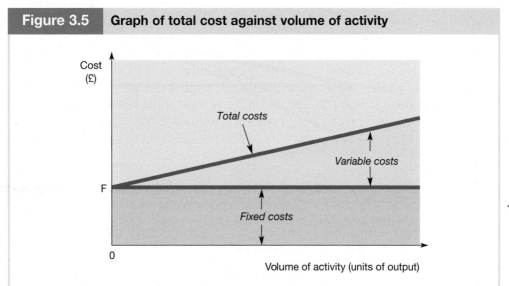

The bottom part of the graph represents the fixed cost element. To this is added the wedge-shaped top portion, which represents the variable cost. The two parts together represent total cost. At zero activity, the variable cost is zero, so total cost equals fixed cost. As activity increases so does total cost, but only because variable cost increases. We are assuming that there are no steps in the fixed cost.

The bottom part of Figure 3.5 shows the fixed-cost area. Added to this is the variable cost, the wedge-shaped portion at the top of the graph. The uppermost line represents the total cost over a range of volume of activity. For any particular volume, the total cost can be measured by the vertical distance between the graph's horizontal axis and the relevant point on the uppermost line.

Logically, the total cost at zero activity is the amount of the fixed cost. This is because, even where there is nothing going on, the business will still be paying rent, salaries and so on, at least in the short term. As the volume of activity increases from zero, the fixed cost is augmented by the relevant variable cost to give the total cost.

If we take this total cost graph in Figure 3.5, and superimpose on it a line representing total revenue over the range of volume of activity, we obtain the **break-even chart**. This is shown in Figure 3.6.

Note in Figure 3.6 that, at zero volume of activity (zero sales), there is zero sales revenue. The profit (loss), which is the difference between total sales revenue and total cost, for a particular volume of activity is the vertical distance between the total sales revenue line and the total cost line at that volume of activity. Where there is no vertical distance between these two lines (total sales revenue equals total cost) the volume of activity is at **break-even point (BEP)**. At this point there is neither profit nor loss: that is, the activity *breaks even*. Where the volume of activity is below BEP, a loss will be incurred because total cost exceeds total sales revenue. Where the business operates at a volume of activity above BEP, there will be a profit because total sales revenue will

---

Figure 3.6 | **Break-even chart**

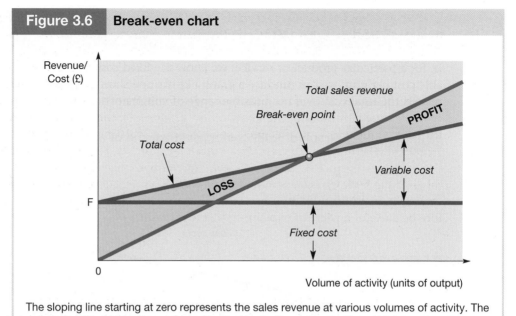

The sloping line starting at zero represents the sales revenue at various volumes of activity. The point at which this finally catches up with the sloping total cost line, which starts at F, is the break-even point (BEP). Below this point a loss is made, above it a profit.

---

exceed total cost. The further below BEP, the higher the loss; the further above BEP, the higher the profit.

Deducing BEPs by graphical means is a laborious business. Since, however, the relationships in the graph are all linear (that is, the lines are all straight), it is easy to calculate the BEP.

We know that at BEP (but not at any other point)

Total sales revenue = Total cost

(At all other points except the BEP, either total sales revenue will exceed total cost or the other way round. Only at BEP are they equal.) The above formula can be expanded so that

Total sales revenue = Fixed cost + Total variable cost

If we call the number of units of output at BEP b, then

$$b \times \text{Sales revenue per unit} = \text{Fixed cost} + (b \times \text{Variable cost per unit})$$

so

$$(b \times \text{Sales revenue per unit}) - (b \times \text{Variable cost per unit}) = \text{Fixed cost}$$

and

$$b \times (\text{Sales revenue per unit} - \text{Variable cost per unit}) = \text{Fixed cost}$$

giving

$$b = \frac{\text{Fixed cost}}{\text{Sales revenue per unit} - \text{Variable costs per unit}}$$

If we look back at the break-even chart in Figure 3.6, this formula seems logical. The total cost line starts off at point F, higher than the starting point for the total sales revenues line (zero) by amount F (the amount of the fixed cost). Because the sales revenue per unit is greater than the variable cost per unit, the sales revenue line will gradually catch up with the total cost line. The rate at which it will catch up is dependent on the relative steepness of the two lines and the amount that it has to catch up (the fixed cost). Bearing in mind that the slopes of the two lines are the variable cost per unit and the selling price per unit, the above equation for calculating b looks perfectly logical.

Though the BEP can be calculated quickly and simply without resorting to graphs, this does not mean that the break-even chart is without value. The chart shows the relationship between cost, volume and profit over a range of activity and in a form that can easily be understood by non-financial managers. The break-even chart can therefore be a useful device for explaining this relationship.

Example 3.1

Cottage Industries Ltd makes baskets. The fixed costs of operating the workshop for a month total £500. Each basket requires materials that cost £2. Each basket takes one hour to make, and the business pays the basket makers £10 an hour. The basket makers are all on contracts such that if they do not work for any reason, they are not paid. The baskets are sold to a wholesaler for £14 each.

What is the BEP for basket making for the business?

Solution

The BEP (in number of baskets)

$$= \frac{\text{Fixed cost}}{(\text{Sales revenue per unit} - \text{Variable cost per unit})}$$

$$= \frac{£500}{£14 - (£2 + £10)}$$

$$= 250 \text{ baskets per month}$$

Note that the BEP must be expressed with respect to a period of time.

Real World 3.1 shows information on the BEPs of three well-known businesses.

REAL WORLD 3.1

BE at BA, Ryanair and easyJet

Commercial airlines seem to pay a lot of attention to their BEPs and their 'load factors', that is, their actual level of activity. Figure 3.7 shows the BEP and load factor for three well-known airlines operating from the UK. British Airways (BA) is a traditional airline. Ryanair and easyJet are both 'no-frills' carriers, which means that passengers receive lower levels of service in return for lower fares. All three operate flights within the UK and from the UK

$\rightarrow$

Real World 3.1 continued

to other countries. BA offers a much wider range of destinations than the other two airlines. We can see that all three airlines were making operating profits as each had a load factor greater than its BEP.

Figure 3.7 **Break-even and load factors in the airline industry**

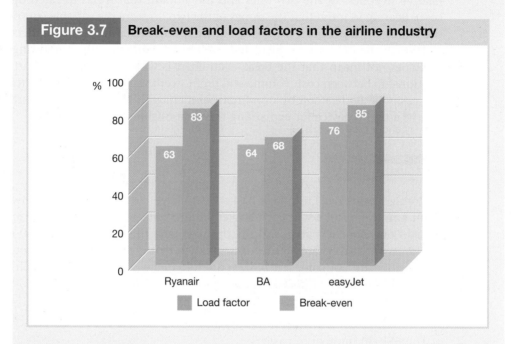

Source: Based on information contained in Binggeli, U. and Pompeo, L., 'The battle for Europe's low-fare flyers', *The McKinsey Quarterly*, August 2005 (www.mckinseyquarterly.com). The data in the article are based on the year ended 31 March 2004.

Activity 3.5

Can you think of reasons why the managers of a business might find it useful to know the BEP of some activity that they are planning to undertake?

....

By knowing the BEP, it is possible to compare the expected, or planned, volume of activity with the BEP and so make a judgement about risk. If the volume of activity is expected to only just exceed the break-even point, this may suggest that it is a risky venture. Only a small fall from the expected volume of activity could lead to a loss.

Activity 3.6

Cottage Industries Ltd (see Example 3.1) expects to sell 500 baskets a month. The business has the opportunity to rent a basket-making machine. Doing so would increase the total fixed cost of operating the workshop for a month to £3,000. Using the machine would reduce the labour time to half an hour per basket. The basket makers would still be paid £10 an hour.

(a) How much profit would the business make each month from selling baskets
    1 assuming that the basket-making machine is not rented; and
    2 assuming that it is rented?
(b) What is the BEP if the machine is rented?
(c) What do you notice about the figures that you calculate?

(a) Estimated monthly profit from basket making:

	Without the machine		With the machine	
	£	£	£	£
Sales revenue (500 × £14)		7,000		7,000
Materials (500 × £2)	(1,000)		(1,000)	
Labour (500 × 1 × £10)	(5,000)			
(500 × ½ × £10)			(2,500)	
Fixed cost	(500)		(3,000)	
		(6,500)		(6,500)
Profit		500		500

(b) The BEP (in number of baskets) with the machine

$$= \frac{\text{Fixed cost}}{\text{Sales revenue per unit} - \text{Variable cost per unit}}$$

$$= \frac{£3,000}{£14 - (£2 + £5)}$$

$$= 429 \text{ baskets a month}$$

The BEP without the machine is 250 baskets per month (see Example 3.1).

(c) There seems to be nothing to choose between the two manufacturing strategies regarding profit, at the estimated sales volume. There is, however, a distinct difference between the two strategies regarding the BEP. Without the machine, the actual volume of sales could fall by a half of that which is expected (from 500 to 250) before the business would fail to make a profit. With the machine, however, just a 14 per cent fall (from 500 to 429) would be enough to cause the business to fail to make a profit. On the other hand, for each additional basket sold above the estimated 500, an additional profit of only £2 (that is, £14 − (£2 + £10)) would be made without the machine, whereas £7 (that is, £14 − (£2 + £5)) would be made with the machine. (Note that knowledge of the BEP and the planned volume of activity gives some basis for assessing the riskiness of the activity.)

Achieving a target profit

In the same way as we can derive the number of units of output necessary to break even, we can calculate the volume of activity required to achieve a particular level of profit. We can expand the equation shown on p. 62 above so that

Total sales revenue = Fixed cost + Total variable cost + Target profit

If we let *t* be the required number of units of output to achieve the target profit, then

$t \times$ Sales revenue per unit = Fixed cost + ($t \times$ Variable cost per unit) + Target profit

so

($t \times$ Sales revenue per unit) − ($t \times$ Variable cost per unit) = Fixed cost + Target profit

and

$t \times$ (Sales revenue per unit − Variable cost per unit) = Fixed cost + Target profit

giving

$$t = \frac{\textbf{Fixed cost + Target profit}}{\textbf{(Sales revenue per unit − Variable cost per unit)}}$$

Activity 3.7

What volume of activity is required by Cottage Industries Ltd (see Example 3.1 and Activity 3.6) in order to make a profit of £4,000 a month
(a) assuming that the basket-making machine is not rented; and
(b) assuming that it is rented?

(a) Using the formula above, the required volume of activity without the machine is

$$\frac{\text{Fixed cost + Target profit}}{\text{(Sales revenue per unit − Variable cost per unit)}}$$

$$= \frac{£500 + £4,000}{£14 − (£2 + £10)} = 2,250 \text{ baskets a month}$$

(b) The required volume of activity with the machine is

$$= \frac{£3,000 + £4,000}{£14 − (£2 + £5)} = 1,000 \text{ baskets a month}$$

We shall take a closer look at the relationship between fixed cost, variable cost and profit together with any advice that we might give the management of Cottage Industries Ltd after we have briefly considered the notion of contribution.

Contribution

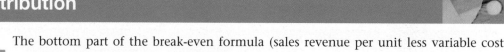

The bottom part of the break-even formula (sales revenue per unit less variable cost per unit) is known as the **contribution per unit**. Thus for the basket-making activity, without the machine the contribution per unit is £2, and with the machine it is £7. This can be quite a useful figure to know in a decision-making context. It is called 'contribution' because it contributes to meeting the fixed cost and, if there is any excess, it then contributes to profit.

We shall see, a little later in this chapter, how knowing the amount of the contribution generated by a particular activity can be valuable in making short-term decisions of various types, as well as being useful in the BEP calculation.

Contribution margin ratio

→ The **contribution margin ratio** is the contribution from an activity expressed as a percentage of the sales revenue, thus:

$$\text{Contribution margin ratio} = \frac{\text{Contribution}}{\text{Sales revenue}} \times 100\%$$

Contribution and sales revenue can both be expressed in per-unit or total terms. For Cottage Industries Ltd (see Example 3.1 and Activity 3.6), the contribution margin ratios are:

● without the machine, $\frac{14 - 12}{14} \times 100\% = 14\%$

● with the machine, $\frac{14 - 7}{14} \times 100\% = 50\%$

The ratio can provide an impression of the extent to which sales revenue is eaten away by variable cost.

Margin of safety

→ The **margin of safety** is the extent to which the planned volume of output or sales lies above the BEP. Going back to Activity 3.6, we saw that the following situation exists:

	Without the machine (number of baskets)	With the machine (number of baskets)
Expected volume of sales	500	500
BEP	250	429
Difference (margin of safety):		
Number of baskets	250	71
Percentage of estimated volume of sales	50%	14%

Activity 3.8

What advice would you give Cottage Industries Ltd about renting the machine, on the basis of the values for margin of safety?

It is a matter of personal judgement, which in turn is related to individual attitudes to risk, as to which strategy to adopt. Most people, however, would prefer the strategy of not renting the machine, since the margin of safety between the expected volume of activity and the BEP is much greater. Thus, for the same level of return, the risk will be lower without renting the machine.

The relative margins of safety are directly linked to the relationship between the selling price per basket, the variable cost per basket and the fixed cost per month. Without the machine the contribution (selling price less variable cost) per basket is £2; with the machine it is £7. On the other hand, without the machine the fixed cost is £500 a month; with the machine it is £3,000. This means that, with the machine, the contributions have more fixed cost to 'overcome' before the activity becomes profitable.

However, the rate at which the contributions can overcome fixed cost is higher with the machine, because variable cost is lower. Thus, one more, or one less, basket sold has a greater impact on profit than it does if the machine is not rented. The contrast between the two scenarios is shown graphically in Figures 3.8(a) and 3.8(b).

| Figure 3.8 | Break-even charts for Cottage Industries' basket-making activities (a) without the machine and (b) with the machine |

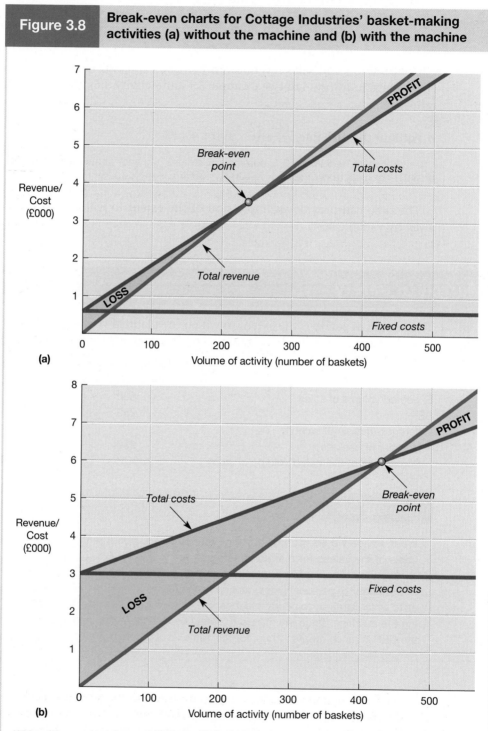

Without the machine the contribution per basket is low. Thus, each additional basket sold does not make a dramatic difference to the profit or loss. With the machine, however, the opposite is true, and small increases or decreases in the sales volume will have a great effect on the profit or loss.

If we look back to Real World 3.1 (page 63), we can see that Ryanair had a much larger margin of safety than either BA or easyJet.

Real World 3.2 goes into more detail on the margin of safety and operating profit, over recent years, of one of the three airlines featured in Real World 3.1.

REAL WORLD 3.2

BA's margin of safety

As we saw in Real World 3.1, commercial airlines pay a lot of attention to BEPs. They are also interested in their margin of safety (the difference between load factor and BEP).

Figure 3.9 shows BA's margin of safety and its operating profit over a seven-year period. Note that in 2002, BA had a load factor that was below its break-even point and this caused an operating loss. In the other years, the load factors were comfortably greater than the BEP. This led to operating profits.

Figure 3.9	BA's margin of safety

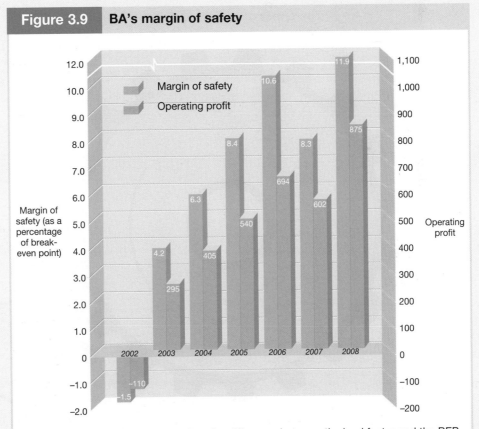

The margin of safety is expressed as the difference between the load factor and the BEP (for each year), expressed as a percentage of the BEP. Generally, the higher the margin of safety, the higher the operating profit.

Source: British Airways plc Annual Reports 2002 to 2008.

Operating gearing

 The relationship between contribution and fixed cost is known as **operating gearing** (or **operational gearing**). An activity with a relatively high fixed cost compared with its variable cost is said to have high operating gearing. Thus, Cottage Industries Ltd has higher operating gearing using the machine than it has if not using it. Renting the machine increases the level of operating gearing quite dramatically because it causes an increase in fixed cost, but at the same time it leads to a reduction in variable cost per basket.

The effect of gearing on profit

The reason why the word 'gearing' is used in this context is that, as with intermeshing gear wheels of different circumferences, a circular movement in one of the factors (volume of output) causes a more-than-proportionate circular movement in the other (profit) as illustrated by Figure 3.10.

| Figure 3.10 | **The effect of operating gearing** |

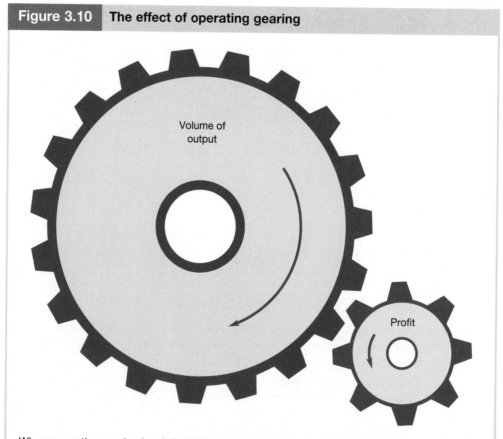

Where operating gearing is relatively high, as in the diagram, a small amount of circular motion in the volume wheel causes a relatively large amount of circular motion in the profit wheel. An increase in volume would cause a disproportionately greater increase in profit. The equivalent would also be true of a decrease in activity, however.

Increasing the level of operating gearing makes profits more sensitive to changes in the volume of activity. We can demonstrate operating gearing with Cottage Industries Ltd's basket-making activities as follows:

	Without the machine			With the machine		
Volume (number of baskets)	500	1,000	1,500	500	1,000	1,500
	£	£	£	£	£	£
Contribution*	1,000	2,000	3,000	3,500	7,000	10,500
Fixed cost	(500)	(500)	(500)	(3,000)	(3,000)	(3,000)
Profit	500	1,500	2,500	500	4,000	7,500

* £2 per basket without the machine and £7 per basket with it.

Note that, without the machine (low operating gearing), a doubling of the output from 500 to 1,000 units brings a trebling of the profit. With the machine (high operating gearing), doubling output causes profit to rise by eight times. At the same time, reductions in the volume of output tend to have a more damaging effect on profit where the operating gearing is higher.

Activity 3.9

Generally speaking, what types of business activity are likely to have high operating gearing? (*Hint*: Cottage Industries Ltd might give you some idea.)

Activities that are capital-intensive tend to have high operating gearing This is because renting or owning capital equipment gives rise to additional fixed cost, but it can also give rise to lower variable cost.

Real World 3.3 shows how a very well-known business has benefited from high operating gearing.

REAL WORLD 3.3

Check out operating gearing

After several years of disappointing trading and loss of market share, in 2004, the UK supermarket company J Sainsbury plc set a plan to improve its profitability and gain market share. During the period from 2005 to 2008, Sainsbury's increased its sales revenue by 16 per cent, but this fed through to a 105 per cent increase in profit. This was partly due to relatively high operating gearing, which caused the profit to increase at a much greater rate than the sales revenue. Quite a lot of retailers' costs are fixed – rent, salaries, heat and light, training and advertising for example.

In its 2008 annual report Sainsbury's Chief Executive, Justin King, said 'Our sales growth is reflected in substantially improved profits and operational gearing is coming through.'

Source: J Sainsbury plc Annual Report 2008, page 4.

Profit–volume charts

A slight variant of the break-even chart is the **profit–volume (PV) chart**. A typical PV chart is shown in Figure 3.11.

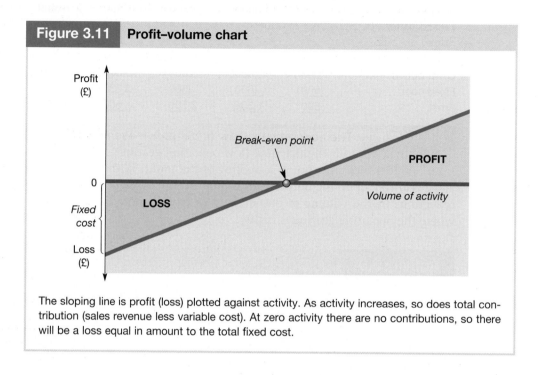

Figure 3.11 Profit–volume chart

The sloping line is profit (loss) plotted against activity. As activity increases, so does total contribution (sales revenue less variable cost). At zero activity there are no contributions, so there will be a loss equal in amount to the total fixed cost.

The profit–volume chart is obtained by plotting loss or profit against volume of activity. The slope of the graph is equal to the contribution per unit, since each additional unit sold decreases the loss, or increases the profit, by the sales revenue per unit less the variable cost per unit. At zero volume of activity there are no contributions, so there is a loss equal to the amount of the fixed cost. As the volume of activity increases, the amount of the loss gradually decreases until BEP is reached. Beyond BEP a profit is made, which increases as activity increases.

As we can see, the profit–volume chart does not tell us anything not shown by the break-even chart. It does, however, highlight key information concerning the profit (loss) arising at any volume of activity. The break-even chart shows this as the vertical distance between the total cost and total sales revenue lines. The profit–volume chart, in effect, combines the total sales revenue and total variable cost lines, which means that profit (or loss) is directly readable.

The economist's view of the break-even chart

So far in this chapter we have treated all the relationships as linear – that is, all of the lines in the graphs have been straight. This is typically the approach taken in management accounting, though it may not be strictly valid.

Consider, for example, the variable cost line in the break-even chart; accountants would normally treat this as being a straight line. Strictly, however, the line should

→ probably not be straight because at high levels of output **economies of scale** may be available to an extent not available at lower levels. For example, a raw material (a typical variable cost) may be able to be used more efficiently with higher volumes of activity. Similarly, buying large quantities of material and services may enable the business to benefit from bulk discounts and so lower its costs.

There is also a tendency for sales revenue per unit to reduce as volume is increased. To sell more of a particular product or service, it will usually be necessary to lower the price per unit.

Economists recognise that, in real life, the relationships portrayed in the break-even chart are usually non-linear. The typical economist's view of the chart is shown in Figure 3.12.

Figure 3.12	**The economist's view of the break-even chart**

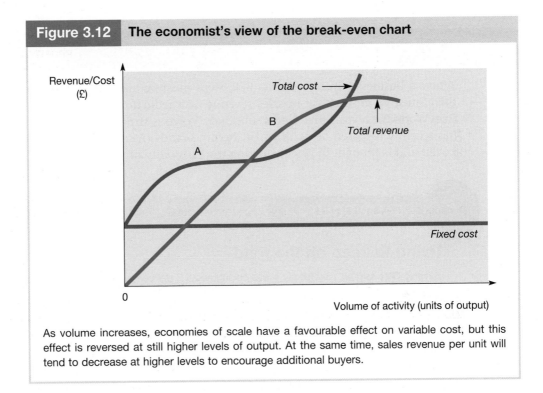

As volume increases, economies of scale have a favourable effect on variable cost, but this effect is reversed at still higher levels of output. At the same time, sales revenue per unit will tend to decrease at higher levels to encourage additional buyers.

Note, in Figure 3.12, that the total variable cost line starts to rise quite steeply with volume but, around point A, economies of scale start to take effect. With further increases in volume, total variable cost does not rise as steeply because variable cost *for each additional unit of output* is lowered. These economies of scale continue to have a benign effect on cost until a point is reached where the business is operating towards the end of its efficient range. Beyond this range, problems will emerge that adversely affect variable cost. For example, the business may be unable to find cheap supplies of the variable-cost elements, or may suffer production difficulties such as machine breakdowns. As a result, the total variable cost line starts to rise more steeply

At low levels of output, sales may be made at a relatively high price per unit. To increase sales output beyond point B, however, it may be necessary to lower the average sales price per unit. This will mean that the total revenue line will not rise as steeply, and may even curve downwards.

Note how this 'curvilinear' representation of the break-even chart can easily lead to the existence of two break-even points.

Accountants justify their approach to this topic by the fact that, though the lines may not, in practice, be perfectly straight, this defect is probably not worth taking into account in most cases. This is partly because all of the information used in the analysis is based on estimates of the future. As this will inevitably be flawed, it seems pointless to be pedantic about minor approximations, such as treating the total cost and total revenue lines as straight when strictly this is not so. Only where significant economies or diseconomies of scale are involved should the non-linearity of the variable cost be taken into account. Also, for most businesses, the range of possible volumes of activity at which they are capable of operating (the **relevant range**) is pretty narrow. Over very short distances, it is perfectly reasonable to treat a curved line as being straight.

Failing to break even

Where a business fails to reach its BEP, steps must be taken to remedy the problem: there must be an increase in sales revenue or a reduction in cost, or both of these. **Real World 3.4** reveals that Ford's subsidiary Volvo is struggling to reach its BEP. Ford has recently disposed of its three UK luxury brands (Aston Martin, Jaguar and Land Rover) and is thought to be considering the possibility of selling off Volvo as well.

REAL WORLD 3.4

Trying to keep on the road   **FT**

Volvo Cars said on Wednesday it was cutting about 8 per cent of its global staff in response to soaring raw material costs and weaker sales on the US and European markets.

The axing of 2,000 jobs is the largest in the history of the premium brand, owned by Ford Motor, and created a stir in Sweden, where other exporters have also been hurt by the weak dollar.

Volvo reported a net loss of $151m in the first quarter of this year, compared with a profit of $94m a year ago.

Volvo has been hit harder than most other carmakers by the weakening of the dollar because it produces no cars in the US, unlike Japanese and Korean manufacturers or Germany's BMW and Mercedes-Benz brands. The brand sold 458,000 cars worldwide last year and the US is its largest market.

The pain at Volvo adds to mounting problems at Ford, which has abandoned pledges to break even next year and return to profit in 2010 due to a sharp contraction in US sales of its profitable large pick-ups and sport utility vehicles.

Source: Extracts from Reed, J. and Anderson, R., 'Volvo to cut 8 per cent of global staff', ft.com, 25 June 2008.

Weaknesses of break-even analysis

As we have seen, break-even analysis can provide some useful insights concerning the important relationship between fixed cost, variable cost and the volume of activity. It does, however, have its weaknesses. There are three general problems:

● *Non-linear relationships*. The management accountant's normal approach to break-even analysis assumes that the relationships between sales revenues, variable cost and volume are strictly straight-line ones. In real life, this is unlikely to be the case. This is probably not a major problem, since, as we have just seen,

  – break-even analysis is normally conducted in advance of the activity actually taking place. Our ability to predict future cost, revenue and so on is somewhat limited, so what are probably minor variations from strict linearity are unlikely to be significant, compared with other forecasting errors; and

  – most businesses operate within a narrow range of volume of activity; over short ranges, curved lines tend to be relatively straight.

● *Stepped fixed cost.* Most types of fixed cost are not fixed over all volumes of activity. They tend to be 'stepped' in the way depicted in Figure 3.2. This means that, in practice, great care must be taken in making assumptions about fixed cost. The problem is heightened because most activities will probably involve various types of fixed cost (for example rent, supervisory salaries, administration costs), all of which are likely to have steps at different points.

● *Multi-product businesses.* Most businesses do not offer just one product or service. This is a problem for break-even analysis since it raises the question of the effect of additional sales of one product or service on sales of another of the business's products or services. There is also the problem of identifying the fixed cost of one particular activity. Fixed cost tends to relate to more than one activity – for example, two activities may be carried out in the same rented premises. There are ways of dividing the fixed cost between activities, but these tend to be arbitrary, which calls into question the value of the break-even analysis and any conclusions reached.

Activity 3.10

We saw above that, in practice, relationships between costs, revenues and volumes of activity are not necessarily straight-line ones.
Can you think of at least three reasons, with examples, why that may be the case?

We thought of the following:

● *Economies of scale with labour.* A business may do things more economically where there is a high volume of activity than is possible at lower levels of activity. It may, for example, be possible for employees to specialise.

● *Economies of scale with buying goods or services.* A business may find it cheaper to buy in goods and services where it is buying in bulk, as discounts are often given.

● *Diseconomies of scale.* This may mean that the per-unit cost of output is higher at higher levels of activity. For example, it may be necessary to pay higher rates of pay to workers to recruit the additional staff needed at higher volumes of activity.

● *Lower sales prices at high levels of activity.* Some consumers may only be prepared to buy the particular product or service at a lower price. Thus, it may not be possible to achieve high levels of sales activity without lowering the selling price.

Despite some practical problems, break-even analysis and BEP seem to be widely used. The media frequently refer to the BEP for businesses and activities. For example, there is seemingly constant discussion about Eurotunnel's BEP and whether it will ever be reached. Similarly, the number of people regularly needed to pay to watch a football team so that the club breaks even is often mentioned. This is illustrated in **Real World 3.5**, which is an extract from an article discussing the failure of Plymouth Argyle FC, the Coca-Cola Championship football club, to spend all of its player transfer income on new players.

REAL WORLD 3.5

Pilgrims not progressing through the turnstiles

This year, Argyle have raked in plenty of income, in addition to their gate receipts. The sale of players has brought in over £8 million. Their expenditure has been nowhere near that sum.

The failure to sign adequate replacements for the departed players could put Argyle's Championship status in jeopardy. Yes, the Pilgrims have to retain some of their transfer income to help them cope with running costs – they do not break even on current gates – but the best way to increase attendances is to provide an attractive and successful team.

Source: Metcalf, R., 'Argyle viewpoint', *Western Morning News*, 15 September 2008.

Real World 3.6 shows specific references to break-even point for three well-known businesses.

REAL WORLD 3.6

Breaking even is breaking out all over   **FT**

Setanta sets its break-even target

Setanta Sports Holdings Ltd, the satellite TV broadcaster and rival of BSkyB, has a break-even point of about 1.5 million subscribers. By April 2009, Setanta plans to have 4 million subscribers.

Source: Fenton, B., 'Setanta chases fresh targets', *Financial Times*, 23 July 2008.

Superjumbo break-even point grows

German industrial group EADS is developing the Airbus A380 aircraft. The aircraft can carry up to 555 passengers on each flight. When EADS approved development of the plane in 2000, it was estimated that the business would need to sell 250 of them to break even. By 2005, the break-even number had increased to 270, but by early 2008 the cost of development had increased to the point where it was estimated that it would require sales of 400 of the aircraft for it to break even. Expected total sales of the aircraft could be about 1,000 over its commercial lifetime.

Source: 'EADS and the A380', *Financial Times*, 27 February 2008.

City Link to break even

City Link, the parcel delivery business owned by Rentokil Initial plc, was expected only to break even in 2008. This was as a result of inadequate management information systems, which led to loss of customers.

Source: Davoudi, S. and Urry, M., 'Rentokil plunge spurs break-up fears', *Financial Times*, 28 February 2008.

Real World 3.7 provides a more formal insight into the extent to which managers in practice use break-even analysis.

REAL WORLD 3.7

Break-even analysis in practice

A survey of management accounting practice in the United States was conducted in 2003. Nearly 2,000 businesses replied to the survey. These tended to be larger businesses, of which about 40 per cent were manufacturers and about 16 per cent financial services; the remainder were across a range of other industries.

The survey revealed that 62 per cent use break-even analysis extensively, with a further 22 per cent considering using the technique in the future.

Though the survey relates to the US, in the absence of UK evidence it provides some insight into what is likely also to be practice in the UK and elsewhere in the developed world.

Source: 2003 Survey of Management Accounting, Ernst and Young, 2003.

Using contribution to make decisions – marginal analysis

If we cast our minds back to Chapter 2, where we discussed relevant costs for decision making, we should recall that when we are trying to decide between two or more possible courses of action, *only costs that vary with the decision should be included in the decision analysis.*

For many decisions that involve relatively small variations from existing practice, and/or relatively limited periods of time, fixed cost is not relevant to the decision, because it will be the same irrespective of the decision made.

This is because either

● fixed cost elements tend to be impossible to alter in the short term

or

● managers are reluctant to alter them in the short term.

Activity 3.11

Ali plc owns premises from which it provides a PC repair and maintenance service. There is a downturn in demand for the service, and it would be possible for Ali plc to carry on the business from smaller, cheaper premises.

Can you think of any reasons why the business might not immediately move to smaller, cheaper premises?

We thought of broadly three reasons:

1 It is not usually possible to find a buyer for existing premises at very short notice and it may be difficult to find available alternative premises quickly.
2 It may be difficult to move premises quickly where there is, say, delicate equipment to be moved.
3 Management may feel that the downturn might not be permanent, and would thus be reluctant to take such a dramatic step and deny itself the opportunity to benefit from a possible revival of trade.

We shall now consider some types of decisions where fixed cost can be regarded as irrelevant. In making these decisions, we should have as our key strategic objective the enhancement of owners' (shareholders') wealth. Since these decisions are short-term in nature, this means that wealth will normally be increased by trying to generate as much net cash inflow as possible.

In **marginal analysis** we concern ourselves just with costs and revenues that vary with the decision and so this usually means that fixed cost is ignored. This is because marginal analysis is usually applied to minor alterations in the level of activity, so it tends to be true that the variable cost per unit will be equal to the **marginal cost**, which is the additional cost of producing one more unit of output. Whilst this is normally the case, there may be times when producing one more unit will involve a step in the fixed cost. If this occurs, the marginal cost is not just the variable cost; it will include the increment, or step, in the fixed cost as well.

Marginal analysis may be used in four key areas of decision making:

- accepting/rejecting special contracts;
- determining the most efficient use of scarce resources;
- make-or-buy decisions;
- closing or continuation decisions.

We shall now consider each of these areas in turn.

Accepting/rejecting special contracts

To understand how marginal analysis may be used in decisions as to whether to accept or reject special contracts, let us consider the following activity.

Activity 3.12

Cottage Industries Ltd (see Example 3.1 and Activity 3.6) has spare capacity in that its basket makers have some spare time. An overseas retail chain has offered the business an order for 300 baskets at a price of £13 each.

Without considering any wider issues, should the business accept the order? (Assume that the business does not rent the machine.)

Since the fixed cost will be incurred in any case, it is not relevant to this decision. All we need to do is see whether the price offered will yield a contribution. If it will, the business will be better off by accepting the contract than by refusing it.

	£
Additional revenue per unit	13
Additional cost per unit	(12)
Additional contribution per unit	1

For 300 units, the additional contribution will be £300 (that is, 300 × £1). Since no fixed-cost increase is involved, irrespective of what else is happening to the business, it will be £300 better off by taking this contract than by refusing it.

As ever with decision making, there are other factors that are either difficult or impossible to quantify. These should be taken into account before reaching a final decision. In the case of Cottage Industries Ltd's decision concerning the overseas customer, these could include the following:

- The possibility that spare capacity will have been 'sold off' cheaply when there might be another potential customer who will offer a higher price, but, by the time they do so, the capacity will be fully committed. It is a matter of commercial judgement as to how likely this will be.
- Selling the same product, but at different prices, could lead to a loss of customer goodwill. The fact that a different price will be set for customers in different countries (that is, in different markets) may be sufficient to avoid this potential problem.
- If the business is going to suffer continually from being unable to sell its full production potential at the 'usual' price, it might be better, in the long run, to reduce capacity and make fixed-cost savings. Using the spare capacity to produce marginal benefits may lead to the business failing to address this issue.
- On a more positive note, the business may see this as a way of breaking into the overseas market. This is something that might be impossible to achieve if the business charges its usual price.

The most efficient use of scarce resources

Normally, the output of a business is determined by customer demand for particular goods or services. In some cases, however, output will be determined by the productive capacity of the business. Limited productive capacity might stem from a shortage of any factor of production – labour, raw materials, space, machine capacity and so on. Such scarce factors are often known as *key* or *limiting* factors.

Where productive capacity acts as a brake on output, management must decide on how best to meet customer demand. That is, it must decide which products, from the range available, should be produced and how many of each should be produced. Marginal analysis can be useful to management in such circumstances. The guiding principle is that the most profitable combination of products will occur where the *contribution per unit of the scarce factor* is maximised. Example 3.2 illustrates this point.

Example 3.2

A business provides three different services, the details of which are as follows:

Service (code name)	AX107	AX109	AX220
Selling price per unit (£)	50	40	65
Variable cost per unit (£)	(25)	(20)	(35)
Contribution per unit (£)	25	20	30
Labour time per unit (hours)	5	3	6

Within reason, the market will take as many units of each service as can be provided, but the ability to provide the service is limited by the availability of labour, all of which needs to be skilled. Fixed cost is not affected by the choice of service provided because all three services use the same facilities.

The most profitable service is AX109 because it generates a contribution of £6.67 (£20/3) an hour. The other two generate only £5.00 each an hour (£25/5 and £30/6). So, to maximise profit, priority should be given to the production that maximises the contribution per unit of limiting factor.

Our first reaction might be that the business should provide only service AX220, as this is the one that yields the highest contribution per unit sold. If so, we would have been making the mistake of thinking that it is the ability to sell that is the limiting factor. If the above analysis is not convincing, we can take a random number of available labour hours and ask ourselves what is the maximum contribution (and, therefore, profit) that could be made by providing each service exclusively. Bear in mind that there is no shortage of anything else, including market demand, just a shortage of labour.

Activity 3.13

A business makes three different products, the details of which are as follows:

Product (code name)	B14	B17	B22
Selling price per unit (£)	25	20	23
Variable cost per unit (£)	10	8	12
Weekly demand (units)	25	20	30
Machine time per unit (hours)	4	3	4

Fixed cost is not affected by the choice of product because all three products use the same machine. Machine time is limited to 148 hours a week.

Which combination of products should be manufactured if the business is to produce the highest profit?

Product (code name)	B14	B17	B22
Selling price per unit (£)	25	20	23
Variable cost per unit (£)	(10)	(8)	(12)
Contribution per unit (£)	15	12	11
Machine time per unit (hours)	4	3	4
Contribution per machine hour	£3.75	£4.00	£2.75
Order of priority	2nd	1st	3rd

Therefore produce:

20 units of product B17 using	60 hours
22 units of product B14 using	88 hours
	148 hours

This leaves unsatisfied the market demand for a further 3 units of product B14 and 30 units of product B22.

Activity 3.14

What steps could be taken that might lead to a higher level of contribution for the business in Activity 3.13?

The possibilities for improving matters that occurred to us are as follows:

- Consider obtaining additional machine time. This could mean obtaining a new machine, subcontracting the machining to another business or, perhaps, squeezing a few more hours a week out of the business's own machine. Perhaps a combination of two or more of these is a possibility.
- Redesign the products in a way that requires less time per unit on the machine.
- Increase the price per unit of the three products. This might well have the effect of dampening demand, but the existing demand cannot be met at present, and it may be more profitable in the long run to make a greater contribution on each unit sold than to take one of the other courses of action to overcome the problem.

Activity 3.15

Going back to Activity 3.13, what is the maximum price that the business concerned would logically be prepared to pay to have the remaining B14s machined by a subcontractor, assuming that no fixed or variable cost would be saved as a result of not doing the machining in-house?

Would there be a different maximum if we were considering the B22s?

If the remaining three B14s were subcontracted at no cost, the business would be able to earn a contribution of £15 a unit, which it would not otherwise be able to gain. Therefore, any price up to £15 a unit would be worth paying to a subcontractor to undertake the machining. Naturally, the business would prefer to pay as little as possible, but anything up to £15 would still make it worthwhile subcontracting the machining.

This would not be true of the B22s because they have a different contribution per unit; £11 would be the relevant figure in their case.

Real World 3.8 contains information from a *Financial Times* article about the price for using a new high-speed rail line.

REAL WORLD 3.8

Fast track   **FT**

Rail freight operators will have to pay a premium rate for using the new 'High Speed 1' (HS1) line that links London to the Channel tunnel. With other lines on the UK rail network, freight operators are required to pay only the marginal cost of running each train. This would comprise the cost of the electricity, signalling and wear to the track that would not have been incurred had the train not run. For using the HS1 line, operators will be asked to pay twice the marginal cost of using the other lines. This is partly because HS1 has a higher maintenance cost, but also so that the owner of the line, London and Continental Railways, can make some profit from freight operations.

Source: Information taken from Wright, R., 'Row over freight charges on fast rail line', *Financial Times*, 14 July 2008.

Make-or-buy decisions

Businesses are frequently confronted by the need to decide whether to produce the product or service that they sell themselves, or to buy it in from some other business. Thus, a producer of electrical appliances might decide to subcontract the manufacture of one of its products to another business, perhaps because there is a shortage of production capacity in the producer's own factory, or because it believes it to be cheaper to subcontract than to make the appliance itself.

It might be just part of a product or service that is subcontracted. For example, the producer may have a component for the appliance made by another manufacturer. In principle, there is hardly any limit to the scope of make-or-buy decisions. Virtually any part, component or service that is required in production of the main product or service, or the main product or service itself, could be the subject of a make-or-buy decision. So, for example, the personnel function of a business, which is normally performed in-house, could be subcontracted. At the same time, electrical power, which is typically provided by an outside electrical utility business, could be generated in-house. Obtaining services or products from a subcontractor is often called **outsourcing**.

Real World 3.9 provides an example of outsourcing by a well-known communications business.

REAL WORLD 3.9

Vodafone subcontracts IT work

Vodafone is in the process of outsourcing all of its IT development and maintenance operations to a specialist organisation based in India. It is also outsourcing its internal helpdesks.

Source: Vodafone Group plc Annual Report 2008.

Activity 3.16

Shah Ltd needs a component for one of its products. It can subcontract production of the component to a subcontractor who will provide the components for £20 each. Shah Ltd can produce the components internally for total variable cost of £15 per component. Shah Ltd has spare capacity.

Should the component be subcontracted or produced internally?

The answer is that Shah Ltd should produce the component internally, since the variable cost of subcontracting is greater by £5 (£20 – £15) than the variable cost of internal manufacture.

Activity 3.17

Now assume that Shah Ltd (Activity 3.16) has no spare capacity, so it can only produce the component internally by reducing its output of another of its products. While it is making each component, it will lose contributions of £12 from the other product.

Should the component be subcontracted or produced internally?

The answer is to subcontract. In this case, both the variable cost of production and the opportunity cost of lost contributions must be taken into account.

Thus, the relevant cost of internal production of each component is:

	£
Variable cost of production of the component	15
Opportunity cost of lost production of the other product	12
	27

This is obviously more costly than the £20 per component that will have to be paid to the subcontractor.

Activity 3.18

What factors, other than the immediately financially quantifiable, would you consider when making a make-or-buy decision?

We feel that there are two major factors:

1 The general problems of subcontracting, particularly
   (a) loss of control of quality;
   (b) potential unreliability of supply.
2 Expertise and specialisation. Generally, businesses should focus on their core competences. It is possible for most businesses, with sufficient determination, to do virtually everything in-house. This may, however, require a level of skill and facilities that most businesses neither have nor feel inclined to acquire. For example, though it is true that most businesses could generate their own electricity, their managements tend to take the view that this is better done by a specialist generator business. Specialists can often do things more cheaply, with less risk of things going wrong.

Closing or continuation decisions

It is quite common for businesses to produce separate financial statements for each department or section, to try to assess their relative performance. Example 3.3 below considers how marginal analysis can help decide how to respond where it is found that a particular department underperforms.

Example 3.3

Goodsports Ltd is a retail shop that operates through three departments, all in the same premises. The three departments occupy roughly equal-sized areas of the premises. The trading results for the year just finished showed the following:

	Total	Sports equipment	Sports clothes	General clothes
	£000	£000	£000	£000
Sales revenue	534	254	183	97
Cost	(482)	(213)	(163)	(106)
Profit/(loss)	52	41	20	(9)

It would appear that if the general clothes department were to close, the business would be more profitable, by £9,000 a year, assuming last year's performance to be a reasonable indication of future performance.

When the cost is analysed between that part that is variable and that part that is fixed, however, the contribution of each department can be deduced and the following results obtained:

→

Example 3.3 continued

	Total	Sports equipment	Sports clothes	General clothes
	£000	£000	£000	£000
Sales revenue	534	254	183	97
Variable cost	(344)	(167)	(117)	(60)
Contribution	190	87	66	37
Fixed cost (rent and so on)	(138)	(46)	(46)	(46)
Profit/(loss)	52	41	20	(9)

Now it is obvious that closing the general clothes department, without any other developments, would make the business worse off by £37,000 (the department's contribution). The department should not be closed, because it makes a positive contribution. The fixed cost would continue whether the department was closed or not. As can be seen from the above analysis, distinguishing between variable and fixed cost, and deducing the contribution, can make the picture a great deal clearer.

Activity 3.19

In considering Goodsports Ltd (in Example 3.3), we saw that the general clothes department should not be closed 'without any other developments'.

What 'other developments' could affect this decision, making continuation either more attractive or less attractive?

The things that we could think of are as follows:

● Expansion of the other departments or replacing the general clothes department with a completely new activity. This would make sense only if the space currently occupied by the general clothes department could generate contributions totalling at least £37,000 a year.

● Sub-letting the space occupied by the general clothes department. Once again, this would need to generate a net rent greater than £37,000 a year to make it more financially beneficial than keeping the department open.

● Keeping the department open, even if it generated no contribution whatsoever (assuming that there is no other use for the space), may still be beneficial. If customers are attracted into the shop because it has general clothing, they may then buy something from one of the other departments. In the same way, the activity of a sub-tenant might attract customers into the shop. (On the other hand, it might drive them away!)

Self-assessment question 3.1

Khan Ltd can render three different types of service (Alpha, Beta and Gamma) using the same staff. Various estimates for next year have been made as follows:

Service	Alpha	Beta	Gamma
Selling price (£/unit)	30	39	20
Variable material cost (£/unit)	15	18	10
Other variable costs (£/unit)	6	10	5
Share of fixed cost (£/unit)	8	12	4
Staff time required (hours)	2	3	1

Fixed cost for next year is expected to total £40,000.

Required:

(a) If the business were to render only service Alpha next year, how many units of the service would it need to provide in order to break even? (Assume for this part of the question that there is no effective limit to market size and staffing level.)

(b) If the business has a maximum of 10,000 staff hours next year, in which order of preference would the three services come?

(c) If the maximum market for next year for the three services is

Alpha	3,000 units
Beta	2,000 units
Gamma	5,000 units

what quantities of which service should the business provide next year and how much profit would this be expected to yield?

The answer to this question can be found in Appendix B at the back of the book.

SUMMARY

The main points in this chapter may be summarised as follows:

Cost behaviour

- Fixed cost is independent of the level of activity (an example is rent).
- Variable cost varies with the level of activity (an example is raw materials).
- Semi-fixed (semi-variable) cost is a mixture of fixed and variable cost (an example is electricity).

Break-even analysis

- The break-even point (BEP) is the level of activity (in units of output or sales revenue) at which total (fixed + variable) cost = total sales revenue.
- Calculation of the BEP is as follows:

$$\text{BEP (in units of output)} = \frac{\text{Fixed cost for the period}}{\text{Contribution per unit}}$$

- Knowledge of the BEP for a particular activity can be used to help assess risk.
- Calculation of the volume of activity (t) required to achieve a target profit is as follows:

$$t = \frac{\text{Fixed cost} + \text{Target profit}}{(\text{Sales revenue per unit} - \text{Variable cost per unit})}$$

- Contribution per unit = sales revenue per unit less variable cost per unit.
- Contribution margin ratio = $\dfrac{\text{contribution}}{\text{sales revenue}}$ $(\times\ 100\%)$
- Margin of safety = excess of planned volume of activity over BEP.
- Operating gearing = the extent to which the total cost of some activity is fixed rather than variable.
- Profit–volume (PV) chart is an alternative approach to BE chart, which is easier to understand.
- Economists tend to take a different approach to BE, taking account of economies (and diseconomies) of scale and of the fact that, generally, to be able to sell large volumes, price per unit tends to fall.

Weaknesses of break-even analysis

- There are non-linear relationships between costs, revenues and volume.
- There may be stepped fixed costs. Most fixed costs are not fixed over all volumes of activity.
- Multi-product businesses have problems in allocating fixed costs to particular activities.

Marginal analysis (ignores fixed cost where these are not affected by the decision)

- Accepting/rejecting special contracts – we consider only the effect on contributions.
- Using scarce resources – the limiting factor is most effectively used by maximising its contribution per unit.
- Make-or-buy decisions – we take the action that leads to the highest total contributions.
- Closing/continuing an activity – should be assessed by net effect on total contributions.

→ Key terms

Further reading

If you would like to explore the topics covered in this chapter in more depth, we recommend the following books:

Drury, C., *Management and Cost Accounting*, 7th edn, Cengage Learning, 2007, chapter 8.

Hilton, R., *Managerial Accounting*, 6th edn. McGraw-Hill Irwin, 2005, chapter 8.

Horngren, C., Foster, G., Datar, S., Rajan, M. and Ittner, C., *Cost Accounting: A Managerial Emphasis*, 13th edn, Prentice Hall International, 2008, chapter 3.

McWatters, C., Zimmerman, J. and Morse, D., *Management Accounting: Analysis and Interpretation*, FT Prentice Hall, 2008, chapter 5.

REVIEW QUESTIONS

Answers to these questions can be found in Appendix C at the back of the book.

3.1 Define the terms *fixed cost* and *variable cost.* Explain how an understanding of the distinction between fixed cost and variable cost can be useful to managers.

3.2 What is meant by the *BEP* for an activity? How is the BEP calculated? Why is it useful to know the BEP?

3.3 When we say that some business activity has *high operating gearing*, what do we mean? What are the implications for the business of high operating gearing?

3.4 If there is a scarce resource that is restricting sales, how will the business maximise its profit? Explain the logic of the approach that you have identified for maximising profit.

EXERCISES

Exercises 3.4 to 3.8 are more advanced than 3.1 to 3.3. Those exercises with coloured numbers have answers in Appendix D at the back of the book.

3.1 The management of a business is concerned about its inability to obtain enough fully trained labour to enable it to meet its present budget projection.

Service:	Alpha £000	Beta £000	Gamma £000	Total £000
Variable cost				
Materials	6	4	5	15
Labour	9	6	12	27
Expenses	3	2	2	7
Allocated fixed cost	6	15	12	33
Total cost	24	27	31	82
Profit	15	2	2	19
Sales revenue	39	29	33	101

The amount of labour likely to be available amounts to £20,000. All of the variable labour is paid at the same hourly rate. You have been asked to prepare a statement of plans ensuring that at least 50 per cent of the budgeted sales revenues are achieved for each service, and the balance of labour is used to produce the greatest profit.

Required:
(a) Prepare the statement, with explanations, showing the greatest profit available from the limited amount of skilled labour available, within the constraint stated. *Hint*: Remember that all labour is paid at the same rate.
(b) What steps could the business take in an attempt to improve profitability, in the light of the labour shortage?

3.2   Lannion and Co. is engaged in providing and marketing a standard advice service. Summarised results for the past two months reveal the following:

	October	November
Sales (units of the service)	200	300
Sales revenue (£)	5,000	7,500
Operating profit (£)	1,000	2,200

There were no price changes of any description during these two months.

Required:

(a) Deduce the BEP (in units of the service) for Lannion and Co.

(b) State why the business might find it useful to know its BEP.

3.3   A hotel group prepares financial statements on a quarterly basis. The senior management is reviewing the performance of one hotel and making plans for next year.

   The managers have in front of them the results for this year (based on some actual results and some forecasts to the end of this year):

Quarter	Sales revenue	Profit/(loss)
	£000	£000
1	400	(280)
2	1,200	360
3	1,600	680
4	800	40
Total	4,000	800

The total estimated number of visitors (guest nights) for this year is 50,000. The results follow a regular pattern; there are no unexpected cost fluctuations beyond the seasonal trading pattern shown above. For next year, management anticipates an increase in unit variable cost of 10 per cent and a profit target for the hotel of £1 million. These will be incorporated into its plans.

Required:

(a) Calculate the total variable and total fixed cost of the hotel for this year. Show the provisional annual results for this year in total, showing variable and fixed cost separately. Show also the revenue and cost per visitor.

(b) 1 If there is no increase in visitors for next year, what will be the required revenue rate per hotel visitor to meet the profit target?

   2 If the required revenue rate per visitor is not raised above this year's level, how many visitors will be required to meet the profit target?

(c) Outline and briefly discuss the assumptions that are made in typical PV or break-even analysis, and assess whether they limit its usefulness.

3.4   Motormusic Ltd makes a standard model of car radio, which it sells to car manufacturers for £60 each. Next year the business plans to make and sell 20,000 radios. The business's costs are as follows:

Manufacturing	
Variable materials	£20 per radio
Variable labour	£14 per radio
Other variable costs	£12 per radio
Fixed cost	£80,000 per year
Administration and selling	
Variable	£3 per radio
Fixed	£60,000 per year

Required:

(a) Calculate the break-even point for next year, expressed both in quantity of radios and sales value.

(b) Calculate the margin of safety for next year, expressed both in quantity of radios and sales value.

3.5 A business makes three products, A, B and C. All three products require the use of two types of machine: cutting machines and assembling machines. Estimates for next year include the following:

Product	A	B	C
Selling price (£ per unit)	25	30	18
Sales demand (units)	2,500	3,400	5,100
Material cost (£ per unit)	12	13	10
Variable production cost (£ per unit)	7	4	3
Time required per unit on cutting machines (hours)	1.0	1.0	0.5
Time required per unit on assembling machines (hours)	0.5	1.0	0.5

Fixed cost for next year is expected to total £42,000. It is the business's policy for each unit of production to absorb these in proportion to its total variable cost.

The business has cutting-machine capacity of 5,000 hours a year and assembling-machine capacity of 8,000 hours a year.

Required:

(a) State, with supporting workings, which products in which quantities the business should plan to make next year on the basis of the above information. *Hint*: First determine which machines will be a limiting factor (scarce resource).

(b) State the maximum price per product that it would be worth the business paying to a sub-contractor to carry out that part of the work that could not be done internally.

3.6 Darmor Ltd has three products, which require the same production facilities. Information about the production cost for one unit of its products is as follows:

Product	X	Y	Z
	£	£	£
Labour: Skilled	6	9	3
Unskilled	2	4	10
Materials	12	25	14
Other variable costs	3	7	7
Fixed cost	5	10	10

All labour and materials are variable costs. Skilled labour is paid £12 an hour, and unskilled labour is paid £8 an hour. All references to labour cost above are based on basic rates of pay. Skilled labour is scarce, which means that the business could sell more than the maximum that it is able to make of any of the three products.

Product X is sold in a regulated market, and the regulators have set a price of £30 per unit for it.

Required:

(a) State, with supporting workings, the price that must be charged for products Y and Z, such that the business would find it equally profitable to make and sell any of the three products.

(b) State, with supporting workings, the maximum rate of overtime premium that the business would logically be prepared to pay its skilled workers to work beyond the basic time.

3.7 Intermediate Products Ltd produces four types of water pump. Two of these (A and B) are sold by the business. The other two (C and D) are incorporated, as components, into another of the business's products. Neither C nor D is incorporated into A or B. Costings (per unit) for the products are as follows:

	A £	B £	C £	D £
Variable materials	15	20	16	17
Variable labour	25	10	10	15
Other variable costs	5	3	2	2
Fixed costs	20	8	8	12
	65	41	36	46
Selling price (per unit)	£70	£45		

There is an outside supplier who is prepared to supply unlimited quantities of products C and D to the business, charging £40 per unit for product C and £55 per unit for product D.

Next year's estimated demand for the products, from the market (in the case of A and B) and from other production requirements (in the case of C and D), is as follows:

	Units
A	5,000
B	6,000
C	4,000
D	3,000

For strategic reasons, the business wishes to supply a minimum of 50 per cent of the above demand for products A and B.

Manufacture of all four products requires the use of a special machine. The products require time on this machine as follows:

	Hours per unit
A	0.5
B	0.4
C	0.5
D	0.3

Next year there are expected to be a maximum of 6,000 special-machine hours available. There will be no shortage of any other factor of production.

Required:
(a) State, with supporting workings and assumptions, which quantities of which products the business should plan to make next year.
(b) Explain the maximum amount that it would be worth the business paying per hour to rent a second special machine.
(c) Suggest ways, other than renting an additional special machine, that could solve the problem of the shortage of special-machine time.

3.8 Gandhi Ltd renders a promotional service to small retailing businesses. There are three levels of service: the 'basic', the 'standard' and the 'comprehensive'. On the basis of past experience, the business plans next year to work at absolutely full capacity as follows:

Service	Number of units of the service	Selling price £	Variable cost per unit £
Basic	11,000	50	25
Standard	6,000	80	65
Comprehensive	16,000	120	90

The business's fixed cost totals £660,000 a year. Each service takes about the same length of time, irrespective of the level.

One of the accounts staff has just produced a report that seems to show that the standard service is unprofitable. The relevant extract from the report is as follows:

Standard service cost analysis

	£	
Selling price per unit	80	
Variable cost per unit	(65)	
Fixed cost per unit	(20)	(£660,000/(11,000 + 6,000 + 16,000))
Loss	(5)	

The producer of the report suggests that the business should not offer the standard service next year.

Required:

(a) Should the standard service be offered next year, assuming that the quantity of the other services could not be expanded to use the spare capacity?

(b) Should the standard service be offered next year, assuming that the released capacity could be used to render a new service, the 'nova', for which customers would be charged £75, and which would have variable cost of £50 and take twice as long as the other three services?

(c) What is the minimum price that could be accepted for the basic service, assuming that the necessary capacity to expand it will come only from not offering the standard service?

4

Full costing

INTRODUCTION

Full (absorption) costing is a widely used approach that takes account of all of the cost of producing a particular product or service. In this chapter, we shall see how this approach can be used to deduce the cost of some productive activity, such as producing a unit of product (for example a tin of baked beans), providing a unit of service (for example, a car repair) or creating a facility (for example, building an Olympic athletics stadium). The precise approach taken to deducing full cost will depend on whether each product or service is identical to the next or whether each job has its own individual characteristics. It will also depend on whether the business accounts for overheads on a segmental basis. We shall look at how full (or absorption) costing is carried out and we shall also consider its usefulness for management purposes.

This chapter considers the traditional, but still very widely used, form of full costing. In Chapter 5 we shall consider activity-based costing, which is a more recently developed approach.

LEARNING OUTCOMES

When you have completed this chapter, you should be able to:

- Deduce the full (absorption) cost of a cost unit in a single-product environment.

- Deduce the full (absorption) cost of a cost unit in a multi-product environment.

- Discuss the problems of deducing full (absorption) cost in practice.

- Discuss the usefulness of full (absorption) cost information to managers.

Why do managers want to know the full cost?

As we saw in Chapter 1, the only point in providing management accounting information is to help managers make more informed decisions. There are broadly four areas where managers use information concerning the full cost of the business's products or services. These are:

1 *Pricing and output decisions.* Having full cost information can help managers to make decisions on the price to be charged to customers for the business's products or services. Linked to the pricing decisions are also decisions on the number of products or services that the business should seek to provide to the market.

2 *Exercising control.* Managers need information to help them make decisions that are aimed at getting the business back on course if plans are not being met. Budgets are typically expressed in full cost terms. This means that periodic reports that compare actual performance with budgets need to be expressed in the same full cost terms.

3 *Assessing relative efficiency.* Full cost information helps managers to compare the cost of doing something in one way, or place, with its cost if done in a different way, or place. For example, a car manufacturer may find it useful to compare the cost of building a particular model of car in one of its plants, rather than another. This could help them decide on where to locate future production.

4 *Assessing performance.* The level of profit, or income, generated over a period is an important measure of business performance. To measure profit, or income, we need to compare sales revenue with the associated expenses. Where a business produces a product or renders a service, a major expense will be the cost of making the product or rendering the service. Logically this is the full cost of whatever was sold. Measuring income provides managers (and other users) with information that can help them make a whole range of decisions.

Later in the chapter we shall consider some of the issues surrounding these four purposes. Figure 4.1 shows the four uses of full cost information.

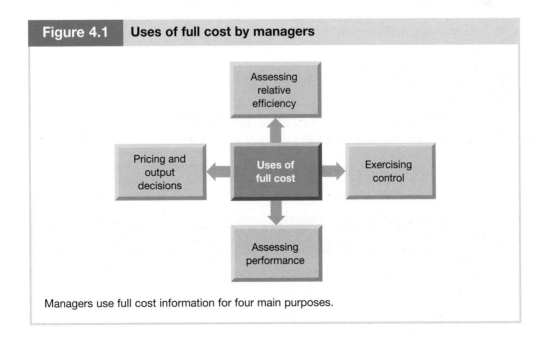

Figure 4.1   Uses of full cost by managers

Managers use full cost information for four main purposes.

Now let us consider **Real World 4.1**.

REAL WORLD 4.1

Operating cost

An interesting example of the use of full cost for pricing decisions is occuring in the National Health Service (NHS). In recent years, the funding of hospitals has radically changed. A new system of Payment by Results (PBR) requires the Department of Health to produce a list of prices for an in-patient spell in hospital that covers different types of procedures. This list, which is revised annually, reflects the prices that hospitals will be paid by the government for carrying out the different procedures.

For 2007/8, the price list included the following figures:

£4,967 for carrying out a hip replacement operation
£4,293 for treating a stroke

These figures are based on the full cost of undertaking each type of procedure in 2006/7 (but adjusted for inflation). Full cost figures were submitted by all NHS hospitals for that year as part of their annual accounting process and an average for each type of procedure was then calculated. Figures for other procedures on the price list were derived in the same way.

Source: Cole, A. and Robjent, G., 'Payment by results – Policy in focus', Chartered Society of Physiotherapists, 20 June 2007.

When considering the information in **Real World 4.1**, an important question that arises is 'what does the full cost of each type of procedure include?' Does it simply include the cost of the salaries earned by doctors and nurses during the time spent with the patient or does it also include the cost of other items? If the cost of other items is included, how is it determined? Would it include, for example, a charge for

- the artificial hip and drugs provided for the patient
- equipment used in the operating theatre
- administrative and support staff within the hospital
- heating and lighting
- maintaining the hospital buildings
- laundry and cleaning?

If the cost of such items is included, how can an appropriate charge be determined? If, on the other hand, it is not included, are the figures of £4,967 and £4,293 potentially misleading?

These questions are the subject of this chapter.

What is full costing?

 Full cost is the total amount of resources, usually measured in monetary terms, sacrificed to achieve a particular objective. It takes account of all resources sacrificed to achieve that objective. Thus, if the objective were to supply a customer with a product or service, the cost of all aspects relating to the production of the product or provision of the service would be included as part of the full cost. To derive the full cost figure, we must accumulate the elements of cost incurred and then assign them to the particular product or service.

➡ The logic of **full costing** is that the entire cost of running a particular facility, say an office, is part of the cost of the output of that office. For example, the rent may be a cost that will not alter merely because we provide one more unit of the service, but if the office were not rented there would be nowhere for the staff who provide the service to work, so rent is an important element of the cost of each cost unit of that
➡ service. A **cost unit** is one unit of whatever is having its cost determined. This is usually one unit of output of a particular product or service.

In the sections that follow we shall first see how full costing is applied to a single-product business and then consider how it is done for a multi-product one.

Single-product businesses

The simplest case for which to deduce the full cost per unit is where the business has only one product or service, that is, each unit of its production is identical. Here it is simply a question of adding up all of the elements of cost of production incurred in a particular period (materials, labour, rent, fuel, power and so on) and dividing this total by the total number of units of output for that period.

Activity 4.1

Fruitjuice Ltd has just one product, a sparkling orange drink that is marketed as Orange Fizz. During last month the business produced 7,300 litres of the drink. The cost incurred was made up as follows:

	£
Ingredients (oranges and so on)	390
Fuel	85
Rent of premises	350
Depreciation of equipment	75
Labour	880

What is the full cost per litre of producing Orange Fizz?

This figure is found by simply adding together all of the elements of cost incurred and then dividing by the number of litres produced:

£(390 + 85 + 350 + 75 + 880)/7,300 = £0.24 per litre

In practice, there can be problems in deciding exactly how much cost was incurred. In the case of Fruitjuice Ltd, for example, how is the cost of depreciation deduced? It is certainly an estimate, and so its reliability is open to question. The cost of raw materials may also be a problem. Should we use the *relevant* cost of the raw materials (in this case, almost certainly the replacement cost), or the actual price paid for it (historic cost)? If the cost per litre is to be used for some decision-making purpose (which it should be), the replacement cost is probably more logical. In practice, however, it seems that historic cost is more often used to deduce full cost. It is not clear why this should be the case.

There can also be problems in deciding precisely how many units of output were produced. If making Orange Fizz is not a very fast process, some of the drink will probably be in the process of being made at any given moment. This, in turn, means that some of the cost incurred last month was for some Orange Fizz that was work in progress at the end of the month, so is not included in last month's output quantity of 7,300 litres. Similarly, part of the 7,300 litres might well have been started and incurred cost in the previous month, yet all of those litres were included in the 7,300 litres that we used in our calculation of the cost per litre. Work in progress is not a serious problem, but some adjustment for the value of opening and closing work in progress for the particular period needs to be made if reliable full cost information is to be obtained.

This approach to full costing, which can be taken where all of the output consists of identical, or near identical items (of goods or services), is often referred to as **process costing**.

Multi-product businesses

Most businesses produce more than one type of product or service. In this situation, the units of output of the product, or service, will not be identical and so the approach used with litres of Orange Fizz in Activity 4.1 is inappropriate. Although it is reasonable to assign an identical cost to units of output that are identical, it is not reasonable to do this where the units of output are obviously different. It would not be reasonable, for example, to assign the same cost to each car repair carried out by a garage, irrespective of the complexity and size of the repair.

Direct and indirect cost

To provide full cost information, we need to have a systematic approach to accumulating the elements of cost and then assigning this total cost to particular cost units on some reasonable basis. Where cost units are not identical, the starting point is to separate cost into two categories: direct cost and indirect cost.

- **Direct cost**. This is the type of cost that can be identified with specific cost units. That is to say, the effect of the cost can be measured in respect of each particular cost unit. The main examples of a direct cost are direct materials and direct labour. Thus, in determining the cost of a motor car repair by a garage, both the cost of spare parts used in the repair and the cost of the mechanic's time would be part of the direct cost of that repair. Collecting elements of direct cost is a simple matter of having a cost-recording system that is capable of capturing the cost of direct materials used on each job and the cost, based on the hours worked and the rate of pay, of direct workers.
- **Indirect cost** (or **overheads**). These are all other elements of cost, that is, those that cannot be directly measured in respect of each particular cost unit (job). Thus, the rent of the garage premises would be an indirect cost of a motor car repair.

We shall use the terms 'indirect cost' and 'overheads' interchangeably for the remainder of this book. Indirect cost is also sometimes known as **common cost** because it is common to all of the output of the production unit (for example, factory or department) for the period.

Real World 4.2 gives some indication of the relative importance of direct and indirect costs in practice.

REAL WORLD 4.2

Counting the cost

A recent survey of 176 UK businesses operating in various industries, all with an annual turnover of more than £50 million, was conducted by Al-Omiri and Drury. They discovered that the total cost of the businesses' output, on average, is split between direct and indirect costs as follows:

	Direct cost Per cent	Indirect cost Per cent
All 176 businesses	69	31
Manufacturing businesses (91)	75	25
Service and retail businesses (85)	49	51

For the manufacturers, the 75 per cent direct cost was, on average, made up as follows:

	Per cent
Direct materials	52
Direct labour	14
Other direct costs	9

Source: Al-Omiri, M. and Drury, C., 'A survey of factors influencing the choice of product costing systems in UK organisations', *Management Accounting Research*, December 2007, pp. 399–424.

A more extensive recent survey of management accounting practice in the US, with nearly 2,000 responses, showed similar results. Like the UK survey (above), this tended to relate to larger businesses. About 40% were manufacturers and about 16% financial services; the remainder were from a range of other industries.

This survey revealed that, of total cost, indirect cost accounted for between 34 per cent for retailers (lowest) and 42 per cent for manufacturers (highest), with other industries' proportion of indirect cost falling within the 34 per cent to 42 per cent range. Financial and commercial businesses showed an average indirect cost percentage of 38 per cent.

Source: 2003 Survey of Management Accounting, Ernst and Young, 2003.

Activity 4.2

A garage bases its prices on the direct cost of each job (car repair) that it carries out. How could the garage collect the direct cost (labour and materials) information concerning a particular job?

Usually, direct workers are required to record how long was spent on each job. Thus, the mechanic doing the job would record the length of time worked on the car by direct workers (that is, the mechanic concerned and any colleagues). The stores staff would normally be required to keep a record of the cost of parts and materials used on each job.

A 'job sheet' will normally be prepared – perhaps on the computer – for each individual job. Staff must get into the routine of faithfully recording all elements of direct labour and materials applied to the job.

Job costing

→ The term **job costing** is used to describe the way in which we identify the full cost per cost unit (unit of output or 'job') where the cost units differ. To cost (that is, deduce the full cost of) a particular cost unit, we first identify the direct cost of the cost unit, which, by the definition of direct cost, is fairly straightforward. We then seek to 'charge' each cost unit with a fair share of indirect cost (overheads). Put another way,

→ cost units will absorb overheads. This leads to full costing also being called **absorption costing**. The absorption process is shown graphically in Figure 4.2.

Figure 4.2	The relationship between direct cost and indirect cost

The full cost of any particular job is the sum of those costs that can be measured specifically in respect of the job (direct costs) and a share of those costs that create the environment in which production (of an object or service) can take place, but which do not relate specifically to any particular job (overheads).

Activity 4.3

Sparky Ltd is a business that employs a number of electricians. The business undertakes a range of work for its customers, from replacing fuses to installing complete wiring systems in new houses.

In respect of a particular job done by Sparky Ltd, into which category (direct or indirect) would each of the following cost elements fall?

- the wages of the electrician who did the job
- depreciation of the tools used by the electrician
- the salary of Sparky Ltd's accountant
- the cost of cable and other materials used on the job
- rent of the premises where Sparky Ltd stores its inventories of cable and other materials

Only the electrician's wages earned while working on the particular job and the cost of the materials used on the job are included in direct cost. This is because it is possible to measure how much time (and therefore the direct labour cost) was spent on the particular job and the amount of materials used (and therefore the direct material cost) in the job.

All of the others are included in the general cost of running the business and, as such, must form part of the indirect cost of doing the job, but they cannot be directly measured in respect of the particular job.

It is important to note that whether a cost is direct or indirect depends on the item being costed – the cost objective. To refer to indirect cost without identifying the cost objective is incorrect.

Activity 4.4

Into which category, direct or indirect, would each of the elements of cost listed in Activity 4.3 fall, if we were seeking to find the cost of operating the entire business of Sparky Ltd for a month?

....

The answer is that all of them will form part of the direct cost, since they can all be related to, and measured in respect of, running the business for a month.

Naturally, broader-reaching cost objectives, such as operating Sparky Ltd for a month, tend to include a higher proportion of direct cost than do more limited ones, such as a particular job done by Sparky Ltd. As we shall see shortly, this makes costing broader cost objectives rather more straightforward than costing narrower ones. It is generally the case that direct cost is easier to deal with than indirect cost.

Full (absorption) costing and the behaviour of cost

We saw in Chapter 3 that the full cost of doing something (or total cost, as it is usually known in the context of marginal analysis) can be analysed between the fixed and the variable elements. This is illustrated in Figure 4.3.

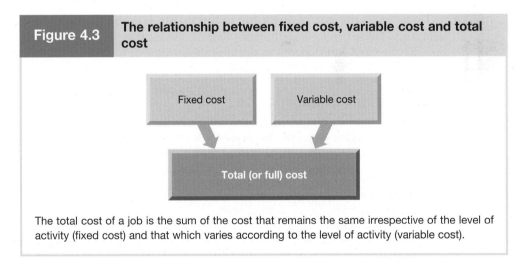

| Figure 4.3 | The relationship between fixed cost, variable cost and total cost |

The total cost of a job is the sum of the cost that remains the same irrespective of the level of activity (fixed cost) and that which varies according to the level of activity (variable cost).

The apparent similarity of Figure 4.3 to Figure 4.2 seems to lead some people to believe that variable cost and direct cost are the same and that fixed cost and indirect cost (overheads) are the same. This is incorrect.

The notions of fixed and variable are concerned with **cost behaviour** in the face of changes in the volume of activity. The notions of direct and indirect, on the other hand, are concerned with the extent to which cost elements can be measured in respect of particular cost units (jobs). The two sets of notions are entirely different. Though it may be true that there is a tendency for fixed cost elements to be indirect (overheads) and for variable cost elements to be direct, there is no link, and there are many exceptions to this tendency. Most activities, for example, have variable indirect cost. Furthermore, labour is a significant element of direct cost in most types of business activity (14 per cent of the total cost of manufacture – see Real World 4.2) but is usually a fixed cost.

The relationship between the reaction of cost to volume changes (cost behaviour), on the one hand, and how cost elements need to be gathered to deduce the full cost (cost collection), on the other, in respect of a particular job is shown in Figure 4.4.

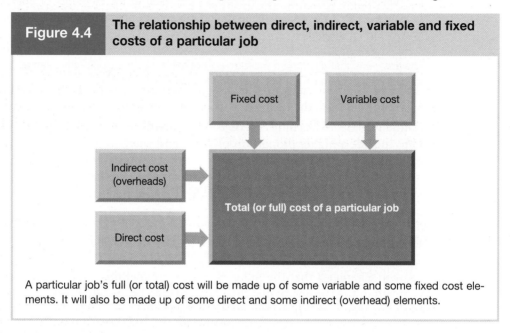

| Figure 4.4 | **The relationship between direct, indirect, variable and fixed costs of a particular job** |

A particular job's full (or total) cost will be made up of some variable and some fixed cost elements. It will also be made up of some direct and some indirect (overhead) elements.

Total cost is the sum of direct and indirect costs. It is also the sum of fixed and variable costs. These two facts are independent of one another. Thus a particular element of cost may be fixed, but that tells us nothing about whether it is a direct or an indirect cost.

The problem of indirect cost

It is worth emphasising that the distinction between direct and indirect cost is only important in a job-costing environment, that is, where units of output differ. When we were considering costing a litre of Orange Fizz in Activity 4.1, whether particular elements of cost were direct or indirect was of no consequence, because all elements of cost were shared equally between the individual litres of Orange Fizz. Where we have units of output that are not identical, however, we have to look more closely at the make-up of the cost to achieve a fair measure of the full cost of a particular job.

Although the indirect cost of any activity must form part of the cost of each cost unit, it cannot, by definition, be directly related to individual cost units. This raises a major practical issue: how is the indirect cost to be apportioned to individual cost units?

Overheads as service renderers

It is reasonable to view the indirect cost (overheads) as rendering a service to the cost units. A legal case, undertaken by a firm of solicitors for a particular client, can be seen as being rendered a service by the office in which the work is done. In this sense, it is reasonable to charge each case (cost unit) with a share of the cost of running the office (rent, lighting, heating, cleaning, building maintenance and so on). It also seems reasonable to relate the charge for the 'use' of the office to the level of service that the particular case has received from the office.

The next step is the difficult one. How might the cost of running the office, which is a cost of all work done by the firm, be divided between individual cases that are not similar in size and complexity?

One possibility is sharing this overhead cost equally between each case handled by the firm within the period. This method, however, has little to commend it unless the cases were close to being identical in terms of the extent to which they had 'benefited' from the overheads.

If we are not to propose equal shares, we must identify something observable and measurable about the cases that we feel provides a reasonable basis for distinguishing between one case and the next. In practice, time spent working on each particular cost unit by direct labour is the most popular basis. It must be stressed that this is not the 'correct' way, and it certainly is not the only way.

Job costing: a worked example

To see how job costing (as it is usually called) works, let us consider Example 4.1.

Example 4.1

Johnson Ltd, a business that provides a personal computer maintenance and repair service to its customers, has overheads of £10,000 each month. Each month 1,000 direct labour hours are worked and charged to cost units (jobs carried out by the business). A particular PC repair undertaken by the business used direct materials costing £15. Direct labour worked on the repair was 3 hours and the wage rate is £16 an hour. Overheads are charged to jobs on a direct labour hour basis. What is the full (absorption) cost of the repair?

Solution

First, let us establish the **overhead absorption (recovery) rate**, that is, the rate at which individual repairs will be charged with overheads. This is £10 (that is, £10,000/1,000) per direct labour hour.

Thus, the full cost of the repair is:

	£
Direct materials	15
Direct labour (3 × £16)	48
	63
Overheads (3 × £10)	30
Full cost of the job	93

Note, in Example 4.1, that the number of labour hours (3 hours) appears twice in deducing the full cost: once to deduce the direct labour cost and a second time to deduce the overheads to be charged to the repair. These are really two separate issues, though they are both based on the same number of labour hours.

Note also that, if all the jobs undertaken during the month are assigned overheads in a similar manner, all £10,000 of overheads will be charged to the jobs between them. Jobs that involve a lot of direct labour will be assigned a large share of overheads, and jobs that involve little direct labour will be assigned a small share of overheads.

Activity 4.5

Can you think of reasons why direct labour hours are regarded as the most logical basis for sharing overheads between cost units?

The reasons that occurred to us are as follows:

- Large jobs should logically attract large amounts of overheads because they are likely to have been rendered more 'service' by the overheads than small ones. The length of time that they are worked on by direct labour may be seen as a rough and ready way of measuring relative size, though other means of doing this may be found – for example, relative physical size, where the cost unit is a physical object, like a manufactured product.
- Most overheads are related to time. Rent, heating, lighting, non-current asset depreciation, supervisors' and managers' salaries and interest on borrowings, which are all typical overheads, are all more or less time-based. That is to say that the overheads for one week tends to be about half of that for a similar two-week period. Thus, a basis of allotting overheads to jobs that takes account of the length of time that the units of output benefited from the 'service' rendered by the overheads seems logical.
- Direct labour hours are capable of being measured for each job. They will normally be measured to deduce the direct labour element of cost in any case. Thus, a direct labour hour basis of dealing with overheads is practical to apply in the real world.

It cannot be emphasised enough that there is no 'correct' way to allot overheads to jobs. Overheads, by definition, do not naturally relate to individual jobs. If, nevertheless, we wish to take account of the fact that overheads are part of the cost of all jobs, we must find some acceptable way of including a share of the total overheads in each job. If a particular means of doing this is accepted by those who use the full cost deduced, then the method is as good as any other method. Accounting is concerned only with providing useful information to decision makers. In practice, the method that seems to be regarded as being the most useful is the direct labour hour method. Real World 4.4, which we shall consider later in the chapter, provides some evidence of this.

Now let us consider **Real World 4.3**, which gives an example of one well-known organisation that does not use direct labour hours to cost its output.

REAL WORLD 4.3

Operating cost

As we saw in **Real World 4.1**, the UK National Health Service (NHS) seeks to ascertain the cost of various medical and surgical procedures that it undertakes for its patients. In determining the costs of a procedure that requires time in hospital as an in-patient, the NHS identifies the total direct cost of the particular procedure (staff time, medication and so on). To this it adds a share of the hospital overheads. The total cost of overheads is absorbed by individual procedures by taking this overheads total and dividing it by the number of 'bed-days' throughout the hospital for the period, to establish a 'bed-day rate'. A bed-day is one patient spending one day occupying a bed in the hospital. To cost the procedure for a particular patient, the bed-day rate is applied to the cost of the procedure according to how many bed-days the particular patient had.

Note that the NHS does not use the direct labour hour basis of absorption. However, the bed-day rate alternative is also a logical, time-based approach.

Source: NHS Costing Manual, Department of Health Gateway reference 9367, February 2008.

Activity 4.6

Marine Suppliers Ltd undertakes a range of work, including making sails for small sailing boats on a made-to-measure basis.

The business expects the following to arise during the next month:

Direct labour cost	£60,000
Direct labour time	6,000 hours
Indirect labour cost	£9,000
Depreciation of machinery	£3,000
Rent and rates	£5,000
Heating, lighting and power	£2,000
Machine time	2,000 hours
Indirect materials	£500
Other miscellaneous indirect cost (overhead) elements	£200
Direct materials cost	£3,000

The business has received an enquiry about a sail. It is estimated that the particular sail will take 12 direct labour hours to make and will require 20 square metres of sailcloth, which costs £2 per square metre.

The business normally uses a direct labour hour basis of charging indirect cost (overheads) to individual jobs.

What is the full (absorption) cost of making the sail?

. . . .

The direct cost of making the sail can be identified as follows:

	£
Direct materials (20 × £2)	40.00
Direct labour (12 × (£60,000/6,000))	120.00
	160.00

To deduce the indirect cost (overhead) element that must be added to derive the full cost of the sail, we first need to total these cost elements as follows:

Activity 4.6 continued

	£
Indirect labour	9,000
Depreciation	3,000
Rent and rates	5,000
Heating, lighting and power	2,000
Indirect materials	500
Other miscellaneous indirect cost (overhead) elements	200
Total indirect cost (overheads)	19,700

Since the business uses a direct labour hour basis of charging indirect cost to jobs, we need to deduce the indirect cost (or overhead) recovery rate per direct labour hour. This is simply

$$£19,700/6,000 = £3.28 \text{ per direct labour hour}$$

Thus, the full cost of the sail would be expected to be:

	£
Direct materials (20 × £2)	40.00
Direct labour (12 × (£60,000/6,000))	120.00
Indirect cost (12 × £3.28)	39.36
Full cost	199.36

Figure 4.5 shows the process for applying indirect cost (overheads) and direct cost to the sail that was the subject of Activity 4.6.

Figure 4.5 **Deriving the full cost of the sail made by Marine Supplies Ltd**

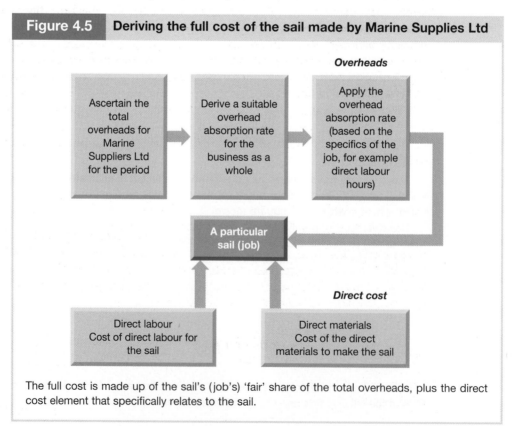

The full cost is made up of the sail's (job's) 'fair' share of the total overheads, plus the direct cost element that specifically relates to the sail.

Activity 4.7

Suppose that Marine Suppliers Ltd (see Activity 4.6) used a machine hour basis of charging overheads to jobs. What would be the cost of the job detailed if it was expected to take 5 machine hours (as well as 12 direct labour hours)?

The total overheads of the business will of course be the same irrespective of the method of charging them to jobs. Thus, the overhead recovery rate, on a machine hour basis, will be

$$£19,700/2,000 = £9.85 \text{ per machine hour}$$

Thus, the full cost of the sail would be expected to be:

	£
Direct materials (20 × £2)	40.00
Direct labour (12 × (£60,000/6,000))	120.00
Indirect cost (5 × £9.85)	49.25
Full cost	209.25

Selecting a basis for charging overheads

We saw earlier that there is no single correct way of charging overheads. The final choice is a matter of judgement. It seems reasonable to say, however, that the nature of the overheads should influence the choice of the basis of charging the overheads to jobs. Where production is capital-intensive and overheads are primarily machine-based (depreciation, machine maintenance, power and so on), machine hours might be favoured. Otherwise direct labour hours might be preferred.

It would be irrational to choose one of these bases in preference to the other simply because it apportions either a higher or a lower amount of overheads to a particular job. The total overheads will be the same irrespective of the method of dividing that total between individual jobs and so a method that gives a higher share of overheads to one particular job must give a lower share to the remaining jobs. There is one cake of fixed size: if one person receives a relatively large slice, others must on average receive relatively small slices. To illustrate further this issue of apportioning overheads, consider Example 4.2.

Example 4.2

A business, that provides a service, expects to incur overheads totalling £20,000 next month. The total direct labour time worked is expected to be 1,600 hours and machines are expected to operate for a total of 1,000 hours.

During the next month, the business expects to do just two large jobs. Information concerning each job is as follows:

	Job 1	Job 2
Direct labour hours	800	800
Machine hours	700	300

How much of the total overheads will be charged to each job if overheads are to be charged on:

Example 4.2 continued

(a) a direct labour hour basis; and
(b) a machine hour basis?

What do you notice about the two sets of figures that you calculate?

Solution

(a) Direct labour hour basis
Overhead recovery rate = £20,000/1,600 = £12.50 per direct labour hour.

$$\begin{array}{lll}
\text{Job 1} & £12.50 \times 800 = & \underline{£10,000} \\
\text{Job 2} & £12.50 \times 800 = & \underline{£10,000}
\end{array}$$

(b) Machine hour basis
Overhead recovery rate = £20,000/1,000 = £20.00 per machine hour.

$$\begin{array}{lll}
\text{Job 1} & £20.00 \times 700 = & \underline{£14,000} \\
\text{Job 2} & £20.00 \times 300 = & £\underline{\ 6,000}
\end{array}$$

It is clear from these calculations that the total overheads charged to jobs is the same (that is, £20,000) whichever method is used. So, whereas the machine hour basis gives Job 1 a higher share than does the direct labour hour method, the opposite is true for Job 2.

It is not practical to charge overheads on one basis to one job and on the other basis to the other job. This is because either total overheads will not be fully charged to the jobs, or the jobs will be overcharged with overheads. For example, using the direct labour hour method for Job 1 (£10,000) and the machine hour basis for Job 2 (£6,000) will mean that only £16,000 of a total £20,000 of overheads will be charged to jobs. As a result, the objective of full (absorption) costing, which is to charge all overheads to jobs done, will not be achieved. In this particular case, if selling prices are based on full cost, the business may not charge high enough prices to cover all of its costs.

Figure 4.6 shows the effect of the two different bases of charging overheads to Jobs 1 and 2.

Figure 4.6	**The effect of different bases of charging overheads to jobs in Example 4.2**

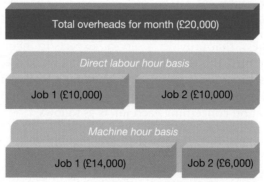

The share of the total overheads for the month charged to jobs can differ significantly depending on the basis used.

Activity 4.8

The point was made above that it would normally be irrational to prefer one basis of charging overheads to jobs simply because it apportions either a higher or a lower amount of overheads to a particular job. This is because the total overheads are the same irrespective of the method of charging the total to individual jobs. Can you think of any circumstances where it would not necessarily be so irrational?

This might apply where, for a particular job, a customer has agreed to pay a price based on full cost plus an agreed fixed percentage for profit. Here it would be beneficial to the producer for the total cost of the job to be as high as possible. This would be relatively unusual, but sometimes public sector organisations, particularly central and local government departments, have entered into contracts to have work done, with the price to be deduced, after the work has been completed, on a cost-plus basis. Such contracts are pretty rare these days, probably because they are open to abuse in the way described. Usually, contract prices are agreed in advance, typically in conjunction with competitive tendering.

Real World 4.4 provides some insight into the basis of overhead recovery in practice.

REAL WORLD 4.4

Overhead recovery rates in practice

A survey of 303 UK manufacturing businesses, published in 1993, showed that the direct labour hour basis of charging indirect cost (overheads) to cost units was overwhelmingly the most popular, used by 73 per cent of the respondents to the survey. Where the work has a strong labour element this seems reasonable, but the survey also showed that 68 per cent of businesses used this basis for automated activities. It is surprising that direct labour hours should have been used as the basis of charging overheads in an environment dominated by machines and machine-related cost.

Though this survey is not very recent and applied only to manufacturing businesses, in the absence of other information it provides some impression of what happens in practice. There is no reason to believe that current practice is very different from that which applied at the beginning of the 1990s.

Source: Based on information taken from Drury, C., Braund, S., Osborne, P. and Tayles, M., *A Survey of Management Accounting Practices in UK Manufacturing Companies*, Chartered Association of Certified Accountants, 1993.

Segmenting the overheads

As we have just seen, charging the same overheads to different jobs on different bases is not logical. It is perfectly reasonable, however, to charge one segment of the total overheads on one basis and another segment (or other segments) on another basis (or bases).

Activity 4.9

Taking the same business as in Example 4.2, on closer analysis we find that of the overheads totalling £20,000 next month, £8,000 relates to machines (depreciation, maintenance, rent of the space occupied by the machines and so on) and the remaining £12,000 to more general overheads. The other information about the business is exactly as it was before.

How much of the total overheads will be charged to each job if the machine-related overheads are to be charged on a machine hour basis and the remaining overheads are charged on a direct labour hour basis?

Direct labour hour basis

Overhead recovery rate = £12,000/1,600 = £7.50 per direct labour hour

Machine hour basis

Overhead recovery rate = £8,000/1,000 = £8.00 per machine hour

Overheads charged to jobs

	Job 1 £	Job 2 £
Direct labour hour basis		
£7.50 × 800	6,000	
£7.50 × 800		6,000
Machine hour basis		
£8.00 × 700	5,600	
£8.00 × 300		2,400
Total	11,600	8,400

We can see from this that the expected overheads of £20,000 are charged in total.

Segmenting the overheads in this way may well be seen as providing a better basis of charging overheads to jobs. This is quite often found in practice, usually by dividing a business into separate 'areas' for costing purposes, charging overheads differently from one area to the next, according to the nature of the work done in each.

Remember that there is no correct basis of charging overheads to jobs, so our frequent reference to the direct labour and machine hour bases should not be taken to imply that these are the correct methods. However, it should be said that these two methods do have something to commend them and they are popular in practice. As we have already seen, a sensible method does need to identify something about each job that can be measured and which distinguishes it from other jobs. There is also a lot to be said for methods that are concerned with time, because most overheads are time-related.

Dealing with overheads on a cost centre basis

In general, as we saw in Chapter 1, all but the smallest businesses are divided into departments. Normally, each department deals with a separate activity. The reasons for dividing a business into departments include the following:

- *Size and complexity.* Many businesses are too large and complex to be managed as a single unit. It is usually more practical to operate each business as a series of relatively independent units with each one having its own manager.
- *Expertise.* Each department normally has its own area of specialism and is managed by a specialist.
- *Accountability.* Each department can have its own accounting records that enable its performance to be assessed. This can lead to greater management control and motivation among the staff.

As is shown in **Real World 4.5**, which we shall consider shortly, most businesses charge overheads to cost units on a department-by-department basis. They do this because they expect that it will give rise to a more useful way of charging overheads. It is probably only in a minority of cases that it leads to any great improvement in the usefulness of the resulting full cost figures. Though it may not be of enormous benefit in many cases, it is probably not an expensive exercise to apply overheads on a departmental basis. Since cost elements are collected department by department for other purposes (particularly control), to apply overheads on a department-by-department basis is a relatively simple matter.

We shall now take a look at how the departmental approach to deriving full cost works, in a service-industry context, through Example 4.3.

Example 4.3

Autosparkle Ltd offers a motor vehicle paint-respray service. The jobs that it undertakes range from painting a small part of a saloon car, usually following a minor accident, to a complete respray of a double-decker bus.

Each job starts life in the Preparation Department, where it is prepared for the Paintshop. In the Preparation Department the job is worked on by direct workers, in most cases taking some direct materials from the stores with which to treat the old paintwork to render the vehicle ready for respraying. Thus the job will be charged with direct materials, direct labour and a share of the Preparation Department's overheads. The job then passes into the Paintshop Department, already valued at the cost that it picked up in the Preparation Department.

In the Paintshop, the staff draw direct materials (mainly paint) from the stores, and direct workers spend time respraying the job, using sophisticated spraying apparatus as well as working by hand. So, in the Paintshop, the job is charged with direct materials, direct labour and a share of that department's overheads. The job now passes into the Finishing Department, valued at the cost of the materials, labour and overheads that it accumulated in the first two departments.

In the Finishing Department, jobs are cleaned and polished ready to go back to the customers. Further direct labour and, in some cases, materials are added. All jobs also pick up a share of that department's overheads. The job, now complete, passes back to the customer.

Figure 4.7 shows graphically how this works for a particular job.

→

Example 4.3 continued

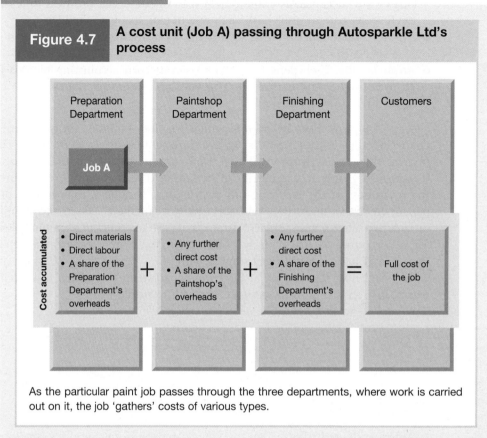

Figure 4.7 A cost unit (Job A) passing through Autosparkle Ltd's process

As the particular paint job passes through the three departments, where work is carried out on it, the job 'gathers' costs of various types.

The basis of charging overheads to jobs (for example, direct labour hours) might be the same for all three departments, or it might be different from one department to another. It is possible that spraying apparatus cost elements dominate the Paintshop cost, so that department's overheads might well be charged to jobs on a machine hour basis. The other two departments are probably labour-intensive, so that direct labour hours may be seen as being appropriate there.

The passage of a job through the departments, picking up cost as it goes, can be compared to a snowball being rolled across snow: as it rolls, it picks up more and more snow.

Where cost determination is dealt with departmentally, each department is known as a **cost centre**. This can be defined as a particular physical area or some activity or function for which the cost is separately identified. Charging direct cost to jobs, in a departmental system, is exactly the same as where the whole business is one single cost centre. It is simply a matter of keeping a record of

- the number of hours of direct labour worked on the particular job and the grade of labour, assuming that there are different grades with different rates of pay;
- the cost of the direct materials taken from stores and applied to the job; and
- any other direct cost elements, for example some subcontracted work, associated with the job.

This record keeping will normally be done cost centre by cost centre in a departmental system.

It is obviously necessary to break down the production overheads of the entire business on a cost centre basis. This means that the total overheads of the business must be divided between the cost centres, such that the sum of the overheads of all of the cost centres equals the overheads for the entire business. By charging all of their overheads to jobs, the cost centres will, between them, charge all of the overheads of the business to jobs. **Real World 4.5** provides an indication of the number of different cost centres that businesses tend to use in practice.

REAL WORLD 4.5

Cost centres in practice

It is not unusual for businesses to have several cost centres. A recent survey by Drury and Tayles of 186 larger UK businesses involved in various activities showed the following:

Figure 4.8	Analysis of the number of cost centres within a business

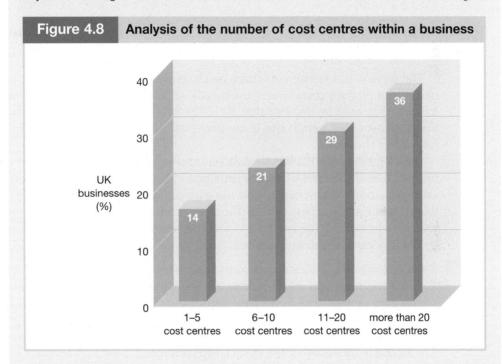

We can see from Figure 4.8 that 86 per cent of businesses surveyed had 6 or more cost centres and that 36 per cent of businesses had more than 20 cost centres. Only 3 per cent of businesses surveyed had a single cost centre (that is, there was a business-wide or overall overhead rate used). Clearly, businesses that deal with overheads on a business-wide basis are very rare.

Source: Based on information taken from Drury, C. and Tayles, M., 'Profitability analysis in UK organisations', *British Accounting Review*, December 2006.

 For purposes of cost assignment, it is necessary to distinguish between **product cost centres** and **service cost centres**. Product cost centres are those in which jobs are worked on by direct workers and/or where direct materials are added. Here jobs can be charged with a share of their overheads. The Preparation, Paintshop and Finishing Departments, discussed above in Example 4.3, are all examples of product cost centres.

Activity 4.10

Can you guess what the definition of a service cost centre is? Can you think of an example of a service cost centre?

A service cost centre is one where no direct cost is involved. It renders a service to other cost centres. Examples include:

- General administration
- Accounting
- Stores
- Maintenance
- Personnel
- Catering.

All of these render services to product cost centres and, possibly, to other service cost centres.

The service cost centre cost must be charged to product cost centres, and become part of the product cost centres' overheads, so that those overheads can be recharged to jobs. This must be done so that all of the overheads of the business find their way into the cost of the jobs. If this is not done, the 'full' cost derived will not really be the full cost of the jobs.

Logically, the cost of a service cost centre should be charged to product cost centres on the basis of the level of service provided to the product cost centre concerned. For example, a product cost centre that has a lot of machine maintenance carried out relative to other product cost centres should be charged with a larger share of the maintenance cost centre's (department's) cost than should those other product cost centres.

The process of dividing overheads between cost centres is as follows:

- **Cost allocation**. Allocate cost elements that are specific to particular cost centres. These are items that relate to, and are specifically measurable in respect of, individual cost centres, that is, they are part of the direct cost of running the cost centre. Examples include:
  - salaries of indirect workers whose activities are wholly within the cost centre, for example the salary of the cost centre manager;
  - rent, where the cost centre is housed in its own premises for which rent can be separately identified;
  - electricity, where it is separately metered for each cost centre.
- **Cost apportionment**. Apportion the more general overheads to the cost centres. These are overheads that relate to more than one cost centre, perhaps to them all. They would include:
  - rent, where more than one cost centre is housed in the same premises;
  - electricity, where it is not separately metered;
  - salaries of cleaning staff who work in a variety of cost centres.

  These overheads would be apportioned to cost centres on the basis of the extent to which each cost centre benefits from the overheads concerned. For example, the rent cost might be apportioned on the basis of the square metres of floor area occupied by each cost centre. With electricity used to power machinery the basis of apportionment might be the level of mechanisation of each cost centre. As with charging overheads to individual jobs, there is no correct basis of apportioning general overheads to cost centres.

● Having totalled, allocated and apportioned the cost to all cost centres, it is now necessary to apportion the total cost of service cost centres to product cost centres. Logically, the basis of apportionment should be the level of service rendered by the individual service cost centre to the individual production cost centre. With personnel cost centre (department) cost, for example, the basis of apportionment might be the number of staff in each product cost centre, because it could be argued that the higher the number of staff, the more benefit the particular product cost centre has derived from the personnel cost centre. This is, of course, rather a crude approach. A particular product cost centre may have severe personnel problems and a high staff turnover rate, which may make it a user of the personnel service that is way out of proportion to the number of staff in the product cost centre.

The final total for each product cost centre is that cost centre's overheads. These can be charged to jobs as they pass through. The process of applying overheads to cost units on a cost centre (departmental) basis is shown in Figure 4.9.

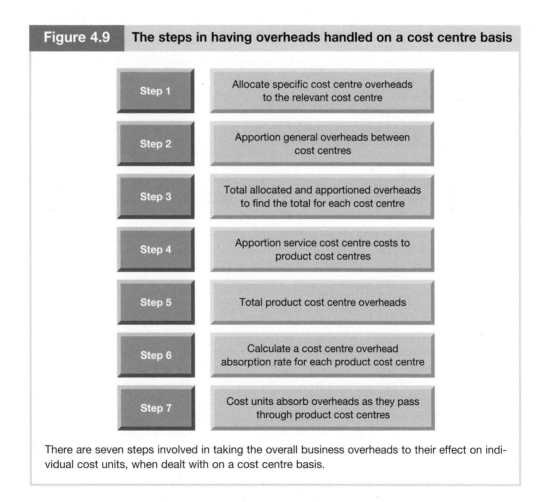

Figure 4.9 The steps in having overheads handled on a cost centre basis

Step 1	Allocate specific cost centre overheads to the relevant cost centre
Step 2	Apportion general overheads between cost centres
Step 3	Total allocated and apportioned overheads to find the total for each cost centre
Step 4	Apportion service cost centre costs to product cost centres
Step 5	Total product cost centre overheads
Step 6	Calculate a cost centre overhead absorption rate for each product cost centre
Step 7	Cost units absorb overheads as they pass through product cost centres

There are seven steps involved in taking the overall business overheads to their effect on individual cost units, when dealt with on a cost centre basis.

We shall now go on to consider Example 4.4, which deals with overheads on a cost centre (departmental) basis.

Example 4.4

A business consists of four cost centres:

● Preparation department
● Machining department
● Finishing department
● General administration (GA) department.

The first three are product cost centres and the last renders a service to the other three. The level of service rendered is thought to be roughly in proportion to the number of employees in each product cost centre.

Overheads, and other data, for next month are expected to be as follows:

	£000
Rent	10,000
Electricity to power machines	3,000
Electricity for heating and lighting	800
Insurance of premises	200
Cleaning	600
Depreciation of machines	2,000

Total salaries to be paid to indirect workers next month are as follows:

	£000
Preparation department	200
Machining department	240
Finishing department	180
General administration department	180

The General administration department has a staff consisting of only indirect workers (including managers). The other departments have both indirect workers (including managers) and direct workers. There are 100 indirect workers within each of the four departments and none does any 'direct' work.

Each direct worker is expected to work 160 hours next month. The number of direct workers in each department is:

Preparation department	600
Machining department	900
Finishing department	500

Machining department direct workers are paid £12 an hour; other direct workers are paid £10 an hour.

All of the machinery is in the machining department. Machines are expected to operate for 120,000 hours next month.

The floorspace (in square metres) occupied by the departments is as follows:

Preparation department	16,000
Machining department	20,000
Finishing department	10,000
General administration department	2,000

Deducing the overheads, cost centre by cost centre, can be done, using a schedule, as follows:

	Total £000	Prep'n £000	Mach'g £000	Fin'g £000	GA £000
	£000				
Allocated cost:					
Machine power		3,000		3,000	
Machine depreciation		2,000		2,000	
Indirect salaries		800	200	240	180	180
Apportioned cost					
Rent	10,000				
Heating and lighting	800				
Insurance of premises	200				
Cleaning	600				
Apportioned by floor area		11,600	3,867	4,833	2,417	483
Cost centre overheads		17,400	4,067	10,073	2,597	663
Reapportion GA cost by number of staff (including the indirect workers)			202	288	173	(663)
		17,400	4,269	10,361	2,770	–

Assume that the machining department overheads (in Example 4.4) are to be charged to jobs on a machine hour basis, but that the direct labour hour basis is to be used for the other two departments. What will be the full (absorption) cost of a job with the following characteristics?

	Preparation	Machining	Finishing
Direct labour hours	10	7	5
Machine hours	–	6	–
Direct materials (£)	85	13	6

Hint: This should be tackled as if each cost centre were a separate business, then departmental cost elements are added together for the job so as to arrive at the total full cost.

First, we need to deduce the indirect (overhead) recovery rates for each cost centre:

Preparation department (direct labour hour based):

$$\frac{£4,269,000}{600 \times 160} = £44.47$$

Machining department (machine hour based):

$$\frac{£10,361,000}{120,000} = £86.34$$

Finishing department (direct labour hour based):

$$\frac{£2,770,000}{500 \times 160} = £34.63$$

→

Activity 4.11 continued

The cost of the job is as follows:

	£	£
Direct labour:		
Preparation department (10 × £10)	100.00	
Machining department (7 × £12)	84.00	
Finishing department (5 × £10)	50.00	
		234.00
Direct materials:		
Preparation department	85.00	
Machining department	13.00	
Finishing department	6.00	
		104.00
Overheads:		
Preparation department (10 × £44.47)	444.70	
Machining department (6 × £86.34)	518.04	
Finishing department (5 × £34.63)	173.15	
		1,135.89
Full cost of the job		1,473.89

Activity 4.12

The manufacturing cost for Buccaneers Ltd for next year is expected to be made up as follows:

	£000
Direct materials:	
Forming department	450
Machining department	100
Finishing department	50
Direct labour:	
Forming department	180
Machining department	120
Finishing department	75
Indirect materials:	
Forming department	40
Machining department	30
Finishing department	10
Administration department	10
Indirect labour:	
Forming department	80
Machining department	70
Finishing department	60
Administration department	60
Maintenance cost	50
Rent and rates	100
Heating and lighting	20
Building insurance	10
Machinery insurance	10
Depreciation of machinery	120
Total manufacturing cost	1,645

The following additional information is available:

(i)   Each of the four departments is treated as a separate cost centre.
(ii) All direct labour is paid £6 an hour for all hours worked.
(iii) The administration department renders personnel and general services to the production departments.
(iv) The area of the premises in which the business manufactures amounts to 50,000 square metres, divided as follows:

	Sq m
Forming department	20,000
Machining department	15,000
Finishing department	10,000
Administration department	5,000

(v) The maintenance employees are expected to divide their time between the production departments as follows:

	%
Forming department	15
Machining department	75
Finishing department	10

(vi) Machine hours are expected to be as follows:

	Hours
Forming department	5,000
Machining department	15,000
Finishing department	5,000

On the basis of this information:

(a) Allocate and apportion overheads to the three product cost centres.
(b) Deduce overhead recovery rates for each product cost centre using two different bases for each cost centre's overheads.
(c) Calculate the full cost of a job with the following characteristics:

Direct labour hours:	
Forming department	4 hours
Machining department	4 hours
Finishing department	1 hour
Machine hours:	
Forming department	1 hour
Machining department	2 hours
Finishing department	1 hour
Direct materials:	
Forming department	£40
Machining department	£9
Finishing department	£4

Use whichever of the two bases of overhead recovery, deduced in (b), that you consider more appropriate.

(d) Explain why you consider the basis used in (c) to be the more appropriate.

Activity 4.12 continued

(a) Overheads can be allocated and apportioned as follows:

Cost	Basis of apport't	Total £000	Forming £000	Machining £000	Finishing £000	Admin. £000
Indirect materials	Specifically allocated	90	40	30	10	10
Indirect labour	Specifically allocated	270	80	70	60	60
Maintenance	Staff time	50	7.5	37.5	5	–
Rent/rates		100				
Heat/light		20				
Buildings insurance		10				
	Area	130	52	39	26	13
Machine insurance		10				
Machine depreciation		120				
	Machine hours	130	26	78	26	–
		670	205.5	254.5	127	83
Admin.	Direct labour		39.84	26.56	16.6	(83)
		670	245.34	281.06	143.6	–

Note: The direct cost is not included in the above because it is allocated *directly* to jobs.

(b) Overhead recovery rates are as follows:
Basis 1: direct labour hours

$$\text{Forming} = \frac{£245,340}{£(180,000/6)} = £8.18 \text{ per direct labour hour}$$

$$\text{Machining} = \frac{£281,060}{£(120,000/6)} = £14.05 \text{ per direct labour hour}$$

$$\text{Finishing} = \frac{£143,600}{£(75,000/6)} = £11.49 \text{ per direct labour hour}$$

Basis 2: machine hours

$$\text{Forming} = \frac{£245,340}{5,000} = £49.07 \text{ per machine hour}$$

$$\text{Machining} = \frac{£281,060}{15,000} = £18.73 \text{ per machine hour}$$

$$\text{Finishing} = \frac{£143,600}{5,000} = £28.72 \text{ per machine hour}$$

(c) Full cost of job – on direct labour hour basis of overhead recovery

	£	£
Direct labour cost (9 × £6)		54.00
Direct materials (£40 + £9 + £4)		53.00
Overheads:		
Forming (4 × £8.18)	32.72	
Machining (4 × £14.05)	56.20	
Finishing (1 × £11.49)	11.49	100.41
Full cost		207.41

(d) The reason for using the direct labour hour basis rather than the machine hour basis was that labour is more important, in terms of the number of hours applied to output, than is machine time. Strong arguments could have been made for the use of the alternative basis; certainly, a machine hour basis could have been justified for the machining department.

It would be possible, and it may be reasonable, to use one basis in respect of one product cost centre's overheads and a different one for those of another. For example, machine hours could have been used for the machining department and a direct labour hours basis for the other two.

Batch costing

The production of many types of goods and services (particularly goods) involves producing in a batch of identical, or nearly identical, units of output, but where each batch is distinctly different from other batches. For example, a theatre may put on a production whose nature (and therefore cost) is very different from that of other productions. On the other hand, ignoring differences in the desirability of the various types of seating, all of the individual units of output (tickets to see the production) are identical.

In these circumstances, the cost per ticket would normally be deduced by using a job costing approach (taking account of direct and indirect costs and so on) to find the cost of mounting the production, and then dividing the cost of mounting the production by the expected number of tickets to be sold to find the cost per ticket. This is known as **batch costing**.

Figure 4.10 shows the process for deriving the cost of one cost unit (product) in a batch.

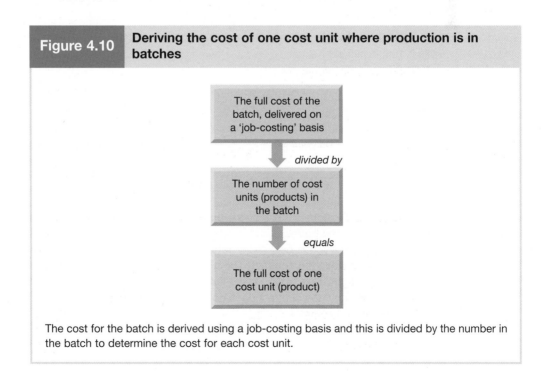

Figure 4.10	**Deriving the cost of one cost unit where production is in batches**

The full cost of the batch, delivered on a 'job-costing' basis

divided by

The number of cost units (products) in the batch

equals

The full cost of one cost unit (product)

The cost for the batch is derived using a job-costing basis and this is divided by the number in the batch to determine the cost for each cost unit.

Full (absorption) cost as the break-even price

For decision-making purposes, it can be helpful to allocate non-manufacturing costs, as well as manufacturing costs, to products using some sensible basis of allocation. When this is done and everything goes according to plan (so that direct cost and overheads prove to be as expected), selling the output for its full cost should cause the business to break even exactly. Therefore, whatever profit (in total) is loaded onto full cost to set actual selling prices will, if plans are achieved, result in that level of profit being earned for the period.

The forward-looking nature of full (absorption) costing

Though deducing full cost can be done after the work has been completed, it is often done in advance. In other words, cost is frequently predicted. Where, for example, full cost is needed as a basis on which to set selling prices, it is usually the case that prices need to be set before the customer will accept the job being done. Even where no particular customer has been identified, some idea of the ultimate price will need to be known before the business will be able to make a judgement as to whether potential customers will buy the product, and in what quantities. There is a risk, of course, that the actual outcome will differ from that which was predicted. If this occurs, corrections are subsequently made to the full cost originally calculated.

Self-assessment question 4.1

Hector and Co. Ltd has been invited to tender for a contract to produce 1,000 clothes hangers. The following information relates to the contract.

Materials
The clothes hangers are made of metal wire covered with a padded fabric. Each hanger requires 2 metres of wire and 0.5 square metres of fabric.

Direct labour
Skilled: 10 minutes per hanger
Unskilled: 5 minutes per hanger

The business already holds sufficient of each of the materials required to complete the contract. Information on the cost of the materials is as follows:

	Metal wire £ per metre	Fabric £ per sq metre
Historic cost	2.20	1.00
Current buying-in cost	2.50	1.10
Scrap value	1.70	0.40

The metal wire is in constant use by the business for a range of its products. The fabric has no other use for the business and is scheduled to be scrapped.

Unskilled labour, which is paid at the rate of £7.50 an hour, will need to be taken on specifically to undertake the contract. The business is fairly quiet at the moment, which means that a pool of skilled labour exists that will still be employed at full pay of £12.00 an hour to do nothing if the contract does not proceed. The pool of skilled labour is sufficient to complete the contract.

The business charges jobs with overheads on a direct labour hour basis. The production overheads of the entire business for the month in which the contract will be undertaken are estimated at £50,000. The estimated total direct labour hours that will be worked are 12,500. The business tends not to alter the established overhead recovery rate to reflect increases or reductions to estimated total hours arising from new contracts. The total overheads are not expected to increase as a result of undertaking the contract.

The business normally adds 12.5 per cent profit loading to the job cost to arrive at a first estimate of the tender price.

Required:
(a) Price this job on a traditional job-costing basis.
(b) Indicate the minimum price at which the contract could be undertaken such that the business would be neither better nor worse off as a result of doing it.

Using full (absorption) cost information

We saw at the beginning of the chapter that full (absorption) cost information may be used for four main purposes. Now that we have seen how full cost is deduced, let us consider in more detail how this information may be used.

- *Pricing and output decisions.* Full cost can be used as the starting point for determining prices. An amount is simply added to the full cost of a product or service for profit in order to derive the selling price. The amount of profit is often calculated as a percentage of the full (absorption) cost figure. This approach to pricing is known as **cost-plus pricing**. Garages carrying out vehicle repairs typically operate in this way. Solicitors and accountants doing work for clients often use this approach as well. Where there is a competitive market, however, it is not possible to set prices on a cost-plus basis. Businesses will usually have to accept the price that the market is prepared to pay. Thus, they are usually *price takers* rather than *price makers*. The prices at which businesses are able to sell their output will usually be a major determinant of the quantity that they make available to the market. We shall take a closer look at pricing and its relationship to cost and output in Chapter 5.
- *Exercising control.* Full (absorption) cost seems often to be used as the basis of budgeting and comparing actual outcomes with budgets, enabling action to be taken to exercise control. It can be useful in this context, though care needs to be taken to try to ensure that individual managers are not being held responsible for cost elements, say overhead costs, that they are unable to control. This point will be raised again in Chapter 5, where we consider another approach to dealing with overheads in full costing. We shall look at budgeting and control in some detail in Chapters 6 and 7.
- *Assessing relative efficiency.* Full cost seems to be used as the basis of comparing relative efficiency in terms of the comparative cost of doing similar things. For example, as we saw in **Real World 4.1** (p. 94), the cost of carrying out a standard surgical procedure seems often to be compared on the basis of full cost between one hospital and another. The objective of this may well be to identify the cheaper hospital and encourage other hospitals to take steps to copy the cheaper hospital's approach.

As we saw in Chapters 2 and 3, including all aspects of cost (as full costing does) can lead to incorrect decisions. It is necessary to identify that part of the cost that is strictly relevant to a decision and ignore the rest, be it direct or indirect in the full-costing context. Similarly, comparing the full cost of doing something, particularly when the two things are being done in different organisations, can be confusing and lead to bad decisions.

● *Assessing performance.* The conventional approach to measuring a business's income for a period requires that expenses must be matched with the sales revenue to which they relate *in the same accounting period*. Thus, where a service is partially rendered in one accounting period but the revenue is recognised in the next, or where manufactured inventories are made, or partially made, in one period but sold in the next, the full cost (including an appropriate share of overheads) must be carried from the first accounting period to the second one. Deducing full cost is important because, unless we know the full cost of work done in one period that is sold in the next, the profit figures for each of the two periods concerned will be meaningless. Managers and others will not have a reliable means of assessing the effectiveness of the business as a whole, or the effectiveness of individual parts of it. We shall take a quick look at an alternative approach to income measurement, where full cost is not used, shortly.

The way in which full cost information is used to measure income can be illustrated by Example 4.5.

Example 4.5

During the accounting year that ended on 31 December last year, IT Modules Ltd developed a special piece of computer software for a customer, Kingsang Ltd. At the beginning of this year, after having a series of tests successfully completed by a subcontractor, the software was passed to Kingsang Ltd. IT Modules's normal practice (which is typical of most businesses) is to take account of sales revenue when the product passes to the customer. The sale price of the Kingsang software was £45,000.

During last year, subcontract work costing £3,500 was used in developing the Kingsang software and 1,200 hours of direct labour, costing £24,300, were worked on it. The business uses a direct labour hour basis of charging overheads to jobs, which is believed to be fair because most of its work is labour-intensive. The total production overheads for the business for last year were £77,000, and the total direct labour hours worked were 22,000. Testing the Kingsang software this year cost £1,000.

How much profit or loss did IT Modules make on the Kingsang software during last year? How much profit or loss did it make on the software during this year? At what value should IT Modules have included the software on its statement of financial position (balance sheet) at the end of last year so that the correct profit will be recorded for each of the two years?

The answers to these questions are as follows:

● No profit or loss was made during last year. This is because of IT Modules's (and the generally accepted) approach to recognising revenues (sales) and the need to match expenses with the revenues to which they relate. The cost incurred during last year is carried forward to this year, which is the year of sale.

● As the sale is recognised this year, the cost of developing the software is treated as expenses in this year. This cost will include a reasonable share of overheads. Were IT Modules to draw up a 'mini' income statement for the Kingsang contract for this year, it would be as follows:

Kingsang software	£	£
Sales price		45,000
Cost:		
Direct labour	(24,300)	
Subcontract	(3,500)	
Overheads (1,200 × (£77,000/22,000))	(4,200)	
Total incurred last year	(32,000)	
Testing cost	(1,000)	
Total cost		(33,000)
This year's profit from the software		12,000

● The software needs to be shown as an asset of the business (valued at £32,000) in the statement of financial position (balance sheet) as at 31 December last year. It represents the work in progress that is carried forward to this year.

Criticisms of full (absorption) costing

Full costing has been criticised because, in practice, it tends to use past cost and to restrict its consideration of future cost to outlay cost. It can be argued that past cost is irrelevant, irrespective of the purpose for which the information is to be used. This is basically because it is not possible to make decisions about the past, only about the future. Similarly, it is argued that it is wrong to ignore opportunity costs. Advocates of full costing would argue, however, that it provides a useful guide to long-run average cost.

Despite the criticisms that are made of full costing, it is, according to research evidence, very widely practised. An international accounting standard (IAS2 *Inventories*) requires that all inventories, including work in progress, be valued at full cost in the published financial statements. This means that virtually all businesses that have work in progress and/or inventories of finished goods at the end of their financial periods are obliged to apply full costing for income measurement purposes. This will include the many service providers that tend to have work in progress. Whether they use full cost information for other purposes is not clear.

Full (absorption) costing versus variable costing

→ An alternative to full (absorption) costing is **variable (marginal) costing**. We may recall from Chapter 3 that this approach distinguishes between fixed and variable costs, and this distinction may be helpful when making short-term decisions. Where a business divides its cost between fixed and variable, it will measure its income differently to that described so far in this chapter. A variable-costing approach will only include variable cost, including any variable indirect elements, as part of the cost of the goods or service. Fixed cost, both direct and indirect elements, is treated as a cost of the period in which it is incurred. Part of the philosophy of variable costing is that fixed cost is not linked to cost units in the way that it is with full costing. Thus, inventories of finished products, or work in progress, carried from one accounting period to the next, are valued only on the basis of their variable cost.

As we have seen, full costing includes in product cost not only the direct cost (whether fixed or variable) but also a 'fair' share of the indirect cost (both fixed and variable) that was incurred during the time that the product was being made or developed.

To illustrate the difference between the two approaches, let us consider Example 4.6.

Example 4.6

Lahore Ltd commenced operations on 1 June and makes a single product, which sells for £14 per unit. In the first two months of operations, the following results were achieved:

	June	July
	(Number of units)	(Number of units)
Production output	6,000	6,000
Sales volume	4,000	5,000
Opening inventories	–	2,000
Closing inventories	2,000	3,000

The fixed manufacturing cost is £18,000 per month and variable manufacturing cost is £5 per unit. There is also a monthly fixed non-manufacturing cost (marketing and administration) of £5,000. There was no work in progress at the end of either June or July.

The operating profit for each month is calculated below, first using a marginal costing approach and then a full costing approach.

Marginal costing

In this case, only the variable costs are charged to the units produced and all the fixed cost (manufacturing and non-manufacturing) is charged to the period. Inventories will be carried forward at their variable cost.

	June		July	
	£	£	£	£
Sales revenue				
(4,000 × £14)		56,000		
(5,000 × £14)				70,000
Opening inventories				
(2,000 × £5)	–		10,000	
Cost of units produced				
(6,000 × £5)	30,000		30,000	
Closing inventories				
(2,000 × £5)	(10,000)	(20,000)		
(3,000 × £5)			(15,000)	(25,000)
Contribution margin		36,000		45,000
Fixed cost				
Manufacturing	(18,000)		(18,000)	
Non-manufacturing	(5,000)	(23,000)	(5,000)	(23,000)
Operating profit		13,000		22,000

Full costing

In this case, fixed manufacturing cost becomes part of the product cost and inventories are carried forward to the next period at their full cost (that is variable cost *plus* an appropriate fixed manufacturing cost element). There are 6,000 units produced in each period and the fixed manufacturing cost for each period is £18,000. Hence, the fixed manufacturing cost element per unit is £3 (that is, £18,000/6,000). The full cost per unit will therefore be £8 (that is, £5 + £3)

	June		July	
	£	£	£	£
Sales revenue				
(4,000 × £14)		56,000		
(5,000 × £14)				70,000
Opening inventories		–		
(2,000 × £8)			16,000	
Cost of units produced				
(6,000 × £8)	48,000		48,000	
Closing inventories				
(2,000 × £8)	(16,000)	(32,000)		
(3,000 × £8)			(24,000)	(40,000)
Gross profit		24,000		30,000
Non-manufacturing cost		(5,000)		(5,000)
Operating profit		19,000		25,000

We can see that the total operating profit over the two months is £35,000 (that is, £13,000 + £22,000) when derived on a marginal cost basis. On a full cost basis it is £44,000 (that is, £19,000 + £25,000). This is a difference of £9,000 (that is £44,000 – £35,000). This is accounted for by the fact that the fixed manufacturing cost element of the inventories valuation at the end of July, on the full cost basis (that is, 3,000 × £3), has yet to be treated as an expense.

Which method is better?

In practice, the recorded profit of a particular business for each period is unlikely to be greatly affected by the choice of costing approach. If the level of fixed cost stays broadly the same from one year to the next and there are similar amounts of inventories and work in progress at year ends, reported profit will be similar regardless of which method is used. This is because the same amount of fixed cost will be treated as an expense each year; all of it originates from the current year in the case of variable costing, while some of it originates from past years in the case of full costing.

The significant differences in operating profit that we saw in Example 4.6 stem from the fact that that inventories levels altered quite severely, from zero at the beginning of June to 2,000 units at the end of June to 3,000 units by the end of July. In practice, businesses do not tend to alter inventories levels so radically, which means that the choice between full and variable costing may not make very much difference to operating profit levels.

Over the entire life of a particular business the total operating profit will be the same irrespective of which costing method has been applied. This is because, ultimately, all of the fixed costs will be charged as an expense.

Proponents of variable costing might argue that it is a very prudent approach to measuring profit, as all fixed production costs are charged to the period in which they are incurred. Perhaps more importantly, they would argue that only variable cost is relevant to decision makers (as we discussed in Chapters 2 and 3) and that considering fixed cost obscures the issue.

Proponents of full (absorption) costing might counter that full costing provides a fairer measure of profit, job by job. Furthermore, in the long run, all elements of cost can be avoided and so to concentrate on only those that can be avoided in the short term (the variable costs) could be misleading.

In practice, management accountants can prepare their income statements taking either, or even both, approaches. We have already seen, however, that accounting rules insist that a full-costing approach is taken when preparing published financial statements.

Real World 4.6 provides some indication of the extent to which variable costing is used in practice.

REAL WORLD 4.6

Variable costing in practice

A recent survey of 41 UK manufacturing businesses found that 68 per cent of them used a variable-costing approach to management reporting.

Many would find this surprising. It seemed to be widely believed that the requirement for financial statements in published annual reports to be in full cost terms has led those businesses to use a full cost approach for management reporting as well. This seems not, however, to be the case.

It should be added that many of those that used variable costing quite possibly mis-used it. For example, three-quarters of those that used it treated labour cost as variable. Possibly in some cases the cost of labour is variable (with the level of output), but it seems likely that this is not true for most of these businesses. At the same time, most of the 68 per cent treat all overheads as a fixed cost. It seems likely that, for most businesses, overheads have a variable element.

Source: Dugdale, D., Jones, C. and Green, S., *Contemporary Management Accounting Practices in UK Manufacturing*, Elsevier, 2006.

SUMMARY

The main points in this chapter may be summarised as follows:

Full (absorption) cost = the total amount of resources sacrificed to achieve a particular objective.

Uses of full (absorption) cost information

● Pricing and output decisions.
● Exercising control.
● Assessing relative efficiency.
● Income measurement.

Single-product businesses

● Where all the units of output are identical, the full cost can be calculated as follows:

$$\text{Cost per unit} = \frac{\text{Total cost of output}}{\text{Number of units produced}}$$

Multi-product businesses – job costing

- Where units of output are not identical, it is necessary to divide the cost into two categories: direct cost and indirect cost (overheads).
- Direct cost = cost that can be identified with specific cost units (for example, labour of a garage mechanic, in relation to a particular job).
- Indirect cost (overheads) = cost that cannot be directly measured in respect of a particular job (for example, the rent of a garage).
- Full (absorption) cost = direct cost + indirect cost.
- Direct/indirect is not linked to variable/fixed.
- Indirect cost is difficult to relate to individual cost units – arbitrary bases are used and there is no single correct method.
- Traditionally, indirect cost is seen as the cost of providing a 'service' to cost units.
- Direct labour hour basis of applying indirect cost to cost units is the most popular in practice.

Dealing with indirect cost on a cost centre (departmental) basis

- Indirect cost (overheads) can be segmented – usually on cost centre basis – each product cost centre has its own overhead recovery rate.
- Cost centres are areas, activities or functions for which cost is separately determined.
- Overheads must be allocated or apportioned to cost centres.
- Service cost centre cost must then be apportioned to product cost centres and product cost centre overheads absorbed by cost units (jobs).

Batch costing

- A variation of job costing where each job consists of a number of identical (or near identical) cost units:

$$\text{Cost per unit} = \frac{\text{Cost of the batch (direct + indirect)}}{\text{Number of units in the batch}}$$

If the full (absorption) cost is charged as the sales price and things go according to plan, the business will break even.

Full cost information is seen by some as not very useful because it can be backward-looking: it includes information irrelevant to decision making, but excludes some relevant information.

Full (absorption) costing versus variable costing

- With full costing, both fixed and variable costs are included in product cost and treated as expenses when the product is sold.
- With variable costing, only the variable product cost is linked to the products in this way; fixed cost is treated as an expense of the period in which it was incurred.
- Variable costing tends to be more straightforward and, according to proponents, more relevant for decision making.
- Supporters of full costing argue that it gives a more complete measure of the income generated from the sale of each unit of the product.
- Such evidence as there is about the use of variable costing in practice suggests that it is widely used. The evidence implies, however, that the values tend to be miscalculated in a large proportion of cases.

→ **Key terms**

Full cost p. 94
Full costing p. 95
Cost unit p 95
Process costing p. 96
Direct cost p. 96
Indirect cost p. 96
Overheads p. 96
Common cost p. 96
Job costing p. 98
Absorption costing p. 98
Cost behaviour p. 99

Total cost p. 100
Overhead absorption (recovery)
  rate p. 101
Cost centre p. 110
Product cost centre p. 111
Service cost centre p. 111
Cost allocation p. 112
Cost apportionment p. 112
Batch costing p. 119
Cost-plus pricing p. 121
Variable costing p. 123

Further reading

If you would like to explore the topics covered in this chapter in more depth, we recommend the following books:

Atkinson, A., Kaplan R., Young, S. M. and Matsumura, E., *Management Accounting*, 5th edn, Prentice Hall, 2007, chapter 3.

Drury, C., *Management and Cost Accounting*, 7th edn, Cengage Learning, 2007, chapters 3, 4 and 5.

Hilton, R., *Managerial Accounting*, 6th edn, McGraw-Hill Irwin, 2005, chapters 2 and 3.

Horngren, C., Foster, G., Datar, S., Rajan, M. and Ittner, C., *Cost Accounting: A Managerial Emphasis*, 13th edn, Prentice Hall International, 2008, chapter 4.

REVIEW QUESTIONS

Answers to these questions can be found in Appendix C at the back of the book.

4.1 What problem does the existence of work in progress cause in process costing?

4.2 What is the point of distinguishing direct cost from indirect cost? Why is this not necessary in process-costing environments?

4.3 Are direct cost and variable cost the same thing? Explain your answer.

4.4 It is sometimes claimed that the full cost of pursuing some objective represents the long-run break-even selling price. Why is this said, and what does it mean?

EXERCISES

Exercises 4.4 to 4.8 are more advanced than 4.1 to 4.3. Answers to those exercises with coloured numbers can be found in Appendix D at the back of the book.

4.1 Bodgers Ltd, a business that provides a market research service, operates a job-costing system. Towards the end of each financial year, the overhead recovery rate (the rate at which indirect cost will be absorbed by jobs) is established for the forthcoming year.

(a) Why does the business bother to predetermine the recovery rate in the way outlined?
(b) What steps will be involved in predetermining the rate?
(c) What problems might arise with using a predetermined rate?

4.2 Athena Ltd is an engineering business doing work for its customers to their particular requirements and specifications. It determines the full cost of each job taking a 'job-costing' approach, accounting for overheads on a cost centre (departmental) basis. It bases its prices to customers on this full cost figure. The business has two departments (both of which are cost centres): a Machining Department, where each job starts, and a Fitting Department, which completes all of the jobs. Machining Department overheads are charged to jobs on a machine hour basis and those of the Fitting Department on a direct labour hour basis. The budgeted information for next year is as follows:

Heating and lighting	£25,000	(allocated equally between the two departments)
Machine power	£10,000	(all allocated to the Machining Department)
Direct labour	£200,000	(£150,000 allocated to the Fitting Department and £50,000 to the Machining Department; all direct workers are paid £10 an hour)
Indirect labour	£50,000	(apportioned to the departments in proportion to the direct labour cost)
Direct materials	£120,000	(all applied to jobs in the Machining Department)
Depreciation	£30,000	(all relates to the Machining Department)
Machine time	20,000 hours	(all worked in the Machining Department)

Required:

(a) Prepare a statement showing the budgeted overheads for next year, analysed between the two cost centres. This should be in the form of three columns: one for the total figure for each type of overhead and one column each for the two cost centres, where each type of overhead is analysed between the two cost centres. Each column should also show the total of overheads for the year.

(b) Derive the appropriate rate for charging the overheads of each cost centre to jobs (that is, a separate rate for each cost centre).

(c) Athena Ltd has been asked by a customer to specify the price that it will charge for a particular job that will, if the job goes ahead, be undertaken early next year. The job is expected to use direct materials costing Athena Ltd £1,200, to need 50 hours of machining time, 10 hours of Machine Department direct labour and 20 hours of Fitting Department direct labour. Athena Ltd charges a profit loading of 20% to the full cost of jobs to determine the selling price.

Show workings to derive the proposed selling price for this job.

4.3 Pieman Products Ltd makes road trailers to the precise specifications of individual customers. The following are predicted to occur during the forthcoming year, which is about to start:

Direct materials cost	£50,000
Direct labour cost	£160,000
Direct labour time	16,000 hours
Indirect labour cost	£25,000
Depreciation of machine	£8,000
Rent and rates	£10,000
Heating, lighting and power	£5,000
Indirect materials	£2,000
Other indirect cost (overhead) elements	£1,000
Machine time	3,000 hours

All direct labour is paid at the same hourly rate.

A customer has asked the business to build a trailer for transporting a racing motorcycle to race meetings. It is estimated that this will require materials and components that will cost £1,150. It will take 250 direct labour hours to do the job, of which 50 will involve the use of machinery.

Required:

Deduce a logical cost for the job, and explain the basis of dealing with overheads that you propose.

4.4 Promptprint Ltd, a printing business, has received an enquiry from a potential customer for the quotation of a price for a job. The pricing policy of the business is based on the plans for the next financial year shown below.

	£
Sales revenue (billings to customers)	196,000
Materials (direct)	(38,000)
Labour (direct)	(32,000)
Variable overheads	(2,400)
Advertising (for business)	(3,000)
Depreciation	(27,600)
Administration	(36,000)
Interest	(8,000)
Profit (before taxation)	49,000

A first estimate of the direct cost for the particular job is:

	£
Direct materials	4,000
Direct labour	3,600

Required:

(a) Prepare a recommended price for the job based on the plans, commenting on your method, ignoring the information given in the Appendix (below).

(b) Comment on the validity of using financial plans in pricing, and recommend any improvements you would consider desirable for the pricing policy used in (a).

(c) Incorporate the effects of the information shown in the Appendix (below) into your estimates of the direct material cost, explaining any changes you consider it necessary to make to the above direct material cost of £4,000.

Appendix to Exercise 4.4

Based on historic cost, direct material cost was computed as follows:

	£
Paper grade 1	1,200
Paper grade 2	2,000
Card (zenith grade)	500
Inks and other miscellaneous items	300
	4,000

Paper grade 1 is regularly used by the business. Enough of this paper to complete the job is currently held. Because it is imported, it is estimated that if it is used for this job, a new purchase order will have to be placed shortly. Sterling has depreciated against the foreign currency by 25 per cent since the last purchase.

Paper grade 2 is purchased from the same source as grade 1. The business holds exactly enough of it for the job, but this was bought in for a special order. This order was cancelled, although the defaulting customer was required to pay £500 towards the cost of the paper. The accountant has offset this against the original cost to arrive at the figure of £2,000 shown above. This paper is rarely used, and due to its special chemical coating will be unusable if it is not used on the job in question.

The card is another specialist item currently held by the business. There is no use foreseen, and it would cost £750 to replace if required. However, the inventories controller had planned to spend £130 on overprinting to use the card as a substitute for other materials costing £640.

Inks and other items are in regular use in the print shop.

4.5 Bookdon plc manufactures three products, X, Y and Z, in two product cost centres: a machine shop and a fitting section; it also has two service cost centres: a canteen and a machine maintenance section. Shown below are next year's planned production data and manufacturing cost for the business.

	X	Y	Z
Production	4,200 units	6,900 units	1,700 units
Direct materials	£11/unit	£14/unit	£17/unit
Direct labour			
Machine shop	£6/unit	£4/unit	£2/unit
Fitting section	£12/unit	£3/unit	£21/unit
Machine hours	6 hr/unit	3 hr/unit	4 hr/unit

Planned overheads are as follows:

	Machine shop	Fitting section	Canteen	Machine maintenance section	Total
Allocated overheads	£27,660	£19,470	£16,600	£26,650	£90,380
Rent, rates, heat and light					£17,000
Depreciation and insurance of equipment					£25,000

Additional data:

	Machine shop	Fitting section	Canteen	Machine maintenance section
Gross book value of equipment	£150,000	£75,000	£30,000	£45,000
Number of employees	18	14	4	4
Floor space occupied	3,600 sq m	1,400 sq m	1,000 sq m	800 sq m

All machining is carried out in the machine shop. It has been estimated that approximately 70 per cent of the machine maintenance section's cost is incurred servicing the machine shop and the remainder servicing the fitting section.

Required:
(a) Calculate the following planned overhead absorption rates:
   (i) A machine hour rate for the machine shop.
   (ii) A rate expressed as a percentage of direct wages for the fitting section.
(b) Calculate the planned full cost per unit of product X.

4.6 Shown below is an extract from next year's plans for a business manufacturing three products, A, B and C, in three product cost centres.

	A	B	C
Production	4,000 units	3,000 units	6,000 units
Direct material cost	£7 per unit	£4 per unit	£9 per unit
Direct labour requirements:			
Cutting department:			
Skilled operatives	3 hr/unit	5 hr/unit	2 hr/unit
Unskilled operatives	6 hr/unit	1 hr/unit	3 hr/unit
Machining department	$1/2$ hr/unit	$1/4$ hr/unit	$1/3$ hr/unit
Pressing department	2 hr/unit	3 hr/unit	4 hr/unit
Machine requirements:			
Machining department	2 hr/unit	$1^1/2$ hr/unit	$2^1/2$ hr/unit

The skilled operatives employed in the cutting department are paid £16 an hour and the unskilled operatives are paid £10 an hour. All the operatives in the machining and pressing departments are paid £12 an hour.

	Product cost centres			Service cost centres	
	Cutting	Machining	Pressing	Engineering	Personnel
Planned total overheads	£154,482	£64,316	£58,452	£56,000	£34,000
Service cost centre cost incurred for the benefit of other cost centres, as follows:					
Engineering services	20%	45%	35%	–	–
Personnel services	55%	10%	20%	15%	–

The business operates a full absorption costing system.

Required:

Derive the total planned cost of:

(a) One completed unit of product A.

(b) One incomplete unit of product B, which has been processed by the cutting and machining departments but which has not yet been passed into the pressing department.

4.7 Consider this statement:

'In a job costing system, it is necessary to divide up the business into departments. Fixed costs (or overheads) will be collected for each department. Where a particular fixed cost relates to the business as a whole, it must be divided between the departments. Usually this is done on the basis of area of floor space occupied by each department relative to the entire business. When the total fixed cost for each department has been identified, this will be divided by the number of hours that were worked in each department to deduce an overhead recovery rate. Each job that was worked on in a department will have a share of fixed cost allotted to it according to how long it was worked on. The total cost for each job will therefore be the sum of the variable cost of the job and its share of the fixed cost. It is essential that this approach is taken in order to deduce a selling price for the business's output.'

Required:

Prepare a table of two columns. In the first column you should show any phrases or sentences in the above statement with which you do not agree, and in the second column you should show your reason for disagreeing with each one.

4.8 Many businesses charge overheads to jobs on a cost centre basis.

Required:

(a) What is the advantage that is claimed for charging overheads to jobs on a cost centre basis, and why is it claimed?

(b) What circumstances need to exist for it to make a difference to the costing of a particular job whether overheads are charged on a business-wide basis or on a cost centre basis? (Note that the answer to this part of the question is not specifically covered in the chapter. You should, nevertheless, be able to deduce the reason from what you know.)

5

Costing and pricing in a competitive environment

INTRODUCTION

We saw in Chapter 1 that major changes have occurred in the business world in recent years, including deregulation, privatisation, the growing expectations of shareholders and the impact of new technology. These have led to a much more fast-changing and competitive environment that has radically altered the way that businesses need to be managed. In this chapter, we consider some of the management accounting techniques that have been developed to help businesses maintain their competitiveness in this new era.

We begin by considering the impact of this new, highly competitive environment on the full-costing approach that we considered in Chapter 4. We shall see that activity-based costing (ABC), which is a development of the traditional full-costing approach, takes a much more enquiring, much less accepting attitude towards indirect cost (overheads). Some other recent approaches to costing that can help lower costs and, therefore, increase the ability of a business to compete on price will also be examined.

Managers must approach pricing decisions with care because of the significant impact they can have on the profitability of a business. We shall see how, in theory and in practice, prices may be set in a competitive environment. In setting prices, managers are likely to be guided by product-costing information. We shall examine this point and, in so doing, pick up other points on relevant cost and cost–volume–profit relationships that were considered in Chapters 2 and 3.

LEARNING OUTCOMES

When you have completed this chapter, you should be able to:

● Describe the nature of the modern product costing and pricing environment.

● Discuss the principles and practicalities of activity-based costing.

● Explain how new developments such as total life-cycle costing and target costing can be used to manage product costs.

● Explain the theoretical underpinning of pricing decisions and discuss the issues involved in reaching a pricing decision in real-world situations.

Cost determination in the changed business environment

Costing and pricing products in the traditional way

The traditional, and still widely used, approach to job costing and product pricing developed when the notion of trying to determine the cost of industrial production first emerged. This was around the time of the UK Industrial Revolution when industry displayed the following characteristics:

- *Direct-labour-intensive and direct-labour-paced production.* Labour was at the heart of production. To the extent that machinery was used, it was to support the efforts of direct labour, and the speed of production was dictated by direct labour.
- *A low level of indirect cost relative to direct cost.* Little was spent on power, personnel services, machinery (leading to low depreciation charges) or other areas typical of the indirect cost (overheads) of modern businesses.
- *A relatively uncompetitive market.* Transport difficulties, limited industrial production worldwide and a lack of knowledge by customers of competitors' prices meant that businesses could prosper without being too scientific in costing and pricing their output. Customers would have tended to accept what the supplier had to offer, rather than demanding precisely what they wanted.

Since overheads at that time represented a pretty small element of total cost, it was acceptable and practical to deal with them in a fairly arbitrary manner. Not too much effort was devoted to trying to control overheads because the potential rewards of better control were relatively small, certainly when compared with the benefits from firmer control of direct labour and material costs. It was also reasonable to charge overheads to individual jobs on a direct labour hour basis. Most of the overheads were incurred directly in support of direct labour: providing direct workers with a place to work, heating and lighting the workplace, employing people to supervise the direct workers, and so on. Direct workers, perhaps aided by machinery, carried out all production.

At that time, service industries were a relatively unimportant part of the economy and would have largely consisted of self-employed individuals. These individuals would probably have been uninterested in trying to do more than work out a rough hourly or daily rate for their time and to try to base prices on this.

Costing and pricing products in the new environment

As mentioned in Chapter 1, the world of industrial production has undergone fundamental change. Most of it is now characterised by:

- *Capital-intensive and machine-paced production.* Machines are at the heart of much production, including both the manufacture of goods and the rendering of services. Most labour supports the efforts of machines, for example, technically maintaining them. Also, machines often dictate the pace of production. According to evidence provided in Real World 4.2 (page 97), direct labour accounts on average for just 14 per cent of manufacturers' total cost.
- *A high level of indirect costs relative to direct costs.* Modern businesses tend to have very high depreciation, servicing and power costs. There are also high costs of personnel and staff welfare, which were scarcely envisaged in the early days of industrial

production. At the same time, there are very low (sometimes no) direct labour costs. Although direct material cost often remains an important element of total cost, more efficient production methods lead to less waste and, therefore, to a lower total material cost, again tending to make indirect cost (overheads) more dominant. Again, according to Real World 4.2, overheads account for 25 per cent of manufacturers' total cost and 51 per cent of service sector total cost.

● *A highly competitive international market.* Production, much of it highly sophisticated, is carried out worldwide. Transport, including fast airfreight, is relatively cheap. Fax, the telephone and, particularly, the internet ensure that potential customers can quickly and cheaply find the prices of a range of suppliers. Markets now tend to be highly price competitive. Customers increasingly demand products custom made to their own requirements. This means that businesses need to know their product costs with a greater degree of accuracy than historically has been the case. Businesses also need to take a considered and informed approach to pricing their output.

In the UK, as in many developed countries, service industries now dominate the economy, employing the great majority of the workforce and producing most of the value of productive output. Though there are many self-employed individuals supplying services, many service providers are vast businesses such as banks, insurance companies and cinema operators. For most of these larger service providers, the activities very closely resemble modern manufacturing activity. They too are characterised by high capital intensity, overheads dominating direct costs and a competitive international market.

Cost management systems

Changes in the competitive environment mean that businesses must now manage costs much more effectively than in the past. This, in turn, places an obligation on the cost management systems employed to provide the information that will enable managers to do this. Traditional cost management systems have often proved inadequate for the task and, in recent years, new systems have gained in popularity. We shall now take a look at some of these systems.

Activity-based costing

In Chapter 4 we considered the traditional approach to job costing (deriving the full cost of output where one unit of output differs from another). We may recall that this approach involves collecting, for each job, those costs that can be clearly linked to, and measured in respect of, the particular job (direct costs). All indirect costs (overheads) are allocated or apportioned to product cost centres and then charged to individual jobs according to some formula. The evidence suggests that this formula is usually based on the number of direct labour hours worked on each particular job.

In the past, this approach has worked reasonably well, largely because overhead recovery rates (that is, rates at which overheads are absorbed by jobs) were typically of a much lower value for each direct labour hour than the rate paid to direct workers as wages or salaries. It is now, however, becoming increasingly common for overhead recovery rates to be between five and ten times the hourly rate of pay, because overheads are now much more significant. When production is dominated by direct labour paid, say, £8 an hour, it might be reasonable to have an overhead recovery rate of, say, £1 an hour. When, however, direct labour plays a relatively small part in production, to have an overhead recovery rate of, say, £50 for each direct labour hour is likely to lead to very arbitrary product costing. Even a small change in the amount of direct labour worked on a job could massively affect the total cost deduced – not because the direct worker is very highly paid, but because of the effect of the direct labour hours on the overhead cost loading. A further problem is that overheads are still typically charged on a direct labour hour basis even though the overheads may not be closely related to direct labour.

Real World 5.1 provides a rather disturbing view of costing and cost control in large banks.

REAL WORLD 5.1

Bank accounts   **FT**

In a study of the cost structures of 52 international banks, the German consultancy firm, Droege, found that indirect cost (overheads) could represent as much as 85 per cent of total cost. However, whilst direct costs were generally under tight management control, overheads were not. The overheads, which include such items as IT development, risk control, auditing, marketing and public relations, were often not allocated between operating divisions or were allocated in a rather arbitrary manner.

Source: Based on information in A. Skorecki, '*Banks have not tackled indirect costs*', ft.com, 7 January 2004.

An alternative approach to full costing

The changes in the competitive environment discussed above have led to much closer attention being paid to the issue of overheads, what causes them and how they are charged to jobs. Historically, businesses have been content to accept that overheads exist and, therefore, for job (product) costing purposes they must be dealt with in as practical a way as possible. In recent years, however, there has been increasing recognition of the fact that overheads do not just happen; something must be causing them. To illustrate this point, let us consider Example 5.1.

Example 5.1

Modern Producers Ltd has a storage area that is set aside for its inventories of finished goods. The cost of running the stores includes a share of the factory rent and other establishment costs, such as heating and lighting. It also includes the salaries of staff employed to look after the inventories, and the cost of financing the inventories held in the stores.

The business has two product lines: A and B. Product A tends to be made in small batches and low levels of finished inventories are held. The business prides itself on its ability to supply Product B in relatively large quantities, instantly. As a consequence, most of the space in the finished goods store is filled with finished Product Bs, ready to be despatched immediately an order is received.

Example 5.1 continued

Traditionally, the whole cost of operating the stores would have been treated as a part of general overheads and included in the total of overheads charged to jobs, probably on a direct labour hour basis. This means that, when assessing the cost of Products A and B, the cost of operating the stores has fallen on them according to the number of direct labour hours worked on manufacturing each one; a factor that has nothing to do with storage. In fact, most of the stores' cost should be charged to Product B, since this product causes (and benefits from) the stores' cost much more than Product A.

Failure to account more precisely for the cost of running the stores is masking the fact that Product B is not as profitable as it seems to be. It may even be leading to losses as a result of the relatively high stores-operating cost that it causes. However, much of this cost is charged to Product A, without regard to the fact that Product A causes little of it.

What drives the costs?

Activity-based costing (ABC) aims to overcome the kind of problem just described by tracing the cost of all support activities directly to particular products or services. For a manufacturing business, these support activities may include materials ordering, materials handling, storage, inspection and so on. The cost of the support activities makes up the total overheads cost. The outcome of this tracing exercise is to provide a more realistic, and more finely measured, account of the overhead cost element for a particular product or service.

To implement a system of ABC, managers must begin by carefully examining the business's operations. They will need to identify:

1 Each of the various support activities involved in the process of making products or providing services;
2 The costs to be attributed to each support activity; and
3 The factors that cause a change in the costs of each support activity, that is, the **cost drivers**.

Identifying the cost drivers is a vital element of a successful ABC system. They have a cause-and-effect relationship with activity costs and so are used as a basis for attaching activity costs to a particular product or service. This point is discussed further below.

Attributing overheads

Once the various support activities, their costs and the factors that drive these costs, have been identified, ABC requires:

1 An overhead **cost pool** to be established for each activity. Thus, the business in Example 5.1 will create a cost pool for operating the finished goods store.
2 The total cost associated with each support activity to be allocated to the relevant cost pool.
3 The total cost in each pool to then be charged to output (Products A and B, in the case of Example 5.1) using the relevant cost driver.

The final step identified involves dividing the amount in each cost pool by the estimated total usage of the cost driver to derive a cost per unit of the cost driver. This unit cost figure is then multiplied by the number of units of the cost driver used by a particular product, or service, to determine the amount of overhead cost to be attached to it.

The following example should make this last step clear.

Example 5.2

The management accountant at Modern Producers Ltd (see Example 5.1) has estimated that the cost of running the finished goods stores for next year will be £90,000. This will be the amount allocated to the 'finished goods stores cost pool'.

It is estimated that each Product A will spend an average of one week in the stores before being sold. With Product B, the equivalent period is four weeks. Both products are of roughly similar size and have very similar storage needs. It is felt, therefore, that period spent in the stores ('product weeks') is the cost driver.

Next year, 50,000 Product As and 25,000 Product Bs are expected to pass through the stores. The estimated total usage of the cost driver will be the total number of 'product weeks' that the products will be in store. For next year, this will be:

$$
\begin{array}{llll}
\text{Product A} & 50{,}000 \times 1\ \text{week} & = & 50{,}000 \\
\text{Product B} & 25{,}000 \times 4\ \text{weeks} & = & \underline{100{,}000} \\
& & & \underline{150{,}000}
\end{array}
$$

The cost per unit of cost driver is the total cost of the stores divided by the number of 'product weeks', as calculated above. This is:

$$\text{£90,000/150,000} = \text{£0.60}$$

To determine the cost to be attached to a particular unit of product, the figure of £0.60 must be multiplied by the number of 'product weeks' that a product stays in the finished goods store. Thus, each unit of Product A will be charged with £0.60 (that is, £0.60 × 1), and each Product B with £2.40 (that is, £0.60 × 4).

Benefits of ABC

Through the direct tracing of cost to products in the way described, ABC seeks to establish more accurate costs for each unit of product or service. This should help managers in assessing product profitability and in making decisions concerning pricing and the appropriate product mix. Other benefits, however, may also flow from adopting an ABC approach.

Activity 5.1

Can you think of any other benefits that an ABC approach to costing may provide?

By identifying the various support activities' costs and analysing what causes them to change, managers should gain a better understanding of the business. This, in turn, should help them in controlling costs and improving efficiency. It should also help them in forward planning. They may, for example, be in a better position to assess the likely effect of new products and processes on activities and costs.

ABC versus the traditional approach

We can see that there is a basic philosophical difference between the traditional and the ABC approaches. The traditional approach views overheads as *rendering a service to cost units*, the cost of which must be charged to those units. ABC, on the other hand, views overheads as being *caused by activities*, and so it is the cost units that cause these activities that must be charged with the costs that they cause.

With the traditional approach, overheads are apportioned to product cost centres. Each product cost centre would then derive an overhead recovery rate, typically overheads per direct labour hour. Overheads would then be applied to units of output according to how many direct labour hours were worked on them.

With ABC, the overheads are analysed into cost pools, with one cost pool for each cost-driving activity. The overheads are then charged to units of output, through activity cost driver rates. These rates are an attempt to represent the extent to which each particular cost unit is believed to cause the particular part of the overheads.

Cost pools are much the same as cost centres, except that each cost pool is linked to a particular *activity* (operating the stores in Examples 5.1 and 5.2), rather than being more general, as is the case with cost centres in traditional job (or product) costing.

The two different approaches are illustrated in Figure 5.1.

ABC and service industries

Much of our discussion of ABC has concentrated on the manufacturing industry, perhaps because early users of ABC were manufacturing businesses. In fact, ABC is possibly even more relevant to service industries because, in the absence of a direct material element, a service business's total cost is likely to be largely made up of overheads. There is certainly evidence that ABC has been adopted more readily by businesses that sell services rather than products, as we shall see later.

Activity 5.2

What is the difference in the way in which direct costs are accounted for when using ABC, relative to their treatment taking a traditional approach to full costing?

The answer is no difference at all. ABC is concerned only with the way in which overheads are charged to jobs to derive the full cost.

Example 5.3 provides an example of activity-based costing and brings together the points that have been raised so far.

Figure 5.1	**Traditional versus activity-based costing**

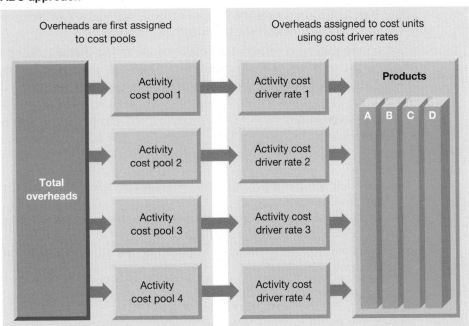

With the traditional approach, overheads are first assigned to product cost centres and then absorbed by cost units based on an overhead recovery rate (using direct labour hours worked on the cost units or some other approach) for each cost centre. With activity-based costing, overheads are assigned to cost pools and then cost units are charged with overheads to the extent that they drive the costs in the various pools.

Source: Adapted from Innes, J. and Mitchell, F., *Activity Based Costing: A Review with Case Studies*, CIMA Publishing, 1990.

Example 5.3

Comma Ltd manufactures two types of Sprizzer – Standard and Deluxe. Each product requires the incorporation of a difficult-to-handle special part (one of them for a Standard and four for a Deluxe). Both of these products are made in batches (large batches for Standards and small ones for Deluxes). Each new batch requires that the production facilities are 'set up'.

Details of the two products are:

	Standard	Deluxe
Annual production and sales – units	12,000	12,000
Sales price per unit	£65	£87
Batch size – units	1,000	50
Direct labour time per unit – hours	2	2½
Direct labour rate per hour	£8	£8
Direct material cost per unit	£22	£32
Number of special parts per unit	1	4
Number of set-ups per batch	1	3
Number of separate material issues from stores per batch	1	1
Number of sales invoices issued per year	50	240

In recent months, Comma Ltd has been trying to persuade customers who buy the Standard to purchase the Deluxe instead. An analysis of overhead costs for Comma Ltd has provided the following information.

Overhead cost analysis	£	Cost driver
Set-up cost	73,200	Number of set-ups
Special part handling cost	60,000	Number of special parts
Customer invoicing cost	29,000	Number of invoices
Material handling cost	63,000	Number of batches
Other overheads	108,000	Labour hours

Required:

(a) Calculate the profit per unit and the return on sales for Standard and Deluxe Sprizzers using
   (i) the traditional direct-labour-hour based absorption of overheads;
   (ii) activity-based costing methods.

(b) Comment on the managerial implications for Comma Ltd of the results in (a) above.

Solution

Using the traditional full (absorption) costing approach that we considered in Chapter 4, the overheads are added together and an overheads recovery rate deduced as follows:

Overheads	£
Set-up cost	73,200
Special part handling cost	60,000
Customer invoicing cost	29,000
Material handling cost	63,000
Other overheads	108,000
	333,200

$$\text{Overhead recovery rate} = \frac{\text{Total overheads}}{\text{Number of labour hours}}$$

$$= \frac{£333,200}{[(12,000 \times 2) + (12,000 \times 2\frac{1}{2})]}$$

$$= \frac{£333,200}{54,000}$$

$$= £6.17 \text{ per hour}$$

The total cost per unit of each type of Sprizzer is calculated by adding the direct cost to the overheads cost per unit. The overheads cost per unit is calculated by multiplying the number of direct labour hours spent on the product (2 hours for each Standard and $2\frac{1}{2}$ hours for each Deluxe) by the overheads recovery rate calculated above. Hence:

	Standard £	Deluxe £
Direct cost		
Labour	16.00	20.00
Material	22.00	32.00
Indirect cost		
Overheads (£6.17 per hour)	12.34	15.43
Total cost per unit	50.34	67.43

The return on sales is calculated as follows:

	Standard £ per unit	Deluxe £ per unit
Selling price	65.00	87.00
Total cost (see above)	50.34	67.43
Profit	14.66	19.57
Return on sales [(profit/sales) × 100%]	22.55%	22.49%

Using the ABC costing approach, the activity cost driver rates will be calculated as follows:

Overhead cost pool	Driver	(a) Standard driver volume	(b) Deluxe driver volume	(c) Total driver volume (a + b)	(d) Costs £	(e) Driver rate £ (d/c)
Set-up	Set-ups per batch	12	720	732	73,200	100
Special part	Special parts per unit	12,000	48,000	60,000	60,000	1
Customer invoices	Invoices per year	50	240	290	29,000	100
Material handling	Number of batches	12	240	252	63,000	250
Other overheads	Labour hours	24,000	30,000	54,000	108,000	2

→

Example 5.3 continued

The activity-based costs are derived as follows:

Overhead cost pool	(f) Total costs Standard (a × e) £	(g) Total costs Deluxe (b × e) £	Unit costs Standard (f/12,000) £	Unit costs Deluxe (g/12,000) £
Set-up	1,200	72,000	0.10	6.00
Special part	12,000	48,000	1.00	4.00
Customer invoices	5,000	24,000	0.42	2.00
Material handling	3,000	60,000	0.25	5.00
Other overheads	48,000	60,000	4.00	5.00
Total overheads			5.77	22.00

The total cost per unit is calculated as follows:

	Standard £ per unit	Deluxe £ per unit
Direct cost:		
Labour	16.00	20.00
Material	22.00	32.00
Indirect cost		
See above	5.77	22.00
Total cost per unit	43.77	74.00

The return on sales is calculated as follows:

	Standard £ per unit	Deluxe £ per unit
Selling price	65.00	87.00
Total cost (see above)	43.77	74.00
Profit	21.23	13.00
Return on sales [(profit/sales) × 100%]	32.67%	14.94%

The figures show that under the traditional approach the returns on sales appear broadly equal. However, the ABC approach shows that the Standard product is far more profitable. Hence, the business should reconsider its policy of trying to persuade customers to switch to the Deluxe product.

Criticisms of ABC

Although many businesses now adopt a system of ABC, its critics point out that ABC can be time-consuming and costly. Set-up costs as well as costs of running and updating the ABC system must be incurred. These costs can be very high, particularly where the business's operations are complex and involve a large number of activities and cost drivers. Furthermore, ABC information produced under the scenario just described may be complex. If managers find ABC reports difficult to understand, there is a risk that the potential benefits of ABC will be lost.

Not all businesses are likely to benefit from ABC. Where a business sells products or services that all have similar levels of output and involve similar activities and processes, it is unlikely that the finer measurements provided by ABC will lead to strikingly different results from those gained under the traditional approach. As a result, opportunities for better pricing, planning and cost control may not be great and may not justify the cost of switching to an ABC system.

Measurement and tracing problems can arise with ABC, which may undermine any potential benefits. Not all costs can be easily identified with a particular activity and some may have to be allocated to cost pools. This can often be done on some sensible basis. For example, factory rent may be allocated on the basis of square metres of space used. In some cases, however, a lack of data concerning a particular cost may lead to fairly arbitrary cost allocations between activities. There is also the problem that the relationship between activity costs and their cost drivers may be difficult to determine. Identifying a cause-and-effect relationship can be difficult where a large proportion of activity costs are fixed and so do not vary with changes in usage.

ABC is also criticised for the same reason that full costing generally is criticised: because it does not provide very relevant information for decision making. The point was made in Chapter 4 that full costing tends to use past costs and to ignore opportunity costs. Since past costs are always irrelevant in decision making and opportunity costs can be significant, full costing information is an expensive irrelevance. In contrast, advocates of full costing claim that it *is* relevant, in that it provides a long-run average cost, whereas 'relevant costing', which we considered in Chapter 2, relates only to the specific circumstances of the short term. The use of ABC, rather than the traditional approach to job (or product) costing, does not affect the validity of this irrelevance argument.

Real World 5.2 shows how ABC came to be used at the Royal Mail.

REAL WORLD 5.2

Delivering ABC

Early in the 2000s the publicly-owned Royal Mail adopted ABC and used it to find the cost of making postal deliveries. Royal Mail identified 340 activities that gave rise to costs, created a cost pool and identified a cost driver for each of these.

Roger Tabour, Royal Mail's Enterprise Systems Programme Director, explained, 'A new regulatory and competitive environment, plus a down-turned economy, led management to seek out more reliable sources of information on performance and profitability,' and this led to the introduction of ABC.

The Royal Mail is a public sector organisation that is subject to supervision by Postcomm, the UK government appointed regulatory body. The government requires the Royal Mail to operate on a commercial basis and to make profits.

Source: www.sas.com.

Real World 5.3 provides some indication of the extent to which ABC is used in practice.

REAL WORLD 5.3

ABC in practice

A recent survey of 176 UK businesses operating in various industries, all with an annual turnover of more than £50 million, was conducted by Al-Omiri and Drury. This indicated that 29 per cent of larger UK businesses use ABC.

The adoption of ABC in the UK varies widely between industries, as is shown in Figure 5.2.

Figure 5.2   ABC in practice

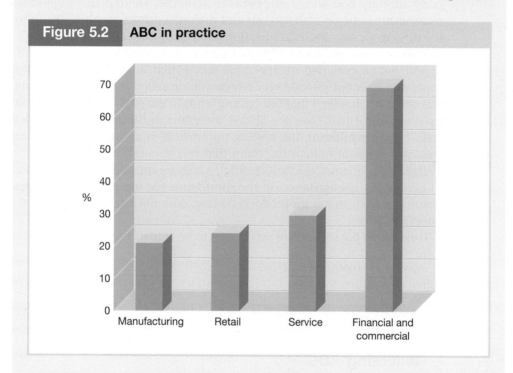

Al-Omiri and Drury took their analysis a step further by looking at the factors that apparently tend to lead a particular business to adopt ABC. They found that businesses that used ABC tended to be:

- Large
- Sophisticated, in terms of using advanced management accounting techniques generally
- In an intensely competitive market for their products
- Operating in a service industry, particularly in the financial services.

All of these findings are broadly in line with other recent research evidence involving businesses from around the world.

Source: Al-Omiri, M. and Drury, C., 'A survey of factors influencing the choice of product costing systems in UK organisations', *Management Accounting Research*, December 2007.

Self-assessment question 5.1

Psilis Ltd makes a product in two qualities, called 'Basic' and 'Super'. The business is able to sell these products at a price that gives a standard profit mark-up of 25 per cent of full cost. Management is concerned by the lack of profit.

Full cost for one unit of a product is calculated by charging overheads to each type of product on the basis of direct labour hours. The costs are as follows:

	Basic £	Super £
Direct labour (all £10/hour)	40	60
Direct material	15	20

The total overheads are £1,000,000.

Based on experience over recent years, in the forthcoming year the business expects to make and sell 40,000 Basics and 10,000 Supers.

Recently, the business's management accountant has undertaken an exercise to try to identify activities and cost drivers in an attempt to be able to deal with the overheads on a more precise basis than had been possible before. This exercise has revealed the following analysis of the annual overheads:

Activity (and cost driver)	Cost £000	Annual number of activities		
		Total	Basic	Super
Number of machine set-ups	280	100	20	80
Number of quality-control inspections	220	2,000	500	1,500
Number of sales orders processed	240	5,000	1,500	3,500
General production (machine hours)	260	500,000	350,000	150,000
Total	1,000			

The management accountant explained the analysis of the £1,000,000 overheads as follows:

- The two products are made in relatively small batches, so that the amount of the finished product held in inventories is negligible. The Supers are made in very small batches because demand for them is relatively low. Each time a new batch is produced, the machines have to be reset by skilled staff. Resetting for Basic production occurs about 20 times a year and for Supers about 80 times: about 100 times in total. The cost of employing the machine-setting staff is about £280,000 a year. It is clear that the more set-ups that occur, the higher the total set-up costs; in other words, the number of set-ups is the factor that drives set-up costs.
- All production has to be inspected for quality and this costs about £220,000 a year. The higher specifications of the Supers mean that there is more chance that there will be quality problems. Thus the Supers are inspected in total 1,500 times annually, whereas the Basics only need about 500 inspections. The number of inspections is the factor that drives these costs.
- Sales order processing (dealing with customers' orders, from receiving the original order to despatching the products) costs about £240,000 a year. Despite the larger amount of Basic production, there are only 1,500 sales orders each year because the Basics are sold to wholesalers in relatively large-sized orders. The Supers are sold mainly direct to the public by mail order, usually in very small-sized orders. It is believed that the number of orders drives the costs of processing orders.

Self-assessment question 5.1 continued

Required:
(a) Deduce the full cost of each of the two products on the basis used at present and, from these, deduce the current selling price.
(b) Deduce the full cost of each product on an ABC basis, taking account of the management accountant's recent investigations.
(c) What conclusions do you draw? What advice would you offer the management of the business?

The answer to this question can be found in Appendix B at the back of the book.

Other approaches to cost management in the modern environment

The increasingly competitive environment in which modern businesses operate is leading to greater effort being applied in trying to manage costs. Businesses need to keep costs to a minimum so that they can supply goods and services at a price that customers will be prepared to pay and, at the same time, generate a level of profit necessary to meet the businesses' objectives of enhancing shareholder wealth. We have just seen how ABC can help manage costs. We shall now go on to outline some other techniques that have recently emerged in an attempt to meet these goals of competitiveness and profitability. These can be used in conjunction with ABC.

Total (or whole) life-cycle costing

This method of costing starts from the premise that the total (or whole) life cycle of a product or service has three phases. These are:

1 The *pre-production phase*. This is the period that precedes production of the product or service for sale. During this phase, research and development – both of the product or service and of the market – is conducted. The product or service is invented/ designed and so is the means of production. The phase culminates with acquiring and setting up the necessary production facilities and with advertising and promotion.
2 The *production phase* comes next, being the one in which the product is made and sold or the service is rendered to customers.
3 The *post-production phase* comes last. During this phase, any costs necessary to correct faults that arose with products or services that have been sold (after-sales service) are incurred. There would also be the costs of closing production at the end of the product's or service's life cycle, such as the cost of decommissioning production facilities. Since after-sales service will tend to arise from as early as the first product or service being sold and probably, therefore, well before the last one is sold, this phase would typically overlap with the manufacturing/service-rendering phase.

Businesses often seem to consider environmental costs alongside the more obvious financial costs involved in the life of a product.

The total life cycle is shown in Figure 5.3.

Figure 5.3	The total life cycle of a product or service

Research and development,
production set-up,
pre-production
marketing costs

**Total life cycle of a
product or service**

Pre-production
phase

Manufacturing and
marketing costs

Production
phase

After-sales service
and production facility
decommissioning costs

Post-production
phase

From the producer's viewpoint, the life of a product can be seen as having three distinct phases. During the first the product is developed and everything is prepared so that production and marketing can start. Next comes production and sales. Lastly, dealing with post-production activities is undertaken.

In some types of business, particularly those engaged in an advanced manufacturing environment, it is estimated that a very high proportion (as much as 80 per cent) of the total costs that will be incurred over the total life of a particular product are either incurred or committed at the pre-production phase. For example, a car manufacturer, when designing, developing and setting up production of a new model, incurs a high proportion of the total costs that will be incurred on that model during the whole of its life. Not only are pre-production costs specifically incurred during this phase, but the need to incur particular costs during the production phase is also established. This is because the design will incorporate features that will lead to particular manufacturing costs. Once the design of the car has been finalised and the manufacturing plant set up, it may be too late to 'design out' a costly feature without incurring another large cost.

Activity 5.3

A decision taken at the design stage could well commit the business to costs after the manufacture of the product has taken place. Can you suggest a potential cost that could be built in at the design stage that will show itself *after* the manufacture of the product?

After-sales service costs could be incurred as a result of some design fault. Once the manufacturing facilities have been established, it may not be economic to revise the design; it may be better to deal with the problem through after-sales service procedures.

Total life-cycle costing seeks to focus management's attention on the fact that it is not just during the production phase that attention needs to be paid to cost management. By the start of the production phase it may be too late to try to manage a large element of the product's or service's total life-cycle cost. Efforts need to be made to assess the costs of alternative designs.

There needs to be a review of the product or service over its entire life cycle, which could be a period of 20 or more years. Traditional management accounting, however, tends to be concerned with assessing performance over periods of just one year or less.

Real World 5.4 provides some idea of the extent to which total life-cycle costing is used in practice.

REAL WORLD 5.4

Total (whole) life-cycle costing in practice

A survey of management accounting practice in the US was conducted in 2003. Nearly 2,000 businesses replied to the survey. These tended to be larger businesses, of which about 40 per cent were manufacturers and about 16 per cent financial services; the remainder were across a range of other industries.

The survey revealed that 22 per cent extensively use a total life-cycle approach to cost control, with a further 37 per cent considering using the technique in the future.

Though the survey relates to the US, in the absence of UK evidence it provides some insight to what is likely also to be practised in the UK and elsewhere in the developed world.

Source: 2003 Survey of Management Accounting, Ernst and Young, 2003.

Real World 5.5 shows how a well-known international carmaker uses total life-cycle costing.

REAL WORLD 5.5

Total life-cycle costing at Renault

According to Renault, the French motor vehicle manufacturer:

The life of a vehicle is long and comprises several phases:

design: Creating a vehicle
manufacturing: Extracting and producing materials, manufacturing and assembling the components, and then the whole vehicle
distribution: Transition between the vehicle's departure from the production plant and its purchase by a customer
vehicle service life: The use by the motorist, the longest phase
recycling.

These phases make up the life cycle. Why the word 'cycle'? Because the end of a vehicle's service life is factored in right from the design phase.

Source: www.renault.com.

Note that Renault divides the *production phase* into two sections: manufacturing and distribution. It also divides the *post-production phase* into vehicle service life and recycling.

Target costing

With traditional cost-plus pricing, costs are totalled for a product or service and a percentage is added for profit to arrive at a selling price. This is not a very practical basis on which to price output for many businesses – certainly not those operating in a price-competitive market. The cost-plus price may well be totally unacceptable to the market. (We shall take another look at this later in this chapter.)

 Target costing approaches the problem from the other direction. First, with the help of market research or other means, a unit selling price and sales volume are established. From the unit selling price is taken an amount for profit. This unit profit figure must be such as to be acceptable to meet the business's profit objective. The resulting figure is the target cost. The target cost may well be less than the 'current' cost; there may be a 'cost gap'. Efforts are then made to bridge this gap, that is, to provide the service or make the product in such a way as to enable the target cost to be met. These efforts may involve revising the design, finding more efficient means of production or requiring suppliers of goods and services to supply more cheaply.

Target costing is seen as a part of a total life-cycle costing approach, in that cost savings are sought at a very early stage in the life cycle, during the pre-production phase.

Real World 5.6 indicates the level of usage of target costing.

REAL WORLD 5.6

On target

The Ernst and Young survey of management accounting practice in the US conducted in 2003 revealed that 27 per cent use target costing extensively, with a further 41 per cent considering using the technique in the future.

Source: 2003 Survey of Management Accounting, Ernst and Young, 2003.

This shows quite a low level of usage in the US. In contrast, survey evidence shows that target costing is very widely used by Japanese manufacturing businesses.

Activity 5.4

Though target costing seems effective and has its enthusiasts, some people feel it has its problems. Can you suggest what these problems might be?

There seem to be three main problem areas:

● It can lead to various conflicts – for example, between the business, its suppliers and its own staff.

● It can cause a great deal of stress for employees who are trying to meet target costs that are sometimes extremely difficult to meet.

● Although, in the end, ways may be found to meet a target cost (through product or service redesign, negotiating lower prices with suppliers, and so on), the whole process can be very expensive.

We shall discuss total life-cycle costing and target costing more in Chapter 9 when we consider the strategic aspects of management accounting.

Costing quality control

Such is the importance that their customers place on quality that businesses are forced to make sure that their output is of a high quality. In the competitive environment in which most businesses operate, a failure to deliver quality will lead to customers going to another supplier. Businesses, therefore, need to establish procedures that promote the quality of their output, either by preventing quality problems in the first place or by dealing with them when they occur. These procedures have a cost. It has been estimated that these **quality costs** can amount to up to 30 per cent of total processing costs. These costs tend to be incurred during the *production phase* of the product life cycle. They have been seen as falling into four main categories:

1 *Prevention costs.* These are involved with procedures to try to prevent items being produced that are not up to the required quality. Such procedures might include staff training on quality issues. Some types of prevention costs might be incurred during the *pre-production phase* of the product life cycle, where the production process could be designed in such a way as to avoid potential quality problems with the output.
2 *Appraisal costs.* These are concerned with monitoring raw materials, work in progress and finished products to try to avoid substandard products from reaching the customer.
3 *Internal failure costs.* These include the costs of rectifying substandard products before they pass to the customer and the costs of scrap arising from quality failures.
4 *External failure costs.* These are involved with rectifying quality problems with products that have passed to the customer. There is also the cost to the business of its loss of reputation from having passed substandard products to the customer.

Figure 5.4 sets these out in diagram form.

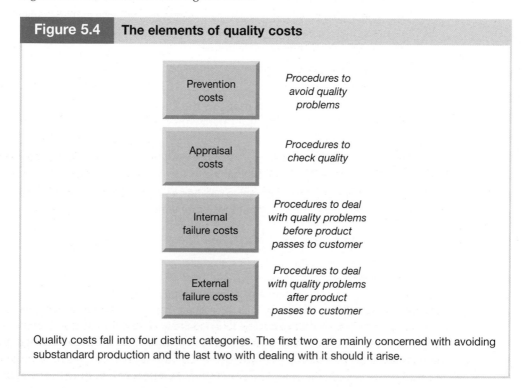

Figure 5.4	The elements of quality costs

Quality costs fall into four distinct categories. The first two are mainly concerned with avoiding substandard production and the last two with dealing with it should it arise.

Kaizen costing

 Kaizen **costing** is linked to total life-cycle costing and focuses on cost saving during the production phase. The Japanese word *kaizen* implies 'continuous changes'. The application of the *kaizen* costing approach involves continuous improvement, in terms of cost saving, throughout the production phase. Since this phase is at a relatively late stage in the life cycle (from a cost control point of view) only relatively small cost savings can usually be made. The major production-phase cost savings should already have been made through target costing.

With *kaizen* costing, efforts are made to reduce the unit manufacturing cost of the particular product or service under review, if possible taking it below the unit cost in the previous period. Target percentage reductions can be set. Usually, production workers are encouraged to identify ways of reducing costs. This is something that the 'hands on' experience of these workers may enable them to do. Even though the scope to reduce costs is limited at the production stage, valuable savings can still be made.

Real World 5.7 explains how a major UK manufacturer used *kaizen* costing to advantage.

REAL WORLD 5.7

Kaizen costing is part of the package

Kappa Packaging is a major UK packaging business. It has a factory at Stalybridge where it makes, among other things, packaging (cardboard cartons) for glass bottles containing alcoholic drinks. In 2002, Kappa introduced a new approach to reducing the amount of waste paper and cardboard. Before this the business wasted 14.6 per cent of the raw materials it used. This figure was taken as the base against which improvements would be measured.

Improvements were made at Kappa as a result of:

● making staff more aware of the waste problem;
● requiring staff to monitor the amount of waste for which they were individually responsible; and
● establishing a *kaizen* team to find ways of reducing waste.

As a result of *kaizen* savings, Kappa was able to reduce waste from 14.6 per cent to 13.1 per cent in 2002 and 11 per cent in 2003. The business estimates that each 1 per cent waste saving was worth £110,000 a year. So by the end of 2003, Kappa was saving about £400,000 a year, relative to 2001: that is, over £2,000 per employee each year.

Source: Taken from 'Accurate measurement of process waste leads to reduced costs', www.envirowise.gov.uk, 2003.

Benchmarking

 Benchmarking is an activity – usually a continuing one – where a business, or one of its divisions, seeks to emulate a successful business or division and so achieve a similar level of success. The successful business or division provides a benchmark against which the business can measure its own performance, as well as examples of approaches that can lead to success. Sometimes the benchmark business will help with the activity, but even where no co-operation is given, outside observers can still learn quite a lot about what makes that business successful.

Businesses are under no statutory obligation to benchmark and are understandably reluctant to divulge commercially sensitive information to competitor businesses. They may, however, benchmark internally, with one division or department comparing itself with another part of the same business. They may also benchmark with businesses with which they are not directly competing but which may have similar functions.

Real World 5.8 provides an example of two well-known divisions of an equally well-known parent business that are able to benchmark, one against the other.

REAL WORLD 5.8

Tracking the Jaguar   **FT**

The solid off-road qualities of Land Rover vehicles inspire devotion among many of their owners, who include members of Britain's royal family.

But the brand has been plagued by quality problems, setting spurious warning lights flashing in some of its vehicles and putting it last in consultancy JD Power's 2007 Initial Quality Study in the US.

Land Rover is now benchmarking the quality levels of Jaguar, its sister brand, and clawing its way back up the league tables.

'They're still below the average, but improving relative to the competition,' said Brian Walters, JD Power's vice-president of European operations.

Lewis Booth, head of Ford Motor's premium-brands group, told the *Financial Times*: 'We want to get Land Rover to Jaguar quality levels.'

The problems owe something to the complexity of the vehicles, packed with electronic control units aimed at keeping them stable off road.

Land Rover, formerly owned by BMW and now up for sale by Ford, has seen a flurry of new vehicle launches in recent years, even as it changed owners.

Source: Royal following but quality issues remain, *Financial Times* (Reed, J.), © The Financial Times Limited, 3 October 2007.

Ford sold Jaguar and Land Rover to the Indian motor business Tata in March 2008, but the inter-divisional benchmarking still continues, no doubt.

Pricing

As we saw in Chapter 4, full costs can be used as a basis for setting prices for the business's output. We also saw that it can be criticised in that role. In this section we are going to take a closer look at pricing. We shall begin by considering some theoretical aspects of the subject before going on to look at some more practical issues, particularly the role of management accounting information in pricing decisions.

Economic theory

In most market conditions found in practice, the price charged by a business will determine the number of units sold. This is shown graphically in Figure 5.5.

Figure 5.5	Graph of quantity demanded against price for Commodity A

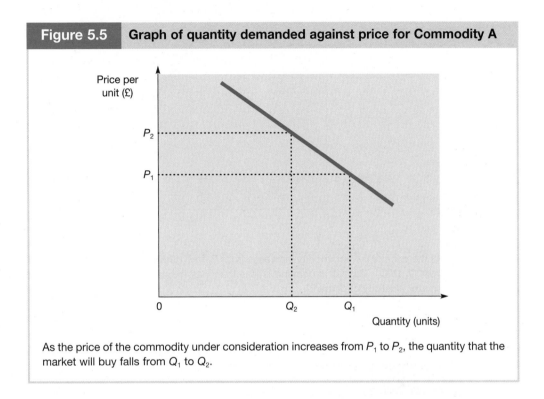

As the price of the commodity under consideration increases from P_1 to P_2, the quantity that the market will buy falls from Q_1 to Q_2.

Figure 5.5 shows the number of units of output that the market would demand at various prices. As price increases, people are less willing to buy the commodity (call it Commodity A). Note that the commodity might be a physical product or a service. At a relatively low price per unit (P_1), the quantity of units demanded by the market (Q_1) is fairly high. When the price is increased to P_2, the demand decreases to Q_2. The graph shows a linear (straight-line) relationship between the price and demand. In practice, the relationship, though broadly similar, may not be quite so straightforward.

Not all commodities show exactly the same slope of line. Figure 5.6 shows the demand/ price relationship for Commodity B, a different commodity from the one depicted in Figure 5.5.

Though a rise in price of Commodity B, from P_1 to P_2, causes a fall in demand, the fall in demand is much smaller than is the case for Commodity A with a similar rise in price. As a result, we say that Commodity A has a higher **elasticity of demand** than Commodity B. Demand for A reacts much more dramatically to price changes (stretches more) than does demand for B. Elastic demand tends to be associated with commodities that are not essential, perhaps because there is a ready substitute.

It is very helpful for those involved with pricing decisions to have some feel for the elasticity of demand of the commodity that will be the subject of a decision. The sensitivity of the demand to the pricing decision is obviously much greater (and the pricing decision more crucial) with commodities whose demand is elastic than with commodities whose demand is relatively inelastic.

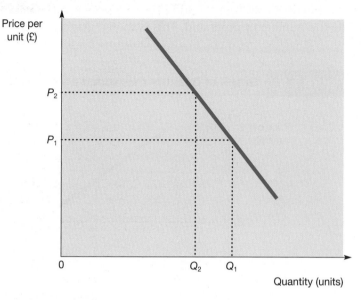

| Figure 5.6 | Graph of quantity demanded against price for Commodity B |

As the price of the commodity increases from P_1 to P_2, the quantity that the market will buy falls from Q_1 to Q_2. This fall in demand is less than was the case for Commodity A, which has the greater elasticity of demand.

Activity 5.5

Which would have the more elastic demand – a particular brand of chocolate bar, or Mains electricity supply?

A branded chocolate bar seems likely to have a fairly *elastic* demand. This is for several reasons, including the following:

- Few buyers of the bar would feel that chocolate bars are essentials.
- Other chocolate bars, probably quite similar to the one in question, will be easily available.

Mains electricity probably has a relatively *inelastic* demand. This is because:

- Many users of electricity would find it very difficult to manage without fuel of some description.
- For neither household nor business users of electricity is there an immediate, practical substitute. For some uses of electricity – for example, powering machinery – there is probably no substitute. Even for a purpose such as heating, where there are substitutes such as gas and oil, it may be impractical to switch to the substitute because gas and oil heating appliances are not immediately available and are costly to acquire.

Real World 5.9 is an extract from a *Financial Times* article that suggests that patterns of elasticity of demand can be modified by an economic recession in the US.

REAL WORLD 5.9

Elasticity of demand affected by the downturn   FT

The signs of an imminent recession are all around us. Spillover from the subprime mortgage crisis is weakening both consumer confidence and the consumer spending – much of it on credit – that has buoyed the US economy.

Don't cut the market research budget. You need to know more than ever how consumers are redefining value and responding to the recession. Price elasticity curves are changing. Consumers take longer searching for durable goods and negotiate harder at point of sale. They are more willing to postpone purchases, trade down or buy less. Must-have features of yesterday are today's can-live-withouts. Trusted brands are especially valued and can still launch products successfully, but interest in new brands and categories fades. Conspicuous consumption becomes less prevalent.

Source: Quelch, J. 'Family comes first when marketing faces tougher times', *Financial Times*, 18 February 2008.

As we saw in Chapter 1, the objective of most businesses is to enhance the wealth of their owners. Broadly speaking, this will be best achieved by seeking to maximise profits – that is, having the largest possible difference between total cost and total revenue. Thus, prices should be set in a way that is likely to have this effect. To do this, the price decision maker needs to have some insight to the way in which cost and price relate to volume of output.

Figure 5.7 shows the relationship between cost and volume of output, which we have already met in Chapter 3.

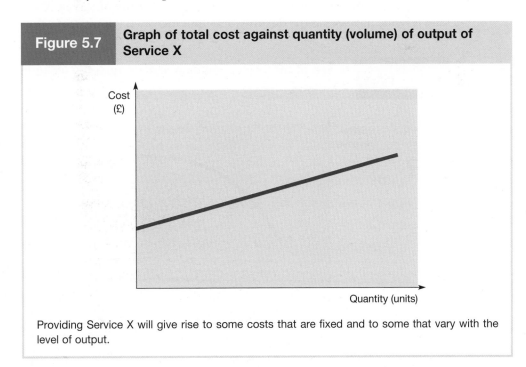

Figure 5.7 Graph of total cost against quantity (volume) of output of Service X

Providing Service X will give rise to some costs that are fixed and to some that vary with the level of output.

The figure shows that the total cost of providing a particular commodity (Service X) increases as the quantity of output increases. It is shown here as a straight line. In practice, it may be curved, either curving upwards (tending to become closer to the vertical) or flattening out (tending to become closer to the horizontal). The figure assumes that the marginal cost of each unit is constant over the range shown.

Activity 5.6

What general effect would tend to cause the total cost line in Figure 5.7 to (a) curve towards the vertical, and (b) curve towards the horizontal? (You may recall that we considered this issue in Chapter 3.)

(a) Curving towards the vertical would mean that the marginal cost (additional cost of making one more) of each successive unit of output would become greater. This would probably imply that increased activity would be causing a shortage of supply of some factor of production, which has the effect of increasing cost prices. This might be caused by a shortage of labour, meaning that overtime payments would need to be made to encourage people to work the hours necessary for increased production. It might also/alternatively be caused by a shortage of raw materials. Perhaps normal supplies were exhausted at lower levels of output and more expensive sources had to be used to expand output.

(b) Curving towards the horizontal might be caused by the business being able to exploit the economies of scale at higher levels of output, making the marginal cost of each successive unit of output cheaper. Perhaps higher volumes of output enable division of labour or more mechanisation. Possibly, suppliers of raw materials offer better deals for larger orders.

Figure 5.8 shows the total sales revenue against quantity of Service X sold. The total sales revenue increases as the quantity of output increases, but often at a decreasing rate.

Figure 5.8   **Graph of total sales revenue against quantity (volume) sold of Service X**

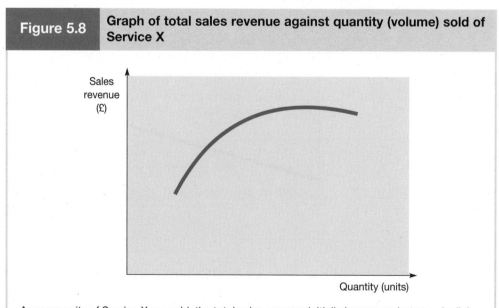

As more units of Service X are sold, the total sales revenue initially increases, but at a declining rate. This is because, to persuade people to buy increasing quantities, the price must be reduced. Eventually the price will have to be reduced so much, to encourage additional sales, that the total sales revenue will fall as the number of units sold increases.

Activity 5.7

What assumption does Figure 5.8 make about the price for a unit of Service X at which output can be sold as the number of units sold increases?

The graph suggests that, to sell more units, the price must be lowered, meaning that the average price for each unit of output reduces as volume sold increases. As we discussed earlier in this section, this is true of most markets found in practice.

Figure 5.8 implies that there will come a point where, to make increased sales, prices will have to be reduced so much that total sales revenue will not increase by much for each additional sale.

In Chapter 3, when we considered break-even analysis, we assumed a steady price per unit over the range that we were considering. Now we are saying that, in practice, it does not work like this. How can these two positions be reconciled? The answer is that, when using break-even analysis, we are normally considering only a relatively small range of output, namely the relevant range (see p. 74). It may well be that over a small range, particularly at low levels of output, a constant sales price per unit is a reasonable assumption. That is to say that, to the left of the curve in Figure 5.8, there may be a straight line from zero up to the start of the curve.

There is nothing in break-even analysis that demands that the assumption about steady selling prices is made, but making it does mean that the analysis becomes very straightforward.

Figure 5.9 combines information about total sales revenue and total cost for Service X over a range of output levels.

Figure 5.9	Graph of total sales revenue and total cost against quantity (volume) of output of Service X

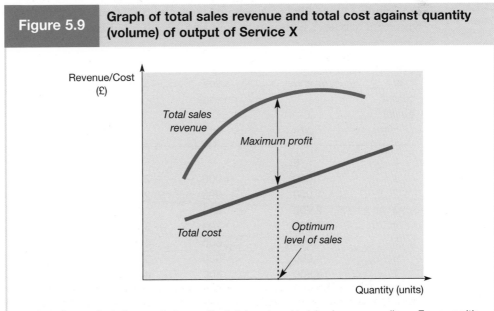

Profit is the vertical distance between the total cost and total sales revenue lines. For a wealth-maximising business, the optimum level of sales will occur when this is at a maximum.

The total sales revenue increases, but at a decreasing rate, and the total cost of production increases as the quantity of output increases. The maximum profit is made where the total sales revenue and total cost lines are vertically furthest apart. At the left-hand end of the graph, we are clearly above break-even point because the total sales revenue line has already gone above the total cost line. At the lower levels of volume of sales and output, the total sales revenue line is climbing faster than the total cost line. The business will wish to keep expanding output as long as this continues to be the case, because profit is the vertical distance between the two lines. A point will be reached where the total sales revenue line will become only as steep as the total cost line. After this it will become less steep; expanding further will reduce overall profit, because in this area of the graph the marginal cost is greater than the marginal revenue.

The point at which profit is maximised is where the two lines stop diverging, that is, the point at which the two lines are climbing at exactly the same rate. Thus we can say that profit is maximised at the point where

Marginal sales revenue = Marginal cost of production

that is,

$$\begin{bmatrix} \text{Increase in total sales} \\ \text{revenue from selling} \\ \text{one more unit} \end{bmatrix} = \begin{bmatrix} \text{Increase in total costs} \\ \text{that will result from} \\ \text{selling one more unit} \end{bmatrix}$$

To see how this approach can be applied, consider Example 5.4.

Example 5.4

A schedule of predicted total sales revenue and total costs at various levels of provision for Service Y is shown in columns (a) and (c) of the table.

Quantity of output (units)	Total sales revenue £ (a)	Marginal sales revenue £ (b)	Total cost £ (c)	Marginal cost £ (d)	Profit (loss) £ (e)
0	0		0		0
1	1,000	1,000	2,300	2,300	(1,300)
2	1,900	900	2,600	300	(700)
3	2,700	800	2,900	300	(200)
4	3,400	700	3,200	300	200
5	4,000	600	3,500	300	500
6	4,500	500	3,800	300	700
7	4,900	400	4,100	300	800
8	5,200	300	4,400	300	800
9	5,400	200	4,700	300	700
10	5,500	100	5,000	300	500

Column (b) is deduced by taking the total sales revenue for one less unit sold from the total sales revenue at the sales level under consideration (column (a)). For example, the marginal sales revenue of the fifth unit of the service sold (£600) is deduced by taking the total sales revenue for four units sold (£3,400) away from the total sales revenue for five units sold (£4,000).

Column (d) is deduced similarly, but using total cost figures from column (c). Column (e) is found by deducting column (c) from column (a).

It can be seen by looking at the profit (loss) column that the maximum profit (£800) occurs with an output of seven or eight units. Thus the maximum output should be eight units of the service. This is the point where marginal cost and marginal revenue are equal (at £300).

Figure 5.10 shows the total cost and total revenue for Service Y in Example 5.4.

Figure 5.10   Total cost and total revenue for Service Y

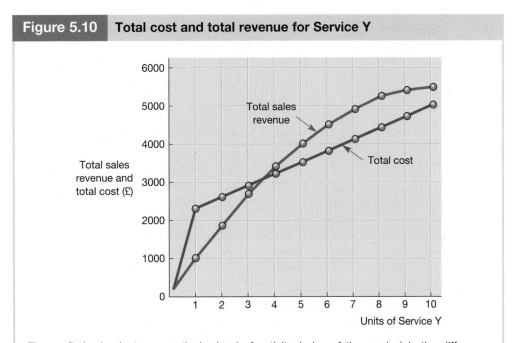

The profit (or loss) at any particular level of activity (sales of the service) is the difference between the total sales revenue and the total cost. On the graph, the vertical distance between the two curves gives this. Note that the highest profit occurs where the marginal cost equals the marginal sales revenue, that is where the two curves run parallel to one another.

Activity 5.8

Specialist Ltd makes a very specialised machine that is sold to manufacturing businesses. The business is about to commence production of a new model of machine for which facilities exist to produce a maximum of 10 machines each week. To assist management in a decision on the price to charge for the new machine, two pieces of information have been collected:

Activity 5.8 continued

- *Market demand*. The business's marketing staff believe that, at a price of £3,000 a machine, the demand would be zero. Each £100 reduction in unit price below £3,000 would generate one additional sale a week. Thus, for example, at a price of £2,800 each, two machines could be sold each week.
- *Manufacturing costs*. Fixed costs associated with manufacture of the machine are estimated at £3,000 a week. Since the work is highly labour-intensive and labour is in short supply, unit variable costs are expected to be progressive. The manufacture of one machine each week is expected to have a variable cost of £1,100, but each additional machine produced will increase the variable cost for the entire output by £100 a machine. For example, if the output were three machines a week, the variable cost for each machine (for all three machines) would be £1,300.

It is the policy of the business always to charge the same price for its entire output of a particular model. What is the most profitable level of output of the new machine?

Output (number of machines)	Unit sales revenue £	Total sales revenue £	Marginal sales revenue £	Unit variable cost £	Total variable cost £	Total cost £	Marginal cost £	Profit/ (loss) £
0	0	0	0	0	0	3,000	3,000	(3,000)
1	2,900	2,900	2,900	1,100	1,100	4,100	1,100	(1,200)
2	2,800	5,600	2,700	1,200	2,400	5,400	1,300	200
3	2,700	8,100	2,500	1,300	3,900	6,900	1,500	1,200
4	2,600	10,400	2,300	1,400	5,600	8,600	1,700	1,800
5	2,500	12,500	2,100	1,500	7,500	10,500	1,900	2,000
6	2,400	14,400	1,900	1,600	9,600	12,600	2,100	1,800
7	2,300	16,100	1,700	1,700	11,900	14,900	2,300	1,200
8	2,200	17,600	1,500	1,800	14,400	17,400	2,500	200
9	2,100	18,900	1,300	1,900	17,100	20,100	2,700	(1,200)
10	2,000	20,000	1,100	2,000	20,000	23,000	2,900	(3,000)

An output of five machines each week will maximise profit at £2,000 a week.

The additional cost of producing the fifth machine compared with the cost of producing the first four (£1,900) is just below the marginal revenue (the amount by which the total revenue from five machines exceeds that from selling four (£2,100)).

The additional cost of producing the sixth machine compared with the cost of producing the first five (£2,100) is just above the marginal revenue (the amount by which the total revenue from six machines exceeds that from selling five (£1,900)).

Some practical considerations

Despite the analysis in Activity 5.8, in practice the answer of five machines a week may prove not to be the best answer. This might be for one or more of several reasons:

- Demand is notoriously difficult to predict, even assuming no changes in the environment.

- The effect of sales of the new machine on the business's other products may mean that the machine cannot be considered in isolation. Five machines a week may be the optimum level of output if sales were being taken from a rival business or a new market were being created, but possibly not in other circumstances.
- Costs are difficult to estimate.
- Since labour is in short supply, the relevant labour cost should probably include an element for opportunity cost. This is because staff may have to be taken away from some other profitable activity to put them on to production of this new machine.
- The optimum level of sales volume is derived on the assumption that short-run profit maximisation is the goal of the business. Unless this is consistent with wealth enhancement in the longer term, it may not be in the business's best interests.

These points highlight some of the weaknesses of the theoretical approaches to pricing, particularly the fact that costs and demands are difficult to predict. It would be wrong, however, to dismiss the theory. The fact that the theory does not work perfectly in practice does not mean that it cannot offer helpful insights on the nature of markets, how profit relates to volume, and the notion of an optimum level of output.

Full cost (cost-plus) pricing

Now that we have considered pricing theory, let us return to the subject of using full cost as the basis for setting prices. We saw in Chapter 4 that one of the reasons that some businesses deduce full costs is to base selling prices on them. This is a perfectly logical approach. If a business charges the full cost of its output as a selling price, the business will, in theory, break even, because the sales revenue will exactly cover all of the costs. Charging something above full cost will yield a profit.

If a **full cost (cost-plus) pricing** approach is to be used, the required profit from each unit sold must be determined. This must logically be based on the total profit required for the period. In practice, this required profit is often set in relation to the amount of capital invested in the business. In other words, businesses seek to generate a target return on capital employed. It seems, therefore, that the profit loading on full cost should reflect the business's target profit and that the target should itself be based on a target return on capital employed.

Activity 5.9

A business has just completed a service job whose full cost has been calculated at £112. For the current period, the total costs (direct and indirect) are estimated at £250,000. The profit target for the period is £100,000.
  Suggest a selling price for the job.

....

If the profit is to be earned by jobs in proportion to their full cost, then the profit for each pound of full cost must be £0.40 (that is, £100,000/250,000). Thus, the target profit on the job must be

$$£0.40 \times 112 = £44.80$$

This means that the target price for the job must be

$$£112 + £44.80 = £156.80$$

Other ways could be found for apportioning a share of profit to jobs – for example, direct labour or machine hours. Such bases may be preferred where it is believed that these factors are better representatives of effort and, therefore, profitworthiness. It is clearly a matter of judgement as to how profit is apportioned to units of output.

Price makers and price takers

An obvious problem with cost-plus pricing is that the market may not agree with the price. Put another way, cost-plus pricing takes no account of the market demand function (the relationship between price and quantity demanded, which we considered above). A business may fairly deduce the full cost of some product and then add what might be regarded as a reasonable level of profit, only to find that a rival producer is offering a similar product for a much lower price, or that the market simply will not buy at the cost-plus price.

Most suppliers are not strong enough in the market to dictate pricing. Most are 'price takers', not 'price makers'. They must accept the price offered by the market or they do not sell any of their products. Cost-plus pricing may be appropriate for price makers, but it has less relevance for price takers.

Real World 5.10 illustrates how adopting a cost-plus approach to pricing may lead to a situation where falling demand leads to price rises, which, in turn, lead to falling demand.

REAL WORLD 5.10

A vicious circle in the library   **FT**

Librarians have long complained about the price rises of academic journals and Derek Haan, chairman and chief executive of Elsevier Science, which publishes more than 1,600 journals, admits that journal price inflation has been a problem for the industry. He says the problem is due to falling subscription numbers as more readers make photocopies or use interlibrary lending. With fewer subscribers to share the cost of each publication, publishers have to increase prices. To stay within budgets, libraries start cancelling titles, which creates a vicious circle of dwindling subscriber numbers, soaring prices and reduced collections. Naturally, with fixed budgets, there is significant price elasticity of demand as far as the libraries are concerned.

Source: Adapted from 'Case study: Elsevier', ft.com, © The Financial Times Limited, 19 June 2002.

Use of cost-plus information by price takers

The cost-plus price is not entirely without use to price takers. When contemplating entering a market, knowing the cost-plus price will give useful information. It will tell the price taker whether it can profitably enter the market or not. As mentioned earlier, the full cost can be seen as a long-run break-even selling price. If entering a market means that this break-even price, plus an acceptable profit, cannot be achieved, then the business might be better to stay out. Having a breakdown of the full cost may put the business in a position to examine where costs might be capable of being cut in order to bring the full cost plus profit within a figure acceptable to the market. Here, the market would be providing the target price to which a target costing approach would be applied.

It is not necessary for a business to dominate a particular market for it to be a price maker. Many small businesses are, to some extent, price makers. This tends to be where buyers find it difficult to make clear distinctions between the prices offered by various suppliers. An example of this might be a car repair. Where the nature and/or extent of the problem is not clear. As a result, garages normally charge cost-plus prices for car repairs.

In its 'pure' sense, cost-plus pricing implies that the seller sets the price which is then accepted by the customer. Often the price will not be finalised until after the product or service has been completed, as, for example, with a car repair or with work done by a firm of accountants. Sometimes, however, cost-plus is used as a basis of negotiating a price in advance, which then becomes the fixed price. This is often the case with contracts with central or local government departments. Typically, with such public contracts, the price is determined by competitive tendering. Here each potential supplier offers a price for which it will perform the subject of the contract, and the department concerned selects the supplier offering the lowest price, subject to quality safeguards. In some cases, however, particularly where only one supplier is capable of doing the work, a fixed cost-plus approach is used.

Cost-plus is also often the approach taken when monopoly suppliers of public utility services are negotiating a price which they are legally allowed to charge their customers with the government-appointed regulator. For example, the UK mains water suppliers, when agreeing the prices that they can charge customers, argue their case with Ofwat, the water industry regulator, on the basis of cost-plus information.

Real World 5.11 discusses how one business sees itself as partly protected from the recession that hit the UK from 2008 as a result of having contracts with its customers on a cost-plus price basis.

REAL WORLD 5.11

Adding Spice to cost-plus pricing   **FT**

Spice plc is a business that undertakes consultancy and other subcontract (outsourced) work for various UK public utilities (water and electricity suppliers). The business started when a group of managers bought Yorkshire Electricity's maintenance division to run it as a separate, independent unit.

Simon Rigby, Spice's chief executive, was very relaxed about the prospect of an economic recession. He said:

> I would not wish a recession on anybody, but if we have a recession it is going to throw Spice into very sharp focus. How do you think my 10-year cost-plus contracts are going to be affected by recession? The answer is not at all.

Source: Jansson, E., 'Flexible business models helps Spice Holdings power ahead in outsource market', *Financial Times*, 12 March 2008.

Real World 5.12 considers the extent to which cost-plus pricing seems to be used in practice.

REAL WORLD 5.12

Counting the cost plus

A fairly recent study surveyed 267 large UK and Australian businesses during the period 1999 to 2002. Their findings were broadly as follows:

- Cost plus is regarded as important in determining selling prices by most of the businesses, but many businesses only use it for a small percentage of their total sales.
- Retailers base most of their sales prices on their costs. This is not surprising; we might expect that retailers add a mark-up on their cost prices to arrive at selling prices.
- Retailers and service businesses (both financial services and others) attach more importance to cost-plus pricing than do manufacturers and others.
- Cost-plus pricing tends to be more important in industries where competition is most intense. This is perhaps surprising, because we might have expected less 'price makers' in more competitive markets.
- The extent of the importance of cost-plus pricing seems to have nothing to do with the size of the business. We might have imagined that larger businesses would have more power in the market and be more likely to be price makers, but the evidence does not support this. The reason could be that many larger businesses are, in effect, groups of smaller businesses. These smaller subsidiaries may not be bigger players in their markets than are small independent businesses. Also, cost-plus pricing tends to be particularly important in retailing and service businesses, where many businesses are quite small.

Source: Guilding, C., Drury, C. and Tayles, M., 'An empirical investigation of the importance of cost-plus pricing', *Management Auditing Journal*, Vol. 20, No. 2, 2005.

Pricing on the basis of relevant/marginal cost

The relevant/marginal cost approach deduces the minimum price for which the business can offer the product for sale. This minimum price will leave the business better off as a result of making the sale than it would have been had it pursued the next best opportunity. We considered the more general approach to relevant cost pricing in Chapter 2. In Chapter 3, we looked at the more restricted case of relevant cost pricing: **marginal cost pricing**. Here it is assumed that fixed costs will not be affected by the decision to produce and, therefore, only the variable cost element need be considered.

It would normally be the case that a relevant/marginal cost approach would only be used where there is not the opportunity to sell at a price that will cover the full cost. The business can sell at any price above the marginal cost and still be better off, simply because it happens to find itself in the position that certain costs will be incurred in any case.

Activity 5.10

A commercial aircraft is due to take off in one hour's time with 20 seats unsold. What is the minimum price at which these seats could be sold such that the airline would be no worse off as a result?

The answer is that any price above the additional cost of carrying one more passenger would represent an acceptable minimum. If there are no such costs, the minimum price is zero.

This is not to say that the airline will seek to charge the minimum price; it will presumably seek to charge the highest price that the market will bear. The fact that the market will not bear the full cost, plus a profit margin, should not, in principle, be sufficient for the airline to refuse to sell seats, where there is spare passenger capacity.

In practice, airlines are major users of a relevant/marginal costing approach. They often offer low-priced tickets for off-peak travel, where there are not sufficient customers willing to pay 'normal' prices. By insisting on a Saturday stopover for return tickets, they tend to exclude 'business' travellers, who are probably forced to travel, but for whom a Saturday stopover may be unattractive. UK train operators often offer substantial discounts for off-peak travel, particularly through Apex tickets. Similarly, hotels often charge very low rates for off-peak rooms. A hotel mainly used by business travellers may well offer very low room rates for Friday and Saturday occupancy.

Relevant/marginal pricing must be regarded as a short-term or limited approach that can be adopted because a business finds itself in a particular position, for example that of having spare aircraft seats. Ultimately, if the business is to be profitable, all costs must be covered by sales revenue.

Activity 5.11

When we considered marginal costing in Chapter 3, we identified three problems with its use. Can you remember what these problems are?

The three problems are as follows:

- The possibility that spare capacity will be 'sold off' cheaply when there is another potential customer who will offer a higher price, but, by the time they do so, the capacity will be fully committed. It is a matter of commercial judgement as to how likely this will be. With reference to Activity 5.10, would an hour before take-off be sufficiently close for the airline to be fairly confident that no 'normal' passenger will come forward to buy a seat?
- The problem that selling the same product but at different prices could lead to a loss of customer goodwill. Would a 'normal' passenger be happy to be told by another passenger that the latter had bought his or her ticket very cheaply, compared with the normal price?
- If the business is going to suffer continually from being unable to sell its full production potential at the 'regular' price, it might be better, in the long run, to reduce capacity and make fixed-cost savings. Using the spare capacity to produce marginal benefits may lead to the business failing to address this issue. Would it be better for the airline to operate smaller aircraft or to have fewer flights, either of these leading to fixed-cost savings, than to sell off surplus seats at marginal prices?

Real World 5.13 provides an unusual example where humanitarian issues are the driving force for adopting marginal pricing.

REAL WORLD 5.13

Drug prices in developing countries   **FT**

Large pharmaceutical businesses have recently been under considerable pressure to provide cheap drugs to developing countries. It has been suggested that life-saving thera-
peutic drugs should be sold to these countries at a price that is close to their marginal
cost. Indeed the Department for International Development would like to see HIV drugs
sold at marginal cost in the poorest countries. However, a number of obstacles to such a
pricing policy have been identified:

1 It may lead to customer revolts in the West (the 'loss of customer goodwill' referred to
   above).
2 There is a concern that the drugs may not reach their intended patients and could be
   re-exported to Western countries. A major cost of producing a new drug is the research
   and development costs incurred, and marginal costs of production are usually very low.
   Thus, a selling price based on marginal cost is likely to be considerably lower than the
   normal (full-cost) selling price in the West. This, it is feared, may lead to the cheap drugs
   provided leaking back into the West. Acquiring drugs at a price near to their marginal
   cost and reselling them at a figure close to the selling price in the West offers unscrupulous individuals an opportunity to make huge profits.
3 Compensation for any adverse consequences that may arise from the drugs sold will
   be sought in courts in the West, thereby creating the risk of huge payouts. This would
   make the risk to the pharmaceutical businesses of selling the drugs out of proportion
   to the benefits to them, in terms of the prices that would be charged.

The above problems are not insurmountable and are not the only problems surrounding
this issue, but they do appear to have slowed progress towards a speedier response to a
humanitarian crisis.

Source: Based on information from Jack, A., 'GSK varies prices to raise sales', ft.com, 16 March 2008; Epstein, R., 'Drug pricing is a
social problem', ft.com, 16 June 2005; 'Pressure builds to cut price of HIV medicine', ft.com, 11 March 2006; and 'Patent nonsense',
Financial Times, 24 August 2001.

Target pricing

We saw earlier in the chapter (pp. 151–152) that, as the starting point of the target-
costing approach to cost management, a target selling price needs to be identified.
Using market research, and so on, a target unit selling price and a planned sales volume
are set. This is the combination of price and quantity demanded that the business
would derive from its estimation of the product's demand function (see pp. 155–158).
Thus the target price is the market-determined price that the business seeks to meet, in
terms of costs and profit margin.

Pricing strategies

Cost and the market-demand function are not the only determinants of price.
Businesses often employ pricing strategies that, in the short term, may not maximise
profit. They do this in the expectation that they will gain in the long term. An example of such a strategy is **penetration pricing**. Here, the product is sold relatively cheaply
in order to sell in quantity and to gain a large share of the market. This would tend to
have the effect of dissuading competitors from entering the market. Subsequently,

once the business has established itself as the market leader, prices would be raised to more profitable levels. By its nature, penetration pricing often applies to new products.

It has been argued that some subscription TV broadcasters have charged low prices while they establish themselves and gain market share. Having achieved this they increase prices to what becomes their 'normal' price.

→ **Price skimming** is almost the opposite of penetration pricing. It seeks to exploit the notion that the market can be stratified according to resistance to price. Here a new product is initially priced highly and sold only to those buyers in the stratum that is fairly unconcerned by high prices. Once this stratum of the market is saturated, the price is lowered to attract the next stratum. The price is gradually lowered as each stratum is saturated. This strategy tends only to be able to be employed where there is some significant barrier to entry for other potential suppliers, such as patent protection.

DVD players provide a good example of a price-skimming strategy. When they first emerged in the 1990s, DVD players would typically cost over £400. They can now be bought for less than £30. Advancing technology, the economies of scale and increasing competition have undoubtedly contributed to this fall in price, but price skimming almost certainly was a major factor. Certain customers would have regarded a DVD player as a 'must-have' product. These 'early adopters' would have been prepared to pay a high price to have one. Once the early adopters had bought their DVD player, the price was gradually reduced, until we reached today's price.

The initial high price can help to recover research and development and production set-up costs quickly. It can also keep demand within manageable levels while production capacity is being built up.

Televisions, CD players, home computers and mobile telephones are also examples of where a price-skimming strategy has been applied.

SUMMARY

The main points of this chapter may be summarised as follows:

Activity-based costing is an approach to dealing with overheads (in full costing) that treats all costs as being caused or 'driven' by activities. Advocates argue that it is more relevant to the modern commercial environment than is the traditional approach.

- It involves identifying the support activities and their costs and then analysing these costs to see what drives them.
- The costs of each support activity enter a cost pool and the relevant cost drivers are used to attach an amount of overheads from this pool to each unit of output.
- ABC should help provide more accurate costs for each unit of output and should help in better control of overheads.
- ABC is, however, time-consuming and costly, can involve measurement problems and is not likely to suit all businesses.

Total (whole) life-cycle costing takes account of all of the costs incurred over a product's entire life.

- The life cycle of a product can be broken down into three phases: pre-production, production and post-production.
- A high proportion of costs is incurred and/or committed during the pre-production phase.

- Target costing attempts to reduce costs so that the market price covers the cost plus an acceptable profit.
- Ensuring quality output has costs, known as *quality costs*, typically divided into four aspects: prevention costs, appraisal costs, internal failure costs and external failure costs.
- *Kaizen* costing attempts to reduce costs at the production stage.
- Since most costs will have been saved at the pre-production phase and through target costing, only small cost savings are likely to be possible.
- Benchmarking attempts to emulate a successful aspect of, for example, another business or division.

Pricing output

- In theory, profit is maximised where the price is such that

$$\text{Marginal sales revenue} = \text{Marginal cost of production}$$

- Elasticity of demand indicates the sensitivity of demand to price changes.
- Full cost (cost-plus) pricing takes the full cost and adds a mark-up for profit;
  - It is popular.
  - The market may not accept the price (most businesses are 'price takers').
  - It can provide a useful benchmark.
- Relevant/marginal cost pricing takes the relevant/marginal cost and adds a mark-up for profit.
  - It can be useful in the short term, but in the longer term it may be better to charge a full cost-plus price.
- Target sales prices are those established as the first step in the target costing process. They are market-determined.
- Various pricing strategies can be used, including penetration pricing and price skimming.

→ Key terms

Further reading

If you would like to explore the topics covered in this chapter in more depth, we recommend the following books:

Atkinson, A., Banker, R., Kaplan, R. and Young, S. M., *Management Accounting*, 5th edn, Prentice Hall, 2007, chapters 4, 5, 6 and 9.

Drury, C., *Management and Cost Accounting*, 7th edn, Cengage Learning, 2007, chapters 10 and 11.

Hilton, R., *Managerial Accounting*, 6th edn, McGraw-Hill Irwin, 2005, chapters 4, 5, 6 and 15.

Horngren, C., Foster, G., Datar, S., Rajan, M. and Ittner, C., *Cost Accounting: A Managerial Emphasis*, 13th edn, Prentice Hall International, 2008, chapters 5 and 12.

REVIEW QUESTIONS

Answers to these questions can be found in Appendix C at the back of the book.

5.1   How does activity-based costing (ABC) differ from the traditional approach? What is the underlying difference in the philosophy of each of them?

5.2   The use of activity-based costing in helping to deduce full costs has been criticised. What has tended to be the basis of this criticism?

5.3   What is meant by elasticity of demand? How does knowledge of the elasticity of demand affect pricing decisions?

5.4   According to economic theory, at what point is profit maximised? Why is it at this point?

EXERCISES

Exercises 5.6 to 5.8 are more advanced than 5.1 to 5.5. Those with a coloured number have answers in Appendix D at the back of the book. If you wish to try more exercises, visit the students' side of the Companion Website at www.pearsoned.co.uk/atrillmclaney.

5.1   Woodner Ltd provides a standard service. It is able to provide a maximum of 100 units of this service each week. Experience shows that at a price of £100, no units of the service would be sold. For every £5 below this price, the business is able to sell 10 more units. For example, at a price of £95, 10 units would be sold, at £90, 20 units would be sold, and so on. The business's fixed costs total £2,500 a week. Variable costs are £20 per unit over the entire range of possible output. The market is such that it is not feasible to charge different prices to different customers.

Required:
What is the most profitable level of output of the service?

5.2   It appears from research evidence that a cost-plus approach influences many pricing decisions in practice. What is meant by cost-plus pricing and what are the problems of using this approach?

5.3   Kaplan plc makes a range of suitcases of various sizes and shapes. There are 10 different models of suitcase produced by the business. In order to keep inventories of finished suitcases to a minimum, each model is made in a small batch. Each batch is costed as a separate job and the cost for each suitcase is deduced by dividing the batch cost by the number of suitcases in the batch.

At present, the business derives the cost of each batch using a traditional job-costing approach. Recently, however, a new management accountant was appointed, who is advocating the use of activity-based costing (ABC) to deduce the cost of the batches. The management accountant claims that ABC leads to much more reliable and relevant costs and that it has other benefits.

Required:
(a)   Explain how the business deduces the cost of each suitcase at present.
(b)   Discuss the purposes to which the knowledge of the cost for each suitcase, deduced on a traditional basis, can be put and how valid the cost is for the purpose concerned.

(c) Explain how ABC could be applied to costing the suitcases, highlighting the differences between ABC and the traditional approach.

(d) Explain what advantages the new management accountant probably believes ABC to have over the traditional approach.

5.4 Comment critically on the following statements that you have overheard:

(a) 'To maximise profit you need to sell your output at the highest price.'
(b) 'Elasticity of demand deals with the extent to which costs increase as demand increases.'
(c) 'Provided that the price is large enough to cover the marginal cost of production, the sale should be made.'
(d) 'According to economic theory, profit is maximised where total cost equals total revenue.'
(e) 'Price skimming is charging low prices for the output until you have a good share of the market, and then putting up your prices.'

Explain clearly all technical terms.

5.5 Comment critically on the following statements that you have overheard:

(a) 'Direct labour hours are the most appropriate basis to use to charge indirect cost (overheads) to jobs in the modern manufacturing environment where people are so important.'
(b) 'Activity-based costing is a means of more accurately accounting for direct labour cost.'
(c) 'Activity-based costing cannot really be applied to the service sector because the 'activities' that it seeks to analyse tend to be related to manufacturing.'
(d) '*Kaizen* costing is an approach where great efforts are made to reduce the costs of developing a new product and setting up its production processes.'
(e) 'Benchmarking is an approach to job costing where each direct worker keeps a record of the time spent on each job on his or her workbench before it is passed on to the next direct worker or into finished inventories stores.'

5.6 The GB Company manufactures a variety of electric motors. The business is currently operating at about 70 per cent of capacity and is earning a satisfactory return on investment.

International Industries (II) has approached the management of GB with an offer to buy 120,000 units of an electric motor. II manufactures a motor that is almost identical to GB's motor, but a fire at the II plant has shut down its manufacturing operations. II needs the 120,000 motors over the next four months to meet commitments to its regular customers; II is prepared to pay £19 each for the motors, which it will collect from the GB plant.

GB's product cost, based on current planned cost for the motor, is:

	£
Direct materials	5.00
Direct labour (variable)	6.00
Manufacturing overheads	9.00
Total	20.00

Manufacturing overheads are applied to production at the rate of £18.00 a direct labour hour. This overheads rate is made up of the following components:

	£
Variable factory overhead	6.00
Fixed factory overhead – direct	8.00
– allocated	4.00
Applied manufacturing overhead rate	18.00

Additional costs usually incurred in connection with sales of electric motors include sales commissions of 5 per cent and freight expense of £1.00 a unit.

In determining selling prices, GB adds a 40 per cent mark-up to the product cost. This provides a suggested selling price of £28 for the motor. The marketing department, however, has set the current selling price at £27.00 to maintain market share. The order would, however, require additional fixed factory overheads of £15,000 a month in the form of supervision and clerical costs. If management accepts the order, 30,000 motors will be manufactured and delivered to II each month for the next four months.

Required:

(a) Prepare a financial evaluation showing the impact of accepting the International Industries order. What is the minimum unit price that the business's management could accept without reducing its operating profit?

(b) State clearly any assumptions contained in the analysis of (a) above and discuss any other organisational or strategic factors that GB should consider.

5.7 Sillycon Ltd is a business engaged in the development of new products in the electronics industry. Subtotals on the spreadsheet of planned overheads reveal:

	Electronics department	Testing department	Service department
Overheads: variable (£000)	1,200	600	700
fixed (£000)	2,000	500	800
Planned activity: Direct labour hours ('000)	800	600	

The three departments are cost centres.

For the purposes of reallocation of service department's overheads, it is agreed that variable overhead costs vary with the direct labour hours worked in each cost centre. Fixed overheads of the service cost centre are to be reallocated on the basis of maximum practical capacity of the two product cost centres, which is the same for each.

The business has a long-standing practice of marking up full manufacturing costs by between 25 per cent and 35 per cent in order to establish selling prices.

It is hoped that one new product, which is in a final development stage, will offer some improvement over competitors' products, which are currently marketed at between £90 and £110 each. Product development engineers have determined that the direct material content is £7 a unit. The product will take 2 labour hours in the electronics department and $1\frac{1}{2}$ hours in testing. Hourly labour rates are £20 and £12, respectively.

Management estimates that the fixed costs that would be specifically incurred in relation to the product are: supervision £13,000, depreciation of a recently acquired machine £100,000, and advertising £37,000 a year. These fixed costs are included in the table above.

Market research indicates that the business could expect to obtain and hold about 25 per cent of the market or, optimistically, 30 per cent. The total market is estimated at 20,000 units.

Note: It may be assumed that the existing plan has been prepared to cater for a range of products and no single product decision will cause the business to amend it.

Required:

(a) Prepare a summary of information that would help with the pricing decision for the new product. Such information should include marginal cost and full cost implications after allocation of service department overheads.

(b) Explain and elaborate on the information prepared.

5.8 A business manufactures refrigerators for domestic use. There are three models: Lo, Mid and Hi. The models, their quality and their price are aimed at different markets.

Product costs are computed on a blanket (business-wide) overhead-rate basis using a labour-hour method. Prices as a general rule are set based on cost plus 20 per cent. The following information is provided:

	Lo	Mid	Hi
Material cost (£/unit)	25	62.5	105
Direct labour hours (per unit)	$1/2$	1	1
Budget production/sales (units)	20,000	1,000	10,000

The budgeted overheads for the business amount to £4,410,000. Direct labour is costed at £8 an hour.

The business is currently facing increasing competition, especially from imported goods. As a result, the selling price of Lo has been reduced to a level that produces a very low profit margin. To address this problem, an activity-based costing approach has been suggested. The overheads are examined and these are grouped around main business activities of machining (£2,780,000), logistics (£590,000) and establishment (£1,040,000) costs. It is maintained that these costs could be allocated based respectively on cost drivers of machine hours, material orders and space, to reflect the use of resources in each of these areas. After analysis, the following proportionate statistics are available in relation to the total volume of products:

	Lo %	Mid %	Hi %
Machine hours	40	15	45
Material orders	47	6	47
Space	42	18	40

Required:

(a) Calculate for each product the full cost and selling price determined by
   1 the original costing method
   2 the activity-based costing method.
(b) What are the implications of the two systems of costing in the situation given?
(c) What business/strategic options exist for the business in the light of the new information?

6

Budgeting

INTRODUCTION

In this chapter we consider the role and nature of budgets. We shall see that budgets set out short-term plans that help managers to run the business. They provide the means to assess whether actual performance has gone as planned and, where it has not, to identify the reasons for this.

It is important to recognise that budgets do not exist in a vacuum; they are an integral part of a planning framework that is adopted by well-run businesses. To understand fully the nature of budgets we must, therefore, understand the strategic planning framework within which they are set.

We shall also see how budgets are prepared. Preparing budgets relies on an understanding of many of the issues relating to the behaviour of costs and full costing, topics that we explored in Chapters 3 and 4. The chapter begins with a discussion of the budgeting framework and then goes on to consider detailed aspects of the budgeting process.

LEARNING OUTCOMES

When you have completed this chapter, you should be able to:

● Define a budget and show how budgets, strategic objectives and strategic plans are related.

● Explain the budgeting process and the interlinking of the various budgets within the business.

● Indicate the uses of budgeting and construct various budgets, including the cash budget, from relevant data.

● Discuss the criticisms that are made of budgeting.

How budgets link with strategic plans and objectives

It is vital that businesses develop plans for the future. Whatever a business is trying to achieve, it is unlikely to come about unless its managers are clear what the future direction of the business is going to be. As we saw in Chapter 1 (pp. 7–11), the development of plans involves five key steps:

1 *Establish mission and objectives*

The *mission statement* sets out the ultimate purpose of the business. (See Real World 1.4 (p. 7) for the mission statements of easyJet and Starbucks.) It is a broad statement of intent, whereas the strategic objectives are more specific and will usually include quantifiable goals.

2 *Undertake a position analysis*

This involves an assessment of where the business is currently placed in relation to where it wants to be, as set out in its mission and strategic objectives.

3 *Identify and assess the strategic options*

The business must explore the various ways in which it might move from where it is now (identified in Step 2) to where it wants to be (identified in Step 1).

4 *Select strategic options and formulate plans*

 This involves selecting what seems to be the best of the courses of action or strategies (identified in Step 3) and formulating a long-term strategic plan. This strategic plan is then normally broken down into a series of short-term plans, one for each element of the business. These plans are the budgets. Thus, a **budget** is a business plan for the short term – typically one year – and is expressed mainly in financial terms. Its role is to convert the strategic plans into actionable blueprints for the immediate future. Budgets will define precise targets concerning such things as
- cash receipts and payments
- sales volumes and revenues, broken down into amounts and prices for each of the products or services provided by the business
- detailed inventories requirements
- detailed labour requirements
- specific production requirements.

5 *Perform, review and control*

Here the business pursues the budgets derived in step 4. By comparing the actual outcome with the budgets, managers can see if things are going according to plan or not. Action would be taken to exercise control where actual performance appears not to be matching the budgets.

Activity 6.1

The approach described in Step 3 above suggests that managers will systematically collect information and then carefully evaluate all the options available. Do you think this is what managers really do?

In practice, managers may not be as rational and capable as implied in the process described. They may find it difficult to handle a wealth of information relating to a wide range of options. To avoid becoming overloaded, they may restrict their range of possible options and/or discard some information. Managers may also adopt rather simple approaches to evaluating the mass of information provided. These approaches might not lead to the best decisions being made.

From the above description of the planning process, we can see that the relationship between the mission, strategic objectives, strategic plans and budgets can be summarised as follows:

- the mission sets the overall direction and, once set, is likely to last for quite a long time – perhaps throughout the life of the business;
- the strategic objectives, which are also long-term, will set out how the mission can be achieved;
- the strategic plans identify how each objective will be pursued; and
- the budgets set out, in detail, the short-term plans and targets necessary to fulfil the strategic objectives.

An analogy might be found in terms of a student enrolling on a course of study. His or her mission might be to have a happy and fulfilling life. A key strategic objective flowing from this mission might be to embark on a career that will be rewarding in various ways. He or she might have identified the particular study course as the most effective way to work towards this objective. Successfully completing the course would then be the strategic plan. In working towards this strategic plan, passing a particular stage of the course might be identified as the target for the forthcoming year. This short-term target is analogous to the budget. Having achieved the 'budget' for the first year, the budget for the second year becomes passing the second stage.

Collecting information on performance and exercising control

However well planned the activities of a business might be, they will come to nothing unless steps are taken to try to achieve them in practice. The process of making planned events actually occur is known as **control**. This is part of step 5 (above).

Control can be defined as compelling events to conform to plan. This definition is valid in any context. For example, when we talk about controlling a car, we mean making the car do what we plan that it should do. In a business context, management accounting is very useful in the control process. This is because it is possible to state many plans in accounting terms (as budgets). Since it is also possible to state *actual* outcomes in the same terms, making comparison between actual and planned outcomes is a relatively simple matter. Where actual outcomes are at variance with budgets, this variance should be highlighted by accounting information. Managers can then take steps to get the business back on track towards the achievement of the budgets. We shall be looking quite closely at the control aspect of budgeting in Chapter 7.

Figure 6.1 shows the planning and control process in diagrammatic form.

It should be emphasised that planning (including budgeting) is the responsibility of managers rather than accountants. Though accountants should play a role in the planning process, by supplying relevant information to managers and by contributing to decision making as part of the management team, they should not dominate the process. In practice, it seems that the budgeting aspect of planning is often in danger of being dominated by accountants, perhaps because most budgets are expressed in financial terms. However, managers are failing in their responsibilities if they allow this to happen.

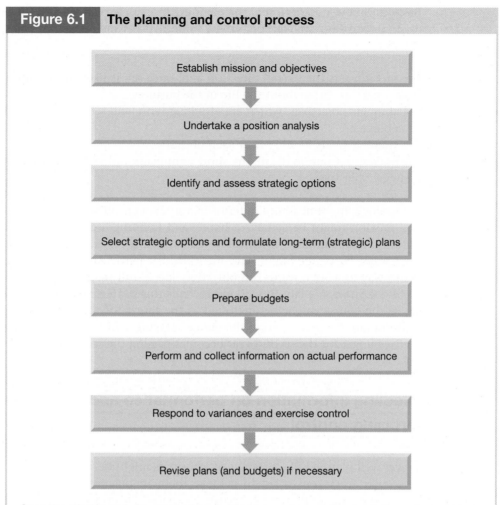

Figure 6.1   The planning and control process

Establish mission and objectives

Undertake a position analysis

Identify and assess strategic options

Select strategic options and formulate long-term (strategic) plans

Prepare budgets

Perform and collect information on actual performance

Respond to variances and exercise control

Revise plans (and budgets) if necessary

Once the mission and objectives of the business have been determined, the various strategic options available must be considered and evaluated in order to derive a strategic plan. The budget is a short-term financial plan for the business that is prepared within the framework of the strategic plan. Control can be exercised through the comparison of budgeted and actual performance. Where a significant divergence emerges, some form of corrective action should be taken. If the budget figures prove to be based on incorrect assumptions about the future, it might be necessary to revise the budget.

Time horizon of plans and budgets

Setting strategic plans is typically a major exercise performed about every five years, and budgets are usually set annually for the forthcoming year. It need not necessarily be the case that strategic plans are set for five years and that budgets are set for one year: it is up to the management of the business concerned. Businesses involved in certain industries – say, information technology – may feel that five years is too long a planning period since new developments can, and do, occur virtually overnight. Here, a planning horizon of two or three years is more feasible. Similarly, a budget need not be set for one year, although this appears to be a widely used time horizon.

Activity 6.2

Can you think of any reason why most businesses prepare detailed budgets for the forthcoming year, rather than for a shorter or longer period?

....

The reason is probably that a year represents a long enough time for the budget preparation exercise to be worthwhile, yet short enough that it is possible to make detailed plans. As we shall see later in this chapter, the process of formulating budgets can be a time-consuming exercise, but there are economies of scale – for example, preparing the budget for the next year would not normally take twice as much time and effort as preparing the budget for the next six months.

An annual budget sets targets for the forthcoming year for all aspects of the business. It is usually broken down into monthly budgets, which define monthly targets. Indeed, in many instances, the annual budget will be built up from monthly figures. For example, the sales staff may be required to set sales targets for each month of the budget period. Other budgets will be set for each month of the budget period, as we shall explain below.

Limiting factors

There will always be some aspect of the business that will stop it achieving its objectives to the maximum extent. This is often a limited ability of the business to sell its products. Sometimes, it is some production shortage (such as labour, materials or plant) that is the **limiting factor**, or, linked to this, a shortage of funds. Often, production shortages can be overcome by an increase in funds – for example, more plant can be bought or leased. This is not always a practical solution, because no amount of money will buy certain labour skills or increase the world supply of some raw material.

It is sometimes possible to ease an initial limiting factor. For example, subcontracting can eliminate a plant capacity problem. This means that some other factor, perhaps sales, will replace the production problem, though at a higher level of output. Ultimately, however, the business will hit a ceiling; some limiting factor will prove impossible to ease.

It is important that the limiting factor is identified. Ultimately, most, if not all, budgets will be affected by the limiting factor, and so, if it can be identified at the outset, all managers can be informed of the restriction early in the process. When preparing the budgets, account can then be taken of the limiting factor.

Budgets and forecasts

As we have seen, a budget may be defined as a business plan for the short term. Budgets are, to a great extent, expressed in financial terms. Note particularly that a budget is a *plan*, not a forecast. To talk of a plan suggests an intention or determination to achieve the targets; **forecasts** tend to be predictions of the future state of the environment.

Clearly, forecasts are very helpful to the planner/budget-setter. If, for example, a reputable forecaster has predicted the number of new cars to be purchased in the UK during next year, it will be valuable for a manager in a car manufacturing business to take account of this information when setting next year's sales budgets. However, a forecast and a budget are distinctly different.

Periodic and continual budgets

Budgeting can be undertaken on a periodic or a continual basis. A **periodic budget** is prepared for a particular period (usually one year). Managers will agree the budget for the year and then allow the budget to run its course. Although it may be necessary to revise the budget on occasions, preparing the budget is in essence a one-off exercise during each financial year. A **continual budget**, as the name suggests, is continually updated. We have seen that an annual budget will normally be broken down into smaller time intervals (usually monthly periods) to help control the activities of a business. A continual budget will add a new month to replace the month that has just passed, thereby ensuring that, at all times, there will be a budget for a full planning period. Continual budgets are also referred to as **rolling budgets**.

Activity 6.3

Which method of budgeting do you think is likely to be more costly and which method is likely to be more beneficial for forward planning?

Periodic budgeting will usually take less time and effort to prepare and will therefore be less costly. However, as time passes, the budget period shortens, and towards the end of the financial year managers will be working to a very short planning period indeed. Continual budgeting, on the other hand, will ensure that managers always have a full year's budget to help them make decisions. It is claimed that continual budgeting ensures that managers plan throughout the year rather than just once each year. In this way it encourages a forward-looking attitude.

While continual budgeting encourages a forward-looking attitude, there is a danger that budgeting will become a mechanical exercise, as managers may not have time to step back from their other tasks each month and consider the future carefully. It may be unreasonable to expect them to take this future-oriented perspective on a continual basis.

Continual budgets do not appear to be very popular in practice. A recent BPM Forum study of 340 senior financial staff of small, medium and large businesses in North America revealed that only 9 per cent of businesses use them (see reference 1 at the end of the chapter).

How budgets link to one another

A business will prepare more than one budget for a particular period. Each budget prepared will relate to a specific aspect of the business. The ideal situation is probably that there should be a separate operating budget for each person who is in a managerial position, no matter how junior. The contents of all of the individual operating budgets will be summarised in **master budgets**, usually consisting of a budgeted income statement and statement of financial position (balance sheet). The cash budget (in summarised form) is considered by some to be a third master budget.

Figure 6.2 illustrates the interrelationship and interlinking of individual operating budgets, in this particular case using a manufacturing business as an example.

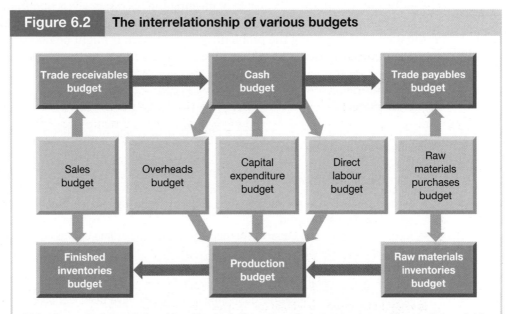

| **Figure 6.2** | **The interrelationship of various budgets** |

This shows the interrelationship of budgets for a manufacturing business. The starting point is usually the sales budget. The expected level of sales normally defines the overall level of activity for the business, and the other operating budgets will be drawn up in accordance with this. Thus, the sales budget will largely define the finished inventories requirements, and from this we can define the production requirements and so on.

The sales budget is usually the first one to be prepared (at the left of Figure 6.2), as the level of sales often determines the overall level of activity for the forthcoming period. This is because it is probably the most common limiting factor (see p. 179). The finished inventories requirement tends to be set by the level of sales, though it would also be dictated by the policy of the business on the level of the finished products inventories. The requirement for finished inventories will define the required production levels, which will, in turn, dictate the requirements of the individual production departments or sections. The demands of manufacturing, in conjunction with the business's policy on how long it holds raw materials before they enter production, define the raw materials inventories budget. The purchases budget will be dictated by the materials inventories budget, which will, in conjunction with the policy of the business on taking credit from suppliers, dictate the trade payables budget. One of the determinants of the cash budget will be the trade payables budget; another will be the trade receivables budget, which itself derives, through the business's policy on credit periods granted to credit customers, from the sales budget. Cash will also be affected by overheads and direct labour costs (themselves linked to production) and by capital expenditure. The factors that affect policies on matters such as inventories holding and trade receivables collection and trade payables payment periods will be discussed in some detail in Chapter 11.

A manufacturing business has been used as the example in Figure 6.2 simply because it has all of the types of budgets found in practice. Service businesses have similar arrangements of budgets, but obviously do not have inventories budgets. All of the issues relating to budgets apply equally well to all types of business.

It may happen that it is not sales demand that is the limiting factor. Assuming that the budgeting process takes the order just described, it might be found in practice that there is some constraint other than sales demand. For example, the production capacity of the business may be incapable of meeting the necessary levels of output to match the sales budget for one or more months. In this case, it might be reasonable to look at the ways of overcoming the problem. As a last resort, it might be necessary to revise the sales budget to a lower level to enable production to meet the target.

Activity 6.4

Can you think of any ways in which a short-term shortage of production facilities of a manufacturer might be overcome?

We thought of the following:

- Higher production in previous months and increasing inventories (stockpiling) to meet periods of higher demand.
- Increasing production capacity, perhaps by working overtime and/or acquiring (buying or leasing) additional plant.
- Subcontracting some production.
- Encouraging potential customers to change the timing of their buying by offering discounts or other special terms during the months that have been identified as quiet.

You might well have thought of other approaches.

There will be the horizontal relationships between budgets, which we have just looked at, but there will usually be vertical ones as well. For example, the sales budget may be broken down into a number of subsidiary budgets, perhaps one for each regional sales manager. The overall sales budget will be a summary of the subsidiary ones. The same may be true of virtually all of the other budgets, most particularly the production budget.

Figure 6.3 shows the vertical relationship of the sales budgets for a business. The business has four geographical sales regions, each one the responsibility of a separate manager, who is probably located in the region concerned. Each regional manager is responsible to the overall sales manager of the business. The overall sales budget is the sum of the budgets for the four sales regions.

Figure 6.3 Vertical relationship of a business's sales budgets

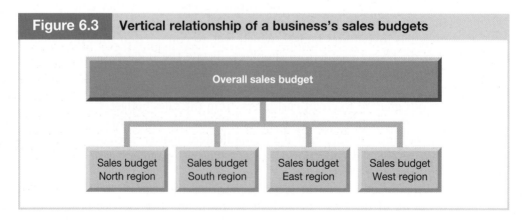

Though sales are often managed on a geographical basis and so their budgets reflect this, sales may be managed on some other basis. For example, a business that sells a range of products may manage sales on a product-type basis, with a specialist manager responsible for each type of product. Thus, an insurance business may have separate sales managers, and so separate sales budgets, for life insurance, household insurance, motor insurance, and so on. Very large businesses may even have separate product-type managers for each geographical region. Each of these managers would have a separate budget, which would combine to form the overall sales budget for the business as a whole.

All of the operating budgets that we have just reviewed must mesh with the master budgets, that is, the budgeted income statement and statement of financial position (balance sheet).

How budgets help managers

Budgets are generally regarded as having five areas of usefulness. These are:

1 *Budgets tend to promote forward thinking and the possible identification of short-term problems.* We saw above that a shortage of production capacity might be identified during the budgeting process. Making this discovery in good time could leave a number of means of overcoming the problem open to exploration. If the potential production problem is picked up early enough, all of the suggestions in the answer to Activity 6.4 and, possibly, other ways of overcoming the problem can be explored. Identifying the potential problem early gives managers time for calm and rational consideration of the best way of overcoming it. The best solution to the potential problem may only be feasible if action can be taken well in advance. This would be true of all of the suggestions made in the answer to Activity 6.4.

2 *Budgets can be used to help co-ordination between the various sections of the business.* It is crucially important that the activities of the various departments and sections of the business are linked so that the activities of one are complementary to those of another. For example, the activities of the purchasing/procurement department of a manufacturing business should dovetail with the raw materials needs of the production departments. If this is not the case, production could run out of raw materials, leading to expensive production stoppages. Possibly, and just as undesirably, excessive amounts of raw materials could be bought, leading to large and unnecessary inventories holding costs. We shall see how this co-ordination tends to work in practice later in this chapter.

3 *Budgets can motivate managers to better performance.* Having a stated task can motivate managers and staff in their performance. Simply, to tell a manager to do his or her best is not very motivating, but to define a required level of achievement is more likely to be so. Managers will be better motivated by being able to relate their particular role in the business to its overall objectives. Since budgets are directly derived from strategic objectives, budgeting makes this possible. It is clearly not possible to allow managers to operate in an unconstrained environment. Having to operate in a way that matches the goals of the business is a price of working in an effective business. We shall consider the role of budgets as motivators in more detail in Chapter 7.

4 *Budgets can provide a basis for a system of control.* As mentioned earlier in the chapter, control is concerned with ensuring that events conform to plans. If senior management wishes to control and to monitor the performance of more junior staff, it needs some yardstick against which to measure and assess performance. Current performance could possibly be compared with past performance or perhaps with what happens in another business. However, planned performance is usually the most logical yardstick. If there is information available concerning the actual performance for a period, and this can be compared with the planned performance, then a basis for control will have been established. Such a basis will enable the use of **management by exception**, a technique where senior managers can spend most of their time dealing with those staff or activities that have failed to achieve the budget (the exceptions). This means that the senior managers do not have to spend too much time on those that are performing well. It also allows junior managers to exercise self-control. By knowing what is expected of them and what they have actually achieved, they can assess how well they are performing and take steps to correct matters where they are failing to achieve. We shall consider the effect of making plans and being held accountable for their achievement in Chapter 7.

5 *Budgets can provide a system of authorisation for managers to spend up to a particular limit.* Some activities (for example, staff development and research expenditure) are allocated a fixed amount of funds at the discretion of senior management. This provides the authority to spend.

Figure 6.4 shows the benefits of budgets in diagrammatic form.

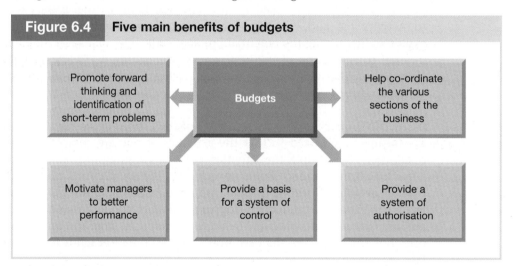

Figure 6.4 **Five main benefits of budgets**

The following two activities pick up issues that relate to some of the uses of budgets.

Activity 6.5

The third on the above list of the uses of budgets (motivation) implies that managers are set stated tasks. Do you think there is a danger that requiring managers to work towards such predetermined targets will stifle their skill, flair and enthusiasm?

If the budgets are set in such a way as to offer challenging yet achievable targets, the manager is still required to show skill, flair and enthusiasm. There is the danger, however, that if targets are badly set (either unreasonably demanding or too easy to achieve), they could be demotivating and have a stifling effect.

Activity 6.6

The fourth on the above list of the uses of budgets (control) implies that current management performance is compared with some yardstick. What is wrong with comparing actual performance with past performance, or the performance of others, in an effort to exercise control?

There is no automatic reason to believe that what happened in the past, or is happening elsewhere, represents a sensible target for this year in this business. Considering what happened last year, and in other businesses, may help in the formulation of plans, but past events and the performance of others should not automatically be seen as the target.

The five identified uses of budgets can conflict with one another on occasions. Where, for example, a budget is being used as a system of authorisation, managers may be motivated to spend to the limit of their budget, even though this may be wasteful. This may occur where the managers are not allowed to carry over unused funds to the next budget period or where they believe that the budget for the next period will be reduced because not all the funds for the current period were spent. The wasting of resources in this way conflicts with the role of budgets as a means of exercising control.

Another example of a conflict between budget uses is where the budget is being used as a motivational device. Some businesses set the budget targets at a more difficult level than the managers are expected to achieve in an attempt to motivate managers to strive to reach their targets. For control purposes, however, the budget becomes less meaningful as a benchmark against which to compare actual performance.

Conflict between the different uses will mean that managers must decide which particular uses for budgets should be given priority; managers must be prepared, if necessary, to trade off the benefits resulting from one particular use for the benefits of another.

The budget-setting process

Budgeting is such an important area for businesses, and other organisations, that it tends to be approached in a fairly methodical and formal way. This usually involves a number of steps, as follows:

Step 1: Establish who will take responsibility

It is usually seen as crucial that those responsible for the budget-setting process have real authority within the organisation.

Activity 6.7

Why would those responsible for the budget-setting process need to have real authority?

One of the crucial aspects of the process is establishing co-ordination between budgets so that the plans of one department match and are complementary to those of other departments. This usually requires compromise where adjustment of initial budgets must be undertaken. This in turn means that someone on the board of directors (or a senior manager) has to be closely involved; only people of this rank are likely to have the necessary moral and, if needed, formal managerial authority to force departmental managers to compromise.

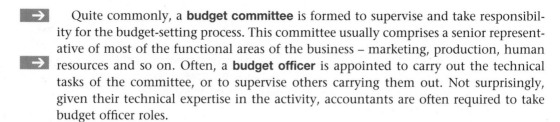

Quite commonly, a **budget committee** is formed to supervise and take responsibility for the budget-setting process. This committee usually comprises a senior representative of most of the functional areas of the business – marketing, production, human resources and so on. Often, a **budget officer** is appointed to carry out the technical tasks of the committee, or to supervise others carrying them out. Not surprisingly, given their technical expertise in the activity, accountants are often required to take budget officer roles.

Step 2: Communicate budget guidelines to relevant managers

Budgets are intended to be the short-term plans that seek to work towards the achievement of strategic plans and to the overall objectives of the business. It is therefore important that, in drawing up budgets, managers are well aware of what the strategic plans are and how the forthcoming budget period is intended to work towards them. Managers also need to be made well aware of the commercial/economic environment in which they will be operating. This may include awareness of market trends, future rates of inflation, predicted changes in technology and so on. It is the responsibility of the budget committee to see that managers have all the necessary information.

Step 3: Identify the key, or limiting, factor

As we saw earlier in the chapter (p. 179), there will be a limiting factor that will restrict the business from achieving its objectives to the maximum extent. It can be very helpful if the limiting factor can be identified at the earliest stage in the budget-setting process.

Step 4: Prepare the budget for the area of the limiting factor

The limiting factor will determine the overall level of activity for the business. We have already seen that the limiting-factor budget will usually be the sales budget, since the ability to sell is normally the constraint on future growth. (When discussing the interrelationship of budgets earlier in the chapter, we started with the sales budget for this reason.) Sales demand, however, is not always the limiting factor.

Real World 6.1 looks at the methods favoured by businesses of different sizes to determine their sales budgets.

REAL WORLD 6.1

Sources of the sales budget in practice

Determining the future level of sales can be a difficult problem. In practice, a business may rely on the judgements of sales staff, statistical techniques or market surveys (or some combination of these) to arrive at a sales budget. A survey of UK manufacturing businesses provides the following insights concerning the use of such techniques and methods.

	All respondents	Small businesses	Large businesses
Number of respondents	281	47	46
	%	%	%
Technique			
Statistical forecasting	31	19	29
Market research	36	13	54
Subjective estimates based on sales staff experience	85	97	80

We can see that the most popular approach by far is the opinion of sales staff. We can also see that there are differences between the largest and smallest businesses surveyed, particularly concerning the use of market surveys. This evidence is now pretty old, but in the absence of more up-to-date research, it provides some idea of how businesses determine their sales targets.

Source: Drury, C., Braund, S., Osborne, P. and Tayles, M., *A Survey of Management Accounting Practices in UK Manufacturing Companies*, Chartered Association of Certified Accountants, 1993.

Step 5: Prepare draft budgets for all other areas

The other budgets are prepared, complementing the budget for the area of the limiting factor. In all budget preparation, the computer has become an almost indispensable tool. Much of the work of preparing budgets is repetitive and tedious, yet the resultant budget has to be a reliable representation of the plans made. Computers are ideally suited to such tasks and human beings are not. It is often the case that budgets have to be redrafted several times because of some minor alteration, and computers do this without complaint.

There are two broad approaches to setting individual budgets. The *top-down approach* is where the senior management of each budget area originates the budget targets, perhaps discussing them with lower levels of management and, as a result, refining them before the final version is produced. With the *bottom-up approach*, the targets are fed upwards from the lowest level. For example, junior sales managers will be asked to set their own sales targets, which then become incorporated into the budgets of higher levels of management until the overall sales budget emerges.

Where the bottom-up approach is adopted, it is usually necessary to haggle and negotiate at different levels of authority to achieve agreement. This may be because the plans of some departments do not fit in with those of others or because the targets set by junior managers are not acceptable to their superiors. This approach seems rarely to be found in practice.

Activity 6.8

What are the advantages and disadvantages of each type of budgeting approach (bottom-up and top-down)?

The bottom-up approach allows greater involvement among managers in the budgeting process and this, in turn, may increase the level of commitment to the targets set. It also allows the business to draw more fully on the local knowledge and expertise of its

→

Activity 6.8 continued

managers. However, this approach can be time-consuming and may result in some managers setting undemanding targets for themselves in order to have an easy life.

The top-down approach enables senior management to communicate plans to employees and to co-ordinate the activities of the business more easily. It may also help in establishing more demanding targets for managers. However, the level of commitment to the budget may be lower as many of those responsible for achieving the budgets will have been excluded from the budget-setting process.

There will be further discussion of the benefits of participation in target setting in Chapter 7.

Step 6: Review and co-ordinate budgets

A business's budget committee must at this stage review the various budgets and satisfy itself that the budgets complement one another. Where there is a lack of co-ordination, steps must be taken to ensure that the budgets mesh. Since this will require that at least one budget must be revised, this activity normally benefits from a diplomatic approach. Ultimately, however, the committee may be forced to assert its authority and insist that alterations are made.

Step 7: Prepare the master budgets

The master budgets are the budgeted income statement and budgeted statement of financial position (balance sheet), and perhaps a summarised cash budget. All of the information required to prepare these statements should be available from the individual operating budgets that have already been prepared. The budget committee usually undertakes the task of preparing the master budgets.

Step 8: Communicate the budgets to all interested parties

The formally agreed operating budgets are now passed to the individual managers who will be responsible for their implementation. This is, in effect, senior management formally communicating to the other managers the targets that they are expected to achieve.

Step 9: Monitor performance relative to the budget

Much of the budget-setting activity will have been pointless unless each manager's actual performance is compared with the benchmark of planned performance, which is embodied in the budget. This issue is examined in detail in Chapter 7.

The steps in the budget-setting process are shown in diagrammatic form in Figure 6.5.

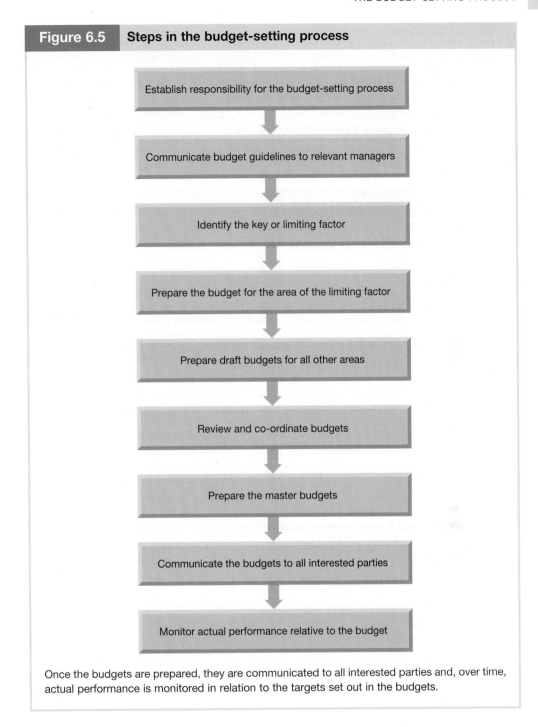

Figure 6.5 **Steps in the budget-setting process**

Establish responsibility for the budget-setting process

Communicate budget guidelines to relevant managers

Identify the key or limiting factor

Prepare the budget for the area of the limiting factor

Prepare draft budgets for all other areas

Review and co-ordinate budgets

Prepare the master budgets

Communicate the budgets to all interested parties

Monitor actual performance relative to the budget

Once the budgets are prepared, they are communicated to all interested parties and, over time, actual performance is monitored in relation to the targets set out in the budgets.

Where the established budgets are proving to be unrealistic, it is usually helpful to revise them. They may be unrealistic because certain assumptions made when the budgets were first set have turned out to be incorrect. This may occur where managers (budget setters) have made poor judgements or where the environment has changed unexpectedly from what was, quite reasonably, assumed. Irrespective of the cause, unrealistic budgets are of little value and revising them may be the only logical approach to take. Nevertheless, revising budgets should be regarded as exceptional and only undertaken after very careful consideration.

Using budgets in practice

This section attempts to give a flavour of how budgets are used, the extent to which they are used, and their level of accuracy.

Real World 6.2 shows how the UK-based international engineering and support services business Babcock International Group plc undertakes its budgeting process.

REAL WORLD 6.2

Budgeting at Babcock

According to its annual report, Babcock has the following arrangements:

> Comprehensive systems are in place to develop annual budgets and medium-term financial plans. The budgets are reviewed by central management before being submitted to the Board for approval. Updated forecasts for the year are prepared at least quarterly. The Board is provided with details of actual performance each month compared with budgets, forecasts and the prior year, and is given a written commentary on significant variances from approved.

Source: Babcock International Group plc Annual Report 2008.

There is quite a lot of recent survey evidence that reveals the extent to which budgeting is used by businesses in practice. **Real World 6.3** reviews some of this evidence, which shows that most businesses prepare and use budgets.

REAL WORLD 6.3

Budgeting in practice

A fairly recent survey of 41 UK manufacturing businesses found that 40 of the 41 prepared budgets.

Source: Dugdale, D., Jones, C. and Green, S., *Contemporary Management Accounting Practices in UK Manufacturing*, Elsevier, 2006.

Another fairly recent survey of UK businesses, but this time businesses involved in the food and drink sector, found that virtually all of them used budgets.

Source: Abdel-Kader, M. and Luther, R., 'An empirical investigation of the evolution of management accounting practices', University of Essex Working paper no. 04/06, October 2004.

A survey of the opinions of senior finance staff at 340 businesses of various sizes and operating in a wide range of industries in North America, which has been mentioned earlier, revealed that 97 per cent of those businesses had a formal budgeting process.

Source: 'Perfect how you project', BPM Forum, 2008.

Though these three surveys relate to UK and North American businesses, they provide some insights about what is likely also to be practice elsewhere in the developed world.

Real World 6.4 below gives some insight to the accuracy of budgets.

REAL WORLD 6.4

Budget accuracy

In the survey of North American businesses mentioned in Real World 6.3 above, senior finance staff were asked to compare the actual revenues with the budgeted revenues for 2007. Figure 6.6 shows the results.

| Figure 6.6 | The accuracy of revenue budgets for 2007 |

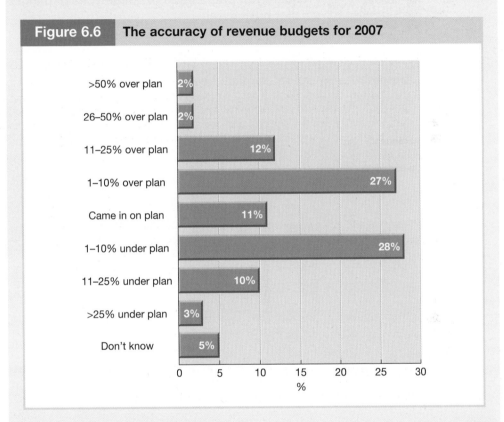

We can see that 66 per cent of revenue budgets were accurate within 10 per cent. The survey revealed that budgets for expenses were generally more accurate, with 74 per cent being accurate within 10 per cent.

Source: 'Perfect how you project', BPM Forum, 2008.

A survey of budgeting practice in small and medium-sized enterprises (SMEs) (see **Real World 6.5**) revealed that not all such businesses fully use budgeting. It seems that some smaller businesses prepare budgets only for what they see as key areas. The budget that is most frequently prepared by such businesses is the sales budget, followed by the budgeted income statement and the overheads budget. Perhaps surprisingly, the cash budget is prepared by less than two-thirds of the small businesses surveyed.

REAL WORLD 6.5

Preparation of budgets in SMEs

A study of budgeting practice in small and medium-sized enterprises (SMEs) revealed that the budget that the most businesses prepare is the sales budget (78 per cent prepared it), followed by the budgeted income statement and the overheads budget as is shown in Figure 6.7.

Figure 6.7	**Frequency of preparation of some types of budget by smaller businesses**

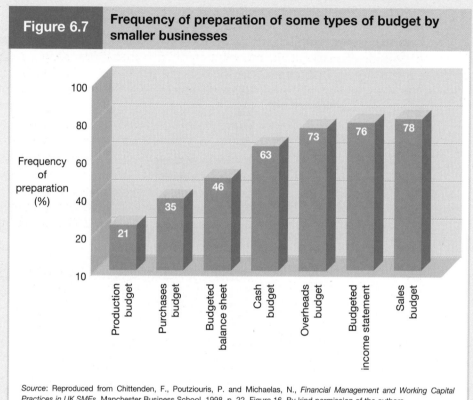

Source: Reproduced from Chittenden, F., Poutziouris, P. and Michaelas, N., *Financial Management and Working Capital Practices in UK SMEs*, Manchester Business School, 1998, p. 22, Figure 16. By kind permission of the authors.

Incremental and zero-base budgeting

Budget setting is often done on the basis of what happened last year, with some adjustment for any changes in factors that are expected to affect the forthcoming budget period (for example, inflation). This approach is known as **incremental budgeting** and is often used for 'discretionary' budgets, such as research and development and staff training. With this type of budget, the **budget holder** (the manager responsible for the budget) is allocated a sum of money to be spent in the area of activity concerned. Budgets of this type are referred to as **discretionary budgets** because the sum allocated is normally at the discretion of senior management. These budgets are very common in local and central government (and in other public bodies), but are also used in commercial businesses to cover the types of activity that we have just referred to.

Discretionary budgets are often found in areas where there is no clear relationship between inputs (resources applied) and outputs (benefits). Compare this with, say, a raw materials usage budget in a manufacturing business, where the amount of material used and, therefore, the amount of funds involved, is clearly related to the level of production and, ultimately, to sales volumes. It is easy for discretionary budgets to eat up funds with no clear benefit being derived. It is often only the proposed periodic increases in these budgets that are closely scrutinised.

Zero-base budgeting (ZBB) rests on the philosophy that all spending needs to be justified. Thus, when establishing, say, the training budget each year, it is not automatically accepted that training courses should be financed in the future simply because they were undertaken this year. The training budget will start from a zero base (that is, no resources at all) and will only be increased above zero if a good case can be made for the scarce resources of the business to be allocated to this form of activity. Top management will need to be convinced that the proposed activities represent 'value for money'.

ZBB encourages managers to adopt a more questioning approach to their areas of responsibility. To justify the allocation of resources, they are often forced to think carefully about particular activities and the ways in which they are undertaken. This questioning approach should result in a more efficient use of business resources. With an increasing portion of the total costs of most businesses being in areas where the link between outputs and inputs is not always clear, and where commitment of resources is discretionary rather than demonstrably essential to production, ZBB is increasingly relevant.

Activity 6.9

Can you think of any disadvantages of using ZBB?

The principal problems with ZBB are:

- It is time-consuming and therefore expensive to undertake.
- Managers whose sphere of responsibility is subjected to ZBB can feel threatened by it.

The benefits of a ZBB approach can be gained to some extent – perhaps at not too great a cost – by using the approach on a selective basis. For example, a particular budget area could be subjected to ZBB-type scrutiny only every third or fourth year. In any case, if ZBB is used more frequently, there is the danger that managers will use the same arguments each year to justify their activities. The process will simply become a mechanical exercise and the benefits will be lost. For a typical business, some areas are likely to benefit from ZBB more than others. ZBB could, in these circumstances, be applied only to those areas that will benefit from it, and not to the others. The areas that are most likely to benefit from ZBB are ones, such as training, advertising, and research and development, where spending is discretionary.

If senior management is aware of the potentially threatening nature of this form of budgeting, care can be taken to apply ZBB with sensitivity. However, in the quest for cost control and value for money, the application of ZBB can result in some tough decisions being made.

Real World 6.6 provides some insight into the extent to which ZBB is used in practice.

REAL WORLD 6.6

ZBB is not food and drink to many businesses

A fairly recent survey of businesses in the UK food and drink sector found that ZBB is not much used by them. Only 48 per cent ever use it and only 16 per cent use it 'often' or 'very often'.

ZBB seems to be most appropriate, however, with 'spending' budgets, such as those for training and advertising. Such budgets probably represent a minority for the types of business in this survey.

Source: Abdel-Kader, M. and Luther, R., 'An empirical investigation of the evolution of management accounting practices', University of Essex Working paper no. 04/06, October 2004.

Preparing the cash budget

We shall now look in some detail at how the various budgets used by the typical business are prepared, starting with the cash budget and then looking at the others. It is helpful for us to start with the cash budget because:

● It is a key budget (some people see it as a 'master budget' along with the budgeted income statement and statement of financial position (balance sheet)); most economic aspects of a business are reflected in cash sooner or later, so that for a typical business the cash budget reflects the whole business more comprehensively than any other single budget.
● Very small, unsophisticated businesses (for example, a corner shop) may feel that full-scale budgeting is not appropriate to their needs, but almost certainly they should prepare a cash budget as a minimum (despite the survey evidence mentioned in Real World 6.5 above).

Since budgets are documents that are to be used only internally by a business, their style is a question of management choice and will vary from one business to the next. However, as managers, irrespective of the business, are likely to be using budgets for similar purposes, some consistency of approach tends to be found. In most businesses, the cash budget will probably possess the following features:

1 The budget period would be broken down into shorter periods, typically months.
2 The budget would be in columnar form, with one column for each month.
3 Receipts of cash would be identified under various headings and a total for each month's receipts shown.
4 Payments of cash would be identified under various headings and a total for each month's payments shown.
5 The surplus of total cash receipts over payments, or of payments over receipts, for each month would be identified.
6 The running cash balance would be identified. This would be achieved by taking the balance at the end of the previous month and adjusting it for the surplus or deficit of receipts over payments (or payments over receipts) for the current month.

Typically, all of the pieces of information in points 3 to 6 in this list would be useful to management for one reason or another.

Probably the best way to deal with this topic is through an example.

Example 6.1

Vierra Popova Ltd is a wholesale business. The budgeted income statements for each of the next six months are as follows:

	Jan £000	Feb £000	Mar £000	Apr £000	May £000	June £000
Sales revenue	52	55	55	60	55	53
Cost of goods sold	(30)	(31)	(31)	(35)	(31)	(32)
Salaries and wages	(10)	(10)	(10)	(10)	(10)	(10)
Electricity	(5)	(5)	(4)	(3)	(3)	(3)
Depreciation	(3)	(3)	(3)	(3)	(3)	(3)
Other overheads	(2)	(2)	(2)	(2)	(2)	(2)
Total expenses	(50)	(51)	(50)	(53)	(49)	(50)
Profit for the month	2	4	5	7	6	3

The business allows all of its customers one month's credit (this means, for example, that cash from January sales will be received in February). Sales revenue during December totalled £60,000.

The business plans to maintain inventories at their existing level until some time in March, when they are to be reduced by £5,000. Inventories will remain at this lower level indefinitely. Inventories purchases are made on one month's credit. December purchases totalled £30,000. Salaries, wages and 'other overheads' are paid in the month concerned. Electricity is paid quarterly in arrears in March and June. The business plans to buy and pay for a new delivery van in March. This will cost a total of £15,000, but an existing van will be traded in for £4,000 as part of the deal.

The business expects to have £12,000 in cash at the beginning of January. The cash budget for the six months ending in June is as follows:

	Jan £000	Feb £000	Mar £000	Apr £000	May £000	June £000
Receipts						
Trade receivables (Note 1)	60	52	55	55	60	55
Payments						
Trade payables (Note 2)	(30)	(30)	(31)	(26)	(35)	(31)
Salaries and wages	(10)	(10)	(10)	(10)	(10)	(10)
Electricity	–	–	(14)	–	–	(9)
Other overheads	(2)	(2)	(2)	(2)	(2)	(2)
Van purchase	–	–	(11)	–	–	–
Total payments	(42)	(42)	(68)	(38)	(47)	(52)
Cash surplus/(deficit) for the month	18	10	(13)	17	13	3
Opening balance (Note 3)	12	30	40	27	44	57
Closing balance	30	40	27	44	57	60

Notes:

1 The cash receipts from trade receivables lag a month behind sales because customers are given a month in which to pay for their purchases. So, December sales will be paid for in January, and so on.

Example 6.1 continued

2　In most months, the purchases of inventories will equal the cost of goods sold. This is because the business maintains a constant level of inventories. For inventories to remain constant at the end of each month, the business must replace exactly the amount that has been used. During March, however, the business plans to reduce its inventories by £5,000. This means that inventories purchases will be lower than inventories usage in that month. The payments for inventories purchases lag a month behind purchases because the business expects to be allowed a month to pay for what it buys.

3　Each month's cash balance is the previous month's figure plus the cash surplus (or minus the cash deficit) for the current month. The balance at the start of January is £12,000 according to the information provided earlier.

4　Depreciation does not give rise to a cash payment. In the context of profit measurement (in the income statement), depreciation is a very important aspect. Here, however, we are interested only in cash.

Activity 6.10

Looking at the cash budget of Vierra Popova Ltd (Example 6.1), what conclusions do you draw and what possible course of action do you recommend regarding the cash balance over the period concerned?

There appears to be a fairly large cash balance, given the size of the business, and it seems to be increasing. Management might give consideration to putting some of the cash into an income-yielding deposit. Alternatively, it could be used to expand the trading activities of the business by, for example, increasing the investment in non-current (fixed) assets.

Activity 6.11

Vierra Popova Ltd (Example 6.1) now wishes to prepare its cash budget for the second six months of the year. The budgeted income statements for each month of the second half of the year are as follows:

	July £000	Aug £000	Sept £000	Oct £000	Nov £000	Dec £000
Sales revenue	57	59	62	57	53	51
Cost of goods sold	(32)	(33)	(35)	(32)	(30)	(29)
Salaries and wages	(10)	(10)	(10)	(10)	(10)	(10)
Electricity	(3)	(3)	(4)	(5)	(6)	(6)
Depreciation	(3)	(3)	(3)	(3)	(3)	(3)
Other overheads	(2)	(2)	(2)	(2)	(2)	(2)
Total expenses	(50)	(51)	(54)	(52)	(51)	(50)
Profit for the month	7	8	8	5	2	1

The business will continue to allow all of its customers one month's credit.

It plans to increase inventories from the 30 June level by £1,000 each month until, and including, September. During the following three months, inventories levels will be decreased by £1,000 each month. Inventories purchases, which had been made on one month's credit until the June payment, will, starting with the purchases made in June, be made on two months' credit.

Salaries, wages and 'other overheads' will continue to be paid in the month concerned. Electricity is paid quarterly in arrears in September and December.

At the end of December, the business intends to pay off part of some borrowings. This payment is to be such that it will leave the business with a cash balance of £5,000 with which to start next year.

Prepare the cash budget for the six months ending in December. (Remember that any information you need that relates to the first six months of the year, including the cash balance that is expected to be brought forward on 1 July, is given in Example 6.1.)

The cash budget for the six months ended 31 December is:

	July £000	Aug £000	Sept £000	Oct £000	Nov £000	Dec £000
Receipts						
Trade receivables	53	57	59	62	57	53
Payments						
Trade payables (Note 1)	–	(32)	(33)	(34)	(36)	(31)
Salaries and wages	(10)	(10)	(10)	(10)	(10)	(10)
Electricity	–	–	(10)	–	–	(17)
Other overheads	(2)	(2)	(2)	(2)	(2)	(2)
Borrowings repayment (Note 2)	–	–	–	–	–	(131)
Total payments	(12)	(44)	(55)	(46)	(48)	(191)
Cash surplus for the month	41	13	4	16	9	(138)
Opening balance	60	101	114	118	134	143
Closing balance	101	114	118	134	143	5

Notes:
1 There will be no payment to suppliers (trade payables) in July because the June purchases will be made on two months' credit and will therefore be paid in August. The July purchases, which will equal the July cost of sales figure plus the increase in inventories made in July, will be paid for in September, and so on.
2 The borrowings repayment is simply the amount that will cause the balance at 31 December to be £5,000.

Preparing other budgets

Though each one will have its own particular features, other budgets will tend to follow the same sort of pattern as the cash budget, that is, they will show inflows and outflows during each month and the opening and closing balances in each month.

Example 6.2

To illustrate some of the other budgets, we shall continue to use the example of Vierra Popova Ltd that we considered in Example 6.1. To the information given there, we need to add the fact that the inventories balance at 1 January was £30,000.

Trade receivables budget

This would normally show the planned amount owed to the business by credit customers at the beginning and at the end of each month, the planned total credit sales revenue for each month and the planned total cash receipts from credit customers (trade receivables). The layout would be something like the following:

	Jan £000	Feb £000	Mar £000	Apr £000	May £000	June £000
Opening balance	60	52	55	55	60	55
Sales revenue	52	55	55	60	55	53
Cash receipts	(60)	(52)	(55)	(55)	(60)	(55)
Closing balance	52	55	55	60	55	53

The opening and closing balances represent the amount that the business plans to be owed (in total) by credit customers (trade receivables) at the beginning and end of each month, respectively.

Trade payables budget

Typically this shows the planned amount owed to suppliers by the business at the beginning and at the end of each month, the planned credit purchases for each month and the planned total cash payments to trade payables. The layout would be something like the following:

	Jan £000	Feb £000	Mar £000	Apr £000	May £000	June £000
Opening balance	30	30	31	26	35	31
Purchases	30	31	26	35	31	32
Cash payment	(30)	(30)	(31)	(26)	(35)	(31)
Closing balance	30	31	26	35	31	32

The opening and closing balances represent the amount planned to be owed (in total) by the business to suppliers (trade payables), at the beginning and end of each month respectively.

Inventories budget

This would normally show the planned amount of inventories to be held by the business at the beginning and at the end of each month, the planned total inventories purchases for each month and the planned total monthly inventories usage. The layout would be something like the following:

	Jan £000	Feb £000	Mar £000	Apr £000	May £000	June £000
Opening balance	30	30	30	25	25	25
Purchases	30	31	26	35	31	32
Inventories used	(30)	(31)	(31)	(35)	(31)	(32)
Closing balance	30	30	25	25	25	25

The opening and closing balances represent the amount of inventories, at cost, planned to be held by the business at the beginning and end of each month respectively.

A *raw materials inventories budget*, for a manufacturing business, would follow a similar pattern, with the 'inventories usage' being the cost of the inventories put into production. A *finished inventories budget* for a manufacturer would also be similar to the above, except that 'inventories manufactured' would replace 'purchases'. A manufacturing business would normally prepare both a raw materials inventories budget and a finished inventories budget. Both of these would typically be based on the full cost of the inventories (that is, including overheads). There is no reason why the inventories should not be valued on the basis of either variable cost or direct costs, should managers feel that this would provide more useful information.

The inventories budget will normally be expressed in financial terms, but may also be expressed in physical terms (for example, kg or metres) for individual inventories items.

Note how the trade receivables, trade payables and inventories budgets in Example 6.2 link to one another, and to the cash budget for the same business in Example 6.1. Note particularly that:

- The purchases figures in the trade payables budget and in the inventories budget are identical.
- The cash payments figures in the trade payables budget and in the cash budget are identical.
- The cash receipts figures in the trade receivables budget and in the cash budget are identical.

Other values would link different budgets in a similar way. For example, the row of sales revenue figures in the trade receivables budget would be identical to the sales revenue figures that will be found in the sales budget. This is how the linking (co-ordination), which was discussed earlier in this chapter, is achieved.

Activity 6.12

Have a go at preparing the trade receivables budget for Vierra Popova Ltd for the six months from July to December (see Activity 6.11).

The trade receivables budget for the six months ended 31 December is:

	July £000	Aug £000	Sept £000	Oct £000	Nov £000	Dec £000
Opening balance (Note 1)	53	57	59	62	57	53
Sales revenue (Note 2)	57	59	62	57	53	51
Cash receipts (Note 3)	(53)	(57)	(59)	(62)	(57)	(53)
Closing balance (Note 4)	57	59	62	57	53	51

Notes:
1 The opening trade receivables figure is the previous month's sales revenue figure (sales are on one month's credit).
2 The sales revenue is the current month's figure.
3 The cash received each month is equal to the previous month's sales revenue figure.
4 The closing balance is equal to the current month's sales revenue figure.
  Note that if we knew any three of the four figures each month, we could deduce the fourth.

  This budget could be set out in any manner that would have given the sort of information that management would require in respect of planned levels of trade receivables and associated transactions.

Activity 6.13

Have a go at preparing the trade payables budget for Vierra Popova Ltd for the six months from July to December (see Activity 6.11). (*Hint*: Remember that the trade payables' payment period alters from the June purchases onwards.)

The trade payables budget for the six months ended 31 December is:

	July £000	Aug £000	Sept £000	Oct £000	Nov £000	Dec £000
Opening balance	32	65	67	70	67	60
Purchases	33	34	36	31	29	28
Cash payments	–	(32)	(33)	(34)	(36)	(31)
Closing balance	65	67	70	67	60	57

This, again, could be set out in any manner that would have given the sort of information that management would require in respect of planned levels of trade payables and associated transactions.

Activity-based budgeting

→ **Activity-based budgeting (ABB)** extends the principles of activity-based costing (ABC), which we discussed in Chapter 5, to budgeting. Under a system of ABB, the budgeted sales of products or services are determined and the activities necessary to achieve the budgeted sales are then identified. Budgets for each of the various activities are prepared by multiplying the budgeted usage of the cost driver for a particular activity (as determined by the sales budget) by the budgeted rate for the relevant cost driver. The following example should help to make the process clear.

Example 6.3

Danube Ltd produces two products, Gamma and Delta. The sales budget for next year shows that 60,000 units of Gamma and 80,000 units of Delta are expected to be sold. Each type of product spends time in the finished goods stores and so a budget for this activity is created. It is estimated that Product Gamma will spend an average of two weeks in the stores before being sold and, for Product Delta, the average period is five weeks.

Both products are of roughly similar size and have very similar storage needs. It is felt, therefore, that the period spent in the stores (measured in 'product-weeks') is the cost driver. Based on previous years' data, the budgeted rate for the cost driver has been set at £1.50 per unit.

To calculate the activity budget for the finished goods stores, the estimated total usage of the cost driver must be calculated. This will be the total number of 'product-weeks' that the products will be in store.

Product	Delta	60,000 × 2 weeks =	120,000
	Gamma	80,000 × 5 weeks =	400,000
			520,000

The number of product weeks will then be multiplied by the budgeted rate for the cost driver to derive the activity budget figure. That is:

$$520,000 × £1.50 = £780,000$$

The same process will be carried out for the other activities identified.

Note that budgets are prepared according to activity rather than function as is normally the case. Note also that, when applying ABC principles, ABB begins with output (the sales budget) and then works through to find the activity costs. With ABC, however, it is the other way around. It begins by establishing activity costs and then attaches those costs to units of output.

Through the application of ABC principles, the factors that cause costs are known and there is a direct tracing of costs with outputs. This means that ABB should provide a better understanding of future resource needs and more accurate budgets. It should also provide a better understanding of the effect on budgeted costs of changes in the usage of the cost driver because of the explicit relationship between cost drivers, activities and costs.

Control should be improved within an ABB environment for two reasons. First, by developing more accurate budgets, managers should be provided with demanding yet achievable targets. Second, ABB ensures that costs are closely linked to responsibilities. Managers who have control over particular cost drivers will become accountable for the costs that are caused. An important principle of effective budgeting is that those responsible for meeting a particular budget (budget holders) should have control over the events that affect performance in their area.

Real World 6.7 provides some indication of the extent to which ABB is used in practice.

REAL WORLD 6.7

ABB is not often on the menu

The survey of UK food and drink businesses mentioned earlier found that ABB is not much used by them. Only 19 per cent use it 'often' or 'very often'. Not surprisingly, businesses that use ABC are much more likely to use ABB as well.

Interestingly, ABB seems to be used by more businesses than those that use ABC for product costing. This implies that the 'activity-based' approach is more used in cost management than in determining product costs.

Source: Abdel-Kader, M. and Luther, R., 'An empirical investigation of the evolution of management accounting practices', University of Essex Working paper no. 04/06, October 2004.

Self-assessment question 6.1 should pull together what we have just seen about preparing budgets.

Self-assessment question 6.1

Antonio Ltd has planned production and sales for the next nine months as follows:

	Production Units	Sales Units
May	350	350
June	400	400
July	500	400
August	600	500
September	600	600
October	700	650
November	750	700
December	750	800
January	750	750

During the period, the business plans to advertise so as to generate these increases in sales. Payments for advertising of £1,000 and £1,500 will be made in July and October respectively.

The selling price per unit will be £20 throughout the period. Forty per cent of sales are normally made on two months' credit. The other 60 per cent are settled within the month of the sale.

Raw materials will be held for one month before they are taken into production. Purchases of raw materials will be on one month's credit (buy one month, pay the next). The cost of raw materials is £8 per unit of production.

Other direct production expenses, including labour, are £6 per unit of production. These will be paid in the month concerned.

Various production overheads, which during the period to 30 June had run at £1,800 a month, are expected to rise to £2,000 each month from 1 July to 31 October. These are expected to rise again from 1 November to £2,400 a month and to remain at that level for the foreseeable future. These overheads include a steady £400 each month for depreciation. Overheads are planned to be paid 80 per cent in the month of production and 20 per cent in the following month.

To help to meet the planned increased production, a new item of plant will be bought and delivered in August. The cost of this item is £6,600; the contract with the supplier will specify that this will be paid in three equal amounts in September, October and November.

Raw materials inventories are planned to be 500 units on 1 July. The balance at the bank on the same day is planned to be £7,500.

Required:

(a) Draw up the following for the six months ending 31 December:
1 A raw materials inventories budget, showing both physical quantities and financial values.
2 A trade payables budget.
3 A cash budget.

(b) The cash budget reveals a potential cash deficiency during October and November. Can you suggest any ways in which a modification of plans could overcome this problem?

The answer to this question can be found in Appendix B at the back of the book.

Non-financial measures in budgeting

The efficiency of internal operations and customer satisfaction levels have become of critical importance to businesses striving to survive in an increasingly competitive environment. Non-financial performance indicators have an important role to play in assessing performance in such key areas as customer/supplier delivery times, set-up times, defect levels and customer satisfaction levels.

There is no reason why budgeting need be confined to financial targets and measures. Non-financial measures can also be used as the basis for targets and can be incorporated into the budgeting process and reported alongside the financial targets for the business. We shall have a closer look at non-financial performance indicators in Chapter 10.

Budgets and management behaviour

All accounting statements and reports are intended to affect the behaviour of at least one group of people. Budgets are intended to affect the behaviour of managers, for example, to encourage them to work towards the business's objectives and to do this in a co-ordinated manner.

Whether budgets seem to be effective and how they can be made more effective are crucial issues for managers. We shall examine this topic in detail in the next chapter, after we have seen how budgets can be used to help managers to exercise control.

Who needs budgets?

Until recently it would have been a heresy to suggest that budgeting was not of central importance to any business. The benefits of budgeting, mentioned earlier in this chapter, have been widely recognised and the vast majority of businesses prepare annual budgets. However, there is increasing concern that, in today's highly dynamic and competitive environment, budgets may actually be harmful to the achievement of business objectives. This has led a small but growing number of businesses to abandon traditional budgets as a tool of planning and control.

Various charges have been levelled against the conventional budgeting process. It is claimed that budgets

- cannot deal with a fast-changing environment, and are often out of date before the start of the budget period;
- focus too much management attention on the achievement of short-term financial targets. Instead, managers should focus on the things that create value for the business (for example, innovation, building brand loyalty, responding quickly to competitive threats, and so on);
- reinforce a 'command and control' structure that concentrates power in the hands of senior managers and prevents junior managers from exercising autonomy. This may be particularly true where a top-down approach, that allocates budgets to managers, is being used. Where managers feel constrained, attempts to retain and recruit able managers can be difficult;
- take up an enormous amount of management time that could be better used. In practice, budgeting can be a lengthy process that may involve much negotiation, reworking and updating, and may add little to the achievement of business objectives;
- are based around business functions (sales, marketing, production, and so on). However, to achieve the business's objectives, the focus should be on business processes that cut across functional boundaries and reflect the needs of the customer;
- encourage incremental thinking by employing a 'last year plus *x* per cent' approach to planning. This can inhibit the development of 'break-out' strategies that may be necessary in a fast-changing environment;
- can protect costs rather than lower costs. In some cases, a fixed budget for an activity, such as research and development, is allocated to a manager. If the amount is not spent, the budget may be taken away and, in future periods, the budget for this activity may be either reduced or eliminated. Such a response to unused budget allocations can encourage managers to spend the whole of the budget, irrespective of need, in order to protect the allocations they receive;
- promote 'sharp' practice among managers. In order to meet budget targets, managers may try to negotiate lower sales targets or higher cost allocations than they feel is really necessary. This helps them to build some 'slack' into the budgets and so meeting the budget becomes easier (see reference 2 at the end of the chapter).

Although some people believe that many of the problems identified can be solved by better budgeting systems such as activity-based budgeting and zero-base budgeting and by taking a more flexible approach, others believe that a more radical solution is required.

Beyond conventional budgeting

In recent years, a few businesses have abandoned budgeting, although they still recognise the need for forward planning. No one seriously doubts that there must be appropriate systems in place to steer a business towards its objectives. It is claimed, however, that the systems adopted should reflect a broader, more integrated approach to planning. The new systems that have been implemented are often based around a 'leaner' financial planning process that is more closely linked to other measurement and reward systems. Emphasis is placed on the use of rolling forecasts, key performance indicators (such as market share, customer satisfaction and innovations) and/or 'score-cards' (like the balanced scorecard, which we shall meet in Chapter 9) that identify both monetary and non-monetary targets to be achieved over the long term and short term. These are often very demanding ('stretch') targets, based on benchmarks that have been set by world-class businesses.

The new 'beyond budgeting' model promotes a more decentralised, participative approach to managing the business. It is claimed that the traditional hierarchical management structure, where decision making is concentrated at the higher levels of the hierarchy, encourages a culture of dependency where meeting the budget targets set by senior managers is the key to managerial success. This traditional structure is replaced by a network structure where decision making is devolved to 'front-line' managers. In the new structure a more open, questioning attitude among employees is encouraged. There is a sharing of knowledge and best practice, and protective behaviour by managers is discouraged. In addition, rewards are linked to targets based on improvement in relative performance rather than to meeting the budget. It is claimed that this new approach allows greater adaptability to changing conditions, improves performance and increases motivation among staff.

Figure 6.8 sets out the main differences between the traditional and 'beyond budgeting' planning models.

Real World 6.8 looks at the management planning systems at Toyota, the well-known Japanese motor vehicle business, a business that does not use conventional budgets.

REAL WORLD 6.8

Steering Toyota

Peter Bunce is at the forefront of those who argue that budgeting systems have an adverse effect on the ability of businesses to compete effectively. The following is an outline of Toyota's planning and control systems, written by him:

> Toyota is a well-known example of a sense-and-respond organisation. Instead of pushing products through rigid processes to meet sales targets, its operating systems start from the customer – it is the customer order that drives operating processes and the work that people do. The point is that in sense-and-respond companies, predetermined plans and performance contracts are an anathema and represent insurmountable barriers; which is why adaptive organisations like Toyota don't have them. However, in industries such as manufacturing, planning has a vital role to play as they have to ensure that they will have sufficient capacity for expected levels of customer orders and they have to manage and coordinate the supply chain. Every year Toyota Motor Europe develops what it calls its Original Business Plan (OBP). The OBP is just a forecast (or financial plan) for the year and provides a baseline for understanding actuals and changes, for communicating, discussion and reaching consensus (a key element of Toyota's way of working) and also for

Real World 6.8 continued

management reviews. The OBP doesn't have any of the toxic elements of a traditional budget such as agreeing and coordinating fixed targets, rewards and resources for the year ahead, and the measuring and controlling performance against such an agreement. Nor is it a reference for bonuses as it doesn't contain any targets or goals (aspirational goals are set separately by Toyota). Toyota Motors Europe also undertakes quarterly forecasts to update the OBP. These are much lighter than the OBP and don't go into much detail.

Source: Bunce, P., 'Transforming financial planning', www.bbrt.org, June 2007.

| Figure 6.8 | Traditional versus 'beyond budgeting' planning model |

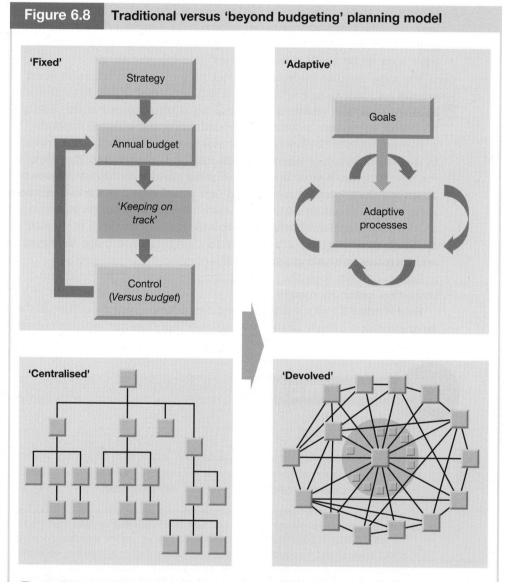

The traditional model is based on the use of fixed targets, which determine the future actions of managers. The 'beyond budgeting' model, on the other hand, is based on the use of stretch targets that can be adapted. The traditional hierarchical management structure is replaced by a network structure.

Source: 'Beyond budgeting', www.beyondbudgeting.plus.com.

It is perhaps too early to predict whether or not the trickle of businesses that are now seeking an alternative to budgets will turn into a flood. However, it is clear that in today's highly competitive environment a business must be flexible and responsive to changing conditions. Management systems that in any way hinder these attributes will not survive.

Long live budgets!

It is worth remembering that, despite the criticisms, budgeting remains a very widely used technique. **Real World 6.3** provides evidence for this. Furthermore, a glance through the annual report of virtually any well-known business will reveal that budgeting is used and is not, therefore, regarded as an impediment to success. **Real World 6.9** is an account of a round table discussion at a Better Budgeting forum held in 2004.

REAL WORLD 6.9

Alive and kicking

A round table discussion at a Better Budgeting Forum held in London in March 2004 was attended by representatives of 32 large organisations, including BAA (the airport operator), the BBC, Ford Motors, Sainsbury (the supermarket business) and Unilever (the household goods group).

The report of the forum discussions said:

> If you were to believe all that has been written in recent years, you'd be forgiven for thinking that budgeting is on its way to becoming extinct. Various research reports allude to the widespread dissatisfaction with the bureaucratic exercise in cost cutting that budgeting is accused of having become. Budgets are pilloried as being out of touch with the needs of modern business and accused of taking too long, costing too much and encouraging all sorts of perverse behaviour.
>
> Yet if there was one conclusion to emerge from the day's discussions it was that budgets are in fact alive and well. Not only did all the organisations present operate a formal budget but all bar two had no interest in getting rid of it. Quite the opposite – although aware of the problems it can cause, the participants by and large regarded the budgeting system and the accompanying processes as indispensable.

and later, in what could have been a reference to the use of 'rolling forecasts' among businesses that claim to have abandoned budgeting, it said:

> It quickly became obvious that, as one participant put it, 'one man's budget is another man's rolling forecast'. What people refer to when they talk about budgeting could in reality be very different things.

This presumably meant that businesses that abandon 'budgets' reintroduce them under another name.

Source: The Chartered Institute of Management Accountants and The Faculty of Finance and Management of the Institute of Chartered Accountants in England and Wales, *Better Budgeting*, March 2004.

It could be argued that Toyota's 'Original Business Plan' (see **Real World 6.8**) is really a budget by another name. The definition of a budget is a business plan, as we saw earlier in the chapter.

Real World 6.10 provides survey evidence of senior finance staff that reveals considerable support for budgets. Nevertheless, many recognised that budgeting is not always well managed and acknowledged some of the criticisms of budgets that were mentioned earlier.

REAL WORLD 6.10

Problems with budgets

The survey of the opinions of senior finance staff at 340 businesses of various sizes and operating in a wide range of industries in North America that was mentioned earlier showed that 86 per cent of those surveyed regarded the budget process as either 'essential' or 'very important'. However,

● 66 per cent thought that budgeting in their business was not agile or flexible enough.
● 59 per cent were not very confident that budget targets would be met in 2008.
● 67 per cent felt that their business devoted inappropriate amounts of time to budgeting (51 per cent felt it was too much and 16 per cent too little).
● 76 per cent felt that their businesses used inappropriate software in the budgeting process (generally using a spreadsheet rather than custom-designed software).

Source: 'Perfect how you project', BPM Forum, 2008.

In the next chapter we shall look in some detail at how budgets can be adapted for use as devices for exercising management control.

SUMMARY

The main points of this chapter may be summarised as follows:

A budget is a short-term business plan, mainly expressed in financial terms.

● Budgets are the short-term means of working towards the business's objectives.
● They are usually prepared for a one-year period with sub-periods of a month.
● There is usually a separate budget for each key area.

Uses of budgets

● Promote forward thinking.
● Help co-ordinate the various aspects of the business.
● Motivate performance.
● Provide the basis of a system of control.
● Provide a system of authorisation.

The budget-setting process

● Establish who will take responsibility.
● Communicate guidelines.
● Identify key factor.
● Prepare budget for key factor area.
● Prepare draft budgets for all other areas.
● Review and co-ordinate.
● Prepare master budgets (income statement and statement of financial position (balance sheet)).
● Communicate the budgets to interested parties.
● Monitor performance relative to budget.

Preparing budgets

- There is no standard style – practicality and usefulness are the key issues.
- They are usually prepared in columnar form, with a column for each month (or other period).
- Each budget must link (co-ordinate) with others.

Criticisms of budgets

- Cannot deal with rapid change.
- Focus on short-term financial targets, rather than on value creation.
- Encourage a 'top-down' management style.
- Time-consuming.
- Based around traditional business functions and do not cross boundaries.
- Encourage incremental thinking (last year's figure, plus x per cent).
- Protect rather than lower costs.
- Promote 'sharp' practice among managers.

Budgeting is very widely regarded as useful and is extensively practised despite the criticisms.

→ Key terms

Budget p. 176	**Management by exception** p. 184
Control p. 177	**Budget committee** p. 186
Limiting factor p. 179	**Budget officer** p. 186
Forecast p. 179	**Incremental budgeting** p. 192
Periodic budget p. 180	**Budget holder** p. 192
Continual budget p. 180	**Discretionary budget** p. 192
Rolling budget p. 180	**Zero-base budgeting (ZBB)** p. 193
Master budget p. 181	**Activity-based budgeting (ABB)** p. 201

References

1 BPM Forum, 'Perfect how you project', BPM Forum, 2008.
2 'Beyond budgeting', www.beyondbudgeting.plus.com.

Further reading

If you would like to explore the topics covered in this chapter in more depth, we recommend the following books:

Atkinson, A., Banker, R., Kaplan, R. and Young, S. M., *Management Accounting*, 5th edn, Prentice Hall, 2007, chapter 11.

Drury, C., *Management and Cost Accounting*, 7th edn, Cengage Learning, 2007, chapter 15.

Hilton, R., *Managerial Accounting*, 6th edn, McGraw-Hill Irwin, 2005, chapter 9.

Horngren, C., Foster, G., Datar, S., Rajan, M. and Ittner, C., *Cost Accounting: A Managerial Emphasis*, 13th edn, Prentice Hall International, 2008, chapter 6.

REVIEW QUESTIONS

Answers to these questions can be found in Appendix C at the back of the book.

6.1 Define a budget. How is a budget different from a forecast?

6.2 What were the five uses of budgets that were identified in the chapter?

6.3 What do budgets have to do with control?

6.4 What is a budget committee? What purpose does it serve?

EXERCISES

Exercises 6.5 to 6.8 are more advanced than 6.1 to 6.4. Those with coloured numbers have answers in Appendix D at the back of the book. If you wish to try more exercises, visit the students' side of the Companion Website at www.pearsoned.co.uk/atrillmclaney.

6.1 Daniel Chu Ltd, a new business, will start production on 1 April, but sales will not start until 1 May. Planned sales for the next nine months are as follows:

	Sales units
May	500
June	600
July	700
August	800
September	900
October	900
November	900
December	800
January	700

The selling price of a unit will be a consistent £100 and all sales will be made on one month's credit. It is planned that sufficient finished goods inventories for each month's sales should be available at the end of the previous month.

Raw materials purchases will be such that there will be sufficient raw materials inventories available at the end of each month precisely to meet the following month's planned production. This planned policy will operate from the end of April. Purchases of raw materials will be on one month's credit. The cost of raw material is £40 a unit of finished product.

The direct labour cost, which is variable with the level of production, is planned to be £20 a unit of finished production. Production overheads are planned to be £20,000 each month, including £3,000 for depreciation. Non-production overheads are planned to be £11,000 a month, of which £1,000 will be depreciation.

Various non-current (fixed) assets costing £250,000 will be bought and paid for during April.

Except where specified, assume that all payments take place in the same month as the cost is incurred.

The business will raise £300,000 in cash from a share issue in April.

Required:
Draw up the following for the six months ending 30 September:
(a) A finished inventories budget, showing just physical quantities.
(b) A raw materials inventories budget showing both physical quantities and financial values.
(c) A trade payables budget.
(d) A trade receivables budget.
(e) A cash budget.

6.2   You have overheard the following statements:

(a) 'A budget is a forecast of what is expected to happen in a business during the next year.'
(b) 'Monthly budgets must be prepared with a column for each month so that you can see the whole year at a glance, month by month.'
(c) 'Budgets are OK but they stifle all initiative. No manager worth employing would work for a business that seeks to control through budgets.'
(d) 'Activity-based budgeting is an approach that takes account of the planned volume of activity in order to deduce the figures to go into the budget.'
(e) 'Any sensible person would start with the sales budget and build up the other budgets from there.'

Required:
Critically discuss these statements, explaining any technical terms.

6.3   A nursing home, which is linked to a large hospital, has been examining its budgetary control procedures, with particular reference to overhead costs.

The level of activity in the facility is measured by the number of patients treated in the budget period. For the current year, the budget stands at 6,000 patients and this is expected to be met.

For months 1 to 6 of this year (assume 12 months of equal length), 2,700 patients were treated. The actual variable overhead costs incurred during this six-month period are as follows:

Expense	£
Staffing	59,400
Power	27,000
Supplies	54,000
Other	8,100
Total	148,500

The hospital accountant believes that the variable overhead costs will be incurred at the same rate during months 7 to 12 of the year.

Fixed overheads are budgeted for the whole year as follows:

Expense	£
Supervision	120,000
Depreciation/financing	187,200
Other	64,800
Total	372,000

Required:
(a) Present an overheads budget for months 7 to 12 of the year. You should show each expense, but should not separate individual months. What is the total overheads cost for each patient that would be incorporated into any statistics?
(b) The home actually treated 3,800 patients during months 7 to 12, the actual variable overheads were £203,300, and the fixed overheads were £190,000. In summary form, examine how well the home exercised control over its overheads.
(c) Interpret your analysis and point out any limitations or assumptions.

6.4 Linpet Ltd is to be incorporated on 1 June. The opening statement of financial position (balance sheet) of the business will then be as follows:

Assets	£
Cash at bank	60,000
Share capital	
£1 ordinary shares	60,000

During June, the business intends to make payments of £40,000 for a leasehold property, £10,000 for equipment and £6,000 for a motor vehicle. The business will also purchase initial trading inventories costing £22,000 on credit.

The business has produced the following estimates:

1 Sales revenue for June will be £8,000 and will increase at the rate of £3,000 a month until September. In October, sales revenue will rise to £22,000 and in subsequent months will be maintained at this figure.
2 The gross profit percentage on goods sold will be 25 per cent.
3 There is a risk that supplies of trading inventories will be interrupted towards the end of the accounting year. The business therefore intends to build up its initial level of inventories (£22,000) by purchasing £1,000 of inventories each month in addition to the monthly purchases necessary to satisfy monthly sales requirements. All purchases of inventories (including the initial inventories) will be on one month's credit.
4 Sales revenue will be divided equally between cash and credit sales. Credit customers are expected to pay two months after the sale is agreed.
5 Wages and salaries will be £900 a month. Other overheads will be £500 a month for the first four months and £650 thereafter. Both types of expense will be payable when incurred.
6 80 per cent of sales revenue will be generated by salespeople who will receive 5 per cent commission on sales revenue. The commission is payable one month after the sale is agreed.
7 The business intends to purchase further equipment in November for £7,000 cash.
8 Depreciation will be provided at the rate of 5 per cent a year on property and 20 per cent a year on equipment. (Depreciation has not been included in the overheads mentioned in 5 above.)

Required:
(a) State why a cash budget is required for a business.
(b) Prepare a cash budget for Linpet Ltd for the six-month period to 30 November.

6.5 Lewisham Ltd manufactures one product line – the Zenith. Sales of Zeniths over the next few months are planned to be as follows:

1 *Demand*

	Units
July	180,000
August	240,000
September	200,000
October	180,000

Each Zenith sells for £3.
−2 *Receipts from sales.* Credit customers are expected to pay as follows:

● 70 per cent during the month of sale
● 28 per cent during the following month.

The remaining trade receivables are expected to go bad (that is, to be uncollectable).

Credit customers who pay in the month of sale are entitled to deduct a 2 per cent discount from the invoice price.

3 *Finished goods inventories*. Inventories of finished goods are expected to be 40,000 units at 1 July. The business's policy is that, in future, the inventories at the end of each month should equal 20 per cent of the following month's planned sales requirements.

4 *Raw materials inventories*. Inventories of raw materials are expected to be 40,000 kg on 1 July. The business's policy is that, in future, the inventories at the end of each month should equal 50 per cent of the following month's planned production requirements. Each Zenith requires 0.5 kg of the raw material, which costs £1.50/kg. Raw materials purchases are paid in the month after purchase.

5 *Labour and overheads*. The direct labour cost of each Zenith is £0.50. The variable overhead element of each Zenith is £0.30. Fixed overheads, including depreciation of £25,000, total £47,000 a month. All labour and overheads are paid during the month in which they arise.

6 *Cash in hand*. At 1 August the business plans to have a bank balance (in funds) of £20,000.

Required:

Prepare the following budgets:

(a) Finished inventories budget (expressed in units of Zenith) for each of the three months July, August and September.

(b) Raw materials inventories budget (expressed in kilograms of the raw material) for the two months July and August.

(c) Cash budget for August and September.

6.6 Newtake Records Ltd owns a chain of 14 shops selling compact discs. At the beginning of June the business had an overdraft of £35,000 and the bank had asked for this to be eliminated by the end of November. As a result, the directors have recently decided to review their plans for the next six months.

The following plans were prepared for the business some months earlier:

	May £000	June £000	July £000	August £000	Sept £000	Oct £000	Nov £000
Sales revenue	180	230	320	250	140	120	110
Purchases	135	180	142	94	75	66	57
Administration expenses	52	55	56	53	48	46	45
Selling expenses	22	24	28	26	21	19	18
Taxation payment				22			
Finance payments	5	5	5	5	5	5	5
Shop refurbishment	–	–	14	18	6	–	–

Notes:

1 The inventories level at 1 June was £112,000. The business believes it is preferable to maintain a minimum inventories level of £40,000 of goods over the period to 30 November.

2 Suppliers allow one month's credit. The first three months' purchases are subject to a contractual agreement, which must be honoured.

3 The gross profit margin is 40 per cent.

4 Cash from all sales is received in the month of sale. However, 50 per cent of customers pay with a credit card. The charge made by the credit card business to Newtake Records Ltd is 3 per cent of the sales revenue value. These charges are in addition to the selling expenses identified above. The credit card business pays Newtake Records Ltd in the month of sale.

5 The business has a bank loan, which it is paying off in monthly instalments of £5,000. The interest element represents 20 per cent of each instalment.

6 Administration expenses are paid when incurred. This item includes a charge of £15,000 each month in respect of depreciation.

7 Selling expenses are payable in the following month.

Required (working to the nearest £1,000):

(a) Prepare a cash budget for the six months ending 30 November which shows the cash balance at the end of each month.

(b) Compute the inventories levels at the end of each month for the six months to 30 November.

(c) Prepare a budgeted income statement for the whole of the six-month period ending 30 November. (A monthly breakdown of profit is *not* required.)

(d) What problems is Newtake Records Ltd likely to face in the next six months? Can you suggest how the business might deal with these problems?

6.7   Prolog Ltd is a small wholesaler of high-specification personal computers. It has in recent months been selling 50 machines a month at a price of £2,000 each. These machines cost £1,600 each. A new model has just been launched and this is expected to offer greatly enhanced perform-ance. Its selling price and cost will be the same as for the old model. From the beginning of January, sales are planned to increase at a rate of 20 machines each month until the end of June, when sales will amount to 170 units a month. They are planned to continue at that level thereafter. Operating costs including depreciation of £2,000 a month are planned as follows:

	January	February	March	April	May	June
Operating costs (£000)	6	8	10	12	12	12

Prolog expects to receive no credit for operating costs. Additional shelving for storage will be bought, installed and paid for in April, costing £12,000. Corporation tax of £25,000 is due at the end of March. Prolog anticipates that trade receivables will amount to two months' sales rev-enue. To give its customers a good level of service, Prolog plans to hold enough inventories at the end of each month to fulfil anticipated demand from customers in the following month. The computer manufacturer, however, grants one month's credit to Prolog. Prolog Ltd's statement of financial position (balance sheet) appears below.

Statement of financial position (balance sheet) at 31 December

	£000
Non-current assets	80
Current assets	
Inventories	112
Trade receivables	200
Cash	–
	312
Total assets	392
Equity	
Share capital (25p ordinary shares)	10
Retained profit	177
	187
Current liabilities	
Trade payables	112
Taxation	25
Overdraft	68
	205
Total equity and liabilities	392

Required:

(a) Prepare a cash budget for Prolog Ltd showing the cash balance or required overdraft for the six months ending 30 June.

(b) State briefly what further information a banker would require from Prolog Ltd before granting additional overdraft facilities for the anticipated expansion of sales.

6.8 Brown and Jeffreys, a West Midlands business, makes one standard product for use in the motor trade. The product, known as the Fuel Miser, for which the business holds the patent, when fitted to the fuel system of production model cars has the effect of reducing petrol consumption.

Part of the production is sold direct to a local car manufacturer, which fits the Fuel Miser as an optional extra to several of its models, and the rest of the production is sold through various retail outlets, garages, and so on.

Brown and Jeffreys assemble the Fuel Miser, but all three components are manufactured by local engineering businesses. The three components are codenamed A, B and C. One Fuel Miser consists of one of each component.

The planned sales for the first seven months of the forthcoming accounting period, by channels of distribution and in terms of Fuel Miser units, are as follows:

	Jan	Feb	Mar	Apr	May	June	July
Manufacturers	4,000	4,000	4,500	4,500	4,500	4,500	4,500
Retail, and so on	2,000	2,700	3,200	3,000	2,700	2,500	2,400
	6,000	6,700	7,700	7,500	7,200	7,000	6,900

The following further information is available:

1 There will be inventories of finished units at 1 January of 7,000 Fuel Misers.
2 The inventories of raw materials at 1 January will be:
 A 10,000 units
 B 16,500 units
 C 7,200 units
3 The selling price of Fuel Misers is to be £10 each to the motor manufacturer and £12 each to retail outlets.
4 The maximum production capacity of the business is 7,000 units a month. There is no possibility of increasing this output.
5 Assembly of each Fuel Miser will take 10 minutes of direct labour. Direct labour is paid at the rate of £7.20 an hour during the month of production.
6 The components are each expected to cost the following:
 A £2.50
 B £1.30
 C £0.80
7 Indirect costs are to be paid at a regular rate of £32,000 each month.
8 The cash at the bank at 1 January will be £2,620.

The planned sales volumes must be met and the business intends to pursue the following policies for as many months as possible, consistent with meeting the sales targets:

● Finished inventories at the end of each month are to equal the following month's total sales to retail outlets, and half the total of the following month's sales to the motor manufacturer.
● Raw materials at the end of each month are to be sufficient to cover production requirements for the following month. The production for July will be 6,800 units.
● Suppliers of raw materials are to be paid during the month following purchase. The payment for January will be £21,250.
● Customers will pay in the month of sale, in the case of sales to the motor manufacturer, and the month after sale, in the case of retail sales. Retail sales during December were 2,000 units at £12 each.

Required:
Prepare the following budgets in monthly columnar form, both in terms of money and units (where relevant), for the six months of January to June inclusive:

(a) Sales budget.*

(b) Finished inventories budget (valued at direct cost).†

(c) Raw materials inventories budget (one budget for each component).†

(d) Production budget (direct costs only).*

(e) Trade receivables budget.†

(f)   Trade payables budget.†

(g) Cash budget.†

* The sales and production budgets should merely state each month's sales or production in units and in money terms.

† The other budgets should all seek to reconcile the opening balance of inventories, trade receivables, trade payables or cash with the closing balance through movements of the relevant factors over the month.

7

Accounting for control

INTRODUCTION

This chapter deals with the role of budgets in management control. We therefore continue some of the themes that we discussed in Chapter 6. We shall consider how a budget can be used to help control a business, and we shall see that, by collecting information on actual performance and comparing it with a revised budget, it is possible to identify those activities that are in control and those that are not.

Budgets are designed to influence the behaviour of managers, and we shall explore some of the issues relating to budgets and management behaviour. We shall also take a look at standard costing and its relationship with budgeting. We shall see that standards provide the building blocks for budgets.

LEARNING OUTCOMES

When you have completed this chapter, you should be able to:

● Discuss the role and limitations of budgets for performance evaluation and control.

● Undertake variance analysis and discuss possible reasons for the variances calculated.

● Discuss the issues that should be taken into account when designing an effective system of budgetary control.

● Explain the nature, role and limitations of standard costing.

Budgeting for control

In Chapter 6, we saw that budgets provide a useful basis for exercising control over a business. Control involves making events conform to a plan and, since the budget is a short-term plan, making events conform to it is an obvious way to try to control the business. We saw in Chapter 6 that, for most businesses, the routine is as shown in Figure 7.1.

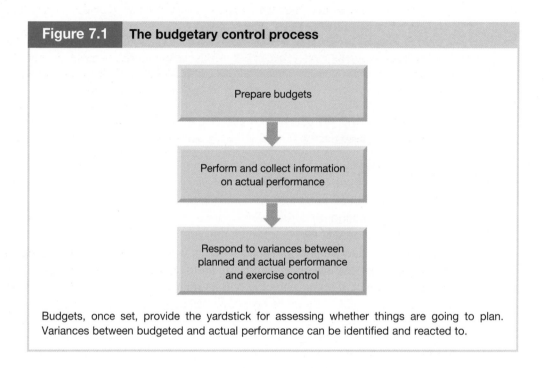

Figure 7.1	The budgetary control process

Budgets, once set, provide the yardstick for assessing whether things are going to plan. Variances between budgeted and actual performance can be identified and reacted to.

If plans are drawn up sensibly, we have a basis for exercising control over the business. We must, however, measure actual performance in the same terms as those in which the budget is stated. If they are not in the same terms, proper comparison will not be possible.

Exercising control involves finding out where and why things did not go according to plan and then seeking ways to put them right for the future. One reason why things may not have gone according to plan is that the budget targets were unachievable. In this case, it may be necessary to revise the budgets for future periods so that targets become achievable.

This last point should not be taken to mean that budget targets can simply be ignored if the going gets tough, but rather that they should be adaptable. Unrealistic budgets cannot form a basis for exercising control, and little can be gained by sticking with them. Budgets may become unrealistic for a variety of reasons, including unexpected changes in the commercial environment (for example, an unexpected collapse in demand for services of the type that the business provides).

Real World 7.1 reveals how one important budget had to be dramatically revised because it had become unrealistic.

REAL WORLD 7.1

No medals for budgeting   **FT**

The government's dramatic increase this spring in the budget for the 2012 Olympic games, almost tripling the £3.3bn cost to the taxpayer estimated at the time of winning the 2005 bid, has put the event on a 'firmer financial footing', says a report by the National Audit Office (NAO).

Nevertheless, the revised £9.3bn London Olympics budget contains 'significant areas of uncertainty' that could drive costs up, unless effective controls are exercised. Sir John Bourn, head of the NAO, warned the government it still had to 'work to contain funding and achieve value for money'. He highlighted areas of uncertainty affecting costs, including the design specifications and future use of the Olympic venues, the level of price inflation in the construction sector and the contracts negotiated by suppliers.

The NAO, in effect, gives the revised budget its seal of approval, saying it 'should be sufficient' to cover the estimated costs of the games, provided – a 'most important proviso' – the assumptions on which the budget is based hold good. But its report calls for action by the government to ensure proper controls over the huge project.

Source: Adapted from Watchdog warns on Olympic costs by Jean Eaglesham, ft.com, © The Financial Times Limited, 20 July 2007.

When there is system of budgetary control, decision making and responsibility can be delegated to junior management, yet senior management can still retain control. This is because senior managers can use the budgetary control system to find out which junior managers are meeting targets and therefore working towards achieving the objectives of the business. (We should remember that budgets are the short-term plans for achieving the business's objectives.) This enables a *management-by-exception* environment to be created where senior management can focus on areas where things are *not* going according to plan (the exceptions – it is to be hoped). Junior managers who are performing to budget can be left to get on with their jobs.

Types of control

→ The control process just outlined is known as **feedback control**. Its main feature is that steps are taken to get operations back on track as soon as there is a signal that they have gone wrong. This is similar to the thermostatic control that is a feature of most central heating systems. The thermostat incorporates a thermometer that senses when the temperature has fallen below a pre-set level (analogous to the budget). The thermostat then takes action to correct matters by activating the heating device that restores the required minimum temperature. Figure 7.2 depicts the stages in a feedback control system using budgets.

→ There is an alternative type of control, known as **feedforward control**. Here predictions are made as to what can go wrong and steps taken to avoid any undesirable outcome. The preparation of budgets, which we discussed in Chapter 6, provides an example of this type of control. Preparing a particular budget may reveal a problem

Figure 7.2   Feedback control

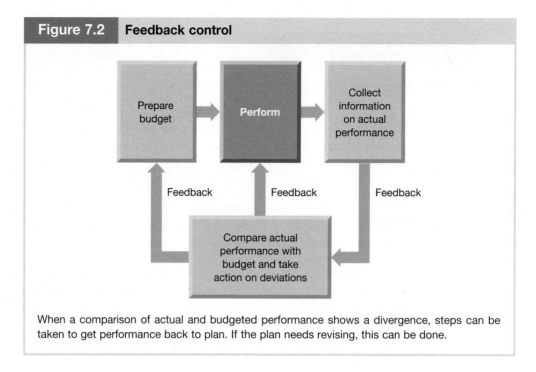

When a comparison of actual and budgeted performance shows a divergence, steps can be taken to get performance back to plan. If the plan needs revising, this can be done.

that will arise unless the business changes its plans. For example, preparing the cash budget may reveal that if the original plans are followed, there will be a negative cash balance for part of the budget period. Having identified the problem, the plans can then be revised to deal with it.

We can see that feedforward controls try to anticipate future problems, whereas feedback controls react to problems that have already occurred. Budgeting embraces both forms of control. Preparing a budget is a form of feedforward control while comparing the budget with actual results is a form of feedback control. Generally speaking, feedforward controls are preferable: things are less likely to go wrong in the first place if steps have been taken to anticipate problems and plan accordingly. It is not always possible, however, to establish effective feedforward control.

Variances from budget

We saw in Chapter 1 that the key financial objective of a business is to increase the wealth of its owners (shareholders). Since profit is the net increase in wealth from business operations, the most important budget target to meet is the profit target. We shall therefore take this as our starting point when comparing the budget with the actual results. Example 7.1 shows the budgeted and actual income statements for Baxter Ltd for the month of May.

Example 7.1

The following are the budgeted and actual income statements for Baxter Ltd, a manufacturing business, for the month of May:

	Budget	Actual
Output (production and sales)	1,000 units	900 units
	£	£
Sales revenue	100,000	92,000
Raw materials	(40,000) (40,000 metres)	(36,900) (37,000 metres)
Labour	(20,000) (2,500 hours)	(17,500) (2,150 hours)
Fixed overheads	(20,000)	(20,700)
Operating profit	20,000	16,900

From these figures, it is clear that the budgeted profit was not achieved. As far as May is concerned, this is a matter of history. However, the business (or at least one aspect of it) is out of control. Senior management must discover where things went wrong during May and try to ensure that these mistakes are not repeated in later months. It is not enough to know that things went wrong overall. We need to know where and why. The approach taken is to compare the budgeted and actual figures for the various items (sales revenue, raw materials and so on) in the above statement.

Activity 7.1

Can you see any problems in comparing the various items (sales revenue, raw materials and so on) for the budget with the actual performance of Baxter Ltd in an attempt to draw conclusions as to which aspects were out of control?

The problem is that the actual level of output was not as budgeted. The actual level of output was 10 per cent less than budget. This means that we cannot, for example, say that there was a labour cost saving of £2,500 (that is, £20,000 − £17,500) and conclude that all is well in that area.

Flexing the budget

One practical way to overcome our difficulty is to 'flex' the budget to what it would have been had the planned level of output been 900 units rather than 1,000 units. **Flexing the budget** simply means revising it, assuming a different volume of output.

To exercise control, the budget is usually flexed to reflect the volume that actually occurred, where this is higher or lower than that originally planned. This means that we need to know which revenues and costs are fixed and which are variable relative to the volume of output. Once we know this, flexing is a simple operation. We shall assume that sales revenue, material cost and labour cost vary strictly with volume. Fixed overheads, by definition, will not. Whether, in real life, labour cost does vary with the volume of output is not so certain, but it will serve well enough as an assumption for our purposes. Were labour actually fixed, we should simply take this into account in the flexing process.

On the basis of our assumptions regarding the behaviour of revenues and costs, the flexed budget would be as follows:

	Flexed budget
Output (production and sales)	900 units
	£
Sales revenue	90,000
Raw materials	(36,000) (36,000 metres)
Labour	(18,000) (2,250 hours)
Fixed overheads	(20,000)
Operating profit	16,000

This is simply the original budget, with the sales revenue, raw materials and labour cost figures scaled down by 10 per cent (the same factor as the actual output fell short of the budgeted one).

Putting the original budget, the flexed budget and the actual for May together, we obtain the following:

	Original budget	*Flexed budget*	*Actual*
Output	1,000 units	900 units	900 units
(production and sales)			
	£	£	£
Sales revenue	100,000	90,000	92,000
Raw materials	(40,000)	(36,000) (36,000 m)	(36,900) (37,000 m)
Labour	(20,000)	(18,000) (2,250 hr)	(17,500) (2,150 hr)
Fixed overheads	(20,000)	(20,000)	(20,700)
Operating profit	20,000	16,000	16,900

→   **Flexible budgets** allow us to make a more valid comparison between the budget (using the flexed figures) and the actual results. Key differences, or variances, between budgeted and actual results for each aspect of the business's activities can then be calculated. In the rest of this section we consider some of the variances that may be calculated.

Sales volume variance

Let us begin by dealing with the shortfall in sales volume. It may seem as if we are saying that this does not matter, because we just revise the budget and carry on as if all is well. However, this is not the case, because losing sales volume generally means losing profit. The first point we must pick up, therefore, is the loss of profit arising from the loss of sales of 100 units of the product.

Activity 7.2

What will be the loss of profit arising from the sales volume shortfall, assuming that everything except sales volume was as planned?

The answer is simply the difference between the original and flexed budget profit figures. The only difference between these two profit figures is the volume of sales; everything else was the same. (That is to say that the flexing was carried out assuming that the per-unit sales revenue, raw material cost and labour cost were all as originally budgeted.) This means that the figure for the loss of profit due to the volume shortfall, taken alone, is £4,000 (that is, £20,000 − £16,000).

When we considered the relationship between cost, volume and profit in Chapter 3, we saw that selling one unit less will result in one less contribution to profit. The contribution is sales revenue less variable cost. We can see from the original budget that the unit sales revenue is £100 (that is, £100,000/1,000), raw material cost is £40 a unit (that is, £40,000/1,000) and labour cost is £20 a unit (that is, £20,000/1,000). Thus the contribution is £40 a unit (that is, £100 − (£40 + £20)).

If, therefore, 100 units of sales are lost, £4,000 (that is, 100 × £40) of contributions, and therefore profit, are forgone. This would be an alternative means of finding the sales volume variance, rather than taking the difference between the original and flexed budget profit figures. Once we have produced the flexed budget, however, it is generally easier to compare the two profit figures.

The difference between the original and flexed budget profit figures is called the **sales volume variance**. In this case, it is an **adverse variance** because, taken alone, it has the effect of making the actual profit lower than the budgeted profit. A variance that has the effect of increasing profit beyond the budgeted profit is known as a **favourable variance**. We can therefore say that a **variance** is the effect of that factor (taken alone) on the budgeted profit. Later we shall consider other forms of variance, some of which may be favourable and some adverse. The difference between the sum of all the various favourable and adverse variances will represent the difference between the budgeted and actual profit. This is shown in Figure 7.3.

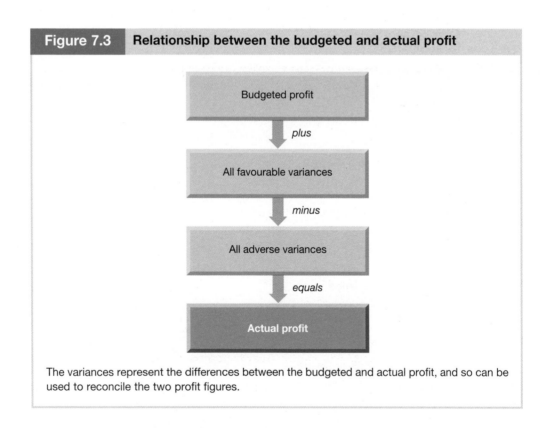

Figure 7.3   Relationship between the budgeted and actual profit

The variances represent the differences between the budgeted and actual profit, and so can be used to reconcile the two profit figures.

When calculating a particular variance, such as sales volume, we assume that all other factors went according to plan.

Activity 7.3

What else do the relevant managers of Baxter Ltd need to know about the May sales volume variance?

They need to know why the volume of sales fell below the budgeted figure. Only by discovering this information will managers be in a position to try to ensure that it does not occur again.

Who should be held accountable for this sales volume variance? The answer is probably the sales manager, who should know precisely why this has occurred. This is not the same, however, as saying that it was the sales manager's fault. The problem may have been that the business failed to produce the budgeted quantities so that not enough items were available to sell. Nevertheless, the sales manager should know the reason for the problem.

The budget and actual figures for Baxter Ltd for June are given in Activity 7.4 and will be used as the basis for a series of Activities that provide an opportunity to calculate and assess the variances. We shall continue to use the May figures for explaining the variances.

Note that the business had budgeted for a higher level of output for June than it did for May.

Activity 7.4

	Budget for June	*Actual for June*
Output	1,100 units	1,150 units
(production and sales)		
	£	£
Sales revenue	110,000	113,500
Raw materials	(44,000) (44,000 metres)	(46,300) (46,300 metres)
Labour	(22,000) (2,750 hours)	(23,200) (2,960 hours)
Fixed overheads	(20,000)	(19,300)
Operating profit	24,000	24,700

Try flexing the June budget, comparing it with the original June budget, and so find the sales volume variance.

	Flexed budget
Output (production and sales)	1,150 units
	£
Sales revenue	115,000
Raw materials	(46,000) (46,000 metres)
Labour	(23,000) (2,875 hours)
Fixed overheads	(20,000)
Operating profit	26,000

The sales volume variance is £2,000 (favourable) (that is, £26,000 − £24,000). It is favourable because the original budget profit was lower than the flexed budget profit. This arises from more sales actually being made than were budgeted.

For the month of May, we have already identified one reason why the budgeted profit of £20,000 was not achieved and that the actual profit was only £16,900. This was the £4,000 loss of profit (adverse variance) that arose from the sales volume short-fall. Now that the budget is flexed, we can compare like with like and reach further conclusions about May's trading.

The fact that the sales revenue, raw materials, labour and fixed overheads figures differ between the flexed budget and the actual results (see p. 222) suggests that the adverse sales volume variance was not the only problem area. To identify the problem areas relating to each of the revenue and cost items mentioned, we need to calculate further variances. This is done in the sections below.

Sales price variance

Starting with the sales revenue figure, we can see that, for May, there is a difference of £2,000 (favourable) between the flexed budget and the actual figures. This can only arise from higher prices being charged than were envisaged in the original budget, because any variance arising from the volume difference has already been 'stripped out' in the flexing process. This price difference is known as the **sales price variance**. Higher sales prices will, all other things being equal, mean more profit. So there is a favourable variance.

When senior management is trying to identify the reason for a sales price variance, it would normally be the sales manager that should be able to offer an explanation. As we shall see later in the chapter, favourable variances of significant size will normally be investigated.

Activity 7.5

Using the figures in Activity 7.4, what is the sales price variance for June?

The sales price variance for June is £1,500 (adverse) (that is, £115,000 − £113,500). Actual sales prices, on average, must have been lower than those budgeted. The actual price averaged £98.70 (that is, £113,500/1,150) whereas the budgeted price was £100. Selling output at a lower price than that budgeted will have an adverse effect on profit, hence an adverse variance.

Let us now move on to look at the cost variances, starting with materials variances.

Materials variances

In May, there was an overall or **total direct materials variance** of £900 (adverse) (that is, £36,900 − £36,000). It is adverse because the actual material cost was higher than the budgeted one, which has an adverse effect on operating profit.

Who should be held accountable for this variance? The answer depends on whether the difference arises from excess usage of the raw material, in which case it is the production manager, or whether it is a higher-than-budgeted cost per metre being paid, in which case it is the responsibility of the buying manager. Fortunately, we can go beyond this total variance to examine the effect of changes in both usage and cost. We can see from the figures that in May there was a 1,000 metre excess usage of the raw material (that is, 37,000 metres − 36,000 metres). All other things being equal, this alone would have led to a profit shortfall of £1,000, since clearly the budgeted cost per metre is £1. The £1,000 (adverse) variance is known as the **direct materials usage variance**. Normally, this variance would be the responsibility of the production manager.

Activity 7.6

Using the figures in Activity 7.4, what was the direct material usage variance for June?

The direct material usage variance for June was £300 (adverse) (that is, (46,300 metres – 46,000 metres) × £1). It is adverse because more material was used than was budgeted, for an output of 1,150 units. Excess usage of material will tend to reduce profit.

The other aspect of direct materials is their cost. The **direct materials price variance** simply takes the actual cost of materials used and compares it with the cost that was allowed, given the quantity used. In May the actual cost of direct materials used was £36,900, whereas the allowed cost of the 37,000 metres was £37,000. Thus we have a favourable variance of £100. Paying less than the budgeted cost will have a favourable effect on profit, hence a favourable variance.

Activity 7.7

Using the figures in Activity 7.4, what was the direct materials price variance for June?

The direct materials price variance for June was zero (that is, £46,300 – (46,300 × £1)).

As we have just seen, the total direct materials variance is the sum of the usage variance and the price variance. The relationship between the direct materials variances for May is shown in Figure 7.4.

Figure 7.4 Total, usage and price variances for direct materials for May

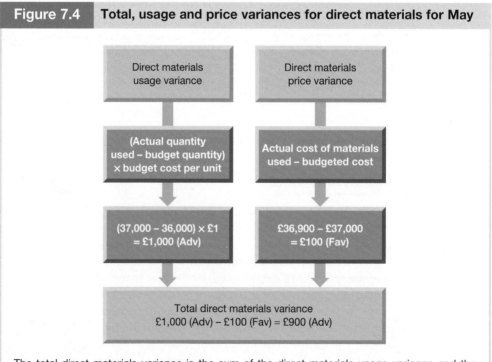

The total direct materials variance is the sum of the direct materials usage variance and the price variance, and can be analysed into these two.

Labour variances

Direct labour variances are similar in form to those for direct materials. The **total direct labour variance** for May was £500 (favourable) (that is, £18,000 – £17,500). It is favourable because £500 less was spent on labour than was budgeted for the actual level of output achieved.

Again, this total variance is not particularly helpful and needs to be analysed further into its usage and cost elements. We should bear in mind that the number of hours used to complete a particular quantity of output is the responsibility of the production manager, whereas the responsibility for the rate of pay lies primarily with the human resources manager.

The **direct labour efficiency variance** compares the number of hours that would be allowed for the achieved level of production with the actual number of hours used. It then costs this difference at the allowed hourly rate. Thus, for May, it was (2,250 hours – 2,150 hours) × £8 = £800 (favourable). We know that the budgeted hourly rate is £8 because the original budget shows that 2,500 hours were budgeted to cost £20,000. The variance is favourable because fewer hours were used than would have been allowed for the actual level of output. Working more quickly would tend to lead to higher profit.

Activity 7.8

Using the figures in Activity 7.4, what was the direct labour efficiency variance for June?

The direct labour efficiency variance for June was £680 (adverse) (that is, (2,960 hours – 2,875 hours) × £8). It is adverse because the work took longer than the budget allowed and so will have an adverse effect on profit.

The **direct labour rate variance** compares the actual cost of the hours worked with the allowed cost. For 2,150 hours worked in May, the allowed cost would be £17,200 (that is, 2,150 × £8). So, the direct labour rate variance is £300 (adverse) (that is, £17,500 – £17,200).

The relationship between the direct labour variances for May is shown in Figure 7.5.

Activity 7.9

Using the figures in Activity 7.4, what was the direct labour rate variance for June?

The direct labour rate variance for June was £480 (favourable) (that is, (2,960 × £8) – £23,200). It is favourable because a lower rate was paid than the budgeted one. Paying a lower wage rate will have a favourable effect on profit.

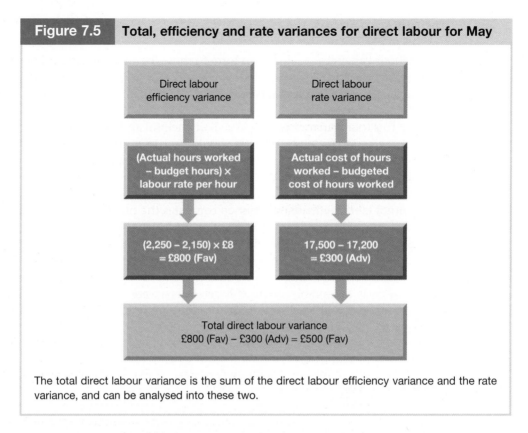

Figure 7.5   **Total, efficiency and rate variances for direct labour for May**

The total direct labour variance is the sum of the direct labour efficiency variance and the rate variance, and can be analysed into these two.

Fixed overhead variance

The final area is that of overheads. In our example, we have assumed that all of the overheads are fixed. Variable overheads certainly exist in practice, but they have been omitted here simply to restrict the amount of detailed coverage. Variances involving variable overheads are similar in style to labour and material variances.

The **fixed overhead spending variance** is simply the difference between the flexed (or original – they will be the same) budget and the actual figures. For May, this was £700 (adverse) (that is, £20,700 – £20,000). It is adverse because more overhead cost was actually incurred than was budgeted. This would tend to lead to less profit. In theory, this is the responsibility of whoever controls overhead expenditure.

In practice, overheads tend to be a very slippery area, and one that is notoriously difficult to control. Of course fixed overheads (and variable ones) are usually made up of more than one type of cost. Typically, they would include such things as rent, administrative costs, salaries of managerial staff, cleaning, electricity and so on. These could be individually budgeted and the actuals recorded. This would enable individual spending variances to be identified for each element of overheads, which in turn would enable managers to identify any problem areas.

Activity 7.10

Using the figures in Activity 7.4, what was the fixed overhead spending variance for June?

The fixed overhead spending variance for June was £700 (favourable) (that is, £20,000 – £19,300). It was favourable because less was spent on overheads than was budgeted, thereby having a favourable effect on profit.

We are now in a position to reconcile the original May budgeted operating profit with the actual operating profit, as follows:

	£	£
Budgeted operating profit		20,000
Add **Favourable variances**		
Sales price	2,000	
Direct materials price	100	
Direct labour efficiency	800	2,900
		22,900
Less **Adverse variances**		
Sales volume	4,000	
Direct materials usage	1,000	
Direct labour rate	300	
Fixed overhead spending	700	6,000
Actual operating profit		16,900

Activity 7.11

If you were the chief executive of Baxter Ltd, what attitude would you take to the overall difference between the budgeted profit and the actual one?

How would you react to the individual variances that are the outcome of the analysis shown in the solution to Activity 7.10?

You would probably be concerned about how large the variances are and their direction (favourable or adverse). In particular you may have thought of the following:

- The overall adverse profit variance is £3,100 (that is £20,000 – £16,900). This represents 15.5 per cent of the budgeted profit (that is £3,100/£20,000 × 100%) and you (as chief executive) would almost certainly see it as significant and worrying.
- The £4,000 adverse sales volume variance represents 20 per cent of budgeted profit and would be a particular cause of concern.
- The £2,000 favourable sales price variance represents 10 per cent of budgeted profit. Since this is favourable it might be seen as a cause for celebration rather than concern. On the other hand it means that Baxter Ltd's output was, on average, sold at prices 10 per cent above the planned price. This could have been the cause of the worrying adverse sales volume variance. Baxter Ltd may have sold fewer units because it charged higher prices.
- The £100 favourable direct materials price variance is very small in relation to budgeted profit – only 0.5 per cent. It would be unrealistic to expect the actual figures to hit the precise budgeted figures each month and so this is unlikley to be regarded as significant. The direct materials usage variance, however, represents 5 per cent of the budgeted profit. The chief executive may feel this is cause for concern.
- The £800 favourable direct labour efficiency variance represents 4 per cent of budgeted profit. Although it is a favourable variance, the reasons for it may be worth investigating.The £300 adverse direct labour rate variance represents only 1.5 per cent of the budgeted profit and may not be regarded as significant.
- The £700 fixed overhead adverse variance represents 3.5 per cent of budgeted profit. The chief executive may feel that this is too low to cause real concern.

The chief executive will now need to ask some questions as to why things went so badly wrong in several areas and what can be done to improve future performance.

Activity 7.12

Using the figures in Activity 7.4, try reconciling the original operating profit figure for June with the actual June figure.

	£	£
Budgeted operating profit		24,000
Add **Favourable variances**		
Sales volume	2,000	
Direct labour rate	480	
Fixed overhead spending	700	3,180
		27,180
Less **Adverse variances**		
Sales price	1,500	
Direct materials usage	300	
Direct labour efficiency	680	2,480
Actual operating profit		24,700

Activity 7.13

The following are the budgeted and actual income statements for Baxter Ltd for the month of July:

	Budget	Actual
Output	1,000 units	1,050 units
(production and sales)		
	£	£
Sales revenue	100,000	104,300
Raw materials	(40,000) (40,000 metres)	(41,200) (40,500 metres)
Labour	(20,000) (2,500 hours)	(21,300) (2,600 hours)
Fixed overheads	(20,000)	(19,400)
Operating profit	20,000	22,400

Produce a reconciliation of the budgeted and actual operating profit, going into as much detail as possible with the variance analysis.

The original budget, the flexed budget and the actual are as follows:

	Original budget	Flexed budget	Actual
Output	1,000 units	1,050 units	1,050 units
(production and sales)			
	£	£	£
Sales revenue	100,000	105,000	104,300
Raw materials	(40,000)	(42,000) (42,000 m)	(41,200) (40,500 m)
Labour	(20,000)	(21,000) (2,625 hrs)	(21,300) (2,600 hrs)
Fixed overheads	(20,000)	(20,000)	(19,400)
Operating profit	20,000	22,000	22,400

Reconciliation of the budgeted and actual operating profits for July

	£	£
Budgeted operating profit		20,000
Add **Favourable variances:**		
Sales volume (22,000 – 20,000)	2,000	
Direct materials usage [(42,000 – 40,500) × £1]	1,500	
Direct labour efficiency [(2,625 – 2,600) × £8]	200	
Fixed overhead spending (20,000 – 19,400)	600	4,300
		24,300
Less **Adverse variances:**		
Sales price (105,000 – 104,300)	700	
Direct materials price [(40,500 × £1) – 41,200]	700	
Direct labour rate [(2,600 × £8) – 21,300]	500	1,900
Actual operating profit		22,400

Real World 7.2 shows how two UK-based businesses, the retailer Next and airline British Airways, use variance analysis to exercise control over their operations. Many businesses explain in their annual reports how they operate systems of budgetary control.

REAL WORLD 7.2

Variance analysis in practice

What Next?

According to its annual report Next has the following arrangements:

> The Board is responsible for approving semi-annual Group budgets. Performance against budget is reported to the Board monthly and any substantial variances are explained.

BA at the controls

BA makes it clear that it too uses budgets and variance analysis to help keep control over its activities. The annual report says:

> A comprehensive management accounting system is in place providing management with financial and operational performance measurement indicators. Detailed management accounts are prepared monthly to cover each major area of the business. Variances from plan are analysed, explained and acted on in a timely manner.

The boards of directors of these businesses will not seek explanations of variances arising at each branch/flight/department, but they will be looking at figures for the businesses as a whole or the results for major divisions of them.

Equally certainly, branch/department managers will receive a monthly (or perhaps more frequent) report of variances arising within their area of responsibility alone.

Sources: Next plc Annual Report 2008, p. 24, and British Airways plc Annual Report 2008, p. 61.

Real World 7.3 gives some indication of the importance of flexible budgeting in practice.

REAL WORLD 7.3

Flexing the budgets

A recent study of the UK food and drinks industry by Abdel-Kader and Luther provides us with some insight as to the importance attached by management accountants to flexible budgeting. The study asked those in charge of the management accounting function to rate the importance of flexible budgeting by selecting one of three possible categories – 'not important', 'moderately important' or 'important'. Figure 7.6 sets out the results, from the sample of 117 respondents.

Figure 7.6	Degree of importance attached to flexible budgeting

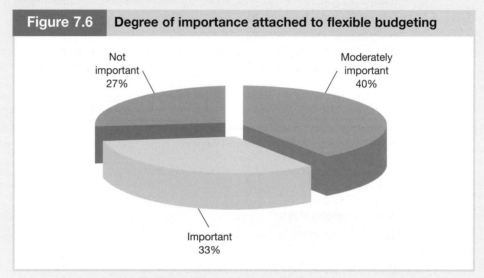

Respondents were also asked to state the frequency with which flexible budgeting was used within the business, using a five-point scale ranging from 1 (never) through to 5 (very often). Figure 7.7 sets out the results.

Figure 7.7	Frequency of use of flexible budgets

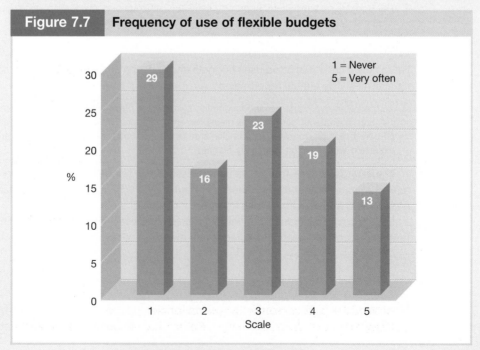

We can see that, whilst flexible budgeting is regarded as important by a significant proportion of management accountants and is being used in practice, not all businesses use it.

Source: Taken from information appearing in Abdel-Kader, M. and Luther, R., 'An empirical investigation of the evolution of management accounting practices', University of Essex Working paper no. 04/06, October 2004.

Reasons for adverse variances

One reason why adverse variances may occur is that the budgets against which performance is being measured are unachievable. This is always a possibility that should be considered when examining variances. Unless budgets are achievable, they are not a useful means of exercising control. However, there are certainly other reasons that may lead actual performance to deviate from budgeted performance.

Activity 7.14

The variances that we have considered are:

- sales volume
- sales price
- direct materials usage
- direct materials price
- direct labour efficiency
- direct labour rate
- fixed overhead spending.

Assuming that the budget targets are reasonable, jot down some possible reasons for adverse variances for each of the above occurring.

....

The reasons that we thought of included the following:

Sales volume
- Poor performance by sales staff.
- Deterioration in market conditions between the time that the budget was set and the actual event.
- Lack of goods or services to sell as a result of some production problem.

Sales price
- Poor performance by sales staff.
- Deterioration in market conditions between the time of setting the budget and the actual event.

Direct materials usage
- Poor performance by production department staff, leading to high rates of scrap.
- Substandard materials, leading to high rates of scrap.
- Faulty machinery, causing high rates of scrap.

Direct materials price
- Poor performance by the buying department staff.
- Using higher quality material than was planned.
- Change in market conditions between the time that the budget was set and the actual event.

Activity 7.14 continued

Labour efficiency
- Poor supervision.
- A worker with a low skill grade taking longer to do the work than was envisaged for the correct skill grade.
- Low-grade materials, leading to high levels of scrap and wasted labour time.
- Problems with a customer for whom a service is being rendered.
- Problems with machinery, leading to labour time being wasted.
- Dislocation of materials supply, leading to workers being unable to proceed with production.

Labour rate
- Poor performance by the human resources department.
- Using a higher grade of worker than was planned.
- Change in labour market conditions between the time of setting the budget and the actual event.

Fixed overheads
- Poor supervision of overheads.
- General increase in costs of overheads not taken into account in the budget.

Variance analysis in service industries

Although we have mainly used the example of a manufacturing business to explain variance analysis, this should not be taken to imply that variance analysis is not relevant and useful to service sector businesses. It is simply that manufacturing businesses tend to have all of the variances found in practice. Service businesses, for example, may not have material variances.

Real World 7.2 shows that BA, a very well-known service provider, uses budgets and variance analysis to help it to manage this complex organisation.

Non-operating profit variances

There are many areas of business that have a budget but where a failure to meet the budget does not have a direct effect on profit. Frequently, however, it has an indirect effect on profit and, sometimes, a profound effect. For example, the cash budget sets out the planned receipts, payments and resultant cash balance for the period. If the person responsible for the cash budget gets things wrong, or is forced to make unplanned expenditures, this could lead to unplanned cash shortages and accompanying costs. These costs might be limited to lost interest on possible investments, which could otherwise have been made, or to the need to pay overdraft interest. If the cash shortage cannot be covered by some form of borrowing, the consequences could be more profound, such as the loss of profits on business that was not able to be undertaken because of the lack of funds.

It is clearly necessary that control be exercised over areas such as cash management as well as over those like production and sales in an attempt to avoid adverse **non-operating profit variances**.

Investigating variances

It is unreasonable to expect budget targets to be met precisely each month and so variances will usually arise. Whatever the reason for a variance, finding out what went wrong can be costly. Reports and other information will have to be scrutinised, and discussions with individuals and groups may have to be carried out. In some cases, production may have to be stopped to discover what went wrong. Since small variances are almost inevitable, and investigating variances can be expensive, management needs to establish a policy concerning which variances to investigate and which to accept.

Activity 7.15

What broad approach do you feel should be taken as to whether to spend money investigating a particular variance?

The general approach to this policy must be concerned with cost and benefit. The benefit likely to be gained from knowing why a variance arose needs to be balanced against the cost of obtaining that knowledge. The issue of balancing the benefit of having information against its cost was discussed in Chapter 1, on p. 18. Unfortunately, however, both the cost of investigation and the value of the benefit are often difficult to assess in advance of the investigation.

Knowing the reason for a variance is valuable only in so far as it helps management to bring things back under control, thereby enabling future targets to be met. It should be borne in mind that variances should be either zero, or very close to zero. In other words, achieving targets, give or take small variances, should be the norm.

Broadly, we suggest the following approach to investigating variances:

1 Significant *adverse* variances should be investigated because the continuation of the fault that they represent could be very costly. Management must decide what 'significant' means. A certain amount of science, in the form of statistical models, can be used in making this decision. Ultimately, however, it must be a matter of managerial judgement as to what is significant. Perhaps variances above a threshold of around 5 per cent of the budgeted figure would be considered significant.

2 Significant *favourable* variances should probably be investigated as well as those that are unfavourable. Though such variances would not cause such immediate management concern as adverse ones, they still represent things not going according to plan. If actual performance is significantly better than target, it may well mean that the target is unrealistically low.

3 Insignificant variances, though not triggering immediate investigation, should be kept under review. For each aspect of operations, the cumulative sum of variances, over a series of control periods, should be zero, with small adverse variances in some periods being compensated for by small favourable ones in others. This is because small variances caused by random factors will not necessarily recur.

Where a variance is caused by systemic (non-random) factors, which will recur over time, the cumulative sum of the periodic variances will not be zero but an increasing figure. Even though the individual variances may be insignificant, the cumulative effect of these variances may not. Thus, an investigation may well be worthwhile, particularly if the variances are adverse.

To illustrate the cumulative effect of relatively small systemic variances, let us consider Example 7.2.

Example 7.2

Indisurers Ltd finds that the variances for direct labour efficiency for processing motor insurance claims, since the beginning of the year, are as follows:

	£
January	25 (adverse)
February	15 (favourable)
March	5 (favourable)
April	20 (adverse)
May	22 (adverse)
June	8 (favourable)
July	20 (adverse)
August	15 (favourable)
September	23 (adverse)
October	15 (favourable)
November	5 (favourable)
December	26 (adverse)

The average total cost of labour performing this task is about £1,200 a month. Management believes that none of these variances, taken alone, is significant given the monthly labour cost. The question is, are they significant when taken together? If we add them together, taking account of the signs, we find that we have a net adverse variance for the year of £73. Of itself this, too, is probably not significant, but we should expect the cumulative total to be close to zero where the variances are random. We might feel that a pattern is developing and, given long enough, a net adverse variance of significant size might build up.

Investigating the labour efficiency might be worth doing. Finding the cause of the variance would put management in a position to correct a systemic fault, which could lead to future cost savings. (We should note that twelve periods are probably not enough to reach a statistically sound conclusion on whether the variances are random or not, but it provides an illustration of the point.)

Plotting the cumulative variances, from month to month, as in Figure 7.8, makes it clear what is happening as time proceeds.

Figure 7.8	The cumulative variances for labour efficiency in motor insurance claim handling at Indisurers Ltd

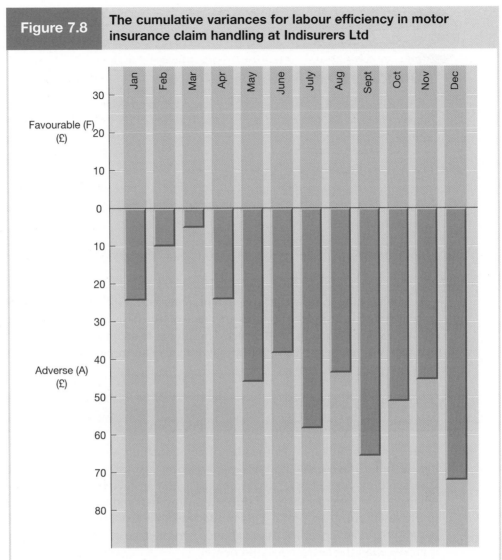

Starting at zero at the beginning of January, each month the cumulative variance is plotted. This is the sum taking account of positive and negative signs. The January figure is £25 (A). The February one is £10 (A) (that is, £25 (A) plus £15 (F)) and so on. The graph seems to show an overall trend of adverse variances, but with several favourable variances involved.

It is important to emphasise that the guidelines proposed for investigating variances are subject to the cost-benefit issues discussed at the beginning of this section. Thus, where the cost of investigating a variance, or the cost of correcting the underlying problem, is expected to be very high, managers may decide against investigating even a significant variance. They may calculate that it would be cheaper to live with the problem and so adjust the budget.

Real World 7.4 provides some insight to how managers determine whether to investigate variances in practice.

REAL WORLD 7.4

Deciding whether to investigate

The table shows the methods used by respondents to decide whether to investigate a particular variance. It is based on a research survey of UK manufacturing businesses by Drury and others.

	% 'Often' or 'Always'
Decisions based on managerial judgement	75
Variance exceeds a specific monetary amount	41
Variance exceeds a given percentage of the budgeted figure	36
Statistical models	3

Source: Reproduced from Drury, C., Braund, S., Osborne, P. and Tayles, M., *A Survey of Management Accounting Practices in UK Manufacturing Companies*, Chartered Association of Certified Accountants, 1993, p. 39, table 5.7.

It is interesting to note the large extent, revealed by this survey, to which decisions on whether to investigate variances are made on the basis of some, presumably subjective, judgement. We might have expected businesses to adopt a more systematic approach. The survey is not very recent, but it may well give an impression of current practice.

Compensating variances

There is superficial appeal in the idea of **compensating variances**. This involves trading off linked favourable and adverse variances against each other, without further consideration. For example, a sales manager may believe that it would be possible to sell more of a particular service if prices were lowered, and that this would feed through to increased operating profit. This would lead to a favourable sales volume variance, but also to an adverse sales price variance. On the face of it, provided that the former is greater than the latter, all would be well.

Activity 7.16

What possible reason is there why the sales manager mentioned above should not go ahead with the price reduction?

The change in policy will have ramifications for other areas of the business, including the following:

● The need for more provision of the service to be available to sell. Staff and other resources may not be available to supply this increase.
● Increased sales volumes would involve an increased need for finance to pay for increased activity, for example to pay additional staff costs.

Thus 'trading off' variances is not automatically acceptable, without a more far-reaching consultation and revision of plans.

Making budgetary control effective

→ It should be clear from what we have seen of **budgetary control** that a system, or a set of routines, must be put in place to enable the potential benefits to be gained. Most businesses that operate successful budgetary control systems tend to share some common features. These include the following:

1 *A serious attitude taken to the system.* This should apply to all levels of management, right from the very top. For example, senior managers need to make clear to junior managers that they take notice of the monthly variance reports and base some of their actions and decisions upon them.

2 *Clear demarcation between areas of managerial responsibility.* It needs to be clear which manager is responsible for each business area so that accountability can more easily be ascribed for any area that seems to be going out of control.

3 *Budget targets that are challenging yet achievable.* Setting unachievable targets is likely to have a demotivating effect. There may be a case for getting managers to participate in establishing their own targets to help create a sense of ownership. This, in turn, can increase the managers' commitment and motivation. We shall consider this in more detail shortly.

4 *Established data collection, analysis and reporting routines.* These should take the actual results and the budget figures, and calculate and report the variances. This should be part of the business's regular accounting information system, so that the required reports are automatically produced each month.

5 *Reports aimed at individual managers, rather than general-purpose documents.* This avoids managers having to wade through reams of reports to find the part that is relevant to them.

6 *Fairly short reporting periods.* These would typically be one month long, so that things cannot go too far wrong before they are picked up.

7 *Timely variance reports.* Reports should be produced and made available to managers shortly after the end of the relevant reporting period. If it is not until the end of June that a manager is informed that the performance in May was below the budgeted level, it is quite likely that the performance for June will be below target as well. Reports on the performance in May ideally need to emerge in early June.

8 *Action being taken to get operations back under control if they are shown to be out of control.* The report will not change things by itself. Managers need to take action to try to ensure that the reporting of significant adverse variances leads to action to put things right for the future.

Behavioural issues

Budgets are prepared with the objective of affecting the attitudes and behaviour of managers. The point was made in Chapter 6 that budgets are intended to motivate managers, and research evidence generally shows that budgets can be effective in achieving this. More specifically, the research shows:

● The existence of budgets can improve job satisfaction and performance. Where a manager's role is ill-defined or ambiguous, budgets can help bring structure and certainty. Budgets provide clear, quantifiable targets that must be pursued. This can be reassuring to managers and can increase their level of commitment.

- Demanding, yet achievable, budget targets tend to motivate better than less demanding targets. It seems that setting the most demanding targets that are acceptable to managers is a very effective way to motivate them.
- Unrealistically demanding targets tend to have an adverse effect on managers' performance. Once managers begin to view the budget targets as being too difficult to achieve, their level of motivation and performance declines. The relationship between the level of performance and the perceived degree of budget difficulty is shown in Figure 7.9.

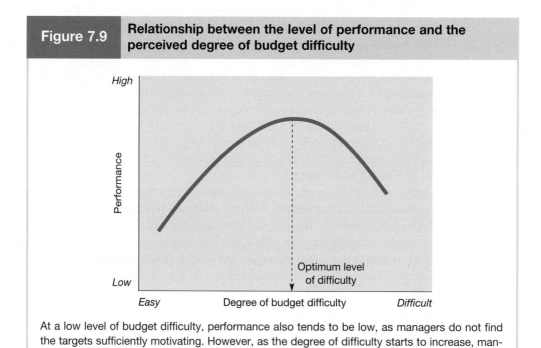

Figure 7.9 **Relationship between the level of performance and the perceived degree of budget difficulty**

At a low level of budget difficulty, performance also tends to be low, as managers do not find the targets sufficiently motivating. However, as the degree of difficulty starts to increase, managers rise to the challenge and improve their performance. Beyond a certain point, however, budgets are seen by managers as being too difficult to achieve, and so motivation and performance decline.

- The participation of managers in setting their targets tends to improve motivation and performance. This is probably because those managers feel a sense of commitment to the targets and a moral obligation to achieve them.

It has been suggested that allowing managers to set their own targets will lead to slack (that is, easily achievable targets) being introduced. This would make achievement of the target that much easier. On the other hand, in an effort to impress, a manager may select a target that is not really achievable. These points imply that care must be taken in the extent to which managers have unfettered choice of their own targets.

Conflict can occur in the budget-setting process, as different groups may well have different agendas. For example, junior managers may be keen to build slack into their budgets while their senior managers may seek to impose unrealistically demanding budget targets. Sometimes, such conflict can be constructive and can result in better decisions being made. To resolve the conflict over budget targets, negotiations may have to take place and other options may have to be explored. This may lead to a better understanding by all parties of the issues involved and final agreement may result in demanding, yet achievable, targets.

The impact of management style

There has been a great deal of discussion among experts on the way in which managers use information generated by the budgeting system and the impact of its use on the attitudes and behaviour of subordinates (that is, the staff). A pioneering study by Hopwood (see reference 1 at the end of the chapter) examined the way that managers working within a manufacturing environment used budget information to evaluate the performance of subordinates. He argued that three distinct styles of management could be observed. These are:

● *Budget-constrained style.* This management style focuses rigidly on the ability of subordinates to meet the budget. Other factors relating to the performance of subordinates are not given serious consideration even though they might include improving the long-term effectiveness of the area for which the subordinate has responsibility.
● *Profit-conscious style.* This management style uses budget information in a more flexible way and often in conjunction with other data. The main focus is on the ability of each subordinate to improve long-term effectiveness.
● *Non-accounting style.* In this case, budget information plays no significant role in the evaluation of a subordinate's performance.

Activity 7.17

How might a manager respond to budget information indicating that a subordinate has not met the budget targets for the period, assuming the manager adopts

(a) a budget-constrained style?
(b) a profit-conscious style?
(c) a non-accounting style?

....

(a) A manager adopting a budget-constrained style is likely to take the budget information very seriously. This may result in criticism of the subordinate and, perhaps, some form of sanction.
(b) A manager adopting a profit-conscious style is likely to take a broader view when examining the budget information and so will take other factors into consideration (for example, factors that could not have been anticipated at the time of preparing the budgets), before deciding whether criticism or punishment is justified.
(c) A manager adopting a non-accounting style will regard the failure to meet the budget as being relatively unimportant and so no action may be taken.

Hopwood found that subordinates working for a manager who adopts a budget-constrained style had unfortunate experiences. They suffered higher levels of job-related stress and had poorer working relationships, with both their colleagues and their manager, than those subordinates whose manager adopted one of the other two styles. Hopwood also found that the subordinates of a budget-constrained style of manager were more likely to manipulate the budget figures, or to take other undesirable actions, to ensure the budgets were met.

Reservations about the Hopwood study

Though Hopwood's findings are interesting, subsequent studies have cast doubt on their universal applicability. Later studies confirm that human attitudes and behaviour are complex and can vary according to the particular situation. For example, it has been found that the impact of different management styles on such factors as job-related stress and the manipulation of budget figures seems to vary. The impact is likely to depend on such factors as the level of independence enjoyed by the subordinates and the level of uncertainty associated with the tasks to be undertaken.

It seems that where there is a high level of interdependence between business divisions, subordinate managers are more likely to feel that they have less control over their performance, because the performance of staff in other divisions could be an important influence on the final outcome. In such a situation, rigid application of the budget could be viewed as being unfair and may lead to undesirable behaviour. However, where managers have a high degree of independence, the application of budgets as a measure of performance is likely to be more acceptable. In this case, the managers are likely to feel that the final outcome is much less dependent on the performance of others.

Later studies have also shown that where a subordinate is undertaking a task that has a high degree of uncertainty concerning the outcome (for example, developing a new product), budget targets are unlikely to be an adequate measure of performance. In such a situation, other factors and measures should be taken into account in order to derive a more complete assessment of performance. However, where a task has a low degree of uncertainty concerning the outcome (for example, producing a standard product using standard equipment and an experienced workforce), budget measures may be regarded as more reliable indicators of performance. Thus, it appears that a budget-constrained style is more likely to work where subordinates enjoy a fair amount of independence and where the tasks set have a low level of uncertainty concerning their outcomes.

Failing to meet the budget

The existence of budgets gives senior managers a ready means to assess the performance of their subordinates (that is, junior managers). If a junior manager fails to meet a budget, this must be dealt with carefully by the relevant senior manager. Adverse variances may imply that the manager needs help. If this is the case, a harsh, critical approach would have a demotivating effect and would be counterproductive.

 Real World 7.5 gives some indication of the effects of the **behavioural aspects of budgetary control** in practice.

 REAL WORLD 7.5

Behavioural issues explored

The survey by Drury and others referred to earlier indicates that there is a large degree of participation in setting budgets by those who will be expected to perform to the budget (the budget holders). It also indicates that senior managers have greater influence in setting the targets than their junior manager budget holders.

Where there is a conflict between the cost estimates submitted by the budget holders and their senior managers, in 40 per cent of respondent businesses the senior manager's view would prevail without negotiation, but in nearly 60 per cent of cases there would be a reduction that would be negotiated between the budget holder and the senior manager. The general philosophy of the businesses that responded to the survey, regarding budget holders influencing the setting of their own budgets, is:

- 23 per cent of respondents believe that budget holders should not have too much influence since they will seek to obtain easy budgets (build in slack) if they do;
- 69 per cent of respondents take an opposite view.

The general view on how senior managers should judge their subordinates is:

- 46 per cent of respondent businesses think that senior managers should judge junior managers mainly on their ability to achieve the budget;
- 40 per cent think otherwise.

Though this research is not very recent (1993), in the absence of more recent evidence it provides some feel for budget setting in practice.

Source: Drury, C., Braund, S., Osborne, P. and Tayles, M., *A Survey of Management Accounting Practices in UK Manufacturing Companies*, Chartered Association of Certified Accountants, 1993.

Self-assessment question 7.1

Toscanini Ltd makes a standard product, which is budgeted to sell at £4.00 a unit, in a competitive market. It is made by taking a budgeted 0.4 kg of material, budgeted to cost £2.40/kg, which is worked on by hand by an employee, paid a budgeted £8.00/hour, for a budgeted 6 minutes. Monthly fixed overheads are budgeted at £4,800. The output for May was budgeted at 4,000 units.

The actual results for May were as follows:

	£
Sales revenue (3,500 units)	13,820
Materials (1,425 kg)	(3,420)
Labour (345 hours)	(2,690)
Fixed overheads	(4,900)
Actual operating profit	2,810

No inventories of any description existed at the beginning and end of the month.

Required:
(a) Deduce the budgeted profit for May and reconcile it, through variances, with the actual profit in as much detail as the information provided will allow.
(b) State which manager should be held accountable, in the first instance, for each variance calculated.
(c) Assuming that the budget was well set and achievable, suggest at least one feasible reason for each of the variances that you identified in (a), given what you know about the business's performance for May.
(d) If it were discovered that the actual total world market demand for the business's product was 10 per cent lower than estimated when the May budget was set, explain how and why the variances that you identified in (a) could be revised to provide information that would be potentially more useful.

The answer to this question appears in Appendix B at the back of the book.

Standard quantities and costs

We have already seen that a budget is a business plan for the short term – typically one year – that is expressed mainly in financial terms. A budget is often constructed from standards. **Standard quantities and costs** (or revenues) are those planned for an individual unit of input or output and provide the building blocks for budgets.

We can say about Baxter Ltd's operations (see Example 7.1 on page 221) that:

● The standard selling price is £100 for one unit of output.
● The standard marginal cost for one manufactured unit is £60.
● The standard raw materials cost is £40 for one unit of output.
● The standard raw materials usage is 40 metres for one unit of output.
● The standard raw materials price is £1 a metre (that is, for one unit of input).
● The standard labour cost is £20 for one unit of output.
● The standard labour time is 2.5 hours for one unit of output.
● The standard labour rate is £8 an hour (that is, for one unit of input).

Standards, like the budgets to which they are linked, represent targets against which actual performance is measured. To maintain their usefulness for planning and control purposes, they should be subject to frequent review and, where necessary, revision. Standards provide the basis for variance analysis, which, as we have seen, helps managers to identify where deviations from planned, or standard, performance have occurred and the extent of those deviations.

Standard costs may be helpful to derive the planned cost for units of output (products or services) that are much larger than those produced by Baxter Ltd. For example, a firm of accountants may find standard costing useful. It may set standard costs for each grade of staff (audit manager, audit senior, trainee and so on). When planning a particular audit of a client business, it can assess how many hours each grade of staff should spend on the audit and, using the standard cost per hour for each grade of staff, it can derive a standard cost or 'budget' for the job as a whole. These standards can subsequently be compared with the actual hours and hourly rates.

Setting standards

When setting standards various points have to be considered. We shall now explore some of the more important of these.

Who sets the standards?

Standards often result from the collective effort of various individuals including management accountants, industrial engineers, human resource managers, production managers and employees. The manager responsible for meeting a particular standard will usually be involved and may be relied on to provide specialised knowledge. The manager may, therefore, have some influence over the final decision, which brings with it the risk that 'slack' may be built into the standard in order to make it easier to achieve. The same problem was mentioned earlier in relation to budgets.

How is information gathered?

Setting standards involves gathering information concerning how much material should be used, how much machine time should be required, how much direct labour time should be spent and so on. Two possible ways of collecting information for standard setting are available.

Activity 7.18

Can you think what these might be?

The first is to examine the particular processes and tasks involved in producing the product or service and to develop suitable estimates. Standards concerning material usage, machine time and direct labour hours may be established by carrying out dummy production runs, time-and-motion studies and so on. This will require close collaboration between the management accountant, industrial engineers and those involved in the production process.

The second approach is to collect information relating to past costs, times and usage for the same, or similar, products and to use this information as a basis for predicting the future. This information may have to be adjusted to reflect changes in price, changes in the production process and so on.

Where the product or service is entirely new or involves entirely new processes, the first approach will probably have to be used, even though it is usually more costly.

What kind of standards should be used?

There are basically two types of standards that may be used: **ideal standards** and **practical standards**. Ideal standards, as the name suggests, assume perfect operating conditions where there is no inefficiency due to lost production time, defects and so on. The objective of setting ideal standards, which are attainable in theory at least, is to encourage employees to strive towards excellence. Practical standards, also as the name suggests, do not assume ideal operating conditions. Although they demand a high level of efficiency, account is taken of possible lost production time, defects and so on. They are designed to be challenging yet achievable.

There are two major difficulties with using ideal standards.

1 They do not provide a useful basis for exercising control. Unless the standards set are realistic, any variances computed are extremely difficult to interpret.
2 They may not achieve their intended purpose of motivating managers: indeed, the opposite may occur. We saw earlier that the evidence suggests that where managers regard a target as beyond their grasp, it is likely to have a demotivating effect.

Given these problems, it is not surprising that practical standards seem to enjoy more widespread support than ideal standards.

Real World 7.6 provides some evidence on the use of ideal standards in practice.

REAL WORLD 7.6

Setting the standard

The study of UK manufacturers by Drury and others showed that only 5 per cent of respondents to the survey set standards at a level that could be achieved if everything went perfectly all of the time. Although the study is a little dated now (1993), it represents the most recent survey and is worth noting.

Source: Drury, C., Braund, S., Osborne, P. and Tayles, M., *A Survey of Management Accounting Practices in UK Manufacturing Companies*, Chartered Association of Certified Accountants, 1993.

The learning-curve effect

Where an activity undertaken by direct workers has been unchanged for some time, and the workers are experienced at performing it, the standard labour time will normally stay unchanged. However, where a new activity is introduced, or new workers are involved with performing an existing activity, a **learning-curve** effect will normally occur. This is shown in Figure 7.10.

Figure 7.10	The learning-curve effect

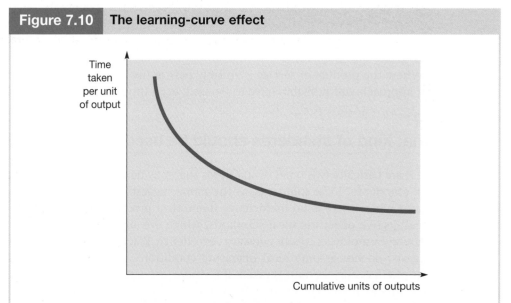

Each time a particular task is performed, people become quicker at it. This learning-curve effect becomes less and less significant until, after the task has been performed a number of times, no further learning occurs.

The first unit of output takes a long time to produce. As experience is gained, the worker takes less time to produce each unit of output. The rate of reduction in the time taken will, however, decrease as experience is gained. Thus, for example, the reduction in time taken between the first and second unit produced will be much bigger than the reduction between, say, the ninth and the tenth. Eventually, the rate of reduction in time taken will reduce to zero so that each unit will take as long as the preceding one.

At this point, the point where the curve in Figure 7.10 becomes horizontal (the bottom right of the graph), the learning-curve effect will have been eliminated and a steady, long-term standard time for the activity will have been established.

The learning-curve effect seems to have little to do with whether workers are skilled or unskilled; if they are unfamiliar with the task, the learning-curve effect will arise. Practical experience shows that learning curves show remarkable regularity and, therefore, predictability from one activity to another.

The learning curve effect applies equally well to activities involved with providing a service (such as dealing with an insurance claim, in an insurance business) as to manufacturing-type activities (for example, upholstering an armchair by hand, in a furniture-making business).

Clearly, the learning-curve effect must be taken into account when setting standards, and when interpreting any adverse labour efficiency variances, where a new process and/or new staff are involved.

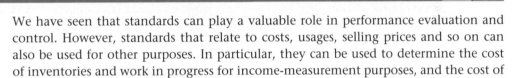

Other uses for standard costing

We have seen that standards can play a valuable role in performance evaluation and control. However, standards that relate to costs, usages, selling prices and so on can also be used for other purposes. In particular, they can be used to determine the cost of inventories and work in progress for income-measurement purposes, and the cost of items for use in pricing decisions.

Real World 7.7 provides some information on the use of standards in practice.

REAL WORLD 7.7

Standards in practice

The survey by Drury and others showed that respondent businesses found standards to be useful for the following purposes:

	Percentage of respondents
Cost control and performance evaluation	72
Valuing inventories and work in progress	80
Deducing costs for decision-making purposes	62
To help in constructing budgets	69

Source: Drury, C., Braund, S., Osborne, P. and Tayles, M., *A Survey of Management Accounting Practices in UK Manufacturing Companies*, Chartered Association of Certified Accountants, 1993.

Some problems . . .

Although standards and variances may be useful for decision-making purposes, they have limited application. Many business and commercial activities do not have direct relationships between inputs and outputs as is the case with, say, the number of direct labour hours worked and the number of products manufactured. Many expenses of modern business are in areas such as human resource development and advertising, where the expense is discretionary and there is no direct link to the level of output.

There are also potential problems when applying standard costing techniques. These include the following:

1 Standards can quickly become out of date as a result of both changes in the production process and price changes. Standards should, therefore, be frequently monitored and updated where necessary. Although this can be costly, it is essential if standards are to be effective for control purposes. When standards become outdated, performance can be adversely affected. For example, a human resources manager who recognises that it is impossible to meet targets on rates of pay for labour, because of general labour cost rises, may have less incentive to minimise costs.

2 Factors over which a particular manager has no control may affect a variance for which that manager is held accountable. When assessing the manager's performance, these uncontrollable factors should be taken into account but there is always a risk that they will not.

3 In practice, creating clear lines of demarcation between the areas of responsibility of various managers may be difficult. In this case, one of the prerequisites of effective standard costing is lost.

4 Once a standard has been met, there is no incentive for employees to improve the quality or quantity of output further. There are usually no additional rewards for doing so; only additional work. Indeed, employees may have a disincentive for exceeding a standard as it may then be viewed by managers as too loose and therefore in need of tightening. However, simply achieving a standard, and no more, may not be enough in highly competitive and fast-changing markets. To compete effectively, a business may need to strive for continuous improvement, and standard costing techniques may impede this process.

5 Standard costing may create incentives for managers and employees to act in undesirable ways. It may, for example, encourage the build up of excess inventories, leading to significant storage and financing costs. This problem can arise where there are opportunities for discounts on bulk purchases of materials, which the purchasing manager then exploits to achieve a favourable direct materials price variance. One way to avoid this problem might be to impose limits on the level of inventories held.

Activity 7.19

Can you think of another example of how a manager may achieve a favourable direct materials price variance but in doing so would create problems for a business?

A manager may buy cheaper, but lower quality, materials. Although this may lead to a favourable price variance, it may also lead to additional inspection and reworking costs, and perhaps lost sales.

To avoid this problem, the manager may be required to buy material of a particular quality or from particular sources.

A final example of the perverse incentives created by standard costing relates to labour efficiency variances. Where these variances are calculated for individual employees, and form the basis for their rewards, there is little incentive for them to work co-operatively. However, co-operative working may be in the best interests of the business. To avoid this problem, some businesses calculate labour efficiency variances for groups of employees rather than individual employees. This, however, creates the risk that some individuals will become 'free riders' and will rely on the more conscientious employees to carry the load.

Activity 7.20

How might the business try to eliminate the 'free-rider' problem just mentioned?

One way would be to carry out an evaluation, perhaps by the group members themselves, of individual contributions to group output, as well as evaluating group output as a whole.

The new business environment

The traditional standard costing approach was developed during an era when business operations were characterised by few product lines, long production runs and heavy reliance on direct labour. More recently, the increasingly competitive environment and the onward march of technology have changed the business landscape. Now, many business operations are characterised by a wide range of different products, shorter product life cycles (leading to shorter production runs) and automated production processes. The effect of these changes has resulted in

● More frequent development of standards to deal with frequent changes to the product range.
● A change in the focus for control. Where manufacturing systems are automated, for example, direct labour becomes less important than direct materials.
● A decline in the importance of monitoring from cost and usage variances. Where manufacturing systems are automated, deviations from standards relating to costs and usage become less frequent and less significant.

Thus, where a business has highly automated production systems, traditional standard costing, with its emphasis on costs and usage, is likely to take on less importance. Other elements of the production process such as quality, production levels, product cycle times, delivery times and the need for continuous improvement become the focus of attention. This does not mean, however, that a standards-based approach is not useful for the new manufacturing environment. It can still provide valuable control information and there is no reason why standard costing systems cannot be redesigned to reflect a concern for some of the elements mentioned earlier. Nevertheless, other measures, including non-financial ones, may help to augment the information provided by the standard costing system. We shall consider this issue in more detail in Chapter 10.

Real World 7.8 indicates that, despite the problems mentioned above, standard costing is used by businesses. However, the extent to which particular standard costing variances are calculated and considered appears to vary.

REAL WORLD 7.8

Standard practice

A study was carried out involving interviews with senior financial managers of businesses. Standard costing was used by 30 of the businesses in the study, which represented most of the businesses that might be expected to do so. The popularity among these businesses of standards for each of the main cost items is set out in Figure 7.11.

Figure 7.11	The popularity of standards in practice

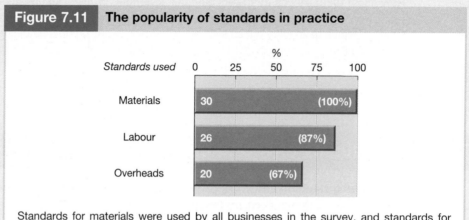

Standards for materials were used by all businesses in the survey, and standards for labour were used by nearly all businesses.

Despite the universal use of materials standards, the study found that four businesses calculated the total direct materials variance only and that only two-thirds of businesses calculated both the direct materials price and usage variances. For labour standards, the variance analysis is even less complete. The study found that 15 businesses calculated the total direct labour variance only and only one-third of businesses calculated both the direct labour and efficiency variances. It seems, therefore, that standard costing was not extensively employed by the businesses.

Source: Figure based on information in Dugdale, D., Jones, C. and Green, S., *Contemporary Management Accounting Practices in UK Manufacturing*, Elsevier, 2006.

SUMMARY

The main points of this chapter may be summarised as follows:

Controlling through budgets

● Budgets act as a system of both feedback and feedforward control.
● To exercise control, budgets can be flexed to match actual volume of output.

Variance analysis

● Variances may be favourable or adverse according to whether they result in an increase to, or decrease from, the budgeted profit figure.

- Budgeted profit plus all favourable variances less all adverse variances equals actual profit.
- Commonly calculated variances:
  - Sales volume variance = difference between the original and flexed budget profit figures.
  - Sales price variance = difference between actual sales revenue and actual volume at the standard sales price.
  - Total direct materials variance = difference between the actual direct materials cost and the direct materials cost according to the flexed budget.
  - Direct materials usage variance = difference between actual usage and budgeted usage, for the actual volume of output, multiplied by the standard materials cost.
  - Direct materials price variance = difference between the actual materials cost and the actual usage multiplied by the standard materials cost.
  - Total direct labour variance = The difference between the actual direct labour cost and the direct labour cost according to the flexed budget.
  - Direct labour efficiency variance = difference between actual labour time and budgeted time, for the actual volume of output, multiplied by the standard labour rate.
  - Direct labour rate variance = difference between the actual labour cost and the actual labour time multiplied by the standard labour rate.
  - Fixed overhead spending variance = difference between the actual and budgeted spending on fixed overheads.
- Significant and/or persistent variances should normally be investigated to establish their cause. However, the costs and benefits of investigating variances must be considered.
- Trading off favourable variances against linked adverse variances should not be automatically acceptable.
- Not all activities can usefully be controlled through traditional variance analysis.

Effective budgetary control

- Good budgetary control requires establishing systems and routines to ensure such things as a clear distinction between individual managers' areas of responsibility; prompt, frequent and relevant variance reporting; and senior management commitment.
- There are behavioural aspects of control relating to management style, participation in budget setting and the failure to meet budget targets that should be taken into account by senior managers.

Standard costing

- Standards = budgeted physical quantities and financial values for one unit of inputs and outputs.
- There are two types of standards: ideal standards and practical standards.
- Information necessary for developing standards can be gathered by analysing the task or by using past data.
- There tends to be a learning-curve effect: routine tasks are performed more quickly with experience.
- Standards are useful in providing data for income measurement and pricing decisions.
- Standards have their limitations, particularly in modern manufacturing environments, however, they are still widely used.

→ **Key terms**

References

1 Hopwood, A. G., 'An empirical study of the role of accounting data in performance evaluation', *Empirical Research in Accounting*, a supplement to the *Journal of Accounting Research*, 1972, pp. 156–82.

Further reading

If you would like to explore the topics covered in this chapter in more depth, we recommend the following books:

Atkinson, A., Kaplan, R., Young, S. M. and Matsumura, E., *Management Accounting*, 5th edn, Prentice Hall, 2007, chapter 12.

Drury C., *Management and Cost Accounting*, 7th edn, Thomson Learning Business Press, 2008, chapters 16–18.

Bhimani, A., Horngren, C., Datar, S. and Foster, G., *Management and Cost Accounting*, 4th edn, FT Prentice Hall 2008, chapters 14–16.

Hilton, R., *Managerial Accounting*, 6th edn, McGraw-Hill Irwin, 2005, chapter 10.

REVIEW QUESTIONS

Answers to these questions can be found in Appendix D at the back of the book.

7.1 Explain what is meant by feedforward control and distinguish it from feedback control.

7.2 What is meant by a variance? What is the point in analysing variances?

7.3 What is the point in flexing the budget in the context of variance analysis? Does flexing imply that differences between budget and actual in the volume of output are ignored in variance analysis?

7.4 Should all variances be investigated to find their cause? Explain your answer.

EXERCISES

Exercises 7.4 to 7.8 are more advanced than 7.1 to 7.3. Those with coloured numbers have answers in Appendix D at the back of the book. If you wish to try more exercises, visit the students' side of the Companion Website at www.pearsoned.co.uk/atrillmclaney.

7.1 You have recently overheard the following remarks:

(a) 'A favourable direct labour rate variance can only be caused by staff working more efficiently than budgeted.'

(b) 'Selling more units than budgeted, because the units were sold at less than standard price, automatically leads to a favourable sales volume variance.'

(c) 'Using below-standard materials will tend to lead to adverse materials usage variances but cannot affect labour variances.'

(d) 'Higher-than-budgeted sales could not possibly affect the labour rate variance.'

(e) 'An adverse sales price variance can only arise from selling a product at less than standard price.'

Required:
Critically assess these remarks, explaining any technical terms.

7.2 Pilot Ltd makes a standard product, which is budgeted to sell at £5.00 a unit. It is made by taking a budgeted 0.5 kg of material, budgeted to cost £3.00 a kilogram, and working on it by hand by an employee, paid a budgeted £10.00 an hour, for a budgeted $7^1/_2$ minutes. Monthly fixed overheads are budgeted at £6,000. The output for March was budgeted at 5,000 units.

The actual results for March were as follows:

	£
Sales revenue (5,400 units)	26,460
Materials (2,830 kg)	(8,770)
Labour (650 hours)	(6,885)
Fixed overheads	(6,350)
Actual operating profit	4,455

No inventories existed at the start or end of March.

Required:
(a) Deduce the budgeted profit for March and reconcile it with the actual profit in as much detail as the information provided will allow.

(b) State which manager should be held accountable, in the first instance, for each variance calculated.

7.3 Antonio plc makes Product X, the standard costs of which are:

	£
Sales revenue	31
Direct labour (1 hour)	(11)
Direct materials (1 kg)	(10)
Fixed overheads	(3)
Standard profit	7

The budgeted output for March was 1,000 units of Product X; the actual output was 1,100 units, which was sold for £34,950. There were no inventories at the start or end of March. The actual production costs were:

	£
Direct labour (1,075 hours)	12,210
Direct materials (1,170 kg)	11,630
Fixed overheads	3,200

Required:
Calculate the variances for March as fully as you are able from the available information, and use them to reconcile the budgeted and actual profit figures.

7.4 You have recently overheard the following remarks:

(a) 'When calculating variances, we in effect ignore differences of volume of output, between original budget and actual, by flexing the budget. If there were a volume difference, it is water under the bridge by the time that the variances come to be calculated.'
(b) 'It is very valuable to calculate variances because they will tell you what went wrong.'
(c) 'All variances should be investigated to find their cause.'
(d) 'Research evidence shows that the more demanding the target, the more motivated the manager.'
(e) 'Most businesses do not have feedforward controls of any type, just feedback controls through budgets.'

Required:
Critically assess these remarks, explaining any technical terms.

7.5 Bradley-Allen Ltd makes one standard product. Its budgeted operating statement for May is as follows:

		£	£
Sales (volume and revenue):	800 units		64,000
Direct materials:	Type A	(12,000)	
	Type B	(16,000)	
Direct labour:	skilled	(4,000)	
	unskilled	(10,000)	
Overheads:	(all fixed)	(12,000)	
			(54,000)
Budgeted operating profit			10,000

The standard costs were as follows:

- Direct materials: Type A   £50/kg
                         Type B   £20/m
- Direct labour: skilled   £10/hour
                    unskilled   £8/hour

During May, the following occurred:

(1) 950 units were sold for a total of £73,000.
(2) 310 kilos (costing £15,200) of Type A material were used in production.
(3) 920 metres (costing £18,900) of Type B material were used in production.
(4) Skilled workers were paid £4,628 for 445 hours.
(5) Unskilled workers were paid £11,275 for 1,375 hours.
(6) Fixed overheads cost £11,960.

There were no inventories of finished production or of work in progress at either the beginning or end of May.

Required:
(a) Prepare a statement that reconciles the budgeted to the actual profit of the business for May, through variances. Your statement should analyse the difference between the two profit figures in as much detail as you are able.
(b) Explain how the statement in (a) might be helpful to managers.

7.6   Mowbray Ltd makes and sells one product, the standard costs of which are as follows:

	£
Direct materials (3 kg at £2.50/kg)	(7.50)
Direct labour (15 minutes at £9.00/hr)	(2.25)
Fixed overheads	(3.60)
	(13.35)
Selling price	20.00
Standard profit margin	6.65

The monthly production and sales are planned to be 1,200 units.
   The actual results for May were as follows:

	£
Sales revenue	18,000
Direct materials	(7,400) (2,800 kg)
Direct labour	(2,300) (255 hr)
Fixed overheads	(4,100)
Operating profit	4,200

There were no inventories at the start or end of May. As a result of poor sales demand during May, the business reduced the price of all sales by 10 per cent.

Required:
Calculate the budgeted profit for May and reconcile it to the actual profit through variances, going into as much detail as is possible from the information available.

7.7   Varne Chemprocessors is a business that specialises in plastics. It uses a standard costing system to monitor and report its purchases and usage of materials. During the most recent month, accounting period six, the purchase and usage of chemical UK194 were as follows:

Purchases/usage:	28,100 litres
Total price:	£51,704

Because of fire risk and the danger to health, no inventories are held by the business.
   UK194 is used solely in the manufacture of a product called Varnelyne. The standard cost specification shows that, for the production of 5,000 litres of Varnelyne, 200 litres of UK194 are needed at a total standard cost of £392. During period six, 637,500 litres of Varnelyne were produced.

Price variances, over recent periods, for two other raw materials used by the business are as follows:

Period	UK500		UK800	
	£		£	
1	301	F	298	F
2	251	A	203	F
3	102	F	52	A
4	202	A	98	A
5	153	F	150	A
6	103	A	201	A

where F = favourable variance and A = adverse variance.

Required:

(a) Calculate the price and usage variances for UK194 for period six.

(b) The following comment was made by the production manager:

'I knew at the beginning of period six that UK194 would be cheaper than the standard cost specification, so I used rather more of it than normal; this saved £4,900 on other chemicals.'

What changes do you need to make in your analysis for (a) as a result of this comment?

(c) Calculate for both UK500 and UK800, the cumulative price variances and comment briefly on the results.

7.8 Brive plc has the following standards for its only product:

Selling price:	£110/unit
Direct labour:	1 hour at £10.50/hour
Direct material:	3 kg at £14.00/kg
Fixed overheads:	£27.00/unit, based on a budgeted output of 800 units/month

During May, there was an actual output of 850 units and the operating statement for the month was as follows:

	£
Sales revenue	92,930
Direct labour (890 hours)	(9,665)
Direct materials (2,410 kg)	(33,258)
Fixed overheads	(21,365)
Operating profit	28,642

There were no inventories of any description at the beginning or end of May.

Required:

Prepare the original budget and a budget flexed to the actual volume. Use these to compare the budgeted and actual profits of the business for the month, going into as much detail with your analysis as the information given will allow.

8

Making capital investment decisions

INTRODUCTION

This chapter looks at how proposed investments in new plant, machinery, buildings and other long-term assets should be evaluated. This is a very important area for businesses; expensive and far-reaching consequences can flow from bad investment decisions.

We shall also consider the problem of risk and how this may be taken into account when evaluating investment proposals. Finally, we shall discuss the ways that managers can oversee capital investment projects and how control may be exercised throughout the life of a project.

LEARNING OUTCOMES

When you have completed this chapter, you should be able to:

- Explain the nature and importance of investment decision making.

- Identify the four main investment appraisal methods found in practice.

- Discuss the strengths and weaknesses of various techniques for dealing with risk in investment appraisal.

- Explain the methods used to monitor and control investment projects.

The nature of investment decisions

The essential feature of investment decisions is *time*. Investment involves making an outlay of something of economic value, usually cash, at one point in time, which is expected to yield economic benefits to the investor at some other point in time. Usually, the outlay precedes the benefits. Also, the outlay is typically one large amount and the benefits arrive as a series of smaller amounts over a fairly protracted period.

Investment decisions tend to be of profound importance to the business because

- *Large amounts of resources are often involved.* Many investments made by businesses involve laying out a significant proportion of their total resources (see **Real World 8.2**). If mistakes are made with the decision, the effects on the businesses could be significant, if not catastrophic.
- *It is often difficult and/or expensive to bail out of an investment once it has been undertaken.* It is often the case that investments made by a business are specific to its needs. For example, a hotel business may invest in a new, custom-designed hotel complex. The specialist nature of this complex will probably lead to its having a rather limited second-hand value to another potential user with different needs. If the business found, after having made the investment, that room occupancy rates were not as buoyant as was planned, the only possible course of action might be to close down and sell the complex. This would probably mean that much less could be recouped from the investment than it had originally cost, particularly if the costs of design are included as part of the cost, as they logically should be.

Real World 8.1 gives an illustration of a major investment by a well-known business operating in the UK.

REAL WORLD 8.1

Brittany Ferries launches an investment

Brittany Ferries, the cross-Channel ferry operator, recently had a new ship built, to be named *Armorique*. The ship cost the business about €81m and is used on the Plymouth to Roscoff route as from Spring 2009. Although Brittany Ferries is a substantial business, this level of expenditure was significant. Clearly, the business believed that acquisition of the new ship would be profitable for it, but how would it have reached this conclusion? Presumably the anticipated future cash flows from passengers and freight operators will have been major inputs to the decision. The ship was specifically designed for Brittany Ferries, so it would be difficult for the business to recoup a large proportion of its €81m should these projected cash flows not materialise.

Source: 'New €81m passenger cruise-ferry to be named "Armorique" ', www.brittany-ferries.co.uk.

The issues raised by Brittany Ferries' investment will be the main subject of this chapter.

Real World 8.2 indicates the level of annual net investment for a number of randomly selected, well-known UK businesses. It can be seen that the scale of investment varies from one business to another. (It also tends to vary from one year to the next for a particular business.) In nearly all of these businesses the scale of investment is very significant.

REAL WORLD 8.2

The scale of investment by UK businesses

	Expenditure on additional non-current assets as a percentage of:	
	Annual sales revenue	End-of-year non-current assets
BT plc (telecommunications)	15.9	17.5
Babcock International Group plc (support services)	6.8	20.6
Tesco plc (supermarkets)	5.5	11.6
J D Wetherspoon plc (pub operator)	12.5	9.0
Marks and Spencer plc (stores)	7.6	14.4
National Grid plc (utilities)	48.0	19.8
J. Sainsbury plc (supermarkets)	4.0	8.9
First Group plc (passenger transport)	5.7	13.1

Source: Annual reports of the businesses concerned for the financial year ending in 2007.

Real World 8.2 is limited to considering the non-current asset investment, but most non-current asset investment also requires a level of current asset investment to support it (additional inventories, for example), meaning that the real scale of investment is even greater, typically considerably so, than indicated above.

Activity 8.1

When managers are making decisions involving capital investments, what should the decisions seek to achieve?

Investment decisions must be consistent with the objectives of the particular business. For a private sector business, maximising the wealth of the owners (shareholders) is usually assumed to be the key financial objective.

Investment appraisal methods

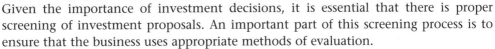

Given the importance of investment decisions, it is essential that there is proper screening of investment proposals. An important part of this screening process is to ensure that the business uses appropriate methods of evaluation.

Research shows that there are basically four methods used in practice by businesses throughout the world to evaluate investment opportunities. They are:

- accounting rate of return (ARR)
- payback period (PP)
- net present value (NPV)
- internal rate of return (IRR).

It is possible to find businesses that use variants of these four methods. It is also possible to find businesses, particularly smaller ones, that do not use any formal appraisal method but rely instead on the 'gut feeling' of their managers. Most businesses, however, seem to use one (or more) of these four methods.

We are going to assess the effectiveness of each of these methods and we shall see that only one of them (NPV) is a wholly logical approach. The other three all have flaws. We shall also see how popular these four methods seem to be in practice.

To help us to examine each of the methods, it might be useful to consider how each of them would cope with a particular investment opportunity. Let us consider the following example.

Example 8.1

Billingsgate Battery Company has carried out some research that shows that the business could provide a standard service that it has recently developed.

Provision of the service would require investment in a machine that would cost £100,000, payable immediately. Sales of the service would take place throughout the next five years. At the end of that time, it is estimated that the machine could be sold for £20,000.

Inflows and outflows from sales of the service would be expected to be as follows:

Time		£000
Immediately	Cost of machine	(100)
1 year's time	Operating profit before depreciation	20
2 years' time	Operating profit before depreciation	40
3 years' time	Operating profit before depreciation	60
4 years' time	Operating profit before depreciation	60
5 years' time	Operating profit before depreciation	20
5 years' time	Disposal proceeds from the machine	20

Note that, broadly speaking, the operating profit before deducting depreciation (that is, before non-cash items) equals the net amount of cash flowing into the business. Apart from depreciation, all of this business's expenses cause cash to flow out of the business. Sales revenues lead to cash flowing in. If, for the time being, we assume that inventories, trade receivables and trade payables remain constant, operating profit before depreciation will equal the cash inflow.

To simplify matters, we shall assume that the cash from sales and for the expenses of providing the service are received and paid, respectively, at the end of each year. This is clearly unlikely to be true in real life. Money will have to be paid to employees (for salaries and wages) on a weekly or a monthly basis. Customers will pay within a month or two of buying the service. On the other hand, making the assumption probably does not lead to a serious distortion. It is a simplifying assumption that is often made in real life, and it will make things more straightforward for us now. We should be clear, however, that there is nothing about any of the four methods that *demands* that this assumption is made.

Having set up the example, we shall now go on to consider how each of the appraisal methods works.

Accounting rate of return (ARR)

→ The **accounting rate of return (ARR)** method takes the average accounting operating profit that the investment will generate and expresses it as a percentage of the average investment made over the life of the project. Thus:

$$\text{ARR} = \frac{\textbf{Average annual operating profit}}{\textbf{Average investment to earn that profit}} \times 100\%$$

We can see from the equation that, to calculate the ARR, we need to deduce two pieces of information about the particular project:

● the annual average operating profit; and
● the average investment.

In our example, the average annual operating profit *before depreciation* over the five years is £40,000 (that is, £000(20 + 40 + 60 + 60 + 20)/5). Assuming 'straight-line' depreciation (that is, equal annual amounts), the annual depreciation charge will be £16,000 (that is, £(100,000 – 20,000)/5). Thus the average annual operating profit *after depreciation* is £24,000 (that is, £40,000 – £16,000).

The average investment over the five years can be calculated as follows:

$$\text{Average investment} = \frac{\text{Cost of machine} + \text{Disposal value}}{2}$$

$$= \frac{£100,000 + £20,000}{2}$$

$$= £60,000$$

Thus, the ARR of the investment is

$$\text{ARR} = \frac{£24,000}{£60,000} \times 100\% = 40\%$$

Users of ARR should apply the following decision rules:

● For any project to be acceptable it must achieve a target ARR as a minimum.
● Where there are competing projects that all seem capable of exceeding this minimum rate (that is, where the business must choose between more than one project), the one with the higher (or highest) ARR would normally be selected.

To decide whether the 40 per cent return is acceptable, we need to compare this percentage return with the minimum rate required by the business.

Activity 8.2

Chaotic Industries is considering an investment in a fleet of ten delivery vans to take its products to customers. The vans will cost £15,000 each to buy, payable immediately. The annual running costs are expected to total £20,000 for each van (including the driver's salary). The vans are expected to operate successfully for six years, at the end of which period they will all have to be sold, with disposal proceeds expected to be about £3,000 a van. At present, the business uses a commercial carrier for all of its deliveries. It is expected that this carrier will charge a total of £230,000 each year for the next six years to undertake the deliveries.

What is the ARR of buying the vans? (Note that cost savings are as relevant a benefit from an investment as are net cash inflows.)

The vans will save the business £30,000 a year (that is, £230,000 – (£20,000 × 10)), before depreciation, in total. Thus, the inflows and outflows will be:

Time		£000
Immediately	Cost of vans (10 × £15,000)	(150)
1 year's time	Net saving before depreciation	30
2 years' time	Net saving before depreciation	30
3 years' time	Net saving before depreciation	30
4 years' time	Net saving before depreciation	30
5 years' time	Net saving before depreciation	30
6 years' time	Net saving before depreciation	30
6 years' time	Disposal proceeds from the vans (10 × £3,000)	30

The total annual depreciation expense (assuming a straight-line method) will be £20,000 (that is, (£150,000 – £30,000)/6). Thus, the average annual saving, after depreciation, is £10,000 (that is, £30,000 – £20,000).

The average investment will be

$$\text{Average investment} = \frac{£150,000 + £30,000}{2} = £90,000$$

and the ARR of the investment is

$$\text{ARR} = \frac{£10,000}{£90,000} \times 100\% = 11.1\%$$

ARR and ROCE

We should note that ARR and the return on capital employed (ROCE) ratio take the same approach to performance measurement, in that they both relate accounting profit to the cost of the assets invested to generate that profit. ROCE is a popular means of assessing the performance of a business, as a whole, *after* it has performed. ARR is an approach that assesses the potential performance of a particular investment, taking the same approach as ROCE, but *before* it has performed.

As we have just seen, managers using ARR will require that any investment undertaken should achieve a target ARR as a minimum. Perhaps the minimum target ROCE would be based on the rate that previous investments had actually achieved (as measured by ROCE). Perhaps it would be the industry-average ROCE.

Since private sector businesses are normally seeking to increase the wealth of their owners, ARR may seem to be a sound method of appraising investment opportunities. Operating profit can be seen as a net increase in wealth over a period, and relating it to the size of investment made to achieve it seems a logical approach.

ARR is said to have a number of advantages as a method of investment appraisal. It was mentioned earlier that ROCE seems to be a widely used measure of business performance. Shareholders seem to use this ratio to evaluate management performance, and sometimes the financial objective of a business will be expressed in terms of a target ROCE. It therefore seems sensible to use a method of investment appraisal that is consistent with this overall approach to measuring business performance. It also gives the result expressed as a percentage. It seems that many managers feel comfortable using measures expressed in percentage terms.

Problems with ARR

Activity 8.3

ARR suffers from a very major defect as a means of assessing investment opportunities. Can you reason out what this is? Consider the three competing projects whose profits are shown below. All three involve investment in a machine that is expected to have no residual value at the end of the five years. Note that all of the projects have the same total operating profits over the five years.

Time		Project A £000	Project B £000	Project C £000
Immediately	Cost of machine	(160)	(160)	(160)
1 year's time	Operating profit after depreciation	20	10	160
2 years' time	Operating profit after depreciation	40	10	10
3 years' time	Operating profit after depreciation	60	10	10
4 years' time	Operating profit after depreciation	60	10	10
5 years' time	Operating profit after depreciation	20	160	10

(*Hint*: The defect is not concerned with the ability of the decision maker to forecast future events, although this too can be a problem. Try to remember the essential feature of investment decisions, which we identified at the beginning of this chapter.)

The problem with ARR is that it almost completely ignores the time factor. In this example, exactly the same ARR would have been computed for each of the three projects.

Since the same total operating profit over the five years (£200,000) arises in all three of these projects, and the average investment in each project is £80,000 (that is, £160,000/2), this means that each case will give rise to the same ARR of 50 per cent (that is, £40,000/ £80,000).

Given a financial objective of maximising the wealth of the owners of the business, any rational decision maker faced with a choice between the three projects set out in Activity 8.3 would strongly prefer Project C. This is because most of the benefits from the investment arise within twelve months of investing the £160,000 to establish the project. Project A would rank second and Project B would come a poor third. Any appraisal technique that is not capable of distinguishing between these three situations is seriously flawed. We shall look at why timing is so important later in the chapter.

There are further problems associated with the use of ARR. One of these problems concerns the approach taken to derive the average investment in a project.

Example 8.2 illustrates the daft result that ARR can produce.

Example 8.2

George put forward an investment proposal to his boss. The business uses ARR to assess investment proposals using a minimum 'hurdle' rate of 27 per cent. Details of the proposal were as follows:

Cost of equipment	£200,000
Estimated residual value of equipment	£40,000
Average annual operating profit before depreciation	£48,000
Estimated life of project	10 years
Annual straight-line depreciation charge	£16,000 (that is, (£200,000 – £40,000)/10)

The ARR of the project will be:

$$ARR = \frac{48,000 - 16,000}{(200,000 + 40,000)/2} \times 100\% = 26.7\%$$

The boss rejected George's proposal because it failed to achieve an ARR of at least 27 per cent. Although George was disappointed, he realised that there was still hope. In fact, all that the business had to do was to give away the piece of equipment at the end of its useful life rather than to sell it. The residual value of the equipment then became zero and the annual depreciation charge became ([£200,000 – £0]/10) = £20,000 a year. The revised ARR calculation was then as follows:

$$ARR = \frac{48,000 - 20,000}{(200,000 + 0)/2} \times 100\% = 28\%$$

ARR is based on the use of accounting profit. When measuring performance over the whole life of a project, however, it is cash flows rather than accounting profits that are important. Cash is the ultimate measure of the economic wealth generated by an investment. This is because it is cash that is used to acquire resources and for distribution to owners. Accounting profit, on the other hand is more appropriate for reporting achievement on a periodic basis. It is a useful measure of productive effort for a relatively short period, such as a year or half year. It is really a question of 'horses for courses'. Accounting profit is fine for measuring performance over short periods, but cash is the appropriate measure when considering the performance over the life of a project.

The ARR method can also create problems when considering competing investments of different size.

Activity 8.4

Sinclair Wholesalers plc is currently considering opening a new sales outlet in Coventry. Two possible sites have been identified for the new outlet. Site A has an area of 30,000 sq m. It will require an average investment of £6m, and will produce an average operating profit of £600,000 a year. Site B has an area of 20,000 sq m. It will require an average investment of £4m, and will produce an average operating profit of £500,000 a year.

What is the ARR of each investment opportunity? Which site would you select, and why?

The ARR of Site A is £600,000/£6m = 10 per cent. The ARR of Site B is £500,000/£4m = 12.5 per cent. Thus, Site B has the higher ARR. However, in terms of the absolute operating profit generated, Site A is the more attractive. If the ultimate objective is to increase the wealth of the shareholders of Sinclair Wholesalers plc, it might be better to choose Site A even though the percentage return is lower. It is the absolute size of the return rather than the relative (percentage) size that is important. This is a general problem of using comparative measures, such as percentages, when the objective is measured in absolute ones, like an amount of money. If businesses were seeking through their investments to generate a percentage rate of return on investment, ARR would be more helpful. The problem is that most businesses seek to achieve increases in their absolute wealth (measured in pounds, euros, dollars and so on) through their investment decisions.

Real World 8.3 illustrates how using percentage measures can lead to confusion.

REAL WORLD 8.3

Increasing road capacity by sleight of hand

During the 1970s, the Mexican government wanted to increase the capacity of a major four-lane road. It came up with the idea of repainting the lane markings so that there were six narrower lanes occupying the same space as four wider ones had previously done. This increased the capacity of the road by 50 per cent (that is, $^2/_4 \times 100$). A tragic outcome of the narrower lanes was an increase in deaths from road accidents. A year later the Mexican government had the six narrower lanes changed back to the original four wider ones. This reduced the capacity of the road by 33 per cent (that is, $^2/_6 \times 100$). The Mexican government reported that, overall, it had increased the capacity of the road by 17 per cent (that is, 50% − 33%), despite the fact that its real capacity was identical to that which it had been originally. The confusion arose because each of the two percentages (50 per cent and 33 per cent) is based on different bases (four and six).

Source: Gigerenzer, G., *Reckoning with Risk*, Penguin, 2002.

Payback period (PP)

→ The **payback period (PP)** is the length of time it takes for an initial investment to be repaid out of the net cash inflows from a project. Since it takes time into account, the PP method seems to go some way towards overcoming the timing problem of ARR – or at first glance it does.

It might be useful to consider PP in the context of the Billingsgate Battery example. We should recall that essentially the project's cash flows are:

Time		£000
Immediately	Cost of machine	(100)
1 year's time	Operating profit before depreciation	20
2 years' time	Operating profit before depreciation	40
3 years' time	Operating profit before depreciation	60
4 years' time	Operating profit before depreciation	60
5 years' time	Operating profit before depreciation	20
5 years' time	Disposal proceeds	20

Note that all of these figures are amounts of cash to be paid or received (we saw earlier that operating profit before depreciation is a rough measure of the cash flows from the project).

As the payback period is the length of time it takes for the initial investment to be repaid out of the net cash inflows, it will be three years before the £100,000 outlay is covered by the inflows. This is still assuming that the cash flows occur at year ends. The payback period can be derived by calculating the cumulative cash flows as follows:

Time		Net cash flows £000	Cumulative cash flows £000	
Immediately	Cost of machine	(100)	(100)	
1 year's time	Operating profit before depreciation	20	(80)	(−100 + 20)
2 years' time	Operating profit before depreciation	40	(40)	(−80 + 40)
3 years' time	Operating profit before depreciation	60	20	(−40 + 60)
4 years' time	Operating profit before depreciation	60	80	(20 + 60)
5 years' time	Operating profit before depreciation	20	100	(80 + 20)
5 years' time	Disposal proceeds	20	120	(100 + 20)

We can see that the cumulative cash flows become positive at the end of the third year. Had we assumed that the cash flows arise evenly over the year, the precise payback period would be

$$2 \text{ years} + (^{40}/_{60}) \text{ years} = 2^2/_3 \text{ years}$$

where 40 represents the cash flow still required at the beginning of the third year to repay the initial outlay, and 60 is the projected cash flow during the third year.

We must now ask how to decide whether three years is an acceptable payback period. The decision rule for using PP is:

- For a project to be acceptable it would need to have a payback period shorter than a maximum payback period set by the business.
- If there were two (or more) competing projects whose payback periods were all shorter than the maximum payback period requirement, the project with the shorter (or shortest) payback period should be selected.

If, for example, Billingsgate Battery had a maximum acceptable payback period of four years, the project would be undertaken. A project with a longer payback period than four years would not be acceptable.

Activity 8.5

What is the payback period of the Chaotic Industries project from Activity 8.2?

The inflows and outflows are expected to be:

Time		Net cash flows £000	Cumulative net cash flows £000	
Immediately	Cost of vans	(150)	(150)	
1 year's time	Net saving before depreciation	30	(120)	(−150 + 30)
2 years' time	Net saving before depreciation	30	(90)	(−120 + 30)
3 years' time	Net saving before depreciation	30	(60)	(−90 + 30)
4 years' time	Net saving before depreciation	30	(30)	(−60 + 30)
5 years' time	Net saving before depreciation	30	0	(−30 + 30)
6 years' time	Net saving before depreciation	30	30	(0 + 30)
6 years' time	Disposal proceeds from the vans	30	60	(30 + 30)

The payback period here is five years; that is, it is not until the end of the fifth year that the vans will pay for themselves out of the savings that they are expected to generate.

The PP method has certain advantages. It is quick and easy to calculate, and can be easily understood by managers. The logic of using PP is that projects that can recoup their cost quickly are economically more attractive than those with longer payback periods, that is, it emphasises liquidity. PP is probably an improvement on ARR in respect of the timing of the cash flows. PP is not, however, the whole answer to the problem.

Problems with PP

Activity 8.6

In what respect is PP not the whole answer as a means of assessing investment opportunities? Consider the cash flows arising from three competing projects:

Time		Project 1 £000	Project 2 £000	Project 3 £000
Immediately	Cost of machine	(200)	(200)	(200)
1 year's time	Operating profit before depreciation	70	20	70
2 years' time	Operating profit before depreciation	60	20	100
3 years' time	Operating profit before depreciation	70	160	30
4 years' time	Operating profit before depreciation	80	30	200
5 years' time	Operating profit before depreciation	50	20	440
5 years' time	Disposal proceeds	40	10	20

(*Hint*: Again, the defect is not concerned with the ability of the manager to forecast future events. This is a problem, but it is a problem whatever approach we take.)

The PP for each project is three years and so the PP method would regard the projects as being equally acceptable. It cannot distinguish between those projects that pay back a significant amount early in the three-year payback period and those that do not.

Activity 8.6 continued

In addition, this method ignores cash flows after the payback period. A decision maker concerned with increasing owners' wealth would prefer Project 3 because the cash flows come in earlier (most of the initial cost of making the investment has been repaid by the end of the second year) and they are greater in total.

The cumulative cash flows of each project in Activity 8.6 are set out in Figure 8.1.

Figure 8.1　**The cumulative cash flows of each project in Activity 8.6**

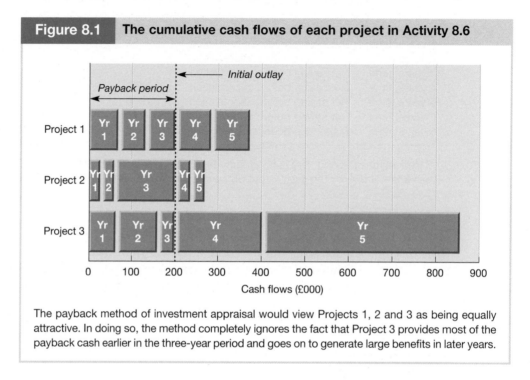

The payback method of investment appraisal would view Projects 1, 2 and 3 as being equally attractive. In doing so, the method completely ignores the fact that Project 3 provides most of the payback cash earlier in the three-year period and goes on to generate large benefits in later years.

We can see that the PP method is not concerned with the profitability of projects; it is concerned simply with their payback period. Thus cash flows arising beyond the payback period are ignored. While this neatly avoids the practical problems of forecasting cash flows over a long period, it means that relevant information could be ignored.

We may feel that, by favouring projects with a short payback period, the PP method does at least provide a means of dealing with the problems of risk and uncertainty. However, this is a fairly crude approach to the problem. It looks only at the risk that the project will end earlier than expected. However, this is only one of many risk areas. What, for example, about the risk that the demand for the product may be less than expected? There are more systematic approaches to dealing with risk that can be used and we shall look at these later in the chapter.

PP takes some note of the timing of the costs and benefits from the project. Its key deficiency, however, is that it is not linked to promoting increases in the wealth of the business and its owners. PP will tend to recommend undertaking projects that pay for themselves quickly.

The PP method requires the managers of a business to select a maximum acceptable payback period. This maximum period, in practice, will vary from one business to the next. **Real World 8.4** provides some evidence of the length of payback period required by small to medium-sized businesses when investing in new forms of energy generation.

REAL WORLD 8.4

Payback time

When it comes to self-generation of renewable energy, UK SMEs (small and medium size enterprises) want an unrealistically quick return on investment according to research carried out by energy consultancy energyTEAM. Nearly three quarters would need payback within three years in order to justify introducing such measures. Only four per cent are prepared for this process to take over five years despite growing concern over commercial energy usage. EnergyTEAM's study revealed that 40 per cent of enterprises with 50 to 500 employees would have to be convinced of a return on investment in just one year before they would proceed down the route of self-generation.

When asked which method of self-generation they would be most inclined to choose, over half of respondents highlighted solar power as the preferred method. This is despite the fact that solar has one of the largest payback times, at around ten years.

Brian Rickerby, joint Managing Director of energyTEAM, said 'I can understand that seeking a quick return is a pragmatic, business-like approach, but unfortunately this is not realistic when it comes to energy issues. Self-generation technologies must be viewed as a long-term strategy that will have a significant positive impact for many years to come.'

Source: 'SMEs' unrealistic demands on renewables', *Sustain*, Vol. 8, Issue 5, 2007, p. 74.

Net present value (NPV)

From what we have seen so far, it seems that to make sensible investment decisions, we need a method of appraisal that both considers *all* of the costs and benefits of each investment opportunity, and makes a logical allowance for the *timing* of those costs and benefits. The **net present value (NPV)** method provides us with this.

Consider the Billingsgate Battery example's cash flows, which we should recall can be summarised as follows:

Time		£000
Immediately	Cost of machine	(100)
1 year's time	Operating profit before depreciation	20
2 years' time	Operating profit before depreciation	40
3 years' time	Operating profit before depreciation	60
4 years' time	Operating profit before depreciation	60
5 years' time	Operating profit before depreciation	20
5 years' time	Disposal proceeds	20

Given that the principal financial objective of the business is to increase owners' wealth, it would be very easy to assess this investment if all of the cash inflows and outflows were to occur now (all at the same time). All that we should need to do would be to add up the cash inflows (total £220,000) and compare them with the cash outflows (£100,000). This would lead us to the conclusion that the project should go ahead because the business, and its owners, would be better off by £120,000. Of course, it is not as easy as this because time is involved. The cash outflow (payment) will occur immediately if the project is undertaken. The inflows (receipts) will arise at a range of later times.

The time factor is an important issue because people do not normally see £100 paid out now as equivalent in value to £100 receivable in a year's time. If we were to be offered £100 in 12 months' time in exchange for paying out £100 now, we should not be prepared to accept the offer unless we wished to do someone a favour.

Activity 8.7

Why would you see £100 to be received in a year's time as not equal in value to £100 to be paid immediately? (There are basically three reasons.)

The reasons are:

- interest lost
- risk
- effects of inflation.

We shall now take a closer look at these three reasons in turn.

Interest lost

If we are to be deprived of the opportunity to spend our money for a year, we could equally well be deprived of its use by placing it on deposit in a bank or building society. In this case, at the end of the year we could have our money back and have interest as well. Thus, by investing the funds in some other way, we shall be incurring an *opportunity cost*. We should remember from Chapter 2 that an opportunity cost occurs where one course of action, for example making an investment, deprives us of the opportunity to derive some benefit from an alternative action, for example putting the money in the bank and earning interest.

From this we can see that any investment opportunity must, if it is to make us wealthier, do better than the returns that are available from the next best opportunity. Thus, if Billingsgate Battery Company sees putting the money in the bank on deposit as the alternative to investment in the machine, the return from investing in the machine must be better than that from investing in the bank. If the bank offered a better return, the business, and its owners, would become wealthier by putting the money on deposit.

Risk

All investments expose their investors to **risk**. For example, buying a machine to manufacture a product, or to provide a service, to be sold in the market, on the strength of various estimates made in advance of buying the machine, exposes the business to risk. Things may not turn out as expected.

Activity 8.8

Can you suggest some areas where things could go other than according to plan in the Billingsgate Battery Company example?

We have come up with the following:

- The machine might not work as well as expected; it might break down, leading to loss of the business's ability to provide the service.
- Sales of the service may not be as buoyant as expected.
- Labour costs may prove to be higher than expected.
- The sale proceeds of the machine could prove to be less than were estimated.

It is important to remember that the decision whether to invest in the machine must be taken *before* any of these things are known. For example, it is only after the machine has been purchased that we could discover that the level of sales which had been estimated before the event is not going to be achieved. It is not possible to wait until we know for certain whether the market will behave as we expected before we buy the machine. We can study reports and analyses of the market. We can commission sophisticated market surveys, and these may give us more confidence in the likely outcome. We can advertise widely and try to promote sales. Ultimately, however, we have to decide whether to jump off into the dark and accept the risk if we want the opportunity to make profitable investments.

Real World 8.5 gives some some impression of the extent to which businesses believe that investment outcomes turn out as expected.

REAL WORLD 8.5

Size matters

Ninety-nine manufacturing businesses in the Cambridge area of the UK were asked the extent to which past investments performed in line with earlier expectations. The results, broken down according to business size, are set out below.

	Size of business			
	Large %	Medium %	Small %	All %
Underperformed	8	14	32	14
Performed as expected	82	72	68	77
Overperformed	10	14	0	9

It seems that smaller businesses are much more likely to get it wrong than medium-sized or larger businesses. This may be because small businesses are often younger and, therefore, less experienced both in the techniques of forecasting and in managing investment projects. They are also likely to have less financial expertise. It also seems that small businesses have a distinct bias towards overoptimism and do not take full account of the possibility that things will turn out worse than expected.

Source: Baddeley, M., 'Unpacking the black box: an econometric analysis of investment strategies in real world firms', CEPP Working Paper No. 08/05, University of Cambridge, p. 14.

Normally, people expect to receive greater returns where they perceive risk to be a factor. Examples of this in real life are not difficult to find. One such example is that banks tend to charge higher rates of interest to borrowers whom the bank perceives as more risky. Those who can offer good security for a loan, and who can point to a regular source of income, tend to be charged lower rates of interest.

Going back to Billingsgate Battery Company's investment opportunity, it is not enough to say that we should not advise making the investment unless the returns from it are as high as those from investing in a bank deposit. Clearly we should want returns above the level of bank deposit interest rates, because the logical equivalent of investing in the machine is not putting the money on deposit but making an alternative investment that is risky.

We have just seen that investors tend to expect a higher rate of return from investment projects where the risk is perceived as being higher. How risky a particular project is, and therefore how large this **risk premium** should be, are, however, matters that are difficult to handle. It is usually necessary to make some judgement on these questions. We shall come back to the size of the risk premium later in the chapter when we consider how the level of risk can be assessed.

Inflation

If we are to be deprived of £100 for a year, when we come to spend that money it will not buy as much as it would have done a year earlier. Generally, we shall not be able to buy as many tins of baked beans or loaves of bread or bus tickets as we could have done a year earlier. This is because of the loss in the purchasing power of money, or **inflation**, which occurs over time. Clearly, the investor needs compensating for this loss of purchasing power if the investment is to be made. This compensation is on top of a return that takes account of what could have been gained from an alternative investment of similar risk.

In practice, interest rates observable in the market tend to take inflation into account. Rates that are offered to potential building society and bank depositors include an allowance for the rate of inflation that is expected in the future.

What will a logical investor do?

As we have seen, logical investors who are seeking to increase their wealth will only be prepared to make investments that will compensate for the loss of interest and purchasing power of the money invested and for the fact that the returns expected may not materialise (risk). This is usually assessed by seeing whether the proposed investment will yield a return that is greater than the basic rate of interest (which would include an allowance for inflation) plus a risk premium.

These three factors (interest lost, risk and inflation) are set out in Figure 8.2.

Naturally, investors need at least the minimum returns before they are prepared to invest. However, it is in terms of the effect on their wealth that they should logically assess an investment project. Usually it is the investment with the highest percentage return that will make the investor most wealthy, but we shall see later in this chapter that this is not always the case. For the time being, therefore, we shall concentrate on wealth.

Let us now return to the Billingsgate Battery Company example. We should recall that the cash flows expected from this investment are:

Figure 8.2	The factors influencing the returns required by investors from a project

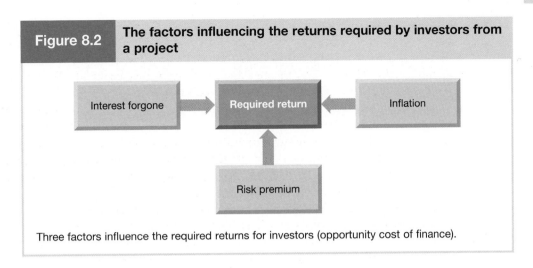

Three factors influence the required returns for investors (opportunity cost of finance).

Time		£000
Immediately	Cost of machine	(100)
1 year's time	Operating profit before depreciation	20
2 years' time	Operating profit before depreciation	40
3 years' time	Operating profit before depreciation	60
4 years' time	Operating profit before depreciation	60
5 years' time	Operating profit before depreciation	20
5 years' time	Disposal proceeds	20

We have already seen that it is not sufficient just to compare the basic cash inflows and outflows for the investment. It would be useful if we could express each of these cash flows in similar terms, so that we could make a direct comparison between the sum of the inflows over time and the immediate £100,000 investment. Fortunately, we can do this.

Let us assume that, instead of making this investment, the business could make an alternative investment with similar risk and obtain a return of 20 per cent a year.

Activity 8.9

We know that Billingsgate Battery Company could alternatively invest its money at a rate of 20 per cent a year. How much do you judge the present (immediate) value of the expected first year receipt of £20,000 to be? In other words, if instead of having to wait a year for the £20,000, and being deprived of the opportunity to invest it at 20 per cent, you could have some money now, what sum to be received now would you regard as exactly equivalent to getting £20,000 but having to wait a year for it?

We should obviously be happy to accept a lower amount if we could get it immediately than if we had to wait a year. This is because we could invest it at 20 per cent (in the alternative project). Logically, we should be prepared to accept the amount that, with a year's income, will grow to £20,000. If we call this amount PV (for present value) we can say

$$PV + (PV \times 20\%) = £20,000$$

– that is, the amount plus income from investing the amount for the year equals the £20,000.

Activity 8.9 continued

If we rearrange this equation we find

$$PV \times (1 + 0.2) = £20,000$$

(Note that 0.2 is the same as 20 per cent, but expressed as a decimal.) Further rearranging gives

$$PV = £20,000/(1 + 0.2) = £16,667$$

Thus, rational investors who have the opportunity to invest at 20 per cent a year would not mind whether they have £16,667 now or £20,000 in a year's time. In this sense we can say that, given a 20 per cent alternative investment opportunity, the present value of £20,000 to be received in one year's time is £16,667.

If we derive the present value (PV) of each of the cash flows associated with Billingsgate's machine investment, we could easily make the direct comparison between the cost of making the investment (£100,000) and the various benefits that will derive from it in years 1 to 5.

We can make a more general statement about the PV of a particular cash flow. It is:

PV of the cash flow of year n = actual cash flow of year n divided by $(1 + r)^n$

where n is the year of the cash flow (that is, how many years into the future) and r is the opportunity investing rate expressed as a decimal (instead of as a percentage).

We have already seen how this works for the £20,000 inflow for year 1 for the Billingsgate project. For year 2 the calculation would be:

$$\text{PV of year 2 cash flow (that is, £40,000)} = £40,000/(1 + 0.2)^2 = £40,000/(1.2)^2$$
$$= £40,000/1.44 = £27,778$$

Thus the present value of the £40,000 to be received in two years' time is £27,778.

Activity 8.10

See if you can show that an investor would find £27,778, receivable now, as equally acceptable to receiving £40,000 in two years' time, assuming that there is a 20 per cent investment opportunity.

The reasoning goes like this:

	£
Amount available for immediate investment	27,778
Add Income for year 1 (20% × 27,778)	5,556
	33,334
Add Income for year 2 (20% × 33,334)	6,667
	40,001

(The extra £1 is only a rounding error.)

This is to say that since the investor can turn £27,778 into £40,000 in two years, these amounts are equivalent. We can say that £27,778 is the present value of £40,000 receivable after two years (given a 20 per cent rate of return).

Now let us calculate the present values of all of the cash flows associated with the Billingsgate machine project and from them the *net present value (NPV)* of the project as a whole.

The relevant cash flows and calculations are as follows:

Time	Cash flow £000	Calculation of PV	PV £000
Immediately (time 0)	(100)	$(100)/(1 + 0.2)^0$	(100.00)
1 year's time	20	$20/(1 + 0.2)^1$	16.67
2 years' time	40	$40/(1 + 0.2)^2$	27.78
3 years' time	60	$60/(1 + 0.2)^3$	34.72
4 years' time	60	$60/(1 + 0.2)^4$	28.94
5 years' time	20	$20/(1 + 0.2)^5$	8.04
5 years' time	20	$20/(1 + 0.2)^5$	8.04
Net present value (NPV)			24.19

Note that $(1 + 0.2)^0 = 1$.

Once again, we must ask how we can decide whether the machine project is acceptable to the business. In fact, the decision rule for NPV is simple:

- If the NPV is positive the project should be accepted; if it is negative the project should be rejected.
- If there are two (or more) competing projects that have positive NPVs, the project with the higher (or highest) NPV should be selected.

In this case, the NPV is positive, so we should accept the project and buy the machine. The reasoning behind this decision rule is quite straightforward. Investing in the machine will make the business, and its owners, £24,190 better off than they would be by taking up the next best opportunity available to it. The gross benefits from investing in this machine are worth a total of £124,190 today, and since the business can 'buy' these benefits for just £100,000 today, the investment should be made. If, however, the present value of the gross benefits were below £100,000, it would be less than the cost of 'buying' those benefits and the opportunity should, therefore, be rejected.

Activity 8.11

What is the *maximum* the Billingsgate Battery Company should be prepared to pay for the machine, given the potential benefits of owning it?

The business would logically be prepared to pay up to £124,190 since the wealth of the owners of the business would be increased up to this price – although the business would prefer to pay as little as possible.

Using discount tables

Deducing the present values of the various cash flows is a little laborious using the approach that we have just taken. To deduce each PV we took the relevant cash flow and multiplied it by $1/(1 + r)^n$. There is a slightly different way to do this. Tables exist

→ that show values of this **discount factor** for a range of values of r and n. Such a table appears at the end of this book, on pp. 521–522. Take a look at it.

Look at the column for 20 per cent and the row for one year. We find that the factor is 0.833. This means that the PV of a cash flow of £1 receivable in one year is £0.833. So the present value of a cash flow of £20,000 receivable in one year's time is £16,660 (that is, 0.833 × £20,000), the same result as we found doing it manually.

Activity 8.12

What is the NPV of the Chaotic Industries project from Activity 8.2, assuming a 15 per cent opportunity cost of finance (discount rate)? You should use the discount table on pp. 521–522.

Remember that the inflows and outflow are expected to be:

Time		£000
Immediately	Cost of vans	(150)
1 year's time	Net saving before depreciation	30
2 years' time	Net saving before depreciation	30
3 years' time	Net saving before depreciation	30
4 years' time	Net saving before depreciation	30
5 years' time	Net saving before depreciation	30
6 years' time	Net saving before depreciation	30
6 years' time	Disposal proceeds from the vans	30

The calculation of the NPV of the project is as follows:

Time	Cash flows £000	Discount factor (15% – from the table)	Present value £000
Immediately	(150)	1.000	(150.00)
1 year's time	30	0.870	26.10
2 years' time	30	0.756	22.68
3 years' time	30	0.658	19.74
4 years' time	30	0.572	17.16
5 years' time	30	0.497	14.91
6 years' time	30	0.432	12.96
6 years' time	30	0.432	12.96
		NPV	(23.49)

Activity 8.13

How would you interpret this result?

The fact that the project has a negative NPV means that the present values of the benefits from the investment are worth less than the cost of entering into it. Any cost up to £126,510 (the present value of the benefits) would be worth paying, but not £150,000.

The discount table shows how the value of £1 diminishes as its receipt goes further into the future. Assuming an opportunity cost of finance of 20 per cent a year, £1 to be received immediately, obviously, has a present value of £1. However, as the time before it is to be received increases, the present value diminishes significantly, as is shown in Figure 8.3.

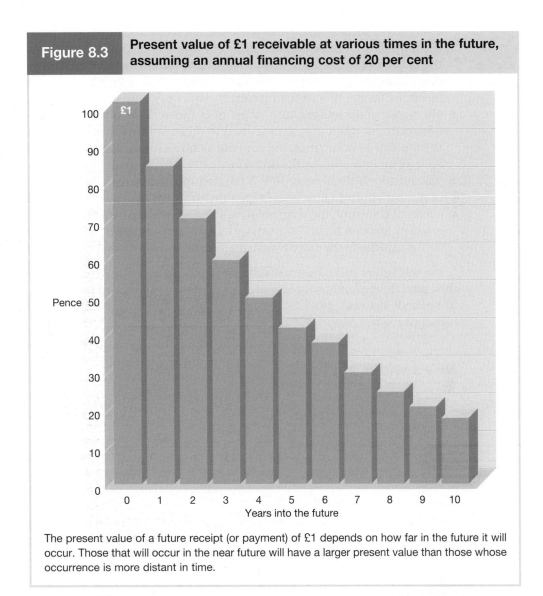

| Figure 8.3 | Present value of £1 receivable at various times in the future, assuming an annual financing cost of 20 per cent |

The present value of a future receipt (or payment) of £1 depends on how far in the future it will occur. Those that will occur in the near future will have a larger present value than those whose occurrence is more distant in time.

The discount rate and the cost of capital

We have seen that the appropriate discount rate to use in NPV assessments is the opportunity cost of finance. This is, in effect, the cost to the business of the finance needed to fund the investment. It will normally be the cost of a mixture of funds (shareholders' funds and borrowings) employed by the business and is often referred to as the **cost of capital**.

Why NPV is better

From what we have seen, NPV seems to be a better method of appraising investment opportunities than either ARR or PP. This is because it fully takes account of each of the following:

- *The timing of the cash flows.* By discounting the various cash flows associated with each project according to when each one is expected to arise, NPV takes account of the time value of money. Associated with this is the fact that by discounting, using the opportunity cost of finance (that is, the return that the next best alternative opportunity would generate), the net benefit *after* financing costs have been met is identified (as the NPV of the project).
- *The whole of the relevant cash flows.* NPV includes *all* of the relevant cash flows irrespective of when they are expected to occur. It treats them differently according to their date of occurrence, but they are all taken into account in the NPV, and they all have an influence on the decision.
- *The objectives of the business.* NPV is the only method of appraisal in which the output of the analysis has a direct bearing on the wealth of the owners of the business (with a limited company, the shareholders). Positive NPVs enhance wealth; negative ones reduce it. Since we assume that private sector businesses seek to increase owners' wealth, NPV is superior to the other two methods (ARR and PP) that we have already discussed.

We saw earlier that a business should take on all projects with positive NPVs, when their cash flows are discounted at the opportunity cost of finance. Where a choice has to be made between projects, the business should normally select the one with the higher or highest NPV.

NPV's wider application

NPV is considered the most logical approach to making business decisions about investments in productive assets. The same logic makes NPV equally valid as the best approach to take when trying to place a value on any economic asset, that is, an asset that seems capable of yielding financial benefits. This would include a share in a limited company and a loan. In fact, when we talk of *economic value*, we mean a value that has been derived by adding together the discounted (present) values of all future cash flows from the asset concerned.

Real World 8.6 provides an estimate of the NPV that is expected from one interesting project.

REAL WORLD 8.6

A real diamond geezer   **FT**

Alan Bond, the disgraced Australian businessman and America's Cup winner, is looking at ways to raise money in London for an African diamond mining project. Lesotho Diamond Corporation (LDC) is a private company in which Mr Bond has a large interest. LDC's main asset is a 93 per cent stake in the Kao diamond project in the southern African kingdom of Lesotho.

Mr Bond says, on his personal website, that the Kao project is forecast to yield 5m carats of diamonds over the next 10 years and could become Lesotho's biggest foreign currency earner.

SRK, the mining consultants, has estimated the net present value of the project at £129m.

It is understood that Mr Bond and his family own about 40 per cent of LDC. Mr Bond has described himself as 'spearheading' the Kao project.

Source: Adapted from *Bond seeks funds in London to mine African diamonds*, by Rebacca Bream, ft.com, © The Financial Times Limited, 23 April 2007.

Internal rate of return (IRR)

This is the last of the four major methods of investment appraisal that are found in practice. It is quite closely related to the NPV method in that, like NPV, it also involves discounting future cash flows. The **internal rate of return (IRR)** of a particular investment is the discount rate that, when applied to its future cash flows, will produce an NPV of precisely zero. In essence, it represents the yield from an investment opportunity.

Activity 8.14

We should recall that, when we discounted the cash flows of the Billingsgate Battery Company machine investment opportunity at 20 per cent, we found that the NPV was a positive figure of £24,190 (see p. 275). What does the NPV of the machine project tell us about the rate of return that the investment will yield for the business (that is, the project's IRR)?

- -

The fact that the NPV is positive when discounting at 20 per cent implies that the rate of return that the project generates is more than 20 per cent. The fact that the NPV is a pretty large figure implies that the actual rate of return is quite a lot above 20 per cent. We should expect increasing the size of the discount rate to reduce NPV, because a higher discount rate gives a lower discounted figure.

It is somewhat laborious to deduce the IRR by hand, since it cannot usually be calculated directly. Iteration (trial and error) is the approach that must usually be adopted. Fortunately, computer spreadsheet packages can deduce the IRR with ease. The package will also use a trial and error approach, but at high speed.

Despite it being laborious, we shall now go on and derive the IRR for the Billingsgate project by hand.

Let us try a higher rate, say 30 per cent, and see what happens.

Time	Cash flow £000	Discount factor (30% – from the table)	PV £000
Immediately (time 0)	(100)	1.000	(100.00)
1 year's time	20	0.769	15.38
2 years' time	40	0.592	23.68
3 years' time	60	0.455	27.30
4 years' time	60	0.350	21.00
5 years' time	20	0.269	5.38
5 years' time	20	0.269	5.38
		NPV	(1.88)

In increasing the discount rate from 20 per cent to 30 per cent, we have reduced the NPV from £24,190 (positive) to £1,880 (negative). Since the IRR is the discount rate that will give us an NPV of exactly zero, we can conclude that the IRR of Billingsgate Battery Company's machine project is very slightly below 30 per cent. Further trials could lead us to the exact rate, but there is probably not much point, given the likely inaccuracy of the cash flow estimates. It is probably good enough, for practical purposes, to say that the IRR is about 30 per cent.

The relationship between the NPV method discussed earlier and the IRR is shown graphically in Figure 8.4 using the information relating to the Billingsgate Battery Company.

Figure 8.4 | **The relationship between the NPV and IRR methods**

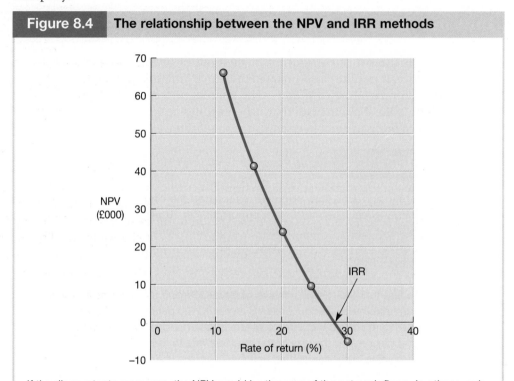

If the discount rate were zero, the NPV would be the sum of the net cash flows. In other words, no account would be taken of the time value of money. However, if we assume increasing discount rates, there is a corresponding decrease in the NPV of the project. When the NPV line crosses the horizontal axis there will be a zero NPV, and the point where it crosses is the IRR.

We can see that, where the discount rate is zero, the NPV will be the sum of the net cash flows. In other words, no account is taken of the time value of money. However, as the discount rate increases there is a corresponding decrease in the NPV of the project. When the NPV line crosses the horizontal axis there will be a zero NPV, and that represents the IRR.

Activity 8.15

What is the internal rate of return of the Chaotic Industries project from Activity 8.2? You should use the discount table on pp. 521–522. (*Hint*: Remember that you already know the NPV of this project at 15 per cent (from Activity 8.12).)

....

Since we know that, at a 15 per cent discount rate, the NPV is a relatively large negative figure, our next trial is using a lower discount rate, say 10 per cent:

Time	Cash flows £000	Discount factor (10% – from the table)	Present value £000
Immediately	(150)	1.000	(150.00)
1 year's time	30	0.909	27.27
2 years' time	30	0.826	24.78
3 years' time	30	0.751	22.53
4 years' time	30	0.683	20.49
5 years' time	30	0.621	18.63
6 years' time	30	0.564	16.92
6 years' time	30	0.564	16.92
			NPV (2.46)

This figure is close to zero NPV. However, the NPV is still negative and so the precise IRR will be a little below 10 per cent.

We could undertake further trials in order to derive the precise IRR. If, however, we have to calculate the IRR manually, further iterations can be time-consuming.

We can get an acceptable approximation to the answer fairly quickly by first calculating the change in NPV arising from a 1 per cent change in the discount rate. This can be done by taking the difference between the two trials (that is, 15 per cent and 10 per cent) that we have already carried out (in Activities 8.12 and 8.15):

Trial	Discount factor %	Net present value £000
1	15	(23.49)
2	10	(2.46)
Difference	5	21.03

The change in NPV for every 1 per cent change in the discount rate will be

$$(21.03/5) = 4.21$$

The reduction in the 10% discount rate required to achieve a zero NPV would therefore be

$$(2.46)/4.21 \times 1\% = 0.58\%$$

The IRR is therefore

$$(10.00 - 0.58)\% = 9.42\%$$

However, to say that the IRR is about 9 or 10 per cent is near enough for most purposes.

Note that this approach assumes a straight-line relationship between the discount rate and NPV. We can see from Figure 8.4 that this assumption is not strictly correct. Over a relatively short range, however, this simplifying assumption is not usually a problem and so we can still arrive at a reasonable approximation using the approach that we took in deriving the 9.42 per cent IRR.

In practice, most businesses have computer software packages that will derive a project's IRR very quickly. Thus, in practice it is not usually necessary either to make a series of trial discount rates or to make the approximation that we have just considered.

Users of the IRR method should apply the following decision rules:

● For any project to be acceptable, it must meet a minimum IRR requirement. This is often referred to as the *hurdle rate* and, logically, this should be the opportunity cost of finance.

● Where there are competing projects (that is, the business can choose only one of two or more viable projects), the one with the higher (or highest) IRR should be selected.

IRR has certain attributes in common with NPV. All cash flows are taken into account, and their timing is logically handled.

Real World 8.7 provides some idea of the IRR for one form of renewable energy.

REAL WORLD 8.7

The answer is blowin' in the wind   **FT**

'Wind farms are practically guaranteed to make returns once you have a licence to operate,' says Bernard Lambilliotte, chief investment officer at Ecofin, a financial group that runs Ecofin Water and Power Opportunities, an investment trust.

'The risk is when you have bought the land and are seeking a licence,' says Lambilliotte. 'But once it is built and you are plugged into the grid it is risk-free. It will give an internal rate of return in the low to mid-teens.' Ecofin's largest investment is in Sechilienne, a French company that operates wind farms in northern France and generates capacity in the French overseas territories powered by sugar cane waste.

Source: Batchelor, C., 'A hot topic, but poor returns', ft.com, 27 August 2005.

Real World 8.8 gives some examples of IRRs sought in practice.

REAL WORLD 8.8

Rates of return

IRR rates for investment projects can vary considerably. Here are a few examples of the expected or target returns from investment projects of large businesses.

● Forth Ports plc, a port operator, concentrates on projects that generate an IRR of at least 15 per cent.

● Rok plc, the builder, aims for a minimum IRR of 15% from new investments.

● Hutchison Whampoa, a large telecommunications business, requires an IRR of at least 25 per cent from its telecom projects.

● Airbus, the plane maker, expects an IRR of 13 per cent from the sale of its A380 super-jumbo aircraft.

● Signet Group plc, the jewellery retailer, requires an IRR of 20 per cent over five years when appraising new stores.

Sources: 'FAQs, Forth Ports plc', www.forthports.co.uk; Numis Broker Research Report www.rokgroup.com, 17 August 2006, p. 31; 'Hutchison Whampoa', Lex column, ft.com, 31 March 2004; 'Airbus hikes A380 break-even target', ft.com, 20 October 2006, 'Risk and other factors', Signet Group plc, www.signetgroupplc.com, 2006.

Problems with IRR

The main disadvantage of IRR, relative to NPV, is the fact that it does not directly address the question of wealth generation. It could therefore lead to the wrong decision being made. This is because IRR will always rank a project with an IRR of 25 per cent above one with an IRR of 20 per cent, assuming an opportunity cost of finance of, say, 15 per cent. Although accepting the project with the higher percentage return will often generate more wealth, this may not always be the case. This is because IRR completely ignores the *scale of investment.*

With a 15 per cent cost of finance, £15 million invested at 20 per cent for one year will make us wealthier by £0.75 million (that is, $15 \times (20 - 15)\% = 0.75$). With the same cost of finance, £5 million invested at 25 per cent for one year will make us only £0.5 million (that is, $5 \times (25 - 15)\% = 0.50$). IRR does not recognise this. It should be acknowledged that it is not usual for projects to be competing where there is such a large difference in scale. Even though the problem may be rare and so, typically, IRR will give the same signal as NPV, a method that is always reliable (NPV) must be better to use than IRR. This problem with percentages is another example of the one illustrated by the Mexican road discussed in Real World 8.3.

A further problem with the IRR method is that it has difficulty handling projects with unconventional cash flows. In the examples studied so far, each project has a negative cash flow arising at the start of its life and then positive cash flows thereafter. However, in some cases, a project may have both positive and negative cash flows at future points in its life. Such a pattern of cash flows can result in there being more than one IRR, or even no IRR at all. This would make the IRR method difficult to use, although it should be said that this is quite rare in practice. This is never a problem for NPV, however.

Some practical points

When undertaking an investment appraisal, there are several practical points that we should bear in mind:

- → ● *Past costs.* As with all decisions, we should take account only of **relevant costs** in our analysis. This means that only costs that vary with the decision should be considered. Thus, all past costs should be ignored as they cannot vary with the decision. In some cases, a business may incur costs (such as development costs and market research costs) *before* the evaluation of an opportunity to launch a new product. As those costs have already been incurred, they should be disregarded, even though the amounts may be substantial. Costs that have already been committed but not yet paid should also be disregarded. Where a business has entered into a binding contract to incur a particular cost, it becomes in effect a past cost even though payment may not be due until some point in the future.
- ● *Common future costs.* It is not only past costs that do not vary with the decision; some future costs may also be the same. For example, the cost of raw materials may not vary with the decision whether to invest in a new piece of manufacturing plant or to continue to use existing plant.
- ● *Opportunity costs.* Opportunity costs arising from benefits forgone must be taken into account. Thus, for example, when considering a decision concerning whether or not

to continue to use a machine already owned by the business, the realisable value of the machine might be an important opportunity cost.

● *Taxation.* Owners will be interested in the after-tax returns generated from the business, and so taxation will usually be an important consideration when making an investment decision. The profits from the project will be taxed, the capital investment may attract tax relief and so on. Tax is levied at significant rates. This means that, in real life, unless tax is formally taken into account, the wrong decision could easily be made. The timing of the tax outflow should also be taken into account when preparing the cash flows for the project.

● *Cash flows not profit flows.* We have seen that for the NPV, IRR and PP methods, it is cash flows rather than profit flows that are relevant to the assessment of investment projects. In an investment appraisal requiring the application of any of these methods we may be given details of the profits for the investment period. These need to be adjusted in order to derive the cash flows. We should remember that the operating profit *before* non-cash items (such as depreciation) is an approximation to the cash flows for the period, and so we should work back to this figure.

When the data are expressed in profit rather than cash flow terms, an adjustment in respect of working capital may also be necessary. Some adjustment should be made to take account of changes in working capital. For example, launching a new product may give rise to an increase in the net investment made in trade receivables and inventories less trade payables, requiring an immediate outlay of cash. This outlay for additional working capital should be shown in the NPV calculations as part of the initial cost. However, at the end of the life of the project, the additional working capital will be released. This divestment results in an effective inflow of cash at the end of the project; it should also be taken into account at the point at which it is received.

● *Year-end assumption.* In the examples and activities that we have considered so far in this chapter, we have assumed that cash flows arise at the end of the relevant year. This is a simplifying assumption that is used to make the calculations easier. (However, it is perfectly possible to deal more precisely with the cash flows.) As we saw earlier, this assumption is clearly unrealistic, as money will have to be paid to employees on a weekly or monthly basis and credit customers will pay within a month or two of buying the product or service. Nevertheless, it is probably not a serious distortion. We should be clear, however, that there is nothing about any of the four appraisal methods that demands that this assumption be made.

● *Interest payments.* When using discounted cash flow techniques (NPV and IRR), interest payments should not be taken into account in deriving the cash flows for the period. The discount factor already takes account of the costs of financing, and so to take account of interest charges in deriving cash flows for the period would be double counting.

● *Other factors.* Investment decision making must not be viewed as simply a mechanical exercise. The results derived from a particular investment appraisal method will be only one input to the decision-making process. There may be broader issues connected to the decision that have to be taken into account but which may be difficult or impossible to quantify.

The reliability of the forecasts and the validity of the assumptions used in the evaluation will also have a bearing on the final decision.

Activity 8.16

The directors of Manuff (Steel) Ltd are considering closing one of the business's factories. There has been a reduction in the demand for the products made at the factory in recent years, and the directors are not optimistic about the long-term prospects for these products. The factory is situated in the north of England, in an area where unemployment is high.

The factory is leased, and there are still four years of the lease remaining. The directors are uncertain whether the factory should be closed immediately or at the end of the period of the lease. Another business has offered to sub-lease the premises from Manuff at a rental of £40,000 a year for the remainder of the lease period.

The machinery and equipment at the factory cost £1,500,000, and have a statement of financial position (balance sheet) value of £400,000. In the event of immediate closure, the machinery and equipment could be sold for £220,000. The working capital at the factory is £420,000, and could be liquidated for that amount immediately, if required. Alternatively, the working capital can be liquidated in full at the end of the lease period. Immediate closure would result in redundancy payments to employees of £180,000.

If the factory continues in operation until the end of the lease period, the following operating profits (losses) are expected:

	Year 1	Year 2	Year 3	Year 4
	£000	£000	£000	£000
Operating profit/(loss)	160	(40)	30	20

The above figures include a charge of £90,000 a year for depreciation of machinery and equipment. The residual value of the machinery and equipment at the end of the lease period is estimated at £40,000.

Redundancy payments are expected to be £150,000 at the end of the lease period if the factory continues in operation. The business has an annual cost of capital of 12 per cent. Ignore taxation.

(a) Determine the relevant cash flows arising from a decision to continue operations until the end of the lease period rather than to close immediately.

(b) Calculate the net present value of continuing operations until the end of the lease period, rather than closing immediately.

(c) What other factors might the directors take into account before making a final decision on the timing of the factory closure?

(d) State, with reasons, whether or not the business should continue to operate the factory until the end of the lease period.

Your answer should be as follows:

(a) Relevant cash flows

	Years				
	0	1	2	3	4
	£000	£000	£000	£000	£000
Operating cash flows (Note 1)		250	50	120	110
Sale of machinery (Note 2)	(220)				40
Redundancy costs (Note 3)	180				(150)
Sub-lease rentals (Note 4)		(40)	(40)	(40)	(40)
Working capital invested (Note 5)	(420)				420
	(460)	210	10	80	380

Activity 8.16 continued

Notes:

1 Each year's operating cash flows are calculated by adding back the depreciation charge for the year to the operating profit for the year. In the case of the operating loss, the depreciation charge is deducted.

2 In the event of closure, machinery could be sold immediately. Thus an opportunity cost of £220,000 is incurred if operations continue.

3 If operations are continued, there will be a saving in immediate redundancy costs of £180,000. However, redundancy costs of £150,000 will be paid in four years' time.

4 If operations are continued, the opportunity to sub-lease the factory will be forgone.

5 Immediate closure would mean that working capital could be liquidated. If operations continue, this opportunity is foregone. However, working capital can be liquidated in four years' time.

(b)

Discount rate 12 per cent	1.000	0.893	0.797	0.712	0.636
Present value	(460)	187.5	8.0	57.0	241.7
Net present value	34.2				

(c) Other factors that may influence the decision include:

- *The overall strategy of the business*. The business may need to set the decision within a broader context. It may be necessary to manufacture the products at the factory because they are an integral part of the business's product range. The business may wish to avoid redundancies in an area of high unemployment for as long as possible.

- *Flexibility*. A decision to close the factory is probably irreversible. If the factory continues, however, there may be a chance that the prospects for the factory will brighten in the future.

- *Creditworthiness of sub-lessee*. The business should investigate the creditworthiness of the sub-lessee. Failure to receive the expected sub-lease payments would make the closure option far less attractive.

- *Accuracy of forecasts*. The forecasts made by the business should be examined carefully. Inaccuracies in the forecasts or any underlying assumptions may change the expected outcomes.

(d) The NPV of the decision to continue operations rather than close immediately is positive. Hence, shareholders would be better off if the directors took this course of action. The factory should therefore continue in operation rather than close down. This decision is likely to be welcomed by employees and would allow the business to maintain its flexibility.

Investment appraisal in practice

Many surveys have been conducted in the UK into the methods of investment appraisal used by businesses. They have shown the following features:

- Businesses tend to use more than one method to assess each investment decision.
- The discounting methods (NPV and IRR) have become increasingly popular over time, with these two becoming the most popular in recent years.
- The continued popularity of PP, and to a lesser extent ARR, despite their theoretical shortcomings.

● A tendency for larger businesses to rely more heavily on discounting methods than smaller businesses.

Real World 8.9 shows the results of a recent survey of UK manufacturing businesses regarding their use of investment appraisal methods.

REAL WORLD 8.9

A survey of UK business practice

A survey of 83 of the UK's largest manufacturing businesses examined the investment appraisal methods used to evaluate both strategic and non-strategic projects. Strategic projects usually aim to increase or change the competitive capabilities of a business, for example by introducing a new manufacturing process. Although a definition was provided, survey respondents were able to decide for themselves what constituted a strategic project. The results of the survey are set out below.

Method	Non-strategic projects Mean score	Strategic projects Mean score
Net present value	3.6829	3.9759
Payback	3.4268	3.6098
Internal rate of return	3.3293	3.7073
Accounting rate of return	1.9867	2.2667

Response scale: 1= never, 2 = rarely, 3 = often, 4 = mostly, 5 = always.

We can see that, for both non-strategic and strategic investments, the NPV method is the most popular. As the sample consists of large businesses (nearly all with total sales revenue in excess of £100 million), a fairly sophisticated approach to evaluation might be expected. Nevertheless, for non-strategic investments, the payback method comes second in popularity. It drops to third place for strategic projects.

The survey also found that 98 per cent of respondents used more than one method and 88 per cent used more than three methods of investment appraisal.

Source: Based on information in Alkaraan, F. and Northcott, D., 'Strategic capital investment decision-making: a role for emergent analysis tools? A study of practice in large UK manufacturing companies', *The British Accounting Review*, No. 38, 2006, p. 159.

A survey of US businesses also shows considerable support for the NPV and IRR methods. There is less support, however, for the payback method and ARR. **Real World 8.10** sets out some of the main findings.

REAL WORLD 8.10

A survey of US practice

A survey of the chief financial officers (CFOs) of 392 US businesses examined the popularity of various methods of investment appraisal. Figure 8.5 shows the percentage of businesses surveyed that always, or almost always, used the four methods discussed in this chapter.

Real World 8.10 continued

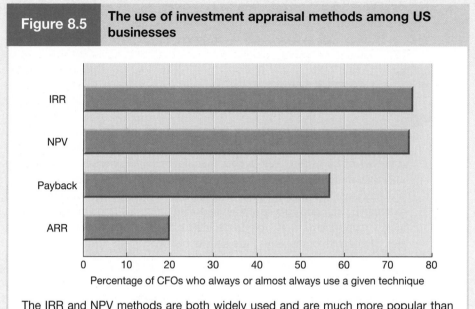

| Figure 8.5 | The use of investment appraisal methods among US businesses |

Percentage of CFOs who always or almost always use a given technique

The IRR and NPV methods are both widely used and are much more popular than the payback and accounting rate of return methods. Nevertheless, the payback method is still used always, or almost always, by a majority of US businesses.

Source: Based on information in Graham, R. and Harvey, C., 'How do CFOs make capital budgeting and capital structure decisions?', *Journal of Applied Corporate Finance*, Vol. 15, No. 1, 2002.

Activity 8.17

Earlier in the chapter we discussed the theoretical limitations of the PP method. Can you explain the fact that it still seems to be a popular method of investment appraisal among businesses?

A number of possible reasons may explain this finding:

● PP is easy to understand and use.
● It can avoid the problems of forecasting far into the future.
● It gives emphasis to the early cash flows when there is greater certainty concerning the accuracy of their predicted value.
● It emphasises the importance of liquidity. Where a business has liquidity problems, a short payback period for a project is likely to appear attractive.

PP can provide a convenient, though rough and ready, assessment of the profitability of a project, in the way that it is used in **Real World 8.11**.

REAL WORLD 8.11

An investment lifts off   **FT**

SES Global is the world's largest commercial satellite operator. This means that it rents satellite capacity to broadcasters, governments, telecommunications groups and internet service providers. It is a risky venture that few are prepared to undertake. As a result, a handful of businesses dominates the market.

Launching a satellite requires a huge initial outlay of capital, but relatively small cash outflows following the launch. Revenues only start to flow once the satellite is in orbit. A satellite launch costs around €250m. The main elements of this cost are the satellite (€120m), the launch vehicle (€80m), insurance (€40m) and ground equipment (€10m).

According to Romain Bausch, president and chief executive of SES Global, it takes three years to build and launch a satellite. However, the average lifetime of a satellite is fifteen years during which time it is generating revenues. The revenues generated are such that the payback period is around four to five years.

Source: Satellites need space to earn, ft.com (Burt, T.), © The Financial Times Limited, 14 July 2003.

The popularity of PP may suggest a lack of sophistication by managers, concerning investment appraisal. This criticism is most often made against managers of smaller businesses. This point is borne out by both of the surveys discussed above, which have found that smaller businesses are much less likely to use discounted cash flow methods (NPV and IRR) than are larger ones. Other surveys have tended to reach a similar conclusion.

IRR may be popular because it expresses outcomes in percentage terms rather than in absolute terms. This form of expression appears to be more acceptable to managers, despite the problems of percentage measures that we discussed earler. This may be because managers are used to using percentage figures as targets (for example, return on capital employed).

Real World 8.12 shows extracts from the 2006 annual report of a well-known business: Rolls-Royce plc, the builder of engines for aircraft and other purposes.

REAL WORLD 8.12

The use of NPV at Rolls-Royce

In its 2007 annual report and accounts, Rolls-Royce plc stated:

> The Group continues to subject all investments to rigorous examination of risks and future cash flows to ensure that they create shareholder value. All major investments require Board approval.
> The Group has a portfolio of projects at different stages of their life cycles. Discounted cash flow analysis of the remaining life of projects is performed on a regular basis.

Source: Rolls-Royce plc Annual Report 2007.

Rolls-Royce makes clear that it uses NPV (the report refers to creating shareholder value and to discounted cash flow, which strongly imply NPV). It is interesting to note that Rolls-Royce not only assesses new projects but also reassesses existing ones. This must be a sensible commercial approach. Businesses should not continue with existing projects unless those projects have a positive NPV based on future cash flows. Just because a project seemed to have a positive NPV before it started does not mean that this will persist in the light of changing circumstances. Activity 8.16 (pp. 285–286) considered a decision on whether to close down a project.

Self-assessment question 8.1

Beacon Chemicals plc is considering buying some equipment to produce a chemical named X14. The new equipment's capital cost is estimated at £100,000. If its purchase is approved now, the equipment can be bought and production can commence by the end of this year. £50,000 has already been spent on research and development work. Estimates of revenues and costs arising from the operation of the new equipment appear below.

	Year 1	Year 2	Year 3	Year 4	Year 5
Sales price (£/litre)	100	120	120	100	80
Sales volume (litres)	800	1,000	1,200	1,000	800
Variable cost (£/litre)	50	50	40	30	40
Fixed cost (£000)	30	30	30	30	30

If the equipment is bought, sales of some existing products will be lost, and this will result in a loss of contribution of £15,000 a year over its life.

The accountant has informed you that the fixed cost includes depreciation of £20,000 a year on the new equipment. It also includes an allocation of £10,000 for fixed overheads. A separate study has indicated that if the new equipment were bought, additional overheads, excluding depreciation, arising from producing the chemical would be £8,000 a year. Production would require additional working capital of £30,000.

For the purposes of your initial calculations ignore taxation.

Required:
(a) Deduce the relevant annual cash flows associated with buying the equipment.
(b) Deduce the payback period.
(c) Calculate the net present value using a discount rate of 8 per cent.

(*Hint*: You should deal with the investment in working capital by treating it as a cash outflow at the start of the project and an inflow at the end.)

The answer to this question can be found in Appendix B at the back of the book.

Investment appraisal and strategic planning

So far, we have tended to view investment opportunities as if they are unconnected, independent entities. In practice, however, successful businesses are those that set out a clear framework for the selection of investment projects. Unless this framework is in place, it may be difficult to identify those projects that are likely to generate a positive NPV. The best investment projects are usually those that match the business's internal strengths (for example, skills, experience, access to finance) with the opportunities available. In areas where this match does not exist, other businesses, for which the match does exist, are likely to have a distinct competitive advantage. This advantage means that they are likely to be able to provide the product or service at a better price and/or quality.

Establishing what is the best area or areas of activity and style of approach for the business is popularly known as *strategic planning*. We saw in Chapter 1 that strategic planning tries to identify the direction in which the business needs to go, in terms of products, markets, financing and so on, to best place it to generate profitable investment opportunities. In practice, strategic plans seem to have a timespan of around five years and generally tend to ask the question: where do we want our business to be in five years' time and how can we get there?

Real World 8.13 shows how easyJet made an investment that fitted its strategic objectives.

REAL WORLD 8.13

easyFit   **FT**

easyJet, the UK budget airline, bought a small rival airline, GB Airways Ltd (GB) in late 2007 for £103m. According to an article in the *Financial Times*:

> GB is a good strategic fit for easyJet. It operates under a British Airways franchise from Gatwick, which happens to be easyJet's biggest base. The deal makes easyJet the single largest passenger carrier at the UK airport. There is plenty of scope for scale economies in purchasing and back office functions. Moreover, easyJet should be able to boost GB's profitability by switching the carrier to its low-cost business model . . . easyJet makes an estimated £4 a passenger, against GB's £1. Assuming easyJet can drag up GB to its own levels of profitability, the company's value to the low-cost carrier is roughly four times its standalone worth.

The article makes the point that this looks like a good investment for easyJet, because of the strategic fit. For a business other than easyJet, the lack of strategic fit might well have meant that buying GB for exactly the same price of £103 million would not have been a good investment.

Source: Easy ride, ft.com (Hughes, C.), © The Financial Times Limited, 26 October 2007.

Dealing with risk

As we discussed earlier, all investments are risky. This means that consideration of risk is an important aspect of financial decision making. Risk, in this context, is the extent and likelihood that what is projected to occur will not actually happen. It is a particularly important issue in the context of investment decisions, because of

1 The relatively long timescales involved. There is more time for things to go wrong between the decision being made and the end of the project.
2 The size of the investment. If things go wrong, the impact can be both significant and lasting.

Various approaches to dealing with risk have been proposed. These fall into two categories: assessing the level of risk and reacting to the level of risk. We now consider formal methods of dealing with risk that fall within each category.

Assessing the level of risk

Sensitivity analysis

One popular way of attempting to assess the level of risk is to carry out a **sensitivity analysis** on the proposed project. This involves an examination of the key input values affecting the project to see how changes in each input might influence the viability of the project.

First, the investment is appraised, using the best estimates for each of the input factors (for example, labour cost, material cost, discount rate and so on). Assuming that the NPV is positive, each input value is then examined to see how far the estimated figure could be changed before the project becomes unviable for that reason alone. Let us suppose that the NPV for an investment in a machine to provide a particular service is a positive value. If we were to carry out a sensitivity analysis on this project, we should consider in turn each of the key input factors:

● initial outlay for the machine;
● sales volume and selling price;
● relevant operating costs;
● life of the project; and
● financing costs (to be used as the discount rate).

We should seek to find the value that each of them could have before the NPV figure would become negative (that is, the value for the factor at which NPV would be zero). The difference between the value for that factor at which the NPV would equal zero and the estimated value represents the margin of safety for that particular input. The process is set out in Figure 8.6.

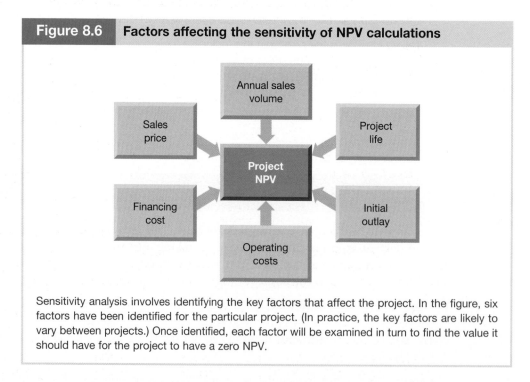

| **Figure 8.6** | **Factors affecting the sensitivity of NPV calculations** |

Sensitivity analysis involves identifying the key factors that affect the project. In the figure, six factors have been identified for the particular project. (In practice, the key factors are likely to vary between projects.) Once identified, each factor will be examined in turn to find the value it should have for the project to have a zero NPV.

A computer spreadsheet model of the project can be extremely valuable for this exercise because it then becomes a very simple matter to try various values for the input data and to see the effect of each. As a result of carrying out a sensitivity analysis, the decision maker is able to get a 'feel' for the project, which otherwise might not be possible. Example 8.3, which illustrates a sensitivity analysis is, however, straightforward and can be undertaken without recourse to a spreadsheet.

Example 8.3

S. Saluja (Property Developers) Ltd intends to bid at an auction, to be held today, for a manor house that has fallen into disrepair. The auctioneer believes that the house will be sold for about £450,000. The business wishes to renovate the property and to divide it into flats, to be sold for £150,000 each. The renovation will be in two stages and will cover a two-year period. Stage 1 will cover the first year of the project. It will cost £500,000 and the six flats completed during this stage are expected to be sold for a total of £900,000 at the end of the first year. Stage 2 will cover the second year of the project. It will cost £300,000 and the three remaining flats are expected to be sold at the end of the second year for a total of £450,000. The cost of renovation will be the subject of a binding contract with local builders if the property is bought. There is, however, some uncertainty over the remaining input values. The business estimates its cost of capital at 12 per cent a year.

(a) What is the NPV of the proposed project?
(b) Assuming none of the other inputs deviates from the best estimates provided,
    (1) What auction price would have to be paid for the manor house to cause the project to have a zero NPV?
    (2) What cost of capital would cause the project to have a zero NPV?
    (3) What is the sale price of each of the flats that would cause the project to have a zero NPV? (Each flat is projected to be sold for the same price: £150,000.)
(c) Is the level of risk associated with the project high or low? Discuss your findings.

Solution

(a) The NPV of the proposed project is as follows:

	Cash flows £	Discount factor 12%	Present value £
Year 1 (£900,000 – £500,000)	400,000	0.893	357,200
Year 2 (£450,000 – £300,000)	150,000	0.797	119,550
Less initial outlay			(450,000)
Net present value			26,750

(b) (1) To obtain a zero NPV, the auction price would have to be £26,750 higher than the current estimate – that is, a total price of £476,750. This is about 6 per cent above the current estimated price.
    (2) As there is a positive NPV, the cost of capital that would cause the project to have a zero NPV must be higher than 12 per cent. Let us try 20 per cent.

	Cash flows £	Discount factor 20%	Present value £
Year 1 (£900,000 – £500,000)	400,000	0.833	333,200
Year 2 (£450,000 – £300,000)	150,000	0.694	104,100
Less initial outlay			(450,000)
Net present value			(12,700)

→

Example 8.3 continued

As the NPV using a 20 per cent discount rate is negative, the 'break-even' cost of capital lies somewhere between 12 per cent and 20 per cent. A reasonable approximation is obtained as follows:

	Discount rate	Net present value
	%	£
	12	26,750
	20	(12,700)
Difference	8	39,450

The change in NPV for every 1 per cent change in the discount rate will be

$$39,450/8 = £4,931$$

The reduction in the 20 per cent discount rate required to achieve a zero NPV would therefore be

$$12,700/4,931 = 2.6\%$$

The cost of capital (that is, the discount rate) would, therefore, have to be 17.4 per cent (20.0 – 2.6) for the project to have a zero NPV.

This calculation is, of course, the same as that used earlier in the chapter, when calculating the IRR of a project. In other words, 17.4 per cent is the IRR of the project.

(3) To obtain a zero NPV, the sale price of each flat must be reduced so that the NPV is reduced by £26,750. In year 1, six flats are sold, and in year 2, three flats are sold. The discount factor at the 12 per cent rate is 0.893 for year 1 and 0.797 for year 2. We can derive the fall in value per flat (Y) to give a zero NPV by using the equation

$$(6Y \times 0.893) + (3Y \times 0.797) = £26,750$$
$$Y = £3,452$$

The sale price of each flat necessary to obtain a zero NPV is therefore

$$£150,000 - £3,452 = £146,548$$

This represents a fall in the estimated price of 2.3 per cent.

(c) These calculations indicate that the auction price would have to be about 6 per cent above the estimated price before a zero NPV is obtained. The margin of safety is, therefore, not very high for this factor. In practice this should not represent a real risk because the business could withdraw from the bidding if the price rises to an unacceptable level.

The other two factors represent serious risks, because only after the project is at a very late stage can the business be sure as to what actual cost of capital and price per flat will prevail. The calculations reveal that the price of the flats would only have to fall by 2.3 per cent from the estimated price before the NPV is reduced to zero. Hence, the margin of safety for this factor is even smaller. However, the cost of capital is less sensitive to changes and there would have to be an increase from 12 per cent to 17.4 per cent before the project produced a zero NPV. It seems from the calculations that the sale price of the flats is the most sensitive factor to consider. A careful re-examination of the market value of the flats seems appropriate before a final decision is made.

There are two major drawbacks with the use of sensitivity analysis:

- It does not give managers clear decision rules concerning acceptance or rejection of the project and so they must rely on their own judgement.
- It is a static form of analysis. Only one input is considered at a time, while the rest are held constant. In practice, however, it is likely that more than one input value will differ from the best estimates provided. Even so, it would be possible to deal with changes in various inputs simultaneously, were the project data put onto a spreadsheet model. This approach, where more than one variable is altered at a time, is known as **scenario building**.

Real World 8.14 describes an evaluation of a mining project that incorporated sensitivity analysis to test the robustness of the findings.

REAL WORLD 8.14

Golden opportunity

In 2006, Eureka Mining plc undertook an evaluation of the opportunity to mine copper and gold deposits at Miheevskoye, which is located in the Southern Urals region of the Russian Federation. Using three investment appraisal methods, the business came up with the following results:

	IRR	Pre-tax NPV	Payback period
	%	US$m	Years
	20.4	178.8	3.8

Sensitivity analysis was carried out on four key variables – the price of copper, the price of gold, operating costs and capital outlay costs – to help assess the riskiness of the project. This was done by assessing the IRR, NPV and PP, making various assumptions regarding the prices of copper and gold and about the percentage change in both the operating and the capital costs. The following table sets out the findings.

Copper price	IRR	Pre-tax NPV	Payback period
	%	US$m	Years
Average spot* copper price US$/lb			
1.10	8.8	(18.4)	8.1
1.20	14.8	80.2	5.0
1.40	25.7	277.3	3.0
1.50	30.8	375.9	2.7
Gold price			
Average spot* gold price US$/oz			
450	18.9	152.0	4.0
500	19.6	165.4	3.9
600	21.2	192.2	3.6
650	21.9	205.6	3.5

Real World 8.14 continued

Operating costs

Percentage change	Average total costs (lb copper equivalent)			
–20	$0.66	26.68	298.5	3.0
–10	$0.72	23.7	238.6	3.3
+10	$0.83	17.1	118.9	4.4
+20	$0.88	13.6	59.0	5.3

Capital costs

	Initial capital (US$m)			
–20	360	28.6	261.8	2.8
–10	405	24.1	220.3	3.2
+10	495	17.3	137.2	4.4
+20	540	14.7	95.7	5.1

* The spot price is the price for immediate delivery of the mineral.

In its report, the business stated:

> This project is most sensitive to percentage changes in the copper price which have the largest impact, whereas movements in the gold price have the least. The impact of changes in operating costs is more significant than capital costs.

Source: Adapted from 'Eureka Mining PLC – drilling report', www.citywire.co.uk, 26 July 2006.

Expected net present value

Another means of assessing risk is through the use of statistical probabilities. It may be possible to identify a range of feasible values for each of the items of input data and to assign a probability of occurrence to each of these values. Using this information, we can derive an **expected net present value (ENPV)**, which is, in effect, a weighted average of the possible outcomes where the probabilities are used as weights. To illustrate this method, let us consider Example 8.4.

Example 8.4

C. Piperis (Properties) Ltd has the opportunity to acquire a lease on a block of flats that has only two years remaining before it expires. The cost of the lease would be £100,000. The occupancy rate of the block of flats is currently around 70 per cent and the flats are let almost exclusively to naval personnel. There is a large naval base located nearby, and there is little other demand for the flats. The occupancy rate of the flats will change in the remaining two years of the lease, depending on the outcome of a defence review. The navy is currently considering three options for the naval base. These are:

● *Option 1*. Increase the size of the base by closing down a base in another region and transferring the personnel to the one located near the flats.
● *Option 2*. Close down the naval base near to the flats and leave only a skeleton staff there for maintenance purposes. The personnel would be moved to a base in another region.
● *Option 3*. Leave the base open but reduce staffing levels by 20 per cent.

The directors of Piperis have estimated the following net cash flows for each of the two years under each option and the probability of their occurrence:

	£	Probability
Option 1	80,000	0.6
Option 2	12,000	0.1
Option 3	40,000	0.3
		1.0

Note that the sum of the probabilities is 1.0 (in other words it is certain that one of the possible options will arise). The business has a cost of capital of 10 per cent. Should the business purchase the lease on the block of flats?

Solution

To calculate the expected NPV of the proposed investment, we must first calculate the weighted average of the expected outcomes for each year, using the probabilities as weights, by multiplying each cash flow by its probability of occurrence. Thus, the expected annual net cash flows will be:

	Cash flows	Probability	Expected cash flows
	£		£
	(a)	(b)	(a × b)
Option 1	80,000	0.6	48,000
Option 2	12,000	0.1	1,200
Option 3	40,000	0.3	12,000
Expected cash flows in each year			61,200

Having derived the expected annual cash flows, we can now discount these using a rate of 10 per cent to reflect the cost of capital:

Year	Expected cash flows	Discount rate	Expected present value
	£	10%	£
1	61,200	0.909	55,631
2	61,200	0.826	50,551
			106,182
Initial investment			(100,000)
Expected NPV			6,182

We can see that the expected NPV is positive. Hence, the wealth of shareholders is expected to increase by purchasing the lease.

The expected NPV approach has the advantage of producing a single numerical outcome and of having a clear decision rule to apply. If the expected NPV is positive, we should invest; if it is negative, we should not.

However, the approach produces an average figure, and it may not be possible for this figure actually to result. This point was illustrated in Example 8.4 where the expected annual cash flow (£61,200) does not correspond to any of the stated options.

Perhaps more importantly, using an average figure can obscure the underlying risk associated with the project. Simply deriving the ENPV, as in Example 8.4, can be misleading. Without some idea of the individual possible outcomes and their probability of occurring, the decision maker is in the dark. In Example 8.4, were either of Options 2 or 3 to occur, the investment would be adverse (wealth-destroying). It is 40 per cent probable that one of these two options will occur, so this is a significant risk. Only should Option 1 arise (60 per cent probable) would investing in the flats represent a good decision. Of course, in advance of making the investment, which option will actually occur is not known. None of this should be taken to mean that the investment in the flats should not be made, simply that the decision maker is better placed to make a judgement where information on the possible outcomes is available. Activity 8.18 further illustrates this point.

Activity 8.18

Qingdao Manufacturing Ltd is considering two competing projects. Details are as follows:

- Project A has a 0.9 probability of producing a negative NPV of £200,000 and a 0.1 probability of producing a positive NPV of £3.8m.
- Project B has a 0.6 probability of producing a positive NPV of £100,000 and a 0.4 probability of producing a positive NPV of £350,000.

What is the expected net present value of each project?

The expected NPV of Project A is

$$[(0.1 \times £3.8m) - (0.9 \times £200,000)] = £200,000$$

The expected NPV of Project B is

$$[(0.6 \times £100,000) + (0.4 \times £350,000)] = £200,000$$

Although the expected NPV of each project in Activity 8.18 is identical, this does not mean that the business will be indifferent about which project to undertake. We can see from the information provided that Project A has a high probability of making a loss whereas Project B is not expected to make a loss under either possible outcome. If we assume that the shareholders dislike risk – which is usually the case – they will prefer the directors to take on Project B as this provides the same level of expected return as Project A but for a lower level of risk.

It can be argued that the problem identified above may not be significant where the business is engaged in several similar projects. This is because a worse than expected outcome on one project may well be balanced by a better than expected outcome on another project. However, in practice, investment projects may be unique events and this argument will not then apply. Also, where the project is large in relation to other projects undertaken, the argument loses its force. There is also the problem that a factor that might cause one project to have an adverse outcome could also have adverse effects on other projects. For example, a large, unexpected increase in the price of oil may have a simultaneous adverse effect on all of the investment projects of a particular business.

Where the expected NPV approach is being used, it is probably a good idea to make known to managers the different possible outcomes and the probability attached to each outcome. By so doing, the managers will be able to gain an insight to the *downside risk* attached to the project. The information relating to each outcome can be presented in the form of a diagram if required. The construction of such a diagram is illustrated in Example 8.5.

Example 8.5

Zeta Computing Services Ltd has recently produced some software for a client organisation. The software has a life of two years and will then become obsolete. The cost of producing the software was £10,000. The client has agreed to pay a licence fee of £8,000 a year for the software if it is used in only one of its two divisions, and £12,000 a year if it is used in both of its divisions. The client may use the software for either one or two years in either division but will definitely use it in at least one division in each of the two years.

Zeta believes there is a 0.6 chance that the licence fee received in any one year will be £8,000 and a 0.4 chance that it will be £12,000. There are, therefore, four possible outcomes attached to this project (where p denotes probability):

- *Outcome 1*. Year 1 cash flow £8,000 ($p = 0.6$) and Year 2 cash flow £8,000 ($p = 0.6$). The probability of both years having cash flows of £8,000 will be

$$0.6 \times 0.6 = 0.36$$

- *Outcome 2*. Year 1 cash flow £12,000 ($p = 0.4$) and Year 2 cash flow £12,000 ($p = 0.4$). The probability of both years having cash flows of £12,000 will be

$$0.4 \times 0.4 = 0.16$$

- *Outcome 3*. Year 1 cash flow £12,000 ($p = 0.4$) and Year 2 cash flow £8,000 ($p = 0.6$). The probability of this sequence of cash flows occurring will be

$$0.4 \times 0.6 = 0.24$$

- *Outcome 4*. Year 1 cash flow £8,000 ($p = 0.6$) and Year 2 cash flow £12,000 ($p = 0.4$). The probability of this sequence of cash flows occurring will be

$$0.6 \times 0.4 = 0.24$$

The information in Example 8.5 can be displayed in the form of a diagram, as in Figure 8.7.

The source of probabilities

As we might expect, assigning probabilities to possible outcomes can often be a problem. There may be many possible outcomes arising from a particular investment project, and to identify each outcome and then assign a probability to it may prove to be an impossible task. When assigning probabilities to possible outcomes, an objective or a subjective approach may be used. **Objective probabilities** are based on information gathered from past experience. Thus, for example, the transport manager of a business operating a fleet of vans may be able to provide information concerning the possible life of a new van based on the record of similar vans acquired in the past. From the information available, probabilities may be developed for different possible lifespans. However, the past may not always be a reliable guide to the future, particularly during a period of rapid change. In the case of the vans, for example, changes in design and technology or changes in the purpose for which the vans are being used may undermine the validity of past data.

Figure 8.7	The different possible project outcomes for the Zeta project (Example 8.5)

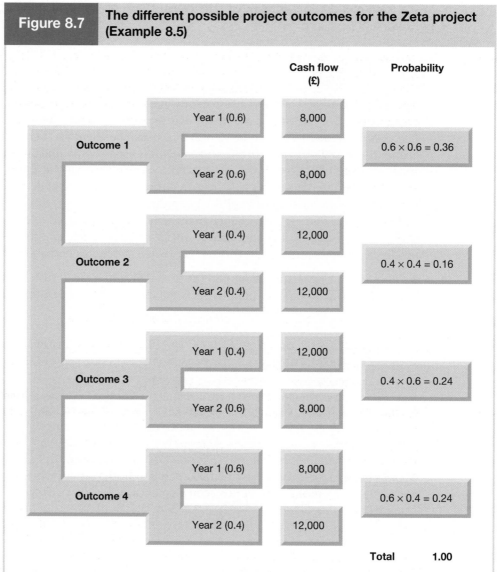

There are four different possible outcomes associated with the project, each with its own probability of occurrence. The sum of the probabilities attached to each outcome must equal 1.00, in other words it is certain that one of the possible outcomes will occur. For example, Outcome 1 would occur where only one division uses the software in each year.

Subjective probabilities are based on opinion and will be used where past data are either inappropriate or unavailable. The opinions of independent experts may provide a useful basis for developing subjective probabilities, though even these may contain bias, which will affect the reliability of the judgements made.

Despite these problems, we should not be dismissive of the use of probabilities. Assigning probabilities can help to make explicit some of the risks associated with a project and should help decision makers to appreciate the uncertainties that have to be faced.

Activity 8.19

Devonia (Laboratories) Ltd has recently carried out successful clinical trials on a new type of skin cream that has been developed to reduce the effects of ageing. Research and development costs incurred relating to the new product amounted to £160,000. In order to gauge the market potential of the new product, independent market research consultants were hired at a cost of £15,000. The market research report submitted by the consultants indicates that the skin cream is likely to have a product life of four years and could be sold to retail chemists and large department stores at a price of £20 per 100 ml container. For each of the four years of the new product's life, sales demand has been estimated as follows:

Number of 100 ml containers sold	Probability of occurrence
11,000	0.3
14,000	0.6
16,000	0.1

If the business decides to launch the new product, it is possible for production to begin at once. The equipment necessary to produce it is already owned by the business and originally cost £150,000. At the end of the new product's life, it is estimated that the equipment could be sold for £35,000. If the business decides against launching the new product, the equipment will be sold immediately for £85,000, as it will be of no further use.

The new product will require one hour's labour for each 100 ml container produced. The cost of labour is £8.00 an hour. Additional workers will have to be recruited to produce the new product. At the end of the product's life, the workers are unlikely to be offered further work with the business and redundancy costs of £10,000 are expected. The cost of the ingredients for each 100 ml container is £6.00. Additional overheads arising from production of the new product are expected to be £15,000 a year.

The new skin cream has attracted the interest of the business's competitors. If the business decides not to produce and sell the skin cream, it can sell the patent rights to a major competitor immediately for £125,000.

Devonia has a cost of capital of 12 per cent.

(a) Calculate the expected net present value (ENPV) of the new product.
(b) State, with reasons, whether or not Devonia should launch the new product.

Ignore taxation.

Your answer should be as follows:

(a) Expected sales volume per year = (11,000 × 0.3) + (14,000 × 0.6) + (16,000 × 0.1)
= 13,300 units
Expected annual sales revenue = 13,300 × £20
= £266,000
Annual labour = 13,300 × £8
= £106,400
Annual ingredient costs = 13,300 × £6
= £79,800

→

Activity 8.19 continued

Incremental cash flows:

	Years				
	0 £	1 £	2 £	3 £	4 £
Sale of patent rights	(125.0)				
Sale of equipment	(85.0)				35.0
Sales revenue		266.0	266.0	266.0	266.0
Cost of ingredients		(79.8)	(79.8)	(79.8)	(79.8)
Labour costs		(106.4)	(106.4)	(106.4)	(106.4)
Redundancy					(10.0)
Additional overheads		(15.0)	(15.0)	(15.0)	(15.0)
	(210.0)	64.8	64.8	64.8	89.8
Discount factor (12%)	1.000	0.893	0.797	0.712	0.636
	(210.0)	57.9	51.6	46.1	57.1
ENPV	2.7				

(b) As the ENPV of the project is positive, accepting the project would increase the wealth of shareholders. However, the ENPV is very low in relation to the size of the project and careful checking of the key estimates and assumptions would be advisable. A relatively small downward revision of sales (volume and/or price) or upward revision of costs could make the project ENPV negative.

It would be helpful to derive the NPV for each of the three possible outcomes regarding sales levels. This would enable the decision maker to have a clearer view of the risk involved with the investment.

Reacting to the level of risk

The logical reaction to a risky project is to demand a higher rate of return. Clear observable evidence shows that there is a relationship between risk and the return required by investors. It was mentioned earlier, for example, that a bank would normally ask for a higher rate of interest on a loan where it perceives the borrower to be less likely to be able to repay the amount borrowed.

When assessing investment projects, it is normal to increase the NPV discount rate in the face of increased risk – that is, to demand a risk premium: the higher the level of risk, the higher the risk premium that will be demanded. The risk premium is added to the 'risk-free' rate of return to derive the total return required (the **risk-adjusted discount rate**). The risk-free rate is normally taken to be equivalent to the rate of return from government loan notes. In practice, a business may divide projects into low-, medium- and high-risk categories and then assign a risk premium to each category. The cash flows from a particular project will then be discounted using a rate based on the risk-free rate plus the appropriate risk premium. Since all investments are risky to some extent, all projects will have a risk premium linked to them.

The relationship between risk and return is illustrated in Figure 8.8.

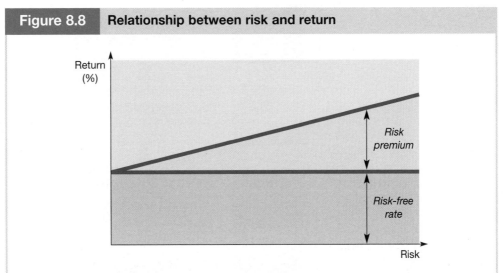

Figure 8.8 | **Relationship between risk and return**

It is logical to take account of the riskiness of projects by changing the discount rate. A risk premium is added to the risk-free rate to derive the appropriate discount rate. A higher return will normally be expected from projects where the risks are higher; thus, the riskier the project, the higher the risk premium.

Activity 8.20

Can you think of any practical problems with estimating an appropriate value for the risk premium for a particular project?

Subjective judgement tends to be required when assigning an investment project to a particular risk category and then in assigning a risk premium to each category. The choices made will reflect the personal views of the managers responsible and these may differ from the views of the shareholders they represent. The choices made can, nevertheless, make the difference between accepting and rejecting a particular project.

Managing investment projects

So far, we have been concerned with the process of carrying out the necessary calculations that enable managers to select among already identified investment opportunities. This topic is given a great deal of emphasis in the literature on investment appraisal. Though the assessment of projects is undoubtedly important, we must bear in mind that it is only *part* of the process of investment decision making. There are other important aspects that managers must also consider.

It is possible to see the investment process as a sequence of five stages, each of which managers must consider. The five stages are set out in Figure 8.9 and described below.

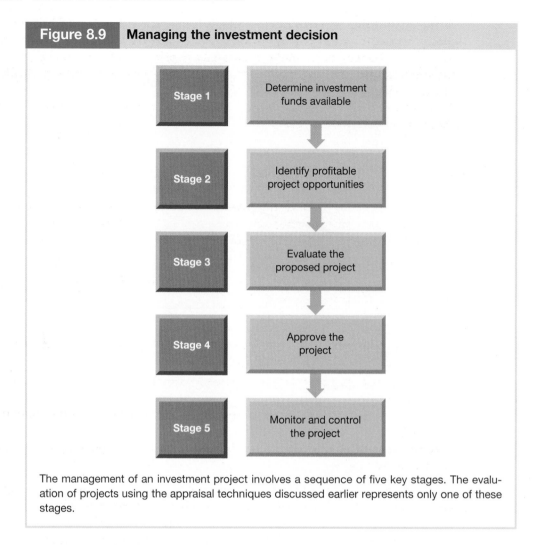

Figure 8.9 **Managing the investment decision**

The management of an investment project involves a sequence of five key stages. The evaluation of projects using the appraisal techniques discussed earlier represents only one of these stages.

Stage 1: Determine investment funds available

The amount of funds available for investment may be determined by the external market for funds or by internal management. In practice, it is often the latter that has the greater influence on the amount available. In either case, it may be that the funds will not be sufficient to finance the profitable investment opportunities available. This shortage of investment funds is known as *capital rationing*. When it arises managers are faced with the task of deciding on the most profitable use of those funds available.

Stage 2: Identify profitable project opportunities

A vital part of the investment process is the search for profitable investment opportunities. The business should carry out methodical routines for identifying feasible projects. This may be done through a research and development department or by some other means. Failure to do so will inevitably lead to the business losing its competitive position with respect to product development, production methods or market penetration. To help identify good investment opportunities, some businesses provide financial incentives to members of staff who come forward with good investment proposals. The search process will, however, usually involve looking outside the business to identify changes in technology, customer demand, market conditions and so on. Information will have to be gathered and this may take some time, particularly for unusual or non-routine investment opportunities.

As we saw earlier in this chapter, it is important that the business's investments should fit in with its strategic plans.

Stage 3: Evaluate the proposed project

If management is to agree to the investment of funds in a project, there must be a proper screening of each proposal. For larger projects, this will involve providing answers to a number of questions, including:

- What are the nature and purpose of the project?
- Does the project align with the overall objectives of the business?
- How much finance is required?
- What other resources (such as expertise, work space and so on) are required for successful completion of the project?
- How long will the project last and what are its key stages?
- What is the expected pattern of cash flows?
- What are the major problems associated with the project and how can they be overcome?
- What is the NPV of the project? How does this compare with other opportunities available?
- Have risk and inflation been taken into account in the appraisal process and, if so, what are the results?

The ability and commitment of those responsible for proposing and managing the project will be vital to its success. This means that, when evaluating a new project, one consideration will be the quality of those proposing it. In some cases, senior managers may decide not to support a project that appears profitable on paper if they lack confidence in the ability of key managers to see it through to completion.

Stage 4: Approve the project

Once the managers responsible for investment decision making are satisfied that the project should be undertaken, formal approval can be given. However, a decision on a project may be postponed if senior managers need more information from those proposing the project, or if revisions to the proposal are required. In some cases, the proposal may be rejected if the project is considered unprofitable or likely to fail. Before rejecting a proposal, however, the implications of not pursuing the project for such areas as market share, staff morale and existing business operations must be carefully considered.

Stage 5: Monitor and control the project

Making a decision to invest in, say, the plant needed to provide a new service does not automatically cause the investment to be made and provision of the service to go smoothly ahead. Managers will need to manage the project actively through to completion. This, in turn, will require further information-gathering exercises.

Management should receive progress reports at regular intervals concerning the project. These reports should provide information relating to the actual cash flows for each stage of the project, which can then be compared against the forecast figures provided when the proposal was submitted for approval. The reasons for significant variations should be ascertained and corrective action taken where possible. Any changes in the expected completion date of the project or any expected variations from budget in future cash flows should be reported immediately; in extreme cases, managers may even abandon the project if circumstances appear to have changed dramatically for the worse. We saw in **Real World 8.12**, on p. 289, that Rolls-Royce undertakes this kind of reassessment of existing projects. No doubt most other well-managed businesses do this too.

Project management techniques (for example, critical path analysis) should be employed wherever possible and their effectiveness reported to senior management.

An important part of the control process is a **post-completion audit** of the project. This is, in essence, a review of the project's performance to see if it lived up to expectations and whether any lessons can be learned from the way that the investment process was carried out. In addition to an evaluation of financial costs and benefits, non-financial measures of performance such as the ability to meet deadlines and levels of quality achieved should also be reported. We should recall that total life-cycle costing, which we discussed in Chapter 5, is based on similar principles.

The fact that a post-completion audit is an integral part of the management of the project should also encourage those who submit projects to use realistic estimates. **Real World 8.15** provides some evidence of a need for greater realism.

REAL WORLD 8.15

Looking on the bright side

McKinsey and Co, the management consultants, surveyed 2,500 senior managers worldwide during the spring of 2007. The managers were asked their opinions on investments made by their businesses in the previous three years. The general opinion is that estimates for the investment decision inputs had been too optimistic. For example, sales levels had been overestimated in about 50 per cent of cases, but underestimated in less than 20 per cent of cases. It is not clear whether the estimates were sufficiently inaccurate to call into question the decision that had been made.

The survey went on to ask about the extent to which investments made seemed, in the light of the actual outcomes, to have been mistakes. Managers felt that 19 per cent of investments that had been made should not have gone ahead. On the other hand, they felt that 31 per cent of rejected projects should have been taken up. Managers also felt that 'good money was thrown after bad' in that existing investments that were not performing well were continuing to be supported in a significant number of cases.

Source: 'How companies spend their money: a McKinsey global survey', www.theglobalmarketer.com, 2007.

Other studies confirm a tendency among managers to use overoptimistic estimates when preparing investment proposals. (See reference 1 at the end of the chapter.) It seems that sometimes this is done deliberately in an attempt to secure project approval.

Where overoptimistic estimates are used, the managers responsible may well find themselves accountable at the post-completion audit stage. Such audits, however, can be difficult and time-consuming to carry out, and so the likely benefits must be weighed against the costs involved. Senior management may feel, therefore, that only projects above a certain size should be subject to a post-completion audit.

Real World 8.16 describes how two large retailers, Tesco plc and Kingfisher plc, use post-completion audit approaches to evaluating past investment projects.

REAL WORLD 8.16

Looking back

In its 2008 corporate governance report, Tesco plc, the supermarket chain, stated:

> All major initiatives require business cases to be prepared, normally covering a minimum period of five years. Post-investment appraisals, carried out by management, determine the reasons for any significant variance from expected performance.

In its 2007/8 financial review, Kingfisher plc, the home improvement retailer, stated:

> An annual post-investment review process will continue to review the performance of all projects above £0.75 million which were completed in the prior year. The findings of this exercise will be considered by both the new Retail Board and the main Board and directly influence the assumptions for similar project proposals going forward.

Sources: The websites of Tesco plc (www.tescocorporate.com) and Kingfisher plc (www.kingfisher.co.uk).

As a footnote to our discussion of business investment decision making, **Real World 8.17** looks at one of the world's biggest investment projects, which has proved to be a commercial disaster, despite being a technological success.

REAL WORLD 8.17

Wealth lost in the chunnel

The tunnel, which runs for 31 miles between Folkestone in the UK and Sangatte in Northern France, was started in 1986 and opened for public use in 1994. From a technological and social perspective it has been a success, but from a financial point of view it has been a disaster. The tunnel was purely a private sector venture for which a new business, Eurotunnel plc, was created. Relatively little public money was involved. To be a commercial success the tunnel needed to cover all of its costs, including interest charges, and leave sufficient to enhance the shareholders' wealth. In fact the providers of long-term finance (lenders and shareholders) have lost virtually all of their investment. Though the main losers were banks and institutional investors, many individuals, particularly in France, bought shares in Eurotunnel.

Key inputs to the pre-1986 assessment of the project were the cost of construction and creating the infrastructure, the length of time required to complete construction and the level of revenue that the tunnel would generate when it became operational.

Real World 8.17 continued

In the event

- Construction cost was £10 billion – it was originally planned to cost £5.6 billion.
- Construction time was seven years – it was planned to be six years.
- Revenues from passengers and freight have been well below those projected – for example, 21 million annual passenger journeys on Eurostar trains were projected; the numbers have consistently remained at around 7 million.

The failure to generate revenues at the projected levels has probably been the biggest contributor to the problem. When preparing the projection, planners failed to take adequate account of two crucial factors:

1 Fierce competition from the ferry operators. At the time (pre-1986), many thought that the ferries would roll over and die.
2 The rise of no-frills, cheap air travel between the UK and the continent.

The commercial failure of the tunnel means that it will be very difficult in future for projects of this nature to be funded by private funds.

Sources: Annual reports of Eurotunnel plc; Randall, J., 'How Eurotunnel went wrong', BBC news, 13 June 2005, www.newsvote.bbc.co.uk.

SUMMARY

The main points of this chapter may be summarised as follows:

Accounting rate of return (ARR) is the average accounting profit from the project expressed as a percentage of the average investment.

- Decision rule – projects with an ARR above a defined minimum are acceptable; the greater the ARR, the more attractive the project becomes.
- Conclusion on ARR:
  - Does not relate directly to shareholders' wealth – can lead to illogical conclusions.
  - Takes almost no account of the timing of cash flows.
  - Ignores some relevant information and may take account of some that is irrelevant.
  - Relatively simple to use.
  - Much inferior to NPV.

Payback period (PP) is the length of time that it takes for the cash outflow for the initial investment to be repaid out of resulting cash inflows.

- Decision rule – projects with a PP up to a defined maximum period are acceptable; the shorter the PP, the more attractive the project.
- Conclusion on PP:
  - Does not relate to shareholders' wealth.
  - Ignores inflows after the payback date.
  - Takes little account of the timing of cash flows.
  - Ignores much relevant information.
  - Does not always provide clear signals and can be impractical to use.
  - Much inferior to NPV, but it is easy to understand and can offer a liquidity insight, which might be the reason for its widespread use.

Net present value (NPV) is the sum of the discounted values of the net cash flows from the investment.

- Money has a time value.
- Decision rule – all positive NPV investments enhance shareholders' wealth; the greater the NPV, the greater the enhancement and the greater the attractiveness of the project.
- PV of a cash flow = cash flow $\times 1/(1 + r)^n$, assuming a constant discount rate.
- Discounting brings cash flows at different points in time to a common valuation basis (their present value), which enables them to be directly compared.
- Conclusion on NPV:
  - Relates directly to shareholders' wealth objective.
  - Takes account of the timing of cash flows.
  - Takes all relevant information into account.
  - Provides clear signals and is practical to use.

Internal rate of return (IRR) is the discount rate that, when applied to the cash flows of a project, causes it to have a zero NPV.

- Represents the average percentage return on the investment, taking account of the fact that cash may be flowing in and out of the project at various points in its life.
- Decision rule – projects that have an IRR greater than the cost of capital are acceptable; the greater the IRR, the more attractive the project.
- Cannot normally be calculated directly; a trial and error approach is often necessary.
- Conclusion on IRR:
  - Does not relate directly to shareholders' wealth. Usually gives the same signals as NPV but can mislead where there are competing projects of different size.
  - Takes account of the timing of cash flows.
  - Takes all relevant information into account.
  - Problems of multiple IRRs when there are unconventional cash flows.
  - Inferior to NPV.

Use of appraisal methods in practice:

- All four methods identified are widely used.
- The discounting methods (NPV and IRR) show a steady increase in usage over time.
- Many businesses use more than one method.
- Larger businesses seem to be more sophisticated in their choice and use of appraisal methods than smaller ones.

Investment appraisal and strategic planning

It is important that businesses invest in a strategic way so as to play to their strengths.

Dealing with risk

- Sensitivity analysis (SA) is an assessment, taking each input factor in turn, of how much each one can vary from estimate before a project is not viable.
  - Provides useful insights to projects.
  - Does not give a clear decision rule, but provides an impression.
  - It can be rather static, but scenario building solves this problem.
- Expected net present value (ENPV) is the weighted average of the possible outcomes for a project, based on probabilities for each of the inputs:
  - Provides a single value and a clear decision rule.
  - The single ENPV figure can hide the real risk.

– Useful for the ENPV figure to be supported by information on the range and dispersion of possible outcomes.
– Probabilities may be subjective (based on opinion) or objective (based on evidence).
● Reacting to the level of risk:
– Logically, high risk should lead to high returns.
– Using a risk-adjusted discount rate, where a risk premium is added to the risk-free rate, is a logical response to risk.

Managing investment projects

● Determine investment funds available – dealing, if necessary, with capital rationing problems.
● Identify profitable project opportunities.
● Evaluate the proposed project.
● Approve the project.
● Monitor and control the project – using a post-completion audit approach.

 Key terms

Accounting rate of return (ARR) p. 261
Payback period (PP) p. 265
Net present value (NPV) p. 269
Risk p. 270
Risk premium p. 272
Inflation p. 272
Discount factor p. 276
Cost of capital p. 277
Internal rate of return (IRR) p. 279

Relevant costs p. 283
Sensitivity analysis p. 292
Scenario building p. 295
Expected net present value (ENPV) p. 296
Objective probabilities p. 299
Subjective probabilities p. 301
Risk-adjusted discount rate p. 302
Post-completion audit p. 306

References

1 Linder, S., 'Fifty years of research on accuracy of capital expenditure project estimates: a review of findings and their validity', Otto Beisham Graduate School of Management, April 2005.

Further reading

If you would like to explore the topics covered in this chapter in more depth, we recommend the following books:

McLaney, E., *Business Finance: Theory and Practice*, 8th edn, Financial Times Prentice Hall, 2009, chapters 4, 5 and 6.

Pike, R. and Neale, B., *Corporate Finance and Investment*, 5th edn, Prentice Hall, 2006, chapters 5, 6 and 7.

Arnold, G., *Corporate Financial Management*, 3rd edn, Financial Times Prentice Hall, 2005, chapters 2, 3 and 4.

Drury, C., *Management and Cost Accounting*, 8th edn, Thomson Learning, 2009, chapters 13 and 14.

REVIEW QUESTIONS

Answers to these questions can be found in Appendix C at the back of the book.

8.1 Why is the net present value (NPV) method of investment appraisal considered to be theoretically superior to other methods that are found in practice?

8.2 The payback method has been criticised for not taking the time value of money into account. Could this limitation be overcome? If so, would this method then be preferable to the NPV method?

8.3 Research indicates that the IRR method is extremely popular even though it has shortcomings when compared to the NPV method. Why might managers prefer to use IRR rather than NPV when carrying out discounted cash flow evaluations?

8.4 Why are cash flows rather than profit flows used in the IRR, NPV and PP methods of investment appraisal?

EXERCISES

Exercises 8.3 to 8.8 are more advanced than 8.1 and 8.2. Those with a coloured number have answers in Appendix D at the back of the book. If you wish to try more exercises, visit the students' side of the Companion Website at www.pearsoned.co.uk/atrillmclaney.

8.1 The directors of Mylo Ltd are currently considering two mutually exclusive investment projects. Both projects are concerned with the purchase of new plant. The following data are available for each project:

	Project 1 £000	Project 2 £000
Cost (immediate outlay)	100	60
Expected annual operating profit (loss):		
Year 1	29	18
2	(1)	(2)
3	2	4
Estimated residual value of the plant	7	6

The business has an estimated cost of capital of 10 per cent, and uses the straight-line method of depreciation for all non-current (fixed) assets when calculating operating profit. Neither project would increase the working capital of the business. The business has sufficient funds to meet all capital expenditure requirements.

Required:
(a) Calculate for each project:
  (1) The net present value.
  (2) The approximate internal rate of return.
  (3) The payback period.

(b) State which, if either, of the two investment projects the directors of Mylo Ltd should accept, and why.

8.2   C. George (Controls) Ltd manufactures a thermostat that can be used in a range of kitchen appliances. The manufacturing process is, at present, semi-automated. The equipment used cost £540,000, and has a written-down (balance sheet) value of £300,000. Demand for the product has been fairly stable, and output has been maintained at 50,000 units a year in recent years.

The following data, based on the current level of output, have been prepared in respect of the product:

	Per unit	
	£	£
Selling price		12.40
Labour	(3.30)	
Materials	(3.65)	
Overheads: Variable	(1.58)	
Fixed	(1.60)	
		(10.13)
Operating profit		2.27

Although the existing equipment is expected to last for a further four years before it is sold for an estimated £40,000, the business has recently been considering purchasing new equipment that would completely automate much of the production process. The new equipment would cost £670,000 and would have an expected life of four years, at the end of which it would be sold for an estimated £70,000. If the new equipment is purchased, the old equipment could be sold for £150,000 immediately.

The assistant to the business's accountant has prepared a report to help assess the viability of the proposed change, which includes the following data:

	Per unit	
	£	£
Selling price		12.40
Labour	(1.20)	
Materials	(3.20)	
Overheads: Variable	(1.40)	
Fixed	(3.30)	
		(9.10)
Operating profit		3.30

Depreciation charges will increase by £85,000 a year as a result of purchasing the new machinery; however, other fixed costs are not expected to change.

In the report the assistant wrote:

> The figures shown above that relate to the proposed change are based on the current level of output and take account of a depreciation charge of £150,000 a year in respect of the new equipment. The effect of purchasing the new equipment will be to increase the operating profit to sales revenue ratio from 18.3% to 26.6%. In addition, the purchase of the new equipment will enable us to reduce our inventories level immediately by £130,000.
>
> In view of these facts, I recommend purchase of the new equipment.

The business has a cost of capital of 12 per cent.

Required:

(a) Prepare a statement of the incremental cash flows arising from the purchase of the new equipment.

(b) Calculate the net present value of the proposed purchase of new equipment.

(c) State, with reasons, whether the business should purchase the new equipment.

(d) Explain why cash flow forecasts are used rather than profit forecasts to assess the viability of proposed capital expenditure projects.

Ignore taxation.

8.3 The accountant of your business has recently been taken ill through overwork. In his absence his assistant has prepared some calculations of the profitability of a project, which are to be discussed soon at the board meeting of your business. His workings, which are set out below, include some errors of principle. You can assume that the statement below includes no arithmetical errors.

	Year 1 £000	Year 2 £000	Year 3 £000	Year 4 £000	Year 5 £000	Year 6 £000
Sales revenue		450	470	470	470	470
Less Costs						
Materials		126	132	132	132	132
Labour		90	94	94	94	94
Overheads		45	47	47	47	47
Depreciation		120	120	120	120	120
Working capital	180					
Interest on working capital		27	27	27	27	27
Write-off of development costs		30	30	30		
Total costs	180	438	450	450	420	420
Operating profit/(loss)	(180)	12	20	20	50	50

$$\frac{\text{Total profit (loss)}}{\text{Cost of equipment}} = \frac{(£28,000)}{£600,000} = \text{Return on investment (4.7\%)}$$

You ascertain the following additional information:

● The cost of equipment contains £100,000, being the carrying (balance sheet) value of an old machine. If it were not used for this project it would be scrapped with a zero net realisable value. New equipment costing £500,000 will be purchased on 31 December Year 0. You should assume that all other cash flows occur at the end of the year to which they relate.

● The development costs of £90,000 have already been spent.

● Overheads have been costed at 50 per cent of direct labour, which is the business's normal practice. An independent assessment has suggested that incremental overheads are likely to amount to £30,000 a year.

● The business's cost of capital is 12 per cent.

Required:

(a) Prepare a corrected statement of the incremental cash flows arising from the project. Where you have altered the assistant's figures you should attach a brief note explaining your alterations.

(b) Calculate:

(1) The project's payback period.

(2) The project's net present value as at 31 December Year 0.

(c) Write a memo to the board advising on the acceptance or rejection of the project.

Ignore taxation in your answer.

8.4   Arkwright Mills plc is considering expanding its production of a new yarn, code name X15. The plant is expected to cost £1 million and have a life of five years and a nil residual value. It will be bought, paid for and ready for operation on 31 December Year 0. £500,000 has already been spent on development costs of the product, and this has been charged in the income statement in the year it was incurred.

The following results are projected for the new yarn:

	Year 1 £m	Year 2 £m	Year 3 £m	Year 4 £m	Year 5 £m
Sales revenue	1.2	1.4	1.4	1.4	1.4
Costs, including depreciation	1.0	1.1	1.1	1.1	1.1
Profit before tax	0.2	0.3	0.3	0.3	0.3

Tax is charged at 50 per cent on annual profits (before tax and after depreciation) and paid one year in arrears. Depreciation of the plant has been calculated on a straight-line basis. Additional working capital of £0.6m will be required at the beginning of the project and released at the end of Year 5. You should assume that all cash flows occur at the end of the year in which they arise.

Required:

(a) Prepare a statement showing the incremental cash flows of the project relevant to a decision concerning whether or not to proceed with the construction of the new plant.

(b) Compute the net present value of the project using a 10 per cent discount rate.

(c) Compute the payback period to the nearest year. Explain the meaning of this term.

8.5   Newton Electronics Ltd has incurred expenditure of £5 million over the past three years researching and developing a miniature hearing aid. The hearing aid is now fully developed, and the directors are considering which of three mutually exclusive options should be taken to exploit the potential of the new product. The options are as follows:

1   The business could manufacture the hearing aid itself. This would be a new departure, since the business has so far concentrated on research and development projects. However, the business has manufacturing space available that it currently rents to another business for £100,000 a year. The business would have to purchase plant and equipment costing £9 million and invest £3 million in working capital immediately for production to begin.

A market research report, for which the business paid £50,000, indicates that the new product has an expected life of five years. Sales of the product during this period are predicted as follows:

	Predicted sales for the year ended 30 November				
	Year 1	Year 2	Year 3	Year 4	Year 5
Number of units (000s)	800	1,400	1,800	1,200	500

The selling price per unit will be £30 in the first year but will fall to £22 in the following three years. In the final year of the product's life, the selling price will fall to £20. Variable production costs are predicted to be £14 a unit, and fixed production costs (including depreciation) will be £2.4 million a year. Marketing costs will be £2 million a year.

The business intends to depreciate the plant and equipment using the straight-line method and based on an estimated residual value at the end of the five years of £1 million. The business has a cost of capital of 10 per cent a year.

2   Newton Electronics Ltd could agree to another business manufacturing and marketing the product under licence. A multinational business, Faraday Electricals plc, has offered to undertake the manufacture and marketing of the product, and in return will make a royalty payment to Newton Electronics Ltd of £5 per unit. It has been estimated that the annual

number of sales of the hearing aid will be 10 per cent higher if the multinational business, rather than Newton Electronics Ltd, manufactures and markets the product.

3   Newton Electronics Ltd could sell the patent rights to Faraday Electricals plc for £24 million, payable in two equal instalments. The first instalment would be payable immediately and the second at the end of two years. This option would give Faraday Electricals the exclusive right to manufacture and market the new product.

Required:

(a) Calculate the net present value (as at 1 January Year 1) of each of the options available to Newton Electronics Ltd.

(b) Identify and discuss any other factors that Newton Electronics Ltd should consider before arriving at a decision.

(c) State what you consider to be the most suitable option, and why.

Ignore taxation.

8.6 Chesterfield Wanderers is a professional football club that has enjoyed considerable success in both national and European competitions in recent years. As a result, the club has accumulated £10 million to spend on its further development. The board of directors is currently considering two mutually exclusive options for spending the funds available.

The first option is to acquire another player. The team manager has expressed a keen interest in acquiring Basil ('Bazza') Ramsey, a central defender, who currently plays for a rival club. The rival club has agreed to release the player immediately for £10 million if required. A decision to acquire 'Bazza' Ramsey would mean that the existing central defender, Vinnie Smith, could be sold to another club. Chesterfield Wanderers has recently received an offer of £2.2 million for this player. This offer is still open but will only be accepted if 'Bazza' Ramsey joins Chesterfield Wanderers. If this does not happen, Vinnie Smith will be expected to stay on with the club until the end of his playing career in five years' time. During this period, Vinnie will receive an annual salary of £400,000 and a loyalty bonus of £200,000 at the end of his five-year period with the club.

Assuming 'Bazza' Ramsey is acquired, the team manager estimates that gate receipts will increase by £2.5 million in the first year and £1.3 million in each of the four following years. There will also be an increase in advertising and sponsorship revenues of £1.2 million for each of the next five years if the player is acquired. At the end of five years, the player can be sold to a club in a lower division and Chesterfield Wanderers will expect to receive £1 million as a transfer fee. During his period at the club, 'Bazza' will receive an annual salary of £800,000 and a loyalty bonus of £400,000 after five years.

The second option is for the club to improve its ground facilities. The west stand could be extended and executive boxes could be built for businesses wishing to offer corporate hospitality to clients. These improvements would also cost £10 million and would take one year to complete. During this period, the west stand would be closed, resulting in a reduction of gate receipts of £1.8 million. However, gate receipts for each of the following four years would be £4.4 million higher than current receipts. In five years' time, the club has plans to sell the existing grounds and to move to a new stadium nearby. Improving the ground facilities is not expected to affect the ground's value when it comes to be sold. Payment for the improvements will be made when the work has been completed at the end of the first year. Whichever option is chosen, the board of directors has decided to take on additional ground staff. The additional wages bill is expected to be £350,000 a year over the next five years.

The club has a cost of capital of 10 per cent. Ignore taxation.

Required:

(a) Calculate the incremental cash flows arising from each of the options available to the club.

(b) Calculate the net present value of each of the options.

(c) On the basis of the calculations made in (b) above, which of the two options would you choose and why?

(d) Discuss the validity of using the net present value method in making investment decisions for a professional football club.

8.7 Simtex Ltd has invested £120,000 to date in developing a new type of shaving foam. The shaving foam is now ready for production and it has been estimated that the new product will sell 160,000 cans a year over the next four years. At the end of four years, the product will be discontinued and replaced by a new product.

The shaving foam is expected to sell at £6 a can and the variable cost is estimated at £4 per can. Fixed cost (excluding depreciation) is expected to be £300,000 a year. (This figure includes £130,000 in fixed cost incurred by the existing business that will be apportioned to this new product.)

To manufacture and package the new product, equipment costing £480,000 must be acquired immediately. The estimated value of this equipment in four years' time is £100,000. The business calculates depreciation using the straight-line method, and has an estimated cost of capital of 12 per cent.

Required:
(a) Deduce the net present value of the new product.
(b) Calculate by how much each of the following must change before the new product is no longer profitable:
   (i) the discount rate;
   (ii) the initial outlay on new equipment;
   (iii) the net operating cash flows;
   (iv) the residual value of the equipment.
(c) Should the business produce the new product?

8.8 Kernow Cleaning Services Ltd provides street-cleaning services for local councils in the far south west of England. The work is currently labour-intensive and few machines are used. However, the business has recently been considering the purchase of a fleet of street-cleaning vehicles at a total cost of £540,000. The vehicles have a life of four years and are likely to result in a considerable saving of labour costs. Estimates of the likely labour savings and their probability of occurrence are set out below.

	Estimated savings £	Probability of occurrence
Year 1	80,000	0.3
	160,000	0.5
	200,000	0.2
Year 2	140,000	0.4
	220,000	0.4
	250,000	0.2
Year 3	140,000	0.4
	200,000	0.3
	230,000	0.3
Year 4	100,000	0.3
	170,000	0.6
	200,000	0.1

Estimates for each year are independent of other years. The business has a cost of capital of 10 per cent.

Required:
(a) Calculate the expected net present value (ENPV) of the street-cleaning machines.
(b) Calculate the net present value (NPV) of the worst possible outcome and the probability of its occurrence.

9

Strategic management accounting

INTRODUCTION

Businesses are increasingly being managed along strategic lines. By this we mean that strategies adopted by a business are increasingly providing the basis for both long-term and short-term decisions. If management accounting is to help guide decision making within a strategic framework, the reports provided and techniques used must align closely with the framework that has been put in place. Conventional management accounting has been criticised, however, for failing to address fully the strategic aspects of managing a business. This criticism does not mean that the management accounting techniques discussed so far are obsolete, but it does mean that the subject must continue to develop if it is to retain a high degree of relevance for decision makers.

Strategic management accounting is still a fairly new topic and there is no generally agreed set of concepts and techniques that can help us define precisely what is meant by this term. Nevertheless, some key features of this new topic can be identified, and new accounting techniques which are seen as useful for strategic decision making have emerged.

We shall begin the chapter by discussing the nature of strategic management accounting and then go on to look at some of the techniques and methods of analysis that fall within its scope. In this chapter we shall draw on the understanding of topics covered in many of the preceding chapters of the book, particularly Chapters 1, 5 and 8.

When you have completed this chapter, you should be able to:

● Discuss the nature and role of strategic management accounting.

● Explain how management accounting information can help a business gain a better understanding of its competitors and customers.

● Describe the techniques available for gaining competitive advantage through cost leadership.

● Explain how the balanced scorecard can help monitor and measure progress towards the achievement of strategic objectives.

● Discuss the role of shareholder value analysis and economic value added in strategic decision making.

What is strategic management accounting?

Strategic management accounting is concerned with providing information that will support the strategic plans and decisions made within a business. We saw in Chapter 1 that strategic planning involves five steps:

1 Establishing the mission and objectives of a business.
2 Undertaking a position analysis, such as a SWOT (strengths, weaknesses, opportunities and threats) analysis, to establish how the business is placed in relation to its environment.
3 Identifying and assessing the possible strategic options that will lead the business from its present position (identified in Step 2) to the achievement of its objectives (identified in Step 1).
4 Selecting the most appropriate strategic options (from those identified in Step 3) and formulating long- and short-term plans to pursue them.
5 Reviewing business performance and exercising control by assessing actual performance against planned performance (identified in Step 4).

To some extent, conventional management accounting already supports this strategic process. We have seen in Chapter 7, for example, how budgets can be used to compare actual performance with earlier planned performance. We have also seen in Chapter 8 the role of investment appraisal techniques in evaluating long-term plans. Nevertheless, there is scope for further development. It can be argued that if management accounting is fully to support the strategic planning process, it must develop in three broad areas:

● *It must become more outward looking.* There is general agreement that the conventional approach to management accounting does not give enough consideration to external factors affecting the business. These factors, however, are vitally important to strategic planning and decision making. For example, we need to understand the environment within which the business operates when we are undertaking a position analysis or when we are formulating plans for the future. Management accounting can play a useful role here by providing information relating to the environment, such as the performance of the business's competitors and the profitability of its customers.

- *There must be greater concern for developing and implementing methods through which a business can outperform the competition.* In a competitive environment, a business must be able to gain an advantage over its rivals, so that it can survive and prosper over the longer term. Competitive advantage can be gained in various ways and one important way is through cost leadership: that is, the ability to produce products or services at a lower cost than that of other businesses. Although conventional management accounting provides a number of cost determination and control techniques to help a business operate more efficiently, these techniques are not always enough. Rather than seeking simply to count and manage the costs incurred, costs and cost structures may need to be transformed. Thus, management accounting has a role to play in helping to shape the costs of the business to fit the strategic objectives.

- *There must be a concern for monitoring the strategies of the business and for bringing these strategies to a successful conclusion.* This means that management accounting should place greater emphasis on long-term planning issues and on developing a comprehensive range of performance measures to try to ensure that the objectives of the business are being met. The objectives of a business are often couched in both financial and non-financial terms and so the measures developed must reflect this fact.

Let us now turn our attention to the ways in which management accounting can help in each of the three areas identified.

Facing outwards

If a business is to thrive, it needs to have a good understanding of the environment within which it operates. In particular, it should have a good understanding of the threat posed by its competitors and the benefits obtained from its customers. There is a strong case for reporting certain information relating to competitors and customers, frequently and routinely to managers. By so doing, managers can respond more quickly to any changes in the environment that may occur. In this section we consider some of the techniques and measures that may help managers gain a better understanding of these two important groups.

Competitor analysis

To compete effectively, a business needs to acquire a sound knowledge of its main competitors. As well as helping in strategic planning, this knowledge can also help in pricing and business acquisition decisions. When appraising competitors, a business needs to understand

- what strategies and plans they have developed;
- how they may react to the plans the business has developed; and
- whether they have the capability to pose a serious threat to the business.

To gain this understanding, a careful analysis of each main competitor should be carried out.

To illustrate the benefits of **competitor analysis**, let us say that a business proposes to reduce its sales prices by 10 per cent. What would be the reaction of competitors?

Would this reduction be matched by them and thereby cancel out any advantage to be gained? Would it lead to a price war where sales prices follow a downward spiral? If competitors could not match the price reduction, would they be able to continue to supply, given the likely sales volume reduction that they would suffer? We can see that the proposal to reduce prices cannot be fully evaluated until competitors' likely reaction to the proposal is known.

Real World 9.1 provides an example of how one business came to realise that it had to pay more attention to the competition.

REAL WORLD 9.1

Angling for recovery   FT

House of Hardy is a world-famous manufacturer of fishing rods and tackle. It enjoys an unrivalled reputation for its products and has a highly skilled workforce. In recent years, however, it has experienced problems, which have been partly caused by global competition. The business is trying to recover and, in analysing its past mistakes, has recognised that it has been rather too complacent in its approach to competitors. As part of its recovery plan it is now paying much more attention to what they are doing. It is now analysing the products offered by competitors and reviewing its own pricing policies in an attempt to compete more effectively.

Source: Based on information from 'How Hardy lost the lure of heritage', ft.com, 1 December 2003.

To find out what drives a competitor and how it might act, four key aspects of its business must be analysed. These are:

1 *Objectives*. Where is the competitor going? In particular, what are its profit objectives, what rate of sales growth is it trying to achieve, what market share does it seek?
2 *Strategies*. How does the competitor expect to achieve its objectives? What investments are being made in new technology? What alliances and joint ventures are being created? What new products are to be launched? What mergers and acquisitions are planned? What cost reduction strategies are being developed?
3 *Assumptions*. How do the competitor's managers view the world? What assumptions are held about

- future trends within the industry;
- the competitive strengths of other businesses; and
- the feasibility of launching into new markets?

4 *Resources and capabilities*. How serious is the potential threat? What is the competitor's scale and size? Does it have superior technology? Is it profitable? Does it have a strong liquidity position? What is the quality of its management?

These four features provide the framework for analysing competitors, as shown in Figure 9.1.

Gathering information to answer the questions posed above is not always easy. Businesses are understandably reluctant to release information that may damage their competitive position. Nevertheless, there are sources of information that can be used. We shall now consider some of these and, given the management accounting focus of

Figure 9.1	Framework for competitor analysis

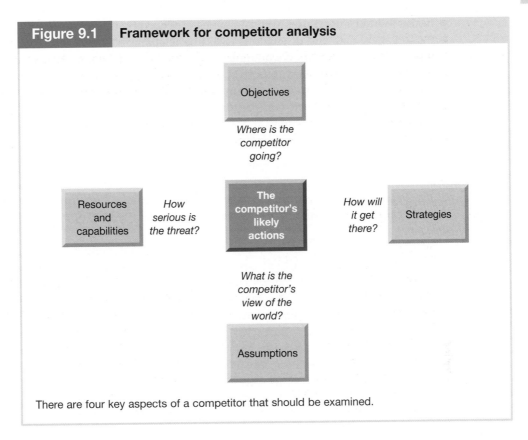

There are four key aspects of a competitor that should be examined.

this book, will concentrate on those sources providing information about the financial resources and capabilities of competitors.

A useful starting point is to examine a competitor's annual report. In the UK, all limited companies are legally obliged to provide information about their business in an annual report that is available to the public. Similar provisions relate to limited companies in most countries in the world. The income statement, cash flow statement and statement of financial position (balance sheet) found in the annual report of a competitor can be examined to gain insights about its financial performance and position. Financial ratios may be used to help gain an impression of the profitability, liquidity, efficiency and financing arrangements of the business. Trends may be detected over time and particular strengths and weaknesses identified.

Where the competitor is not the whole business, but simply an operating division, the annual reports are likely to be less helpful. This is because the results of the relevant division will normally be obscured as a result of its aggregation with the rest of the competitor's operations. Though large businesses operating as limited companies must publish some information about the sales revenues and profits of their various operating divisions, this is often not enough to enable a full picture of the competitor to be built up. Nonetheless, a competitor's annual report should still offer some useful information. Furthermore, a business will have detailed knowledge of its own profitability, liquidity, efficiency and so on, which may well help in compiling a picture of the competitor's position.

It may be possible to gain other information from both published and unpublished sources. This could be from

● press coverage of the competitor's business;
● statements by managers made at conferences or on the competitor's website;

- house journals, brochures and catalogues produced by the competitor;
- market share data and discussions with financial analysts;
- discussions with customers who trade both with the business and with the competitor;
- discussions with suppliers to both the business and its competitor;
- physical observation, such as insights from 'mystery shopping';
- detailed inspection of the competitor's products and prices;
- industry reports; and
- government statistics on such matters as the total size of the market.

By examining such sources, it may be possible to deduce likely capital investments, acquisitions, promotional campaigns, new products and prices, cost structures and so on. It is worth mentioning that specialist agencies can be employed to provide a profile of competitors. These agencies normally rely on the kind of information sources described above.

Of particular value to the business is knowledge of its competitors' cost structures in terms of the extent to which costs are fixed and variable. This would enable the business to make some estimate of the effect on the competitors' profit of an increase or decrease in sales volume. This might, in turn, enable the business to assess how well placed each competitor might be to react to a change in sales volume and/or sales price. For example, a competitor with a high level of fixed costs (high operating gearing) and, consequently, a low margin of safety may not be able to withstand a downturn in sales volume as comfortably as another business with lower operating gearing.

Real World 9.2 concludes this section by revealing that many businesses are not alert to the moves made by competitors and so fail to gain competitive advantage.

REAL WORLD 9.2

Too little, too late

A global survey of 1,825 business executives by McKinsey, the management consultants, found that businesses were not as active as they should be in responding to competitive threats or monitoring the behaviour of competitors. The survey asked executives how their businesses responded to either a significant change in prices or to a significant change in innovation. The answers of executives were strikingly similar across regions and industries.

A majority of executives stated that their businesses found out about the competitive move too late to respond before it hit the market. Thirty-four per cent of those facing an innovation threat and 44 per cent of those facing a pricing change said that they found out about the competitors' moves either when they were announced or when they actually hit the market. An additional 20 per cent of the respondents facing a price change didn't find out until it had been in the market place for at least one or two reporting periods.

These findings suggest that businesses are not conducting an ongoing, sophisticated analysis of their competitors' potential actions. That view was supported by the executives' responses to questions on how they gather information about what competitors might do. Executives most often said that they track information using news reports, industry groups, annual reports, market share data and pricing data. Far fewer respondents obtained information from more complex sources such as detailed examination of the products or mystery shopping.

Source: Adapted from 'How companies respond to competitors: a McKinsey global survey', mckinseyquarterly.com, May 2008.

Customer profitability analysis

Businesses wish to attract and retain customers that produce profitable sales orders. It is, therefore, important to know whether a particular customer, or type of customer, generates profits for the business. Modern businesses are likely to find that much of the cost incurred is not related to the products sold but to the selling and distribution costs associated with those sales. This has led to a shift in emphasis from product profitability to customer profitability.

Customer profitability analysis (CPA) assesses the profitability of each customer or type of customer. In order for CPA to be undertaken, the total costs associated with selling and distributing goods or services to particular customers must be identified. These include the cost of

- *Handling orders from the customer*. This covers the costs involved with receiving the order and activities relating to it up to the point where the goods are despatched, or the service rendered, including the costs of raising invoices and other accounting work.
- *Visiting the customer by the business's sales staff*. Many businesses have a member of staff visit customers, perhaps to take orders, but often to keep the customer up to date with the latest developments in the business's products.
- *Delivering goods to the customer*, using either a delivery service provided by another business, or the business's own transport. Naturally, the distance involved and the size and fragility of the goods will have an effect on this cost.
- *Inventories holding*. Some customers may require a particular level of inventories to be held by the business: for example, a customer operating a 'just-in-time' raw material delivery policy. This can require deliveries to be made frequently and at short notice, in effect putting pressure on the supplier to hold higher inventories levels. (We shall discuss 'just-in-time' inventories management in more detail in Chapter 11.)
- *Offering credit*. The business will have to finance any credit allowed to its customers. This could vary from customer to customer, depending on how promptly they pay.
- *After-sales support*. Technical assistance or servicing may be offered as part of the sales agreement.

These customer-related costs are probably best determined using an activity-based costing approach to cost allocation. This means that, once customer-related costs are identified, cost drivers must be established and appropriate cost driver rates deduced.

Activity 9.1

Imam plc identified the following costs relating to its customers:

- Order handling
- Invoicing and collection
- Shipment processing
- Sales visits
- After-sales service.

Suggest a possible cost driver for each of the items identified.

Activity 9.1 continued

We thought of the following:

Customer-related cost	Possible cost driver
Order handling	Number of orders placed
Invoicing and collection	Number of invoices sent
Shipment processing	Number of shipments made
Sales visits	Number of sales visits made
After-sales service	Number of technical support visits made

These are only suggestions. Other factors may be found that drive each cost.

Once customer-related costs are derived, a CPA statement, which is essentially an abbreviated income statement, can be produced for each customer and/or type of customer. The CPA statement will show the relevant sales revenues and, in addition to the customer-related costs identified earlier, will include the basic cost of creating or buying-in the goods or services supplied (that is, cost of goods sold) and any general selling and administration costs of the business. Example 9.1 illustrates a CPA statement.

Example 9.1

Imam plc – CPA statement for December

	Customer			
	A plc	B plc	C plc	D plc
	£000	£000	£000	£000
Sales revenue	125	75	80	145
Cost of goods sold	(87)	(52)	(56)	(101)
Gross profit	38	23	24	44
General selling and administrative costs	(19)	(11)	(12)	(22)
Customer-related costs				
Order handling	(4)	(2)	(2)	(4)
Invoicing and collection	(4)	(2)	(2)	(4)
Shipment processing	(6)	(4)	(4)	(8)
Sales visits	(7)	(1)	(1)	(2)
After-sales service	(6)	–	(1)	–
Profit/(loss) for the month	(8)	3	2	4

Where all customers are sold products at the same price, the top part of the CPA statement, which is concerned with deducing the gross profit, may be viewed as relating to product profitability. The bottom part of the CPA statement, which is the part below the gross profit figure, may be viewed as relating to customer profitability.

To analyse customer profitability, we can express each of the costs found in this part as a percentage of gross profit. The following table provides the results.

	Customer			
	A plc %	B plc %	C plc %	D plc %
Gross profit	100.0	100.0	100.0	100.0
General selling and administrative costs	50.0	47.8	50.0	50.0
Customer-related costs				
Order handling	10.5	8.7	8.3	9.1
Invoicing and collection	10.5	8.7	8.3	9.1
Shipment processing	15.8	17.4	16.7	18.2
Sales visits	18.4	4.3	4.2	4.5
After-sales service	15.8	–	4.2	–
Profit/(loss) for the month	(21.0)	13.0	8.3	9.1
	100.0	100.0	100.0	100.0

The information generated shows that one customer, A plc, is generating a loss. To find out whether this is a persistent problem, trend analysis can be undertaken which plots the customer-related costs as a percentage of gross profit over time. An example of a trend analysis for A plc is shown in Figure 9.2.

Figure 9.2   Trend analysis for A plc

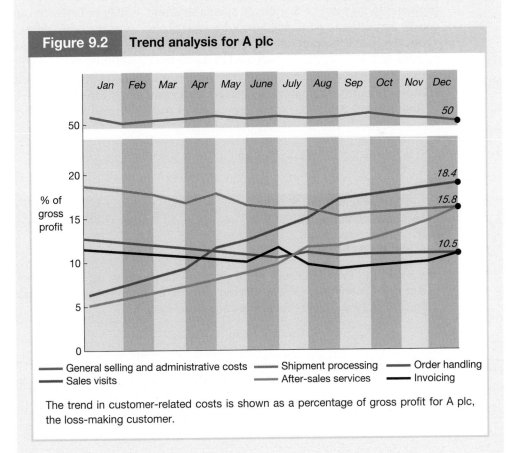

The trend in customer-related costs is shown as a percentage of gross profit for A plc, the loss-making customer.

Activity 9.2

What steps might be taken to deal with the problem of A plc?

The problem appears to be the cost of both sales visits and technical support visits for A plc. They are much higher than for those of other customers, whereas other customer-related costs, when expressed as a percentage of gross profit, are broadly in line with the other three customers. The cost of sales visits and technical support visits have shown a persistent rise over time and do not appear to be due to a unique factor such as the sale of faulty goods. In view of this, the managers may decide to cut down on the number of sales and technical visits or to charge for them, perhaps through increased prices.

In practice, it is often the case that a small proportion of customers generate a large proportion of total profit. Where this occurs, the business may decide to focus its marketing and customer support efforts on these customers. The less profitable customers may then be targeted for price increases or, perhaps, reduced customer support, as we saw in Activity 9.2 above.

Where a business has many customers, the analysis of individual customers' profitability may not be feasible. In such a situation, it may be better to categorise customers according to particular attributes and then to assess the profitability of each category. Thus, the support services division of one large computer business divides its customers into three categories based on technical capabilities, how they use the product and the type of service contract they have (see reference 1 at the end of the chapter). However, identifying appropriate categories for customers can sometimes be difficult.

Real World 9.3 provides some impression of the extent and frequency to which customer profitability is assessed in practice.

REAL WORLD 9.3

CPA in practice

A survey by Tayles and Drury, which elicited responses from 185 management accountants in UK businesses, gives some insight into the extent and frequency of customer profitability analysis. The key findings are shown in Figure 9.3.

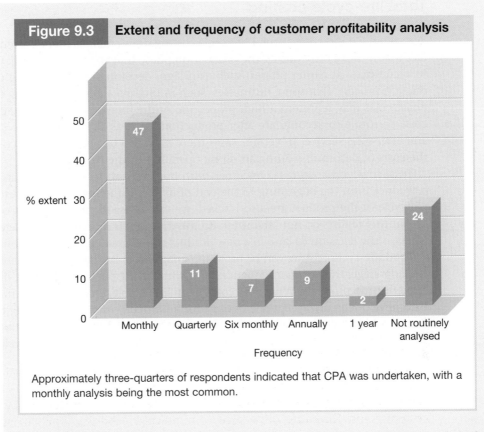

Figure 9.3 **Extent and frequency of customer profitability analysis**

Approximately three-quarters of respondents indicated that CPA was undertaken, with a monthly analysis being the most common.

We can see that there are wide variations to be found in practice. Whereas nearly half the respondents undertake CPA on a monthly basis, nearly a quarter do not undertake CPA analysis at all.

Source: Based on information in Tayles, M. and Drury, C., 'Profiting from profitability analysis?', University of Bradford Working Paper series No. 03/18, June 2003, p. 8.

Competitive advantage through cost leadership

Many businesses try to compete on price: that is, they try to provide goods or services at prices that compare favourably with those of their competitors. To do this success-fully over time, they must also compete on costs: lower prices can only normally be sustained by lower costs. A strategic commitment to competitive pricing must there-fore be accompanied by a strategic commitment to managing the cost base.

In Chapter 5 we saw that, to manage costs in an active way, new forms of costing have been devised. Some of these new costing techniques reflect a concern for long-term cost management and so fall within the broad scope of strategic management accounting. Total life-cycle costing, target costing and *kaizen* costing provide three examples. In this section, we shall briefly review these forms of costing and then go on to consider other ways in which costs may be strategically managed.

Total life-cycle costing

We saw in Chapter 5 that total life-cycle costing draws management's attention to the fact that it is not only during the production phase that costs are incurred. Costs begin to accumulate at earlier phases, such as design, development and setting up the production process. (For some businesses, such as pharmaceutical businesses, these early-phase costs may represent a high proportion of the total costs incurred.) Furthermore, costs continue to accumulate after production, such as those relating to distribution and after-sales service. In certain cases there may also be abandonment costs, such as the costs of decommissioning an oil rig operating in the North Sea.

Total life-cycle costing is concerned with tracking and reporting all costs relating to a product from the beginning to the end of its life. If the revenues generated over the life cycle of the product are also tracked, we can assess its profitability. Conventional accounting reports do not attempt to do this and so it is difficult for managers to know whether the decision to launch a new product will ultimately generate profits or losses.

Total life-cycle costing can be used to manage costs. Managers will be able to see, at an early stage, the cost consequences of incorporating particular designs or particular elements into products. Where the costs are unacceptable, changes may be made. Where a number of equally acceptable designs for a particular product are being considered, knowledge of the total life-cycle costs of each may help decide the final outcome.

Real World 9.4 shows how one well-known business operates a life-cycle approach to both costing and environmental issues.

REAL WORLD 9.4

Life cycle

Rolls-Royce provides engines for use in the air, at sea and on land, and is concerned with the environmental impact as well as the costs over the whole life of its products. Rolls-Royce states:

> The environmental performance of our products has always been a priority for Rolls-Royce. A large part of our research and development has been directed towards new products with increased efficiency, together with reduced emissions and noise.
>
> Our products typically remain in service for many years and consequently much of our business is directed towards the whole life cycle of the product. Our product development processes have evolved to address issues associated with manufacturing, assembly, operation, repair and overhaul. This approach has much in common with the concept of Design for Environment (DfE) which is a process for designing to minimise the overall impact of the product during its whole life. . . .
>
> We are also using Life Cycle Analysis techniques to benchmark the total environmental impact associated with our products and ultimately to inform our decision-making processes. This approach has proved the importance of the 'in service' phase of the life cycle for our products, when the vast majority of the environmental impacts occur. Rolls-Royce has long applied life-cycle management in the form of life-cycle costing to products. We incorporate environmental life-cycle thinking into our design processes alongside cost measurement to ensure that our products are the most cost-effective solutions while protecting the environment as far as possible.

Source: rolls-royce.com.

Target costing

Target costing is a market-based approach to managing costs. We saw in Chapter 5 that the starting point is to set the target price of a product on the basis of market research, which may include an analysis of competitors' prices. The target price, less the required profit from the product, will be the target cost of the product. Target costing places demands on managers because the target cost is usually lower than the current full cost of the product. Thus, to achieve the target cost, a systematic approach to cost reduction is often required.

A team of managers, drawn from each of the main functional areas, such as design, production, purchasing and marketing, will normally be charged with achieving the target cost. Together they will examine all aspects of the product and the production process to try to eliminate anything that does not add value. This can place considerable pressure on designers, as they are likely to be asked to redesign the product to a specification that is more acceptable.

Kaizen costing

Once the product design and the production process have been agreed, the production phase can begin. *Kaizen* costing may be used to manage the efficiency of this phase. We saw in Chapter 5 that *kaizen* costing aims at continual and gradual incremental improvements to the product design and the production process. Like target costing, it also involves target setting: a cost reduction rate will be specified for a period and actual performance will be compared against it. To achieve the required cost reduction, the involvement of employees is normally essential. The suggestions they make can often lead to significant savings. *Kaizen* costing is closely associated with **lean manufacturing**, which is committed to the elimination of waste through continuous improvement.

Figure 9.4 shows the phases of the product life cycle covered by the three forms of costing discussed.

| Figure 9.4 | **The relationship between the three types of costing** |

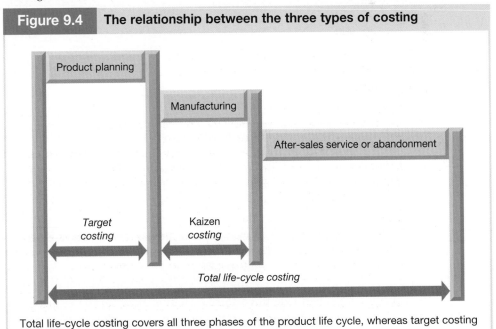

Total life-cycle costing covers all three phases of the product life cycle, whereas target costing and *Kaizen* costing are each concerned with only a single phase.

Value chain analysis

To secure competitive advantage, a business must be able to perform key activities more successfully than its competitors. This means that it must either obtain some cost advantage over its competitors, or differentiate itself in some way from them. To help identify particular ways in which competitive advantage may be achieved, it is useful to analyse a business into a sequence of value-creating activities. This sequence is known as the value chain, and **value chain analysis** examines the potential for each link in the chain to add value.

For a manufacturing business, the value-creating sequence begins with the acquisition of inputs, such as raw materials and energy, and ends with the sale of completed goods and after-sales service. Figure 9.5 sets out the main 'links' in the value chain for a manufacturing business. We can see that five primary activities are supported by four secondary activities.

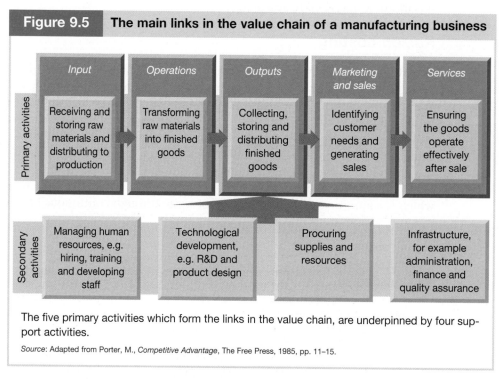

| Figure 9.5 | The main links in the value chain of a manufacturing business |

The five primary activities which form the links in the value chain, are underpinned by four support activities.

Source: Adapted from Porter, M., *Competitive Advantage*, The Free Press, 1985, pp. 11–15.

Value chain analysis applies as much to service-providing businesses as it does to manufacturers. Service providers similarly have a sequence of activities leading to provision of the service to their customers. Analysing these activities in an attempt to identify and eliminate non-value-added activities is very important.

Each link in the value chain represents an activity that will incur costs and affect profits. Ideally, each will add value – that is, the customer will be prepared to pay more for the activity than it costs to carry out. If, however, a business is to outperform its rivals, it must ensure that the value chain is configured in such a way that it leads either to a cost advantage or to differentiation.

To achieve a cost advantage, the costs associated with each link in the chain must be identified and then examined to see whether they can be reduced or eliminated. For example, a business may identify a non-value-added activity, such as the inspection of the completed product by a quality controller. The introduction of a 'quality' culture in the business could lead to all output being reliable. As a result, inspection would no longer be needed and therefore this cost can be eliminated. To achieve differentiation from its rivals, a business must achieve uniqueness in at least one part of the value chain. A large baker, for example, may try to differentiate its products by moving production facilities to its retail shops to ensure that the products are freshly available to customers.

In some cases, value chain analysis may result in significant operational changes such as the introduction of new manufacturing or service-provision technology, or the development of new sales policies. In other cases it may result in significant strategic shifts. A manufacturing business, for example, may find that it is unable to match the manufacturing costs achieved by its rivals. Nevertheless, it has competitive strengths in the areas of marketing and distribution. In such circumstances, a decision may be made to focus on the business's core competencies. This may lead it to outsource the manufacturing function and to concentrate on the marketing and distribution of the goods.

Real World 9.5 provides an example of how focusing on the value chain may help transform the performance of a business.

REAL WORLD 9.5

What a sauce   **FT**

Ahold is a major Dutch retailer that has recently been recovering its fortunes, under its chief executive Anders Moberg. The business has a recovery plan that involves 're-engineering the value chain' and according to Mr Moberg, the key is a detailed analysis of the cost of goods sold.

'That is probably the single biggest opportunity [for savings] that we have.'

Take a bottle of tomato ketchup. 'What are the costs of the growers of the tomatoes? What are the components of the value chain, production, marketing, packaging and distribution? Can you add a component in a different way, for example with standardised bottles? You are looking at how to re-engineer the value chain [in order] to lower the price.'

Manufacturers' brands do this, he says, 'but they keep the savings, hence they have a better return on capital'. With supermarket own-label brands on the rise – they account for 50 per cent of Ahold Dutch store sales, and 15 per cent in the US – Mr Moberg can reduce what it costs him to make products while at the same time lowering prices, attracting more shoppers to Ahold stores and thereby raising volumes. . . .

Armed with intricate knowledge of supply chain costs, Ahold can press big brand manufacturers to cut the prices they ask of the retailer. It is a delicate balancing act. Both Grolsch, the Dutch brewer, and Peijnenburg, a bakery group, have quarrelled with Ahold about the damage inflicted on their brands by pricing policy, while Unilever, the consumer goods group, took Ahold to court, claiming it had copied its packaging.

It appears, however, to be a battle Mr Moberg is winning. Not only is customer perception of the quality of own-label products rising – a fact confirmed by independent industry research – but Ahold has a strong position with big consumer brands through its control of distribution channels, especially in the Netherlands, where its Albert Heijn chain is market leader and has 700 stores.

Source: Bickerton, I., 'It is all about the value chain', ft.com, 23 February 2006.

An alternative view

Whilst the costing methods just described are used and are regarded as useful by many businesses, some believe that they fail to provide the key to successful strategic cost management. It has been suggested that undue emphasis on costing methods, such as total life-cycle costing, is misplaced and what is really needed is for businesses to develop ways of learning and adapting to their changing environment. To manage costs successfully, businesses should continually review them in the face of new threats and pressures rather than relying on particular techniques to provide solutions.

Hopwood (see reference 2 at the end of the chapter) suggests that to transform costs over time in order to fit the strategic objectives, businesses do not need very sophisticated techniques or highly bureaucratic systems. Rather, they need to change the ways in which costs are viewed and dealt with. He suggests that the following broad principles should be adopted.

1 Spread the responsibility

Employees throughout the business should share responsibility for managing costs. Thus, design experts, engineers, store managers, sales managers, and so on. should all contribute towards managing costs and should see this as part of their job. The involvement of non-accountants is, of course, a feature of target costing and *kaizen* costing, and so this point already appears to be widely accepted.

Hopwood suggests that employees should be provided with a basic understanding of costing ideas such as fixed and variable costs, relevant costs and so on, to enable them to contribute fully. As cost-consciousness permeates the business, and non-accounting employees become more involved in costing issues, the role of the accountants will change. They will often facilitate, rather than initiate, cost management proposals and will become part of the multi-skilled teams engaged in creatively managing them.

2 Spread the word

Throughout the business, costs and cost management should become everyday topics for discussion. Managers should seize every opportunity to raise these topics with employees, as talking about costs can often lead to ideas being developed and action being taken to manage costs.

3 Think local

Emphasis should be placed on managing costs within specific sites and settings. Managers of departments, product lines or local offices are more likely to become engaged in managing costs if they are allowed to take initiatives in areas over which they have control. Local managers tend to have local knowledge not possessed by managers at head office. They are more likely to be able to spot cost-saving opportunities than are their more senior colleagues. Business-wide initiatives for cost management which have been developed by senior management are unlikely to have the same beneficial effect.

4 Benchmark continually

Benchmarking should be a never-ending journey. There should be regular, as well as special-purpose, reporting of cost information for benchmarking purposes. The costs of competitors may provide a useful basis for comparison, as we saw earlier. In addition, costs that may be expected as a result of moving to new technology or work patterns may be helpful.

5 Focus on managing rather than reducing costs

Conventional management accounting tends to focus on cost reduction, which is, essentially, taking a short-term perspective on costs. Strategic cost management, however, means that in some situations costs should be increased rather than reduced.

Activity 9.3

Under what kind of circumstances might it be a good idea to increase costs?

This may include situations that could lead to

- additional revenues being generated
- lower costs being incurred over the longer term
- lower costs being incurred in other areas of the business.

Hopwood argues that the above principles, when used in conjunction with overall financial controls, provide the best way to manage costs strategically.

Real World 9.6 gives an example of how local managers who are not accountants can identify potential cost savings and not resent their implementation.

REAL WORLD 9.6

Costing problem? Call a doctor   **FT**

One research study contrasts the difference in approach to cost management in UK and Finnish hospitals. In the UK, cost management is seen as the domain of financial staff. This can lead to problems as financial systems that have been introduced to manage costs have led to more complex organisational structures. In addition there is often an emphasis on cost savings, which can lead to conflict between financial staff and medical staff. The latter often resent cost cuts being imposed on them by the financial staff.

In contrast, medical staff in Finnish hospitals share responsibility for cost management. Doctors and other medical professionals recognise the need to use resources in an efficient way and are committed to ensuring that resources are not wasted. Rather than fighting cost-cutting initiatives from financial staff, they see both medical knowledge and cost awareness as being necessary to successful medical practice.

Source: Based on information in Hopwood, A., 'Costs count in the strategic agenda', ft.com, 13 August 2002.

Translating strategy into action

Once the strategic objectives of a business have been set, progress towards these objectives must be monitored. This means that there must be appropriate measures by which progress can be assessed. Financial measures have long been seen as the most important ones for a business. They provide us with a valuable means of summarising and evaluating business achievement and there is no real doubt about the continued importance of financial measures in this role. In recent years, however, there has been increasing recognition that financial measures alone will not provide managers with sufficient information to manage a business effectively. Non-financial measures must also be used to gain a deeper understanding of the business and to achieve the objectives of the business, including the financial objectives.

Financial measures portray various aspects of business achievement (for example, sales revenues, profits and return on capital employed) that can help managers determine whether the business is increasing the wealth of its owners. These measures are vitally important but, in an increasingly competitive environment, managers also need to understand what drives the creation of wealth. These **value drivers** may be such things as employee satisfaction, customer loyalty and the level of product innovation. Often they do not lend themselves to financial measurement, although non-financial measures may provide some means of assessment.

Activity 9.4

How might we measure:

(a) employee satisfaction?
(b) customer loyalty?
(c) the level of product innovation?

....

(a) Employee satisfaction may be measured through the use of an employee survey. This could examine attitudes towards various aspects of the job, the degree of autonomy that is permitted, the level of recognition and reward received, the level of participation in decision making, the degree of support received in carrying out tasks and so on. Less direct measures of satisfaction may include employee turnover rates and employee productivity. However, other factors may have a significant influence on these measures.

(b) Customer loyalty may be measured through the proportion of total sales generated from existing customers, the number of repeat sales made to customers, the percentage of customers renewing subscriptions or other contracts, and so on.

(c) The level of product innovation may be measured through the number of innovations during a period compared to those of competitors, the percentage of sales attributable to recent product innovations, the number of innovations that are brought successfully to market, and so on.

Financial measures are normally 'lag' indicators, in that they tell us about outcomes. In other words, they measure the consequences arising from management decisions that were made earlier. Non-financial measures can also be used as lag indicators, of course. However, they can also be used as 'lead' indicators by focusing on those things that drive performance. It is argued that if we measure changes in these value drivers, we may be able to predict changes in future financial performance. For example, a business may find from experience that a 10 per cent fall in levels of product innovation during one period will lead to a 20 per cent fall in sales revenues over the next three periods. In this case, the levels of product innovation can be regarded as a lead indicator that can alert managers to a future decline in sales unless corrective action is taken. Thus, by using this lead indicator, managers can identify key changes at an early stage and can respond quickly.

The balanced scorecard

One of the most impressive attempts to integrate the use of financial and non-financial measures has been the **balanced scorecard**, developed by Robert Kaplan and David

Norton (see reference 3 at the end of the chapter). The balanced scorecard is both a management system and a measurement system. In essence, it provides a framework that translates the aims and objectives of a business into a series of key performance measures and targets. This framework is intended to make the strategy of the business more coherent by tightly linking it to particular targets and initiatives. As a result, managers should be able to see more clearly whether the objectives that have been set have actually been achieved.

The balanced scorecard approach involves setting objectives and developing appropriate measures and targets in four main areas:

1 *Financial.* This area will specify the financial returns required by shareholders and may involve the use of financial measures such as return on capital employed, operating profit margin, percentage sales revenue growth and so on.
2 *Customer.* This area will specify the kind of customer and/or markets that the business wishes to service and will establish appropriate measures such as customer satisfaction, new customer growth levels and so on.
3 *Internal business process.* This area will specify those business processes (for example, innovation, types of operation, and after-sales service) that are important to the success of the business, and will establish appropriate measures such as percentage of sales from new products, time to market for new products, product cycle times, and speed of response to customer complaints.
4 *Learning and growth.* This area will specify the kind of people, the systems and the procedures that are necessary to deliver long-term business growth. This area is often the most difficult for the development of appropriate measures. However, examples of measures may include employee motivation, employee skills profiles and information systems capabilities. These four areas are shown in Figure 9.6.

The balanced scorecard approach does not prescribe the particular objectives, measures or targets that a business should adopt; this is a matter for the individual business to decide upon. There are differences between businesses in terms of technology employed, organisational structure, management philosophy and business environment, so each business should develop objectives and measures that reflect its unique circumstances. The balanced scorecard simply sets out the framework for developing a coherent set of objectives for the business and for ensuring that these objectives are then linked to specific targets and initiatives.

A balanced scorecard will be prepared for the business as a whole or, in the case of large, diverse businesses, for each strategic business unit. However, having prepared an overall scorecard, it is then possible to prepare a balanced scorecard for each sub-unit, such as a department, within the business. Thus, the balanced scorecard approach can cascade down the business and can result in a pyramid of balanced scorecards that are linked to the 'master' balanced scorecard through an alignment of the objectives and measures employed.

Though a very large number of measures, both financial and non-financial, exist and so could be used in a balanced scorecard, only a handful of measures should be employed. A maximum of 20 measures will normally be sufficient to enable the factors that are critical to the success of the business to be captured. (If a business has come up with more than 20 measures, it is usually because the managers have not thought hard enough about what the key measures really are.) The key measures developed should be a mix of lagging indicators (those relating to outcomes) and lead indicators (those relating to the things that drive performance).

Although the balanced scorecard employs measures across a wide range of business activity, it does not seek to dilute the importance of financial measures and objectives.

Figure 9.6	The balanced scorecard – for translating a strategy into operational processes

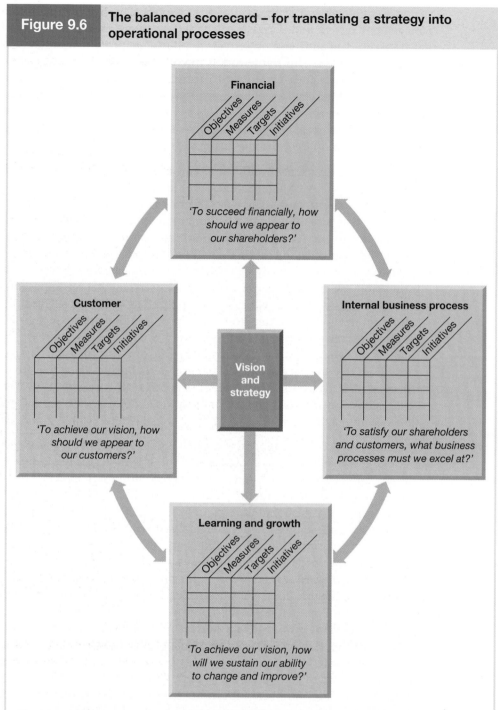

There are four main areas covered by the balanced scorecard. Note that, for each area, a fundamental question must be addressed. By answering these questions, managers should be able to develop the key objectives of the business. Once this has been done, suitable measures and targets can be developed that are relevant to those objectives. Finally, appropriate management initiatives will be developed to achieve the targets set.

In fact, the opposite is true. Kaplan and Norton (see reference 3 at the end of the chapter) emphasise the point that a balanced scorecard must reflect a concern for the financial objectives of the business and so measures and objectives in the other three areas that have been identified must ultimately be related back to the financial objectives. There must be a cause-and-effect relationship. So, for example, an investment in staff development (in the learning and growth area) may lead to improved levels of after-sales service (internal business process area), which, in turn, may lead to higher levels of customer satisfaction (customer area) and, ultimately, higher sales revenues and profits (financial area). At first, cause-and-effect relationships may not be very clearly identified. However, by gathering information over time, the business can improve its understanding of the linkages and thereby improve the effectiveness of the scorecard.

Figure 9.7 shows the cause-and-effect relationship between the investment in staff development and the business's financial objectives.

| Figure 9.7 | The cause-and-effect relationship |

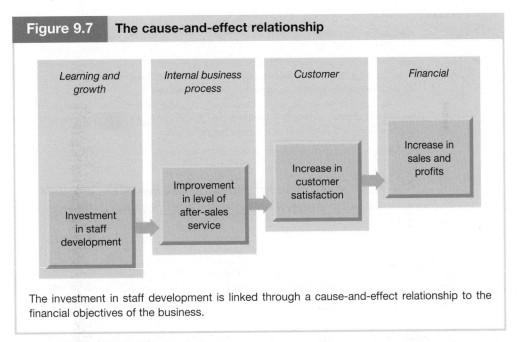

The investment in staff development is linked through a cause-and-effect relationship to the financial objectives of the business.

Activity 9.5

Do you think this is a rather hard-nosed approach to dealing with staff development? Should staff development always have to be justified in terms of the financial results achieved?

This approach may seem rather hard-nosed. However, Kaplan and Norton argue that unless this kind of link between staff development and increased financial returns can be demonstrated, managers are likely to become cynical about the benefits of staff development and so the result may be that there will be no investment in staff.

Why is this framework referred to as a *balanced* scorecard? According to Kaplan and Norton, there are various reasons. First, it is because it aims to strike a balance between *external* measures relating to customers and shareholders, and *internal* measures relating to business process, learning and growth. Secondly, it aims to strike a balance between the measures that reflect *outcomes* (lag indicators) and measures that help *predict future performance* (lead indicators). Finally, the framework aims to strike a balance between *hard* financial measures and *soft* non-financial measures.

It is possible to adapt the balanced scorecard to fit the needs of the particular business. **Real World 9.7** shows how this has been done by Tesco plc, the large retailer.

REAL WORLD 9.7

Every little helps

Tesco plc has modified the balanced scorecard approach to meet its particular needs. It has added a fifth dimension, the community, to demonstrate its commitment to the communities that it serves. There is frequent monitoring of the various performance measures against the scorecard targets. The business states:

> We operate a balanced scorecard approach which is known within the Group as our Steering Wheel. This unites the Group's resources around our customers, people, operations, community and finance. The scorecard operates at every level within the Group, from ground level business units, through to country level operations. It enables the business to be operated and monitored on a balanced basis with due regard for all stakeholders. . . .
>
> The Steering Wheel is reviewed quarterly. Steering Wheels are operated in business units across the Group, and reports are prepared of performance against target KPIs on a quarterly basis enabling management to measure performance.

Source: Tesco plc, 'Internal control and risk management', 2008, tesco.com.

As a footnote to our consideration of the balanced scorecard, **Real World 9.8** provides an interesting analogy with aeroplane pilots limiting themselves to just one control device.

(UN)REAL WORLD 9.8

Fear of flying

Kaplan and Norton invite us to imagine the following conversation between a passenger and the pilot of a jet aeroplane during a flight:

> Q: I'm surprised to see you operating the plane with only a single instrument. What does it measure?
> A: Airspeed. I'm really working on airspeed this flight.
> Q: That's good. Airspeed certainly seems important. But what about altitude? Wouldn't an altimeter be helpful?
> A: I worked on altitude for the last few flights and I've gotten pretty good on it. Now I have to concentrate on proper airspeed.
> Q: But I notice you don't even have a fuel gauge. Wouldn't that be useful?
> A: You're right; fuel is significant, but I can't concentrate on doing too many things well at the same time. So on this flight I'm focusing on airspeed. Once I get to be excellent at airspeed, as well as altitude, I intend to concentrate on fuel consumption on the next set of flights.

The point they are trying to make (apart from warning against flying with a pilot like this!) is that to fly an aeroplane, which is a complex activity, a wide range of navigation instruments is required. A business, however, can be even more complex to manage than an aeroplane and so a wide range of measures, both financial and non-financial, is necessary. Reliance on financial measures is not enough and so the balanced scorecard aims to provide managers with a more complete navigation system.

Source: Kaplan and Norton (see reference 3 at the end of the chapter).

The above story makes the point that, if one concentrates only on a few areas of performance, other important areas may be ignored. Too narrow a focus can adversely affect behaviour and distort performance. This may, in turn, mean that the business fails to meet its strategic objectives. Perhaps we should bear in mind another apocryphal story concerning a factory in Russia which, under the former communist regime, produced nails. The factory had its output measured according only to the weight of nails manufactured. For one financial period, it achieved its output target by producing one very large nail!

Scorecard problems

Not all attempts to embed the balanced scorecard approach within a business are successful. Why do things go wrong? It has been suggested that often too many measures are employed, thereby making the scorecard too complex and unwieldy. It has also been suggested that managers are confronted with trade-off decisions between the four different dimensions, and struggle because they lack a clear compass. Imagine a manager who has a limited budget and therefore has to decide whether to invest in staff training or product innovation. If both add value to the business, which choice will be optimal for the business?

Whilst such problems exist, David Norton believes that there are two main reasons why the balanced scorecard fails to take root within a business, as **Real World 9.9** explains.

REAL WORLD 9.9

When misuse leads to failure　　　**FT**

There are two main reasons why companies go wrong with the widely used balanced scorecard, according to David Norton, the consultant who created the concept with Robert Kaplan, a Harvard Business School Professor.

'The number one cause of failure is that you don't have leadership at the executive levels of the organisation,' says Mr Norton. 'They don't embrace it and use it for managing their strategy.'

The second is that some companies treat it purely as a measurement tool, a problem he admits stems partly from its name. The concept has evolved since its inception, he says. The latest Kaplan–Norton thinking is that companies need a unit at corporate level – they call it an 'office of strategy management' – dedicated to ensuring that strategy is communicated to every employee and translated into plans, targets and incentives in each business unit and department.

Incentives are crucial, Mr Norton believes. Managers who have achieved breakthroughs in performance with the scorecard say they would tie it to executive compensation sooner if they were doing it again. 'There's so much change in organisations that managers don't always believe you mean what you say. The balanced scorecard may just be "flavour of the month". Tying it to compensation shows that you mean it.'

Source: When misuse leads to failure, ft.com, © The Financial Times Limited, 24 May 2006.

Measuring shareholder value

Traditional measures of financial performance have been subject to much criticism in recent years and new measures have been advocated to guide and to assess strategic management decisions. In this section we shall consider two new measures, both of which are based on the idea of increasing shareholder value. Before examining each method, we shall first consider why increasing shareholder value is regarded as the ultimate financial objective of a business.

The quest for shareholder value

For some years, shareholder value has been a 'hot' issue among managers. Many leading businesses now claim that the quest for shareholder value is the driving force behind their strategic and operational decisions. As a starting point, we shall consider what is meant by the term 'shareholder value', and in the sections that follow we shall look at two of the main approaches to measuring shareholder value.

In simple terms, 'shareholder value' is about putting the needs of shareholders at the heart of management decisions. It is argued that shareholders invest in a business with a view to maximising their financial returns in relation to the risks that they are prepared to take. As managers are appointed by the shareholders to act on their behalf, management decisions and actions should therefore reflect a concern for maximising shareholder returns. Though the business may have other 'stakeholder' groups, such as employees, customers and suppliers, it is the shareholders that should be seen as the most important group.

This, of course, is not a new idea. As we discussed in Chapter 1, maximising shareholder wealth is assumed to be the key objective of a business. However, not everyone accepts this idea. Some believe that a balance must be struck between the competing claims of the various stakeholders. A debate concerning the merits of each viewpoint is beyond the scope of this book; however, it is worth pointing out that, in recent years, the business environment has radically changed.

In the past, shareholders have been accused of being too passive and of accepting too readily the profits and dividends that managers have delivered. However, this has changed. Shareholders are now much more assertive, and, as owners of the business, are in a position to insist that their needs are given priority. Since the 1980s we have witnessed the deregulation and globalisation of business, as well as enormous changes in technology. The effect has been to create a much more competitive world. This has meant not only competition for products and services but also competition for funds. Businesses must now compete more strongly for shareholder funds and so must offer competitive rates of return.

Thus, self-interest may be the most powerful reason for managers to commit themselves to maximising shareholder returns. If they do not do this, there is a real risk that shareholders will either replace them with managers who will, or allow the business to be taken over by another business that has managers who are dedicated to maximising shareholder returns.

How can shareholder value be created?

Creating shareholder value involves a four-stage process. The first stage is to set objectives for the business that recognise the central importance of maximising shareholder returns. This will set a clear direction for the business. The second stage is to establish an appropriate means of measuring the returns, or value, that have been generated for shareholders. For reasons that we shall discuss later, the traditional methods of measuring returns to shareholders are inadequate for this purpose. The third stage is to manage the business in such a manner as to ensure that shareholder returns are maximised. This means setting demanding targets and then achieving them through the best possible use of resources, the use of incentive systems and the embedding of a shareholder value culture throughout the business. The final stage is to measure the shareholder returns over a period of time to see whether the objectives have actually been achieved.

Figure 9.8 shows the shareholder value creation process.

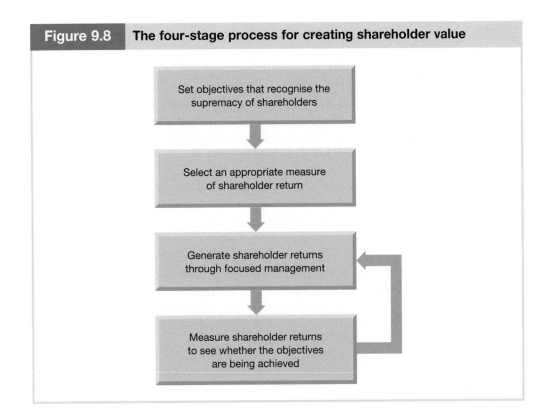

Figure 9.8   The four-stage process for creating shareholder value

The need for new measures

Given a commitment to maximise shareholder returns, we must select an appropriate measure that will help us assess the returns to shareholders over time. It is argued that the traditional methods for measuring shareholder returns are seriously flawed and so should not be used for this purpose.

Activity 9.6

What are the traditional methods of measuring shareholder returns?

The traditional approach is to use accounting profit or some ratio that is based on accounting profit, such as return on shareholders' funds or earnings per share.

There are broadly four problems with using accounting profit, or a ratio based on profit, to assess shareholder returns. These are:

● *Profit is measured over a relatively short period of time* (usually one year). However, when we talk about maximising shareholder returns, we are concerned with maximising returns over the *long term*. It has been suggested that using profit as the key measure will run the risk that managers will take decisions that improve performance in the short term, but which may have an adverse effect on long-term performance. For example, profits may be increased in the short term by cutting back on staff training and research expenditure. However, this type of expenditure may be vital to long-term survival.

● *Risk is ignored.* A fundamental business reality is that there is a clear relationship between the level of returns achieved and the level of risk that must be taken to achieve those returns. The higher the level of returns required, the higher the level of risk that must be taken. A management strategy that produces an increase in profits can reduce shareholder value if the increase in profits achieved is not commensurate with the increase in the level of risk. Thus, profit alone is not enough.

● *Accounting profit does not take account of all of the costs of the capital invested by the business.* The conventional approach to measuring profit will deduct the cost of borrowing (that is, interest charges) in arriving at profit for the period, but there is no similar deduction for the cost of shareholder funds. Critics of the conventional approach point out that a business will not make a profit, in an economic sense, unless it covers the cost of all capital invested, including shareholder funds. Unless the business achieves this, it will operate at a loss and so shareholder value will be reduced.

● *Accounting profit reported by a business can vary according to the particular accounting policies that have been adopted.* The way that accounting profit is measured can vary from one business to another. Some businesses adopt a very conservative approach, which would be reflected in particular accounting policies such as immediately treating some intangible assets (for example, research and development and goodwill) as expenses ('writing them off') rather than retaining them on the statement of financial position as assets. Similarly, the use of the reducing-balance method of depreciation (which means high depreciation charges in the early years) reduces profit in those early years.

Businesses that adopt less conservative accounting policies would report higher profits in the early years of owning depreciating assets. Writing off intangible assets over a long time period (or, perhaps, not writing off intangible assets at all), the use of the straight-line method of depreciation and so on will have this effect. In addition, there may be some businesses that adopt particular accounting policies or carry out particular transactions in a way that paints a picture of financial health that is in line with what those who prepared the financial statements would like shareholders and other users to see, rather than what is a true and fair view of financial performance and position. This practice is referred to as 'creative accounting' and has been a major problem for accounting rule makers and for society generally.

Real World 9.10 provides some examples of creative accounting methods that have recently been found in practice.

REAL WORLD 9.10

Dirty laundry: how businesses fudge the numbers

The ways in which managers can manipulate the financial statements are many and varied. The methods below have come to light in the recent wave of accounting scandals that have been reported in the US and UK.

- *Hollow swaps*: telecoms businesses sell useless fibre optic capacity to each other in order to generate revenues on their income statements.
- *Channel stuffing*: a business floods the market with more products than its distributors can sell, artificially boosting its sales revenue. An international condom maker shifted £60m in excess inventory on to trade customers. Also known as 'trade loading'.
- *Round tripping*: also known as 'in-and-out trading'. Used to notorious effect by Enron. Two or more traders buy and sell energy among themselves for the same price and at the same time. Inflates trading volumes and makes participants appear to be doing more business than they really are.
- *Pre-despatching*: goods such as carpets are marked as 'sold' as soon as an order is placed. This inflates sales revenues and profits.
- *Off-balance-sheet activities*: businesses use special-purpose entities and other devices such as leasing to push assets and liabilities off their statements of financial position.

Net present value (NPV) analysis

To summarise the points made above, we can say that, to enable us to assess changes in shareholder value fairly, we need a measure that will consider the long term, take account of risk, acknowledge the cost of shareholders' funds, and will not be affected by accounting policy choices. Fortunately, we have a measure that can, in theory, do this.

Net present value analysis was discussed in Chapter 8. We saw that if we want to know the net present value (NPV) of an asset (whether this is a physical asset such as a machine or a financial asset such as a share in a business) we must discount the future cash flows generated by the asset over its life. Thus:

$$NPV = \frac{C_1}{(1+r)^1} + \frac{C_2}{(1+r)^2} + \frac{C_3}{(1+r)^3} + \cdots + \frac{C_n}{(1+r)^n}$$

where C_1, C_2, C_3 and C_n are cash flows after one year, two years, three years and n years, respectively, and r is the required rate of return.

Shareholders have a required rate of return, and managers must strive to generate long-term cash flows for shares (in the form of dividends or proceeds from the sale of the shares) that meet this rate of return. The expectation that the managers will, in the future, fail to generate the minimum required cash flows will have the effect of reducing the value of the business as a whole and, therefore, of the individual shares in it. If a business is to create value for its shareholders, it must be expected to generate cash flows that exceed the required returns of shareholders. We should bear in mind here that the value of a business and its shares is entirely dependent on two factors:

1 expectations of future cash flows; and
2 the shareholders' required rate of return.

Past successes are not relevant.

The NPV approach fulfils the criteria that we mentioned earlier as a means of fairly assessing changes in shareholder value because:

● It considers the long term. The returns from an investment, such as shares, are considered over the whole of its life.
● It takes account of the cost of capital and risk. Future cash flows are discounted using the required rates of returns from investors (that is, both long-term lenders and shareholders). Moreover, this required rate of return will reflect the level of risk associated with the investment. The higher the level of risk, the higher the required level of return.
● It is not sensitive to the choice of accounting policies. Cash rather than profit is used in the calculations and is a more objective measure of return.

Extending NPV analysis: shareholder value analysis (SVA)

We know from our consideration of NPV in Chapter 8 that, when evaluating an investment project, shareholder wealth will be maximised if we maximise the net present value of the cash flows generated from the project. Leading on from this, the business as a whole can be viewed as simply a portfolio of investment projects and so to maximise the wealth of shareholders the same principles should apply. **Shareholder value analysis (SVA)** is founded on this basic idea.

The SVA approach involves evaluating strategic decisions according to their ability to maximise value, or wealth, for shareholders.

To enable a business to assess the effect of a particular set of strategies on shareholder value, it needs a means of measuring shareholder value both before and after adopting the strategy and comparing the two values. We shall now go on to see how this can be done.

Measuring free cash flows

The cash flows used to measure total business value are the **free cash flows**. These are the cash flows generated by the business that are available to ordinary shareholders and long-term lenders. In other words, they are equivalent to the net cash flows from operations after deducting tax paid and cash for additional investment. These free cash flows can be deduced from information contained within the income statement and statement of financial position of a business.

It is probably worth going through a simple example to illustrate how the free cash flows are calculated in practice.

Example 9.2

Sagittarius plc generated sales revenue of £220m during the year and has an operating profit margin of 25 per cent of sales revenue. The depreciation charge for the year was £8.0m and the effective tax rate for the year was 20 per cent of operating profit. During the year £11.3m was invested in additional working capital and £15.2m was invested in additional non-current assets. A further £8.0m was invested in the replacement of existing non-current assets.

The free cash flows are calculated as follows:

	£m	£m
Sales revenue		220.0
Operating profit (25% × £220m)		55.0
Depreciation charge		8.0
Operating cash flows		63.0
Tax (20% × £55m)		(11.0)
Operating cash flows after tax		52.0
Additional working capital	(11.3)	
Additional non-current assets	(15.2)	
Replacement non-current assets	(8.0)	(34.5)
Free cash flows		17.5

We can see that to derive the operating cash flows, the depreciation charge is added back to the operating profit figure. We can also see that the cost of replacement of existing non-current assets is deducted from the operating cash flows to deduce the free cash flow figure. When we are trying to predict future free cash flows, one way of arriving at an approximate figure for the cost of replacing existing assets is to assume that the depreciation charge for the year is equivalent to the replacement charge for non-current assets. This would mean that the two adjustments mentioned cancel each other out. In other words, the calculation above could be shortened to:

	£m	£m
Sales revenue		220.0
Operating profit (25% × £220m)		55.0
Tax (20% × £55m)		(11.0)
		44.0
Additional working capital	(11.3)	
Additional non-current assets	(15.2)	(26.5)
Free cash flows		17.5

This shortened approach leads us to identify the key variables in determining free cash flows as being

- sales revenue
- operating profit margin
- tax rate
- additional investment in working capital
- additional investment in non-current assets.

These are value drivers of the business that reflect key business decisions. These decisions convert into free cash flows and finally into shareholder value. Any actions that management can take to

- boost sales revenue; and/or
- increase the operating profit margin; and/or
- reduce the effective tax rate; and/or
- reduce the investment in working capital; and/or
- reduce the investment in non-current assets

will have the effect of increasing shareholders' wealth.

Figure 9.9 shows the process of measuring free cash flows.

Figure 9.9	Measuring free cash flows

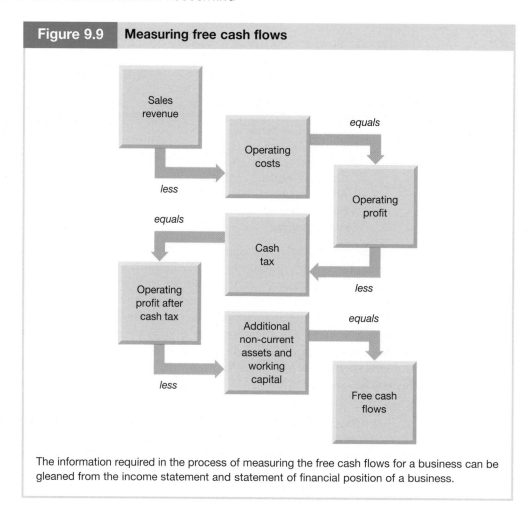

The information required in the process of measuring the free cash flows for a business can be gleaned from the income statement and statement of financial position of a business.

Business value and shareholder value

We have just seen how SVA measures the value of the business as a whole through discounting the free cash flows. The value of the business as a whole is not necessarily, however, that part which is available to the shareholders.

Activity 9.7

If the net present value of future cash flows generated by the business represents the value of the business as a whole, how can we derive that part of the value of the business that is available to shareholders?

A business will normally be financed by a combination of borrowing and ordinary shareholders' funds. Thus lenders will also have a claim on the total value of the business. That part of the total business value that is available to ordinary shareholders can therefore be derived by deducting from the total value of the business (total NPV) the market value of any borrowings outstanding. Hence:

Shareholder value = total business value − market value of outstanding borrowings

At this point, it is probably worth going through an example to illustrate the way in which we might calculate shareholder value for a business.

Example 9.3

The directors of United Pharmaceuticals plc are considering making a takeover bid for Bortex plc, which produces vitamins and health foods. It will do this by offering to buy all of the shares in Bortex plc. It is expected that the Bortex plc shareholders will reject any bid that values the shares at less than £11 each.

Bortex plc generated sales revenue for the most recent year of £3,000m. Extracts from the business's statement of financial position at the end of the most recent year are as follows:

	£m
Equity	
Share capital £1 ordinary shares	400
Reserves	380
	780
Non-current liabilities	
Loan notes	120

Forecasts that have been prepared by the business planning department of Bortex plc are as follows:

- Sales revenue will grow at 10 per cent a year for the next five years.
- The operating profit margin is currently 15 per cent and is likely to be maintained at this rate in the future.
- The cash tax rate is 25 per cent.
- Replacement non-current asset investment (RNCAI) will be in line with the annual depreciation charge each year.
- Additional non-current asset investment (ANCAI) for each year over the next five years will be 10 per cent of sales revenue growth.
- Additional working capital investment (AWCI) for each year over the next five years will be 5 per cent of sales revenue growth.

After five years, the business's sales revenues will stabilise at their Year 5 level. The business has a cost of capital of 10 per cent and the loan notes figure in the statement of financial position reflects its current market value.

The free cash flow calculation will be as follows:

	Year 1 £m	Year 2 £m	Year 3 £m	Year 4 £m	Year 5 £m	After Year 5 £m
Sales revenue	3,300.0	3,630.0	3,993.0	4,392.3	4,831.5	4,831.5
Operating profit (15%)	495.0	544.5	599.0	658.8	724.7	724.7
Less Cash tax (25%)	(123.8)	(136.1)	(149.8)	(164.7)	(181.2)	(181.2)
Operating profit after cash tax	371.2	408.4	449.2	494.1	543.5	543.5
Less						
ANCAI*	(30.0)	(33.0)	(36.3)	(39.9)	(43.9)	–
AWCI†	(15.0)	(16.5)	(18.2)	(20.0)	(22.0)	–
Free cash flows	326.2	358.9	394.7	434.2	477.6	543.5

Notes:
* The additional non-current asset investment is 10 per cent of sales revenue growth. In the first year, sales revenue growth is £300m (that is, £3,300m – £3,000m). Thus, the investment will be 10% × £300m = £30m. Similar calculations are carried out for the following years.
† The additional working capital investment is 5 per cent of sales revenue growth. In the first year the investment will be 5% × £300m = £15m. Similar calculations are carried out in following years.

Example 9.3 continued

Having derived the free cash flows (FCF), the total business value can be calculated as follows:

Year	FCF £m	Discount factor @ 10%	Present value £m
1	326.2	0.909	296.5
2	358.9	0.826	296.5
3	394.7	0.751	296.4
4	434.2	0.683	296.6
5	477.6	0.621	296.6
Terminal value: 543.5/0.10 (see Note)	5,435.0	0.621	3,375.1
Total business value			4,857.7

Note: After Year 5 there is no further sales expansion, so no increase in assets will be involved. Also, since the shareholders require a 10 per cent return, they will place a value of £5,435m on the future returns after Year 5. This is a value on which £543.5m represents a 10 per cent return.

Activity 9.8

What is the shareholder value figure for the business in Example 9.3?

Would the sale of the shares at £11 per share add value for the shareholders of Bortex plc?

Shareholder value will be the total business value less the market value of the loan notes. Hence, shareholder value is

$$£4,857.7m - £120m = £4,737.7m$$

The proceeds from the sale of the shares to United Pharmaceuticals would yield

$$400m \times £11 = £4,400.0m$$

Thus, from the point of view of the shareholders of Bortex plc, the sale of the business, at the share price mentioned, would not increase shareholder value.

Managing with SVA

We saw earlier that the adoption of SVA indicates a commitment to managing the business in such a way as to maximise shareholder returns. Those who support this approach argue that SVA can be a powerful tool for strategic planning. For example, SVA can be extremely useful when considering major shifts of direction such as

- acquiring new businesses
- selling existing businesses
- developing new products or markets
- reorganising or restructuring the business

because it takes account of all the elements that determine shareholder value.

Figure 9.10 shows how shareholder value is derived.

| Figure 9.10 | **Deriving shareholder value** |

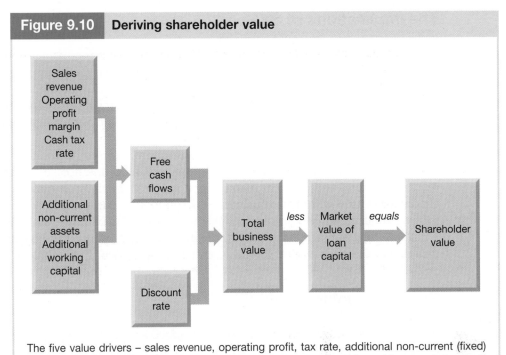

The five value drivers – sales revenue, operating profit, tax rate, additional non-current (fixed) assets and additional working capital – will determine the free cash flows. These cash flows will be discounted using the investors' required rate of return from investors to determine the total value of the business. If we deduct the market value of any borrowings from this figure, we are left with a measure of shareholder value.

SVA is useful in focusing attention on the value drivers that create shareholder wealth. For example, we saw earlier that the key variables in determining free cash flows were

- sales revenue
- operating profit margin
- cash tax rate
- additional investment in working capital
- additional investment in non-current assets.

In order to improve free cash flows and, in turn, shareholder value, management targets can be set for improving performance in relation to each value driver and responsibility assigned for achieving these targets.

Activity 9.9

Can you suggest what might be the practical problems of adopting an SVA approach?

Two practical problems spring to mind:

1 Forecasting future cash flows lies at the heart of this approach. In practice, forecasting can be difficult, and simplifying assumptions will usually have to be made.
2 SVA requires more comprehensive information (for example, information concerning the value drivers) than the traditional measures discussed earlier.

You may have thought of other problems.

The implications of SVA

It is worth emphasising that supporters of SVA believe that this measure should replace the traditional accounting measures of value creation such as profit, earnings per share and return on ordinary shareholders' funds. Thus, only if shareholder value increases over time can we say that there has been an increase in shareholder wealth. Any change over time can be measured by comparing shareholder value at the beginning and the end of a particular period.

We can see that SVA is really a radical departure from the conventional approach to managing a business. It will require different performance indicators, different financial reporting systems and different management incentive methods. It may also require a change of culture within the business to accommodate the shareholder value philosophy. Not all employees may be focused on the need to maximise shareholder wealth.

If SVA is implemented, it can provide the basis of targets for managers to work towards, on a day-to-day basis, which should promote maximisation of shareholder value.

Economic value added (EVA®)

→ **Economic value added (EVA®)** has been developed and trademarked by a US management consultancy firm, Stern Stewart. However, EVA® is based on the idea of economic profit, which has been around for many years. The measure reflects the point made earlier that, for a business to be profitable in an economic sense, it must generate returns that exceed the required returns of investors. It is not enough simply to make an accounting profit, because this measure does not take full account of the returns required by investors.

EVA® indicates whether or not the returns generated exceed the required returns by investors. The formula is as follows:

$$\text{EVA}^® = \text{NOPAT} - (R \times C)$$

where
NOPAT = net operating profit after tax
R = required returns of investors
C = capital invested (that is, the net assets of the business).

Only when EVA® is positive can we say that the business is increasing shareholder wealth. To maximise shareholder wealth, managers must increase EVA® by as much as possible.

Activity 9.10

Can you suggest what managers might do in order to increase EVA®? (*Hint*: Use the formula shown above as your starting point.)

The formula suggests that in order to increase EVA® managers may try to:

- Increase NOPAT. This may be done either by reducing expenses or by increasing sales revenue.
- Reduce capital invested by using assets more efficiently. This means selling off any assets that are not generating adequate returns and investing in assets that are generating a satisfactory NOPAT.

● Reduce the required rates of return for investors. This may be achieved by changing the capital structure in favour of borrowing (which tends to be cheaper to service than share capital). However, this strategy can create problems.

EVA® relies on conventional financial statements (income statement and statement of financial position) to measure the wealth created for shareholders. However, the NOPAT and capital figures shown on these statements are used only as a starting point. They have to be adjusted because of the problems and limitations of conventional measures. According to Stern Stewart, the major problem is that both profit and capital tend to be understated because of the conservative bias in accounting measurement.

Profit is understated as a result of judgemental write-offs (such as goodwill written off or research and development expenditure written off) and as a result of excessive provisions being created (such as an allowance for trade receivables (bad debt provision)). Both of these stem from taking an unrealistically pessimistic view of the value of some of the business's assets.

Capital is also understated because assets are reported at their original cost (less amounts written off for depreciation and so on), which can produce figures considerably below current market values. In addition, certain assets, such as internally generated goodwill and brand names, are omitted from the financial statements because no external transactions have occurred.

Stern Stewart has identified more than 100 adjustments that could be made to the conventional financial statements in order to eliminate the conservative bias. However, it is believed that, in practice, only a handful of adjustments will usually have to be made to the accounting figures of any particular business. Unless an adjustment is going to have a significant effect on the calculation of EVA® it is really not worth making. The adjustments made should reflect the nature of the particular business. Each business is unique and so must customise the calculation of EVA® to its particular circumstances. (This aspect of EVA® can be seen as either indicating flexibility or as being open to manipulation depending on whether or not you support this measure.)

Common adjustments that have to be made include:

1 *Research and development (R&D) costs and marketing costs.* These costs should be written off over the period that they benefit. In practice, however, they are often written off in the period in which they are incurred. This means that any amounts written off immediately should be added back to the assets on the statement of financial position, thereby increasing invested capital, and then written off over time.

2 *Restructuring costs.* This item can be viewed as an investment in the future rather than an expense to be written off. Supporters of EVA® argue that by restructuring, the business is better placed to meet future challenges and so any amounts incurred should be added back to assets.

3 *Marketable investments.* Investment in shares and loan notes of other businesses are not included as part of the capital invested in the business. This is because the income from marketable investments is not included in the calculation of operating profit. (Income from this source will be added in the income statement *after* operating profit has been calculated.)

Let us now consider a simple example to show how EVA® may be calculated.

Example 9.4

Scorpio plc was established two years ago and has produced the following statement of financial position and income statement at the end of the second year of trading.

Statement of financial position as at the end of the second year

	£m
Non-current assets	
Plant and equipment	80.0
Motor vehicles	12.4
Marketable investments	6.6
	99.0
Current assets	
Inventories	34.5
Receivables	29.3
Cash	2.1
	65.9
Total assets	164.9
Equity	
Share capital	60.0
Retained earnings	23.7
	83.7
Non-current liabilities	
Loan notes	50.0
Current liabilities	
Trade payables	30.3
Taxation	0.9
	31.2
Total equity and liabilities	164.9

Income statement for the second year

	£m
Sales revenue	148.6
Cost of sales	(76.2)
Gross profit	72.4
Wages	(24.5)
Depreciation of plant and equipment	(12.8)
Marketing costs	(22.5)
Allowances for trade receivables	(4.5)
Operating profit	8.1
Income from investments	0.4
	8.5
Interest payable	(0.5)
Ordinary profit before taxation	8.0
Restructuring costs	(2.0)
Profit before taxation	6.0
Tax	(1.8)
Profit for the year	4.2

Discussions with the finance director reveal the following:

1 Marketing costs relate to the launch of a new product. The benefits of the marketing campaign are expected to last for three years (including this most recent year).

2 The allowance for trade receivables was created this year and the amount is considered to be very high. A more realistic figure for the allowance would be £2.0 million.

3 Restructuring costs were incurred as a result of a collapse in a particular product market. By restructuring the business, benefits are expected to flow for an infinite period.

4 The business has a 10 per cent required rate of return for investors.

The first step in calculating EVA® is to adjust the net operating profit after tax to take account of the various points revealed by the discussion with the finance director. The revised figure is calculated as follows:

NOPAT adjustment

	£m	£m
Operating profit		8.1
Tax		(1.8)
		6.3

EVA® adjustments (to be added back to profit)

	£m	£m
Marketing costs (2/3 × 22.5)	15.0	
Excess allowance	2.5	17.5
Adjusted NOPAT		23.8

The next step is to adjust the net assets (as represented by equity and loan notes) to take account of the points revealed.

Adjusted net assets (or capital invested)

	£m	£m
Net assets (from statement of financial position)		133.7
Marketing costs (Note 1)	15.0	
Allowance for trade receivables	2.5	
Restructuring costs (Note 2)	2.0	19.5
		153.2
Marketable investments (Note 3)		(6.6)
Adjusted net assets		146.6

Notes:

1 The marketing costs represent two years' benefits added back (2/3 × £22.5m).

2 The restructuring costs are added back to the net assets as they provide benefits over an infinite period. (Note that they were not added back to the operating profit as these costs were deducted after arriving at operating profit in the income statement.)

3 The marketable investments do not form part of the operating assets of the business, and the income from these investments is not part of the operating income.

Activity 9.11

Can you work out the EVA® for the second year of the business in Example 9.4?

EVA® can be calculated as follows:

$$\text{EVA}^® = \text{NOPAT} - (R \times C) = £23.8m - (10\% \times £146.6m)$$
$$= £9.1m \text{ (to one decimal place)}$$

We can see that EVA® is positive and so the business increased shareholder wealth during the year.

Although EVA® is used by many large businesses, both in the US and Europe, it tends to be used for management purposes only: few businesses report this measure to shareholders. One business that does, however, is Whole Foods Market, a leading retailer of natural and organic foods, which operates more than 270 stores in the US and the UK. **Real World 9.11** describes the way in which the business uses EVA® and the results of doing so.

REAL WORLD 9.11

The whole picture

Whole Foods Market aims to improve its business by achieving improvements to EVA®. To encourage managers along this path, an incentive plan, based on improvements to EVA®, has been introduced. The plan embraces senior executives, regional managers and store managers, and the bonuses awarded form a significant part of their total remuneration. To make the incentive plan work, measures of EVA® based on the whole business, the regional level and the store level are calculated. More than five hundred managers are already included in the incentive plan and this number is expected to increase in the future.

EVA® is used to evaluate capital investment decisions such as the acquisition of new stores and the refurbishment of existing stores. Unless there is clear evidence that value will be added, investment proposals are rejected. EVA® is also used to improve operational efficiency. It was mentioned earlier that one way in which EVA® can be increased is through an improvement in NOPAT. The business is, therefore, continually seeking ways to improve sales and profit margins and to bear down on costs.

EVA® figures for 2005 and 2006 are shown below. The relevant tax rate for each year was 40% and the cost of capital was 9%.

Years ended:	24 September 2006	25 September 2005
	$000	$000
NOPAT	215,281	165,579
Capital cost	(150,871)	(139,793)
EVA®	64,410	25,786
Improvement in EVA®	38,624	

Source: www.wholefoodsmarket.com.

One often-mentioned limitation of EVA® is that it can be difficult to allocate revenues, costs and capital easily between different business units (individual stores in the case of Whole Food Markets). As a result, this technique cannot always be applied to individual business units. We have just seen, however, that Whole Food Markets seems able to do this.

The main advantage of this measure is the discipline to which managers are subjected as a result of the charge for capital that has been invested. Before any increase in shareholder wealth can be recognised, an appropriate deduction is made for the use of business resources. Thus, EVA® encourages managers to use these resources efficiently. Where managers are focused simply on increasing profits, there is a danger that the resources used to achieve any increase in profits will not be taken into proper account.

The benefits of EVA® may be undermined, however, if a short-term perspective is adopted. **Real World 9.12** describes the problems of a large engineering business that is using EVA® and where it is claimed that the technique may be distorting management behaviour.

REAL WORLD 9.12

Hard times   **FT**

Klaus Kleinfeld, Siemens' chief executive, is stuck in an unfortunate position after a deeply testing period at the helm of Europe's largest engineering group.

On the one side he is receiving pressure from investors fed up with a stagnating share price and profitability that continues to lag behind most of the German group's main competitors. But from the other he is under attack from the powerful IG Metall union aimed at holding him back from doing any serious restructuring. . . .

'He is having to walk a tightrope,' says a former senior Siemens director. 'His focus right now has to be on fixing the problem areas and very quickly.' . . .

Ben Uglow, an analyst at Morgan Stanley, . . . says 'I think the real question now in Siemens is one of management incentivisation. I think Kleinfeld has done a good job in the last year of refocusing the portfolio but some of his big chiefs have let him down.' Many investors are concerned that the margin targets that Mr Kleinfeld set last year for all his divisions to reach by April 2007 are distorting matters by making managers relax if they have already exceeded them.

Mr Kleinfeld and other directors disagree vehemently. Management pay is based on the 'economic value added' each division provides against each year's budget, not on specific margin targets. But a former senior director says this has led to a lack of investment in some parts of the business as managers look to earn as much as possible.

Source: Siemens chief finds himself in a difficult balancing act, ft.com (Milne, R.), © The Financial Times Limited, 6 November 2006.

EVA® and SVA compared

Although at first glance it may appear that EVA® and SVA are worlds apart, in fact the opposite is true. EVA® and SVA are closely related and, in theory at least, should produce the same figure for shareholder value. The way in which shareholder value is calculated using SVA has already been described. The EVA® approach to calculating shareholder value adds the capital invested to the present value of future EVA® flows and then deducts the market value of any borrowings. Figure 9.11 illustrates the two approaches to determining shareholder value.

Figure 9.11 | **Two approaches to determining shareholder value**

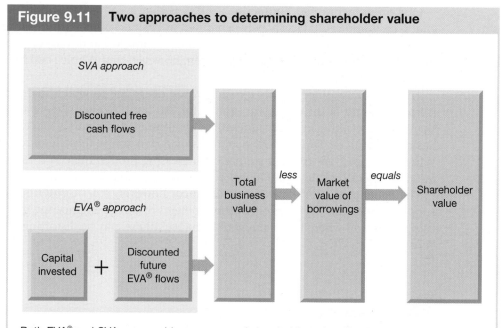

Both EVA® and SVA can provide a measure of shareholder value. Total business value can be derived either by discounting the free cash flows over time or by discounting the EVA® flows over time and adding the capital invested. Whichever approach is used, the market value of borrowings must then be deducted to derive shareholder value.

Let us go through a simple example to illustrate this point.

Example 9.5

Leo Ltd has just been formed and has been financed by a £20 million issue of share capital and a £10 million issue of loan notes. The proceeds of the issue have been invested in non-current (fixed) assets with a life of three years and during this period these assets will depreciate by £10 million per year. The operating profit after tax is expected to be £15 million each year. There will be no replacement of non-current assets during the three-year period and no investment in working capital. At the end of the three years, the business will be wound up and the non-current assets will have no residual value.

The required rate of return by investors is 10 per cent.

The SVA approach to determining shareholder value will be as follows:

Year	Free cash flows £m	Discount rate 10%	Present value £m
1	25.0*	0.91	22.8
2	25.0	0.83	20.7
3	25.0	0.75	18.7
		Total business value	62.2
		Loan notes	(10.0)
		Shareholder value	52.2

* The free cash flows will be the operating profit after tax *plus* the depreciation charge (that is, £15m + £10m). In this case, there are no replacement non-current assets against which the depreciation charge can be netted off. It must therefore be added back.

The EVA® approach to determining shareholder value will be as follows:

Year	Opening capital invested (C) £m	Capital charge (10% × C) £m	Operating profit after tax £m	EVA® £m	Discount rate 10%	Present value of EVA® £m
1	30.0*	3.0	15.0	12.0	0.91	10.9
2	20.0	2.0	15.0	13.0	0.83	10.8
3	10.0	1.0	15.0	14.0	0.75	10.5
						32.2
				Opening capital		30.0
						62.2
				Loan notes		(10.0)
				Shareholder value		52.2

* The capital invested decreases each year by the depreciation charge (that is, £10 million).

EVA® or SVA?

Although both EVA® and SVA are consistent with the objective of maximising shareholder wealth and, in theory, should produce the same decisions and results, the supporters of EVA® claim that this measure has a number of practical advantages over SVA. One such advantage is that EVA® sits more comfortably with the conventional financial reporting systems and financial reports. There is no need to develop entirely new systems to implement EVA® as it can be calculated by making a few adjustments to the conventional income statement and statement of financial position.

It is also claimed that EVA® is more useful as a basis for rewarding managers. Both EVA® and SVA support the idea that management rewards should be linked to increases in shareholder value. This should ensure that the interests of managers are closely aligned to the interests of shareholders. Under the SVA approach, management rewards will be determined on the basis of the contribution made to the generation of long-term cash flows. However, there are practical problems in using SVA for this purpose.

Activity 9.12

What are the practical problems that may arise when using SVA calculations to reward managers? (*Hint:* Think about how SVA is calculated.)

The SVA approach measures changes in shareholder value by reference to predicted changes in future cash flows and it is unwise to pay managers on the basis of predicted rather than actual achievements. If the predictions are optimistic, the effect will be that the business rewards optimism rather than real achievement. There is also a risk that unscrupulous managers will manipulate predicted future cash flows in order to increase their rewards.

Under EVA®, managers can receive bonuses based on actual achievement during a particular period. If management rewards are linked to a single period, however, there is a danger that managers will pay undue attention to increasing EVA® during this period rather than over the long term. The objective should be to maximise EVA® over the longer term. Where a business has a stable level of sales revenue, operating assets and borrowing, a current-period focus is likely to be less of a problem than where these elements are unstable over time. A stable pattern of operations minimises the risk that improvements in EVA® during the current period are achieved at the expense of future periods. Nevertheless, any reward system for managers must encourage a long-term perspective and so rewards should be based on the ability of managers to improve EVA® over a number of years rather than a single year.

Real World 9.13 describes the way in which one business uses EVA® to reward its managers.

REAL WORLD 9.13

Rewarding managers

Hanson PLC, a major supplier of heavy building materials, adopts a bonus system for its directors based on EVA®. EVA® generated is accumulated in a 'bonus bank' and the directors are paid a portion of the EVA® bonus bank during a particular year; the remainder is carried forward for payment in future years. The following is an extract from the 2006 annual report of the business.

Annual bonus scheme

The annual bonus scheme for the Executive Directors and other senior executives is aligned with changes in shareholder value through the economic value added methodology. The main principle of economic value added is to recognise that over time a company should generate returns in excess of its cost of capital – the return that lenders and shareholders expect of the Company each year.

The annual bonus scheme is calibrated by reference to target levels of bonus and, for the Executive Directors and other senior executives, works on a bonus banking arrangement whereby each year the improvement in the group's overall economic value added for that year determines whether there is a bonus bank addition or deduction. Following the addition or deduction, the participant receives one-third of the accumulated bonus bank. There is neither a cap (maximum addition into the bonus bank each year) nor a floor (maximum deduction from the bonus bank each year).

The bonus bank has two main functions; firstly it ensures that individuals do not make short-term decisions such as deferring essential expenditure from one year to the next and receive a bonus for doing so; and secondly, the bonus bank can act as a retention tool.

For 2006, the target level of bonus for A J Murray was 62.5% of basic salary and for G Dransfield 37.5% of basic salary. No bonus entitlement arose for J C Nicholls who left the Company on October 31, 2006.

Improvement in the group's overall economic value added for the year to December 31, 2006 determined the bonus bank addition for the Executive Directors. The strong operating and profit performance in 2006 led to improvement in the group's economic value added and resulted in additions to the bonus bank of 69.4% of basic salary for A J Murray and 41.6% of basic salary for G Dransfield. The bonuses paid in respect of the year to December 31, 2006 to the Executive Directors were £509,262 for A J Murray and £161,986 for G Dransfield.

Source: Hanson PLC Annual Report 2006, www.hanson.biz.

It is worth noting that Stern Stewart believes that bonuses, calculated as a percentage of EVA®, should form a very large part of the total remuneration package for managers. Thus, the higher the EVA® figure, the higher the rewards to managers – with no upper limits. The philosophy is that EVA® should make managers wealthy provided it makes shareholders extremely wealthy. A bonus system should encompass as many managers as possible in order to encourage a widespread commitment to implementing EVA®.

Just another fad?

The techniques described in this chapter are all potentially valuable to a business, but their successful implementation is far from certain. According to one source, failure rates are as high as 60 per cent (see reference 4 at the end of the chapter). A depressingly common scenario is that a new technique will be enthusiastically adopted but, within a short while, disillusionment will set in. Managers will decide that the technique does not meet their requirements and so it will be abandoned. In some businesses, a pattern of adoption, disillusionment and abandonment of new techniques may develop. Where this occurs, employees are likely to become sceptical and to dismiss any newly-adopted technique as simply a passing fad.

Introducing a new technique is likely to be costly and can cause considerable upheaval. Managers must, therefore, tread carefully. They must try to identify the potential problems, as well as the benefits, that may accrue from its adoption. The main problems that lie in wait are:

● the excessive optimism that managers often have in their ability to implement a new technique that will quickly yield good results;
● the assumption that others will share the enthusiasm felt for a new technique;
● the failure to acknowledge that there will be losers as well as winners when a new technique is implemented (see reference 4 at the end of the chapter).

Managers must be realistic about what can be achieved from a new technique and must accept that resistance to its introduction is likely. They must not underestimate what it will take to ensure a successful outcome.

Self-assessment question 9.1

You have recently heard a fellow student talking about strategic management accounting as follows:

1 'Identifying cost-saving measures really needs to be left to accountants. Non-experts tend to cause problems when they attempt it.'
2 'Customer profitability analysis is about finding out which of your customers are the more profitable businesses and trying to encourage the ones that are more profitable to place orders. This is to avoid having customers that go bankrupt.'
3 'Shareholder value analysis (SVA) tries to give shareholders their returns in the form that they like. Some shareholders prefer dividends and others prefer profits to be ploughed back.'
4 'EVA® stands for "equity value analysis" and is an alternative name for SVA.'
5 'The "balanced scorecard" is the American name for what people in the UK call a statement of financial position (balance sheet).'

Required:
Critically comment on the student's statements, explaining any technical terms.

The answer to this question can be found in Appendix B at the back of the book.

SUMMARY

The main points in this chapter may be summarised as follows:

Strategic management accounting (SMA)

- SMA is concerned with providing information to support strategic plans and decisions.
- It is more outward looking, more concerned with outperforming the competition and more concerned with monitoring progress towards strategic objectives than conventional management accounting.

Facing outwards

- Competitor analysis examines the objectives, strategies, assumptions and resource capabilities of competitors.
- Customer profitability analysis assesses the profitability of each customer or type of customer to the business.

Competitive advantage through cost leadership

- Total life-cycle costing is concerned with tracking and reporting all costs relating to a product from the beginning to the end of its life.
- Target costing is a market-based approach to managing costs that is used at the planning stage.
  - It attempts to reduce costs so that the market price covers the cost plus an acceptable profit.
  - It distinguishes between activities that add value and those that do not; it may be possible to save costs by eliminating or reducing the cost of the non-value-adding ones.
- *Kaizen* costing is concerned with continual and gradual cost reduction and is used at the production stage.
- Costs may be managed without using sophisticated techniques if:
  - There is a shared responsibility for managing costs.
  - Discussion of costs becomes an everyday activity.
  - Costs are managed locally.
  - Benchmarking is used at regular intervals.
  - The focus is on managing rather than reducing costs.
- Value chain analysis involves analysing the various activities in the product life cycle to identify and try to eliminate non-value-added activities.

Translating strategies into action

- The balanced scorecard is a management tool that uses financial and non-financial measures to assess progress towards objectives.
- It has four aspects: financial, customer, internal business process, and learning and growth.
- It encourages a balanced approach to managing the business.

Measuring shareholder value

- Shareholder value is seen as the key objective of most businesses.
- Two approaches used to measure shareholder value are shareholder value analysis (SVA) and economic value added (EVA®).
- Shareholder value analysis (SVA) is based on the concept of net present value analysis.
- It identifies key value drivers for generating shareholder value.

- Economic value added is a means of measuring whether the returns generated by the business exceed the required returns of investors.

$$EVA^® = NOPAT - (R \times C)$$

where
NOPAT = net operating profit after tax
R = required returns from investors
C = capital invested (that is, the net assets of the business).

→ Key terms

Competitor analysis p. 319
Customer profitability analysis (CPA) p. 323
Lean manufacturing p. 329
Value chain analysis p. 330
Value drivers p. 334

Balanced scorecard p. 334
Shareholder value analysis (SVA) p. 344
Free cash flows p. 344
Economic value added (EVA®) p. 350

References

1 Crawford, D. and Baveja, S., 'In search of new value for the support operation', ft.com, 27 July 2006.
2 Hopwood, A., 'Costs count in the strategic agenda', ft.com, 13 August 2002.
3 Kaplan, R. and Norton, D., *The Balanced Scorecard*, Harvard Business School Press, 1996.
4 Bruce, R., 'Tread a careful path between creative hope and blind faith', ft.com, 2 February 2006.

Further reading

If you would like to explore topics covered in this chapter in more depth, we recommend the following books:

Bhimani, A., Horngren, C., Datar, S. and Foster, G., *Management and Cost Accounting*, 4th edn, FT Prentice Hall, 2008, chapter 22.
McWatters, C., Zimmerman, J. and Morse, D., *Management Accounting: Analysis and Interpretation*, FT Prentice Hall, 2008, chapter 4.
Kaplan, R. and Norton, D., *The Balanced Scorecard*, Harvard Business School Press, 1996.
Mills, R., *The Dynamics of Shareholder Value*, Mars Business Associates, 1998.
Stern, J. and Shelly, J., *The EVA Challenge*, John Wiley, 2001.

REVIEW QUESTIONS

Answers to these questions can be found in Appendix C at the back of the book.

9.1 How does strategic management accounting differ from its more traditional counterpart?

9.2 Both Customer A and Customer B buy 1,000 units of your business's service each year, paying the same price per unit. Why might your business regard Customer A as a desirable customer, but not Customer B?

9.3 What is the principle on which shareholder value analysis is based?

9.4 What are the four main areas on which the balanced scorecard is based?

EXERCISES

Exercises 9.4 to 9.8 are more advanced than 9.1 to 9.3. Those with a coloured number have answers in Appendix D at the back of the book. If you wish to try more exercises, visit the students' side of the Companion Website at www.pearsoned.co.uk/atrillmclaney.

9.1 Aires plc was recently formed and issued 80 million £0.50 shares at nominal value and loan notes of £24m. The business used the proceeds from the capital issues to purchase the remaining lease on some commercial properties that are rented out to small businesses. The lease will expire in four years' time and during that period the operating profits are expected to be £12m each year. At the end of the four years, the business will be wound up and the lease will have no residual value.

The required rate of return by investors is 12 per cent.

Required:

Calculate the expected shareholder value generated by the business over the four years, using
(a) the SVA approach
(b) the EVA® approach.

9.2 You have recently heard someone making the following statement about competitor profitability analysis (CPA).

> 'CPA is an assessment of how profitable competitors are, that is carried out in an attempt to establish a benchmark by which one's own business's success can be measured. Usually most of the information for this can be found in the competitors' annual report and financial statements. Usually competitors are willing to provide information about their financial results so that any gaps in the CPA can be filled in.'

Required:

Comment on this statement.

9.3 Sharma plc makes one standard product for which it charges the same basic price of £20 a unit, though discounts are allowed to certain customers. The business is in the process of carrying out a profitability analysis of all of its customers during the financial year just ended.

Information about Lopez Ltd, one of Sharma's customers, is as follows:

Discount on sales price	5%
Number of products sold	40,000 units
Manufacturing cost	£12 a unit
Number of sales orders	22
Number of deliveries	22
Distance travelled to deliver	120 miles
Number of sales visits from Sharma's staff	30

Sharma uses an activity-based approach to ascribing costs to customers, as follows:

Cost pool	Cost driver	Rate
Order handling	Number of orders	£75 an order
Delivery costs	Miles travelled	£1.50 a mile
Customer sales visits	Number of visits	£230 a visit

Lopez Ltd usually takes two months' credit, of which the cost to Sharma is estimated at 2 per cent per month.

Required:
Calculate the profit that Sharma plc derived from sales to Lopez Ltd during last year.

9.4 (a) The shareholder value approach to managing businesses is different to the stakeholder approach to managing businesses. In the latter case, the different stakeholders of the business (employees, customers, suppliers and so on) are considered as being of equal importance and so the interests of shareholders will not dominate. Is it possible for these two approaches to managing businesses to co-exist in harmony within a particular economy?

(b) It has often been argued that businesses are overcapitalised. If this is true, what might be the reasons for businesses having too much capital and how can EVA® help avoid this problem?

9.5 Virgo plc is considering introducing a system of EVA® and wants its managers to focus on the longer term rather than simply focus on the year-to-year EVA® results. The business is seeking your advice as to how a management bonus system could be arranged so as to ensure that the longer term is taken into account. The business is also unclear as to how much of the managers' pay should be paid in the form of a bonus and when such bonuses should be paid. Finally, the business is unclear as to where the balance between individual performance and corporate performance should be struck within any bonus system.

The finance director has recently produced figures that show that if Virgo plc had used EVA® over the past three years, the results would have been as follows:

2006	£25m (profit)
2007	£20m (loss)
2008	£10m (profit)

Required:
Set out your recommendations for a suitable bonus system for the divisional managers of the business.

9.6 Leo plc is considering entering a new market. A new product has been developed at a cost of £5m and is now ready for production. The market is growing and estimates from the finance department concerning future sales revenue of the new product are as follows:

Year	Sales revenue
	£m
1	30
2	36
3	40
4	48
5	60

After Year 5, sales revenues are expected to stabilise at the Year 5 level.
You are told that:

- The operating profit margin from the new market is likely to be a constant 20 per cent of sales revenue.
- The cash tax rate is 25 per cent of operating profit.
- Replacement non-current asset investment (RNCAI) will be in line with the annual depreciation charge each year.
- Additional non-current asset investment (ANCAI) over the next five years will be 15 per cent of sales revenue growth.
- Additional working capital investment (AWCI) for each year over the next five years will be 10 per cent of sales revenue growth.

The business has a cost of capital of 12 per cent. The new market is considered to be no more risky than the markets in which the business already has a presence.

Required:
Using an SVA approach, indicate the effect of entering the new market on shareholder value. (Workings should be to one decimal place.)

9.7 Pisces plc produced the following statement of financial position (balance sheet) and income statement at the end of the third year of trading:

Statement of financial position as at the end of the third year

	£m
Non-current assets	
Property	40.0
Machinery and equipment	80.0
Motor vans	18.6
Marketable investments	9.0
	147.6
Current assets	
Inventories	45.8
Trade receivables	64.6
Cash	1.0
	111.4
Total assets	259.0
Equity	
Share capital	80.0
Reserves	36.5
	116.5
Non-current liabilities	
Loan notes	80.0
Current liabilities	
Trade payables	62.5
	259.0

Income statement for the third year

	£m
Sales revenue	231.5
Cost of sales	(143.2)
Gross profit	88.3
Wages	(43.5)
Depreciation of machinery and equipment	(14.8)
R&D costs	(40.0)
Allowance for trade receivables	(10.5)
Operating loss	(20.5)
Income from investments	0.6
	(19.9)
Interest payable	(0.8)
Ordinary loss before taxation	(20.7)
Restructuring costs	(6.0)
Loss before taxation	(26.7)
Tax	–
Loss for the year	(26.7)

An analysis of the underlying records reveals the following:

1 R&D costs relate to the development of a new product in the previous year. These costs are written off over a 2-year period (starting last year). However, this is a prudent approach and the benefits are expected to last for 16 years.
2 The allowance for trade receivables (bad debts) was created this year and the amount of the provision is very high. A more realistic figure for the allowance would be £4 million.
3 Restructuring costs were incurred at the beginning of the year and are expected to provide benefits for an infinite period.
4 The business has a 7 per cent required rate of return for investors.

Required:
Calculate the EVA® for the business for the third year of trading.

9.8 Aquarius plc has estimated the following free cash flows for its five-year planning period:

Year	Free cash flows
	£m
1	35
2	38
3	45
4	49
5	53

Required:
How might it be possible to check the accuracy of these figures? What internal and external sources of information might be used to see whether the figures are realistic?

10

Measuring performance

INTRODUCTION

Although small businesses can be managed as a single unit, most large businesses are divided into operating units or divisions. We saw in Chapter 1 that large businesses are likely to work more effectively towards their strategic objectives if managed in this way. Where a divisional structure is in place, selecting appropriate measures to assess divisional performance becomes an important issue. In this chapter, we shall consider the strengths and weaknesses of the main measures that are used.

An operating division may supply products or services to other divisions within the same business. When this occurs, the problem of measuring divisional performance can be more difficult, because the price at which goods and services are transferred to the buying divisions will have an important influence on key performance indicators such as sales revenue and profits. We shall discuss the possible approaches that may be used to set transfer prices and we shall identify the most suitable approach to use.

Finally, we shall examine the role of non-financial measures in helping to assess divisional performance. We shall see why they are important and how they can improve the quality of financial decisions.

Throughout this chapter we shall be picking up some of the points made in earlier chapters, particularly Chapters 3, 8 and 9.

LEARNING OUTCOMES

When you have completed this chapter, you should be able to:

● Discuss the potential advantages and disadvantages for a business of adopting a divisional structure.

● Identify the major methods of measuring the performance of operating divisions and divisional managers, and assess their usefulness.

● Describe the problems of determining transfer prices between divisions, and outline the methods used in practice.

● Explain the increasing importance of non-financial measures in managing a business and how they may be used for decision-making purposes.

Divisionalisation

Why do businesses divisionalise?

Many large businesses supply a wide range of products and services and have operating units located throughout the world. Where business operations are complex, there is usually a need for an extended management hierarchy so that some decisions relating to particular operating units can be devolved from senior managers to those further down the hierarchy. It is not really feasible for those at the top of the hierarchy to know everything that is going on within the various operating units, and it is therefore impractical for them to take all the decisions relating to these units. By creating separate **divisions**, a large business can therefore become more responsive to the market and can operate more effectively.

Types of divisions

Managers of divisions are given discretion over various aspects of divisional operations. The extent of the discretion allowed to divisional managers will vary, however, from one business to another. In practice, divisions tend to fall into two broad categories:

1 **Profit centres.** The divisional manager of a profit centre will have responsibility for production and sales performance and can therefore decide on such matters as pricing, marketing, volume of output, sources of supply and sales mix. Divisional managers will each be assigned non-current assets and working capital by top management and will be expected to generate profits from the effective use of those assets. Any additional capital expenditure relating to the division would have to be agreed by top management.

2 **Investment centres.** The divisional manager of an investment centre has discretion over capital expenditure and working capital decisions as well as production and sales performance. Thus, an investment centre is a profit centre with added authority to make investment decisions. It is, in many respects, a business within a business.

In practice, it appears that top management is more prepared to allow discretion over production and sales decisions than over capital expenditure decisions. Thus, profit centres are more common than investment centres.

Divisional structures

A business may be divided into divisions in any way that top management considers appropriate. We saw in Chapter 1, however, that divisions are usually organised according to

- the services provided or the products made; and/or
- the geographical location.

Within each division, departments are often created and organised along functional lines. However, certain functions, which provide support across the various divisions, may be undertaken at head office to avoid duplication.

Real World 10.1 sets out the organisational chart for a well-known business that has a structure that includes several operating divisions.

REAL WORLD 10.1

Dividing up the cake

Greggs plc is a leading bakery retailer which operates more than 1,200 shops throughout the UK. These shops trade under either the *Greggs* or *Bakers Oven* brand name and serve around 5 million customers each week. The business has a decentralised structure with the Greggs brand having eight divisions and the Bakers Oven brand having three regions. Each division/region is an individual profit centre in an effort to drive local commitment and control.

The Greggs business has central bakeries around the UK supplying shops within their areas, whereas Bakers Oven has shops with in-store bakery and catering facilities. The organisational chart for Greggs plc is set out in Figure 10.1.

Figure 10.1	The organisational chart for Greggs plc

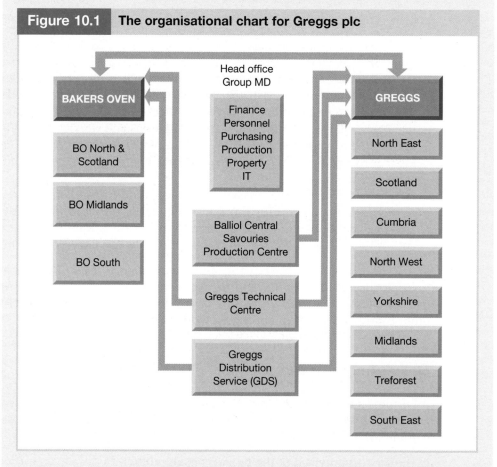

Certain functions, such as finance, personnel and purchasing are provided centrally. Each of the eight divisions and three regions identified in the chart operates as a profit centre.

Source: www.greggs.plc.uk.

Is divisionalisation a good idea?

There are several advantages claimed for dividing business operations into divisions and for allowing divisional managers a measure of autonomy.

Activity 10.1

Try to identify and briefly explain at least three advantages that may accrue to a business that decides to divisionalise. (We have already touched on some possible advantages.)

The following reasons occurred to us:

- *Market information*. Divisional managers will gather an enormous amount of information concerning customers, markets, sources of supply and so on, which may be difficult and costly to transmit to top management. In some cases, they might find it impossible to pass on to management at head office all of the knowledge and experience gathered. Furthermore, as divisional managers are 'in the front line' they can often use this information to best advantage.

- *Management motivation*. Divisional managers are likely to have a greater commitment to their work if they feel they have a significant influence over divisional decisions. Research evidence suggests that participation in decision making encourages a sense of responsibility towards seeing those decisions through. There is a danger that divisional managers will simply lose motivation if decisions concerning the division are made by top management and then imposed on them.

- *Management development*. Allowing divisional managers a degree of autonomy should help in their development. They will become exposed to marketing, production, financial problems and so on. This should help them to gain valuable specialist skills. In addition, the opportunity to run a division more or less as a separate business should develop their ability to think in strategic terms. This can be of great benefit to the business when it is looking for successors to the current generation of top managers.

- *Specialist knowledge*. Where a business offers a wide range of products and services, it would be difficult for top management to have the expertise to make operating decisions concerning each product and service. It is more practical to give divisional managers, with the detailed knowledge of the products and services, responsibility for such matters.

- *Allowing a strategic role for top managers*. If top managers were required to take detailed responsibility for the day-to-day operations of each division, they could become bogged down with making a huge number of relatively small decisions. Even if they were capable of making better operating decisions than the divisional managers, this is unlikely to be the best use of their time. Managers operating at a senior level should develop a strategic role. They must look to the future to identify the opportunities and threats facing the business and make appropriate plans. By taking a broader view of the business and plotting a course to be followed, top managers will be making the most valuable use of their time.

- *Timely decisions*. If information concerning a local division has to be gathered, shaped into a report and then passed up the hierarchy before a decision is made, it is unlikely that the business will be able to act quickly when dealing with changing conditions or emerging issues. In a highly competitive or turbulent environment, the speed of response to market changes can be critical. Divisional managers can usually formulate a response much more quickly than top managers.

The potential advantages of divisionalisation that have been identified are summarised in Figure 10. 2.

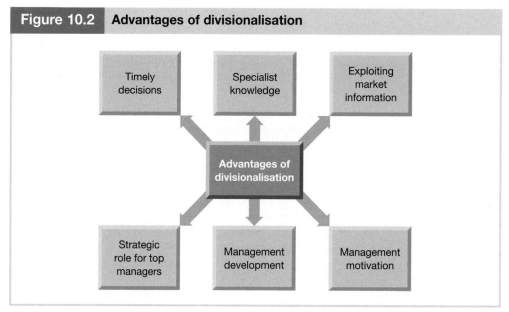

Figure 10.2 **Advantages of divisionalisation**

Real World 10.2 provides an example of a business in which decision making has become highly devolved.

REAL WORLD 10.2

Showing enterprise
FT

Enterprise is the largest car rental business in the US and is expanding its operations into the UK, Germany and Ireland. It is valued at around $8bn and has a fleet of 500,000 cars. It is managed by a network of 5,000 offices and 50,000 employees. An important market for the business is renting replacement cars for people involved in an accident or breakdown and for those whose car is being serviced. It is not an easy market to serve as day-to-day demand is difficult to predict and, often, customers are feeling anxious or distressed. Furthermore, the requirements of insurance companies and garage repair businesses often have to be considered.

To deal with this type of market, decision making has become highly devolved and offices within the network enjoy considerable autonomy. With this high degree of autonomy, however, comes responsibility. Each office is regarded as a profit centre and those who manage an office are accountable for profits (or losses) made. To help managers to monitor performance, the head office issues more than 5,000 financial statements each month. This allows the manager of each office within the network to have frequent feedback on costs, profits and customer satisfaction ratings relating to the office.

Senior management views Enterprise as a confederation of small businesses and the role of head office is that of a 'switching station' for the best ideas.

Source: Based on information from 'Enterprise drives home the service ethic', *Financial Times*, 2 June 2003.

Although most large businesses have separate operating divisions, there are problems that may arise as a result of adopting this type of structure. These include:

● *Goal conflict.* It is possible that the goals of the operating division will be inconsistent with those either of the business as a whole or of other divisions of the business. For example, an operating division of a business may be unable to sell computer equipment to a particular overseas government because another operating division within the business is selling military equipment to a hostile government. The overall profits of the business, however, may be increased if the military equipment sales cease, allowing a new market to develop for the computing equipment sold by the other division.

- *Risk avoidance.* Where managers of a division are faced with a large project, which involves a high level of risk, they may decide against the project even though the potential returns are high. The prospect of losing their jobs and remuneration may be the reason for this. However, the business's shareholders may prefer to take the risks involved because they view the project as just one of a number undertaken by the business. Whilst each particular project will have its risks, there is an expectation by investors that, overall, the expected returns will compensate for the risks involved. Divisional managers may be unable to take such a detached view, as they may not have a diversified portfolio of projects within the division to help reduce the effect of things going badly wrong.

- *Management 'perks'.* If divisional managers are allowed autonomy, there is a danger that they will award themselves substantial perquisites or 'perks'. These perks may include such things as a generous expense allowance, first-class travel and a chauffeur. These additional benefits may mean that divisional managers receive a far better remuneration package than the market requires for their services. The obvious way to avoid this is to monitor divisional managers' behaviour. The costs of monitoring, however, may outweigh any benefits arising from identifying and reducing these perks.

- *Increasing costs.* Additional costs may be borne by the business as a result of organising into divisions. For example, each division may have its own market research department, which may duplicate the efforts of market research departments in other divisions. By organising into smaller operating units, the business may also be unable to take advantage of its size in order to reduce costs. For example, it may be unable to negotiate quantity discounts with suppliers, as each division will be deciding on which supplier it uses and will only be purchasing quantities that are appropriate for its needs.

- *Competition.* Divisions within the same business offering similar or substitute products may find themselves in competition with one another. Where this competition is intense, prices may be reduced which may, in turn, have the effect of reducing profits of the business as a whole. For this reason, divisionalisation often works best where the different divisions do not offer closely related products or services, or where they operate in separate geographical regions.

It is clear from the above that divisionalisation is not without its problems. Although it may not be possible to eliminate these problems, it may be possible to reduce their severity. Thus, an important task of top management is to devise a divisional framework that reaps the benefits of divisional autonomy and yet minimises the problems that divisionalisation brings.

Activity 10.2

Assume that you are the chief executive of a divisionalised business. How might you try to reduce the effects of some of the problems identified above?

The problems of goal conflict and competition may be dealt with by regulating the behaviour of divisional managers. They should be prevented from making decisions that result in an increase in profits for their particular division, but which reduce the profits of

Activity 10.2 continued

the business as a whole. Though such a policy would cut across the autonomy of divisional managers, it is important for them to appreciate that they are not operating completely independent units and that divisional managers also have responsibilities towards the business as a whole.

The problem of risk avoidance by management is a complex one that may be difficult to deal with in practice. It might be possible, however, to encourage divisional managers to take on more risk if the rewards offered reflect the higher levels of risk involved. Observation of real life tells us that individuals will often be prepared to take on greater risk provided that they receive compensation in the form of higher rewards.

If things start to go wrong, it may also be possible for the business, through the use of budget variance reports, to distinguish between those variances that are outside the control of the divisional manager and those that are within the manager's control. Divisional managers would then be accountable only for the variances within their control. It is not always easy, however, to obtain unbiased information for preparing budgets from divisional managers when they know that such information will be used to evaluate their performance.

Management perks may be controlled by central management by setting out clear rules as to what is acceptable. To some extent, observing the behaviour and actions of divisional managers can reveal departures from the rules. Many perks, such as luxury cars, chauffeurs and large offices, are highly visible. Central management should be alert to any signs that divisional managers are rewarding themselves in this way.

Duplication of effort in certain areas can be extremely costly. For this reason, some businesses prefer particular functions, such as administration, accounting, research and development and marketing, to be undertaken by central staff rather than at the divisional level. Again, this means that divisional managers will have to sacrifice some autonomy for the sake of the performance of the business overall.

We can see that divisionalisation poses a major challenge for top management. Somehow, it must encourage management discretion at the divisional level whilst trying to ensure that the divisional objectives are consistent with the overall strategic objectives of the business as a whole. This requires sound judgement, as there are really no techniques or models that can be applied to solve this problem.

A further challenge for top management is to identify valid and reliable performance measures that can help assess both the division and its divisional managers. It is to this challenge that we now turn.

Measuring divisional profit

Businesses operate with the financial objective of increasing shareholders' wealth, which on a short-term basis translates into making a profit. It is not surprising, therefore, that profits and profitability are of central importance in measuring the performance of both the operating divisions and their divisional managers. There are, however, various measures of profit that we can use for these purposes. When deciding on the appropriate measure, it is important to be clear about the purpose for which it is to be used.

To help understand the issues involved, let us take a look at the following divisional income statement. We can see that it incorporates various measures of profit that can be used to assess performance and we shall consider each of these in turn.

Household Appliances
Divisional Income Statement for last year

	£000
Sales revenue	980
Variable expenses	(490)
Contribution	490
Controllable divisional fixed expenses	(130)
Controllable profit	360
Non-controllable divisional fixed expenses	(150)
Divisional profit before common expenses	210
Apportioned cost of common expenses	(80)
Divisional profit (loss) for the period	130

Before looking at the various measures of profit, we should be clear that the words 'controllable' and 'non-controllable' in this income statement refer to the ability of the divisional manager to exert an influence over particular expenses. Thus, an expense that is authorised by a senior manager at head office will not be under the control of the divisional manager, despite the fact that the expense may relate to the division. An expense that arises directly from a decision taken by the divisional manager, on the other hand, is controllable at divisional level.

As is implied by this income statement for the division, there are four measures of profit that could be used to assess performance. These are: contribution; controllable profit; divisional profit before common expenses; and divisional profit for the period.

Contribution

The first measure of profit is the *contribution*, which represents the difference between the total sales revenue of the division and the variable expenses incurred. We considered this measure at length in Chapter 3. There we saw that it can be a useful measure for gaining an insight into the relationship between costs, output levels and profit.

Activity 10.3

Assume that you are the chief executive of a divisionalised business. Would you use contribution as a primary measure of divisional performance?

This measure has its drawbacks for this purpose. The most important drawback is that it only takes account of variable expenses and ignores any fixed expenses incurred. This means that not all aspects of operating performance are considered.

Activity 10.4

Assume now that you are a divisional manager. What might you be encouraged to do if the contribution were used to assess your performance?

As variable expenses are taken into account in this measure and fixed expenses are ignored, it would be tempting to arrange things so that fixed expenses rather than variable expenses are incurred wherever possible. In this way, the contribution will be maximised. For example, you may decide, as divisional manager, to employ less casual labour and to use machines to do the work instead (even though this may be a more expensive option).

Controllable profit

The second measure of profit is the *controllable profit*, which takes account of all expenses that are within the control of divisional managers in arriving at a measure of performance. Many view this as the best measure of performance for divisional managers, as they will be in a position to determine the level of expenses incurred. However, in practice, it may be difficult to categorise costs as being either **controllable costs** or **non-controllable costs**. Some expenses may be capable of being influenced by divisional managers, yet not be entirely under their control.

Depreciation can be one example of such an expense. The divisional manager may be required to purchase a particular type of computer hardware so that the information systems of the division are compatible with the systems used throughout the business. The manager may, however, have some discretion over how often the hardware is replaced, as well as over the purchase of particular hardware models that perform beyond the requirement standards needed for the business. By exercising this discretion, the depreciation charge for the year will be different from the one that would arise if the manager stuck to the minimum standards laid down by central management.

Divisional profit before common expenses

The third measure of profit is *divisional profit before common expenses*, which takes account of all divisional expenses (controllable and non-controllable) that are incurred by the division. This provides us with a measure of how the division contributes to the overall profits of the business.

Activity 10.5

Which one of the three measures that we have discussed so far is most useful for evaluating the performance of divisional managers, and which for evaluating the performance of divisions?

It can be argued that the performance of divisional managers should be judged on the basis of those things that are within their control. Hence, the controllable profit would be the most appropriate measure to use. The contribution measure does not take account of all the expenses that are controllable by divisional managers, whilst the divisional profit before common expenses takes account of some expenses that are not under the control of divisional managers. The latter measure, however, may be appropriate for evaluating the performance of the division, as it deducts all divisional expenses from the divisional revenues earned. It is a fairly comprehensive measure of divisional achievement.

Divisional profit for the period

The final measure of profit is *divisional profit for the period*, which is derived after deducting a proportion of the common expenses incurred for the period. The expenses apportioned to each division will presumably represent what central management believes to be a fair share of the total common expenses incurred. These expenses will typically include such things as marketing, personnel, accounting, planning, information technology and research and development expenses. In practice, the way that these apportionments are made between divisions can be extremely contentious. Some divisional managers may be convinced that they have been apportioned an unfair share of the common expenses. They may also believe that the divisions are being loaded with expenses over which they have little control and that the divisional profit figure derived will not truly represent the achievements of the division. These are often compelling arguments for not apportioning common expenses to the various divisions.

Activity 10.6

Can you think of any arguments for apportioning common expenses to divisions?

The business as a whole will only make a profit after all common expenses have been covered. Apportioning these expenses to the divisions should help make divisional managers more aware of this fact. In addition, top management may wish to compare the results of the division with the results of similar businesses in the same industry that are operating as independent entities. By apportioning common expenses to the divisions, a more valid basis for comparison is provided. Independent businesses will have to bear these kinds of expenses before arriving at *their* profit for the period. The effect of apportioning common expenses may also help to impose an element of control over these expenses. Divisional managers may put pressure on top managers to keep common expenses low so as to minimise the adverse effect on divisional profits.

Real World 10.3 sheds some light on the amount of common expenses assigned to divisions.

REAL WORLD 10.3

Something in common

Drury and El-Shishini conducted a survey of 124 senior financial managers of divisionalised businesses within the manufacturing sector. They found that nearly all managers (95 per cent) stated that the divisions used common resources such as marketing, personnel, accounting and so on. The survey asked those managers to state the approximate cost of using these resources as a percentage of annual divisional sales revenue. Figure 10.3 sets out the findings.

We can see that the costs of using common resources tend to be fairly low. The reasons for this are not entirely clear. One possible explanation is that highly decentralised businesses tend to have divisions that are self-reliant. Hence, the level of dependence on common resources will be low. Another possible explanation is that businesses with a large number of divisions have a greater opportunity to spread the costs of common resources among the various divisions. The study found, however, little or no evidence to support these explanations.

Real World 10.3 continued

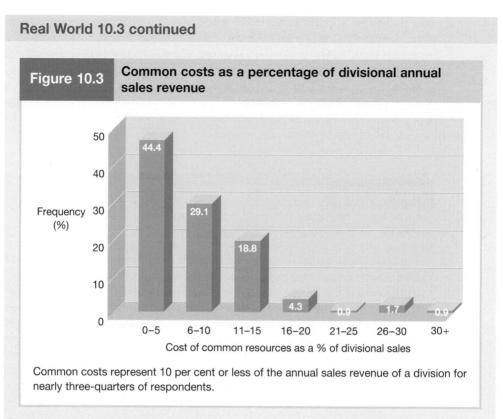

| Figure 10.3 | Common costs as a percentage of divisional annual sales revenue |

Common costs represent 10 per cent or less of the annual sales revenue of a division for nearly three-quarters of respondents.

Source: Drury, C. and El-Shishini, E., 'Divisional performance measurement: an examination of potential explanatory factors', CIMA Research Report, August 2005, p. 32.

Divisional performance measures

Divisional profit, by itself, is an inadequate measure of divisional performance. Some account must be taken of the investment in assets required to generate that profit. Two well-established measures of divisional performance that do this are

● return on investment (ROI), and
● residual income (RI).

We shall deal with both of these measures in turn.

Return on investment (ROI)

Return on investment (ROI) is a well-known method of assessing the profitability of divisions. The ratio is calculated in the following way:

$$\text{ROI} = \frac{\text{Divisional profit}}{\text{Divisional investment (assets employed)}} \times 100\%$$

When defining divisional profit for this ratio, the purpose for which the ratio is to be used must be considered. For evaluating the performance of a divisional manager, the controllable profit is likely to be the most appropriate, whereas for evaluating the performance of a division, the divisional profit for the period is likely to be more appropriate. Various definitions can be used for divisional investment. The total assets (non-current assets plus current assets) or the net assets (non-current assets plus current assets less current liabilities) figure may be used. In addition, non-current assets may be shown at their historic cost, or their historic cost less accumulated depreciation, or on some other basis, such as current market value.

It is important that, whichever definitions of divisional profit and investment are used, there is absolute consistency. It could be very misleading to try to compare the ROIs of two different divisions using one set of definitions for one division and another set for the other division.

The ROI ratio can be broken down into two main elements. These are:

$$\text{ROI} = \frac{\text{Divisional profit}}{\text{Sales revenue}} \times \frac{\text{Sales revenue}}{\text{Divisional investment}}$$

This separation into the two main elements is useful, because it shows that ROI is determined by both the profit margin on each £ of sales revenue and the ability to generate a high level of sales revenue in relation to the investment base.

Activity 10.7

The following data relate to the performance and position of two operating divisions that sell similar products:

	Kuala Lumpur Division £000	Singapore Division £000
Sales revenue	300	750
Divisional profit	30	25
Divisional investment	600	500

What observations can you make about the performance of each division?

First, the ROIs for both divisions are identical at 5 per cent a year (that is, 30/600 and 25/500). The information shows, however, that the divisions appear to be pursuing different strategies. The profit margins for the Kuala Lumpur and Singapore Divisions are 10 per cent (that is, 30/300) and 3.3 per cent (that is, 25/750) respectively. The sales revenue to divisional investment ratios for the Kuala Lumpur and Singapore Divisions are 50 per cent (that is, 300/600) and 150 per cent (that is, 750/500) respectively. Thus, we can see that the Kuala Lumpur Division prefers to sell goods at a higher profit margin than the Singapore Division, resulting in lower sales revenue to assets employed.

ROI is a measure of *profitability*, as it relates profits to the size of the investment made in the division. This relative measure allows comparisons between divisions of different sizes. However, ROI has its drawbacks. Where it is used as the primary measure of performance for divisional managers, there is a danger that it will lead to behaviour that is not really consistent with the interests of the business overall.

Activity 10.8

Russell Francis plc has two divisions, both selling similar products but operating in different geographical areas. The Wessex Division reported a £200,000 controllable profit from a divisional investment of £1m and the Sussex Division a £150,000 controllable profit from a divisional investment of £500,000.

Activity 10.8 continued

The divisional manager of each division has the opportunity to invest £200,000 in the development of a new product line that will boost controllable profit by £50,000. The minimum acceptable ROI for each division is 16 per cent a year.

Which operating division has been the more successful? How might each divisional manager react to the new opportunity?

Although the Wessex Division has achieved a higher profit in absolute terms, it has a lower ROI than the Sussex Division. The ROI for Wessex is 20 per cent a year (that is, £200,000/£1,000,000) compared with 30 per cent (that is, £150,000/£500,000) for the Sussex Division. Using ROI as the measure of performance, the Sussex Division is therefore the better-performing division.

The ROI from the new investment is 25 per cent a year (that is, £50,000/£200,000). Thus, by taking on this investment, the divisional manager of Wessex will increase the ROI of the division, which currently stands at 20 per cent a year. However, the divisional manager of Sussex will reduce the ROI of the division by taking this opportunity as its ROI is below the overall ROI of 30 per cent a year for the division.

If ROI is used as the primary measure of divisional performance, the divisional manager of Sussex may decline the opportunity for fear that a reduction in divisional ROI will reflect poorly on performance. However, the return from the opportunity is 25 per cent a year, which comfortably exceeds the minimum ROI of 16 per cent a year. So failure to exploit the opportunity will mean the profit potential of the division is not fully realised.

This activity illustrates the problems that can arise when using comparative measures, such as percentages.

A further disincentive to invest can result where the divisional investment in assets is measured in terms of the original cost less any accumulated depreciation to date (that is, written-down value or net book value). Where depreciation is being charged each year, the written-down value of the divisional investment will be reduced. Provided that profit stays at the same level, this means that ROI will climb during the lifetime of the depreciating assets.

To illustrate this point consider Example 10.1.

Example 10.1

The following are the profits and investment for a division over a four-year period:

Year	Divisional profit	Divisional investment	ROI at net book value
	£	£	%
1	30,000	200,000	15.0
2	30,000	180,000	16.7
3	30,000	160,000	18.8
4	30,000	140,000	21.4

The investment is an item of equipment that cost £200,000 at the beginning of Year 1. It is being depreciated at the rate of 10 per cent of cost each year.

We can see that the ROI increases over time simply because the investment base is shrinking. This is despite the fact that it is the same equipment, generating as much profit. We saw above that divisional managers may be discouraged from investing in further assets where the ROI is below the existing ROI for the division. In this example, the divisional manager would probably be reluctant to replace the equipment and expose the division to a 15 per cent ROI. This would be the case even though the need for new investment is likely to increase as the existing equipment becomes fully depreciated.

Activity 10.9

How might the problem caused by ROI being boosted simply through a reduction in the investment base, as in Example 10.1, be dealt with?

One way around the problem would be to keep the investment in assets at original cost and not to deduct depreciation for purposes of calculating ROI. However, non-current assets normally lose their productive capacity over time, and this fact should really be recognised. Another way around the problem is to use some measure of current market value, such as replacement cost, for the investment in assets. However, there may be problems in establishing current values for some assets.

Residual income (RI)

The weaknesses of the ROI method, particularly the fact that it ignores the cost of financing a division, has led some businesses to search for a more appropriate measure of divisional performance. An alternative measure is that of **residual income (RI)**. RI is the amount of income, or profit, generated by a division, which is in excess of the minimum acceptable level of income. If we assume that the objective of the business is to increase owners' (shareholders') wealth, the minimum acceptable level of income to be generated is the amount necessary to cover the cost of capital.

Taking the divisional profit figure and then deducting an imputed charge for the capital invested gives the RI. Example 10.2 should make the process clear.

Example 10.2

A division produced a profit of £100,000 and there was a divisional investment of £600,000 with a cost of financing this investment of 15 per cent a year. The residual income would be as follows:

	£
Divisional profit	100,000
Charge for capital invested	
(15% × £600,000)	(90,000)
Residual income	10,000

A positive RI, as in Example 10.2, means that the division is generating returns in excess of the minimum requirements of the business. The higher these excess returns, the better the performance of the division.

Activity 10.10

Does this measure seem familiar to you? Where have we discussed a similar measure to this earlier in the book?

This measure is based on the same idea as the EVA® measure that we discussed in Chapter 9. We shall consider this point in more detail a little later in the chapter.

Activity 10.11

Simonson Pharmaceuticals plc operates the Helena Beauty Care Division, which has reported the following results for last year:

Divisional investment	£2,000,000
Divisional profit	£300,000

The division has the opportunity to invest in a new product. This will require an additional investment in non-current assets of £400,000 and is expected to generate additional profits of £50,000 a year. This business has a cost of capital of 12 per cent a year. Try calculating the residual income of the division for last year. Do you believe that the division should produce the new product? How do you think that the divisional manager might react to the new product opportunity if ROI were used as the means of evaluating performance?

The residual income for last year is:

	£000
Divisional profit	300
Charge for capital invested	
(12% × £2,000,000)	(240)
Residual income	60

The residual income expected from the new product is:

	£000
Additional divisional profit	50
Charge for additional capital	
(12% × £400,000)	(48)
Residual income	2

The residual income is positive and, therefore, it would be worthwhile to produce the new product.

The ROI of the division for last year was 15 per cent a year (that is, £300,000/£2m). However, the new product is only expected to produce an ROI of 12.5 per cent a year (that is, £50,000/£400,000). The effect of producing the new product will be to reduce the overall ROI of the division (assuming similar results from the existing activities next year). The divisional manager may, therefore, reject the new investment opportunity, despite the fact that acceptance would enhance the owners' (shareholders') wealth. The new product would cover all of the costs, including the cost of financing the investment.

Looking to the longer term

A problem of both ROI and RI is that divisional managers may focus on short-term divisional performance at the expense of the longer term. There is a danger that investment opportunities will be rejected because they reduce short-term ROI and RI, even though over the longer term they have a positive NPV. This is illustrated in Example 10.3.

Example 10.3

A division is faced with an investment opportunity that will require an initial investment of £90,000 and produce the following operating cash flows (operating profit before depreciation) over the next five years:

Year	£
1	18,000
2	18,000
3	25,000
4	50,000
5	60,000

Assuming a cost of capital of 16 per cent a year, the NPV of the project will be:

Year	Cash flows £	Discount factor @ 16%	Present value £
1	18,000	0.862	15,516
2	18,000	0.743	13,374
3	25,000	0.641	16,025
4	50,000	0.552	27,600
5	60,000	0.476	28,560
			101,075
Initial investment			(90,000)
Net present value			11,075

This indicates that the NPV is positive and, therefore, it would be in the shareholders' interests to undertake the project.

To calculate ROI and RI, we need to derive the divisional profit for each year (that is, deduct a charge for depreciation from the operating cash flows shown above). Assuming that depreciation is charged equally over the life of the assets acquired and there is no residual value for the assets, the annual depreciation charge will be £18,000 (that is, £90,000/5).

After deducting an annual depreciation charge, the divisional profit for each year will be as follows:

Year	£
1	zero
2	zero
3	7,000
4	32,000
5	42,000

Activity 10.12

Calculate the ROI and RI for each of the five years of the project's life. (Base the ROI calculation on the cost of the assets concerned.)

The ROI for the project will be as follows:

Year	£	ROI %
1	zero/90,000	zero
2	zero/90,000	zero
3	7,000/90,000	7.8
4	32,000/90,000	35.6
5	42,000/90,000	46.7

The RI will be as follows:

Year	Divisional profit £	Capital charge £	RI £
1	zero	14,400*	(14,400)
2	zero	14,400	(14,400)
3	7,000	14,400	(7,400)
4	32,000	14,400	17,600
5	42,000	14,400	27,600
			9,000

* The capital charge is 16% × £90,000 = £14,400.

Activity 10.13

What do you deduce from the calculations resulting from Activity 10.12?

We can see that, in the early years, the ROI and RI calculations do not produce good results, though the situation is reversed in later years. For the first two years the ROI is zero and for the first three years the RI is negative. Divisional managers may, therefore, be discouraged from making investments if they feel that central management would view the results in the early years unfavourably. Given the results of the NPV analysis, however, the managers would not be acting in the shareholders' best interests in rejecting the proposal.

Note, however, that the RI of the project overall is positive and so provides a result that is consistent with the NPV result, over the five years.

Various approaches have been proposed in an attempt to avoid the kind of problem described above. It has been suggested, for example, that for the purpose of calculating divisional ROI and RI, the assets employed in the project should not be included in the divisional investment base until the project is fully established and generating good returns.

Comparing performance

Assessing divisional performance requires some benchmark against which we can compare the chosen measure(s). There are various bases for comparison available, including:

- *Other divisions within the business*. Comparing different divisions within the same business, however, may not be very useful where the divisions operate in different industries. Different types of industries have different levels of risk and this in turn produces different expectations concerning acceptable levels of return. (See pp. 270–272 in Chapter 8.)
- *Previous performance of the division*. It is possible to compare current performance with previous performance to see whether there has been any improvement or deterioration. However, it is often necessary to compare performance against some external standard in order to bring to light operating inefficiencies within the division. Also, the economic environment in previous periods may be different from the current environment and so may invalidate comparisons of this nature.
- *Similar businesses within the same industry*. The performance of similar divisions of other businesses, or whole businesses operating within the same industry, may provide a useful basis for comparison. However, there are often problems associated with this basis. We shall come back to this in Activity 10.14.
- *Budgeted (target) performance*. This should be the best basis for comparison because achievement of the budget should lead the division, and the business as a whole, towards its strategic objectives. In setting the budget, performances elsewhere in the business, previous levels of performance by the division and the performance of competitors may well be considered. Ultimately, however, it is against what the division has planned for that its actual performance should be assessed.

Activity 10.14

What problems are we likely to come across, in practice, when seeking to compare the performance of a particular division with a similar division of another business, or a whole business entity?

We may encounter a number of problems such as:

- *Obtaining the information required*. This is particularly true for a division within another business. This information may not be available to those outside the business.
- *Differences in accounting policies*. Different approaches to such matters as depreciation methods and inventories valuation methods may result in different measures of profit.
- *Differences in asset structure*. The different age of non-current assets employed, the decision to rent rather than buy particular assets and so on, may result in differences in the measures derived.

EVA® revisited

We saw in the previous chapter that EVA® measures the amount of wealth that has been created for the owners (shareholders). We may recall that it is based on the following formula:

$$EVA^® = NOPAT - (R \times C)$$

where

NOPAT = net operating profit after tax

R = required returns of investors (that is, cost of financing)

C = capital invested (that is, the net assets).

This measure, though not specifically designed for assessing divisional performance, may nevertheless be used for this purpose.

There are clear similarities between EVA® and RI. Both recognise that, in economic terms, profit can only be said to have been made after all costs, including financing costs, have been taken into account. Hence, a charge for capital invested should be made. When comparing the two measures, it is tempting to think that there is no real difference between them. However, EVA® is a more rigorous measure. The various elements in the EVA® equation (net operating profit after tax, required returns of investors and net assets) are defined more clearly and in such a way that there is an unambiguous link between EVA® and wealth creation. This is not necessarily the case with RI.

Real World 10.4 provides some insights as to what senior managers consider important when evaluating the performance of divisional managers. It seems that, whatever the theoretical appeal of EVA®, it is not widely used for this purpose.

REAL WORLD 10.4

Ranking the measures

In their survey of senior financial managers of 124 divisionalised businesses within the manufacturing sector, referred to in Real World 10.3, Drury and El-Shishini asked the managers to rank in order of importance the three measures that they considered most important for evaluating managerial performance. The results are set out below.

Financial measure	Most important ranking		Second most important ranking		Third most important ranking	
	Managers		Managers		Managers	
	Number	%	Number	%	Number	%
● Achievement of a target rate of return on capital employed (ROI)	9	7.3	21	18.1	41	41.0
● A target profit after charging interest on capital employed (RI)	18	14.5	11	9.5	5	5.0
● A target profit before charging interest on capital employed	68	54.8	23	19.8	5	5.0
● A target economic value added (EVA®) figure	11	8.9	8	6.9	10	10.0
● A target cash flow figure	10	8.1	45	38.8	27	27.0
● Other	8	6.4	8	6.9	12	12.0
	124	100.0	116	100.0	100	100.0

We can see that target profit *before* charging interest on capital employed was by far the most popular measure. Although ROI and RI are well-known measures, neither were frequently cited as the most important measure by senior financial managers. The limited support for target EVA® may be partially due to the fact that it is a relatively new measure.

Source: Drury, C. and El-Shishini, E., 'Divisional performance measurement: an examination of potential explanatory factors', CIMA Research Report, August 2005, p. 30.

Self-assessment question 10.1

Andromeda International plc has two operating divisions, the managers of which are given considerable autonomy. To assess the performance of divisional managers, senior management uses ROI. For the purposes of this measure the assets employed include both non-current and current assets. The business has a minimum acceptable ROI of 15 per cent a year and uses the straight-line method of depreciation for external reporting purposes.

Extracts from the budgets for each of the two divisions for next year are as follows:

	Jupiter division £000	Mars division £000
Divisional profit	260	50
Non-current assets at cost	940	1,200
Current assets	390	180

Since the budgets were prepared, two investment opportunities have been brought to the attention of the relevant divisional managers. These are as follows:

1 Senior management would like to see the productivity of the Mars division improve. To help achieve this, they have authorised the divisional manager to buy some new equipment costing £300,000. This will have a life of five years and will lead to operating savings of £90,000 each year.
2 A new product can be sold by the Jupiter division. This will increase sales revenue by £250,000 each year over the next five years. It will be necessary to increase marketing costs by £60,000 a year and inventories held will increase by £90,000. The contribution margin ratio (that is, contribution to sales revenue × 100%) for the new product will be 30 per cent.

Required:
(a) Calculate the expected ROI for each division assuming:
    1 the investment opportunities are not taken up,
    2 the investment opportunities are taken up.
(b) Comment on the results obtained in (a) and state how the divisional managers and senior managers might view the investment opportunities.
(c) Discuss the implications of using net book value (that is, after accumulated depreciation) rather than gross book value (that is, before accumulated depreciation) as a basis for valuing non-current assets when calculating ROI.

The answer to this question can be found in Appendix B at the back of the book.

Transfer pricing

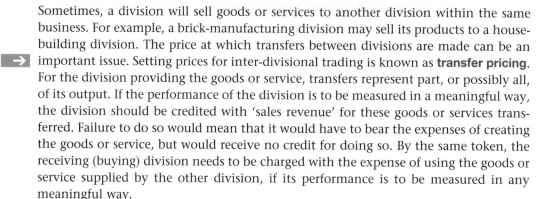

Sometimes, a division will sell goods or services to another division within the same business. For example, a brick-manufacturing division may sell its products to a house-building division. The price at which transfers between divisions are made can be an important issue. Setting prices for inter-divisional trading is known as **transfer pricing**. For the division providing the goods or service, transfers represent part, or possibly all, of its output. If the performance of the division is to be measured in a meaningful way, the division should be credited with 'sales revenue' for these goods or services transferred. Failure to do so would mean that it would have to bear the expenses of creating the goods or service, but would receive no credit for doing so. By the same token, the receiving (buying) division needs to be charged with the expense of using the goods or service supplied by the other division, if its performance is to be measured in any meaningful way.

Where inter-divisional transfers represent a large part of the total sales or purchases of a division, transfer pricing is a very important issue. Small changes in the transfer price of goods or services can result in large changes in profits for the division concerned. As divisional managers are often assessed (and partially remunerated) according to the profits generated by their division, setting transfer prices may be a sensitive issue between divisional managers.

Whilst the particular transfer prices used will affect the profits of individual divisions, the profits of the business as a whole should not be directly affected. An increase in the transfer price of goods or services will lead to an increase in the profits of the selling division, which is normally cancelled out by the decrease in profits of the buying division. However, the transfer prices set between divisions can indirectly lead to a loss of profits to the business as a whole. This is because the level at which they are set may encourage a divisional manager to take actions that would benefit the division but not the business as a whole. For example a divisional manager may choose to buy a particular product or service from an outside supplier because it is cheaper than the established internal transfer price. In such a situation, the profits of the business as a whole may be adversely affected.

Activity 10.15

In what circumstances would the business as a whole not be less profitable, if one division chooses to buy from an external supplier rather than from an internal source?

....

If the internal supplying division is able to sell in the external market

● the same quantity as were bought externally by the buying division; and
● at the same price as the internal division bought at,

the business as a whole will not be worse off.

The objectives of transfer pricing

Transfer pricing may help to achieve various objectives. In particular, setting appropriate transfer prices may help in promoting the following:

- *The independence of divisions.* By allowing divisional managers to set their own transfer prices, and by allowing other divisions to decide whether or not to trade at the prices quoted, the autonomy of individual divisions is encouraged. This, in turn, should help motivate divisional managers.
- *The assessment of divisional performance.* Inter-divisional sales will contribute to total revenues for a division, which in turn influence divisional profit. Setting an appropriate transfer price can, therefore, be important in deriving a valid measure of divisional profit for evaluation purposes. This should be of value in helping to establish incentives for, and promoting accountability of, divisional managers.
- *The optimisation of profits for the business.* Transfer prices may seek to optimise profits for the business as a whole. For example, a division may be prevented from quoting a transfer price for goods that will make buying divisions seek cheaper sources of supply from outside the business.
- *The allocation of divisional resources.* Transfer prices will be important in determining the level of output for particular goods and services. The level of return from inter-divisional sales can be important in deciding on the level of sales and investment relating to a particular product, or group of products.
- *Tax minimisation.* Where a business has operations in various countries, it may be beneficial to set transfer prices such that the bulk of profits are reported in divisions where the host country has low tax rates. However, tax laws operating in many countries will seek to prevent this kind of profit manipulation.

These objectives for transfer pricing are summarised in Figure 10.4.

Figure 10.4	**Objectives of transfer pricing**

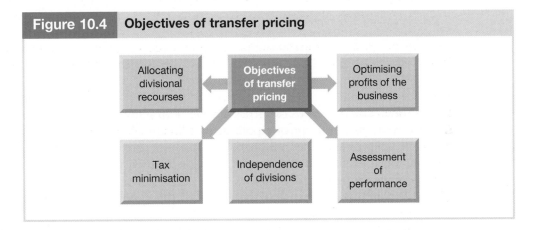

Activity 10.16

Is there a conflict between any of the transfer-pricing objectives identified above? If so, can a single transfer price help achieve all these objectives?

It is quite possible for there to be a conflict between the objectives identified. Thus, a single transfer price is unlikely to achieve all the stated objectives. To optimise the profits for the business as a whole, for example, transfer prices may have to be imposed centrally, which would undermine the autonomy of divisions. In addition, a centrally imposed transfer price may result in inter-divisional sales at artificially low prices, which would disadvantage particular divisions. It may also result in reported profit figures in both the buying and selling divisions becoming meaningless as measures of achievement.

Transfer pricing and tax mitigation

We saw above that transfer prices may be used to reduce the tax liabilities of businesses with international operations. It is often claimed that many of these businesses adopt novel transfer pricing policies, combined with complex organisational structures, to ensure that profits are reported in those countries where tax rates are low. Where there are doubts over the legality of these complicated manoeuvres, the tax authorities must try to unravel them.

Real World 10.5 provides an example of where disappointing tax levies from large businesses has led to the finger of suspicion being pointed at transfer pricing.

REAL WORLD 10.5

A taxing issue   **FT**

A majority of large businesses operating in the US reported no tax liability for at least one year between 1998 and 2005, according to a study released by the Government Accountability Office yesterday.

The finding could raise pressure on the US authorities to crack down more aggressively on abuses of transfer pricing – the price that units of the same company charge each other for internal transactions.

A number of senior US legislators have pointed to transfer-pricing violations as the vehicle by which companies have been shifting profits abroad and leaving US divisions with little or no tax liability.

Source: Transfer pricing abuses criticised, ft.com (Politi, J.), © The Financial Times Limited, 13 August 2008.

Tax authorities in various countries are trying to stamp out transfer pricing abuses. Investigations of transfer pricing policies of individual businesses are becoming more common and cross-border co-operation between tax authorities has increased. Information is exchanged and treaties are signed which set out transfer pricing rules that businesses are expected to follow.

Real World 10.6 suggests that the efforts of the various tax authorities have had some effect.

REAL WORLD 10.6

The tax man cometh

The 2007/8 transfer pricing survey carried out by Ernst and Young covered 850 large international businesses in 24 different countries. It found that nearly 40 per cent of all respondents considered transfer pricing to be their most important tax issue. Furthermore, 52 per cent of all respondents had been subjected to an examination of their transfer pricing policies since 2003, resulting in 27 per cent having their transfer prices adjusted by the tax authorities.

Source: 'Global transfer pricing survey 2007–2008: global pricing trends, practices and analysis', Ernst and Young, 2008.

It is, perhaps, worth mentioning that not all tax authorities have the resources and expertise to investigate what can be complex and opaque practices. Developing countries, for example, may find it hard to mount a serious challenge to transfer pricing abuses.

Transfer pricing policies

There are various approaches to setting a transfer price for goods and services between divisions. In this section we shall explore some of the major approaches. Before doing this, however, it is worth identifying the principle that the best transfer price is one based closely on the opportunity cost of the goods or services concerned. The opportunity cost represents the best alternative forgone. Thus, when examining the various approaches, the extent to which they reflect the opportunity cost of the goods or service should be the appropriate benchmark against which they are measured.

Market prices

→ **Market prices** are the prices that exist in the 'outside' market (that is, outside the business whose divisions are involved in the transfer). Intuition may tell us that market prices should be the appropriate method of setting transfer prices. Using this approach, the transfer price is an objective, verifiable amount that has real economic credibility. Where there is a competitive and active market for the products, the market price will represent the opportunity cost of goods and services. For the selling division, it is the revenue lost by selling to another division rather than to an outside customer. For the buying division, it is the best purchase price available.

The market price, however, may not always be appropriate. Activity 10.17 illustrates why.

Activity 10.17

Wolf Industries plc has an operating division that produces microwave ovens. The ovens are normally sold to retailers for £120. The division is currently producing 3,000 ovens a month (which uses only about 50 per cent of the division's manufacturing capacity). The ovens have the following cost structure:

	Cost for one oven £
Variable cost	70
Fixed cost apportionment	20
Total cost	90

Another division of the business has offered to buy 2,000 ovens for £75 each. How would you respond to such an offer if you were manager of the division making the microwave ovens?

Since the division is operating below capacity, basing the transfer price on market prices may lead to lost sales. Other divisions within the business have no price incentive to buy their microwave ovens internally. This may lead them to buy from outside sources rather than from the selling division and this loss of sales will not be made good by sales to outside customers.

→

Activity 10.17 continued

We saw in Chapter 3 that businesses may base selling prices on the variable cost of the goods or services, rather than on the market price, where there is a short-term problem of excess capacity. Provided that the selling price exceeds the variable cost of the goods or service, a contribution will be made towards the profits of the business. This principle can equally be applied to divisions of businesses. Thus, in such circumstances, a selling price somewhere between the variable cost of the product (£70) and the market price (£120) may be the best price for divisional transfers.

Senior management could intervene to insist that the microwave ovens are bought internally, but this would tend to undermine divisional autonomy and the right of divisions to make their own decisions.

A final point to consider when making inter-divisional transfers at market prices is that the selling division may make savings owing to the fact that selling and distribution costs may be lower. In such a situation, part of these savings may be passed on to the buying division in the form of lower prices. Thus, some adjustment may be made to the market price of the goods being transferred.

Activity 10.18

Apart from the problems that we have just considered, there is another, perhaps more fundamental, problem with trying to use market prices that we may come across in practice. Can you think what it may be?

An external market may simply not exist. It may not be possible for the potential buying division to identify external suppliers, and therefore an external price, for the particular good or service required. Alternatively, there may be no potential external customer for the selling division's output. Particular goods or services may be so tailored to the needs of the buying division that it is the only market available.

Variable cost

→ We have just seen that using **variable cost** is appropriate where the division is operating below capacity. In these particular circumstances, the opportunity cost to the supplying division is not the market price. The division will not have to stop selling to the market in order to supply its fellow division since there is a capacity to do both. In these circumstances, the opportunity cost is equal to the variable cost of producing the good or service. However, this represents an absolute minimum transfer price and a figure above the variable cost is required for a contribution to be made towards fixed costs and profit. Where the division is operating at full capacity and external customers are prepared to pay above the variable cost of the goods, a variable-cost internal transfer price would mean that inter-divisional sales are less profitable than sales to external customers. Managers of the selling division would therefore have no incentive to agree transfer prices on a strictly variable-cost basis (even though the business as a whole may benefit). If top management imposed this pricing method, divisional autonomy would be undermined.

Full cost

→ Transfers can be made at **full cost**. In such circumstances the selling division will make no profit on the transactions. This can hinder an evaluation of divisional performance. It will also lead to more difficulty in making resource allocation decisions concerning the level of output, product mix and investment levels within the division, as profit cannot be used as a measure of efficiency. It is possible to add a mark-up to the full cost of the goods or services to ensure that the selling division makes a profit. However, the amount of the mark-up must be justified in some way or it will become a contentious issue between buying and selling divisions.

A cost-based approach (with or without the use of a mark-up) does not provide any real incentive for managers of a selling division to keep costs down, since they can pass the costs on to the buying division. This will result in selling divisions transferring their operating inefficiencies to buying divisions. Where the mark-up is a percentage of cost, the selling division's profit will be higher if it incurs higher costs. On the other hand, where buying divisions have the ability to go to outside suppliers, pressure can be exerted on the selling divisions to control their costs. Although use of the full cost approach is found in practice, it is not an approach that is particularly logical, since it is not linked to the opportunity cost approach.

Transferring goods or services between divisions can be based on either a standard (budgeted) cost or an actual cost approach. The case for using standard costs appears to be the stronger.

Activity 10.19

What are the arguments in favour of using standard (budgeted) costs rather than actual costs?

Information relating to actual costs may not be available until after the transfer has taken place, which can create planning problems for the buying division. By using standard (budgeted) costs, this problem is overcome. It may also help to impose some discipline on the selling division as adverse variances cannot be simply passed on to the buying division. These arguments apply whether variable costs or full costs are being used as the transfer price.

The way in which standards are set, however, will need to be closely monitored to prevent the resulting transfer prices from becoming a contentious issue. The manager of the buying division may be quick to point out that there is no incentive for the selling division to develop tight standards. Indeed, the opposite is true as loose standards will make it easier to generate favourable variances.

Negotiated prices

It is possible to adopt an approach that allows the divisional managers to arrive at
→ **negotiated prices** for inter-divisional transfers. However, this can lead to serious disputes, and where divisional managers are unable to agree a price, top management will be required to arbitrate. This can be a time-consuming process and may deflect top management from its more strategic role. Furthermore, divisional managers may resent the decisions made by senior managers and see these as undermining the autonomy of their divisions.

Negotiated transfer prices probably work best where there is an external market for the goods supplied by the buying and selling divisions and where divisional managers are free to accept or reject offers made by other divisions. Under such circumstances, the negotiated price is likely to be closely related to the external market price of the products. In other circumstances, the negotiated prices may be artificial and misleading. For example, where a division sells the whole of its output to another division, the selling division may be in a weak bargaining position and the transfer price agreed may not provide a valid measure of divisional performance. Negotiated prices are likely to be influenced by the negotiating skills of managers, which can be a problem where this largely determines the outcome.

Figure 10.5 summarises the various approaches to transfer pricing that have been discussed.

Figure 10.5 Transfer pricing methods

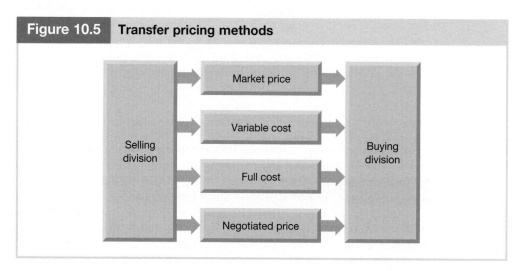

Divisions with mixed sales

A division may sell part of its output to another division within the same business and part to outside customers. For a business with only two divisions, the position will be as set out in Figure 10.6.

Figure 10.6 Relationship between divisions and the external market

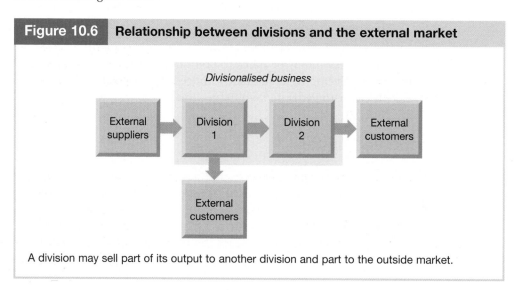

A division may sell part of its output to another division and part to the outside market.

Activity 10.20 requires you to calculate the budgeted divisional profits for a business with divisions that operate in the way illustrated above.

Activity 10.20

Dorset Ltd has two operating divisions: Cornwall and Devon. Cornwall produces a very high quality fabric that is used in making curtains. The budgeted cost of a square metre of the fabric is made up as follows:

	£
Variable cost	
Labour	4
Material	7
	11
Fixed cost	
Overheads	13
Total cost	24

The budgeted output for Cornwall is 300,000 sq m each year and the market price for the fabric is £30 per sq m.

Devon makes curtains and uses 1.1 sq m of this fabric to make 1 sq m of curtains. The management of Dorset Ltd insists that Cornwall must sell to Devon as much of the fabric as is required to meet its needs and any surplus output can then be sold to outside businesses. The management of Dorset Ltd also insists that Devon must buy all its requirements for this fabric from Cornwall. The budgeted output for Devon is 200,000 sq m of curtains. Devon sells its output for £75 per sq m and, in addition to the cost of the fabric, incurs fixed and variable costs totaling £35 per sq m at the budgeted output. What will be the budgeted profit for each operating division, assuming a transfer pricing policy based on

● variable cost
● full cost
● market price?

Comment on your findings.

··

For Cornwall, the budgeted profit under each transfer pricing policy will be:

	Variable cost £000	Full cost £000	Market price £000
Revenue			
Devon (200,000 × 1.1)			
× £11	2,420		
× £24		5,280	
× £30			6,600
External market ([300,000 − (200,000 × 1.1)] × £30)	2,400	2,400	2,400
	4,820	7,680	9,000
Costs			
Variable (300,000 × £11)	(3,300)	(3,300)	(3,300)
Fixed (300,000 × £13)	(3,900)	(3,900)	(3,900)
Budgeted profit (loss)	(2,380)	480	1,800

→

Activity 10.20 continued

For Devon, the budgeted profit under each transfer pricing policy will be:

	Variable cost £000	Full cost £000	Market price £000
Revenue			
200,000 × £75	15,000	15,000	15,000
Costs			
Fabric (200,000 × 1.1)			
× £11	(2,420)		
× £24		(5,280)	
× £30			(6,600)
Other costs (200,000 × £35)	(7,000)	(7,000)	(7,000)
Budgeted profit	5,580	2,720	1,400

We can see that Cornwall will make a significant loss under the variable cost policy. Most of the division's output must be sold to Devon and, whilst the surplus sold to the external market makes a contribution, it is not enough to cover the fixed cost. Cornwall manages to make a small profit under the full cost policy, which is entirely due to the sales to the outside market. If there were no external sales, the division would simply break even. When, however, transfer prices are set at market price, Cornwall makes a significant profit.

For Devon, the situation is reversed. It makes a significant profit under the variable cost policy but when fabric prices are increased under the full cost policy, and then further increased under the market price policy, so the budgeted profit declines. Devon's profits, of course, are unaffected by Cornwall's sales to outside businesses.

Differential transfer prices

There is no reason why, in respect of a particular inter-divisional transaction, there cannot be two different transfer prices. It may be that setting the buying price, for the buying division, at one value and the selling price, for the selling division, at a different value, could lead to both divisions being encouraged to act in the best interests of the business as a whole. This would mean that the overall profit for the business would not equal the sum of the profits of the individual divisions, but this is not necessarily a problem.

Real World 10.7 sets out transfer pricing guidelines for businesses operating in the water industry.

REAL WORLD 10.7

Thinking water

To protect the interests of customers, the UK government regulates the activities of water and sewerage businesses. Many of these businesses are part of a large group with diversified operations, some of which are not regulated. The government regulator, Ofwat, must therefore be assured that any transactions between the regulated water and sewerage activities and other unregulated businesses are not to the disadvantage of customers of the regulated activities. If, for example, water or sewerage services were charged to other unregulated businesses at a price below cost, or services bought in from other businesses were charged at a price above their market value, customers of the regulated water and sewerage services might have to bear an unfair share of the costs of the business as a whole.

To prevent this problem from occurring, the following transfer pricing guidelines are in place:

● transfer prices for goods and services transferred from unregulated businesses to regulated ones should be at market price or less;
● regulated businesses should market test to determine the market prices for works or services to be transferred to unregulated businesses;
● transfer prices for transfers from unregulated to regulated businesses should be based on full cost (direct costs plus indirect costs) for specialised services where no market exists.

It is interesting to note that transfers of goods and services at cost may, at times, be appropriate, as this can protect the interests of water customers.

Source: Guidelines for transfer pricing in the water industry: Regulatory accounting guideline 5.04, ofwat.gov.uk, March 2005.

Real World 10.8 provides detail about the use of transfer pricing in UK manufacturing businesses. This survey evidence is now quite old, but there is no more recent evidence of UK practice.

REAL WORLD 10.8

Transfer pricing in practice

A survey by Drury and others of UK manufacturing businesses found that, amongst divisionalised businesses, the approaches to setting transfer prices were as follows:

Approach used	% of divisionalised respondents	
Variable cost	37	(2)
Full cost	42	(22)
Variable cost plus a profit mark-up	30	(11)
Full cost plus a profit mark-up	52	(27)
Market price	52	(33)
Negotiated price	70	(30)
Other methods	9	(1)

→

Real World 10.8 continued

It is clear from the table that, on average, businesses use more than one method. Some of these percentages include 'used rarely' and 'sometimes'. The bracketed figures are percentages of businesses that use the approach 'often' or 'always'. For example, variable cost is used by 37 per cent of respondents, but of those only 2 per cent of total respondents used it 'often' or 'always'.

Full cost, which has not too much credibility in theory, seems widely used. The more theoretically respectable variable cost and the market-price-based approaches also seem popular, as do negotiated prices.

Source: Drury, C., Braund, S., Osborne, P. and Tayles, M., *A Survey of Management Accounting Practices in UK Manufacturing Companies*, Chartered Association of Certified Accountants, 1993.

Transfer pricing and service industries

There is absolutely no reason why the item being transferred inter-divisionally need be a physical object. A water company, for example, may have separate divisions for services such as IT, scientific testing and customer relations, which then charge the division providing water services for any work undertaken. The transfer pricing issues raised above will equally apply under these circumstances.

Non-financial measures of performance

For both divisions and businesses overall, managers increasingly use non-financial measures to help assess performance. Non-financial measures can help managers to cope with an uncertain environment: the greater the uncertainty of the environment, the greater the extent to which non-financial measures are likely to be of value. This is because they contribute to a broader and more complete range of information for managers, which should, in turn, contribute to a more balanced assessment of performance. It is, therefore, not surprising that these measures have taken on increasing importance in recent years.

The reporting of non-financial measures can provide a useful counterweight to the reporting of financial information. It is often the case that 'the things that count are the things that get counted'. That is, the degree of importance given to items will depend on whether they are reported, irrespective of their real significance. Thus, where managers receive reports based exclusively on short-term financial performance measures, such as sales revenues and profits, these measures become the main focus of attention. As a result, decisions may be made to enhance these reported performance measures, and other aspects of the business may be ignored. The result is likely to be to the detriment of the business. For example, to increase annual profit a decision may be made to cut back on research and development costs, which may be vital to long-term survival. In this kind of situation, reporting non-financial measures concerning the quality and success of research and development would help to provide a more complete picture.

Non-financial measures can also provide managers with insights that are difficult or impossible to gain with purely financial ones. For example, customer satisfaction is difficult to assess simply on the basis of financial values.

We saw in Chapter 9 that financial measures are normally 'lag indicators' that tell us about the outcomes of management decisions. Thus, sales revenues and profits are both examples of lag indicators. Some non-financial measures are also lag indicators, but others may be 'lead indicators' that provide an insight to the elements that drive performance such as product quality, delivery times and innovation levels. It is, therefore, important to identify and measure the non-financial factors that are critical to future success. **Real World 10.9** provides an example of a non-financial measure that is used by one large business. This measure not only serves as a useful measure of customer satisfaction, but is a vital lead indicator.

REAL WORLD 10.9

Is everybody happy?   **FT**

Enterprise (see Real World 10.2) is a car rental business that is committed to high standards of service to its customers. To monitor performance it has developed an Enterprise service quality index (ESQI) that measures customer satisfaction. Experience has shown that those customers who express themselves to be 'completely satisfied' with the service provided are three times more likely to come back. Thus, the index is seen as a key indicator of future growth and success. To demonstrate to staff how seriously the ESQI is taken by the business, no manager can be promoted from a network office where the ESQI score is below average, no matter how impressive the financial performance of that office may be.

According to Andy Taylor, chairman and chief executive, rising ESQI scores give him greater confidence about the future than Enterprise's strong cash flow or increase in market share: 'ESQI doesn't mean we can ignore other things but it will keep us on track.'

Source: Based on information from 'Enterprise drives home the service ethic', *Financial Times*, 2 June 2003.

What is measured?

Some of the main areas covered by non-financial measures include:

- *Research and development (R&D) expenditure.* For some businesses, R&D may be vital to long-term success. Developing suitable measures relating to the quality and success of the R&D effort may therefore be useful. These might include the number of innovations successfully launched, the percentage of total sales revenue arising from new products, and the time taken to bring a new product to market.
- *Staff training and morale.* It is a modern-day mantra that the employees are the most valuable assets of a business. If this is the case, it is useful to know how the managers are cultivating this resource. Staff training may be measured directly by such means as the number of training days per employee, or indirectly through measures of customer satisfaction. Staff morale may be revealed by staff turnover, absenteeism levels and attitude surveys.
- *Product/service quality.* In a competitive environment, the quality of the products and services offered is of vital importance. Measures such as number of product defects, percentage of scrap, number of warranty claims and number of customer complaints may be important.
- *Market share.* The percentage share of total sales generated within a particular market can help to assess the success of the product range.

● *Environmental and social concerns.* In highly industrialised societies, there is increasing pressure on businesses to acknowledge their responsibility towards the environment and to assess the impact of their activities on the communities in which they are based. An assessment of the policies on such matters as pollution, wildlife protection and employment of minorities can be carried out to see whether the business is being a good 'corporate citizen'.

Although this is not an exhaustive list of areas, it nevertheless provides a flavour of what non-financial measures can cover.

Activity 10.21

Bling plc operates a chain of high street shops selling costume jewellery to those in the 18 to 30 age range. The business aims to sell products that are both highly fashionable and of good quality, and tries to ensure that customers are provided with a wide range from which to choose.

Suggest *four* non-financial measures that may help the business to assess its performance in achieving these aims.

....

Possible non-financial measures include:

● the percentage of new products that were 'first to market';
● the percentage of sales revenue from new products;
● the percentage of returned items;
● the number of customer complaints concerning quality;
● customer satisfaction scores;
● the number of different types of product available for sale;
● the percentage of items unable to be supplied due to insufficient inventories;
● the average inventories turnover period; and
● the percentage share of the market in which the business competes.

You may have thought of others.

Real World 10.10 provides some insight into the kind of non-financial measures that are regarded as important by management accountants in manufacturing businesses.

REAL WORLD 10.10

Rank-and-file measures

A study by Abdel-Maksoud and others asked management accountants employed in 313 UK manufacturing businesses to assess the importance of 19 'shop floor' non-financial measures. The accountants were asked to rank the measures on a scale ranging from 1 (low) to 7 (high). The mean importance accorded to each of the 19 measures is set out in Figure 10.7.

We can see that the first three measures relate to customers. This is followed by four measures relating to cost control and the efficiency of processes.

Source: Abdel-Maksoud, A., Dugdale, D. and Luther, R., 'Non-financial performance measurement in manufacturing companies', *The British Accounting Review*, 37, 2005, pp. 261–297.

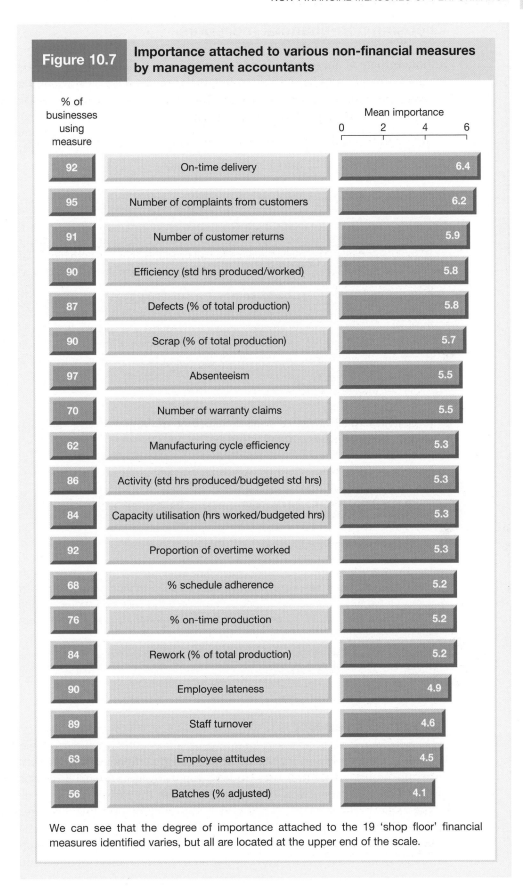

Figure 10.7 Importance attached to various non-financial measures by management accountants

% of businesses using measure	Measure	Mean importance
92	On-time delivery	6.4
95	Number of complaints from customers	6.2
91	Number of customer returns	5.9
90	Efficiency (std hrs produced/worked)	5.8
87	Defects (% of total production)	5.8
90	Scrap (% of total production)	5.7
97	Absenteeism	5.5
70	Number of warranty claims	5.5
62	Manufacturing cycle efficiency	5.3
86	Activity (std hrs produced/budgeted std hrs)	5.3
84	Capacity utilisation (hrs worked/budgeted hrs)	5.3
92	Proportion of overtime worked	5.3
68	% schedule adherence	5.2
76	% on-time production	5.2
84	Rework (% of total production)	5.2
90	Employee lateness	4.9
89	Staff turnover	4.6
63	Employee attitudes	4.5
56	Batches (% adjusted)	4.1

We can see that the degree of importance attached to the 19 'shop floor' financial measures identified varies, but all are located at the upper end of the scale.

Choosing non-financial measures

Although there is an almost infinite number of non-financial measures that may be reported, it would not be sensible to report too many. Managers would become over-loaded, which would undermine rather than improve the quality of decision making. It would also add significantly to the costs of gathering and reporting information. Choices must be made and the measures chosen must demonstrate some logic and coherence. What is needed is a set of non-financial measures that deal with the factors that really matter and fit into a logical framework.

Activity 10.22

Can you suggest how this might be done? (*Hint*: Think back to a particular approach that we discussed in Chapter 9.)

A useful approach would be to employ the balanced scorecard. We may recall that this provides a coherent framework and attempts to translate the aims and objectives of the business into a series of key performance measures and targets. In this way, strategy is linked more closely to particular measures. The choice of measure (either financial or non-financial) would then be determined according to its value in achieving the agreed strategy.

Real World 10.11 provides some evidence of the popularity of the balanced score-card among UK divisionalised businesses.

REAL WORLD 10.11

A question of balance

The study by Drury and El-Shishini mentioned earlier asked senior financial managers of divisionalised businesses about the approaches used to incorporate non-financial mea-sures. Of the 97 respondents, 55 per cent adopted the balanced scorecard approach for the business as a whole; 43 per cent of the 97 respondents also used this approach to evaluate divisional performance.

Source: Drury, C. and El-Shishini, E., 'Divisional performance measurement: an examination of potential explanatory factors', CIMA Research Report, August 2005, p. 31.

Who should report?

We saw in Chapter 1 that management accounting embraces both financial perform-ance and non-financial measures. Indeed, reporting non-financial measures, such as budgeted units of production, can be traced back to the early years of the development of the subject. However, the scale and importance of non-financial measures have increased dramatically in recent years and this has raised questions as to whether it should be the management accountant's responsibility to report such measures. Although many see it as a natural development of the management accountant's role, some believe that it will lead to unbalanced reports. It is feared that financial measures will dominate, resulting in an emphasis on lag indicators rather than lead indicators.

Real World 10.12 provides some evidence to support the view that management accountants consider financial measures to be more important than non-financial measures.

REAL WORLD 10.12

Finance matters

The study by Drury and El-Shishini mentioned earlier asked senior financial managers about the relative importance of financial and non-financial measures for assessing divisional performance. To do this, a seven-point scale was used where 1 represented the view that financial measures were considerably more important than non-financial measures, 7 represented the view that non-financial measures were considerably more important than financial ones, and 4 represented a midpoint which reflected the view that they were of about the same importance. The managers' scores were as follows:

	%
Financial measures more important (scores 1 to 3)	71
Financial and non-financial measures of equal importance (score 4)	18
Non-financial measures more important (scores 5 to 7)	11
	100

Source: Drury, C. and El-Shishini, E., 'Divisional performance measurement: an examination of potential explanatory factors, CIMA Research Report, August 2005, pp. 31–32.

Whilst this may provide support for those who would like others to report non-financial measures, it is worth remembering that, over time, management accountants have strengthened their position at the heart of decision making. This can only have been achieved by responding to the changing needs of business. We should not, therefore, assume that they are unwilling or unable to confront new challenges.

SUMMARY

The main points of this chapter may be summarised as follows:

Divisionalisation

- Many large businesses operate through relatively independent divisions.
- Divisions are typically either:
  - Profit centres, which have responsibility for most aspects except investment.
  - Investment centres, which have responsibility for most aspects including investment.
- Divisionalisation is usually made according to:
  - Product or service.
  - Geographical location.
- Benefits of divisionalisation are said to include:
  - Better access to market information.
  - Motivating middle and junior managers.

- Developing managers through experience.
- Better use of specialised knowledge.
- Allowing senior managers to deal with strategic issues.
- Enabling timely decision making.
● Problems of divisionalisation are said to include:
- Goal conflict between divisions.
- Excessive avoidance of risky courses of action.
- Excessive management 'perks'.
- Costly duplication of facilities and other losses of economies of scale.
- Divisions competing with each other to the detriment of the business as a whole.

Divisional performance measurement

● There are various measures of divisional profit. The most suitable measure must take account of the purpose for which the measure will be used.
● Return on investment (ROI) = (divisional profit/divisional investment) × 100%.
- Resembles the return on capital employed ratio, which seems to be widely used.
- Can be broken down into a profit margin and an asset turnover element.
- Problems of definition of the divisional profit and investment – need to be consistent.
● ROI is a comparative (percentage) measure that can mislead.
- Can lead to the rejection of beneficial activities because they lower the ROI despite generating wealth.
- Tends to focus on the short term.
● Residual income (RI) = divisional profit less a capital charge (investment × cost of capital).
- Relates to wealth generated.
- An absolute measure (£s), not a percentage.
- Tends to focus on the short term.
● RI is generally considered a better performance indicator than ROI.
● Assessing divisional performance requires some basis for comparison. A particular division can be compared with that for:
- Other divisions of the same business.
- Previous performance of the same division.
- Performance of businesses in the same industry as the division.
- Budgeted performance – probably the best basis of comparison.
● EVA® may also be used to measure divisional performance.

Transfer pricing

● Involves setting prices for transfers (sales and purchases) between divisions of the same business.
● An important issue because transfer prices (TPs) have a direct effect on divisional profit and therefore on ROI and RI.
● Transfer pricing has the following objectives:
- Promoting divisional independence, by allowing divisions to act as if they are independent businesses.
- Providing a basis for measuring the effectiveness of divisions through, for example, ROI and RI.
- Promoting the objectives of the business as a whole.
- Allocating resources provided for individual divisions.
- Minimising tax charges by moving profits to low-tax countries.
● The best TPs are based on the opportunity cost for both divisions.

- In practice, the following are found:
  - Market prices – these are usually best because they tend to represent the opportunity cost; however, a market may not exist in practice.
  - Variable cost – will represent the opportunity cost to a supplying division with spare capacity.
  - Full cost, usually plus a profit loading – rarely reflects the opportunity cost and tends to pass on inefficiencies.
  - Negotiated prices – enable the divisions to act as independent businesses but can be unfair.

Non-financial measures

- Non-financial measures have increased in importance due to environmental uncertainty.
- Possible areas for measurement include:
  - Research and development.
  - Staff training and morale.
  - Product/service quality.
  - Market share.
  - Environmental and social concerns.
- Non-financial measures should be integrated with financial measures into a logical framework, such as the balanced scorecard.
- Management accountants usually take responsibility for reporting non-financial measures, although this has raised some concern.

→ Key terms

Divisions p. 367	**Return on investment (ROI)** p. 376
Profit centre p. 367	**Residual income (RI)** p. 379
Investment centre p. 367	**Transfer pricing** p. 386
Controllable costs p. 374	**Market prices** p. 389
Non-controllable costs p. 374	**Negotiated prices** p. 391

Further reading

If you would like to explore the topics covered in this chapter in more depth, we recommend the following books:

McWatters, C., Zimmerman, J. and Morse, D., *Management Accounting: Analysis and Interpretation*, FT Prentice Hall, 2008, chapter 7.

Drury, C., *Management and Cost Accounting*, 7th edn, Thomson Learning Business Press, 2008, chapters 19 and 20.

Bhimani, A., Horngren, C., Datar, S. and Foster, G., *Management and Cost Accounting*, 4th edn, FT Prentice Hall, 2008, chapter 18.

Hilton, R., *Managerial Accounting*, 6th edn, McGraw-Hill Irwin, 2005, chapter 13.

REVIEW QUESTIONS

Answers to these questions can be found in Appendix C at the back of the book.

10.1 What problems might be encountered when a business attempts to incorporate non-financial measures into its management reports?

10.2 Westcott Supplies Ltd has an operating division that produces a single product. In addition to the conventional RI and ROI measures, central management wishes to use other methods of measuring performance and productivity to help assess the division.

Identify four possible measures (financial or non-financial) that top management may decide to use.

10.3 Jerry and Co. is a large computer consultancy business that has a division specialising in robotics. Can you identify three *non-financial measures* that might be used to help assess the performance of this division?

10.4 A UK survey of decentralised businesses revealed that negotiated prices are the most popular form of transfer pricing method.

Is this necessarily the best approach in theory? Why?

EXERCISES

Exercises 10.4 to 10.8 are more advanced than 10.1 to 10.3. Those with a coloured number have answers in Appendix D at the back of the book. If you wish to try more exercises, visit the students' side of the Companion Website at www.pearsoned.co.uk/atrillmclaney.

10.1 In divisionalised organisations, complete autonomy of action is impossible when a substantial level of inter-divisional transfers take place.

Required:
(a) In this context, explain what is meant by 'divisionalised organisation' and 'autonomy of action'.
(b) What are the benefits of this autonomy?
(c) Are there any dangers from permitting autonomy of action and in what ways do inter-divisional transfers make complete autonomy impossible?

10.2 Measures are required to assess the performance of divisions and of divisional managers. Three financial measures are
● contribution;
● controllable profit; and
● return on investment (ROI).

Required:
(a) For each of the above measures explain
  ● the way in which each measure is calculated;
  ● for what purpose they are most suitably applied; and
  ● the weaknesses of each method.

(b) Suggest three different non-financial measures of performance that may be appropriate to an operating division and consider how such measures, in general, offer improvements when used in conjunction with financial measures.

10.3 You have recently taken a management post in a large divisionalised business. A substantial proportion of the business of your division is undertaken through inter-divisional transfers.

Required:
(a) What are the objectives of a system of transfer pricing?
(b) Describe the use of, and problems associated with, transfer prices based on
  ● variable cost; and
  ● full cost.
(c) Where an external market exists, to what extent is market price an improvement on cost?

10.4 The following information applies to the planned operations of Division A of ABC Corporation for next year:

	£
Sales revenue (100,000 units at £12)	1,200,000
Variable cost (100,000 units at £8)	800,000
Fixed cost (including depreciation)	250,000
Division A investment (at original cost)	500,000

The minimum desired rate of return on investment is the cost of capital of 20 per cent a year.

The business is highly profit-conscious and delegates a considerable level of autonomy to divisional managers. As part of a procedure to review planned operations of Division A, a meeting has been convened to consider two options:

Option X
Division A may sell a further 20,000 units at £11 to customers outside ABC Corporation. Variable costs per unit will be the same as budgeted, but to enable capacity to increase by 20,000 units, one extra piece of equipment will be required costing £80,000. The equipment will have a four-year life and the business depreciates assets on a straight-line basis. No extra fixed costs will occur.

Option Y
Included in the current plan of operations of Division A is the sale of 20,000 units to Division B also within ABC Corporation. A competitor of Division A, from outside ABC Corporation, has offered to supply Division B at £10 per unit. Division A intends to adopt a strategy of matching the price quoted from outside ABC Corporation to retain the order.

Required:
(a) Calculate Division A's residual income based on
  1 the original planned operation
  2 Option X only added to the original plan
  3 Option Y only added to the original plan
  and briefly interpret the results of the options as they affect Division A.
(b) Assess the implications for Division A, Division B and the ABC Corporation as a whole of Option Y, bearing in mind that if Division A does not compete on price, it will lose the 20,000 units order from Division B. Make any recommendations you consider appropriate.

10.5 The following information applies to the budgeted operations of the Goodman division of the Telling Company.

	£
Sales revenue (50,000 units at £8)	400,000
Variable cost (50,000 units at £6)	(300,000)
Contribution	100,000
Fixed cost	(75,000)
Divisional profit for the period	25,000
Divisional investment	150,000

The minimum desired return on investment is the cost of capital of 20 per cent a year.

Required:

(a) (1) Calculate the divisional expected ROI (return on investment).
   (2) Calculate the division's expected RI (residual income).
   (3) Comment on the results of (1) and (2).

(b) The division has the opportunity to sell an additional 10,000 units at £7.50. Variable cost per unit would be the same as budgeted, but fixed costs would increase by £5,000. Additional investment of £20,000 would be required. If the manager accepted this opportunity, by how much and in what direction would the residual income change?

(c) Goodman expects to sell 10,000 units of its budgeted volume of 50,000 units to Sharp, another division of the Telling Company. An outside business has promised to supply the 10,000 units to Sharp at £7.20. If Goodman does not meet the £7.20 price, Sharp will buy from the outside business. Goodman will not save any part of the fixed cost if the work goes outside, but the variable cost will be avoided completely.

   (1) Show the effect on the total profit of the Telling Company if Goodman meets the £7.20 price.
   (2) Show the effect on the total profit of the Telling Company if Goodman does not meet the price and the work goes outside.

10.6 Glasnost plc is a large business organised on divisional lines. Two typical divisions are East and West. They are engaged in broadly similar activities and, therefore, central management compares their results to help it to make judgements on managerial performance. Both divisions are regarded as investment centres.

A summary of last year's financial results of the two divisions is as follows:

	West		East	
	£000	£000	£000	£000
Capital employed		2,500		500
Sales revenue		1,000		400
Manufacturing cost:				
Direct	(300)		(212)	
Indirect	(220)		(48)	
Selling and distribution cost	(180)	(700)	(40)	(300)
Divisional profit		300		100
Apportionment of uncontrollable common				
overhead costs		(50)		(20)
Profit for the period		250		80

At the beginning of last year, West division incurred substantial expenditure on automated production lines and new equipment. East has quite old plant. Approximately 50 per cent of the sales revenue of East comes from internal transfers to other divisions within the business. These transfers are based on an unadjusted prevailing market price. The inter-divisional transfers of West are minimal.

Management of the business focuses on return on investment as a major performance indicator. The required minimum rate of return is the business's cost of capital of 10 per cent a year.

Required:

(a) Compute any ratios (or other measures) that you consider will help in an assessment of the costs and performance of the two divisions.

(b) Comment on this performance, making reference to any matters that give cause for concern when comparing the divisions or in divisional performance generally.

10.7 The University of Devonport consists of six faculties and an administration unit. Under the university's management philosophy, each faculty is treated, as far as is reasonable, as an independent entity. Each faculty is responsible for its own budget and financial decision making.

A new course in the Faculty of Geography (FG) requires some input from a member of staff of the Faculty of Modern Languages (FML).

The two faculties are in dispute about the 'price' that FG should pay FML for each hour of the staff member's time. FML argues that the hourly rate should be £97. This is based on the FML budget for this year, which in broad outline is as follows:

	£000
Academic staff salaries (45 staff)	1,062
Faculty overheads (nearly all fixed costs)	903
	1,965

Each academic is expected to teach on average for 15 hours a week for 33 weeks a year.

FML wishes to charge FG an hourly rate which will cover the appropriate proportion of the member of staff's salary plus a 'fair' share of the overheads plus 10 per cent for a small surplus.

FG is refusing to pay this rate. One of FG's arguments is that it should not have to bear any other cost than the appropriate share of the salary. FG also argues that it could find a lecturer who works at the nearby University of Tavistock and is prepared to do the work for £25 an hour, as an additional, spare-time activity.

FML argues that it has deliberately staffed itself at a level which will enable it to cover FG's requirements and that the price must therefore cover the costs.

The university's Vice-Chancellor (its most senior manager) has been asked to resolve the dispute. You are the university's finance manager.

Required:

Make notes in preparation for a meeting with the Vice-Chancellor, where you will discuss the problem with her. The Vice-Chancellor is a historian by background and is not familiar with financial matters. Your notes will therefore need to be expressed in language that an intelligent layperson can understand.

Your notes should deal both with the objectives of effective transfer prices and with the specifics of this case. You should raise any issues which you think might be relevant.

10.8 AB Ltd operates retail stores throughout the country. The business is divisionalised. Included in its business are Divisions A and B. A centralised and automated warehouse that replenishes inventories using computer-based systems supports the work of these divisions.

For many years AB Ltd has given considerable autonomy to divisional managers and has emphasised return on investment (ROI) as a composite performance measure. This is calculated after apportionment of all actual costs and assets of the business and 'its appropriate service facilities', which includes the costs and assets of the warehouse.

The following information is available for last year:

	Division A		Division B	
	Actual	Budget	Actual	Budget
	£m	£m	£m	£m
Sales revenue	30.0	50.0	110.0	96.0
Assets employed	20.0		48.0	
Operating profit	4.3		14.7	

These actual figures do not include the apportioned costs or assets of the automated warehouse shared by the two divisions. The data available for the warehouse facility for last year are:

	Warehouse Actual £m	Budget £m
Despatches (that is, sales revenue)	140.0	146.0
Assets employed at book value	8.0	8.0
Operating cost:		
Depreciation	1.6	1.6
Other elements of fixed cost	1.1	0.9
Variable storage cost	0.6	0.5
Variable handling cost	1.3	1.1
Total operating cost	4.6	4.1

When the warehouse investment was authorised it was agreed that the assets employed and the actual expenses were to be apportioned between the divisions concerned in the proportions originally agreed (50 per cent each). However, it was also pointed out that in the future the situation could be redesigned and there was no need for one single basis to apply. For example, the space occupied by inventories of the two divisions is now A 40 per cent and B 60 per cent. This information could be used in the apportionment of assets and expenses.

Required:

(a) (1) Calculate the actual return on investment (ROI) for Divisions A and B after incorporating the warehouse assets and actual costs apportioned on an equal basis as originally agreed.

(2) What basis of apportionment of assets and actual costs would the manager of Division A argue for, in order to maximise the reported ROI of the division? How would you anticipate that the manager of Division B might react?

(b) It has been pointed out that a combination of bases of apportionment may be used instead of just one, such as the space occupied by inventories (A 40 per cent, B 60 per cent) or the level of actual or budgeted sales revenue. If you were given the freedom to revise the calculation, what bases of apportionment would you recommend in the circumstances? Discuss your approach and recalculate the ROI of Division A on your recommended basis.

Work to two places of decimals only.

11

Managing working capital

INTRODUCTION

This chapter considers the factors that must be taken into account when managing the working capital of a business. Each element of working capital will be identified and the major issues surrounding them will be discussed. Working capital represents a significant investment for many businesses and so its proper management and control can be vital. We saw in Chapter 8 that an investment in working capital is typically an important aspect of new investment proposals.

LEARNING OUTCOMES

When you have completed this chapter, you should be able to:

● Identify the main elements of working capital.

● Discuss the purpose of working capital and the nature of the working capital cycle.

● Explain the importance of establishing policies for the control of working capital.

● Explain the factors that have to be taken into account when managing each element of working capital.

What is working capital?

→ **Working capital** is usually defined as current assets less current liabilities. The major elements of current assets are

- inventories
- trade receivables
- cash (in hand and at bank).

The major elements of current liabilities are

- trade payables
- bank overdrafts.

The size and composition of working capital can vary between industries. For some types of business, the investment in working capital can be substantial. For example, a manufacturing business will typically invest heavily in raw material, work in progress and finished goods, and will normally sell its goods on credit, giving rise to trade receivables. A retailer, on the other hand, will hold only one form of inventories (finished goods), and will usually sell goods for cash. Many service businesses hold no inventories.

Most businesses buy goods and/or services on credit, giving rise to trade payables. Few, if any, businesses operate without a cash balance, though in some cases it is a negative one (a bank overdraft).

Working capital represents a net investment in short-term assets. These assets are continually flowing into and out of the business and are essential for day-to-day operations. The various elements of working capital are interrelated and can be seen as part of a short-term cycle. For a manufacturing business, the working capital cycle can be depicted as shown in Figure 11.1.

Figure 11.1   **The working capital cycle**

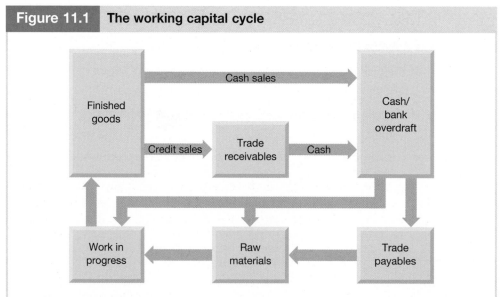

Cash is used to pay trade payables for raw materials, or raw materials are bought for immediate cash settlement. Cash is also spent on labour and other items that turn raw materials into work in progress and, finally, into finished goods. The finished goods are sold to customers either for cash or on credit. In the case of credit customers, there will be a delay before the cash is received from the sales. Receipt of cash completes the cycle.

For a retailer the situation would be as in Figure 11.1 except that there would be only inventories of finished goods and no work in progress or raw materials. For a purely service business, the working capital cycle would also be similar to that depicted in Figure 11.1 except that there would be no inventories of finished goods or raw materials. There may well be work in progress, however, since many services, for example a case handled by a firm of solicitors, will take some time to complete and costs will build up before the client is billed for them.

Managing working capital

The management of working capital is an essential part of the business's short-term planning process. It is necessary for management to decide how much of each element should be held. As we shall see later in this chapter, there are costs associated with holding either too much or too little of each element. Management must be aware of these costs, which include opportunity costs, in order to manage effectively. Hence, potential benefits must be weighed against likely costs in an attempt to achieve the optimum investment.

The working capital needs of a business are likely to vary over time as a result of changes in the business environment. Managers must try to identify these changes to ensure that the level of investment in working capital is appropriate. This means that working capital decisions are frequently being made.

Activity 11.1

What kinds of changes in the business environment might lead to a decision to change the level of investment in working capital? Try to identify four possible changes that could affect the working capital needs of a business.

These may include the following:

- changes in interest rates
- changes in market demand
- seasonal changes
- changes in the state of the economy.

You may have thought of others.

In addition to changes in the external environment, changes arising within the business could alter the required level of investment in working capital. Examples of such internal changes include using different production methods (resulting, perhaps, in a need to hold less inventories) and changes in the level of risk that managers are prepared to take.

The scale of working capital

We might imagine that, compared with the scale of investment in non-current assets by the typical business, the amounts involved with working capital are pretty trivial. However, this is not the case – the scale of the working capital elements for most businesses is vast.

Real World 11.1 gives some impression of the working capital involvement for five very well-known UK businesses. These businesses were randomly selected, except that each is high profile and each is from a different industry. For each business the major items appearing on the statement of financial position (balance sheet) are expressed as a percentage of the total investment by the providers of long-term finance (equity and non-current liabilities).

REAL WORLD 11.1

A summary of the statements of financial position of five UK businesses

Business:	Next plc	British Airways plc	Rolls-Royce plc	Tesco plc	Severn Trent plc
Statement of financial position date:	28.1.07	31.3.07	31.12.07	24.2.07	31.3.07
Non-current assets	71	103	63	122	112
Current assets					
Inventories	34	1	33	12	–
Trade receivables	69	8	34	6	8
Other receivables	–	4	5	–	–
Cash and near cash	15	30	37	9	3
	118	43	109	27	11
Total assets	189	146	172	149	123
Equity and non-current liabilities	100	100	100	100	100
Current liabilities					
Trade payables	75	35	65	36	8
Taxation	10	1	3	3	1
Other short-term liabilities	–	5	3	–	–
Overdrafts and short-term loans	4	5	1	10	14
	89	46	72	49	23
Total equity and liabilities	189	146	172	149	123

The non-current assets, current assets and current liabilities are expressed as a percentage of the total net long-term investment (equity plus non-current liabilities) of the business concerned. Next is a major retail and home shopping business. British Airways (BA) is a major airline. Rolls-Royce makes aero and other engines. Tesco is one of the major UK supermarket chains. Severn Trent is a major supplier of water, sewerage services and waste management, mainly in the UK.

Source: Table constructed from information appearing in the financial statements for the year ending in 2007 for each of the five businesses concerned.

The totals for current assets are pretty large when compared with the total long-term investment. This is particularly true of Next and Rolls-Royce. The amounts vary considerably from one type of business to the next. When we look at the nature of working capital held we can see that Next, Rolls-Royce and Tesco, which produce and/or sell goods, are the only ones that hold significant amounts of inventories. The other two businesses are service providers and so inventories are not a significant item.

We can see from the table that Tesco does not sell a lot on credit and very few of BA's and Severn Trent's sales are on credit as these businesses have little invested in trade receivables. It is interesting to note that Tesco's trade payables are much higher than its inventories. Since most of this money will be due to suppliers of inventories, it means that the business is able, on average, to have the cash from a particular sale in the bank before it needs to pay for the goods concerned.

These types of variation in the amounts and types of working capital elements are typical of other businesses.

In the sections that follow, we shall consider each element of working capital separately and how they might be properly managed. It seems from the evidence presented in **Real World 11.2** that there is much scope for improvement in working capital management among European businesses.

REAL WORLD 11.2

Working capital not working hard enough!

According to a survey of 1,000 of Europe's largest businesses, working capital is not as well managed as it could be. The survey, conducted in 2008 by REL Consultancy Group and CFO Europe, suggests that larger European businesses have €865bn tied up in working capital that could be released through better management of inventories, trade receivables and trade payables. The potential for savings represents a total of 36 per cent of the total working capital invested and is calculated by comparing the results for a particular industry with the results for businesses within the upper quartile of that industry.

The overall working capital invested by large European businesses as a percentage of sales for the five-year period ending in 2007 is shown in Figure 11.2.

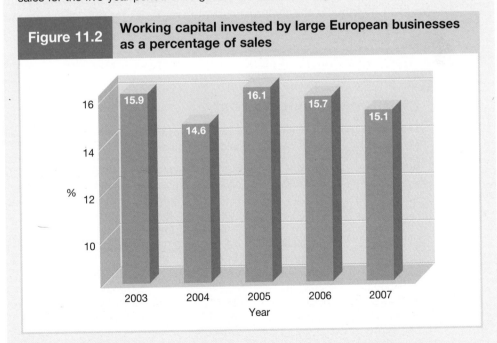

| Figure 11.2 | Working capital invested by large European businesses as a percentage of sales |

The figure shows that there has been little variation in this percentage over time.

Source: Compiled from information in 2008 REL/CFO European Working Capital Survey, www.relconsult.com.

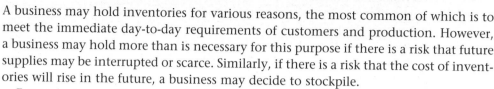

Managing inventories

A business may hold inventories for various reasons, the most common of which is to meet the immediate day-to-day requirements of customers and production. However, a business may hold more than is necessary for this purpose if there is a risk that future supplies may be interrupted or scarce. Similarly, if there is a risk that the cost of inventories will rise in the future, a business may decide to stockpile.

For some types of business, the inventories held may represent a substantial proportion of the total assets held. For example, a car dealership that rents its premises may have nearly all of its total assets in the form of inventories. Inventories levels of manufacturers tend to be higher than in many other types of business as it is necessary to hold three kinds of inventories: raw materials, work in progress and finished goods. Each form of inventories represents a particular stage in the production cycle.

For some types of business, the level of inventories held may vary substantially over the year owing to the seasonal nature of the industry. An example of such a business is a greetings card manufacturer. For other businesses, inventories levels may remain fairly stable throughout the year.

Where a business holds inventories simply to meet the day-to-day requirements of its customers and for production, it will normally seek to minimise the amount of inventories held. This is because there are significant costs associated with holding inventories. These include:

● storage and handling costs
● financing costs
● the costs of pilferage and obsolescence
● the cost of opportunities forgone in tying up funds in this form of asset.

To gain some impression of the level of cost involved in holding inventories, **Real World 11.3** estimates the *financing* cost of inventories for five large businesses.

REAL WORLD 11.3

Inventories financing cost

The financing cost of inventories for each of five large businesses, based on their respective opportunity costs of capital, is calculated below.

Business	Type of operations	Cost of capital (a) %	Average inventories held* (b) £m	Cost of holding inventories (a) × (b) £m	Profit before tax £m	Cost as % of profit before tax %
Rolls-Royce	Engineering	12.75	2,024	258	733	35.2
Rexam	Packaging	11.0	373	41	260	15.8
Carphone Warehouse	Mobile phone retailer	6.8	150	10.2	67	15.2
Kingfisher	Home improvement retailer	7.4	1,443	106.8	338.4	31.6
United Business Media	Media	8.0	6.9	0.6	129.5	0.0

* Based on opening and closing inventories for the financial year ending in 2007.

We can see that for four out of the five businesses listed, inventories financing costs are significant in relation to the profits generated. These figures do not take account of other costs of inventories holding mentioned above, like the cost of providing a secure store for the inventories. Clearly, the efficient management of inventories is an important issue for many businesses.

Source: Annual reports of the businesses for the financial year ended in 2007.

As we have just seen, the cost of holding inventories can be very large. A business must also recognise, however, that, if the level of inventories held is too low, there will also be associated costs.

Activity 11.2

What costs might a business incur as a result of holding too low a level of inventories? Try to jot down at least three types of cost.

In answering this activity you may have thought of the following costs:

- loss of sales, from being unable to provide the goods required immediately;
- loss of customer goodwill, for being unable to satisfy customer demand;
- high transport costs incurred to ensure that inventories are replenished quickly;
- lost production due to shortage of raw materials;
- inefficient production scheduling due to shortages of raw materials;
- purchasing inventories at a higher price than might otherwise have been possible in order to replenish inventories quickly.

Before we go on to deal with the various approaches that can be taken to managing inventories, **Real World 11.4** describes how one large international business has sought to reduce its inventories levels.

REAL WORLD 11.4

Back to basics   **FT**

Wal-Mart has said it will seek further reductions in the levels of backroom inventory it holds at its US stores, in a drive to improve its performance. . . . John Menzer, vice chairman and head of Wal-Mart's US operations, made the retailer's efforts to cut inventory one of the key elements of remarks to reporters this week when he outlined current strategy. Wal-Mart, he said, currently 'has a real focus on reducing our inventory. Inventory that's on trailers behind our stores, in backrooms and on shelves in our stores.' Cutting back on inventory, he said, reduced 'clutter' in the retailer's stores, gave a better return on invested capital, reduced the need to cut prices on old merchandise, and increased the velocity at which goods moved through the stores.

Eduardo Castro-Wright, chief executive of Wal-Mart's US store network, said the inventory reduction marked a return to basics for the retailer, which would be 'getting more disciplined'. Earlier this year, he said Wal-Mart would link inventory reduction to incentive payments to its officers and managers. Wal-Mart is already regarded as one of the most

> **Real World 11.4 continued**
>
> efficient logistical operations in US retailing. It is currently rolling out to all its US stores and distribution centres a new parallel distribution system that speeds the delivery to stores of 5,000 high turnover items. It is also discussing with its suppliers how new RFID radio frequency tagging could be used to further reduce the volume of goods in transit to its stores. But further reductions in its inventory turnover would release working capital that could fund investment in its ongoing initiatives to improve its stores.
>
> Adrienne Shapira, retail analyst at Goldman Sachs, has estimated that the retailer could reduce its annual inventory by 18 per cent, which would lead to a $6bn reduction in working capital needs on a trailing 12-month basis.
>
> *Source*: Wal-Mart aims for further inventory cuts, ft.com (Birchall, J.), © The Financial Times Limited, 19 April 2006.

To try to ensure that the inventories are properly managed, a number of procedures and techniques may be used. These are reviewed below.

Budgeting future demand

One of the best ways to ensure that there will be inventories available to meet future production and sales requirements is to make appropriate plans and budgets. Budgets should deal with each product that the business makes and/or sells. It is important that every attempt is made to ensure that budgets are realistic, as they will determine future ordering and production levels. The budgets may be derived in various ways. They may be developed using statistical techniques such as time series analysis, or they may be based on the judgement of the sales and marketing staff. We considered inventories budgets and their link to production and sales budgets in Chapter 6.

Financial ratios

One ratio that can be used to help monitor inventories levels is the average inventories turnover period. This ratio is calculated as follows:

$$\text{Average inventories turnover period} = \frac{\text{Average inventories held}}{\text{Cost of sales}} \times 365$$

This will provide a picture of the average period for which inventories are held, and can be useful as a basis for comparison. It is possible to calculate the average inventories turnover period for individual product lines as well as for inventories as a whole.

Recording and reordering systems

The management of inventories in a business of any size requires a sound system of recording inventories movements. There must be proper procedures for recording inventories purchases and usages. Periodic inventories checks may be required to ensure that the amount of physical inventories held is consistent with what is indicated by the inventories records.

There should also be clear procedures for the reordering of inventories. Authorisation for both the purchase and the issue of inventories should be confined to a few senior staff. This should avoid problems of duplication and lack of co-ordination. To determine the point at which inventories should be reordered, information will be required concerning the **lead time** (that is, the time between the placing of an order and the receipt of the goods) and the likely level of demand.

Activity 11.3

An electrical retailer stocks a particular type of light switch. The annual demand for the light switch is 10,400 units, and the lead time for orders is four weeks. Demand for the light switch is steady throughout the year. At what quantity of the light switch should the business reorder, assuming that it is confident of the information given above?

The average weekly demand for the switch is 10,400/52 = 200 units. During the time between ordering new switches and receiving them, the quantity sold will be 4 × 200 units = 800 units. So the business should reorder no later than when the level held reaches 800 units, in order to avoid running out of inventories.

In most businesses, there will be some uncertainty surrounding the above factors and so a buffer or safety inventories level may be maintained in case problems occur. The amount of the buffer to be held is really a matter of judgement. This judgement will depend on:

- the degree of uncertainty concerning the above factors;
- the likely costs of running out of the item concerned;
- the cost of holding the buffer inventories.

The effect of holding a buffer will be to raise the inventories level (the reorder point) at which an order for new inventories is placed.

Activity 11.4

Assume the same facts as in Activity 11.3. However, we are also told that the business maintains buffer inventories of 300 units. At what level should the business reorder?

Reorder point = expected level of demand during the lead time plus the level
of buffer inventories
= 800 + 300
= 1,100 units

Carrying buffer inventories will increase the cost of holding inventories; however, this must be weighed against the cost of running out of inventories, in terms of lost sales, production problems and so on.

Real World 11.5 provides an example of how small businesses can use technology in inventories reordering to help compete against their larger rivals.

REAL WORLD 11.5

Taking on the big boys   **FT**

The use of technology in inventories recording and reordering may be of vital importance to the survival of small businesses that are being threatened by larger rivals. One such example is that of small independent bookshops. Technology can come to their rescue in two ways. First, electronic point-of-sale (EPOS) systems can record books as they are sold and can constantly update records of inventories held. Thus, books that need to be reordered can be quickly and easily identified. Second, the reordering process can be improved by using web-based technology, which allows books to be ordered in real time. Many large book wholesalers provide free web-based software to their customers for this purpose and try to deliver books ordered during the next working day. This means that a small bookseller, with limited shelf space, may keep one copy only of a particular book but maintain a range of books that competes with that of a large bookseller.

Source: Information taken from 'Small stores keep up with the big boys', *Financial Times*, 5 February 2003.

Levels of control

Senior managers must make a commitment to the management of inventories. However, the cost of controlling inventories must be weighed against the potential benefits. It may be possible to have different levels of control according to the nature of the inventories held. The **ABC system of inventories control** is based on the idea of selective levels of control.

A business may find that it is possible to divide its inventories into three broad categories: A, B and C. Each category will be based on the value of inventories held, as is illustrated in Example 11.1.

Example 11.1

Alascan Products plc makes door handles and door fittings. It makes them in brass, in steel and in plastic. The business finds that brass fittings account for 10 per cent of the physical volume of the finished inventories that it holds, but represent 65 per cent of their total value. These are treated as Category A inventories. There are sophisticated recording procedures, tight control is exerted over inventories movements and there is a high level of security where the brass inventories are stored. This is economic because the inventories represent a relatively small proportion of the total volume.

The business finds that steel fittings account for 30 per cent of the total volume of finished inventories and represent 25 per cent of their total value. They are treated as Category B inventories, with a lower level of recording and management control being applied.

The remaining 60 per cent of the volume of inventories is plastic fittings, which represent the least valuable items and account for only 10 per cent of the total value of finished inventories held. They are treated as Category C inventories, so the level of recording and management control would be lower still. Applying to these inventories, the level of control that is applied to Category A or even Category B inventories would be uneconomic.

Categorising inventories in this way seeks to direct management effort to the most important areas, and tries to ensure that the costs of controlling inventories are appropriate to their importance.

Figure 11.3 shows the nature of the ABC approach to inventories control.

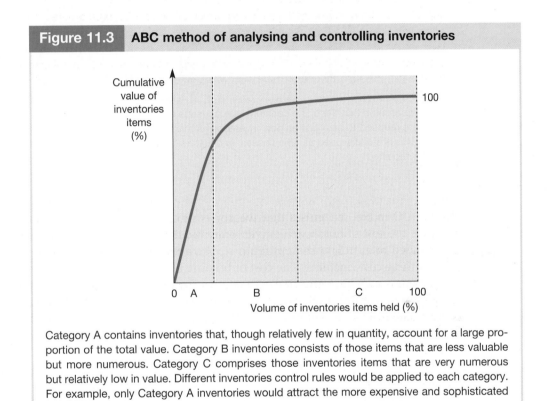

Figure 11.3 **ABC method of analysing and controlling inventories**

Category A contains inventories that, though relatively few in quantity, account for a large proportion of the total value. Category B inventories consists of those items that are less valuable but more numerous. Category C comprises those inventories items that are very numerous but relatively low in value. Different inventories control rules would be applied to each category. For example, only Category A inventories would attract the more expensive and sophisticated controls.

Inventories management models

Economic order quantity

It is possible to use decision models to help manage inventories. The **economic order quantity (EOQ)** model is concerned with answering the question 'How much should be ordered?' In its simplest form, the EOQ model assumes that demand is constant, so that inventories will be depleted evenly over time, and replenished just at the point that they run out. These assumptions would lead to a 'saw-tooth' pattern to represent movements in inventories, as shown in Figure 11.4.

Figure 11.4 **Patterns of inventories movements over time**

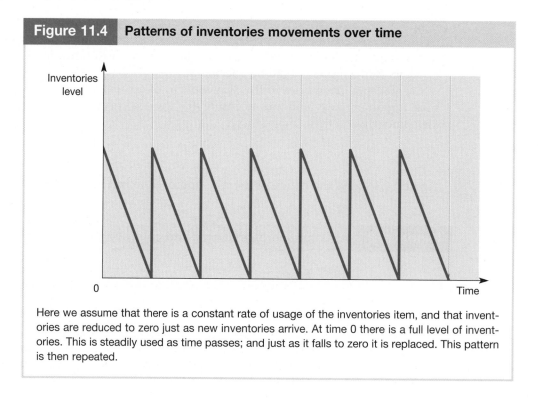

Here we assume that there is a constant rate of usage of the inventories item, and that inventories are reduced to zero just as new inventories arrive. At time 0 there is a full level of inventories. This is steadily used as time passes; and just as it falls to zero it is replaced. This pattern is then repeated.

The EOQ model recognises that the key costs associated with inventories management are the cost of holding the inventories and the cost of ordering them. The model can be used to calculate the optimum size of a purchase order by taking account of both of these cost elements. The cost of holding inventories can be substantial, and so management may try to minimise the average amount of inventories held. However, if the level of inventories held and, therefore, the holding costs, are reduced, there will be a need to increase the number of orders during the period and so ordering costs will rise.

Figure 11.5 shows how, as the level of inventories and the size of inventories orders increase, the annual costs of placing orders will decrease because fewer orders will be placed. However, the cost of holding inventories will increase, as there will be higher average inventories levels. The total costs curve, which is based on the sum of holding costs and ordering costs, will fall until the point E, which represents the minimum total cost. Thereafter, total costs begin to rise. The EOQ model seeks to identify point E at which total costs are minimised. This will represent half of the optimum amount that should be ordered on each occasion. Assuming, as we are doing, that inventories are used evenly over time and that they fall to zero before being replaced, the average inventories level equals half of the order size.

The EOQ model, which can be used to derive the most economic order quantity, is

$$EOQ = \sqrt{\frac{2DC}{H}}$$

where
D = the annual demand for the inventories item (expressed in units of the inventories item);
C = the cost of placing an order;
H = the cost of holding one unit of inventories for one year.

Figure 11.5 **Inventories holding and order costs**

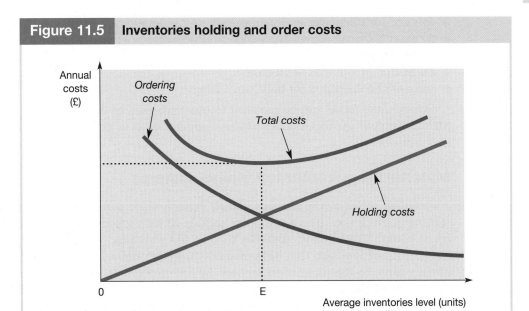

Small inventories levels imply frequent reordering and high annual ordering costs. Small inventories levels also imply relatively low inventories holding costs. High inventories levels imply exactly the opposite. There is, in theory, an optimum order size that will lead to the sum of ordering and holding costs (total costs) being at a minimum.

Activity 11.5

HLA Ltd sells 2,000 bags of cement each year. It has been estimated that the cost of holding one bag of cement for a year is £4. The cost of placing an order for new inventories is estimated at £250.

Calculate the EOQ for bags of cement.

Your answer to this activity should be as follows:

$$EOQ = \sqrt{\frac{2 \times 2,000 \times 250}{4}}$$

$$= 500 \text{ bags}$$

This will mean that the business will have to order bags of cement four (2,000/500) times each year in batches of 500 bags so that sales demand can be met.

Note that the cost of the inventories concerned, which is the price paid to the supplier, does not directly impact on the EOQ model. The EOQ model is concerned only with the administrative costs of placing each order and the costs of looking after the inventories. Where the business operates an ABC system of inventories control, however, more expensive inventories items will have greater holding costs. For example, Category A inventories would tend to have a lower EOQ than Category B ones. So the cost of the inventories may have an indirect effect on the economic order size that the model recommends.

The basic EOQ model has a number of limiting assumptions. In particular, it assumes that:

- demand for the particular inventories item can be predicted with accuracy;
- demand is constant over the period and does not fluctuate through seasonality or for other reasons;
- no 'buffer' inventories are required;
- there are no discounts for bulk purchasing.

However, the model can be modified to overcome each of these limiting assumptions. Many businesses use this model (or a development of it) to help in the management of inventories.

Materials requirement planning systems

A **materials requirement planning (MRP) system** takes planned sales demand as its starting point. It then uses a computer package to help schedule the timing of deliveries of bought-in parts and materials to coincide with production requirements. It is a co-ordinated approach that links materials and parts deliveries to the scheduled time of their input to the production process. By ordering only those items that are necessary to ensure the flow of production, it is possible to reduce inventories levels. MRP is really a 'top-down' approach to inventories management, which recognises that inventories ordering decisions cannot be viewed as being independent of production decisions. In recent years, this approach has been extended to provide a fully integrated approach to production planning. The approach also takes account of other manufacturing resources such as labour and machine capacity.

Just-in-time inventories management

In recent years, many businesses have tried to eliminate the need to hold inventories by adopting **just-in-time (JIT) inventories management**. This approach was first used in the US defence industry during the Second World War, but was first used on a wide scale by Japanese manufacturing businesses. The essence of JIT is, as the name suggests, to have supplies delivered to the business just in time for them to be used in the production process or in a sale. By adopting this approach the inventories holding costs rest with suppliers rather than with the business itself. On the other hand, a failure by a particular supplier to deliver on time could cause enormous problems and costs to the business. Thus JIT can save cost, but it tends to increase risk.

For JIT to be successful, it is important that the business informs suppliers of its inventories requirements in advance. Also suppliers, in their turn, must deliver materials of the right quality at the agreed times. Failure to do so could lead to a dislocation of production or supply to customers and could be very costly. Thus a close relationship is required between the business and its suppliers. This close relationship enables suppliers to schedule their own production to that of their customers. This should mean that between supplier and customer there will be a net saving in the amount of inventories that need to be held, relative to that that would apply were JIT not in operation.

Adopting JIT may well require re-engineering a business's production process. To ensure that orders are quickly fulfilled, factory production must be flexible and responsive. This may require changes both to the production layout and to working practices. Production flows may have to be redesigned and employees may have to be given greater responsibility to allow them to deal with unanticipated problems and to encourage greater commitment. Information systems must also be installed that facilitate an uninterrupted production flow.

Although a business that applies JIT will not have to hold inventories, there may be other costs associated with this approach. As the suppliers may need to hold inventories for the customer, they may try to recoup this additional cost through increased prices. On the other hand, the close relationship between customer and supplier should enable the supplier to predict its customers' inventories needs. This means that suppliers can tailor their own production to that of the customer. The close relationship necessary between the business and its suppliers may also prevent the business from taking advantage of cheaper sources of supply if they become available.

Many people view JIT as more than simply an inventories control system. The philosophy underpinning this approach is concerned with eliminating waste and striving for excellence. There is an expectation that suppliers will always deliver inventories on time and that there will be no defects in the items supplied. There is also an expectation that, for manufacturers, the production process will operate at maximum efficiency. This means there will be no production breakdowns and the queuing and storage times of products manufactured will be eliminated, as only that time spent directly on processing the products is seen as adding value. While these expectations may be impossible to achieve, they do help to create a culture that is dedicated to the pursuit of excellence and quality.

Real World 11.6 and **Real World 11.7** show how two very well-known businesses operating in the UK (one a retailer, the other a manufacturer) use JIT to advantage.

REAL WORLD 11.6

JIT at Boots

The Boots Company plc, the UK's largest healthcare retailer, has improved inventories management at its stores. The business is working towards a JIT system where delivery from its one central warehouse in Nottingham will be made every day to each retail branch, with nearly all of the inventories lines being placed directly on to the sales shelves, not into a branch inventories store room. The business says that this will bring significant savings of stores staff time and lead to significantly lower levels of inventories being held, without any lessening of the service offered to customers. The new system is expected to lead to major economic benefits for the business.

Source: Information taken from The Boots Company plc Annual Report and Accounts 2005.

REAL WORLD 11.7

JIT at Nissan

Nissan Motors UK Limited, the UK manufacturing arm of the world-famous Japanese car business, has a plant in Sunderland in the north east of England. Here it operates a fairly well-developed JIT system. For example, Sommer supplies carpets and soft interior trim from a factory close to the Nissan plant. It makes deliveries to Nissan once every 20 minutes on average, so as to arrive exactly as they are needed in production. This is fairly typical of all of the 200 suppliers of components and materials to the Nissan plant.

The business used to have a complete JIT system. More recently, however, Nissan has drawn back from its total adherence to JIT. By using only local suppliers it had cut itself off from the opportunity to exploit low-cost suppliers, particularly some located in China. Sourcing parts from the Far East has now led the business to feel the need to hold buffer inventories of certain items to guard against disruption of supply arising from transport problems.

Sources: Information taken from Partnership Sourcing Best Practice Case Study, www.pslcbi.com/studies/docnissan.htm, and Tighe, C., 'Nissan reviews just-in-time parts policy', *Financial Times*, 23 October 2006.

Managing receivables
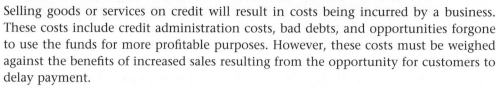

Selling goods or services on credit will result in costs being incurred by a business. These costs include credit administration costs, bad debts, and opportunities forgone to use the funds for more profitable purposes. However, these costs must be weighed against the benefits of increased sales resulting from the opportunity for customers to delay payment.

Selling on credit is very widespread and is the norm outside the retail industry. When a business offers to sell its goods or services on credit, it must have clear policies concerning

- which customers should receive credit;
- how much credit should be offered;
- what length of credit it is prepared to offer;
- whether discounts will be offered for prompt payment;
- what collection policies should be adopted;
- how the risk of non-payment can be reduced.

In this section, we shall consider each of these issues.

Which customers should receive credit and how much credit should they be offered?

A business offering credit runs the risk of not receiving payment for goods or services supplied. Thus, care must be taken over the type of customer to whom credit facilities are offered and how much credit is allowed. When considering a proposal from a customer for the supply of goods or services on credit, the business must take a number of factors into account. The following **five Cs of credit** provide a business with a useful checklist.

- *Capital*. The customer must appear to be financially sound before any credit is extended. Where the customer is a business, its financial statements should be examined. Particular regard should be given to the customer's likely future profitability and liquidity. In addition, any major financial commitments (for example, capital expenditure, contracts with suppliers) must be taken into account.
- *Capacity*. The customer must appear to have the capacity to pay amounts owing. Where possible, the payment record of the customer to date should be examined. If the customer is a business, the type of business operated and the physical resources of the business will be relevant. The value of goods that the customer wishes to buy on credit must be related to the customer's total financial resources.
- *Collateral*. On occasions, it may be necessary to ask for some kind of security for goods supplied on credit. When this occurs, the business must be convinced that the customer is able to offer a satisfactory form of security.
- *Conditions*. The state of the industry in which the customer operates, and the general economic conditions of the particular region or country, may have an important influence on the ability of a customer to pay the amounts outstanding on the due date.
- *Character*. It is important for a business to make some assessment of the customer's character. The willingness to pay will depend on the honesty and integrity of the individual with whom the business is dealing. Where the customer is a business, this

will mean assessing the characters of its senior managers. The selling business must feel satisfied that the customer will make every effort to pay any amounts owing.

It is clear from the above that the business will need to gather information concerning the ability and willingness of the customer to pay the amounts owing at the due dates.

Activity 11.6

Assume that you are the credit manager of a business and that a limited company approaches you with a view to buying goods on credit. What sources of information might you decide to use to help assess the financial health of the potential customer?

There are various possibilities. You may have thought of some of the following:

● *Trade references*. Some businesses ask potential customers to supply them with references from other suppliers who have made sales on credit to them. This may be extremely useful provided that the references supplied are truly representative of the opinions of a customer's suppliers. There is a danger that a potential customer will be selective when giving details of other suppliers, in an attempt to create a more favourable impression than is deserved.

● *Bank references*. It is possible to ask the potential customer for a bank reference. Although banks are usually prepared to supply references, the contents of such references are not always very informative. If customers are in financial difficulties, the bank may be unwilling to add to their problems by supplying poor references. It is worth remembering that the bank's loyalty is likely to be with the customer rather than the enquirer. The bank will usually charge a fee for providing a reference.

● *Published financial statements*. A limited company is obliged by law to file a copy of its annual financial statements with the Registrar of Companies. These financial statements are available for public inspection and provide a useful source of information. Apart from the information contained in the financial statements, company law requires public limited companies to state in the directors' report the average time taken to pay suppliers. The annual reports of many companies are available on their own websites or on computer-based information systems (for example, FAME).

● *The customer*. Interviews with the directors of the customer business and visits to its premises may be carried out to gain an impression of the way that the customer conducts its business. Where a significant amount of credit is required, the business may ask the customer for access to internal budgets and other unpublished financial information to help assess the level of risk involved.

● *Credit agencies*. Specialist agencies exist to provide information that can be used to assess the creditworthiness of a potential customer. The information that a credit agency supplies may be gleaned from various sources, including the financial statements of the customer and news items relating to the customer from both published and unpublished sources. The credit agencies may also provide a credit rating for the business. Agencies will charge a fee for their services.

● *Register of Judgments, Orders and Fines*. Any money judgments given against the business or an individual in a county court will be maintained on the register for six years. This register is available for inspection by any member of the public for a small fee.

● *Other suppliers*. Similar businesses will often be prepared to exchange information concerning slow payers or defaulting customers through an industry credit circle. This can be a reliable and relatively cheap way of obtaining information.

Length of credit period

A business must determine what credit terms it is prepared to offer its customers. The length of credit offered to customers can vary significantly between businesses. It may be influenced by such factors as:

- the typical credit terms operating within the industry;
- the degree of competition within the industry;
- the bargaining power of particular customers;
- the risk of non-payment;
- the capacity of the business to offer credit;
- the marketing strategy of the business.

The last point identified may require some explanation. If, for example, a business wishes to increase its market share, it may decide to be more generous in its credit policy in an attempt to stimulate sales. Potential customers may be attracted by the offer of a longer credit period. However, any such change in policy must take account of the likely costs and benefits arising.

To illustrate this point, consider Example 11.2.

Example 11.2

Torrance Ltd produces a new type of golf putter. The business sells the putter to wholesalers and retailers and has an annual turnover of £600,000. The following data relate to each putter produced.

	£
Selling price	40
Variable costs	(20)
Fixed cost apportionment	(6)
Profit	14

The business's cost of capital is estimated at 10 per cent a year.

Torrance Ltd wishes to expand the sales volume of the new putter. It believes that offering a longer credit period can achieve this. The business's average receivables collection period is currently 30 days. It is considering three options in an attempt to increase sales revenue. These are as follows:

	Option 1	Option 2	Option 3
Increase in average collection period (days)	10	20	30
Increase in sales revenue (£)	30,000	45,000	50,000

To enable the business to decide on the best option to adopt, it must weigh the benefits of the options against their respective costs. The benefits arising will be represented by the increase in profit from the sale of additional putters. From the cost data supplied we can see that the contribution (that is, selling price (£40) less variable costs (£20)) is £20 a putter, that is, 50 per cent of the selling price. So, whatever increase there may be in sales revenue, the additional contributions will be half of that figure. The fixed costs can be ignored in our calculations, as they will remain the same whichever option is chosen.

The increase in contribution under each option will therefore be:

	Option 1	Option 2	Option 3
50% of the increase in sales revenue (£)	15,000	22,500	25,000

The increase in trade receivables under each option will be as follows:

	Option 1 £	Option 2 £	Option 3 £
Projected level of trade receivables			
40 × £630,000/365 (Note 1)	69,041		
50 × £645,000/365		88,356	
60 × £650,000/365			106,849
Current level of trade receivables			
30 × £600,000/365	(49,315)	(49,315)	(49,315)
Increase in trade receivables	19,726	39,041	57,534

The increase in receivables that results from each option will mean an additional finance cost to the business.

The net increase in the business's profit arising from the projected change is:

	Option 1 £	Option 2 £	Option 3 £
Increase in contribution (see above)	15,000	22,500	25,000
Increase in finance cost (Note 2)	(1,973)	(3,904)	(5,753)
Net increase in profits	13,027	18,596	19,247

The calculations show that Option 3 will be the most profitable one.

Notes:

1 If the annual sales revenue totals £630,000 and 40 days' credit is allowed (both of which will apply under Option 1), the average amount that will be owed to the business by its customers, at any point during the year, will be the daily sales revenue (that is, £630,000/365) multiplied by the number of days that the customers take to pay (that is, 40).

Exactly the same logic applies to Options 2 and 3 and to the current level of trade receivables.

2 The increase in the finance cost for Option 1 will be the increase in trade receivables (£19,726) × 10 per cent. The equivalent figures for the other options are derived in a similar way.

Example 11.2 illustrates the way that a business should assess changes in credit terms. However, if there is a risk that, by extending the length of credit, there will be an increase in bad debts, this should also be taken into account in the calculations, as should any additional trade receivables collection costs that will be incurred.

Real World 11.8 shows how the length of credit taken by some larger UK businesses leads to problems for smaller businesses.

REAL WORLD 11.8

Credit where it's due   FT

Late payment to small companies has got progressively worse over the past three years and they need to employ stricter credit management techniques, a survey released today claims.

Siemens Financial Services (SFS), a subsidiary of Siemens, the German engineering group, studied the accounts of thousands of UK companies. It found that smaller firms had to wait for 80 days to get paid by customers in 2006, compared with 69 days in 2004.

In contrast, medium-size and large companies have seen their 'days sales outstanding' hold steady over the period at 62 days and 47 days respectively.

Rod Tonna-Barthet, sales director at SFS, said the results showed that 'small firms are suffering' as a result of medium-size and large companies using competitive pressures to extend payment terms.

Source: Late payments hit small companies, ft.com (Chisholm, J.), © The Financial Times Limited, 29 January 2007.

An alternative approach to evaluating the credit decision

It is possible to view the credit decision as a capital investment decision. Granting trade credit involves an opportunity outlay of resources in the form of cash (which has been temporarily forgone) in the expectation that future cash flows will be increased (through higher sales) as a result. A business will usually have choices concerning the level of investment to be made in credit sales and the period over which credit is granted. These choices will result in different returns and different levels of risk. There is no reason in principle why the net present value (NPV) investment appraisal method, which we considered in Chapter 8, should not be used to evaluate these choices. We have seen that the NPV method takes into account both the time value of money and the level of risk involved.

Approaching the problem as an NPV assessment is not different in principle from the way that we dealt with the decision in Example 11.2. In both approaches the time value of money is considered, but in Example 11.2 we did it by charging a financing cost on the outstanding trade receivables.

Cash discounts

A business may decide to offer a **cash discount** (or discount for prompt payment) in an attempt to encourage prompt payment from its credit customers. The size of any discount will be an important influence on whether a customer decides to pay promptly.

From the business's viewpoint, the cost of offering discounts must be weighed against the likely benefits in the form of a reduction both in the cost of financing receivables and in the amount of bad debts.

In practice, there is always the danger that a customer may be slow to pay and yet may still take the discount offered. Where the customer is important to the business, it may be difficult to insist on full payment. An alternative to allowing the customer to take discounts by reducing payment is to agree in advance to provide discounts for prompt payment through quarterly credit notes. As credit notes will be given only for those debts paid on time, the customer will often make an effort to qualify for the discount.

Self-assessment question 11.1

Williams Wholesalers Ltd at present asks its credit customers to pay by the end of the month after the month of delivery. In practice, customers take rather longer to pay; on average, 70 days. Sales revenue amounts to £4m a year and bad debts to £20,000 a year.

It is planned to offer customers a cash discount of 2 per cent for payment within 30 days. Williams estimates that 50 per cent of customers will accept this facility but that the remaining customers, who tend to be slow payers, will not pay until 80 days after the sale. At present the business has an overdraft facility at an interest rate of 13 per cent a year. If the plan goes ahead, bad debts will be reduced to £10,000 a year and there will be savings in credit administration expenses of £6,000 a year.

Required:

Should Williams Wholesalers Ltd offer the new credit terms to customers? You should support your answer with any calculations and explanations that you consider necessary.

The answer to this question can be found in Appendix B at the back of the book.

Debt factoring and invoice discounting

Trade receivables can, in effect, be turned into cash by either factoring them or having sales invoices discounted. Both are forms of asset-based finance, which involve a financial institution providing a business with an advance up to 80 per cent of the value of the trade receivables outstanding. Both of these methods seem to be fairly popular approaches to managing receivables.

Collection policies and reducing the risk of non-payment

A business offering credit must ensure that amounts owing are collected as quickly as possible so that the risk of non-payment is minimised. Various steps can be taken to achieve this, including the following.

Develop customer relationships

For major customers it is often useful to cultivate a relationship with the key staff responsible for paying sales invoices. By so doing, it may be possible to increase the chances of prompt payment. For less important customers, the business should at least identify key staff responsible for paying invoices, who can be contacted in the event of a payment problem.

Publicise credit terms

The credit terms of the business should be made clear in all relevant correspondence, such as order acknowledgements, invoices and statements. In early negotiations with the prospective customer, credit terms should be openly discussed and an agreement reached.

Issue invoices promptly

An efficient collection policy requires an efficient accounting system. Invoices (bills) must be sent out promptly to customers, as must monthly statements. Reminders must also be despatched promptly to customers who are late in paying. If a customer fails to respond to a reminder, the accounting system should alert managers so that a stop can be placed on further deliveries.

Monitor outstanding debts

Management can monitor the effectiveness of collection policies in a number of ways. One method is to calculate the **average settlement period for trade receivables** ratio. This ratio is calculated as follows:

$$\text{Average settlement period for trade receivables} = \frac{\text{Average trade receivables}}{\text{Credit sales}} \times 365$$

Although this ratio can be useful, it is important to remember that it produces an *average* figure for the number of days for which debts are outstanding. This average may be badly distorted by a few large customers who are very slow or very fast payers.

Produce an ageing schedule of trade receivables

A more detailed and informative approach to monitoring receivables may be to produce an **ageing schedule of trade receivables**. Receivables are divided into categories according to the length of time they have been outstanding. An ageing schedule can be produced, on a regular basis, to help managers see the pattern of outstanding receivables. An example of an ageing schedule is set out in Example 11.3.

Example 11.3

Ageing schedule of trade receivables at 31 December

Customer	Days outstanding				Total
	1 to 30 days	31 to 60 days	61 to 90 days	More than 90 days	
	£	£	£	£	£
A Ltd	20,000	10,000	–	–	30,000
B Ltd	–	24,000	–	–	24,000
C Ltd	12,000	13,000	14,000	18,000	57,000
Total	32,000	47,000	14,000	18,000	111,000

This shows a business's trade receivables figure at 31 December, which totals £111,000. Each customer's balance is analysed according to how long the amount has been outstanding. (This business has just three credit customers.)

Thus we can see from the schedule, for example, that A Ltd has £20,000 outstanding for 30 or fewer days (that is, arising from sales during December) and £10,000 outstanding for between 31 and 60 days (arising from November sales). This information can be very useful for credit control purposes.

Many accounting software packages now include this ageing schedule as one of the routine reports available to managers. Such packages often have the facility to put customers 'on hold' when they reach their credit limits. Putting a customer on hold means that no further credit sales will be made to that customer until amounts owing from past sales have been settled.

Answer queries quickly

It is important for relevant staff to deal quickly and efficiently with customer queries on goods and services supplied. Payment is unlikely to be made by customers until their queries have been dealt with.

Deal with slow payers

It is almost inevitably the case that a business making significant sales on credit will be faced with customers who do not pay. When this occurs, there should be agreed procedures for dealing with the situation. However, the cost of any action to be taken against delinquent credit customers must be weighed against the likely returns. For example, there is little point in taking legal action against a customer, incurring large legal expenses, if there is evidence that the customer does not have the necessary resources to pay. Where possible, an estimate of the cost of bad debts should be taken into account when setting prices for products or services.

Real World 11.9 shows that businesses are not always as efficient as they might be with their management of trade receivables.

REAL WORLD 11.9

Would you credit it?

FT

According to a recent survey of 6,500 UK businesses, 44 per cent of businesses leave it a fortnight, or longer, after the due date for payment before sending reminders to their credit customers, while 13 per cent leave it for a month or more. In other words, many businesses are very slow to react to their customers failing to pay on time.

Intrum Justitia UK, who conducted the survey, said: 'A clear credit policy, consistent checks on overdue payments and robust credit management systems are just some of the critical measures that businesses need to adopt.'

Source: Information taken from Moules, J., 'Late reminders lead to late payments', *Financial Times*, 12 July 2004.

As a footnote to our consideration of managing receivables, **Real World 11.10** outlines some of the excuses that long-suffering credit managers must listen to when chasing payment for outstanding debts.

REAL WORLD 11.10

It's in the post

The Atradius Group provides trade credit insurance and trade receivables collections services worldwide, and has a presence in 40 countries. Its products and services aim to reduce its customers' exposure to buyers who cannot pay for the products and services customers purchase.

In a recent press release Atradius said:

Although it happens rarely, some debtors (credit customers) still manage to surprise even us. These excuses have actually been used by credit customers:
● It's not a valid debt as my vindictive ex-wife ran off with the company credit card.
● I just got back from my luxury holiday, it cost more than I thought so I no longer have the funds to pay.
● I wanted to pay but all the invoices were in my briefcase, which was stolen on the street.
● My wife has been kidnapped, and I need the money to get her back.

Source: www.atradius.us/news/press-releases, 13 August 2008.

Managing cash

Why hold cash?

Most businesses hold a certain amount of cash. The amount of cash held tends to vary considerably between businesses.

Activity 11.7

Why do you think a business may decide to hold at least some of its assets in the form of cash? (*Hint*: There are broadly three reasons.)

The three reasons are:

1 To meet day-to-day commitments, a business requires a certain amount of cash. Payments for wages, overhead expenses, goods purchased and so on must be made at the due dates. Cash has been described as the lifeblood of a business. Unless it circulates through the business and is available for the payment of claims as they become due, the survival of the business will be at risk. Profitability is not enough; a business must have sufficient cash to pay its debts when they fall due.

2 If future cash flows are uncertain for any reason, it would be prudent to hold a balance of cash. For example, a major customer that owes a large sum to the business may be in financial difficulties. Given this situation, the business can retain its capacity to meet its obligations by holding a cash balance. Similarly, if there is some uncertainty concerning future outlays, a cash balance will be required.

3 A business may decide to hold cash to put itself in a position to exploit profitable opportunities as and when they arise. For example, by holding cash, a business may be able to acquire a competitor's business that suddenly becomes available at an attractive price.

How much cash should be held?

Although cash can be held for each of the reasons identified, doing so may not always be necessary. If a business is able to borrow quickly, the amount of cash it needs to hold can be reduced. Similarly, if the business holds assets that can easily be converted to cash (for example, marketable securities such as shares in Stock Exchange listed businesses or government bonds), the amount of cash held can be reduced.

The decision as to how much cash a particular business should hold is a difficult one. Different businesses will have different views on the subject.

Activity 11.8

What do you think are the major factors that influence how much cash a business will hold? See if you can think of five possible factors.

You may have thought of the following:

● *The nature of the business*. Some businesses, such as utilities (for example, water, electricity and gas suppliers), may have cash flows that are both predictable and reasonably certain. This will enable them to hold lower cash balances. For some businesses, cash balances may vary greatly according to the time of year. A seasonal business may accumulate cash during the high season to enable it to meet commitments during the low season.

● *The opportunity cost of holding cash*. Where there are profitable opportunities it may not be wise to hold a large cash balance.

● *The level of inflation*. Holding cash during a period of rising prices will lead to a loss of purchasing power. The higher the level of inflation, the greater will be this loss.

● *The availability of near-liquid assets*. If a business has marketable securities or inventories that may easily be liquidated, high cash balances may not be necessary.

- *The availability of borrowing*. If a business can borrow easily (and quickly) there is less need to hold cash.
- *The cost of borrowing*. When interest rates are high, the option of borrowing becomes less attractive.
- *Economic conditions*. When the economy is in recession, businesses may prefer to hold cash so that they can be well placed to invest when the economy improves. In addition, during a recession, businesses may experience difficulties in collecting trade receivables. They may therefore hold higher cash balances than usual in order to meet commitments.
- *Relationships with suppliers*. Too little cash may hinder the ability of the business to pay suppliers promptly. This can lead to a loss of goodwill. It may also lead to discounts being forgone.

Controlling the cash balance

Several models have been developed to help control the cash balance of the business. One such model proposes the use of upper and lower control limits for cash balances and the use of a target cash balance. The model assumes that the business will invest in marketable investments that can easily be liquidated. These investments will be purchased or sold, as necessary, in order to keep the cash balance within the control limits.

The model proposes two upper and two lower control limits (see Figure 11.6). If the business exceeds an *outer* limit, the managers must decide whether the cash balance is likely to return to a point within the *inner* control limits set, over the next few days.

Figure 11.6	**Controlling the cash balance**

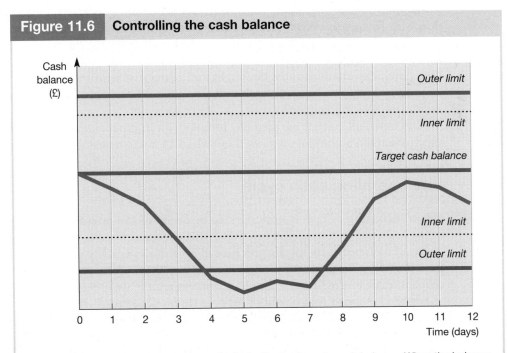

Management sets the upper and lower limits for the business's cash balance. When the balance goes beyond either of these limits, unless it is clear that the balance will return fairly quickly to within the limit, action will need to be taken. If the upper limit is breached, some cash will be placed on deposit or used to buy some marketable securities. If the lower limit is breached, the business will need to borrow some cash or sell some securities.

If this seems likely, then no action is required. If, on the other hand, it does not seem likely, management must change the cash position by either buying or selling marketable investments.

In Figure 11.6 we can see that the lower outer control limit has been breached for four days. If a four-day period is unacceptable, managers must sell marketable investments to replenish the cash balance.

The model relies heavily on management judgement to determine where the control limits are set and the period within which breaches of the control limits are acceptable. Past experience may be useful in helping managers decide on these issues. There are other models, however, that do not rely on management judgement. Instead, these use quantitative techniques to determine an optimal cash policy. One model proposed, for example, is the cash equivalent of the inventories economic order quantity model, discussed earlier in the chapter.

Cash budgets and managing cash

To manage cash effectively, it is useful for a business to prepare a cash budget. This is a very important tool for both planning and control purposes. Cash budgets were considered in Chapter 6, and so we shall not consider them again in detail. However, it is worth repeating that these statements enable managers to see how planned events are expected to affect the cash balance. The projected cash flow statement will identify periods when cash surpluses and cash deficits are expected.

When a cash surplus is expected to arise, managers must decide on the best use of the surplus funds. When a cash deficit is expected, managers must make adequate provision by borrowing, liquidating assets or rescheduling cash payments or receipts to deal with this. Cash budgets are useful in helping to control the cash held. The actual cash flows can be compared with the planned cash flows for the period. If there is a significant divergence between the projected, or forecast, cash flows and the actual cash flows, explanations must be sought and corrective action taken where necessary.

To refresh your memory on cash budgets, it would probably be worth looking back at pp. 194–197 in Chapter 6.

Although cash budgets are prepared primarily for internal management purposes, prospective lenders sometimes require them when a loan to a business is being considered.

The operating cash cycle

→ When managing cash, it is important to be aware of the **operating cash cycle (OCC)** of the business. For a retailer, for example, this may be defined as the period between the outlay of cash necessary for the purchase of inventories and the ultimate receipt of cash from the sale of the goods. In the case of a business that purchases goods on credit for subsequent resale on credit (for example, a wholesaler), the OCC is as shown in Figure 11.7.

Figure 11.7 shows that payment for inventories acquired on credit occurs some time after those inventories have been purchased and, therefore, no immediate cash outflow arises from the purchase. Similarly, cash receipts from credit customers will occur some time after the sale is made and so there will be no immediate cash inflow as a result of the sale. The OCC is the period between the payment made to the supplier for goods concerned and the cash received from the credit customer. Although Figure 11.7 depicts the position for a wholesaling business, the precise definition of the OCC can easily be adapted for other types of business.

The OCC is important because it has a significant influence on the financing requirements of the business. Broadly, the longer the cycle, the greater the financing

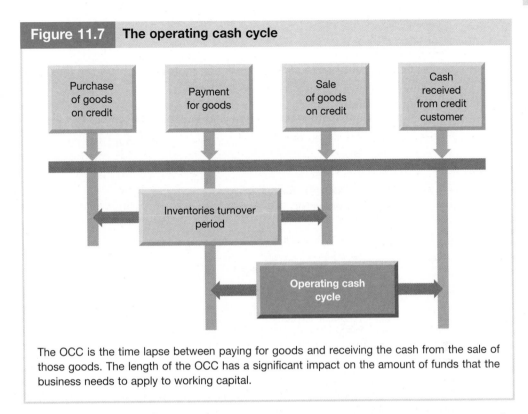

Figure 11.7   The operating cash cycle

The OCC is the time lapse between paying for goods and receiving the cash from the sale of those goods. The length of the OCC has a significant impact on the amount of funds that the business needs to apply to working capital.

requirements of the business and the greater the financial risks. For this reason, the business is likely to want to reduce the OCC to the minimum possible period.

For the type of business mentioned above, which buys and sells on credit, the OCC can be calculated from the financial statements by the use of certain ratios. It is calculated as shown in Figure 11.8.

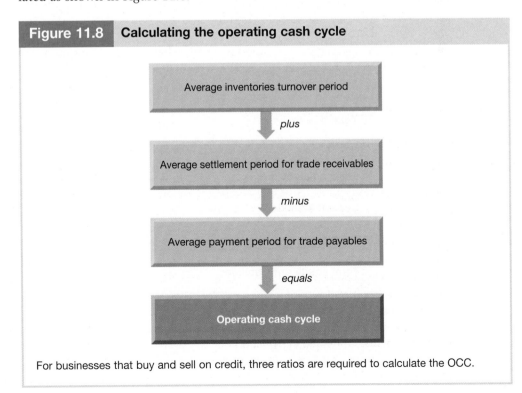

Figure 11.8   Calculating the operating cash cycle

For businesses that buy and sell on credit, three ratios are required to calculate the OCC.

Activity 11.9

The financial statements of Freezeqwik Ltd, a distributor of frozen foods, for the year ended 31 December last year are set out below.

Income statement for the year ended 31 December last year

	£000	£000
Sales revenue		820
Cost of sales		
Opening inventories	142	
Purchases	568	
	710	
Closing inventories	(166)	(544)
Gross profit		276
Administration expenses		(120)
Distribution expenses		(95)
Operating profit		61
Financial expenses		(32)
Profit before taxation		29
Taxation		(7)
Profit for the year		22

Statement of financial position as at 31 December last year

	£000
Non-current assets	
Property, plant and equipment	
Premises at valuation	180
Fixtures and fittings at cost less depreciation	82
Motor vans at cost less depreciation	102
	364
Current assets	
Inventories	166
Trade receivables	264
Cash	24
	454
Total assets	818
Equity	
Ordinary share capital	300
Retained earnings	352
	652
Current liabilities	
Trade payables	159
Taxation	7
	166
Total equity and liabilities	818

All purchases and sales are on credit. There has been no change in the level of trade receivables or payables over the period.

Calculate the length of the OCC for the business and go on to suggest how the business may seek to reduce this period.

The OCC may be calculated as follows:

Number of days

Average inventories turnover period:

$$\frac{\text{(Opening inventories + Closing inventories)/2}}{\text{Cost of sales}} \times 365 = \frac{(142 + 166)/2}{544} \times 365 \qquad 103$$

Average settlement period for trade receivables:

$$\frac{\text{Trade receivables}}{\text{Credit sales}} \times 365 = \frac{264}{820} \times 365 \qquad\qquad 118$$

Average settlement period for trade payables:

$$\frac{\text{Trade payables}}{\text{Credit purchases}} \times 365 = \frac{159}{568} \times 365 \qquad\qquad (102)$$

OCC \underline{119}

The business can reduce the length of the OCC in a number of ways. The average inventories turnover period seems quite long. At present, average inventories held represent more than three months' sales requirements. Lowering the level of inventories held will reduce this. Similarly, the average settlement period for trade receivables seems long, at nearly four months' sales. Imposing tighter credit control, offering discounts, charging interest on overdue accounts and so on may reduce this. However, any policy decisions concerning inventories and trade receivables must take account of current trading conditions.

Extending the period of credit taken to pay suppliers could also reduce the OCC. However, for reasons that will be explained later, this option must be given careful consideration.

Real World 11.11 shows the average operating cash cycle for large European businesses.

REAL WORLD 11.11

Cycling along

The annual survey of working capital by REL Consulting and CFO Europe (see Real World 11.2 above) calculates the average operating cash cycle for the top 1,000 European businesses (excluding the financial sector). Comparative figures for the five-year period ending in 2007 are shown in Figure 11.9.

→

Real World 11.11 continued

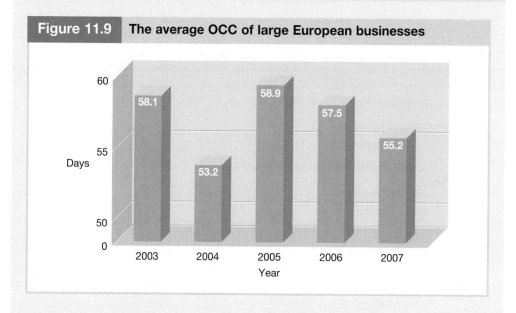

| Figure 11.9 | The average OCC of large European businesses |

The survey calculates the operating cash cycle using year-end figures for trade receivables, inventories and trade payables. We can see that there has been a slight improvement in 2007 compared to the two previous years.

Source: Compiled from information in 2008 REL/CFO European Working Capital Survey, www.relconsult.com.

Cash transmission

A business will normally wish to benefit from receipts from customers at the earliest opportunity. The benefit is immediate where payment is made in cash. However, when payment is made by cheque, there is normally a delay of three to four working days before the cheque can be cleared through the banking system. The business must therefore wait for this period before it can benefit from the amount paid in. In the case of a business that receives large amounts in the form of cheques, the opportunity cost of this delay can be significant.

To avoid this cost, a business could require payments to be made in cash. This is not usually very practical, mainly because of the risk of theft and/or the expense of conveying cash securely. Another option is to ask for payment to be made by standing order or by direct debit from the customer's bank account. This should ensure that the amount owing is always transferred from the bank account of the customer to the bank account of the business on the day that has been agreed.

It is also possible for funds to be transferred directly to a business's bank account. Customers can pay for items by using debit cards, which results in the appropriate account being instantly debited and the seller's bank account being instantly credited with the required amount. This method of payment is widely used by large retail businesses, and can be extended to other types of business.

Bank overdrafts

Bank overdrafts are simply bank current accounts that have a negative balance. They are a type of bank loan and can be a useful tool in managing the business's cash flow requirements.

Real World 11.12 shows how Indesit, a large white-goods manufacturer, managed to improve its cash flows through better working capital management.

REAL WORLD 11.12

Dash for cash

Despite an impressive working capital track record, a 50% plunge in profit at Indesit in 2005 led to the creation of a new three-year plan that meant an even stronger emphasis on cash generation. Operating cash flow was added to the incentive scheme for senior and middle managers, who subsequently released more cash from Indesit's already lean processes by 'attacking the areas that were somehow neglected', Crenna [the chief financial officer] says.

Hidden in the dark corners of the accounts-receivable department in the UK's after-sales service operation, for example, were a host of delinquent, albeit small, payments – in some cases overdue by a year or more. 'If you don't put a specific focus on these receivables, it's very easy for them to become neglected,' Crenna says. 'In theory, nobody worries about collecting £20. In reality, we were sitting on a huge amount of receivables, though each individual bill was for a small amount.'

More trapped cash was found in the company's spare-parts inventory. The inventory is worth around €30m today compared with around €40m three years ago. 'This was a good result that came just from paying the same level of attention to spare parts as to finished products,' Crenna says. In general, Indesit has been able to improve working capital performance through 'fine-tuning rather than launching epic projects'. Over the past two years, according to REL, Indesit has released €115m from its working capital processes.

Source: Karaian, J., 'Dash for Cash', *CFO Europe Magazine*, 8 July 2008, www.CFO.com.

Managing trade payables

Trade credit arises from the fact that most businesses buy their goods and service requirements on credit. In effect, suppliers are lending the business money, interest-free, on a short-term basis. Trade payables are the other side of the coin from trade receivables. One business's trade payable is another one's trade receivable, in respect of a particular transaction. Trade payables are an important source of finance for most businesses. They have been described as a 'spontaneous' source, as they tend to increase in line with the increase in the level of activity achieved by a business. Trade credit is widely regarded as a 'free' source of finance and, therefore, a good thing for a business to use. There may be real costs, however, associated with taking trade credit.

First, customers who take credit may not be as well treated as those who pay immediately. For example, when goods are in short supply, credit customers may receive lower priority when allocating the goods available. In addition, credit customers may be less favoured in terms of delivery dates or the provision of technical support services. Sometimes, the goods or services provided may be more costly if credit is required. However, in most industries, trade credit is the norm. As a result, the above costs will not apply except, perhaps, to customers that abuse the credit facilities. A business that purchases supplies on credit will normally have to incur additional administration and accounting costs in dealing with the scrutiny and payment of invoices, maintaining and updating payables accounts, and so on.

These points are not meant to imply that taking credit represents a net cost to a business. There are, of course, real benefits that can accrue. Provided that trade credit is not abused, it can represent a form of interest-free loan. It can be a much more convenient method of paying for goods and services than paying by cash, and during a period of inflation there will be an economic gain by paying later rather than sooner for goods and services purchased. For most businesses, these benefits will exceed the costs involved.

In some cases, delaying payment can be a sign of financial problems. One such example is given in **Real World 11.13**.

REAL WORLD 11.13

NHS waiting times   FT

The National Health Service is delaying paying bills and cutting orders for supplies as it tries to balance its books, according to the trade associations whose members supply the service with everything from scanners to diagnostic tests.

Ray Hodgkinson, director-general of the British Healthcare Trades Association, said that while the picture was highly variable 'some of our members are having real trouble getting money out of NHS trusts'.

Most had standing orders that said bills should be paid within 30 days, Mr Hodgkinson said. 'But some are not paying for 60 or 90 days and even longer. They are in breach of their standing orders and for a lot of our members who are small businesses this is creating problems with cash flow. There is no doubt there is slow payment on a significant scale.' . . .

Doris-Ann Williams, director-general of the British In-Vitro Diagnostics Association, whose members provide diagnostics supplies and tests, said: 'We are starting to see invoices not being paid and orders not being closed until the start of the new financial year [in April].

'All sorts of measures are being taken to try not to spend money in this financial year.'

Having seen orders dry up and bills not paid this time last year as the NHS headed for a £500m-plus financial deficit, she added that this was 'starting to seem like an annual event'.

Source: NHS paying bills late in struggle to balance books, say suppliers, ft.com (Timmins, N.), © The Financial Times Limited, 13 February 2007.

Taking advantage of cash discounts

Where a supplier offers a discount for prompt payment, the business should give careful consideration to the possibility of paying within the discount period. An example may be useful to illustrate the cost of forgoing possible discounts.

Example 11.4

Hassan Ltd takes 70 days to pay for goods from its supplier. To encourage prompt payment, the supplier has offered the business a 2 per cent discount if payment for goods is made within 30 days.

Hassan Ltd is not sure whether it is worth taking the discount offered.

If the discount is taken, payment could be made on the last day of the discount period (that is, the 30th day). However, if the discount is not taken, payment will be made after 70 days. This means that, by not taking the discount, the business will receive an extra 40 (that is, 70 − 30) days' credit. The cost of this extra credit to the business will be the 2 per cent discount forgone. If we annualise the cost of this discount forgone, we have:

$$365/40 \times 2\% = 18.3\%*$$

We can see that the annual cost of forgoing the discount is very high, and so it may be profitable for the business to pay the supplier within the discount period, even if it means that it will have to borrow to enable it to do so.

* This is an approximate annual rate. For the more mathematically minded, the precise rate is

$$([(1 + 2/98)^{9.125}] - 1) \times 100\% = 20.2\%$$

Controlling trade payables

To help monitor the level of trade credit taken, management can calculate the **average settlement period for trade payables**. This ratio is:

$$\text{Average settlement period for trade payables} = \frac{\text{Average trade payables}}{\text{Credit purchases}} \times 365$$

Once again, this provides an average figure, which could be misleading. A more informative approach would be to produce an ageing schedule for payables. This would look much the same as the ageing schedule for receivables described earlier in Example 11.3.

We saw earlier that delaying payment to suppliers may create problems for a business. **Real World 11.14**, however, describes how cash-strapped businesses may delay payments and still retain the support of its suppliers.

REAL WORLD 11.14

Credit stretch

According to Gavin Swindell, European managing director of REL, a research and consulting firm, there are 'win-win' ways of extending credit terms. He states:

'A lot of businesses aren't worried about getting paid in 40 or 45 days, but are more interested in the certainty of payment on a specific date.'

Jas Sahota, a partner in Deloitte's UK restructuring practice, says that three-month extensions are common, 'as long as the supplier can see that there is a plan'. In times of stress, he says, it's

Real World 11.14 continued

important to negotiate with only a handful of the most important partners – squeezing suppliers large and small only generates grief and distracts employees with lots of calls.

More fundamentally, the benefits of pulling the payables lever in isolation is 'questionable', notes Andrew Ashby, director of the working capital practice at KPMG in London, 'especially as the impact on the receivables balance is typically a lot more than the payables balance'.

Improving collections, such as achieving longer payment terms, relies on the strength of relationships built over time, notes Robert Hecht, a London-based managing director of turnaround consultancy AlixPartners. 'You can't wait for a crisis, and then expect suppliers to step up and be your best friends.'

Source: Karaian, J., 'Dash for Cash', *CFO Europe Magazine*, 8 July 2008, www.CFO.com.

SUMMARY

The main points of this chapter may be summarised as follows.

Working capital

- Working capital is the difference between current assets and current liabilities.
- That is,

  working capital = inventories + receivables + cash – payables – bank overdrafts.

- An investment in working capital cannot be avoided in practice – typically large amounts are involved.

Inventories

- There are costs of holding inventories, which include:
  - Lost interest.
  - Storage cost.
  - Insurance cost.
  - Obsolescence.
- There are also costs of not holding sufficient inventories, which include:
  - Loss of sales and customer goodwill.
  - Production dislocation.
  - Loss of flexibility – cannot take advantage of opportunities.
  - Reorder costs – low inventories imply more frequent ordering.
- Practical points on inventories management include:
  - Identify optimum order size – models can help with this.
  - Set inventories reorder levels.
  - Use forecasts.
  - Keep reliable inventories records.
  - Use accounting ratios (for example, inventories turnover period ratio).
  - Establish systems for security of inventories and authorisation.
  - Consider just-in-time (JIT) inventories management.

Trade receivables

- When assessing which customers should receive credit, the five Cs of credit can be used:
  - Capital.
  - Capacity.
  - Collateral.
  - Condition.
  - Character.
- The costs of allowing credit include:
  - Lost interest.
  - Lost purchasing power.
  - Costs of assessing customer creditworthiness.
  - Administration cost.
  - Bad debts.
  - Cash discounts (for prompt payment).
- The costs of denying credit include:
  - Loss of customer goodwill.
- Practical points on receivables management:
  - Establish a policy.
  - Assess and monitor customer creditworthiness.
  - Establish effective administration of receivables.
  - Establish a policy on bad debts.
  - Consider cash discounts.
  - Use financial ratios (for example, average settlement period for trade receivables ratio).
  - Use ageing summaries.

Cash

- The costs of holding cash include:
  - Lost interest.
  - Lost purchasing power.
- The costs of holding insufficient cash include:
  - Loss of supplier goodwill if unable to meet commitments on time.
  - Loss of opportunities.
  - Inability to claim cash discounts.
  - Costs of borrowing (should an obligation need to be met at short notice).
- Practical points on cash management:
  - Establish a policy.
  - Plan cash flows.
  - Make judicious use of bank overdraft finance – it can be cheap and flexible.
  - Use short-term cash surpluses profitably.
  - Bank frequently.
  - Operating cash cycle (for a wholesaler) = length of time from buying inventories to receiving cash from receivables less payables' payment period (in days).
  - Transmit cash promptly.
- An objective of working capital management is to limit the length of the operating cash cycle (OCC), subject to any risks that this may cause.

Trade payables

- The costs of taking credit include:
  - Higher price than purchases for immediate cash settlement.
  - Administrative costs.
  - Restrictions imposed by seller.

- The costs of not taking credit include:
  - Lost interest-free borrowing.
  - Lost purchasing power.
  - Inconvenience – paying at the time of purchase can be inconvenient.
- Practical points on payables management:
  - Establish a policy.
  - Exploit free credit as far as possible.
  - Use accounting ratios (for example, average settlement period for trade payables ratio).

→ **Key terms**

Working capital   p. 410
Lead time   p. 417
ABC system of inventories control
   p. 418
Economic order quantity (EOQ)   p. 419
Materials requirement planning (MRP) system   p. 422
Just-in-time (JIT) inventories management   p. 422

Five Cs of credit   p. 424
Cash discount   p. 428
Average settlement period for trade receivables   p. 429
Ageing schedule of trade receivables   p. 429
Operating cash cycle (OCC)   p. 434
Average settlement period for trade payables   p. 441

Further reading

If you would like to explore the topics covered in this chapter in more depth, we recommend the following books:

McLaney, E., *Business Finance: Theory and Practice*, 8th edn, Financial Times Prentice Hall, 2009, chapter 13.

Brealey, B., Myers, S. and Allen, F., *Corporate Finance*, 9th edn, McGraw-Hill, 2008, chapters 30 and 31.

Pike, R. and Neale, B., *Corporate Finance and Investment*, 5th edn, Prentice Hall, 2006, chapters 13 and 14.

Arnold, G., *Corporate Financial Management*, 3rd edn, Financial Times Prentice Hall, 2005, chapter 13.

REVIEW QUESTIONS

Answers to these questions can be found in Appendix C at the back of the book.

11.1 Tariq is the credit manager of Heltex plc. He is concerned that the pattern of monthly cash receipts from credit sales shows that credit collection is poor compared with budget. Heltex's sales director believes that Tariq is to blame for this situation, but Tariq insists that he is not. Why might Tariq not be to blame for the deterioration in the credit collection period?

11.2 How might each of the following affect the level of inventories held by a business?

(a) An increase in the number of production bottlenecks experienced by the business.
(b) A rise in the level of interest rates.
(c) A decision to offer customers a narrower range of products in the future.
(d) A switch of suppliers from an overseas business to a local business.
(e) A deterioration in the quality and reliability of bought-in components.

11.3 What are the reasons for holding inventories? Are these reasons different from the reasons for holding cash?

11.4 Identify the costs of holding:

(a) too little cash;
(b) too much cash.

EXERCISES

Exercises 11.4 to 11.8 are more advanced than 11.1 to 11.3. Those with coloured numbers have an answer in Appendix D at the back of the book. If you wish to try more exercises, visit the students' side of the Companion Website at www.pearsoned.co.uk/atrillmclaney.

11.1 Hercules Wholesalers Ltd has been particularly concerned with its liquidity position in recent months. The most recent income statement and statement of financial position (balance sheet) of the business are as follows:

Income statement for the year ended 31 December last year

	£000	£000
Sales revenue		452
Cost of sales		
Opening inventories	125	
Purchases	341	
	466	
Closing inventories	(143)	(323)
Gross profit		129
Expenses		(132)
Loss for the year		(3)

Statement of financial position as at 31 December last year

	£000
Non-current assets	
Property, plant and equipment	
Premises at valuation	280
Fixtures and fittings at cost less depreciation	25
Motor vehicles at cost less depreciation	52
	357
Current assets	
Inventories	143
Trade receivables	163
	306
Total assets	663
Equity	
Ordinary share capital	100
Retained earnings	158
	258
Non-current liabilities	
Borrowings – Loans	120
Current liabilities	
Trade payables	145
Borrowings – Bank overdraft	140
	285
Total equity and liabilities	663

The trade receivables and payables were maintained at a constant level throughout the year.

Required:

(a) Explain why Hercules Wholesalers Ltd is concerned about its liquidity position.

(b) Calculate the operating cash cycle for Hercules Wholesalers Ltd based on the information above. (Assume a 360-day year.)

(c) State what steps may be taken to improve the operating cash cycle of the business.

11.2 International Electric plc at present offers its customers 30 days' credit. Half the customers, by value, pay on time. The other half take an average of 70 days to pay. The business is considering offering a cash discount of 2 per cent to its customers for payment within 30 days.

The credit controller anticipates that half of the customers who now take an average of 70 days to pay (that is, a quarter of all customers) will pay in 30 days. The other half (the final quarter) will still take an average of 70 days to pay. The scheme will also reduce bad debts by £300,000 a year.

Annual sales revenue of £365m is made evenly throughout the year. At present the business has a large overdraft (£60m) with its bank at an interest cost of 12 per cent a year.

Required:

(a) Calculate the approximate equivalent annual percentage cost of a discount of 2 per cent, which reduces the time taken by credit customers to pay from 70 days to 30 days. (*Hint*: This part can be answered without reference to the narrative above.)

(b) Calculate the value of trade receivables outstanding under both the old and new schemes.

(c) How much will the scheme cost the business in discounts?

(d) Should the business go ahead with the scheme? State what other factors, if any, should be taken into account.

(e) Outline the controls and procedures that a business should adopt to manage the level of its trade receivables.

11.3 The managing director of Sparkrite Ltd, a trading business, has just received summary sets of financial statements for last year and this year:

Sparkrite Ltd
Income statements for years ended 30 September last year and this year

	Last year		This year	
	£000	£000	£000	£000
Sales revenue		1,800		1,920
Cost of sales				
Opening inventories	160		200	
Purchases	1,120		1,175	
	1,280		1,375	
Closing inventories	(200)		(250)	
		(1,080)		(1,125)
Gross profit		720		795
Expenses		(680)		(750)
Profit for the year		40		45

Statements of financial position (balance sheets) as at
30 September last year and this year

	Last year	This year
	£000	£000
Non-current assets	950	930
Current assets		
Inventories	200	250
Trade receivables	375	480
Bank	4	2
	579	732
Total assets	1,529	1,662
Equity		
Fully paid £1 ordinary shares	825	883
Retained earnings	509	554
	1,334	1,437
Current liabilities	195	225
Total equity and liabilities	1,529	1,662

The finance director has expressed concern at the increase in inventories and trade receivables levels.

Required:
(a) Show, by using the data given, how you would calculate ratios that could be used to measure inventories and trade receivables levels during last year and this year.
(b) Discuss the ways in which the management of Sparkrite Ltd could exercise control over:
  1 inventories levels;
  2 trade receivables levels.

11.4 Your superior, the general manager of Plastics Manufacturers Limited, has recently been talking to the chief buyer of Plastic Toys Limited, which manufactures a wide range of toys for young children. At present, Plastic Toys is considering changing its supplier of plastic granules and has offered to buy its entire requirement of 2,000 kg a month from you at the going market rate, provided that you will grant it three months' credit on its purchases. The following information is available:

1 Plastic granules sell for £10 a kg, variable costs are £7 a kg, and fixed costs £2 a kg.
2 Your own business is financially strong, and has sales revenue of £15 million a year. For the foreseeable future it will have surplus capacity, and it is actively looking for new outlets.
3 Extracts from Plastic Toys' financial statements:

	Year 1	Year 2	Year 3
	£000	£000	£000
Sales revenue	800	980	640
Profit before interest and tax	100	110	(150)
Capital employed	600	650	575

	Year 1	Year 2	Year 3
Current assets	£000	£000	£000
Inventories	200	220	320
Trade receivables	140	160	160
	340	380	480
Current liabilities			
Trade payables	180	190	220
Overdraft	100	150	310
	280	340	530
Working capital	60	40	(50)

Required:

(a) Write some short notes suggesting sources of information that you would use to assess the creditworthiness of potential customers who are unknown to you. You should critically evaluate each source of information.

(b) Describe the accounting controls that you would use to monitor the level of your business's trade receivables.

(c) Advise your general manager on the acceptability of the proposal. You should give your reasons and do any calculations you consider necessary. (*Hint*: To answer this question you must weigh the costs of administration and cash discounts against the savings in bad debts and interest charges.)

11.5 Mayo Computers Ltd has annual sales of £20m. Bad debts amount to £0.1m a year. All sales made by the business are on credit and, at present, credit terms are negotiable by the customer. On average, the settlement period for trade receivables is 60 days. Trade receivables are financed by an overdraft bearing a 14 per cent rate of interest per year. The business is currently reviewing its credit policies to see whether more efficient and profitable methods could be employed. Only one proposal has so far been put forward concerning the management of trade credit.

The credit control department has proposed that customers should be given a 2.5 per cent discount if they pay within 30 days. For those who do not pay within this period, a maximum of 50 days' credit should be given. The credit department believes that 60 per cent of customers will take advantage of the discount by paying at the end of the discount period. The remainder will pay at the end of 50 days. The credit department believes that bad debts can be effectively eliminated by adopting the above policies and by employing stricter credit investigation procedures, which will cost an additional £20,000 a year. The credit department is confident that these new policies will not result in any reduction in sales revenue.

Required:

Calculate the net annual cost (savings) to the business of abandoning its existing credit policies and adopting the proposals of the credit control department. (*Hint*: To answer this question you must weigh the costs of administration and cash discounts against the savings in bad debts and interest charges.)

11.6 Boswell Enterprises Ltd is reviewing its trade credit policy. The business, which sells all of its goods on credit, has estimated that sales revenue for the forthcoming year will be £3m under the existing policy. Credit customers representing 30 per cent of trade receivables are expected to pay one month after being invoiced and 70 per cent are expected to pay two months after being invoiced. These estimates are in line with previous years' figures.

At present, no cash discounts are offered to customers. However, to encourage prompt payment, the business is considering giving a 2.5 per cent cash discount to credit customers who pay in one month or less. Given this incentive, the business expects credit customers accounting for 60 per cent of trade receivables to pay one month after being invoiced and those accounting for 40 per cent of trade receivables to pay two months after being invoiced. The business believes that the introduction of a cash discount policy will prove attractive to some customers and will lead to a 5 per cent increase in total sales revenue.

Irrespective of the trade credit policy adopted, the gross profit margin of the business will be 20 per cent for the forthcoming year and three months' inventories will be held. Fixed monthly expenses of £15,000 and variable expenses (excluding discounts) equivalent to 10 per cent of sales revenue will be incurred and will be paid one month in arrears. Trade payables will be paid in arrears and will be equal to two months' cost of sales. The business will hold a fixed cash balance of £140,000 throughout the year, whichever trade credit policy is adopted. Ignore taxation.

Required:

(a) Calculate the investment in working capital at the end of the forthcoming year under:
   (i) the existing policy;
   (ii) the proposed policy.

(b) Calculate the expected profit for the forthcoming year under:
   (i) the existing policy;
   (ii) the proposed policy.

(c) Advise the business as to whether it should implement the proposed policy.
   (*Hint*: The investment in working capital will be made up of inventories, trade receivables and cash, *less* trade payables and any unpaid expenses at the year end.)

11.7 Delphi plc has recently decided to enter the expanding market for minidisc players. The business will manufacture the players and sell them to small TV and hi-fi specialists, medium-sized music stores and large retail chain stores. The new product will be launched next February and predicted sales revenue for the product from each customer group for February and the expected rate of growth for subsequent months are as follows:

Customer type	February sales revenue £000	Monthly compound sales revenue growth %	Credit period months
TV and hi-fi specialists	20	4	1
Music stores	30	6	2
Retail chain stores	40	8	3

The business is concerned about the financing implications of launching the new product, as it is already experiencing liquidity problems. In addition, it is concerned that the credit control department will find it difficult to cope. This is a new market for the business and there are likely to be many new customers who will have to be investigated for creditworthiness.

Workings should be in £000's and calculations made to one decimal place only.

Required:

(a) Prepare an ageing schedule of the monthly trade receivables balance relating to the new product for each of the first four months of the new product's life, and comment on the results. The schedule should analyse the trade receivables outstanding according to customer type. It should also indicate, for each customer type, the relevant percentage outstanding in relation to the total amount outstanding for each month.

(b) Identify and discuss the factors that should be taken into account when evaluating the creditworthiness of the new business customers.

11.8 Goliath plc is a retail business operating in Ireland. The most recent financial statements of the business are as follows:

Income statement for the year to 31 May

	£000	£000
Sales revenue		2,400.0
Cost of sales		
Opening inventories	550.0	
Purchases	1,450.0	
	2,000.0	
Closing inventories	(560.0)	(1,440.0)
Gross profit		960.0
Administration expenses		(300.0)
Selling expenses		(436.0)
Operating profit		224.0
Interest payable		(40.0)
Profit before taxation		184.0
Taxation (25%)		(46.0)
Profit for the period		138.0

Statement of financial position as at 31 May

	£000	£000
Non-current assets		
Property, plant and equipment		
Machinery and equipment at cost	424.4	
Accumulated depreciation	(140.8)	283.6
Motor vehicles at cost	308.4	
Accumulated depreciation	(135.6)	172.8
		456.4
Current assets		
Inventories at cost		560.0
Trade receivables		565.0
Cash at bank		36.4
		1,161.4
Total assets		1,617.8
Equity		
£1 ordinary shares		200.0
Retained earnings		520.8
		720.8
Non-current liabilities		
Borrowings – Loan notes		400.0
Current liabilities		
Trade payables		451.0
Taxation		46.0
		497.0
Total equity and liabilities		1,617.8

All sales and purchases are made on credit.

The business is considering whether to grant extended credit facilities to its customers. It has been estimated that increasing the settlement period for trade receivables by a further 20 days will increase the turnover of the business by 10 per cent. However, inventories will have to be increased by 15 per cent to cope with the increased demand. It is estimated that purchases will have to rise to £1,668,000 during the next year as a result of these changes. To finance the increase in inventories and trade receivables, the business will increase the settlement period taken for suppliers by 15 days and use a loan facility bearing a 10 per cent rate of interest for the remaining balance.

If the policy is implemented, bad debts are likely to increase by £120,000 a year and administration costs will rise by 15 per cent.

Required:

(a) Calculate the increase or decrease to each of the following that will occur in the forthcoming year if the proposed policy is implemented:
   (1) operating cash cycle (based on year-end figures)
   (2) net investment in inventories, trade receivables and trade payables
   (3) net profit after taxation.
(b) Should the business implement the proposed policy? Give reasons for your conclusion.

Appendix A
Glossary of key terms

ABC system of inventories control A method of applying different levels of inventories control, based on the value of each category of inventory. *p. 418*

Absorption costing A method of costing in which a 'fair share' of the total manufacturing/service provision overhead cost is included when calculating the cost of a particular product or service. *p. 98*

Accounting rate of return (ARR) The average profit from an investment, expressed as a percentage of the average investment made. *p. 261*

Activity-based budgeting (ABB) A system of budgeting based on the philosophy of activity-based costing (ABC). *p. 201*

Activity-based costing (ABC) A technique for more accurately relating overheads to specific production or provision of a service. It is based on acceptance of the fact that overheads do not just occur but are caused by activities, such as holding products in stores, which 'drive' the costs. *p. 138*

Adverse variance A difference between planned and actual performance, where the difference will cause the actual profit to be lower than the budgeted one. *p. 223*

Ageing schedule of trade receivables A report analysing receivables into categories, according to the length of time outstanding. *p. 429*

Average settlement period for trade payables The average time taken for a business to pay its trade payables (creditors). *p. 441*

Average settlement period for trade receivables The average time taken for trade receivables (debtors) to pay the amounts owing to a business. *p. 429*

Balanced scorecard A framework for translating the aims and objectives of a business into a series of key performance measures and targets. *p. 334*

Batch costing A technique for identifying full cost, where the production of many types of goods and services, particularly goods, involves producing a batch of identical or nearly identical units of output, but where each batch is distinctly different from other batches. *p. 119*

Behavioural aspects of budgetary control The effect on people's attitudes and behaviour of the various aspects of using budgets as the basis of exercising control over performance. *p. 242*

Benchmarking Identifying a successful business, or part of a business, and measuring the effectiveness of one's own business by comparison with this standard. *p. 153*

Break-even analysis Deducing the break-even point of some activity by analysing the relationship between cost, volume and revenue. *p. 60*

Break-even chart A graphical representation of the cost and sales revenue of some activity, at various levels, which enables the break-even point to be identified. *p. 61*

Break-even point (BEP) A level of activity where revenue will exactly equal total cost, so there is neither profit nor loss. *p. 61*

Budget A financial plan for the short term, typically one year. *p. 176*

Budget committee A group of managers formed to supervise and take responsibility for the budget-setting process. *p. 186*

Budget holder An individual responsible for a particular budget. *p. 192*

Budget officer An individual, often an accountant, appointed to carry out, or take immediate responsibility for having carried out, the tasks of the budget committee. *p. 186*

Budgetary control Using the budget as a yardstick against which the effectiveness of actual performance may be assessed. *p. 239*

Cash discount A reduction in the amount due for goods or services sold on credit in return for prompt payment. *p. 428*

Committed cost A cost incurred that has not yet been paid, but which must, under some existing contract or obligation, be paid. *p. 44*

Common cost Cost that relates to more than one business segment. *p. 96*

Comparability The requirement that items which are basically the same should be treated in the same manner for measurement and reporting purposes. Lack of comparability will limit the usefulness of accounting information. *p. 18*

Compensating variances The situation that exists when two variances, both caused by the same factor, one adverse and the other favourable, are of equal size, and therefore cancel each other out. *p. 238*

Competitor analysis An examination of information relating to competitors to find out what strategies and plans they have developed, how they may react to the plans that the business has developed, and whether they have the capability to pose a serious threat. *p. 319*

Continual (or rolling) budget A budgeting system that continually updates budgets so that there is always a budget for a full planning period. *p. 180*

Contribution margin ratio The contribution from an activity expressed as a percentage of the sales revenue. *p. 67*

Contribution per unit Sales revenue per unit less variable cost per unit. *p. 66*

Control Compelling events to conform to plan. *p. 177*

Controllable cost A cost that is the responsibility of a specific manager. *p. 374*

Cost The amount of resources, usually measured in monetary terms, sacrificed to achieve a particular objective. *p. 38*

Cost allocation Assigning cost to cost centres according to the amount of cost that has been incurred in each centre. *p. 112*

Cost apportionment   Dividing cost between cost centres on a basis that is considered to reflect fairly the cost incurred in each centre. *p. 112*

Cost behaviour   The manner in which cost alters with changes in the level of activity. *p. 99*

Cost centre   Some area, object, person or activity for which elements of cost are separately collected. *p. 110*

Cost driver   An activity that causes cost. *p. 138*

Cost of capital   The cost to a business of the finance needed to fund an investment. *p. 277*

Cost-plus pricing   An approach to pricing output that is based on full cost plus a percentage profit loading. *p. 121*

Cost pool   The sum of the overhead cost associated with a particular support activity. *p. 138*

Cost unit   The objective for which the cost is being deduced, usually a product or service. *p. 96*

Customer profitability analysis (CPA)   An assessment of the profitability to the business of individual customers, or types of customer. *p. 323*

Direct cost   A cost that can be identified with specific cost units, to the extent that the effect of the cost can be measured in respect of each particular unit of output. *p. 96*

Direct labour efficiency variance   The difference between the actual direct labour hours worked and the number of direct labour hours according to the flexed budget (budgeted direct labour hours for the actual output). This figure is multiplied by the budgeted direct labour rate for one hour. *p. 227*

Direct labour rate variance   The difference between the actual cost of the direct labour hours worked and the direct labour cost allowed (actual direct labour hours worked at the budgeted labour rate). *p. 227*

Direct materials price variance   The difference between the actual cost of the direct material used and the direct materials cost allowed (actual quantity of material used at the budgeted direct material cost). *p. 226*

Direct materials usage variance   The difference between the actual quantity of direct materials used and the quantity of direct materials according to the flexed budget (budgeted usage for actual output). This quantity is multiplied by the budgeted direct materials cost for one unit of the direct materials. *p. 225*

Discount factor   The rate applied to future cash flows to derive the present value of those cash flows. *p. 276*

Discretionary budget   A budget based on a sum allocated at the discretion of top management. *p. 192*

Divisions   Business segments, often organised along geographical and/or product lines, through which large businesses are managed. *p. 367*

Economic order quantity (EOQ)   The quantity of inventories that should be purchased in order to minimise total inventories ordering and carrying costs. *p. 419*

Economic value added (EVA®)   A measure of economic, as opposed to accounting, profit. It is said to be more useful than accounting profit as a measure of business performance because it takes full account of the cost of financing the business. *p. 350*

Economies of scale   Cost savings per unit that result from undertaking a large volume of activities; they are due to factors such as division and specialisation of labour, and discounts from bulk buying. *p. 73*

Elasticity of demand   The extent to which the level of demand alters with changes in price. *p. 155*

Expected net present value (ENPV)   A weighted average of the possible present value outcomes, where the probabilities associated with each outcome are used as weights. *p. 296*

Favourable variance   A difference between planned and actual performance where the difference will cause the actual profit to be higher than the budgeted one. *p. 223*

Feedback control   A control device where actual performance is compared with planned performance, and where action is taken to deal with possible future divergences between them. *p. 219*

Feedforward control   A control device where forecast future performance is compared with planned performance, and where action is taken to deal with divergences between them. *p. 219*

Financial accounting   The measuring and reporting of accounting information for external users (those users other than the managers of the business). *p. 29*

Five Cs of credit   A checklist of factors to be taken into account when assessing the creditworthiness of a customer. *p. 424*

Fixed cost   A cost that stays the same when changes occur to the volume of activity. *p. 56*

Fixed overhead spending variance   The difference between the actual fixed overhead cost and the fixed overhead cost, according to the flexed (and the original) budget. *p. 228*

Flexible budget   A budget that is adjusted to reflect the actual level of output achieved. *p. 222*

Flexing the budget   Revising the budget to what it would have been had the planned level of output been different. *p. 221*

Forecast   A prediction of future outcomes or of the future state of the environment. *p. 179*

Free cash flows   The cash flows generated by the business that are available to the shareholders and long-term lenders. This is the net cash flow from operating activities, less tax and funds laid out on additional non-current assets. *p. 344*

Full cost   The total amount of resources, usually measured in monetary terms, sacrificed to achieve a particular objective. *pp. 94, 391*

Full cost (cost-plus) pricing   Pricing output on the basis of its full cost, normally with a loading for profit. *pp. 121, 163*

Full costing   Deducing the total direct and indirect (overhead) costs of pursuing some activity or objective. *p. 95*

Historic cost   What an asset cost when it was originally acquired. *p. 38*

Ideal standards   Standards that assume perfect operating conditions where there is no inefficiency due to lost production time, defects, and so on. The objective of setting ideal standards is to encourage employees to strive towards excellence. *p. 245*

Incremental budgeting   Constructing budgets on the basis of what happened in the previous period, with some adjustment for expected changes in the forthcoming budget period. *p. 192*

Indirect cost (or overheads)   All cost except direct cost: that is, those which cannot be directly measured in respect of each particular unit of output. *p. 96*

Inflation   An increase in the general price of goods and services resulting in a corresponding decline in the purchasing power of the currency. *p. 272*

Internal rate of return (IRR)   The discount rate for a project that will have the effect of producing a zero NPV. *p. 279*

Investment centre   Some area or activity whose manager or activity is responsible and accountable for the profit generated and capital invested. *p. 367*

Irrelevant cost   A cost that is not relevant to a particular decision. *p. 39*

Job costing   A technique for identifying the full cost per unit of output, where that output is not similar to other units of output. *p. 98*

Just-in-time (JIT) inventories management   A system of inventories management that aims to have supplies delivered to production just in time for their required use. *p. 422*

***Kaizen* costing**   An approach to cost control where an attempt is made to control cost by trying continually to make cost savings, often only small ones, from one time period to the next. *p. 153*

Key performance indicators (KPIs)   Financial and/or non-financial measures that reflect the critical success factors of a business. *p. 24*

Lead time   The time lag between placing an order for goods or services and their delivery. *p. 417*

Lean manufacturing   An approach to manufacturing that involves a systematic attempt to identify and eliminate waste in the production process, which may arise from storing excess materials, excess production, delays, defects, and so on. *p. 329*

Learning curve   The tendency for people to carry out tasks more quickly as they become more experienced in doing them. *p. 246*

Limiting factor   Some aspect of the business (for example, lack of sales demand) that will prevent it achieving its objectives to the maximum extent. *p. 179*

Management accounting   The measuring and reporting of accounting information for the managers of a business. *p. 15*

Management accounting information system   The system used within a business to identify, record, analyse and report accounting information. *p. 21*

Management by exception   A system of control, based on a comparison of planned and actual performance, that allows managers to focus on areas of poor performance rather than dealing with areas where performance is satisfactory. *p. 184*

Margin of safety The extent to which the planned level of output or sales lies above the break-even point. *p. 67*

Marginal analysis The activity of decision making through analysing variable cost and revenues, ignoring fixed cost. *p. 78*

Marginal cost The addition to total cost that will be incurred by making/providing one more unit of output. *p. 78*

Marginal cost pricing Pricing output on the basis of its marginal cost, normally with a loading for profit. *p. 166*

Market prices (as transfer prices) Using a price set by the market outside the business as a suitable price for internal, inter-divisional transfers. *p. 389*

Master budget A summary of the individual budgets, usually consisting of a budgeted income statement, a budgeted balance sheet and a cash budget. *p. 181*

Materiality The requirement that material information should be disclosed to users of financial reports. *p. 18*

Materials requirement planning (MRP) system A computer-based system of inventories control that schedules the timing of deliveries of bought-in parts and materials to coincide with production requirements to meet demand. *p. 422*

Mission statement A brief statement setting out the aims of the business. *p. 7*

Negotiated prices Transfer prices that are derived as a result of negotiation between managers of the divisions concerned, possibly with the involvement of the business's central management as well. *p. 391*

Net present value (NPV) A method of investment appraisal based on the present value of all relevant cash flows associated with the project. *p. 269*

Non-controllable cost A cost for which a specific manager is not held responsible. *p. 374*

Non-operating profit variances Differences between budgeted and actual performance which do not lead directly to differences between budgeted and actual operating profit. *p. 235*

Objective probabilities Probabilities based on information gathered from past experience. *p. 299*

Operating cash cycle (OCC) The period between the outlay of cash to purchase supplies and the ultimate receipt of cash from the sale of goods. *p. 434*

Operating gearing (operational gearing) The relationship between the total fixed and the total variable costs for some activity. *p. 70*

Opportunity cost The cost incurred when one course of action prevents an opportunity to derive some benefit from another course of action. *p. 38*

Outlay cost A cost that involves the spending of money or some other transfer of assets. *p. 40*

Outsourcing Subcontracting activities to (sourcing goods or services from) outside organisations. *p. 82*

Overhead absorption (recovery) rate The rate at which overheads are charged to cost units (jobs), usually in a job costing system. *p. 101*

Overheads (or indirect cost) Any cost except a direct cost; a cost that cannot be directly measured in respect of each particular unit of output. *p. 96*

Past cost A cost that has been incurred in the past. *p. 40*

Payback period (PP) The time taken for the initial investment in a project to be repaid from the net cash inflows of the project. *p. 265*

Penetration pricing Setting prices at a level low enough to encourage wide market acceptance of a product or service. *p. 168*

Periodic budget A budget developed on a one-off basis to cover a particular planning period. *p. 180*

Position analysis A step in the strategic planning process in which the business assesses its present position in the light of the commercial and economic environment in which it operates. *p. 8*

Post-completion audit A review of the performance of an investment project to see whether actual performance matched planned performance and whether any lessons can be drawn from the way in which the investment was carried out. *p. 306*

Practical standards Standards that do not assume perfect operating conditions. Although they demand a high level of efficiency, account is taken of possible lost production time, defects, and so on. They are designed to be challenging yet achievable. *p. 245*

Price skimming Setting prices at a high level to make the maximum profit from the product or service before the price is lowered to attract the next segment of the market. *p. 169*

Process costing A technique for deriving the full cost per unit of output, where the units of output are exactly similar or it is reasonable to treat them as being so. *p. 96*

Product cost centre Some area, object, person or activity for which cost is separately collected, in which cost units have cost added. *p. 111*

Profit centre Some area, object, person or activity for which its revenues and expenses are compared to derive a profit figure, for which the manager is held accountable. *p. 367*

Profit–volume (PV) chart A graphical representation of the contributions (revenue less variable cost) of some activity, at various levels, which enables the break-even point, and the profit at various activity levels, to be identified. *p. 72*

Quality costs The cost of establishing procedures which promote the quality of output, either by preventing quality problems in the first place or by dealing with them when they occur. *p. 152*

Relevance The ability of accounting information to influence decisions. Relevance is regarded as a key characteristic of useful accounting information. *p. 17*

Relevant cost A cost that is relevant to a particular decision. *pp. 39, 283*

Relevant range The range of volume of activities that a particular business is expected to operate within. *p. 74*

Reliability The requirement that accounting should be free from material error or bias. Reliability is regarded as a key characteristic of useful accounting information. *p. 17*

Residual income (RI)   A divisional performance measure. The operating profit of a division, less an interest charge based on the business's investment in the division. *p. 379*

Return on investment (ROI)   A divisional performance measure. The operating profit of a division expressed as a percentage of the business's investment in the division. *p. 376*

Risk   The extent and likelihood that what is estimated to occur will not actually occur. *p. 270*

Risk-adjusted discount rate   A discount rate applied to investment projects that is increased (decreased) in the face of increased (decreased) risk. *p. 302*

Risk premium   An extra amount of return required from an investment, owing to a perceived level of risk. The greater the perceived risk, the larger the required risk premium. *p. 272*

Rolling (or continual) budget   A budgeting system which continually updates budgets so that there is always a budget for a full planning period. *p. 180*

Sales price variance   The difference between the actual sales revenue figure for the period and the sales revenue figure as shown in the flexed budget. *p. 225*

Sales volume variance   The difference between the operating profit as shown in the original budget, and the operating profit as shown in the flexed budget for the period. *p. 223*

Scenario building   Creating a model of a business decision, usually on a computer spreadsheet, enabling the decision maker to look at the effect of different assumptions on the decision outcome. *p. 295*

Semi-fixed (semi-variable) cost   A cost that has an element of both fixed and variable cost. *p. 59*

Sensitivity analysis   An examination of the key variables affecting a project, to see how changes in each input might influence the outcome. *p. 292*

Service cost centre   Some area, object, person or activity for which cost is collected separately, in which cost units do not have cost added, because service cost centres only render services to product cost services and to other service cost centres. *p. 112*

Shareholder value analysis (SVA)   Method of measuring and managing business value based on the long-term cash flows generated. *p. 344*

Standard quantities and costs   Planned quantities and costs (or revenues) for individual units of input or output. Standards are the building blocks used to produce the budget. *p. 244*

Stepped fixed cost   A fixed cost that does not remain fixed over all levels of output but which changes in steps as a threshold level of output is reached. *p. 58*

Strategic management   The process of setting a course to achieve the business's objectives, taking account of the commercial and economic environment in which the business operates. *p. 6*

Subjective probabilities   Probabilities based on opinion rather than past data. *p. 301*

Sunk cost   A cost that has been incurred in the past; the same as a past cost. *p. 44*

SWOT analysis   A framework in which many businesses set a position analysis. Here the business lists its strengths, weaknesses, opportunities and threats. *p. 8*

Target costing   Where the business starts with the projected selling price and from it deduces the target cost per unit which must be met to enable the business to meet its profit objectives. *p. 151*

Total cost   The sum of the variable and fixed costs of pursuing some activity. *p. 100*

Total direct labour variance   The difference between the actual direct labour cost and the direct labour cost according to the flexed budget (budgeted direct labour hours for the actual output). *p. 227*

Total direct materials variance   The difference between the actual direct materials cost and the direct materials cost according to the flexed budget. *p. 225*

Total life-cycle costing   Paying attention to all of the cost that will be incurred during the entire life of a product or service. *p. 150*

Transfer pricing   The activity of setting prices at which products or services will be transferred from one division of the business to another division of the same business. *p. 386*

Understandability   The requirement that accounting information should be understood by those for whom the information is primarily compiled. Lack of understandability will limit the usefulness of accounting information. *p. 18*

Value chain analysis   Analysing each activity undertaken by a business to identify any that do not add value to the output of goods or services. *p. 330*

Value drivers   The factors that are seen in shareholder value analysis as being key in generating shareholder value. *p. 334*

Variable cost   A cost that varies according to the volume of activity. *pp. 56, 390*

Variable costing   A method of costing in which only that element of cost that varies with output are included in the product cost. *p. 123*

Variance   The financial effect, usually on the budgeted profit, of the particular factor under consideration being more or less than budgeted. *p. 223*

Working capital   Current assets less current liabilities. *p. 410*

Zero-base budgeting (ZBB)   An approach to budgeting, based on the philosophy that all spending needs to be justified annually and that each budget should start as a clean sheet. *p. 193*

Appendix B

Solutions to self-assessment questions

Chapter 2

2.1 **JB Limited**

(a)

	£	
Material M1		
400 × 3 @ £5.50	6,600	The original cost is irrelevant since any inventories used will need to be replaced
Material P2		
400 × 2 @ £2.00 (that is, £3.60 – £1.60)	1,600	The best alternative use of this material is as a substitute for P4 – an effective opportunity cost of £2.00/kg
Part number 678		
400 × 1 @ £50	20,000	
Labour		
Skilled 400 × 5 @ £12	24,000	The effective cost is £12/hour
Semi-skilled 400 × 5 @ £10	20,000	
Overheads	3,200	It is only the additional cost which is relevant; the method of apportioning total overheads is not relevant
Total relevant cost	75,400	
Potential revenue		
400 @ £200	80,000	

Clearly, on the basis of the information available it would be beneficial for the business to undertake the contract.

(b) There are many possible answers to this part of the question, including:

- If material P2 had not already been held, it may be that it would not have been possible to buy it in and still leave the contract as a beneficial one. In this case the business may be unhappy about accepting a price under the particular conditions that apply, which could not be accepted under other conditions.
- Will the replacement for the skilled worker be able to do the normal work of that person to the necessary standard?
- Is JB Limited confident that the additional semi-skilled employee can be made redundant at the end of this contract without cost to the business?

Chapter 3

3.1   Khan Ltd

(a) The break-even point, if only the Alpha service were rendered, would be:

$$\frac{\text{Fixed costs}}{\text{Sales revenue per unit} - \text{Variable cost per unit}} = \frac{£40,000}{£30 - £(15 + 6)} = 4,445 \text{ units (a year)}$$

(Strictly it is 4,444.44 but 4,445 is the smallest number of units of the service that must be rendered to avoid a loss.)

(b)

	Alpha	Beta	Gamma
Selling price (£/unit)	30	39	20
Variable materials (£/unit)	(15)	(18)	(10)
Variable production costs (£/unit)	(6)	(10)	(5)
Contribution (£/unit)	9	11	5
Staff time (hr/unit)	2	3	1
Contribution/staff hour	£4.50	£3.67	£5.00
Order of priority	2nd	3rd	1st

(c)

	Hours		Contribution £
Render:			
5,000 Gamma using	5,000	generating (that is, 5,000 × £5 =)	25,000
2,500 Alpha using	5,000	generating (that is, 2,500 × £9 =)	22,500
	10,000		47,500
		Less Fixed costs	40,000
		Profit	7,500

This leaves a demand for 500 units of Alpha and 2,000 units of Beta unsatisfied.

Chapter 4

4.1   Hector and Co. Ltd

(a) Job-costing basis

			£
Materials:	Metal wire	1,000 × 2 × £2.20*	4,400
	Fabric	1,000 × 0.5 × £1.00*	500
Labour:	Skilled	1,000 × (10/60) × £12.00	2,000
	Unskilled	1,000 × (5/60) × £7.50	625
Indirect cost		1,000 × (15/60) × (50,000/12,500)	1,000
Total cost			8,525
Add Profit loading		12.5% thereof	1,066
Total tender price			9,591

* In the traditional approach to full costing, historic costs of materials tend to be used. It would not necessarily have been incorrect to used the 'relevant' (opportunity) costs here.

(b) Minimum contract price (relevant cost basis)

			£
Materials:	Metal wire	1,000 × 2 × £2.50 (replacement cost)	5,000
	Fabric	1,000 × 0.5 × £0.40 (scrap value)	200
Labour:	Skilled	(there is no effective cost of skilled staff)	–
	Unskilled	1,000 × 5/60 × £7.50	625
Minimum tender price			5,825

The difference between the two prices is partly that the relevant costing approach tends to look to the future, partly that it considers opportunity costs, and partly that the job-costing basis total has a profit loading.

Chapter 5

5.1   Psilis Ltd

(a) Full cost (present basis)

	Basic £		Super £	
Direct labour (all £10/hour)	40.00	(4 hours)	60.00	(6 hours)
Direct material	15.00		20.00	
Overheads	18.20	(£4.55* × 4)	27.30	(£4.55* × 6)
	73.20		107.30	

* Total direct labour hours worked = (40,000 × 4) + (10,000 × 6) = 220,000 hours. Overhead recovery rate = £1,000,000/220,000 = £4.55 per direct labour hour.

Thus the selling prices are currently:

Basic: £73.20 + 25% = £91.50
Super: £107.30 + 25% = £134.13

(b) Full cost (activity cost basis)
Here, the cost of each cost-driving activity is apportioned between total production of the two products.

Activity	Cost £000	Basis of apportionment	Basic £000		Super £000	
Machine set-ups	280	Number of set-ups	56	(20/100)	224	(80/100)
Quality inspection	220	Number of inspections	55	(500/2,000)	165	(1,500/2,000)
Sales order processing	240	Number of orders processed	72	(1,500/5,000)	168	(3,500/5,000)
General production	260	Machine hours	182	(350/500)	78	(150/500)
Total	1,000		365		635	

The overheads per unit are:

$$\text{Basic:} \quad \frac{£365,000}{40,000} = £9.13$$

$$\text{Super:} \quad \frac{£635,000}{10,000} = £63.50$$

Thus, on an activity basis the full costs are as follows:

	Basic £		Super £	
Direct labour (all £10/hour)	40.00	(4 hours)	60.00	(6 hours)
Direct material	15.00		20.00	
Overheads	9.13		63.50	
Full cost	64.13		143.50	
Current selling price	£91.50		£134.13	

(c) It seems that the Supers are being sold for less than they cost to produce. If the price cannot be increased, there is a very strong case for abandoning this product. At the same time, the Basics are very profitable to the extent that it may be worth considering lowering the price to attract more sales revenue.

The fact that the overhead costs can be related to activities and, more specifically, to products does not mean that abandoning Super production would lead to immediate overhead cost savings. For example, it may not be possible or desirable to dismiss machine-setting staff overnight. It would certainly rarely be possible to release factory space occupied by machine setters and make immediate cost savings. Nevertheless, in the medium term it is possible to avoid these costs, and it may be sensible to do so.

Chapter 6

6.1   Antonio Ltd

(a) (1) Raw materials inventories budget for the six months ending 31 December (physical quantities):

	July Units	Aug Units	Sept Units	Oct Units	Nov Units	Dec Units
Opening inventories (current month's production)	500	600	600	700	750	750
Purchases (balance figure)	600	600	700	750	750	750
	1,100	1,200	1,300	1,450	1,500	1,500
Issues to production (from question)	(500)	(600)	(600)	(700)	(750)	(750)
Closing inventories (next month's production)	600	600	700	750	750	750

Raw material inventories budget for the six months ending 31 December (in financial terms), that is, the physical quantities × £8:

	July £	Aug £	Sept £	Oct £	Nov £	Dec £
Opening inventories	4,000	4,800	4,800	5,600	6,000	6,000
Purchases	4,800	4,800	5,600	6,000	6,000	6,000
	8,800	9,600	10,400	11,600	12,000	12,000
Issues to production	(4,000)	(4,800)	(4,800)	(5,600)	(6,000)	(6,000)
Closing inventories	4,800	4,800	5,600	6,000	6,000	6,000

(2) Trade payables budget for the six months ending 31 December:

	July £	Aug £	Sept £	Oct £	Nov £	Dec £
Opening balance (current month's payment)	4,000	4,800	4,800	5,600	6,000	6,000
Purchases (from raw materials inventories budget)	4,800	4,800	5,600	6,000	6,000	6,000
	8,800	9,600	10,400	11,600	12,000	12,000
Payments	(4,000)	(4,800)	(4,800)	(5,600)	(6,000)	(6,000)
Closing balance (next month's payment)	4,800	4,800	5,600	6,000	6,000	6,000

(3) Cash budget for the six months ending 31 December:

	July £	Aug £	Sept £	Oct £	Nov £	Dec £
Inflows						
Trade receivables (40% of sales revenue of two months previous)	2,800	3,200	3,200	4,000	4,800	5,200
Cash sales revenue (60% of current month's sales revenue)	4,800	6,000	7,200	7,800	8,400	9,600
Total inflows	7,600	9,200	10,400	11,800	13,200	14,800
Outflows						
Payables (from payables budget)	(4,000)	(4,800)	(4,800)	(5,600)	(6,000)	(6,000)
Direct costs	(3,000)	(3,600)	(3,600)	(4,200)	(4,500)	(4,500)
Advertising	(1,000)	–	–	(1,500)	–	–
Overheads: 80%	(1,280)	(1,280)	(1,280)	(1,280)	(1,600)	(1,600)
20%	(280)	(320)	(320)	(320)	(320)	(400)
New plant			(2,200)	(2,200)	(2,200)	
Total outflows	(9,560)	(10,000)	(12,200)	(15,100)	(14,620)	(12,500)
Net inflows/(outflows)	(1,960)	(800)	(1,800)	(3,300)	(1,420)	2,300
Balance c/f	5,540	4,740	2,940	(360)	(1,780)	520

The balances carried forward are deduced by deducting the deficit (net outflows) for the month from (or adding the surplus for the month to) the previous month's balance.

Note how budgets are linked; in this case the inventories budget to the trade payables budget and the payables budget to the cash budget.

(b) The following are possible means of relieving the cash shortages revealed by the budget:

- Make a higher proportion of sales on a cash basis.
- Collect the money from credit customers more promptly, for example during the month following the sale.
- Hold lower inventories, both of raw materials and of finished goods.
- Increase the trade payables payment period.
- Delay the payments for advertising.
- Obtain more credit for the overhead costs; at present only 20 per cent are on credit.
- Delay the payments for the new plant.

Chapter 7

7.1 Toscanini Ltd

(a)

	Budget			Actual	
	Original	Flexed		Actual	
Output (units) (production and sales)	4,000	3,500		3,500	
	£	£		£	
Sales revenue	16,000	14,000		13,820	
Raw materials	(3,840)	(3,360)	(1,400 kg)	(3,420)	(1,425 kg)
Labour	(3,200)	(2,800)	(350 hr)	(2,690)	(345 hr)
Fixed overheads	(4,800)	(4,800)		(4,900)	
Operating profit	4,160	3,040		2,810	

	£	
Sales volume variance (4,160 − 3,040)	(1,120)	(A)
Sales price variance (14,000 − 13,820)	(180)	(A)
Materials price variance (1,425 × 2.40) − 3,420	0	
Materials usage variance [(3,500 × 0.4) − 1,425] × £2.40	(60)	(A)
Labour rate variance (345 × £8) − 2,690	70	(F)
Labour efficiency variance [(3,500 × 0.10) − 345] × £8	40	(F)
Fixed overhead spending variance (4,800 − 4,900)	(100)	(A)
Total net variances	(1,350)	(A)
Budgeted profit	4,160	
Less Total net variance	1,350	
Actual profit	2,810	

(b) Sales volume variance: sales manager; sales price variance: sales manager; materials usage variance: production manager; labour rate variance: personnel manager; labour efficiency variance: production manager; fixed overhead spending variance: various, depending on the nature of the overheads.

(c) Feasible explanations include the following:

- Sales volume   Unanticipated fall in world demand would account for 400 × £2.24 = £896 of this variance (£2.24 is the budgeted contribution per unit). Ineffective marketing probably caused the remainder, though a lack of availability of the finished product to sell may be a reason.
- Sales price   Ineffective selling seems the only logical reason.
- Materials usage   Inefficient usage of material, perhaps because of poor performance by labour, or substandard materials.
- Labour rate   Less overtime worked or lower production bonuses paid as a result of lower volume of activity.
- Labour efficiency   More effective working.
- Overheads   Ineffective control of overheads.

(d) Clearly, not all of the sales volume variance can be attributed to poor marketing, given a 10 per cent reduction in demand.

It will probably be useful to distinguish between that part of the variance that arose from the shortfall in general demand (a planning variance) and a volume variance, which is more fairly attributable to the manager concerned. Thus accountability will be more fairly imposed.

	£
Planning variance (10% × 4,000) × £2.24	896
'New' sales volume variance	
[4,000 – (10% × 4,000) – 3,500] × £2.24	224
Original sales volume variance	1,120

Chapter 8

8.1 Beacon Chemicals plc

(a) Relevant cash flows are as follows:

	Year 0 £000	Year 1 £000	Year 2 £000	Year 3 £000	Year 4 £000	Year 5 £000
Sales revenue		80	120	144	100	64
Loss of contribution		(15)	(15)	(15)	(15)	(15)
Variable costs		(40)	(50)	(48)	(30)	(32)
Fixed costs (Note 1)		(8)	(8)	(8)	(8)	(8)
Operating cash flows		17	47	73	47	9
Working capital	(30)					30
Capital cost	(100)					
Net relevant cash flows	(130)	17	47	73	47	39

Notes:
1. Only the fixed costs that are incremental to the project (only existing because of the project) are relevant. Depreciation is irrelevant because it is not a cash flow.
2. The research and development cost is irrelevant since it has been spent irrespective of the decision on X14 production.

(b)

	Year 0 £000	Year 1 £000	Year 2 £000	Year 3 £000
Cumulative cash flows	(130)	(113)	(66)	7

Thus the equipment will have repaid the initial investment by the end of the third year of operations, that is, the payback period is three years.

(c)

	Year 0 £000	Year 1 £000	Year 2 £000	Year 3 £000	Year 4 £000	Year 5 £000
Discount factor	1.00	0.926	0.857	0.794	0.735	0.681
Present value	(130)	15.74	40.28	57.96	34.55	26.56
Net present value	45.09	(That is, the sum of the present values for years 0 to 5.)				

Chapter 9

9.1 Student's statements

1 The student is not correct in making this statement. Non-experts, in the sense of not being accountants, may well be experts about certain costs because they are involved with costs being incurred as they carry out their work. Many well-managed businesses encourage staff members of all types to look out for and recommend cost-saving measures that could be introduced. Making staff cost-conscious through training, perhaps including some basic costing principles like the difference between fixed and variable costs, could be helpful. This a long way from saying that only accountants can spot cost-saving measures.

2 Customer profitability analysis is concerned with assessing how profitable particular customers are to one's own business, as customers. This involves preparing a 'mini income statement' for each customer or, perhaps, group of customers. Here all of the costs of providing the business's goods or services to the customer are taken into account. This includes not just the cost of providing the basic goods or service, but also other costs that probably vary between customers, such as delivery costs, warehousing (stores) costs and the costs of providing trade credit. The customer's own profitability as a trading business is not the subject of customer profitability analysis, though this would be of interest to the supplying business. The student is therefore incorrect in stating this.

3 SVA is an approach to management that focuses on the generally accepted business objective of maximisation of shareholder wealth. It does this by identifying a number of 'value drivers' that are seen as key to delivering value for shareholders. Plans can be made in respect of each of these key value drivers. These plans can be used as the basis of day-to-day management targets, against which managers can be assessed. SVA has little to do with the preferences of individual shareholders for dividends rather than retained profits.

4 EVA® stands for 'economic value added', not 'equity value analysis'. It tries to measure the extent to which a period of trading has led to value being created for shareholders. It tries to assess whether the profit generated by the business exceeds the minimum required to maintain the shareholders' wealth. The latter is based on the shareholders' required return and a fair assessment of the value of the assets in use in generating that profit. Though SVA and EVA® are quite closely linked, in that they both focus on achieving shareholder wealth maximisation, they approach this in rather different ways.

5 The balanced scorecard is certainly not another name for the statement of financial position (balance sheet). It is an attempt to provide financial and non-financial targets for managing the business. It seeks to strike a balance between financial and non-financial, external and internal, and predictive and historic factors. The statement of financial position (balance sheet) deals only with financial matters and has no connection with the balanced scorecard, except that both use the word 'balance' in their names.

Chapter 10

10.1 Andromeda International plc

(a)

	Jupiter	Mars
(1)	$(260/1,330) \times 100\% = 19.5\%$	$(50/1,380) \times 100\% = 3.6\%$
(2)	$(275/1,420^*) \times 100\% = 19.4\%$	$(80/1,680^\dagger) \times 100\% = 4.8\%$

* The profit will increase by £15,000 ((£250,000 × 0.30) − £60,000). Assets will increase by £90,000.
† Profit will increase by £30,000 (£90,000 − £60,000 depreciation). Assets will increase by £300,000.

(b) The investment opportunity for Jupiter division will result in an ROI of 16.7% (that is, 15/90) which is above the cost of capital for the business. As a result, central management is likely to view the opportunity favourably. However, the effect of taking the opportunity will be to lower the existing ROI of the division. This may mean that the divisional manager will be reluctant to take on the opportunity.

The investment opportunity for the Mars division provides an ROI of 10% (that is, 30/300), which is below the cost of capital of the business. As a result, central management would not wish for this opportunity to be taken up. However, the opportunity will increase the ROI of the Mars division overall and so the divisional manager may be keen to invest in the opportunity.

There may be reasons for investing in each opportunity which are not given in the question but which may be compelling. For example, it may be necessary to introduce the new product into the Jupiter division in order to ensure that the range of products offered to customers is complete. Failure to do so may result in a decline in overall sales. It may be that investment in the Mars division is important to ensure that productivity over the longer term does not slip behind that of its competitors.

(c) Ideally, ROI should be calculated using the current value of the assets employed. By so doing we can see whether or not the returns are satisfactory as compared with the alternative use of those resources. Using cost (or cost less accumulated depreciation) as the basis for ROI will be measuring current performance against past outlays.

Gross book value fails to take account of the age of the assets held. It may be that the assets are all near the end of their useful lives and are, therefore, highly depreciated. In such a case, the gross book value may produce a low ROI and may provide too high a 'hurdle' rate for new investment opportunities. Gross book value in such circumstances would also provide a poor approximation to the current value of the assets.

Using net book value would overcome the problem mentioned above but, during a period of inflation, this measure may be significantly lower than the current value of the assets employed. In addition, there is the problem that ROI can improve over time simply because of the declining value of the assets employed. Divisional managers may be less willing to replace old assets where this will lead to a decline in ROI.

Chapter 11

11.1 Williams Wholesalers Ltd

	£	£
Existing level of trade receivables (£4m × 70/365)		767,123
New level of trade receivables: £2m × 80/365	438,356	
£2m × 30/365	164,384	602,740
Reduction in trade receivables		164,383
Costs and benefits of policy		
Cost of discount (£2m × 2%)		40,000
Less Savings		
Interest payable (£164,383* × 13%)	21,370	
Administration costs	6,000	
Bad debts (20,000 − 10,000)	10,000	37,370
Net cost of policy		2,630

* It could be argued that the interest should be based on the amount expected to be received, that is the value of the trade receivables *after* taking account of the discount.

The above calculations reveal that the business will be worse off by offering the discounts.

Appendix C
Solutions to review questions

Chapter 1

1.1

Students	Whether to enrol on a course of study. This would probably involve an assessment of the university's ability to continue to operate and to fulfil students' needs.
Other universities and colleges	How best to compete against the university. This might involve using the university's performance in various aspects as a 'benchmark' when evaluating their own performance.
Employees	Whether to take up or to continue in employment with the university. Employees might assess this by considering the ability of the university to continue to provide employment and to reward employees adequately for their labour.
Government/ funding authority	How efficient the university is in undertaking its various activities.
Local community representatives	Whether to allow/encourage the university to expand its activities. To assess this, the university's ability to continue to provide employment for the community, to use community resources and to help fund environmental improvements might be considered.
Suppliers	Whether to continue to supply the university at all; also whether to supply on credit. This would involve an assessment of the university's ability to pay for any goods and services supplied.
Lenders	Whether to lend money to the university and/or whether to require repayment of any existing loans. To assess this, the university's ability to meet its obligations to pay interest and to repay the principal would be considered.
Board of governors and other managers (Faculty deans, and so on)	Whether the performance of the university requires improvement. Here current performance would be compared with plans or some other 'benchmark' to decide whether action needs to be taken. Whether there should be a change in the university's future direction. In making such decisions, management will need to look at the university's ability to perform and at the opportunities available to it.

In principle, there is no difference between the ways in which the user groups concerned with a university and those concerned with a private sector business would use accounting information.

1.2   Most businesses are far too large and complex for managers to be able to see and assess everything that is going on in their own areas of responsibility merely by personal observation. Managers need information on all aspects within their control. Management accounting reports can provide them with this information, to a greater or lesser extent. These reports can be seen, therefore, as acting as the eyes and ears of the managers, providing insights not necessarily obvious without them.

1.3   The following accounting information relating to a new service might be useful to a manager:

- the cost of providing the service and the level of profit that will be required;
- the capital investment that will be necessary to enable the business to provide the service; and
- the extent to which the provision of the service would be expected to enhance the business's wealth.

1.4   There is no doubt that the onus is on accountants to make their reports as easy to understand as they can possibly be. A key aspect of accountants' work is communicating to non-accountants, and they should never overlook this. At the same time, accounting information cannot always be expressed in such a way that someone with absolutely no accounting knowledge can absorb it successfully. The onus is also therefore on managers to acquire a working knowledge of the basis on which accounting reports are prepared and what they mean.

Chapter 2

2.1   The two attributes are:

1   They must relate to the objective(s) that the decision is intended to work towards. In most businesses this is taken to be wealth enhancement. This means that any information relating to the decision that does not impact on wealth enhancement is irrelevant, where wealth enhancement is the sole objective. In practice a business may have more than one objective.
2   They must differ between the options under consideration. Where a cost will be the same irrespective of the outcome of the decision that is to be taken it is irrelevant. It is only on the basis of things that differ from one outcome to another that decisions can be made.

2.2   A sunk cost is a past and, therefore, an irrelevant cost in the context of any decision about the future. Thus, for example, the cost of an item of inventories already bought is a sunk cost. It is irrelevant, in any decision involving the use of the inventories, because this cost will be the same irrespective of the decision made.

An opportunity cost is the cost of being deprived of the next best option to the one under consideration. For example, where using an hour of a worker's time on activity A deprives the business of the opportunity to use that time in a profitable activity B, the benefit lost from activity B is an opportunity cost of pursuing activity A.

2.3   Cost may be defined as the amount of resources, usually measured in monetary terms, sacrificed to achieve a particular objective.

2.4   A committed cost is like a past cost in that an irrevocable decision has been made to incur the cost. This might be because the business has entered into a binding contract, for example to rent some premises for the next two years. Thus it is effectively a past cost even though the payment (for rent, in our example) has yet to be made. Since the business cannot avoid a committed cost, committed costs cannot be relevant costs.

Chapter 3

3.1 A fixed cost is one that is the same irrespective of the level of activity or output. Typical examples of costs that are fixed, irrespective of the level of production or provision of a service, include rent of business premises, salaries of supervisory staff and insurance.

A variable cost is one that varies with the level of activity or output. Examples include raw materials and labour, where labour is rewarded in proportion to the level of output.

Note particularly that it is relative to the level of activity that costs are fixed or variable. Fixed costs will be affected by inflation and they will be greater for a longer period than for a shorter one.

For a particular product or service, knowing which costs are fixed and which are variable enables managers to predict the total cost for any particular level of activity. It also enables them to concentrate only on the variable costs in circumstances where a decision will not alter the fixed costs.

3.2 The BEP is the break-even point, that is, the level of activity, measured either in physical units or in value of sales revenue, at which the sales revenue exactly covers all of the costs, both fixed and variable.

Break-even point is calculated as

Fixed costs/(sales revenue per unit – variable costs per unit)

which may alternatively be expressed as

Fixed costs/Contribution per unit

Thus break-even will occur when the contributions for the period are sufficient to cover the fixed costs for the period.

Break-even point tends to be useful as a comparison with planned level of activity in an attempt to assess the riskiness of the activity.

3.3 Operating gearing refers to the extent of fixed cost relative to variable cost in the total cost of some activity. Where the fixed cost forms a relatively high proportion of the total, we say that the activity has high operating gearing.

Typically, high operating gearing is present in environments where there is a relatively high level of mechanisation (that is, capital-intensive environments). This is because such environments tend simultaneously to involve relatively high fixed costs of depreciation, maintenance, and so on and relatively low variable costs.

High operating gearing tends to mean that the effects of increases or decreases in the level of activity have an accentuated effect on operating profit. For example, a 20% decrease in output of a particular service will lead to a greater than 20% decrease in operating profit, assuming no cost or price changes.

3.4 In the face of a restricting scarce resource, profit will be maximised by using the scarce resource on output where the contribution per unit of the scarce resource is maximised.

This means that the contribution per unit of the scarce resource (for example, hour of scarce labour, or unit of scarce raw material) for each competing product or service needs to be identified. It is then a question of allocating the scarce resource to the product or service that provides the highest contribution per unit of the particular scarce resource.

The logic of this approach is that the scarce resource is allocated to the activity that uses it most effectively, in terms of contribution and, therefore, profit.

Chapter 4

4.1 In process costing, the total production cost for a period is divided by the number of completed units of output for the period to deduce the full cost per unit. Where there is work in progress at the beginning and/or the end of the period complications arise.

The problem is that some of the completed output incurred cost in the preceding period. Similarly, some of the cost incurred in the current period leads to completed production in the subsequent period. Account needs to be taken of these facts, if reliable full cost information is to be obtained.

4.2 The only reason for distinguishing between direct and indirect costs is to help to deduce the full cost of a unit of output in a job-costing environment. In an environment where all units of output are identical, or can reasonably be regarded as being so, a process-costing approach will be taken. This avoids the need for identifying direct and indirect costs separately.

Direct cost forms that part of the total cost of pursuing some activity that can, unequivocally, be associated with that particular activity. Examples of direct cost items in the typical job-costing environment include direct labour and direct materials.

Indirect cost is the remainder of the cost of pursuing some activity.

In practice, knowledge of the direct costs tends to provide the basis used to charge overheads to jobs.

The distinction between direct and indirect cost is irrelevant for any other purpose.

Directness and indirectness is dictated by the nature of that which is being costed, as much as the nature of the cost.

4.3 The notion of direct and indirect cost is concerned only with the extent to which particular elements of cost can unequivocally be related to, and measured in respect of, a particular cost unit, usually a product or service. The distinction between direct and indirect costs is made exclusively for the purpose of deducing the full cost of some cost unit, in an environment where each cost unit is not identical, or close enough to being identical for it to be treated as such. Thus, it is typically in the context of job costing, or some variant of it, that the distinction between direct and indirect cost is usefully made.

The notion of variable and fixed cost is concerned entirely with how costs behave in the face of changes in the volume of output. The benefit of being able to distinguish between fixed and variable cost is that predictions can be made of what total cost will be at particular levels of volume and/or what reduction or addition to cost will occur if the volume of output is reduced or increased.

Thus the notion of direct and indirect cost, on the one hand, and that of variable and fixed cost, on the other, are not linked to one another, and, in most contexts, some elements of direct cost are variable, while some are fixed. Similarly, indirect cost might be fixed or variable.

4.4 The full cost includes all of the cost of pursuing the cost objective, including a 'fair' share of the overheads. Generally the full cost represents an average cost of the various elements, rather than a cost that arises because the business finds itself in a particular situation.

The fact that the full cost reflects all aspects of cost should mean that, were the business to sell its output at a price exactly equal to the full cost (manufacturing and non-manufacturing cost), the sales revenues for the period would exactly cover all of the cost and the business would break even, that is make neither profit nor loss.

Chapter 5

5.1 ABC is a means of dealing with charging overheads to units of output to derive full costs in a multi-product (job or batch costing) environment.

The traditional approach tends to accept that once identifiable direct costs, normally labour and materials, have been taken out, all of the other costs (overheads) must be treated as common costs and applied to jobs using the same formula, typically on the basis of direct labour hours.

ABC takes a much more enquiring approach to overheads. It follows the philosophy that overheads do not occur for no reason, but they must be driven by activities. For example, a particular type of product may take up a disproportionately large part of supervisors' time. If that product were not made, in the long run, supervision costs could be cut (fewer supervisors would be needed). Whereas the traditional approach would just accept that supervisory salaries are an overhead, which needs to be apportioned along with other overheads, ABC would seek to charge that part of the supervisors' salaries which is driven by the particular type of product, to that product.

5.2 One criticism is on the issue of the cost/benefit balance. It is claimed that the work necessary to analyse activities and identify the cost drivers tends to be more expensive than is justified by the increased quality of the full costs that emerge.

Linked to this is the belief of many that full cost information is of rather dubious value for most purposes, irrespective of how the full costs are deduced. Many argue that full cost information is flawed by the fact that it takes no account of opportunity costs.

ABC enthusiasts would probably argue that deducing better quality full costs is not the only benefit which is available, if the overhead cost drivers can be identified. Knowing what drives costs can enable management to exercise more control over them. This benefit needs to be taken into account when assessing the cost/benefit of using ABC.

5.3 Generally, a rise in the price of a commodity causes a fall in demand. A commodity is said to have a relatively elastic demand where demand reacts relatively dramatically (stretches more) in the face of a particular price alteration. Elastic demand tends to be associated with commodities that are not essential, perhaps because there is a ready substitute.

It can be very helpful for those involved with pricing decisions to have some feel for the elasticity of demand of the commodity that will be the subject of a decision. The sensitivity of the demand to the decision is obviously much greater (and the pricing decision more crucial) with commodities whose demand is elastic than with commodities whose demand is relatively inelastic.

5.4 A business will make the most profit from one of its products or services at the point where marginal sales revenue equals marginal cost of production, or in other words, the point where the increase in total sales revenue that will result from selling one more unit equals the increase in total costs which will result from selling that unit.

Chapter 6

6.1 A budget can be defined as a financial plan for a future period of time. Thus it sets out the intentions which management has for the period concerned. Achieving the budget plans should help to achieve the long-term plans of the business. Achievement of the long-term plans should mean that the business is successfully working towards its objectives.

A budget differs from a forecast in that a forecast is a statement of what is expected to happen without the intervention of management, perhaps because they cannot intervene (as with a weather forecast). A plan is an intention to achieve.

Normally management would take account of reliable forecasts when making its plans.

6.2 1 Budgets tend to promote forward thinking and the possible identification of short-term problems. Managers must plan and the budgeting process tends to force them to do so. In doing so they are likely to encounter potential problems. If the potential problems can be identified early enough, solutions might be easily found.

2 Budgets can be used to help co-ordination between various sections of the business. It is important that the plans of one area of the business fit in with those of other areas; a lack of co-ordination could have disastrous consequences. Having formal statements of plans for each aspect of the business enables a check to be made that plans are complementary.

3 Budgets can motivate managers to better performance. It is believed that people are motivated by having a target to aim for. Provided that the inherent goals are achievable, budgets can provide an effective motivational device.

4 Budgets can provide a basis for a system of control. Having a plan against which actual performance can be measured provides a potentially useful tool of control.

5 Budgets can provide a system of authorisation. Many managers have 'spending' budgets such as research and development, staff training, and so on. For these people, the size of their budget defines their authority to spend.

6.3 Control can be defined as 'compelling things to occur as planned'. This implies that control can only be achieved if a plan exists. Budgets are financial plans. This means that, if actual performance can be compared with the budget (plan) for each aspect of the business, divergences from plan can be spotted. Steps can then be taken to bring matters back under control where they are going out of control.

6.4 A budget committee is a group of senior staff that is responsible for the budget preparation process within an organisation. The existence of the committee places the budget responsibility clearly with an identifiable group of people. This group can focus on the tasks involved.

Chapter 7

7.1 Feedforward controls try to anticipate what is likely to happen in the future and then assist in making the actual outcome match the desired outcome. They contrast with feedback controls, which simply compare actual to planned outcomes after the event. Feedforward controls are therefore more pro-active.

7.2 A variance is the effect on budgeted profit of the particular cost or revenue item being considered. It represents the difference between the budgeted profit and the actual profit assuming everything, except the item under consideration, had gone according to budget. From this it must be the case that

Budgeted profit + favourable variances – unfavourable variances = actual profit.

The purpose of analysing variances is to identify whether, and if so where, things are not going according to plan. If this can be done, it may be possible to find out the cause of things going out of control. If this can be discovered, it may then be possible to put things right for the future.

7.3 Where the budgeted and actual volumes of output do not coincide it is impossible to make valid comparison of 'allowed' and actual costs and revenues. Flexing the original budget to reflect the actual output level enables a more informative comparison to be made.

Flexing certainly does not mean that output volume differences do not matter. Flexing will show (as the difference between flexed and original budget profits) the effect on profit of output volume differences.

7.4 Deciding whether variances should be investigated involves the use of judgement. Often management will set a threshold of significance, for example 5 per cent of the budgeted figure for each variance relating to revenue or cost items. All variances above this threshold would then be investigated. Even where variances are below the threshold, any sign of a systemic variance, shown, for example, by an increasing cumulative total for the factor, should be investigated.

Knowledge of the cause of a particular variance may well put management in a position to take actions that will be beneficial to the business in the future. Investigating variances, however, is likely to be relatively expensive in staff time. A judgement needs to be made on whether the value or benefit of knowing the cause of the variance will be justified by the cost of this knowledge. As with most investigations of this type, it is difficult to judge the value of the knowledge until after the variance has been investigated.

Chapter 8

8.1 NPV is usually considered the best method of assessing investment opportunities because it takes account of:

- *The timing of the cash flows.* By *discounting* the various cash flows associated with each project according to when it is expected to arise, it recognises the fact that cash flows do not all occur simultaneously. Associated with this is the fact that, by discounting using the opportunity cost of finance (that is, the return which the next best alternative opportunity would generate), it is possible to identify the net benefit after financing costs have been met (as the NPV).
- *The whole of the relevant cash flows.* NPV includes all of the relevant cash flows irrespective of when they are expected to occur. It treats them differently according to their date of occurrence, but they are all taken account of in the NPV and they all have, or can have, an influence on the decision.
- *The objectives of the business.* NPV is the only method of appraisal where the output of the analysis has a direct bearing on the wealth of the business. (Positive NPVs enhance wealth; negative ones reduce it). Since most private sector businesses seek to increase their value and wealth, NPV clearly is the best approach to use, at least out of the methods we have considered so far.

NPV provides clear decision rules concerning acceptance/rejection of projects and the ranking of projects. It is fairly simple to use, particularly with the availability of modern computer software that takes away the need for routine calculations to be done manually.

8.2 The payback method, in its original form, does not take account of the time value of money. However, it would be possible to modify the payback method to accommodate this requirement. Cash flows arising from a project could be discounted, using the cost of finance as the appropriate discount rate, in the same way as with the NPV and IRR methods. The discounted payback approach is used by some businesses and represents an improvement on the original approach described in the chapter. However, it still retains the other flaws of the original payback approach that were discussed: for example, it ignores relevant data after the payback period. Thus, even in its modified form, the PP method cannot be regarded as superior to NPV.

8.3 The IRR method does appear to be preferred to the NPV method among many practising managers. The main reasons for this seem to be as follows:

- A preference for a percentage return ratio rather than an absolute figure as a means of expressing the outcome of a project. This preference for a ratio may reflect the fact that other financial goals of the business are often set in terms of ratios (for example, return on capital employed).

● A preference for ranking projects in terms of their percentage return. Managers feel it is easier to rank projects on the basis of percentage returns (though NPV outcomes should be just as easy for them). We saw in the chapter that the IRR method could provide misleading advice on the ranking of projects, and the NPV method was preferable for this purpose.

8.4   Cash flows are preferred to profit flows because cash is the ultimate measure of economic wealth. Cash is used to acquire resources and for distribution to shareholders. When cash is invested in an investment project an opportunity cost is incurred, as the cash cannot be used in other investment projects. Similarly, when positive cash flows are generated by the project it can be used to reinvest in other investment projects.

Profit, on the other hand, is relevant to reporting the productive effort for a period. This measure of effort may have only a tenuous relationship to cash flows for a period. The conventions of accounting may lead to the recognition of gains and losses in one period and the relevant cash inflows and outflows occurring in another period.

Chapter 9

9.1   The objective of strategic management accounting (SMA) is to provide information to managers that will help them to run the business in a way that will work towards achievement of the business's strategic objectives. Traditional management accounting is not necessarily so much different, but lacks the clear focus on achievement of strategic objectives.

Given its focus, SMA necessarily needs to be more outward looking and more customer oriented than the traditional approach. It also needs to focus on beating the competition. Finally, it must monitor the business's strategies and be concerned with bringing these to a successful conclusion.

9.2   Possible reasons for Customer A being preferred to Customer B include:

● A may place fewer orders than B, so saving the business's order handling costs.
● A may have the service provided in larger quantities than B. This might lead to savings in travel costs or similar, if the service is provided on the customers' premises.
● A may require fewer visits by sales representatives than B.
● A may be a quicker payer than B, assuming that sales are on credit.

There may well be other possibilities.

9.3   Shareholder value analysis is based on the principle that there are just a few key value drivers that generate shareholder value, for example, investment in working capital. If managers are focused on maximising performance with each of these so-called value drivers, the maximum increase in shareholder wealth will be generated. This can be used to relate the objectives of individual managers throughout the business to the primary objective for the business as a whole. This should lead to managers working directly towards shareholder value enhancement. It is claimed that more traditional approaches to management target setting tend not always to lead to the desired outcome for the business as a whole.

9.4   The four main areas in the balanced scorecard are:

1 *Financial.* Here targets for measures such as return on capital employed will be stated.
2 *Customer.* Here the market/customers that the business will aim for is established, as will be targets for such things as measures of customer satisfaction and rate of growth in customer numbers.

3 *Internal business process*. Here the processes that are vital to the business will be established. This might include levels of innovation, types of operation and after-sales service.

4 *Learning and growth*. In this area issues relating to growing the business and development of staff are identified and targets set.

Chapter 10

10.1 Reporting non-financial measures may pose a number of problems. These include:

- resistance to the introduction of new measures (and, by implication, new ways of being assessed);
- scepticism of proposed measures (the latest 'flavour of the month');
- the cost of reporting new measures;
- data integrity (the lack of common measurement bases and objectivity associated with many non-financial measures);
- the difficulty of measuring the benefits (for example, establishing the link between a particular non-financial measure and the achievement of business objectives).

10.2 Four possible measures may include:

- Sales per employee
- Output per employee
- Total output during the period
- Sales to assets employed.

Other measures may have been suggested which are equally valid.

10.3 Three non-financial measures might include:

- Turnover of staff during period
- New clients obtained during period
- Level of client satisfaction during period.

10.4 We saw in the chapter that negotiated prices can create problems for both the efficient use of resources and divisional autonomy. They can also tie up central management in arbitrational matters and deflect them from their more strategic role. This method is best used when there is an external market for the services or goods of both buying and selling divisions and when divisional managers are free to reject offers made by other divisions.

Market-based prices are, generally speaking, more appropriate as they reflect the opportunity cost of the goods. However, where the division is operating below capacity, a variable-cost-based approach is more appropriate.

Chapter 11

11.1 Although the credit manager is responsible for ensuring that receivables pay on time, Tariq may be right in denying blame. Various factors may be responsible for the situation described which are beyond the control of the credit manager. These include:

- a downturn in the economy leading to financial difficulties among trade receivables;
- decisions by other managers within the business to liberalise credit policy in order to stimulate sales;
- an increase in competition among suppliers offering credit, which is being exploited by customers;

- disputes with customers over the quality of goods or services supplied;
- problems in the delivery of goods leading to delays.

You may have thought of others.

11.2 The level of inventories held will be affected in the following ways.

(a) An increase in production bottlenecks is likely to result in an increase in raw materials and work in progress being processed within the plant. Therefore, levels of inventories should rise.

(b) A rise in interest rates will make holding inventories more expensive if they are financed by debt. This may, in turn, lead to a decision to reduce inventory levels.

(c) The decision to reduce the range of products should result in fewer inventories being held. It would no longer be necessary to hold certain items in order to meet customer demand.

(d) Switching to a local supplier may reduce the lead time between ordering an item and receiving it. This should, in turn, reduce the need to carry such high levels of the particular item.

(e) A deterioration in the quality of bought-in items may result in the purchase of higher quantities of inventories in order to take account of the defective element in inventories acquired and, perhaps, an increase in the inspection time for items received. This would lead to a rise in inventory levels.

11.3 Inventories are held:

- to meet customer demand,
- to avoid the problems of running out of inventories, and
- to take advantage of profitable opportunities (for example, buying a product that is expected to rise steeply in price in the future).

The first reason may be described as transactionary, the second precautionary and the third speculative. They are, in essence, the same reasons why a business holds cash.

11.4 (a) The costs of holding too little cash are:

- failure to meet obligations when they fall due which can damage the reputation of the business and may, in the extreme, lead to the business being wound up;
- having to borrow and thereby incur interest charges;
- an inability to take advantage of profitable opportunities.

(b) The costs of holding too much cash are:

- failure to use the funds available for more profitable purposes;
- loss of value during a period of inflation.

Appendix D
Solutions to selected exercises

Chapter 1

1.1 Strategic management involves five steps:

1 *Establish mission and objectives.* The mission statement is usually a brief statement of the overall aims of the business. The objectives are rather more specific than the mission and need to be both quantifiable and consistent with the mission or aims.

2 *Undertake a position analysis.* Here the business is seeking to establish how it is placed relative to its environment (competitors, markets, technology, the economy, political climate and so on), given the business's mission and objectives. This is often approached within the framework of an analysis of the business's strengths, weaknesses, opportunities and threats (a SWOT analysis). Strengths and weaknesses are internal factors that are attributes of the business itself, whereas opportunities and threats are factors expected to be present in the environment in which the business operates. The SWOT framework is not the only possible approach to undertaking a position analysis, but it seems to be a very popular one.

3 *Identify and assess the strategic options.* This involves attempting to identify possible courses of action that will enable the business to reach its objectives in the light of the position analysis undertaken in Step 2.

4 *Select strategic options and formulate plans.* Here the business will select what seems to be the best of the courses of action or strategies (identified in Step 3) and will formulate a strategic plan in the form of long- and short-term budgets.

5 *Perform, review and control.* Here the business pursues the plans derived in Step 4, using the traditional approach to compare actual performance against budgets, seeking to control where actual performance appears not to be matching plans.

1.2 SWOT analysis of Jones Dairy Ltd

Strengths

- A portfolio of identifiable customers who show some loyalty to the business.
- Good cash flow profile. Though credit will be given, a week is the normal credit period.
- An apparently sound distribution system.
- A monopoly of doorstep delivery in the area.
- Barriers to entry. There are probably relatively high fixed costs, which implies a 'critical mass' of volume is necessary.
- Good employees and ease of recruitment.
- Differentiated product; clearly different from what is supplied by the supermarket in that it is delivered to the door.
- Apparently good marketing, since the decline in business is less than the national average.
- Good knowledge of the local market.

- Tendency for people to shop infrequently means that doorstep delivery may be the only practical means of having fresh milk.

Weaknesses

- Ageing managers.
- Success might be dependent on the present management continuing to manage.
- Narrow product range.
- High price necessary to generate acceptable level of profit.
- Available substitute – that is, non-delivered milk.
- High operating gearing (probably) means that profit suffers disproportionately with a downturn in demand. (This point will be considered in Chapter 3.)
- Single supplier.

Opportunities

- Possibility of extending the product range to include other dairy and non-dairy products to existing customers.
- Possible geographical expansion to cover other local towns and villages.
- Possibly move to act as a wholesaler to local stores at differentiated prices. It is probable that the bottlers would supply Jones more cheaply than they would supply individual small stores.
- Using plant for some other purpose, such as leasing cold store facilities.

Threats

- Apparently strong trend against doorstep delivery driven by price differential.
- Trend away from dairy products for health/cultural reasons.
- The probability that Jones is entirely dependent on the only local bottler. More geographically remote bottlers may not be prepared to supply at an acceptable price.
- Increasing strength of supermarket buying power.

Chapter 2

2.1 Lombard Ltd

Relevant costs of undertaking the contract are:

	£
Equipment costs	200,000
Component X (20,000 × 4 × £5)	
Any of these components used will need to be replaced.	400,000
Component Y (20,000 × 3 × £8)	
All of the required units will come from inventories and this	
will be an effective cost of the net realisable value.	480,000
Additional costs (20,000 × £8)	160,000
	1,240,000
Revenue from the contract (20,000 × £80)	1,600,000

Thus, from a purely financial point of view the project is acceptable. (Note that there is no relevant labour cost since the staff concerned will be paid irrespective of whether the contract is undertaken.)

2.2 The local authority

(a) Net benefit of accepting the touring company proposal

	£
Net reduction in ticket revenues (see workings below)	(20,000)
Savings on: Costumes	5,600
Scenery	3,300
Casual staff	3,520
Net deficit	(7,580)

Since there is a net deficit, on financial grounds, the touring company's proposal should be rejected.

Note that all of the following are irrelevant, because they will occur irrespective of the decision:

- non-performing staff salaries
- artistes' salaries
- heating and lighting
- administration costs
- refreshment revenues and costs
- programme advertising.

Workings

Normal ticket sales revenue:

	£
200 @ £24 =	4,800
500 @ £16 =	8,000
300 @ £12 =	3,600
	16,400

Ticket revenue at 50 per cent capacity for 20 performances:

(£16,400 × 50% × 20)   £164,000

Touring company ticket sales:

Total revenue for each performance for a full house:

	£
200 @ £22 =	4,400
500 @ £14 =	7,000
300 @ £10 =	3,000
	14,400

		£
Ticket revenues	(£14,400 × 10 × 50%)	72,000
	(£14,400 × 15 × $\frac{2}{3}$ × 50%)	72,000
		144,000

Net loss of revenue (£164,000 − £144,000) =	£20,000

(b) Other possible factors to consider include:

- The reliability of the estimations, including the assumption that the level of occupancy will not alter programme and refreshment sales revenue.
- A desire to offer theatregoers the opportunity to see another group of players.
- Dangers of loss of morale of staff not employed, or employed to do other than their usual work.

2.3 Andrews and Co. Ltd

Minimum contract price

			£
Materials	Steel core:	10,000 × £2.10	21,000
	Plastic:	10,000 × 0.10 × £0.10	100
Labour	Skilled:		–
	Unskilled:	10,000 × $^5/_{60}$ × £7.50	6,250
	Minimum tender price		27,350

2.6 The local education authority

(a) One-off financial net benefits of closing:

	D only	A and B	A and C
Capacity reduction	800	700	800
	£m	£m	£m
Property developer (A)	–	14.0	14.0
Shopping complex (B)	–	8.0	–
Property developer (D)	9.0	–	–
Safety (C)	–	–	3.0
Adapt facilities	(1.8)	–	–
Total	7.2	22.0	17.0
Ranking based on total one-off benefits	3	1	2

(Note that all past costs of buying and improving the schools are irrelevant.)

Recurrent financial net benefits of closing:

	D only	A and B	A and C
	£m	£m	£m
Rent (C)	–	–	0.3
Administrators	0.2	0.4	0.4
Total	0.2	0.4	0.7
Ranking based on total of recurrent benefits	3	2	1

On the basis of the financial figures alone, closure of either A and B or A and C looks best. It is not possible to add the one-off and the recurring costs directly, but the large one-off cost saving associated with closing schools A and B makes this option look attractive. (In Chapter 8 we shall see that it is possible to add one-off and recurring costs in a way that should lead to sensible conclusions.)

(b) The costs of acquiring and improving the schools in the past are past costs or sunk costs and, therefore, irrelevant. The costs of employing the chief education officer is a future cost, but irrelevant because it is not dependent on outcomes, it is a common cost.

(c) There are many other factors, some of a non-quantifiable nature. These include:

- Accuracy of projections of capacity requirements.
- Locality of existing schools relative to where potential pupils live.
- Political acceptability of selling schools to property developers.
- Importance of purely financial issues in making the final decision.
- The quality of the replacement sporting facilities compared with those at school D.
- Political acceptability of staff redundancies.
- Possible savings/costs of employing fewer teachers, which might be relevant if economies of scale are available by having fewer schools.
- Staff morale.

2.7   Rob Otics Ltd

(a) The minimum price for the proposed contract would be:

	£
Materials	
Component X (2 × 8 × £180)	2,880
If the 16 units of this component are used on the proposed contract, the business will need to buy an additional 16 units at the new price.	
Component Y	0
The history of the components held in inventories is irrelevant because it applies irrespective of the decision made on this contract. Since the alternative to using the units on this contract is to scrap them, the relevant cost is zero.	
Component Z [(75 + 32) × £20] − (75 × £25)	265
The relevant cost here is how much extra the business will pay the supplier as a result of undertaking the contract.	
Other miscellaneous items	250
Labour	
Assembly (25 + 24 + 23 + 22 + 21 + 20 + 19 + 18) × £48	8,256
The assembly labour cost is irrelevant because it will be incurred irrespective of which work the members of staff do. The relevant cost is based on the sales revenue per hour lost if the other orders are lost less the material cost per hour saved; that is £60 − £12 = £48.	
Inspection (8 × 6 × £12 × 150%)	864
Total	12,515

Thus the minimum price is £12,515.

(b) Other factors include:

- Competitive state of the market.
- The fact that the above figure is unique to the particular circumstances at the time – for example, having component Y available but having no use for it. Any subsequent order might have to take account of an outlay cost.
- Breaking even (that is, just covering the costs) on a contract will not fulfil the business's objective.
- Charging a low price may cause marketing problems. Other customers may resent the low price for this contract. The current enquirer may expect a similar price in future.

Chapter 3

3.4   Motormusic Ltd

(a) Break-even point = fixed costs/contribution per unit

$$= (80,000 + 60,000)/[60 − (20 + 14 + 12 + 3)] = 12,727 \text{ radios.}$$

These would have a sales value of £763,620 (that is, 12,727 × £60).

(b) The margin of safety is 7,273 radios (that is, 20,000 − 12,727). This margin would have a sales value of £436,380 (that is, 7,273 × £60).

3.5 Products A, B and C

(a) Total time required on cutting machines is:

$$(2,500 \times 1.0) + (3,400 \times 1.0) + (5,100 \times 0.5) = 8,450 \text{ hours}$$

Total time available on cutting machines is 5,000 hours. Therefore, this is a limiting factor.

Total time required on assembling machines is:

$$(2,500 \times 0.5) + (3,400 \times 1.0) + (5,100 \times 0.5) = 7,200 \text{ hours}$$

Total time available on assembling machines is 8,000 hours. Therefore, this is not a limiting factor.

	A (per unit) £	B (per unit) £	C (per unit) £
Selling price	25	30	18
Variable materials	(12)	(13)	(10)
Variable production costs	(7)	(4)	(3)
Contribution	6	13	5
Time on cutting machines	1.0 hour	1.0 hour	0.5 hour
Contribution per hour on cutting machines	£6	£13	£10
Order of priority	3rd	1st	2nd

Therefore, produce:

3,400 product B using	3,400 hours
3,200 product C using	1,600 hours
	5,000 hours

(b) Assuming that the business would make no saving in variable production costs by sub-contracting, it would be worth paying up to the contribution per unit (£5) for product C, which would therefore be £5 × (5,100 − 3,200) = £9,500 in total.

Similarly it would be worth paying up to £6 per unit for product A – that is, £6 × 2,500 = £15,000 in total.

3.6 Darmor Ltd

(a) Contribution per hour of skilled labour of product X is

$$\frac{£(30 - 6 - 2 - 12 - 3)}{(6/12)} = £14$$

Given the scarcity of skilled labour, if the management is to be indifferent between the products, the contribution per skilled labour hour must be the same. Thus for product Y the selling price must be

$$[£(14 \times (9/12)) + 9 + 4 + 25 + 7] = £55.50$$

(that is, the contribution plus the variable costs), and for product Z the selling price must be

$$[£(14 \times (3/12)) + 3 + 10 + 14 + 7] = £37.50$$

(b) The business could pay up to £26 an hour (£12 + £14) for additional hours of skilled labour. This is the potential contribution per hour, before taking account of the labour rate of £12 an hour.

3.7 Intermediate Products Ltd

(a)

	A	B	C	D
Total costs per unit (£)	(65)	(41)	(36)	(46)
Less Fixed costs (£)	20	8	8	12
Variable cost per unit (£)	(45)	(33)	(28)	(34)
Buying/selling price per unit (£)	70	45	40	55
Contribution per unit (£)	25	12	12	21
Hours on special machine	0.5	0.4	0.5	0.3
Contribution per hour (£)	50	30	24	70
Order of preference	2nd	3rd	4th	1st

Optimum use of hours on special machine	*Balance of hours*
D $3,000 \times 0.3 =$ 900	5,100 (that is, 6,000 – 900)
A $5,000 \times 0.5 = 2,500$	2,600 (that is, 5,100 – 2,500)
B $6,000 \times 0.4 = 2,400$	200 (that is, 2,600 – 2,400)
C $400 \times 0.5 = \underline{\;\;200}$	
$\underline{6,000}$	

Therefore, make all of the demand for Ds, As and Bs plus 400 (of 4,000) Cs.

(b) The contribution per hour from Cs is £24, and so this is the maximum amount per hour that it would be worth paying to rent the machine, for a maximum of 1,800 hours (that is, $3,600 \times 0.5$, the time necessary to make the remaining demand for Cs).

(c) Other possible actions to overcome the shortage of machine time include the following:

● Alter the design of the products to avoid the use of the special machine.
● Increase the selling price of the product so that the demand will fall, making the available machine time sufficient but making production more profitable.

3.8 Gandhi Ltd

(a) Given that the spare capacity could not be used by other services, the standard service should continue to be offered. This is because it renders a positive contribution.

(b) The standard service renders a contribution per unit of £15 (that is, £80 – £65), or £30 during the time it would take to render one unit of the nova service. The nova service would provide a contribution of only £25 (that is, £75 – £50).

The nova service should, therefore, not replace the standard service.

(c) Under the original plans, the following contributions would be rendered by the basic and standard services:

		£
Basic	$11,000 \times (£50 – £25) =$	275,000
Standard	$6,000 \times (£80 – £65) =$	90,000
		365,000

If the basic were to take the standard's place, 17,000 units (that is, 11,000 + 6,000) of them could be produced in total. To generate the same total contribution, each unit of the standard service would need to provide £21.47 (that is, £365,000/17,000) of contribution. Given the basic's variable cost of £25, this would mean a selling price of £46.47 each (that is, £21.47 + £25.00).

Chapter 4

4.4   Promptprint Ltd

(a) The plan (budget) may be summarised as:

	£
Sales revenue	196,000
Direct materials	(38,000)
Direct labour	(32,000)
Total indirect cost	(77,000)
Profit	49,000

(2,400 + 3,000 + 27,600 + 36,000 + 8,000)

The job may be priced on the basis that both indirect cost and profit should be apportioned to it on the basis of direct labour cost, as follows:

	£	
Direct materials	4,000	
Direct labour	3,600	
Overheads	8,663	(£77,000 × 3,600/32,000)
Profit	5,513	(£49,000 × 3,600/32,000)
	21,776	

This answer assumes that variable overheads vary in proportion to direct labour cost.

Various other bases of charging overheads and profit loading the job could have been adopted. For example, materials cost could have been included (with direct labour) as the basis for profit loading, or even apportioning overheads.

(b) This part of the question is, in effect, asking for comments on the validity of 'full cost-plus' pricing. This approach can be useful as an indicator of the effective long-run cost of doing the job. On the other hand, it fails to take account of relevant opportunity costs as well as the state of the market and other external factors. For example, it ignores the price that a competitor printing business may quote.

(c) Revised estimates of direct material cost for the job:

	£	
Paper grade 1	1,500	(£1,200 × 125%) (this item of inventories needs to be replaced)
Paper grade 2	0	(it has no opportunity cost value)
Card	510	(£640 − £130: using the card on another job would save £640, but cost £130 to achieve that saving)
Inks and so on	300	(this item of inventories needs to be replaced)
	2,310	

4.5   Bookdon plc

(a) To answer this question, we need first to allocate and apportion the overheads to product cost centres, as follows:

Cost	Basis of apportionment	Total	Department			
			Machine shop	Fitting section	Canteen	Machine main'ce section
		£	£	£	£	£
Allocated items	Specific	90,380	27,660	19,470	16,600	26,650
Rent, rates, heat, light	Floor area	17,000	9,000	3,500	2,500	2,000
			(3,600/ 6,800)	(1,400/ 6,800)	(1,000/ 6,800)	(800/ 6,800)
Dep'n and insurance	Book value	25,000	12,500	6,250	2,500	3,750
			(150/300)	(75/300)	(30/300)	(45/300)
		132,380	49,160	29,220	21,600	32,400
Canteen	Number of employees	–	10,800	8,400	(21,600)	2,400
			(18/36)	(14/36)		(4/36)
		132,380	59,960	37,620	–	34,800
Machine maintenance section	Specified %	–	24,360	10,440	–	(34,800)
			(70%)	(30%)		
		132,380	84,320	48,060	–	–

Note that the canteen overheads were reapportioned to the other cost centres first because the canteen renders a service to the machine maintenance section but does not receive a service from it.

Calculation of the overhead absorption (recovery) rates can now proceed:

(i) Total budgeted machine hours are:

	Hours
Product X (4,200 × 6)	25,200
Product Y (6,900 × 3)	20,700
Product Z (1,700 × 4)	6,800
	52,700

Overhead absorption rate for the machine shop is:

$$\frac{£84,320}{52,700} = £1.60/\text{machine hour}$$

(ii) Total budgeted direct labour cost for the fitting section is:

	£
Product X (4,200 × £12)	50,400
Product Y (6,900 × £3)	20,700
Product Z (1,700 × £21)	35,700
	106,800

Overhead absorption rate for the fitting section is:

$$\frac{£48,060}{£106,800} \times 100\% = 45\% \text{ or } £0.45 \text{ per £ of direct labour cost.}$$

(b) The cost of one unit of product X is calculated as follows:

	£
Direct materials	11.00
Direct labour	
Machine shop	6.00
Fitting section	12.00
Overheads	
Machine shop (6 × £1.60)	9.60
Fitting section (£12 × 45%)	5.40
	44.00

Therefore, the cost of one unit of product X is £44.00.

4.6 Products A, B and C

Allocation and apportionment of overheads to product cost centres

	Basis of apportionment	Department				
		Cutting £	Machining £	Pressing £	Engineering £	Personnel £
Total		154,482	64,316	58,452	56,000	34,000
Personnel	Specified	18,700 (55%)	3,400 (10%)	6,800 (20%)	5,100 (15%)	(34,000)
		173,182	67,716	65,252	61,100	–
Engineering	Specified	12,220 (20%)	27,495 (45%)	21,385 (35%)	(61,100)	
		185,402	95,211	86,637	–	–

Note that the personnel overheads were reapportioned to the other cost centres first because the canteen renders a service to the engineering department section, but does not receive a service from it.

Calculation of the overhead absorption (recovery) rates
In both the cutting and pressing departments, no machines seem to be used, and so a direct labour hour basis of overhead absorption seems reasonable.

In the machining department, machine hours are far in excess of labour hours and the overheads are probably machine-related. In this department, machine hours seem a fair basis for cost units to absorb overheads.

Total planned direct labour hours for the cutting department are thus:

Product A	4,000 × (3 + 6) =	36,000
Product B	3,000 × (5 + 1) =	18,000
Product C	6,000 × (2 + 3) =	30,000
		84,000

The overhead absorption rate for the cutting department is £185,402/84,000 = £2.21 per direct labour hour.

Total planned machine hours for the machining department are thus:

Product A	4,000 × 2.0 =	8,000
Product B	3,000 × 1.5 =	4,500
Product C	6,000 × 2.5 =	15,000
		27,500

The overhead absorption rate for the machining department is £95,211/27,500 = £3.46 per machine hour.

Total planned direct labour hours for the pressing department are:

Product A	4,000 × 2 =	8,000
Product B	3,000 × 3 =	9,000
Product C	6,000 × 4 =	24,000
		41,000

The overhead absorption rate for the cutting department = £86,637/41,000 = £2.11 per direct labour hour.

(a) Cost of one completed unit of product A:

		£
Direct materials		7.00
Direct labour		
Cutting department – skilled	(3 × £16)	48.00
– unskilled	(6 × £10)	60.00
Machining department	(0.5 × £12)	6.00
Pressing department	(2 × £12)	24.00
Overheads		
Cutting department	(9 × £2.21)	19.89
Machining department	(2 × £3.46)	6.92
Pressing department	(2 × £2.11)	4.22
		176.03

(b) Cost of one uncompleted unit of product B:

		£
Direct materials		4.00*
Direct labour		
Cutting department – skilled	(5 × £16)	80.00
– unskilled	(1 × £10)	10.00
Machining department	(0.25 × £12)	3.00
Overheads		
Cutting department	(6 × £2.21)	13.26
Machining department	(1.5 × £3.46)	5.19
		115.45

* This assumes that all of the materials are added in the cutting or machining departments.

4.7 Offending phrases and explanations

Offending phrase	Explanation
'Necessary to divide up the business into departments'	This can be done but it will not always be of much benefit. Only in quite restricted circumstances will it give significantly different job costs.
'Fixed costs (or overheads)'	This implies that fixed costs and overheads are the same thing. They are not really connected with one another. 'Fixed' is to do with how costs behave as the level of output is raised or lowered; 'overheads' are to do with the extent to which costs can be directly measured in respect of a particular unit of output. Though it is true that many overheads are fixed, not all are. Also, direct labour is usually a fixed cost.

All of the other references to fixed and variable costs are wrong. The person should have referred to indirect and direct costs.

'Usually this is done on the basis of area'	Where overheads are apportioned to departments, they will be apportioned on some logical basis. For certain costs – for example, rent – the floor area may be the most logical; for others, such as machine maintenance costs, the floor area would be totally inappropriate.
'When the total fixed cost for each department has been identified, this will be divided by the number of hours that were worked'	Where overheads are dealt with on a departmental basis, they may be divided by the number of direct labour hours to deduce a recovery rate. However, this is only one basis of applying overheads to jobs. For example, machine hours or some other basis may be more appropriate to the particular circumstances involved.
'It is essential that this approach is taken in order to deduce a selling price'	It is relatively unusual for the 'job cost' to be able to dictate the price at which the manufacturer can price its output. For many businesses, the market dictates the price.

4.8 (a) Charging overheads to jobs on a departmental basis means that overheads are collected 'product' cost centre (department) by 'product' cost centre. This involves picking up the overheads that are direct to each department and adding to them a share of overheads that are general to the business as a whole. The overheads of 'service' cost centres must then be apportioned to the product cost centres. At this point, all of the overheads for the whole business are divided between the 'product' cost centres, such that the sum of the 'product' cost centre overheads equals those for the whole business.

Dealing with overheads departmentally is believed to provide more fair and useful information to decision makers, because different departments may have rather different overheads, and applying overheads departmentally can take account of that and reflect it in job costs.

In theory, dealing with overheads on a departmental basis is more costly than on a business-wide basis. In practice, it possibly does not make too much difference to the cost of collecting the information. This is because, normally, businesses are divided into departments, and the costs are collected departmentally, as part of the normal routine for exercising control over the business.

(b) In order to make any difference to the job cost that will emerge as a result of dealing with overheads departmentally, as compared with doing so on a business-wide basis, the following *both* need to be the case:

- the overheads per unit of the basis of charging (for example direct labour hours) need to be different from one department to the next; and
- the proportion (but not the actual amounts) of total overheads that are charged to jobs must differ from one job to the next.

Assume, for the sake of argument, that direct labour hours are used as the basis of charging overheads in all departments. Also assume that there are three departments, A, B and C.

There will be no difference to the overheads charged to a particular job if the rate of overheads per direct labour hour is the same for all departments. Obviously, if the charging rate is the same in all departments, that same rate must also apply to the business taken as a whole.

Also, even where overheads per direct labour hour differ significantly from one department to another, if all jobs spend, say, about 20 per cent of their time in Department A, 50 per cent in Department B and 30 per cent in Department C, it will not make any difference whether overheads are charged departmentally or overall.

These conclusions are not in any way dependent on the basis of charging overheads or even whether overheads are charged on the same basis in each department.

The statements above combine to mean that, probably in many cases in practice, departmentalising overheads is not providing information that is significantly different from that which would be provided by charging overheads to jobs on a business-wide basis.

Chapter 5

5.1   Woodner Ltd

A Output	B Sales price per unit	C Total sales revenue $(A \times B)$	D Marginal unit sales revenue	E Total variable cost $(A \times £20)$	F Total cost (variable cost + £2,500)	G Marginal cost per unit	H Profit/(loss)
units	£	£	£	£	£	£	£
0	0	0	0	0	2,500	–	(2,500)
10	95	950*	95†	200	2,700	20	(1,750)
20	90	1,800	85	400	2,900	20	(1,100)
30	85	2,550	75	600	3,100	20	(550)
40	80	3,200	65	800	3,300	20	(100)
50	75	3,750	55	1,000	3,500	20	250
60	70	4,200	45	1,200	3,700	20	500
70	65	4,550	35	1,400	3,900	20	650
80	60	4,800	25	1,600	4,100	20	700
90	55	4,950	15	1,800	4,300	20	650
100	50	5,000	5	2,000	4,500	20	500

* $(10 \times £95)$
† $((950 - 0)/(10 - 0))$

An output of 80 units each week will maximise profit at £700 a week. This is the nearest, given the nature of the input data, to the level of output where marginal cost per unit equals marginal revenue per unit. (For the mathematically minded, calculus could have been used to find the point at which slopes of the total sales revenue and total cost lines were equal.)

5.2   Cost-plus pricing

Cost-plus pricing means that prices are based on calculations/assessments of how much it costs to produce the good or service, and includes a margin for profit. 'Cost' in this context might mean relevant cost, variable cost, direct cost or full cost. Usually cost-plus prices are based on full costs. These full costs might be derived using a traditional or an ABC approach.

If a business charges the full cost of its output as a selling price, it will in theory break even. This is because the sales revenue will exactly cover all of the costs. Charging something above full cost will yield a profit. Thus, in theory, cost-plus pricing is logical.

If a cost-plus approach to pricing is to be taken, the issue that must be addressed is the level of profit required from each unit sold. This must logically be based on the total profit that is required for the period. Normally, businesses seek to enhance their wealth through trading. The extent to which they expect to do this is normally related to the amount of wealth that is invested to promote wealth enhancement. Businesses tend to seek to produce a particular percentage increase in wealth. In other words, they seek to generate a particular return on capital employed. It seems logical, therefore, that the profit loading on full cost should reflect the business's target profit and that the target should itself be based on a target return on capital employed.

An obvious problem with cost-plus pricing is that the market may not agree with the price. Put another way, cost-plus pricing takes no account of the market demand function (the relationship between price and quantity demanded). A business may fairly deduce the full cost of some product and then add what might be regarded as a reasonable level of profit, only to find that a rival producer is offering a similar product for a much lower price, or that the market simply will not buy at the cost-plus price.

Most suppliers are not strong enough in the market to dictate pricing; most are 'price takers', not 'price makers'. They must accept the price offered by the market or they do not sell any of their wares. Cost-plus pricing may be appropriate for price makers, but it has less relevance for price takers.

The cost-plus price is not entirely useless to price takers, however. When contemplating entering a market, knowing the cost-plus price will tell the price taker whether it can profitably enter the market or not. As has been said above, the full cost can be seen as a long-run break-even selling price. If entering a market means that this break-even price, plus an acceptable profit, cannot be achieved, then the business should probably stay out. Having a breakdown of the full cost may put the business in a position to examine where costs might be capable of being cut in order to bring the full cost-plus profit to within a figure acceptable to the market.

Being a price maker does not always imply that the business dominates a particular market. Many small businesses are, to some extent, price makers. This tends to be where buyers find it difficult to make clear distinctions between the prices offered by various suppliers. An example of this might be a car repair. Though it may be possible to obtain a series of binding estimates for the work from various garages, most people would not normally do so. As a result, garages normally charge cost-plus prices for car repairs.

5.3   Kaplan plc

(a) The business makes each model of suitcase in a batch. The direct materials and labour costs will be recorded in respect of each batch. To these costs will be added a share of the overheads of the business for the period in which production of the batch takes place. The basis of the batch absorbing overheads is a matter of managerial judgement. Direct labour hours spent working on the batch, relative to total direct labour hours worked during the period, is a popular method. This is not the 'correct' way, however. There is no correct way. If the activity is capital-intensive, some machine hour basis of dealing with overheads might be more appropriate, though still not 'correct'. Overheads might be collected, cost centre by cost centre (department by department), and charged to the batch as it passes through each product cost centre. Alternatively, all of the overheads for the entire production facility might be totalled and the overheads dealt with more globally. It is only in restricted circumstances that overheads charged to batches will be affected by a decision to deal with them by cost centres, rather than globally.

   Once the 'full cost' (direct costs plus a share of indirect costs) has been ascertained for the batch, the cost per suitcase can be established by dividing the batch cost by the number in the batch.

(b) The uses to which full cost information can be put have been identified as:

- *For pricing purposes.* In some industries and circumstances, full costs are used as the basis of pricing. Here the full cost is deduced and a percentage is added on for profit. This is known as cost-plus pricing. A solicitor handling a case for a client probably provides an example of this.

  In many circumstances, however, suppliers are not in a position to deduce prices on a cost-plus basis. Where there is a competitive market, a supplier will probably need to accept the price that the market offers – that is, most suppliers are 'price takers' not 'price makers'.

- *For income-measurement purposes.* To provide a valid means of measuring a business's income, it is necessary to match expenses with the revenue realised in the same accounting period. Where manufactured products are made or partially made in one period but sold in the next, or where a service is partially rendered in one accounting period but the revenue is realised in the next, the full cost (including an appropriate share of overheads) must be carried from one accounting period to the next. Unless we are able to identify the full cost of work done in one period, which is the subject of a sale in the next, the profit figures of the periods concerned will become meaningless.

  Unless all related production costs are charged in the same accounting period as the sale is recognised in the income statement, distortions will occur that will render the income statement much less useful. Thus it is necessary to deduce the full cost of any production undertaken completely or partially in one accounting period but sold in a subsequent one.

- *For budgetary planning and control.* Often budgets are set in terms of full costs. If budgets are to be used as the yardsticks that actual performance is to be assessed, the information on actual performance must also be expressed in the same full-cost terms. Knowing the full cost of the suitcases could be helpful in these activities.

- *General decision making.* Knowing the full cost of the suitcases might be helpful in making a decision as to whether to continue to make all or some of the models. It is argued, however, that relevant costs, which might be just the variable costs, would provide a more helpful basis for the decision.

(c) Whereas the traditional approach to dealing with overheads is just to accept that they exist and deal with them in a fairly broad manner, ABC takes a much more enquiring approach. ABC takes the view that overheads do not just 'occur', but that they are caused or 'driven' by 'activities'. It is a matter of finding out which activities are driving the costs and how much cost they are driving.

For example, a significant part of the costs of making suitcases of different sizes might be resetting machinery to cope with a batch of a different size from its predecessor batch. Where a particular model is made in very small batches, because it has only a small market, ABC would advocate that this model is charged directly with its machine-setting costs. The traditional approach would be to treat machine setting as a general overhead that the individual suitcases (irrespective of the model) might bear equally. ABC, it is claimed, leads to more accurate costing and thus to more accurate assessment of profitability.

(d) The other advantage of pursuing an ABC philosophy and identifying cost drivers is that, once the drivers have been identified, they are likely to become much more susceptible to being controlled. Thus assessment by management of the benefit of certain activities against their cost becomes more feasible.

5.6 GB Company – the International Industries (II) enquiry

(a) The minimum acceptable price of 120,000 motors to be supplied over the next four months is:

	£000	
Direct materials	600	(120,000 × £5.00)
Direct labour	720	(120,000 × £6.00)
Variable manufacturing overheads	360	(120,000 × £3.00 (that is, £3.00 for half an hour))
Fixed manufacturing overheads	60	(4 × £15,000)
Total	1,740	

The offer price is:

$$120{,}000 \times £19.00 = £2{,}280{,}000$$

On this basis, the price of £19 per machine could be accepted, subject to a number of factors identified in (b) below.

(b) The assumptions on which the above analysis and decision in (a) are based include the following:

- That the contract can be accommodated within the 30 per cent spare capacity of GB. If this is not so, then there will be an opportunity cost relating to lost 'normal' production, which must be taken account of in the decision.
- That sales commission and freight costs will not be affected by the contract.
- It is unlikely that work more remunerative to GB than the contract will be available during the period of the contract.

There are also some strategic issues involved in the decision, including:

- The possibility that the contract could lead to other and better-remunerated work from II.
- A problem of selling similar products in the same market at different prices. Other customers, knowing that GB is selling at marginal prices, may make it difficult for the business to resist demand from other customers for similarly priced output.

5.7 Sillycon Ltd

(a)   **Overhead analysis**

	Electronics £000	Testing £000	Service £000
Variable overheads	1,200	600	700
Apportionment of service dept (800:600)	400	300	(700)
	1,600	900	–
Direct labour hours ('000)	800	600	
Variable overheads per direct labour hour	£2.00	£1.50	

	Electronics £000	Testing £000	Service £000
Fixed overheads	2,000	500	800
Apportionment of service dept (equally)	400	400	(800)
	2,400	900	–
Direct labour hours ('000)	800	600	
Fixed overheads per direct labour hour	£3.00	£1.50	

Product cost (per unit)

		£	
Direct materials		7.00	
Direct labour:	Electronics	40.00	(2 × £20.00)
	Testing	18.00	(1½ × £12.00)
Variable overheads:	Electronics	4.00	(2 × £2.00)
	Testing	2.25	(1½ × £1.50)
Total variable cost		71.25	(assuming direct labour to be variable)
Fixed overheads:	Electronics	6.00	(2 × £3.00)
	Testing	2.25	(1½ × £1.50)
Total 'full' cost		79.50	
Add Mark-up, say 30%		23.85	
		103.35	

On the basis of the above, the business could hope to compete in the market at a price that reflects normal pricing practice.

(b) At this price, and only taking account of incremental fixed overheads, the break-even point (BEP) would be given by:

$$\text{BEP} = \frac{\text{Fixed costs}}{\text{Contribution per unit}} = \frac{£150,000^*}{£103.35 - £71.25} = 4,673 \text{ units}$$

* (£13,000 + £100,000 + £37,000) namely the costs specifically incurred.

As the potential market for the business is around 5,000 to 6,000 units a year, the new product looks viable.

Chapter 6

6.3 Nursing Home

(a) The rates per patient for the variable overheads, on the basis of experience during months 1 to 6, are as follows:

Expense	Amount for 2,700 patients	Amount per patient
	£	£
Staffing	59,400	22
Power	27,000	10
Supplies	54,000	20
Other	8,100	3
	148,500	55

Since the expected level of activity for the full year is 6,000, the expected level of activity for the second six months is 3,300 (that is, 6,000 – 2,700).

Thus the budget for the second six months will be:

Variable element:	£	
Staffing	72,600	(3,300 × £22)
Power	33,000	(3,300 × £10)
Supplies	66,000	(3,300 × £20)
Other	9,900	(3,300 × £3)
	181,500	(3,300 × £55)

Fixed element:

Supervision	60,000	6/12 of the annual figure
Depreciation/finance	93,600	ditto
Other	32,400	ditto
	186,000	(per patient = £56.36 (that is £186,000/3,300))
Total (second six months)	367,500	(per patient = £111.36 (that is £56.36 + £55.00))

(b) For the second six months the actual activity was 3,800 patients. For a valid comparison with the actual outcome, the budget will need to be revised to reflect this activity.

	Actual costs	*Budget* *(3,800 patients)*	*Difference*
	£	£	£
Variable element	203,300	209,000 (3,800 × £55)	5,700 (saving)
Fixed element	190,000	186,000	4,000 (overspend)
Total	393,300	395,000	1,700 (saving)

(c) Relative to the budget, there was a saving of nearly 3 per cent on the variable element and an overspend of about 2 per cent on fixed costs. Without further information, it is impossible to deduce much more than this.

    The differences between the budget and the actual may be caused by some assumptions made in framing the budget for 3,800 patients in the second part of the year. There may be some element of economies of scale in the variable costs; that is, the costs may not be strictly linear. If this were the case, basing a relatively large activity budget on the experience of a relatively small activity period would tend to overstate the large activity budget. The fixed-cost budget was deduced by dividing the budget for 12 months by two. In fact, there could be seasonal factors or inflationary pressures at work that might make such a crude division of the fixed cost element unfair.

6.4   Linpet Ltd

(a) Cash budgets are extremely useful for decision-making purposes. They allow managers to see the likely effect on the cash balance of the plans that they have set in place. Cash is an important asset and it is necessary to ensure that it is properly managed. Failure to do so can have disastrous consequences for the business. Where the cash budget indicates a surplus balance, managers must decide whether this balance should be reinvested in the business or distributed to the owners. Where the cash budget indicates a deficit balance, managers must decide how this deficit should be financed or how it might be avoided.

(b) Cash budget for the six months to 30 November

	June £	*July* £	*Aug* £	*Sept* £	*Oct* £	*Nov* £
Receipts						
Cash sales revenue						
(Note 1)	4,000	5,500	7,000	8,500	11,000	11,000
Credit sales revenue						
(Note 2)	–	–	4,000	5,500	7,000	8,500
	4,000	5,500	11,000	14,000	18,000	19,500
Payments						
Purchases						
(Note 3)	–	29,000	9,250	11,500	13,750	17,500
Overheads	500	500	500	500	650	650
Wages	900	900	900	900	900	900
Commission						
(Note 4)	–	320	440	560	680	880

Equipment	10,000	–	–	–	–	7,000
Motor vehicle	6,000	–	–	–	–	
Leasehold	40,000					
	57,400	30,720	11,090	13,460	15,980	26,930
Cash flow	(53,400)	(25,220)	(90)	540	2,020	(7,430)
Opening balance	60,000	6,600	(18,620)	(18,710)	(18,170)	(16,150)
Closing balance	6,600	(18,620)	(18,710)	(18,170)	(16,150)	(23,580)

Notes:

1 50 per cent of the current month's sales revenue.

2 50 per cent of sales revenue of two months previous.

3 To have sufficient inventories to meet each month's sales will require purchases of 75 per cent of the month's sales inventories figures (25 per cent is profit). In addition, each month the business will buy £1,000 more inventories than it will sell. In June, the business will also buy its initial inventories of £22,000. This will be paid for in the following month. For example, June's purchases will be (75% × £8,000) + £1,000 + £22,000 = £29,000, paid for in July.

4 This is 5 per cent of 80 per cent of the month's sales revenue, paid in the following month. For example, June's commission will be 5% × 80% × £8,000 = £320, payable in July.

6.5   Lewisham Ltd

(a) The finished goods inventories budget for the three months ending 30 September (in units of production) is:

	July '000 units	Aug '000 units	Sept '000 units
Opening inventories (Note 1)	40	48	40
Production (Note 2)	188	232	196
	228	280	236
Inventories sold (Note 3)	(180)	(240)	(200)
Closing inventories	48	40	36

(b) The raw materials inventories budget for the two months ending 31 August (in kg) is:

	July '000 kg	Aug '000 kg
Opening inventories (Note 1)	40	58
Purchases (Note 2)	112	107
	152	165
Production (Note 4)	(94)	(116)
Closing inventories	58	49

(c) The cash budget for the two months ending 30 September is:

	Aug £	Sept £
Inflows		
Receivables – current month (Note 5)	493,920	411,600
– preceding month (Note 6)	151,200	201,600
Total inflows	645,120	613,200
Outflows		
Payments to trade payables (Note 7)	168,000	160,500
Labour and overheads (Note 8)	185,600	156,800
Fixed overheads	22,000	22,000
Total outflows	375,600	339,300
Net inflows/(outflows)	269,520	273,900
Balance carried forward	289,520	563,420

Notes:
1 The opening balance is the same as the closing balance from the previous month.
2 This is a balancing figure.
3 This figure is given in the question.
4 This figure derives from the finished inventories budget. [July 188,000 × 0.5 = 94000]
5 This is 98 per cent of 70 per cent of the current month's sales revenue.
6 This is 28 per cent of the previous month's sales revenue.
7 This figure derives from the raw materials inventories budget. [July 112,000 × £1.50 = £168,000]
8 This figure derives from the finished inventories budget. [July 232,000 × £0.80 = £185,600]

6.6 Newtake Records

(a) The cash budget for the period to 30 November is:

	June £000	July £000	Aug £000	Sept £000	Oct £000	Nov £000
Cash receipts						
Sales revenue (Note 1)	227	315	246	138	118	108
Cash payments						
Administration (Note 2)	(40)	(41)	(38)	(33)	(31)	(30)
Goods purchased	(135)	(180)	(142)	(94)	(75)	(66)
Repayments of borrowings	(5)	(5)	(5)	(5)	(5)	(5)
Selling expenses	(22)	(24)	(28)	(26)	(21)	(19)
Tax paid				(22)		
Shop refurbishment		(14)	(18)	(6)		
	(202)	(264)	(253)	(164)	(132)	(120)
Cash surplus (deficit)	25	51	(7)	(26)	(14)	(12)
Opening balance	(35)	(10)	41	34	8	(6)
Closing balance	(10)	41	34	8	(6)	(18)

Notes:
1 (50% of the current month's sales revenue) + (97% × 50% of that sales revenue). For example, the June cash receipts = (50% × £230,000) + (97% × 50% × £230,000) = £226,550.
2 The administration expenses figure for the month, *less* £15,000 for depreciation (a non-cash expense).

(b) The inventories budget for the six months to 30 November is:

	June £000	July £000	Aug £000	Sept £000	Oct £000	Nov £000
Opening balance	112	154	104	48	39	33
Inventories purchased	180	142	94	75	66	57
	292	296	198	123	105	90
Cost of inventories sold (60% sales revenue)	(138)	(192)	(150)	(84)	(72)	(66)
Closing balance	154	104	48	39	33	24

(c) The budgeted income statement for the six months ending 30 November is:

	£000
Sales revenue	1,170
Cost of goods sold	(702)
Gross profit (40%)	468
Selling expenses	(136)
Admin. expenses	(303)
Credit card charges	(18)
Interest charges	(6)
Profit for the period	5

(d) We are told that the business is required to eliminate the bank overdraft by the end of November. However, the cash budget reveals that this will not be achieved. There is a decline in the overdraft of nearly 50 per cent over the period, but this is not enough and ways must be found to comply with the bank's requirements. It may be possible to delay the refurbishment programme that is included in the forecasts or to obtain an injection of funds from the owners or other investors. It may also be possible to stimulate sales in some way. However, there has been a decline in the sales revenue since the end of July and the November sales revenue is approximately one-third of the July sales revenue. The reasons for this decline should be sought.

The inventories levels will fall below the preferred minimum level for each of the last three months. However, to rectify this situation it will be necessary to purchase more inventories, which will, in turn, exacerbate the cash flow problems of the business.

The budgeted income statement reveals a very low net profit for the period. For every £1 of sales revenue, the business is only managing to generate 0.4p in profit. The business should look carefully at its pricing policies and its overhead expenses. The administration expenses, for example, absorb more than one-quarter of the total sales revenue. Any reduction in overhead expenses will have a beneficial effect on cash flows.

6.7 Prolog Ltd

(a) Cash budget for the six months to 30 June

	Jan £000	Feb £000	Mar £000	Apr £000	May £000	June £000
Receipts						
Credit sales revenue (Note 1)	100	100	140	180	220	260
Payments						
Trade payables (Note 2)	112	144	176	208	240	272
Operating expenses	4	6	8	10	10	10
Shelving				12		
Taxation			25			
	116	150	209	230	250	282
Cash flow	(16)	(50)	(69)	(50)	(30)	(22)
Opening balance	(68)	(84)	(134)	(203)	(253)	(283)
Closing balance	(84)	(134)	(203)	(253)	(283)	(305)

Notes:

1 Sales receipts will equal the month's sales revenue, but be received two months later. For example, the January sales revenue = £2,000 × (50 + 20) = £140,000, to be received in March.

2 Payments to suppliers will equal the next month's sales requirements, payable the next month. For example, January purchases = £1,600 × (50 + 40) = £144,000, payable in February.

(b) A banker may require various pieces of information before granting additional overdraft facilities. These may include:

● Security available for the loan.
● Details of past profit performance.
● Profit projections for the next twelve months.
● Cash projections beyond the next six months to help assess the prospects of repayment.
● Details of the assumptions underlying projected figures supplied.
● Details of the contractual commitment between Prolog Ltd and its supplier.
● Details of management expertise. Can they manage the expansion programme?
● Details of the new machine and its performance in relation to competing models.
● Details of funds available from owners to finance the expansion.

Chapter 7

7.1 True or false

(a) A favourable direct labour rate variance can only be caused by something that leads to the rate per hour paid being less than standard. Normally, this would not be linked to efficient working. Where, however, the standard envisaged some overtime working, at premium rates, the actual labour rate may be below standard if efficiency has removed the need for the overtime.

(b) The statement is true. The action will lead to an adverse sales price variance and may well lead to problems elsewhere, but the sales volume variance must be favourable.

(c) It is true that below-standard materials could lead to adverse materials usage variances because there may be more than a standard amount of scrap. This could also cause adverse labour efficiency variances because working on materials that would not form part of the output would waste labour time.

(d) Higher-than-budgeted sales revenue could well lead to an adverse labour rate variance because producing the additional work may require overtime working at premium rates.

(e) The statement is true. Nothing else could cause such a variance.

7.2 Pilot Ltd

(a)

	Budget			Actual	
	Original	Flexed			
Output (units) (production and sales)	5,000	5,400		5,400	
	£	£		£	
Sales revenue	25,000	27,000		26,460	
Raw materials	(7,500)	(8,100)	(2,700 kg)	(8,770)	(2,830 kg)
Labour	(6,250)	(6,750)	(675 hr)	(6,885)	(650 hr)
Fixed overheads	(6,000)	(6,000)		(6,350)	
Operating profit	5,250	6,150		4,455	

	£	
Sales volume variance (5,250 – 6,150)	900	(F)
Sales price variance (27,000 – 26,460)	(540)	(A)
Materials price variance (2,830 × 3) – 8,770	(280)	(A)
Materials usage variance [(5,400 × 0.5) – 2,830] × £3	(390)	(A)
Labour rate variance (650 × £10) – 6,885	(385)	(A)
Labour efficiency variance [(5,400 × $^{7.5}/_{60}$) – 650] × £10	250	(F)
Fixed overhead spending variance (6,000 – 6,350)	(350)	(A)
Total net variances	(795)	(A)

	£
Budgeted profit	5,250
Less Total net variance	(795)
Actual profit	4,455

(b) Sales volume variance: sales manager; sales price variance: sales manager; materials price variance: buyer; materials usage variance: production manager; labour rate variance: personnel manager; labour efficiency variance: production manager; fixed overhead spending variance: various, depending on the nature of the overheads.

7.4   Overheard remarks

(a) Flexing the budget identifies what the profit would have been, had the only difference between the original budget and the actual figures been concerned with the difference in volume of output. Comparing this profit figure with that in the original budget reveals the profit difference (variance) arising solely from the volume difference (sales volume variance). Thus, flexing the budget does not mean at all that volume differences do not matter. Flexing the budget is the means of discovering the effect on profit of the volume difference.

In one sense, all variances are 'water under the bridge', to the extent that the past cannot be undone, and so it is impossible to go back to the last control period and put in a better performance. Identifying variances can, however, be useful in identifying where things went wrong, which should enable management to take steps to ensure that the same things do not to go wrong in the future.

(b) Variances will not tell you what went wrong. They should, however, be a great help in identifying the manager within whose sphere of responsibility things went wrong. That manager should know why it went wrong. In this sense, variances identify relevant questions, but not answers.

(c) Identifying the reason for variances may well cost money, usually in terms of staff time. It is a matter of judgement in any particular situation, of balancing the cost of investigation against the potential benefits. As is usual in such judgements, it is difficult, before undertaking the investigation, to know either the cost or the likely benefit.

In general, significant variances, particularly adverse ones, should be investigated. Persistent (over a period of months) smaller variances should also be investigated. It should not automatically be assumed that favourable variances can be ignored. They indicate that things are not going according to plan, possibly because the plans (budgets) are flawed.

(d) Research evidence does not show this. It seems to show that managers tend to be most motivated by having as a target the most difficult goals that they find acceptable.

(e) Budgets normally provide the basis of feedforward and feedback control. During a budget preparation period, potential problems (for example, a potential inventories shortage) might be revealed. Steps can then be taken to revise the plans in order to avoid the potential problem. This is an example of a feedforward control: potential problems are anticipated and eliminated before they can occur.

Budgetary control is a very good example of feedback control, where a signal that something is going wrong triggers steps to take corrective action for the future.

7.5   Bradley-Allen Ltd

(a)

	Budget		Actual
	Original	Flexed	
Output (units) (production and sales)	800	950	950

	£	£		£	
Sales revenue	64,000	76,000		73,000	
Raw materials – A	(12,000)	(14,250)	(285 kg)	(15,200)	(310 kg)
– B	(16,000)	(19,000)	(950 m)	(18,900)	(920 m)
Labour – skilled	(4,000)	(4,750)	(475 hr)	(4,628)	(445 hr)
– unskilled	(10,000)	(11,875)	(1,484.375 hr)	(11,275)	(1,375 hr)
Fixed overheads	(12,000)	(12,000)		(11,960)	
Operating profit	10,000	14,125		11,037	

Sales variances

Volume: $10,000 - 14,125 = £4,125$ (F)

Price: $76,000 - 73,000 = £3,000$ (A)

Direct materials A variances

Usage: $[(950 \times 0.3) - 310] \times £50 = £1,250$ (A)

Price: $(310 \times £50) - £15,200 = £300$ (F)

Direct materials B variances

Usage: $[(950 \times 1) - 920] \times £20 = £600$ (F)

Price: $(920 \times £20) - £18,900 = £500$ (A)

Skilled direct labour variances

Efficiency: $[(950 \times 0.5) - 445] \times £10 = £300$ (F)

Rate: $(445 \times £10) - £4,628 = £178$ (A)

Unskilled direct labour variances

Efficiency: $[(950 \times 1.5625) - 1,375] \times £8 = £875$ (F)

Rate: $(1,375 \times £8) - £11,275 = £275$ (A)

Fixed overhead variances

Spending: $(12,000 - 11,960) = £40$ (F)

Budgeted profit				£10,000
Sales:	Volume	4,125	(F)	
	Price	(3,000)	(A)	1,125
Direct material A:	Usage	(1,250)	(A)	
	Price	300	(F)	(950)
Direct material B:	Usage	600	(F)	
	Price	(500)	(A)	100
Skilled labour:	Efficiency	300	(F)	
	Rate	(178)	(A)	122
Unskilled labour:	Efficiency	875	(F)	
	Rate	(275)	(A)	600
Fixed overheads:	Expenditure			40
Actual profit				£11,037

(b) The statement in (a) is useful to management because it enables them to see where there have been failures to meet the original budget and to quantify the extent of such failures. This means that junior managers can be held accountable for the performance of their particular area of responsibility.

7.7 **Varne Chemprocessors**

(a) The standard usage rate of UK194 per litre of Varnelyne is 200/5,000 = 0.04. The standard price is £392/200 = £1.96 per litre of UK194.
Materials usage variance (UK194) is

$$[(637,500 \times 0.04) - 28,100] \times £1.96 = £5,096 \text{ (A)}$$

Materials price variance is

$$(28,100 \times £1.96) - £51,704 = £3,372 \text{ (F)}$$

(b) The net variance on UK194 was, from the calculations in (a), £1,724 (A) (that is £5,096 – £3,372). This seems to have led directly to savings elsewhere of £4,900, giving a net cost saving of over £3,000 for the month.

Unfortunately things may not be quite as simple as the numbers suggest. The non-standard mix to make the Varnelyne might lead to a substandard product, which could have very wide-ranging ramifications in terms of potential loss of market goodwill.

There is also the possibility that the material for which the UK194 was used as a substitute was already held in inventories. If this were the case, is there any danger that this material may deteriorate and, ultimately, prove to be unusable?

Other possible adverse outcomes of the non-standard mix could also arise.

The question is raised by the analysis in part (a) (and by the production manager's comment) of why the cost standard for UK194 had not been revised to take account of the lower price prevailing in the market.

(c) The variances, period by period and cumulatively, for each of the two materials are given as follows:

	UK500		UK800	
Period	Period £	Cumulative £	Period £	Cumulative £
1	301 (F)	301 (F)	298 (F)	298 (F)
2	(251) (A)	50 (F)	203 (F)	501 (F)
3	102 (F)	152 (F)	(52) (A)	449 (F)
4	(202) (A)	(50) (A)	(98) (A)	351 (F)
5	153 (F)	103 (F)	(150) (A)	201 (F)
6	(103) (A)	zero	(201) (A)	zero

Without knowing the scale of these variances relative to the actual costs involved, it is not possible to be too dogmatic about how to interpret the above information.

UK500 appears to show a fairly random set of data, with the period variances fluctuating from positive to negative and giving a net variance of zero. This is what would be expected from a situation that is basically under control.

UK800 also shows a zero cumulative figure over the six periods, *but* there seems to be a more systematic train of events, particularly the four consecutive adverse variances from period 3 onwards. This looks as if it may be out of control and worthy of investigation.

Chapter 8

8.1   Mylo Ltd

(a) The annual depreciation of the two projects is:

$$\text{Project 1: } \frac{(£100{,}000 - £7{,}000)}{3} = £31{,}000$$

$$\text{Project 2: } \frac{(£60{,}000 - £6{,}000)}{3} = £18{,}000$$

Project 1

(1)

	Year 0 £000	Year 1 £000	Year 2 £000	Year 3 £000
Operating profit/(loss)		29	(1)	2
Depreciation		31	31	31
Capital cost	(100)			
Residual value				7
Net cash flows	(100)	60	30	40
10% discount factor	1.000	0.909	0.826	0.751
Present value	(100.00)	54.54	24.78	30.04
Net present value	9.36			

(2)   Clearly the IRR lies above 10%; try 15%:

15% discount factor	1.000	0.870	0.756	0.658
Present value	(100.00)	52.20	22.68	26.32
Net present value	1.20			

Thus the IRR lies a little above 15%, perhaps around 16%.

(3)   To find the payback period, the cumulative cash flows are calculated:

Cumulative cash flows	(100)	(40)	(10)	30

Thus the payback will occur after 3 years if we assume year-end cash flows.

Project 2

(1)

	Year 0 £000	Year 1 £000	Year 2 £000	Year 3 £000
Operating profit/(loss)		18	(2)	4
Depreciation		18	18	18
Capital cost	(60)			
Residual value				6
Net cash flows	(60)	36	16	28
10% discount factor	1.000	0.909	0.826	0.751
Present value	(60.00)	32.72	13.22	21.03
Net present value	6.97			

(2) Clearly the IRR lies above 10%; try 15%:

15% discount factor	1.000	0.870	0.756	0.658
Present value	(60.00)	31.32	12.10	18.42
Net present value	1.84			

Thus the IRR lies a little above 15%; perhaps around 17%.

(3) The cumulative cash flows are:

Cumulative cash flows	(60)	(24)	(8)	20

Thus the payback will occur after 3 years (assuming year-end cash flows).

(b) Presuming that Mylo Ltd is pursuing a wealth-enhancement objective, Project 1 is preferable since it has the higher NPV. The difference between the two NPVs is not significant, however.

8.5 Newton Electronics Ltd

(a)

Option 1

	Year 0 £m	Year 1 £m	Year 2 £m	Year 3 £m	Year 4 £m	Year 5 £m
Plant and equipment	(9.0)					1.0
Sales revenue		24.0	30.8	39.6	26.4	10.0
Variable costs		(11.2)	(19.6)	(25.2)	(16.8)	(7.0)
Fixed costs (ex. dep'n)		(0.8)	(0.8)	(0.8)	(0.8)	(0.8)
Working capital	(3.0)					3.0
Marketing costs		(2.0)	(2.0)	(2.0)	(2.0)	(2.0)
Opportunity costs		(0.1)	(0.1)	(0.1)	(0.1)	(0.1)
	(12.0)	9.9	8.3	11.5	6.7	4.1
Discount factor 10%	1.000	0.909	0.826	0.751	0.683	0.621
Present value	(12.0)	9.0	6.9	8.6	4.6	2.5
NPV	19.6					

Option 2

	Year 0 £m	Year 1 £m	Year 2 £m	Year 3 £m	Year 4 £m	Year 5 £m
Royalties	–	4.4	7.7	9.9	6.6	2.8
Discount factor 10%	1.000	0.909	0.826	0.751	0.683	0.621
Present value	–	4.0	6.4	7.4	4.5	1.7
NPV	24.0					

Option 3

	Year 0	Year 2
Instalments	12.0	12.0
Discount factor 10%	1.000	0.826
Present value	12.0	9.9
NPV	21.9	

(b) Before making a final decision, the board should consider the following factors:

(1) The long-term competitiveness of the business may be affected by the sale of the patents.

(2) At present, the business is not involved in manufacturing and marketing products. Would a change in direction be desirable?

(3) The business will probably have to buy in the skills necessary to produce the product itself. This will involve costs, and problems could arise. Has this been taken into account?

(4) How accurate are the forecasts made and how valid are the assumptions on which they are based?

(c) Option 2 has the highest NPV and is therefore the most attractive to shareholders. However, the accuracy of the forecasts should be checked before a final decision is made.

8.6   **Chesterfield Wanderers**

(a) and (b)

Player option

	Year 0 £000	Year 1 £000	Year 2 £000	Year 3 £000	Year 4 £000	Year 5 £000
Sale of player	2,200					1,000
Purchase of Bazza	(10,000)					
Sponsorship, and so on		1,200	1,200	1,200	1,200	1,200
Gate receipts		2,500	1,300	1,300	1,300	1,300
Salaries paid		(800)	(800)	(800)	(800)	(1,200)
Salaries saved		400	400	400	400	600
	(7,800)	3,300	2,100	2,100	2,100	2,900
Discount factor 10%	1.000	0.909	0.826	0.751	0.683	0.621
Present values	(7,800)	3,000	1,735	1,577	1,434	1,801
NPV	1,747					

Ground improvement option

	Year 1 £000	Year 2 £000	Year 3 £000	Year 4 £000	Year 5 £000
Ground improvements	(10,000)				
Increased gate receipts	(1,800)	4,400	4,400	4,400	4,400
	(11,800)	4,400	4,400	4,400	4,400
Discount factor 10%	0.909	0.826	0.751	0.683	0.621
Present values	(10,726)	3,634	3,304	3,005	2,732
NPV	1,949				

(c) The ground improvement option provides the higher NPV and is therefore the preferable option, based on the objective of shareholder wealth maximisation.

(d) A professional football club may not wish to pursue an objective of shareholder wealth enhancement. It may prefer to invest in quality players in an attempt to enjoy future sporting success. If this is the case, the NPV approach will be less appropriate because the club is not pursuing a strict wealth-related objective.

8.7 Simtex Ltd

(a) Net operating cash flows each year will be:

	£000	£000
Sales revenue (160 × £6)		960
Less		
Variable costs (160 × £4)	640	
Relevant fixed costs	170	810
		150

The estimated NPV of the new product can then be calculated:

	£000
Annual cash flows (150 × 3.038*)	456
Residual value of equipment (100 × 0.636)	64
	520
Less Initial outlay	480
Net present value	40

* This is the sum of the 12 per cent discount factors over four years. Where the cash flows are constant, it is a quicker procedure than working out the present value of cash flows for each year and then adding them together.

(b) (i) Assume the discount rate is 18%. The net present value of the project would be:

	£000
Annual cash flows (150 × 2.690)	404
Residual value of equipment (100 × 0.516)	52
	456
Less Initial outlay	480
NPV	(24)

Thus an increase of 6%, from 12% to 18%, in the discount rate causes a fall from +40 to –24 in the NPV, a fall of 64 or 10.67 (that is, 64/6) for each 1% rise in the discount rate. So a zero NPV will occur with a discount rate approximately equal to 12 + (40/11.67) = 15.4%. (This is, of course, the IRR.)

This higher discount rate represents an increase of about 28% on the existing cost of capital figure.

(ii) The initial outlay on equipment is already expressed in present-value terms and so, to make the project no longer viable, the outlay will have to increase by an amount equal to the NPV of the project (that is, £40,000) – an increase of 8.3% on the stated initial outlay.

(iii) The change necessary in the annual net cash flows to make the project no longer profitable can be calculated as follows:

Let Y = change in the annual operating cash flows. Then

$$(Y \times \text{cumulative discount rates for a four-year period}) - \text{NPV} = 0$$

This can be rearranged as

$$Y \times \text{cumulative discount factors for a four-year period} = \text{NPV}$$

$$Y \times 3.038 = £40,000$$

$$Y = £40,000/3.038$$

$$Y = \underline{£13,167}$$

In percentage terms, this is a decrease of 8.8% on the estimated cash flows.

(iv) The change in the residual value required to make the new product no longer profitable can be calculated as follows:

Let V = change in the residual value:

$$(V \times \text{discount factor at end of four years}) - \text{NPV of product} = 0$$

This can be rearranged as follows:

$$V \times \text{discount factor at end of four years} = \text{NPV of product}$$

$$V \times 0.636 = £40,000$$

$$V = £40,000/0.636$$

$$V = \underline{£62,893}$$

This is a decrease of 63.9% in the residual value of the equipment.

(c) The NPV of the product is positive and so it will increase shareholder wealth. Thus, it should be produced. The sensitivity analysis suggests that the initial outlay and the annual cash flows are the most sensitive variables for managers to consider.

8.8 Kernow Cleaning Services Ltd

(a) The first step is to calculate the expected annual cash flows:

	£
Year 1	
£ 80,000 × 0.3	24,000
£160,000 × 0.5	80,000
£200,000 × 0.2	40,000
	144,000
Year 2	£
£140,000 × 0.4	56,000
£220,000 × 0.4	88,000
£250,000 × 0.2	50,000
	194,000
Year 3	£
£140,000 × 0.4	56,000
£200,000 × 0.3	60,000
£230,000 × 0.3	69,000
	185,000
Year 4	£
£100,000 × 0.3	30,000
£170,000 × 0.6	102,000
£200,000 × 0.1	20,000
	152,000

The expected net present value (ENPV) can now be calculated as follows:

Period	Expected cash flow £	Discount rate 10%	Expected PV £
0	(540,000)	1.000	(540,000)
1	144,000	0.909	130,896
2	194,000	0.826	160,244
3	185,000	0.751	138,935
4	152,000	0.683	103,816
ENPV			(6,109)

(b) The worst possible outcome can be calculated by taking the lowest values of savings each year, as follows:

Period	Cash flow £	Discount rate 10%	PV £
0	(540,000)	1.000	(540,000)
1	80,000	0.909	72,720
2	140,000	0.826	115,640
3	140,000	0.751	105,140
4	100,000	0.683	68,300
NPV			(178,200)

The probability of occurrence can be obtained by multiplying together the probability of *each* of the worst outcomes above, that is $0.3 \times 0.4 \times 0.4 \times 0.3 = 0.014$.

Thus, the probability of occurrence is 1.4%, which is very low.

Chapter 9

9.1 Aires plc

(a) The SVA determination of shareholder value will be as follows:

Year	FCF £m	Discount rate 12%	Present value £m
1	28.0*	0.893	25.0
2	28.0	0.797	22.3
3	28.0	0.712	19.9
4	28.0	0.636	17.8
Total business value			85.0
Less Loan notes			24.0
Shareholder value			61.0

* The free cash flows will be the operating profit after tax plus the lease depreciation charge (that is, £12.0m + £16m).

(b) The EVA® determination of shareholder value will be as follows:

Year	Opening capital invested (C) £m	Capital charge (12% × C) £m	Operating profit after tax £m	EVA® £m	Discount rate 12%	PV of EVA® £m
1	64.0	7.7	12.0	4.3	0.893	3.8
2	48.0	5.8	12.0	6.2	0.797	4.9
3	32.0	3.8	12.0	8.2	0.712	5.8
4	16.0	1.9	12.0	10.1	0.636	6.4
						20.9
			Opening capital			64.0
						84.9
			Less Loan notes			24.0
			Shareholder value			60.9

9.3 **Sharma plc**

Analysis of trading with Lopez Ltd during last year

		£
Gross sales revenue	(40,000 × £20)	800,000
Discount allowed	(£800,000 × 5%)	(40,000)
Manufacturing cost	(40,000 × £12)	(480,000)
Sales order handling	(22 × £75)	(1,650)
Delivery costs	(22 × 120 × £1.50)	(3,960)
Customer sales visits	(30 × £230)	(6,900)
Credit costs	[(£800,000 − £40,000) × $^2/_{12}$ × 2%]	(2,533)
		(535,043)
Profit from the customer for the year		264,957

9.4 **Shareholder value and EVA®**

(a) It is difficult for these different approaches to co-exist in a highly competitive economy. The pursuit of shareholder value may be necessary in order to secure funds and for managers to secure their jobs. A stakeholder approach, which is committed to satisfying the needs of a broad group of constituents, may be difficult to sustain in such an environment.

It has been suggested that other stakeholders have been seriously adversely affected by the pursuit of shareholder value. It is claimed that the application of various techniques to improve shareholder value such as hostile takeovers, cost cutting and large management incentive bonuses have badly damaged the interests of certain stakeholders such as employees and local communities. However, a commitment to shareholder value must take account of the needs of other stakeholders if it is to deliver long-term benefits.

(b) If businesses are overcapitalised it is probably because insufficient attention is given to the amount of capital that is required. Management incentive schemes that are geared towards generating a particular level of profits or achieving a particular market share without specifying the level of capital invested can help create such a problem. EVA® can help by highlighting the cost of capital, through the capital charge.

9.5 **Virgo plc**

There is no single correct answer to this problem. The suggestions set out below are based on experiences that some businesses have had in implementing a management bonus system based on EVA® performance.

In order to get the divisional managers to think and act like the owners of the business, it is recommended that divisional performance, as measured by EVA®, should form a significant part of their total rewards. Thus, around 50 per cent of the total rewards paid to managers could be related to the EVA® that has been generated for a period. (In the case of very senior managers it could be more, and for junior managers less.)

The target for managers to achieve could be a particular level of improvement in EVA® for their division over a year. A target bonus can then be set for achievement of the target level of improvement. If this target level of improvement is achieved, 100 per cent of the bonus should be paid. If the target is not achieved, an agreed percentage (below 100 per cent) could be paid according to the amount of shortfall. If, on the other hand, the target is exceeded, an agreed percentage (with no upper limits) may be paid.

The timing of the payment of management bonuses is important. In the question it was mentioned that Virgo plc wishes to encourage a longer-term view among its managers. One approach is to use a 'bonus bank' system whereby the bonus for a period is placed in a 'bank' and a certain proportion (usually one-third) can be drawn in the period in which it is earned. If the target for the following period is not met, there can be a charge against the bonus bank so that the total amount available for withdrawal is reduced. This will ensure that the managers try to maintain improvements in EVA® consistently over the years.

In some cases, the amount of bonus is determined by three factors: the performance of the business as a whole (as measured by EVA®), the performance of the division (as measured by EVA®) and the performance of the particular manager (using agreed indicators of performance). The performance for the business as a whole is often given the most weighting, and individual performance the least weighting. Thus, 50 per cent of the bonus may be for corporate performance, 30 per cent for divisional performance and 20 per cent for individual performance.

9.6 Leo plc

Free cash flows

	Year 1 £m	Year 2 £m	Year 3 £m	Year 4 £m	Year 5 £m	After Year 5 £m
Sales revenue	30.0	36.0	40.0	48.0	60.0	60.0
Operating profit (20%)	6.0	7.2	8.0	9.6	12.0	12.0
Less						
Cash tax (25%)	1.5	1.8	2.0	2.4	3.0	3.0
Operating profit less cash tax	4.5	5.4	6.0	7.2	9.0	9.0
Less						
ANCAI (15%)	(4.5)*	(0.9)	(0.6)	(1.2)	(1.8)	–
AWCI (10%)	(3.0)*	(0.6)	(0.4)	(0.8)	(1.2)	–
Free cash flows	(3.0)	3.9	5.0	5.2	6.0	9.0
12% discount factor	0.893	0.797	0.712	0.636	0.567	0.567
Present value	(2.7)	3.1	3.6	3.3	3.4	42.5†
	53.2					

* In the first year, the additional sales revenue will be £30m and so the calculations for non-current (fixed) assets and working capital must be based on this figure.
† The terminal value is (9.0/0.12 × 0.567) = 42.5.

Total business value will increase by £53.2m. As there has been no change to the level of borrowing, shareholder value should increase by this amount.

Chapter 10

10.1 Divisionalised organisations

(a) A divisionalised organisation is one that divides itself into operating units in order to deliver its range of products or services. Divisionalisation is, in essence, an attempt to deal with the problems of size and complexity.

Autonomy of action relates to the amount of discretion the managers of divisions have been given by central management over the operations of the division. Two popular forms of autonomy are profit centres and investment centres. Though divisionalisation usually leads to decentralisation of decision making, this need not necessarily be the case.

(b) The benefits of allowing divisional managers autonomy include:

● Better use of market information.
● Increase in management motivation.
● Providing opportunities for management development.
● Making full use of specialist knowledge.
● Giving central managers time to focus on strategic issues.
● Permitting a more rapid response to changes in market conditions.

(c) There are certain problems with this approach which include:

- Goal conflict between divisions or between divisions and central management.
- Risk avoidance on the part of divisional managers.
- The growth of management 'perks'.
- Increasing costs due to inability to benefit from economies of scale.

Transfers between divisions can create problems for a business. Managers of the selling division may wish to obtain a high price for the transfers in an attempt to achieve certain profit objectives. However, the managers of the purchasing division may wish to buy as cheaply as possible in order to achieve their own profit objectives. This can create conflict, and central managers may find that they are spending time arbitrating disputes. It may be necessary for central managers to impose a solution on the divisions where agreement cannot be reached, which will, of course, undermine the divisions' autonomy.

10.2 **Financial performance measures**

(a) *Contribution* represents the difference between the total sales revenue of the division and the variable expenses incurred. This is a useful measure for understanding the relationship between costs, output and profit. However, it ignores any fixed expenses incurred and so not all aspects of operating performance are considered.

The *controllable profit* deducts all expenses (variable and fixed) within the control of the divisional manager when arriving at a measure of performance. This is viewed by many as the best measure of performance for divisional managers as they will be in a position to determine the level of expenses incurred. However, in practice, it may be difficult to categorise expenses as being either controllable or non-controllable. This measure also ignores the investment made in assets. For example, a manager may decide to hold very high levels of inventories, which may be an inefficient use of resources.

Return on investment (ROI) is a widely used method of evaluating the profitability of divisions. The ratio is calculated in the following way:

$$\text{ROI} = \frac{\text{Division profit}}{\text{Divisional investment (assets employed)}} \times 100\%$$

The ratio is seen as capturing many of the dimensions of running a division.

When defining divisional profit for this ratio, the purpose for which the ratio is to be used must be considered. When evaluating the performance of a divisional manager, the controllable contribution is likely to be the most appropriate, whereas for evaluating the performance of a division, the divisional contribution is likely to be more appropriate. Different definitions can be employed for divisional investment. The net assets or total assets figure may be used. In addition, assets may be shown at original cost or some other basis such as current replacement cost.

(b) There are several non-financial measures available to evaluate a division's performance. Examples of these measures have been cited in the chapter. Further examples include:

- Plant capacity utilised.
- Percentage of rejects in production runs.
- Ratio of customer visits to customer orders.
- Number of customers visited.

If a broad range of financial and non-financial measures covering different time horizons are used, there is a better chance that all of the major dimensions of management and divisional performance will be properly assessed. Focusing on a few short-term financial objectives incurs the danger that managers will strive to achieve these at the expense of the longer-term objectives. Clearly, ROI can be increased in the short term by cutting back on discretionary expenditure such as staff training and research and development and by not replacing heavily depreciated assets.

10.4   ABC Corporation

(a) (1) Residual income calculation – original plan:

	£000
Sales revenue	1,200
Variable costs	(800)
Contribution	400
Fixed costs	(250)
Divisional profit	150
Capital charge (£500,000 × 20%)	(100)
Residual income	50

(2) Residual income calculation – original plan and Option X:

	£000
Sales revenue [(100,000 × £12) + (20,000 × £11)]	1,420
Variable costs (120,000 × £8)	(960)
Contribution	460
Fixed costs [250,000 + (80,000/4)]	(270)
Divisional profit	190
Capital charge (£580,000 × 20%)	(116)
Residual income	74

(3) Residual income calculation – original plan and Option Y:

	£000
Sales revenue [(80,000 × £12) (20,000 × £10)]	1,160
Variable costs	(800)
Contribution	360
Fixed costs	(250)
Divisional profit	110
Capital charge (£500,000 × 20%)	(100)
Residual income	10

We can see that the highest residual income for Division A arises when only Option X is added to the original plan and that the lowest residual income arises when only Option Y is added to the original plan.

(b) Division A is unlikely to find the price reduction for Division B attractive. Division B, on the other hand, will benefit by £40,000 (20,000 × £2) from the price reduction. However, overall, the total profits of the business will be unaffected as the increase in Division B's profits will be cancelled out by the decrease in Division A's profit.

If an outside supplier is used, the profits of the business overall will fall by the amount of the lost contribution (20,000 × (£10 – £8) = £40,000).

Another option would be to allow the outsiders to supply Division B and to use the released production capacity to sell outside customers 20,000 units at £11 per unit. In this way, additional equipment costs would be avoided.

10.5   Telling Company

(a) (1)

$$\text{ROI} = \frac{\text{Divisional profit}}{\text{Divisional investment (assets employed)}} \times 100\%$$

$$= \frac{25,000}{150,000} \times 100\%$$

$$= 16.7\%$$

		£
(2)	Divisional profit	25,000
	Required return (20% × £150,000)	(30,000)
	Residual income (loss)	(5,000)

(3) The results show that the ROI is less than the required return of 20 per cent and the residual income is negative. The results must therefore be considered unsatisfactory.

(b)

	£
Increase in sales revenue (£7.50 × 10,000)	75,000
Increase in variable costs (£6 × 10,000)	(60,000)
Increase in contribution	15,000
Increase in fixed costs	(5,000)
Increase in divisional profit	10,000
Increase in cost of capital (20% × £20,000)	(4,000)
Increase in RI	6,000

(c) (1) Though the divisional profits of Goodman and Sharp will each be affected by a change in the transfer price, the total profits of Telling Co. will be unaffected. The increase in profit occurring in one division will be cancelled out by the decrease in profit in the other division and so the overall effect will be nil.

(2) If the work goes outside, Goodman would lose £20,000 in contribution (that is, 10,000 × £2) and Sharp would gain £8,000 by the reduction in the buying-in price (that is, 10,000 × (£8 − £7.20)). The net effect on the business as a whole will therefore be a loss of £12,000 (that is, £20,000 − £8,000).

10.6 Glasnost plc

(a)

	West £000	East £000
Residual income:		
300 − (2,500 × 10%)	50	
100 − (500 × 10%)		50
Return on investment (ROI):		
Based on net profit		
(250/2,500) × 100%	10%	
(80/500) × 100%		16%
Based on divisional profit		
(300/2,500) × 100%	12%	
(100/500) × 100%		20%
Expenses to sales revenue ratio:		
Direct manufacturing	30%	53%
Indirect manufacturing	22%	12%
Selling and distribution	18%	10%
Central overhead	5%	5%

(b) The ROI ratios indicate that East is the better performing division. However, we are told in the question that East has older plant than West, which has recently modernised its production lines. This difference in the age of the plant is likely to mean that the ROI of East is higher due, at least in part, to the fact that the plant has been substantially written down. Some common base is required for comparison purposes (for example, unadjusted historical cost).

We are told that ROI is used as the basis for evaluating performance. We can see that, whichever measure of ROI is used, the two divisions meet the minimum returns required. If ROI is being used to assess managerial performance then the divisional profit rather than net profit figure should be used in the calculation. This is because the net profit figure is calculated after non-controllable central overheads have been deducted.

The business should consider the use of RI as another measure of divisional performance. This measure reveals the same level of performance for the current year from each division.

The expenses to sales revenue ratios are revealing. West has a lower direct manufacturing cost to sales revenue ratio but a higher indirect manufacturing cost to sales revenue ratio than East. This is consistent with the introduction of modern labour-saving plant.

West has a higher selling expenses to sales revenue ratio than East. This is probably due to the fact that inter-business transfers are minimal whereas for East they represent 50 per cent of total sales revenue.

Chapter 11

11.1 Hercules Wholesalers Ltd

(a) The business is probably concerned about its liquidity position because:

- it has a substantial overdraft, which together with its non-current borrowings means that it has borrowed an amount roughly equal to its equity (according to values in the statement of financial position);
- it has increased its investment in inventories during the past year (as shown by the income statement); and
- it has a low current ratio (ratio of current assets to current liabilities).

(b) The operating cash cycle can be calculated as follows:

Number of days

Average inventories holding period:

$$\frac{[(\text{Opening inventories} + \text{Closing inventories})/2] \times 360}{\text{Cost of inventories}} = \frac{[(125 + 143/2)] \times 360}{323} = 149$$

Add Average settlement period for receivables:

$$\frac{\text{Trade receivables} \times 360}{\text{Credit sales revenue}} = \frac{163}{452} \times 360 \qquad\qquad = \underline{130}$$

279

Less Average settlement period for payables:

$$\frac{\text{Trade payables} \times 360}{\text{Credit purchases}} = \frac{145}{341} \times 360 \qquad\qquad = \underline{153}$$

Operating cash cycle $\qquad\qquad\qquad\qquad\qquad\qquad\qquad\qquad \underline{126}$

(c) The business can reduce the operating cash cycle in a number of ways. The average inventories holding period seems quite long. At present, average inventories held represent almost five months' sales. Reducing the level of inventories held can reduce this period. Similarly, the average settlement period for receivables seems long at more than four months' sales revenue. Imposing tighter credit control, offering discounts, charging interest on overdue accounts, and so on, may reduce this. However, any policy decisions concerning inventories and receivables must take account of current trading conditions. Extending the period of credit taken to pay suppliers would also reduce the operating cash cycle. However, for the reasons mentioned in the chapter, this option must be considered carefully.

11.5 Mayo Computers Ltd

New proposals from credit control department

	£000	£000
Current level of investment in receivables		
(£20m × (60/365))		3,288
Proposed level of investment in receivables		
((£20m × 60%) × (30/365))	(986)	
((£20m × 40%) × (50/365))	(1,096)	(2,082)
Reduction in level of investment		1,206

The reduction in overdraft interest as a result of the reduction in the level of investment will be £1,206,000 × 14% = £169,000.

	£000	£000
Cost of cash discounts offered (£20m × 60% × 2.5%)		300
Additional cost of credit administration		20
		320
Bad debt savings	(100)	
Interest charge savings (see above)	(169)	(269)
Net cost of policy each year		51

These calculations show that the business would incur additional annual costs if it implemented this proposal. It would therefore be cheaper to stay with the existing credit policy.

11.6 Boswell Enterprises Ltd

(a)

	(i) Current policy		(ii) New policy	
	£000	£000	£000	£000
Receivables				
[(£3m × 1/12 × 30%) + (£3m × 2/12 × 70%)]		425.0		
[(£3.15m × 1/12 × 60%) + (£3.15m × 2/12 × 40%)]				367.5
Inventories				
{[£3m − (£3m × 20%)] × 3/12}		600.0		
{[£3.15m − (£3.15m × 20%)] × 3/12}				630.0
Cash (fixed)		140.0		140.0
		1,165.0		1,137.5
Payables				
{[£3m − (£3m × 20%)] × 2/12}	(400.0)			
{[£3.15m − (£3.15m × 20%)] × 2/12}			(420.0)	
Accrued variable expenses				
[£3m × 1/12 × 10%]	(25.0)			
[£3.15m × 1/12 × 10%]			(26.3)	
Accrued fixed expenses	(15.0)	(440.0)	(15.0)	(461.3)
Investment in working capital		725.0		676.2

(b) The expected profit for the year

	(i) Current policy		(ii) New policy	
	£000	£000	£000	£000
Sales revenue		3,000.0		3,150.0
Cost of goods sold		(2,400.0)		(2,520.0)
Gross profit (20%)		600.0		630.0
Variable expenses (10%)	(300.0)		(315.0)	
Fixed expenses	(180.0)		(180.0)	
Discounts (£3.15m × 60% × 2.5%)	–	(480.0)	(47.3)	(542.3)
Profit for the year		120.0		87.7

(c) Under the proposed policy we can see that the investment in working capital will be slightly lower than under the current policy. However, profits will be substantially lower as a result of offering discounts. The increase in sales revenue resulting from the discounts will not be sufficient to offset the additional costs of making the discounts to customers. It seems that the business should, therefore, stick with its current policy.

11.7 Delphi plc

(a) The receivables ageing schedule is:

	Number of months outstanding							
	1 month or less		1 to 2 months		2 to 3 months		Total receivables	
	£000	%	£000	%	£000	%	£000	%
February								
TV and hi-fi	20.0	(22.2)					20.0	(22.2)
Music	30.0	(33.3)					30.0	(33.3)
Retail	40.0	(44.5)					40.0	(44.5)
	90.0	(100.0)					90.0	(100.0)
March								
TV and hi-fi	20.8	(12.5)					20.8	(12.5)
Music	31.8	(19.2)	30.0	(18.1)			61.8	(37.3)
Retail	43.2	(26.1)	40.0	(24.1)	—	—	83.2	(50.2)
	95.8	(57.8)	70.0	(42.2)	—	—	165.8	(100.0)
April								
TV and hi-fi	21.6	(10.0)					21.6	(10.0)
Music	33.7	(15.6)	31.8	(14.7)			65.5	(30.3)
Retail	46.7	(21.4)	43.2	(19.9)	40.0	(18.4)	129.9	(59.7)
	102.0	(47.0)	75.0	(34.6)	40.0	(18.4)	217.0	(100.0)
May								
TV and hi-fi	22.5	(9.6)					22.5	(9.6)
Music	35.7	(15.4)	33.7	(14.6)			69.4	(30.0)
Retail	50.4	(21.7)	46.7	(20.1)	43.2	(18.6)	140.3	(60.4)
	108.6	(46.7)	80.4	(34.7)	43.2	(18.6)	232.2	(100.0)

We can see that the receivables figure will increase substantially in the first four months. The retail chains will account for about 60 per cent of the total receivables outstanding by May as this group has the fastest rate of growth. There is also a significant decline in the proportion of total receivables outstanding from TV and hi-fi shops over this period.

(b) In answering this part of the question, you should refer to the 'five Cs of credit' that were discussed in detail in the chapter.

11.8 Goliath plc

(a) (1) The existing operating cash cycle can be calculated as follows:

	Number of days
Inventories holding period $= \dfrac{\text{Inventories at year end}}{\text{Cost of sales}} \times 365$	
$= \dfrac{560}{1,440} \times 365 =$	142
Add Receivables settlement period $= \dfrac{\text{Receivables at year end}}{\text{Sales revenue}} \times 365$	
$= \dfrac{565}{2,400} \times 365 =$	86
	228
Less Payables settlement period $= \dfrac{\text{Payables at year end}}{\text{Purchases}} \times 365$	
$= \dfrac{451}{1,450} \times 365 =$	(114)
Operating cash cycle	114

The new operating cash cycle is:

	Number of days
Inventories holding period $= \dfrac{(560 \times 1.15)}{(2,400 \times 1.10) \times 0.60^*} \times 365 =$	148
Receivables settlement period $= 86 + 20$	106
	254
Less Payables settlement period $= 114 + 15$	(129)
	125
New operating cash cycle	125
Existing operating cash cycle	(114)
Increase in operating cash cycle (days)	11

* Cost of sales is 60% of sales revenue (see Income statement).

(2)

	£000
Increase (decrease) in inventories held [(560 × 1.15) − 560]	84.0
Increase (decrease) in receivables {[(2,400 × 1.1) × (106/365)] − 565}	201.7
	285.7
(Increase) decrease in payables [1,668 × (129/365) − 451]	(138.5)
Increase (decrease) in net investment	147.2

(3)

	£000	£000
Gross profit increase [(2,400 × 0.1) × 0.40]		96.0
Adjust for		
Admin. expenses increase (15%)	(45.0)	
Bad debts increase	(120.0)	
Interest (10%) on borrowing for increased net investment in working capital (147.2)	(14.7)	(179.7)
Increase (decrease) in profit before tax		(83.7)
Decrease in tax charge for the period (25% × 83.7)		20.9
Increase (decrease) in profit for the period		(62.8)

(b) There would be an increase in the operating cash cycle and this would have an adverse effect on liquidity. The existing receivables and inventories holding periods already appear to be quite high. Any increase in either of these must be justified. The planned increase in the payables period must also be justified because it may risk the loss of goodwill from suppliers. Though there is an expected increase in sales revenue of £240,000 from adopting the new policy, the net profit after taxation will decrease by £62,800. This represents a substantial decrease when compared with the previous year. (The increase in bad debts is a major reason why the profit for the period is adversely affected.) There is also a substantial increase in the net investment in inventories, receivables and payables, which seem high in relation to the expected increase in sales revenue. The new policy requires a significant increase in investment and is expected to generate lower profits than are currently being enjoyed. It should, therefore, be rejected.

Appendix E

Present value table

Present value of £1, that is, $1/(1 + r)^n$

where r = discount rate

n = number of periods until payment

	Discount rates (r)										
Periods (n)	1%	2%	3%	4%	5%	6%	7%	8%	9%	10%	
1	0.990	0.980	0.971	0.962	0.952	0.943	0.935	0.926	0.917	0.909	1
2	0.980	0.961	0.943	0.925	0.907	0.890	0.873	0.857	0.842	0.826	2
3	0.971	0.942	0.915	0.889	0.864	0.840	0.816	0.794	0.772	0.751	3
4	0.961	0.924	0.888	0.855	0.823	0.792	0.763	0.735	0.708	0.683	4
5	0.951	0.906	0.863	0.822	0.784	0.747	0.713	0.681	0.650	0.621	5
6	0.942	0.888	0.837	0.790	0.746	0.705	0.666	0.630	0.596	0.564	6
7	0.933	0.871	0.813	0.760	0.711	0.665	0.623	0.583	0.547	0.513	7
8	0.923	0.853	0.789	0.731	0.677	0.627	0.582	0.540	0.502	0.467	8
9	0.914	0.837	0.766	0.703	0.645	0.592	0.544	0.500	0.460	0.424	9
10	0.905	0.820	0.744	0.676	0.614	0.558	0.508	0.463	0.422	0.386	10
11	0.896	0.804	0.722	0.650	0.585	0.527	0.475	0.429	0.388	0.350	11
12	0.887	0.788	0.701	0.625	0.557	0.497	0.444	0.397	0.356	0.319	12
13	0.879	0.773	0.681	0.601	0.530	0.469	0.415	0.368	0.326	0.290	13
14	0.870	0.758	0.661	0.577	0.505	0.442	0.388	0.340	0.299	0.263	14
15	0.861	0.743	0.642	0.555	0.481	0.417	0.362	0.315	0.275	0.239	15

(continued over)

Periods (n)	Discount rates (r)												
	11%	12%	13%	14%	15%	16%	17%	18%	19%	20%	25%	30%	
1	0.901	0.893	0.885	0.877	0.870	0.862	0.855	0.847	0.840	0.833	0.800	0.769	1
2	0.812	0.797	0.783	0.769	0.756	0.743	0.731	0.718	0.706	0.694	0.640	0.592	2
3	0.731	0.712	0.693	0.675	0.658	0.641	0.624	0.609	0.593	0.579	0.512	0.455	3
4	0.659	0.636	0.613	0.592	0.572	0.552	0.534	0.516	0.499	0.482	0.410	0.350	4
5	0.593	0.567	0.543	0.519	0.497	0.476	0.456	0.437	0.419	0.402	0.328	0.269	5
6	0.535	0.507	0.480	0.456	0.432	0.410	0.390	0.370	0.352	0.335	0.262	0.207	6
7	0.482	0.452	0.425	0.400	0.376	0.354	0.333	0.314	0.296	0.279	0.210	0.159	7
8	0.434	0.404	0.376	0.351	0.327	0.305	0.285	0.266	0.249	0.233	0.168	0.123	8
9	0.391	0.361	0.333	0.308	0.284	0.263	0.243	0.225	0.209	0.194	0.134	0.094	9
10	0.352	0.322	0.295	0.270	0.247	0.227	0.208	0.191	0.176	0.162	0.107	0.073	10
11	0.317	0.287	0.261	0.237	0.215	0.195	0.178	0.162	0.148	0.135	0.086	0.056	11
12	0.286	0.257	0.231	0.208	0.187	0.168	0.152	0.137	0.124	0.112	0.069	0.043	12
13	0.258	0.229	0.204	0.182	0.163	0.145	0.130	0.116	0.104	0.093	0.055	0.033	13
14	0.232	0.205	0.181	0.160	0.141	0.125	0.111	0.099	0.088	0.078	0.044	0.025	14
15	0.209	0.183	0.160	0.140	0.123	0.108	0.095	0.084	0.074	0.065	0.035	0.020	15

Index